Legends & Legacies

Celebrating a Century of Minnesota Coaches

by
Ross Bernstein

Nodin Press

"Legends & Legacies: Celebrating a Century of Minnesota Coaches"
by Ross Bernstein
(WWW.BERNSTEINBOOKS.COM)

ISBN#: 1-932472-00-2

Published by Nodin Press • 530 North Third Street • Minneapolis, MN 55401 • (612) 333-6300
Printed in Minnesota by Printing Enterprises, New Brighton.
Edited by Joel Rippel

PHOTO CREDITS:
Minnesota Twins: 22,23,25,28,36,40,42,
Minnesota Vikings: 96,100,101,127,150,
David Sherman: 74
Bruce Kluckhohn: 188,206
Minnesota Historical Society: 11,43,67,73,
U.S. Hockey Hall of Fame: 31,176,187,191-93,196,202-03,205,209,213,215,
Jonckowski Archives: 27,33,41,43,53,95,103,113,
Pioneer Press: 116
Tim Cortes: 4
Sandy Thompson: 33
Eric Miller: 84,
Mike Laimey: 207,184
TPG Sports: 231
University of Minnesota: 5,8-9,12,30,37,45,46,54,59,61,63,65,68,70,78,81,87,89,91,104-07,109,114,115,118,121-23,125-26,
129,131,134,137-38,141,149,153,155-56,158,160,164,170-71,180-81,185,190,199,226,230-32,
234,237,242,245,247,251,256,263,269,271,277,282,
University of Minnesota-Duluth: 41,69,90,132-33,189,194,203,205,220,275,
St. Cloud State University: 34,62,73,79,82,173-74,261,272,
Minnesota State Mankato: 14,72,75,105,143,168,237,250,270,280,
Bemidji State University: 183,200,276,
UM-Crookston: 133,
UM-Morris: 79,143,285
MSU-Moorhead: 93,108,267-68,279,
Southwest State: 19,287
Winona State: 24,29,37,94,
St. Scholastica: 15,179,
Augsburg: 47,80,93,140,211,216,217,284
Bethel: 235
Carleton: 55,67,83,157,249,270,
Concordia: 16,57,99,102,281
Gustavus: 75,86,115,131,136,147,149,210,238,243,261,274,
Hamline: 39,51,65,154,219,
Macalester: 239,248
St. Ben's: 52,251,273,
St. John's: 26,88,97,110,145,182,245,267,287-89
St. Mary's: 17,57,112,198,223,233,252,
St. Olaf: 20,142,145,159,231,257,267,
St. Thomas: 18,27,49,56,119,222,269-70,
*Photos from the respective individuals themselves: 32,35,38,44,45,48,50,58,60,64,66,76,92, 96,98,104, 119,120,
124,128,130,146,148,152,172,176-78,186,204,208,212,225,235-36,240-41,244,246,252-55,258-60,262,264,265-66,278,286
Cleveland Browns: 144
San Jose Sharks: 195
University of North Dakota: 53,162,167,207
University of California: 61
University of Washington: 137
University of Wisconsin: 211,214,229
Georgia Tech University: 139
University of Nebraska Omaha: 169
University of Notre Dame: 197,224,
Air Force Academy: 175,218
*(*Some photos were acquired from various university and sports related web-sites, thanks too for your help in acquiring those!)*

ACKNOWLEDGEMENTS:

I would really like to thank all of the people that were kind enough to help me in writing this book. In addition to the countless pro,
college and university Sports Information Directors that I hounded throughout this project I would like to sincerely thank all of the
more than 200 gracious men and women who allowed me to interview them. In addition, I would particularly like to thank my publisher, and friend, Norton Stillman. Thank you for your continued support.

Tim Cortes	Andy Johnson	Ron Christian	Megan Jahnke	Dan McMahon
Todd Fultz	Mike Durbin	Jennifer Foley	Tom Nelson	Ann Johnson
Herb Brooks	Mike Hemmesch	Nick Kornder	Mike Jacobson	Denise Johnson
John Gagliardi	Don Nadeau	Bob Nygaard	Tom West	Sarah Burhau
Joel Rippel	Le Ann Finger	Troy Andre	Nick Garner	Brad Ruiter
Randy Johnson	Gene McGivern	Brian Curtis	Tom Challey	Dave St. Peter
Don Stoner	Paul Allan	Larry Scott	John Gessner	Gordon Slaybau
Greg Peterson	Brian Zins	Kelly Loft	Dan Westby	John Toren
Eric Sieger	Tom Nelson	Mike Herzberg	Bob Hagen	Aaron Sickman
Jim Cella	Anne Abicht	Jen Walter	Tim Trainor	Julie Arthur-Sherman
Tim Kennedy	Andy Bartlett	Ann Johnson	Bob Snyder	Toddler Rendahl
Troy Mallat	Dave Wright	Amber Holloway	Matt Pederson	*H.J. Pieser

For Sara and Campbell, the two loves of my life...

Cover Painting by Artist Tim Cortes

I would especially like to express my gratitude to Minnesota sports artist Tim Cortes and sports publisher Todd Fultz for allowing me the privilege of showcasing their newest masterpiece entitled *"Coaches,"* on the cover of my new book. I couldn't be more pleased with the final product and simply can't them enough for all of their hard work. Tim and Todd are both skilled in what they do, and are also both wonderful friends. *(Contact The National Sports Gallery for information on purchasing a signed and numbered limited edition print of "Coaches," or any other of Tim's amazing works of art.)*

One of the nation's premier photo realism artists, Tim Cortes uses colored pencils as his preferred medium. Hundreds of his collectible lithographs have been sold throughout North America and his clients are a venerable who's-who of American sports. From Shaquille O'Neal to Mark McGwire and from Wayne Gretzky to Troy Aikman, Cortes has been commissioned to create countless commemorative works of art over the past decade.

Cortes' paintings have also been featured in numerous venus around the world, including: the US Hockey Hall of Fame, Franklin Mint, Kelly Russell Studios and Beckett's Magazine, as well as on trading cards, pro sports teams' game-day programs, and in various publications. Known for his impeccable detail, Cortes has dedicated his life to the pursuit of celebrating the life and times of many of the world's most famous athletes and the sporting events in which they play.

Cortes grew up in Duluth, where he later starred as a hockey goaltender at Duluth East High School. After a brief stint in the United States Hockey League, Cortes went on to play between the pipes for two seasons in the mid-1980s for the University of Minnesota's Golden Gophers. Cortes then decided to pursue his passion of art and sports full-time, and enrolled at the prestigious Minneapolis College of Art and Design. He has been painting ever since!

Today Tim lives in Duluth with his wife Kathy and their two children. He continues to play senior hockey and also gives back by coaching both youth football and hockey. In addition, in 2002 Tim was named as the goalie coach for the University of Minnesota-Duluth Women's Hockey program. In 2003 Tim even got to meet President George W. Bush when his three-time NCAA National Champion Lady Bulldogs made their third straight trip to the White House to be honored. Hey, this guy gets around!

THE NATIONAL SPORTS GALLERY

Tim Cortes is one of many talented sporting artists working with publisher Todd Fultz and The National Sports Gallery. Everyone's collective talents have made Todd Fultz Sports Management the Gold Medal Standard in the sports art publishing world. Publisher Todd Fultz's philosophy has and remains to be keeping the edition sizes low to ensure sellouts and collectability. Todd's newest vision of personalization sporting prints has quickly proven to be extremely popular among dedicated athletes and fans alike. The first personalization print available was *"Game Winner"* which enables the clients NAME and NUMBER to be remarqued onto the back of a young goal-scorers hockey jersey. This was followed by another hockey personalization piece *"Prized Possessions"* which features a collection of hockey equipment with the last name of the client remarqued onto the front of the hockey helmet. The latest personalization print concentrates on the game of golf, the vintage golf bag and clubs display a brass member's tag where artist Tim Cortes will remarque the NAME and chosen COURSE! With new Limited Edition Prints as well as Personalization Prints being added every month, visit their gallery in Stillwater or check out their web-site for a complete up-to-date listing. In addition, the National Sports Gallery also offers custom framing packages to showcase all of their fantastic images.

The National Sports Gallery
115 Union Alley
Stillwater, MN 55082
(651) 430-2044

WWW.NATIONALSPORTSGALLERY.COM
&
MAIL@NATIONALSPORTSGALLERY.COM

"Local Legend"

"The Old Ball Game"

"Prized Possessions"

In Memory of Herbie Brooks

A great coach, a great person and a great friend.

1937 — 2003

TABLE OF CONTENTS

FOREWORD BY HERB BROOKS

"Do you believe in miracles?!" "Yes?!" Well... Herb Brooks didn't. That's right. Minnesota's greatest coach, the man who was responsible for that very fabled 1980 Olympic Hockey "Miracle on Ice," instead believed in hard work, commitment and integrity. Nope, there were no short-cuts or divine interventions for this guy. He simply knew how to build teams that could achieve greatness and was a proven winner. A calculating tactician, an innovative strategist, and a superb motivator, Herb Brooks was without question the best of the best. Period. And his story is as amazing as he was.

Herb Brooks grew up on St. Paul's east side loving the game of hockey. After going on to lead his St. Paul Johnson team to the 1955 State High School Hockey Championship, Herb went on to wear the Maroon and Gold at the University of Minnesota. From there he played on two Olympic and five U.S. National teams — more than any player in the history of United States hockey — before coming home to take over as the head coach of his Golden Gophers. The team was in last place in the WCHA at the time Herb took over and in just two years he produced the University of Minnesota's first national championship. Two NCAA National Championships later, Herb had created a dynasty — and more importantly, he did it all with Minnesota kids. Then, in 1980 he fulfilled a life-long dream by becoming the coach of the Olympic team. The historic Gold Medal which ensued would later be named as the "Sports Achievement of the 21st Century," defining a man whose passion for the game has never been equaled.

Herb's coaching success continued into the National Hockey League with the New York Rangers, where he gained 100 victories quicker than any other coach before him and, for his efforts, was named NHL Coach of the Year in 1982. In 1987 Brooks shocked the hockey world yet again, this time by coming came and accepting the head coaching position at St. Cloud State University. He would be revered as the school's savior, ultimately leading them to NCAA Division I status. Herb headed back to the big-time the following season, taking over as the coach of his hometown Minnesota North Stars.

Brooks took some well deserved time away from coaching for a few years after that to embark on a successful business career which included motivational speaking, TV analysis and NHL scouting. In the early 1990s he got the coaching bug again, eventually becoming the head coach of both the New Jersey Devils and Pittsburgh Penguins. He then came full circle in 2002 when he guided the U.S. Olympic team to a silver medal at the Winter Games in Salt Lake City. Once again, Herbie had made America proud.

Tragically, on August 11, 2003, Herb was killed in a one car accident just north of Minneapolis on Interstate 35. Ironically, he was returning home from the U.S. Hockey Hall of Fame Golf Tournament in Northern Minnesota, where he was once again doing his part to promote the growth of American hockey. His funeral was a venerable who's who of the hockey world, with dignitaries, politicians, coaches and fans alike, all coming out to pay their respects to one of the modern patriarchs of the game. One of our nation's most charismatic and innovative coaches, Herbie was a true American hero and a real Minnesota treasure. His legacy will live on forever in the youth of America as they continue to enjoy the fruits of his hard work. In the world of coaching, no one, was larger than Herb Brooks. He was simply the best of the absolute best, and will dearly be missed.

One of our nation's most charismatic and inventive coaches, Herb Brooks was a true American hero. Whether he was competing in the business world, on the ice, or even on the diamond of a world championship fast-pitch softball team, he took the same no-nonsense attitude and intensity to whatever he did, and that's why he was so successful. So, who better to talk about the state-of-the-state of Minnesota's greatest coaches than a true legend with an unbelievable legacy — our very own Herbie Brooks.

"Growing up in St. Paul I was a typical youth hockey player that hung around the rink and just fell in love with the game," said Herb. "I think I was just like any other kid in that when I had a chance to finally make my high school team, it was a big thrill. Then, to win the state championship was very gratifying because it represented the guys I grew up with in the neighborhood. It was a grass-roots type of thrill, and those things stay you for the rest of your life."

"I think that sports really affects the quality of our lives in a positive way here in the state of Minnesota, and I think that what has happened here over the years, has given us a lot to feel good about. We have such a rich sports legacy with so many outstanding athletes, great teams, great fans, great moments, and great people, and that has all gone into making our proud heritage."

"Like so many people, I too am a real Minnesota sports fan. I love to read the sports page and see what is going on. I follow it all, from the amateurs to the college kids to the pros. I am extremely interested in all of our athletes, at all levels, and follow all of our teams very closely. I enjoy reading about our teams and our players and try to keep up with it as much as possible. Of all the athletes I admire I feel that gymnasts are the most unique. They just might be the greatest athletes in the world. Who can do what they can do? I just marvel at them."

"With regards to my own coaching style, I believe in setting high standards for my players. I never wanted to let them slide or have any sort of comfort zone. It is a combination of pushing or pulling them to those standards. I don't think good coaches put greatness into their athletes. You try to create an environment for athletes to pull this greatness out."

"I would also say that I am definitely not a book coach. In fact, I think there are too many book coaches today. You know it's like 'Time-out, I gotta run to the library...' Instead, I would encourage those coaches to study and do research on the academic side of coaching. Then they could try to incorporate that research along with their personality to see how they can best sell those X's and O's to their players. Because really, when you are a coach you are just selling. You are selling team building, you are selling your systems of play, you are selling everything associated with making an individual better, and collectively your team better. I also think they have to be instinctive and be able to react on the turn of a dime, particularly under pressure. Coaching is really a battle for the hearts and minds of your athletes. It is as simple as that."

"I am also a big believer in the philosophy of 'it's not what you say, but how you say it.' I think having the ability to communicate and, once again, having the ability to sell your beliefs is the key to being a successful coach. You have to give your players something to believe in, then they will have something to belong to. Once they have something belong to, then they have something to follow."

"Has coaching has changed over the years? There is no question. I think that every sport has changed, particularly in terms of the knowledge of physiology. Coaches today are also more knowledgeable than ever before as they look at and understand the game. Are they more dynamic? Are they more believable? Are they more personable? Do they have more leadership? I really don't know. But I do think the way they present and prepare for their competition has definitely changed."

"Overall, I think there is a real bright future for hockey in Minnesota. We have the infrastructure in place, we have a lot of wonderful volunteers and we have some very dedicated coaches out there. But I think we have to always remember, at least on the amateur side, what this is for. It is for our young people so that they have a real meaningful environment to play and learn the game. There are a lot of positive things, but we also have to watch out for the 'doing too much too soon for too few' syndrome. Basically, we need to stop narrowing the base of our pyramid. We have to understand that when you have competition without preparation, then there is no real development. Sure, we've got to take care of our elite players by challenging them and bringing them along, but at the same time we can't let other kids, with latent development, fall through the cracks. And these triple A programs, showcase teams, and select programs do little for the real developmental of our players. That is a big concern."

"I also believe that we have more athletes than we have opportunities for them. Sure, we have five division one hockey schools in Minnesota right now, and that is great, but we could easily support another two or three in the area. I think that North Dakota State and Iowa State could make the jump right away for starters. We also have some great division two and three schools here, but overall we have a lot of kids who have the ability to compete at a higher level if given the opportunity."

"Lastly, I feel that we need some changes in high school hockey, particularly at the Minnesota State High School League, which, in my opinion, is really forced mediocrity. There is a lot of room for improvement there. I think that the MSHSL should be asking our coaches one simple question: 'How can we make our student athletes better?'. Nobody knows more what should be done better than our high school coaches and we must listen to them. We should always be looking for new ways to make progress for our athletes. That is the bottom line."

"You know, someone recently asked me at a seminar why I would coach the 2002 Olympic Hockey team after winning the gold medal in 1980, and risk losing credibility. I told him that I was a psychology major in college and asked if he was familiar with Sigmund Freud. Some of Freud's writings dealt with people who avoid stress, competition and anxiety, oftentimes tranquilizing themselves. They wind up sort of sleep-walking through life, never really understanding their true capabilities. So, I guess I never wanted to step away from a challenge, and I am very glad I did it. We came up just short in that gold medal game against Canada, but it was a marvelous experience. I am much better off for having taken on that challenge. That is what life is all about."

"You know, the best coach that I have ever seen would have to be John Wooden. (Wooden built a dynasty at UCLA, leading his teams to a total of 10 NCAA basketball championships throughout the 1960s and '70s.) His philosophy on life, his teaching methods, standards and values were just second to none. He is probably America's greatest coach. He was a man of so much integrity and that is why I admire him so much. I heard him speak once and I was just in awe. He stands for all the right things and has high principles. He is also a fundamentalist but is still able to get his players out of their comfort zones to be better athletes. He was able to build great teams with superstars, and through it all keep them humble. He was able to articulate tremendous values to his players and they respected him for it immensely. He was not just a coach, he was a mentor, a surrogate, and just wore a lot of different hats. For those reasons, I think that is how I would like to be similarly remembered. So, if my legacy to some of my players is similar to how much I respect Coach Wooden, then I would be very honored."

INTRODUCTION

Welcome to "Legends & Legacies," my newest book celebrating more than a century of Minnesota's greatest coaches. Not only does the book include hundreds of biographies of many of our state's greatest coaches, it also features a comprehensive look at just what makes so many of them tick. In many ways this book was somewhat of a departure from my previous coffee-table books in that I wanted to dive in deeper, and really find out the secrets of these people's success. I wanted to know how they motivated their athletes. I wanted to find out what their philosophies on life and see what makes them winners. Hey, we could all use a little coaching wisdom in our lives these days. What I found out was was not only inspiring, it was also fascinating.

While there are many common denominators for achieving success, a good number of these men and women featured in the book have simply found their ways to build a better mouse trap. In fact, what they have to say is oftentimes as shocking as it is enlightening. From the secrets of time management to describing how to build team chemistry — it's all in here. Really, the book is an amalgam of sports history and business self-help, which I hope will make for a very fun read. Regardless of if you are a sports fan, a history buff or just want to read about how to improve your own life, there is something for everybody in here.

I think that all of us have an affinity with coaches, even those of us who weren't athletes. I would say that comes in large part due to the fact that all of us had teachers in grade school and in high school who were also coaches. Many of those teachers stuck around in their communities for 30 or even 40 years, teaching and coaching second and third generations of families along the way. Some of these men and women were like family, and in many instances those relationships were just as paternal or maternal as the ones we had with our own parents.

After more than a year of research and more than 200 lengthy interviews with coaches from all spectrums of the world of sports, the book came to life. What an amazing journey it was to meet and speak to so many truly interesting people. From Ron Gardenhire to Mike Tice and from Jacques Lemaire to Flip Saunders, I heard it all. While their wisdom was sometimes hilarious, other times it was heartwarming and inspiring.

From football to basketball and from baseball to hockey, it's all in here. And I didn't leave out the other sports either. I spoke to a whole bunch of volleyball, softball, wrestling, track & field, cross country, golf, tennis, skiing, swimming, soccer and gymnastics coaches as well.

Each interview I did was an adventure. When you get a chance to ask someone about their life history, it can make for one interesting couple of hours! So, I sat back, turned on my recorder, asked the questions, and then listened. What I heard back was incredible. To hear these people talk about their personal struggles; to follow along as they built their programs into champions; and to listen as they explained the secrets of their success was more than I ever bargained for. After finishing the book, I was truly inspired to be a better, more successful person in my own life.

There were so many fun and interesting things that I was able to uncover. For instance, talking to Bud Grant was awesome. That guy is such a legend and a real hero of mine. He had some really poignant things to say about the state-of-the-state of coaches today and I felt that he added a lot. Other guys, like Gopher Wrestling coach J Robinson, were just as intriguing. The two-time national champion coach has been able to become friends with many of his student-athletes outside of the gym on a social basis, something which is very outside the box in traditional coaching circles — but fascinating nonetheless.

Other things which I thought were interesting included Gopher Basketball coach Jim Dutcher leaving right after his teams' games, because that was what he felt was family time. Find out how former North Stars coach Glen Sonmor really feels about fighting in hockey — I dare you not to laugh yourself silly reading his chapter! Or how about the older guys, who gave up everything to go off and serve our country during World War II. Take Chet Anderson, the wrestling and football coach at Bemidji State, who spent five years as an infantry company commander overseas. His coaching style was no nonsense and full of discipline, as could only be expected from a man who was responsible for the lives of more than 100 young soldiers.

The personal stories were just as unique. Take Oakland Raiders Offensive Coordinator Marc Trestman, from St. Louis Park,

whose 11 year old daughter has already lived in nine different cities. The commitment and sacrifice these people make in pursuit of their dreams is remarkable.

Then, there was Bob Peters, the hockey coach at Bemidji State, who I really enjoyed talking with. Bob is so deep and so well read, that it is hard to believe that he is actually a hockey coach! I mean not many guys in his line of work can talk about hip checks in one breath and then quote Roosevelt in the next. He is great.

What about former Burnsville High School Football coach Dick Hanson, who had no less than 12 VCR's rolling in his basement at all times, recording games non-stop in his lifelong pursuit of finding that one perfect play. I am sure Mrs. Hanson loved that! You know, I was always amazed too at the sacrifice the wives of a lot of these guys made. That was another thing that really struck me. It was a total team effort, and the hours these people put in to be successful was nothing less than epic.

Other coaches were more personal than others. Mike Sertich, the legendary University of Minnesota-Duluth Hockey coach, talked candidly about his relationship with his late father. Others, meanwhile, didn't want to talk at all, like Duluth East Cross Country Coach Dick Skoog, who won a whole bunch of state championships during his tenure in the port city. He just said, "that is personal, and between me and the kids." You know, as much as I wanted to interview that guy, I have to respect his decision.

Other things were just Cliff Claven oddities that I found to be really interesting. For instance, did you know that the 1942 NCAA Basketball Finals between Stanford and Dartmouth featured a pair of former Carleton alums behind the bench? That's right, Everett Dean and Ozzie Cowles, making Minnesota proud. That, is good trivia!

Last, but certainly not least, was Herbie Brooks, who finished writing the foreword for the book just weeks before his tragic death on August 11th. Herbie was a tremendous friend, a great mentor and an unbelievable person. I miss him terribly. In fact, I was with him that unforgettable weekend up at the Hockey Hall of Fame Golf Tournament in Biwabik, and spoke to him just hours before his death. I was actually working with him at the time on writing a series of motivational self-help books. Herb had been approached by some pretty big-time national sports journalists to work with him on the project, but he called me instead. He wanted to keep it local and work with someone he knew and could trust. I was blown away. Herbie is truly a coaching legend with an unbelievable legacy which will live on forever. He was also a good friend, and I will miss our weekly hour-long phone calls dearly. After getting to know him over the years I can see how so many of his former players referred to him as "father-like," he just had that special quality.

All in all, the book came together beautifully, and I couldn't be happier with the finished product. I am truly honored to be able to bring so many wonderful people to life in it and honor their memories. While some of their stories are riveting, others are downright hilarious. And really, the book is as diverse as the people featured in it. That is what makes it so much fun.

You know, nearly every coach I spoke with had one thing in common, and that was the fact that they were interested in helping kids to be better people — both on and off the playing field. Sure, the wins, the championships and the awards were great, but for the most part, these people genuinely cared about helping young people. Just to hear them talk about how great it was for them when their former players would come back and visit with them at school, or for them to see those same kids years later with their own families, all grown up — those were the things that really made it all worth while for these people.

I think back to my old coaches at Fairmont High School, guys I respected so much like Tom Mahoney, who was the all-time winningest football coach in state history; or Freddie Carlson, my hockey coach/dentist, who was just the best. (In Fairmont we didn't have any full-time hockey coaches, they were all volunteers — yet another side of coaches which so often goes unappreciated.) "Doc" and I are great friends to this day and I don't think he will ever know how much fun I had playing hockey for him. All the road-trips to Windom and Luverne, all the nights flooding the rink, and all the Saturday afternoon's out on Hall Lake playing shinny — I certainly didn't learn too much about hockey out there, but I learned a lot about life and had a whole lot of fun — and that was what it was all about.

So, sit back, relax, and enjoy. I hope you have half as much fun reading about these amazing people as I did putting it all together. It was truly an experience of a lifetime.

CAVEAT EMPTOR!

(kâ´vē ât´ emp´tôr)

Hey, this is Latin for "Buyer Beware..."

I feel that it is necessary to issue a caveat of sorts for my new book, and in so doing, explain the parameters as to what it is all about. You know, I will be working on my 30th book this next year, and it seems like every time I write a book like this, I get a whole boat-load of e-mail and letters from people telling me that they were appalled because I forgot to include so-and-so, or that they were shocked because their favorite (*fill in appropriate choice: player, coach, brother, father, sister, fourth cousin, gardener, etc.*) wasn't in my book. With that, I want to formally proclaim right here and now that this book is *not* a list of the greatest coaches of all-time. Period.

Rather, it is a celebration of *many* of our state's greatest coaches. There are so many outstanding men and women deserving of being in a book like this, and for those who I left out, I sincerely apologize. A book which would include all of them would probably take about 10 years to write and would come in at around 10,000 pages. That wouldn't be a book... it would be a major home appliance. Ouch!

So, I chose to highlight a good sampling of local heroes, both native Minnesotans as well as the transplants, at the high school, college, semi-pro and professional levels. Some were obvious choices while others might have been a reach. All of them, however, had a very unique and interesting story to tell, and all of them have touched the lives of countless young people along the way.

In all, I interviewed over 200 current and former coaches for the book. In addition, I featured another several hundred biographies throughout the book as side-bar chapters. I also tried to follow an alphabetical approach as best as possible (*this was really tough due to space constraints*), starting with the big four: baseball, basketball, football and hockey. From there, I hit the other sports, trying to do justice to them all as best as I could. Having said that, I will say that I definitely focused more so on the big four, rather than on the others. And, yes, there are more hockey coaches in the book for obvious reasons... among them being the fact that, yes, it's very, very cold here.

With regards to the criteria for choosing the coaches, I was very open and did not necessarily go by all-time wins or by the most state championships. I tried to include a variety of men and women from across the board who made a difference in their respective sports. So, if your coach, who won hundreds of games and several state championships is not in the book, once again, I am sorry. There were just too many coaches to sift through to make that happen. So, I instead tried to have some fun with a wide variety of outstanding people from the vast world of Minnesota sports.

Now, other than a few basketball sidebars that got thrown into the baseball chapter (*due to space constraints*), for the most part the book follows an alphabetical approach with the main interviewees, with the sidebars just randomly thrown in for good measure. I also tried to follow a question and answer format for the main 200 interviewees as well, which made for some very interesting responses. (*To locate people, there is a table of contents in the front and an index in the back as well.*)

Overall, the book is very fun and informative in nature. I really tried to make it a true blend of sports history and business self-help, and hopefully I succeeded in my mission. I think it is inspirational as well as motivational, and can be picked up or put down on whim — which makes for a very fun read. You know, my books have oftentimes been referred to as the ultimate "bathroom-books," which, as a sports author, you have to take as a compliment!

Most of all, I just tried to honor the countless men and women who have so humbly and graciously coached our moms and dads and sons and daughters, through thick and thin, and for not a lot of money. They do it out of love — a love of the game — and a love of helping others. Coaches are very special people, and I want to honor them for what they do and for what they have done — both for us and for our kids. That is what it is all about. It is not about the wins and losses, it is about the journey. I hope your journey in reading my book was as enjoyable as mine. Thank you. Enjoy!

JOHN ANDERSON
COLLEGE BASEBALL: UNIVERSITY OF MINNESOTA

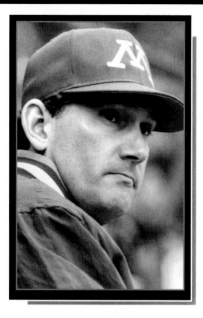

John Anderson was born in Hibbing and went on to graduate from Nashwauk-Keewatin High School in 1973. From there Anderson came down to the University of Minnesota, where he hoped to catch on as a pitcher for legendary baseball coach Dick Siebert's Golden Gophers. After suffering an arm injury that ended his playing career, however, Anderson decided to continue his association with the program as a student coach. So well liked and respected was Anderson, that he was even voted as the team MVP by the players of the 1977 squad — a team that featured Hall of Famer Paul Molitor, and finished sixth at the College World Series. After receiving his degree in Education from Minnesota in 1977, Anderson began his coaching career as a graduate assistant under Siebert in 1978.

That same year, when Coach Siebert tragically died, Anderson was elevated to the position of assistant coach under George Thomas. Upon Thomas' resignation after the 1981 season, Anderson was named as the 13th coach in Golden Gopher history. At just 26 years of age, John Anderson was the youngest baseball coach in Big Ten Conference history. Following in the footsteps of his mentor, Anderson set out to make history in Minnesota, and that is just what he has done. Now entering his 23rd season in the Gopher dugout, Anderson has very quietly become the winningest coach in Gopher history. He surpassed his mentor, Coach Siebert, in 2002 with his 755th career victory, and presently has an overall record of 800-493-3 (.616), including a Big Ten record of 354-171 (.653). Anderson has had 20 straight 30-win seasons in Minnesota — an amazing statistic. Anderson's teams have made appearances in the Big Ten Tournament in 19 of his 22 seasons, winning six Big Ten championships. He has also led Minnesota to 13 NCAA postseason appearances, including the 2000 NCAA Regional, which the Golden Gophers hosted. It was the first time since 1977 that the University of Minnesota played the role of host to a regional tournament. Additionally, Anderson has developed and coached 10 All-Americans and sent 61 players on to professional baseball, including five currently in the major leagues.

Among his many coaching accolades and honors, Anderson has been named Big Ten Coach of the Year on four occasions: 1982, 2000, 2002 and 2003. In addition, Anderson has coached a total of 96 Academic All-Big Ten selections and has coached 182 U of M Scholar-Athlete Award winners. John was also inducted into the 'M' Club Hall of Fame in 2002 as well.

Known for fairness in dealing with his players, Anderson believes his number one responsibility is to prepare his athletes for the next phase of their lives. Providing his players with the necessary opportunities to mature and gain a greater understanding of life's lessons is what it is all about for Anderson. An outstanding recruiter and an overall good friend to the game of baseball, John Anderson is amongst the most respected people in all of baseball. One of the youngest collegiate coaches ever to win 800 games and the only Big Ten coach to ever reach 300 conference victories, John Anderson has had a lifetime of coaching experience — and he is only 48 years old! Now poised to help get a new baseball stadium built on campus, Anderson is just gearing up for his next 800 wins — and with them will most certainly be a national championship. John and his wife Jan have one daughter, Erin Elizabeth, and reside in the Twin Cities.

HOW WOULD YOU DESCRIBE YOUR COACHING STYLE? "I think in the latter stages of my career I have become more of a consultant. I have tried to encourage people to become

interested, accountable and responsible for their own careers and just provide support for them where they need it. Rather than being a person who gets my players out of bed in the morning, walks them to class, makes them show up for study time, and makes it mandatory that they put in X amount of hours outside of the regular practice time, I think I have become more of a person who has tried to teach people how to become internally motivated. I want to help them decide what it is that is important to them and what it is that they want to get out of their careers. Philosophically this has been my new style and approach to coaching and it has worked out well. I want my kids to be independent, critical thinkers who can map out a path for themselves. In the end I think the kids can take some ownership in the process and from what they accomplish. To me it's more about internal motivation versus external motivation based on realistic expectations."

HOW DO YOU MOTIVATE YOUR PLAYERS? "My motivation comes first from finding out what we want to do as a team and then trying to get my players to motivate themselves. I think as a group you are much more effective if the players within the group hold each other accountable for the day to day effort it takes to accomplish their goals. My motivation comes from educating them and helping them agree upon some realistic expectations and goals. I think occasionally players might need a little push every now and then and at that point I sit down with my players and discuss their situation, whether it means helping them reevaluate their goals or just getting them to focus and work harder, that is where I step in. Overall, I would rather motivate people by sitting down with them and getting a sense of who they are, what they want to become and where they want to end up. Then, I can help them set goals and or change their behavior. I am not a yeller or a screamer. I don't believe in making my guys run or doing physical things if they are not working hard enough or are not going to class. I would rather take away their privileges and tell them that until their expectations and responsibilities are raised, then they can't come to practice or maybe play in a game. Some people motivate people by making them dependent upon them, and forcing them to do things by fear or intimidation, but that is just not me at all."

IF YOU COULD MAGICALLY GO BACK IN TIME TO THE FIRST YEAR YOU WERE A HEAD COACH AND GIVE YOURSELF SOME ADVICE FOR THE FUTURE, KNOWING WHAT YOU KNOW NOW, BACK THEN, WHAT WOULD YOU SAY TO YOURSELF? "Sometimes you need to work smarter versus harder and early in my career I was more inclined to just do more. I don't think that I completely understood the process on what it takes to be successful at that point. I think early on in your career you tend to think more is better and now that I have grown as a coach I think you probably get more out of your players if you actually do less or even take a day off. Sometimes we tend to practice harder and push our kids harder before big games and that is not always the best way to go. I just think you need to plan and be organized. Success is a process and a journey, it is not necessarily trying to cram as much as you can into a short period of time. Quality of work is more important than quantity and sometimes less is more. It's also easy when you're a young coach to just blame everything on the kids — I call that 'blame, blame and complain.' You can blame the kids and then complain about it all you want, and that is an easy thing to do, but you need to take a look at yourself first and foremost and how you are contributing to the problem. You have to ask yourself if you have done a good enough job in teaching the kids so that they can perform. Did you spend enough time and prepare them for that particular situation? It's easy to just say that they are not good enough or that they don't care or they don't want to work hard enough. So, it's easy as a young coach to point the blame elsewhere rather than at yourself, and it starts with the person at the top. You have to examine your role in the problem or in the process before you can point fingers."

HOW DO YOU BUILD TEAM UNITY & CHEMISTRY? "I think people assume you can just take 30 or 40 kids and throw them into a room and make them a team. It couldn't be further from the truth. Building chemistry is an ongoing process and first and foremost it starts with an understanding of who you are and what you are all about. Then you need to get people all on the same page and agree on some common goals together. I also think that you have to create a role for everybody on your team, whether they are regulars or not. They have to clearly know what that role is and what their job is to help the team be successful. If they don't want to accept that role then they need to make a decision about going elsewhere. It just starts with getting everybody on the same page and everybody having a clear vision for who they are, what they are all about and what they are trying to accomplish. Then, you need to hold people accountable to their roles. If certain players don't want to fulfill those roles, then they need to be addressed, or even asked to leave. You need to be a team and unless everyone is together, it can't happen. This is something that has to be developed and grown. It changes every season as you get new people, new personalities and different circumstances. The bottom line for a coach, however, is that you need to have the same rules and expectations for all the players. You also can't have different expectations for your stars, you have to be consistent otherwise the players won't respect what you are doing. To create chemistry you have to have people who are willing to talk to one another and challenge others who aren't pulling their weight. It comes from within the group and dealing internally with problems rather than always running to the coaches. I think as coaches we want to jump in and solve all their problems, rather than giving them a chance to figure it out as a group."

WHAT'S THE BIGGEST THING YOU'VE LEARNED FROM COACHING THAT YOU'VE BEEN ABLE TO APPLY TO YOUR EVERYDAY LIFE? "How to solve problems, deal with adversity and overcome failure. I know that I am a good person regardless of whether I win or lose. Also, I have learned so much about people and relationships from coaching and I am a better person because of it."

WHAT ARE THE KEY INGREDIENTS TO CREATING A CHAMPIONSHIP TEAM? "First and foremost you need a group of coaches that compliment one another and respect one another really well. Then, you need talent. I think in any successful business or organization you have those same traits. Then, you need consistency, trust and a solid effort from your players. It is also very important that you learn from your mistakes so that you can always get better."

WHAT'S THE SECRET TO YOUR SUCCESS? "Longevity, perseverance and patience. The greatest teacher in the world is failure and we learn more from failure than we do from our successes. I also think that the more difficult it gets, the better coach you become. I just love the challenge of solving problems that you encounter along the way in the teaching and coaching environment. You know, I learned so much from Dick Siebert. He taught me that you can never think you know it all. You need to enlist as many people as you can, ask questions, seek out advice and study how other successful people do things. I remember a sign he had in his office that read 'The four

most important words: What is your opinion?' Dick used to always listen to anybody who he thought could help him, and I have tried to follow that in my career. You know I don't think you can ever wake up in the morning and say you have all the answers. In our business you either grow or die, you don't stay the same. So you have to remain open minded and flexible."

WHAT WOULD YOU WANT TO SAY TO YOUR FANS, BOOSTERS, AND ALUMNI WHO HAVE SUPPORTED YOU ALL THESE YEARS? "You can't accomplish great things in life without other people helping you and encouraging you along the way. No one can do it all by themselves and I have had so many great assistant coaches, players, fans, alumni and supporters through the years, it has just been wonderful. So many people have supported me through the years and I can't thank them enough. I appreciate their support so much and it has helped immensely to make the Gopher baseball family what it is today. The success doesn't just belong to me, we can all share in it because it wouldn't be possible without them."

HOW DO YOU WANT YOUR COACHING EPITAPH TO READ — HOW DO YOU WANT TO BE REMEMBERED AS A COACH? "I would want to be remembered as a person who made a difference in other people's lives and cared about them as people, not just as baseball players. I also hope that I was someone that my players could trust, respect and lived up to his word."

HAYDEN FOX: THE MINNESOTA STATE "SCREAMING EAGLES"

Craig T. Nelson, A.K.A. "Hayden Fox," was the fictitious head coach of the late 1980s and early 1990s ABC show "Coach," which chronicled the life and times of a bumbling coach, his bone-head assistants, "Luther" and "Dauber," and their mythical college football team — the "Minnesota State Screaming Eagles." The show used old Gopher football video footage from the Metrodome that was even color enhanced to make the maroon jerseys appear as purple. One can only assume that Minnesota State Mankato's decision to change their name from Mankato State University to Minnesota State had anything to do with the television show being cancelled. Or maybe it did! Who knows?

DEAN BOWYER
COLLEGE BASEBALL: UNIVERSITY OF MINNESOTA

Dean Bowyer grew up in Ada and went on to graduate from Ada High School in 1962. From there Bowyer attended Mayville State College, where he was an all-conference football player and also played baseball and basketball. Bowyer then went on to play baseball briefly in the minor leagues in the Baltimore Orioles organization. Bowyer's first coaching stint was at Barnsville High School in 1966, where he coached football and basketball. From there, Bowyer went to Vietnam to serve in the military and upon his discharge, he wound up in Appleton, where he taught at an elementary school and coached baseball in 1969. Bowyer then became a graduate assistant at Minnesota State Mankato, where he got his masters degree in physical education. In 1971 Bowyer went to Benson High School to teach and coach baseball for one year, and in 1972 he got the head baseball coaching position at Minot State, N.D., where he led his teams to a couple of conference titles. Four years later, in 1976, Bowyer took over as the head baseball coach at Minnesota State from Jean McCarthy. Since then, he has become a baseball coaching legend.

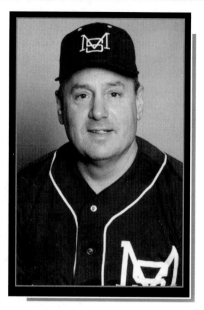

In 2003 Bowyer completed his 27th season at Minnesota State and his 31st as a collegiate head coach. Bowyer, who has led the Mavericks to 19 conference titles and is a nine-time North Central Conference Coach of the Year, owns a 797-396-7 (.667) mark in his tenure at MSU and stands 871-447-7 (.660) as a college head coach. Bowyer now ranks among the top five winningest active NCAA Division II coaches in the country and is 10th for all-time career wins. Bowyer has also led the Mavericks to 18 NCAA post-season appearances and berths in three NCAA Division II World Series, where his teams finished fourth in 1979, third in 1980 and seventh in 1986. Under Bowyer, the Mavericks have won at least 30 games in a season 17 times and during his tenure at MSU 39 players have signed professional contracts — two of which made it all the way to the "show," Todd Revenig with the Oakland A's in 1992 and Gary Mielke with the Texas Rangers from 1987-90.

Bowyer's success can be attributed to his ability to recruit and develop talent. Overall, however, he is a player's coach, and that is why his players love him. And hey, did you know that this guy can bowl? That's right. In addition to teaching four bowling classes per semester in the physical education department at Minnesota State, he is also one of the top bowling instructors in the country. Go figure!

HOW WOULD YOU DESCRIBE YOUR COACHING STYLE? "I think I wear my emotions on my sleeve. I am also not a negative person, I believe in being positive. Sometimes mental mistakes deserve chewing out, but I think you get a lot further with your guys if you are positive instead. A big part of this game is confidence and if you are running the ballplayers down then you are taking away from their ability to perform."

HOW DO YOU MOTIVATE YOUR PLAYERS? "I think it comes down to sense of pride and tradition. Because we don't have a lot of money for scholarships, players that come into our program really love the game and have a passion for the game. I think that is their motivation. Most of our kids have incredible work ethics and that is what has given us the success that we have had throughout the years. I think that they are there to learn and we just try and teach them the game the best that we can. From there, I try to talk to guys individually and work with them on specific things that they need to improve on. Really though, we recruit guys who are pretty self-moti-

vated, so we just have to get them mentally prepared before each game."

WHO ARE YOUR COACHING MENTORS? "My high school coach at Ada, Bill Brady, was a great coach. He was very respected and knew the game well. He demanded a lot from us but was pretty even keeled, he wasn't a yeller or a screamer. Through him I knew that I wanted to become a coach. Then, my college coach at Mayville State was Al Meyer, who is a coaching legend in North Dakota. He really knew the game and I learned a great deal from him too. Then, I would have to say that my biggest mentor was Cal Ripken Sr. I played for him for two years in the minors when I was with Aberdeen, S.D., in the Northern League, and he taught me that you can play hard but you can still have fun. And that has really stuck with me to the point where I have tried to incorporate that same philosophy into my own coaching style."

IF YOU COULD MAGICALLY GO BACK IN TIME TO THE FIRST YEAR YOU WERE A HEAD COACH AND GIVE YOURSELF SOME ADVICE FOR THE FUTURE, KNOWING WHAT YOU KNOW NOW, BACK THEN, WHAT WOULD YOU SAY TO YOURSELF? "I made so many mistakes when I was young, but like anything in life, experience is the greatest teacher. So, I would tell him, 'you don't know what is in store for you tomorrow, so play as hard as you can. Enjoy each day, enjoy the abilities that God gave you and play to the full potential that you have.'"

WHAT ARE THE CHARACTERISTICS OF LEADERS? "A leader is a person who works hard in whatever they do, whether it is conditioning or hitting or what have you. A good leader is one who will lead by example, and that is how they earn the respect of their teammates. My leaders are the 'soul of our team' because they don't let the team lose. I have also had some great quiet leaders too, who led by how hard they worked and by showing how badly they wanted to win. So, there are different types of leaders. You know, the coach can motivate, but you have to have the soul of the team — one guy, usually our captain, who the players really respect. He is there to make sure the guys play as hard as they can and keep it all in perspective by reminding them that they are out there to win. Then, I also think that you need a goofy guy to keep people loose and make sure that the kids are having fun. That is sometimes just as important. I try to recruit both types of players because that will build chemistry."

LOOKING BACK WHAT ARE YOU MOST PROUD OF IN YOUR CAREER? "The consistency of our program has remained outstanding through the years and I am very proud of that because that means as a coach, you have had some great kids. I have always said that if the team does well then the individuals reap the benefits, so I am proud of our 19 conference championships over the past 27 years. It never gets old and I am still having fun."

WHAT IS THE KEY TO RECRUITING? "I try to recruit kids who have the same passion for the game that I do. Then, even if you don't win, you are going to have fun because your kids just want to play the game. Beyond that, you have to do as much homework as you can to find the right kinds of players which will fit in your program. I talk to their coaches, their teammates, their friends, their parents, and even the parents of their friends, to get a better idea of who that person is. If you get a kid who is a good ballplayer but does not have a passion or is lazy, then they are not going to fit in. So, I do a lot of homework to check out their makeup and their work ethic."

HOW DO YOU BUILD TEAM UNITY & CHEMISTRY? "I think you need to have fun out there and we try to do that. You also need to recruit the right kinds of kids who will get along and will play well together. I think that there is a correlation between academics and baseball too. I mean if you get kids who are dedicated and disciplined in the classroom, then they are going to be the same way on the baseball diamond. They pick up things quicker and are students of the game. So, if you get good student-athletes, then you have a much better chance of getting more well rounded players. Beyond that, I think our kids really bond together when they spend time together on road trips and that kind of thing. Chemistry is an odd thing, but it is very important to your team's success."

WHAT MOTIVATES YOU? "I just enjoy working with young people. I am also very happy to see our kids get opportunities to go on and do well after college as well. That is what it is all about. Then, to see them give back to the program after they graduate, that is the most gratifying thing to see. That tells you that they had a great experience here and as a coach you can't help but feel good about that."

WHAT ADVICE WOULD YOU HAVE FOR YOUNG COACHES STARTING OUT TODAY? "I think the most important thing is to just know the game, because if you know the game then your guys are going to respect you. That is so important because they don't have to like you, but they have to respect the knowledge that you have. Then they will work hard for you and work hard to improve their skills. The next thing I would say is to be organized. Beyond that, I would say make sure that your games and practices are fun because baseball is a fun sport. Don't ever forget that."

WHAT'S THE SECRET TO YOUR SUCCESS? "I surround myself with good people. I have never had a full-time assistant coach, but I have had great graduate assistants. I am also lucky that my son has been able to coach with me for several years now as well. He has great knowledge of the game and I am very proud of him. Beyond that I work very hard and truly believe that there are no shortcuts."

WHAT WOULD YOU WANT TO SAY TO YOUR FANS, BOOSTERS, AND ALUMNI WHO HAVE SUPPORTED YOU ALL THESE YEARS? "The support that we have received financially from our alumni has given us the chance to do so many more things now, with regards to traveling, that we couldn't do before and that is just wonderful. Our alumni, supporters, parents and fans are great and that is what allows this tradition to continue. So, thanks to all of you because without you we wouldn't be where we are today."

HOW DO YOU WANT YOUR COACHING EPITAPH TO READ — HOW DO YOU WANT TO BE REMEMBERED AS A COACH? "As a person who knew the game, could teach the game and had a passion for the game. I also hope that I made the people around me better by being a good coach."

TOP 20 ALL-TIME STATE HIGH SCHOOL CHAMPIONSHIPS
(ALL SPORTS COMBINED: 1913-2002)

	SCHOOL	TOTAL
1.	Edina	85
2.	Stillwater Area	46
3.	Apple Valley	40
4.	Duluth Central	37
5.	Minnetonka	34
6.	Bloomington Jefferson	33
6.	Burnsville	33
8.	Blake School	31
8.	Duluth East	31
10.	Rochester Lourdes	29
11.	Hopkins	25
	Virginia	25
13.	Hibbing	23
	Minneapolis Southwest	23
15.	Robbinsdale Armstrong	21
	Wayzata	21
17.	Anoka	20
	Rochester	20
19.	Austin	19
	Minneapolis North	19

Source: MSHSL

JOHN BAGGS: ST. SCHOLASTICA BASEBALL

John Baggs was born in Chicago and grew up playing baseball in Hanover Park. He then went on to play third base at Iowa State University, graduating in 1989. Two years later, Baggs was hired to serve as the head baseball coach at St. Scholastica. At just 24, Baggs immediately became the youngest head collegiate baseball coach in the country. Coach Baggs is credited with turning the CSS baseball team into a nationally-ranked program. The Saints won just 34 games in the five years prior to his arrival in Duluth and since then, his Saints have won 170 games in the last five years. Baggs has also directed the Saints to a Top 20 NAIA national ranking in 1997, 1999, and 2000, and an NCAA Top 20 national ranking in both 1998 and 1999. For his efforts, Baggs earned Louisville Slugger Coach of the Year awards in 1996, 1997, 1998 and 2000, and was named UMAC Coach of the Year in 1997, 1999 and 2000 as well. Earning his highest honors after leading the Saints to 41-11 record and regional championship in 2000, Baggs was also named ABCA Regional Coach of the Year and was a finalist for the NAIA National Coach of the Year award that year as well.

Described by his players as a "demanding player's coach," Baggs also has a 27-3 record coaching USA teams internationally. In 1996, Baggs was selected to coach Team USA II, an NCAA all-star team that won the International Series '96 in Apeldoorn, Holland. The next summer he was chosen to coach Team America and led that team to the first place trophy in Solingen, Germany. In addition, Baggs has been a member of the Pro Baseball-College Baseball relations committee and currently serves on the national rules committee. He has also served as Chairman for the NAIA Midwest Region. Now in his 12th year as Head Baseball Coach at the College of St. Scholastica, John Baggs has built a program that continues to draw attention both at the national and local level. In 1998, Baggs became the winningest coach ever at St. Scholastica, in any sport. Baggs and his wife Colleen live in Duluth and have one son, Maddux.

BUCKY BURGAU
COLLEGE BASEBALL: CONCORDIA

Donald "Bucky" Burgau grew up in Perham, where he learned to love the game of baseball. As a 16-year-old, Bucky played second base alongside his dad and uncle for the Perham Pirates town team, which won the state amateur title in 1966. After graduating from high school in 1969, Bucky went on to play two years of college baseball at Fergus Falls Community College before enrolling at North Dakota State University. There, Burgau played under Coach Arlo Brunsberg, a Concordia graduate and member of the Cobber Athletic Hall of Fame. Upon graduation, Bucky took his first coaching job with the Perham American Legion. In 1973, he became head coach of the Moorhead American Legion Blues, where he would coach for 27 years, compiling a 883-396 record and 18 District Nine titles along the way. (In 1988, his Legion team won the state title, as well as the Central Plains Regional title, and finished fourth in the American Legion World Series.)

In 1977 Burgau came to Concordia to serve as the equipment manager and assistant baseball coach. He became head coach in 1979 and since then, Cobber teams have been consistent contenders for the MIAC crown. Under Burgau the Cobbers won MIAC titles in 1985, 1993 and 1995, and have finished in the league's upper division in 18 of his 24 seasons at Concordia. His teams are 284-169 in the MIAC and overall he is has amassed nearly 500 wins. Bucky and his wife Penny live in Moorhead and they have two daughters; Jennifer and Rachel.

HOW WOULD YOU DESCRIBE YOUR COACHING STYLE? "I think I am a players-coach whereas I try and work within the needs of a player. I try to make it as fun as I possibly can for them within the framework of baseball, which is playing the game the way I think it should be played."

HOW DO YOU MOTIVATE YOUR PLAYERS? "I just come to work every day. That is the biggest thing that I can show my guys. Hard work, discipline and respect. That is how I motivate my players. You know, another thing we do here at Concordia is that we wear our game uniforms everyday for practice. All of the little things like that make a big difference with me and they all add up to big things. I want our kids to be motivated and to be proud of our program."

WHO ARE YOUR COACHING MENTORS? "My first mentor was my college coach at North Dakota State, Arlo Brunsberg, a Concordia grad who went on to play nine years of minor league baseball in the Tigers organization, and he really taught me the ins and outs of baseball. The second guy was Halvor Johnson, the athletic director of the Moorhead American Legion program. I coached the Moorhead Blues for 27 summers and he showed me the importance of good discipline, respect and sportsmanship. Then, when I was growing up, Chuck Shumaker was my B-squad basketball coach and he was like a father-figure to me. My parents were going through a divorce and had no money at that time, and he took me under his wing and would take me out to shoot pool and talk about life with me when at a time when I really needed a friend. Then, I can't forget about Max Molock down at St. Mary's too, he always took care of me as well. Finally, getting to know Jim Christopherson, the legendary football coach here at Concordia, has been so wonderful. Seeing him touch base with his kids has had a profound affect on me and how I go about my daily business. So, I have had some great mentors and they all went into who I am as a coach and as a person."

IF YOU COULD MAGICALLY GO BACK IN TIME TO THE FIRST YEAR YOU WERE A HEAD COACH AND GIVE YOURSELF SOME ADVICE FOR THE FUTURE, KNOWING WHAT YOU KNOW NOW, BACK THEN, WHAT WOULD YOU SAY TO YOURSELF? "I would tell that guy not to puff his chest out so much and to learn from the people that have been in the business for a long time. I would also tell him not to think that he knew more than they did and to learn from each and every one of those coaches who have been there before him along the way."

WHAT ARE THE CHARACTERISTICS OF WINNERS? "It is staying on task every darn day. It is having a love for the game. It is having a love for winning. You know, none of us ever want to lose, but sometimes losing is good because it forces us to learn lessons that we can carry forward in our lives to become better."

LOOKING BACK WHAT ARE YOU MOST PROUD OF IN YOUR CAREER? "I am really proud of my longevity because I think that says something about how I have done it over the long haul. I am always trying to learn as much as I can so that I can help these kids better themselves in baseball and in life. Then, another fun thing that I am proud of is when I was 16 years old I threw the final out of the 1966 state amateur title game for Perham with my father playing next to me at first base. Not many people can say that."

WHAT IS THE KEY TO RECRUITING? "Getting on the phone and working hard. I don't have a travel budget so I have to work hard on the phones. Beyond that it is introducing yourself to the kids and meeting their moms and dads. You have to get to know them and have them get to know you so that they can feel comfortable with you and your program. You know, Concordia, as an academic institution, sells itself, so I just need to sell them on our baseball program. Sure, sometimes the cold northern climate works against us, but we get in our 30-40 ballgames per year. Because of that I really concentrate my recruiting effort to within 200 miles or so, because those kids are already used to cold weather baseball. We also try to get kids who are two-sport athletes. We don't have Spring football in Division III, so kids can play football in the Fall and baseball in the Spring, and that works out great for a lot of kids."

HOW DO YOU BUILD TEAM UNITY & CHEMISTRY? "Through hard work and by me showing the kids that this game is darn important. We set goals and we try to reach them. I try to show my kids that winning and being a keeper of the game is very important and hopefully that will build unity amongst the players. You know, another thing here at the Division III level is that all of the field maintenance at our ballpark is entirely up to us. So, we require all of our kids to put in as much time as possible out on the field after practice to make sure it looks good. That brings us together as a team and gives us great pride in knowing that we are all in this together. That is a fun time too, where we can relax a little big and get to know each other better. All of that goes into building team unity."

WHAT MOTIVATES YOU? "First of all, if there wasn't a fear of losing then winning wouldn't be a whole lot of fun. You know, I just love this game and what it stands for. The blue sky, the green grass, the strategies of the game — all of those things motivate me to be the best I can be. I grew up in Perham loving baseball and I still love it today. It is just a wonderful game."

WHAT ADVICE WOULD YOU HAVE FOR YOUNG COACHES STARTING OUT TODAY? "Listen to your peers and don't worry about punching a time clock because during the season it is from dusk to dawn. I would also tell them to be a keeper of the game, and by that I mean have your guys play baseball the way it was meant to be played. Play it hard from the first pitch of the season to the last. Sprint on and off the field between innings. Make the fans want to come back and see you play. Have your kids wear their uniforms right. Win or lose have your kids go across the field after the game and show the proper respect to the other team and the other coach. Have them do the little things, like respecting the flag when they are singing the National Anthem. That is real important."

WHAT'S THE BIGGEST THING YOU'VE LEARNED FROM COACHING THAT YOU'VE BEEN ABLE TO APPLY TO YOUR EVERYDAY LIFE? "I think that baseball is a great teacher of life because there is so much failure in it. If I have learned anything from baseball it is to be patient, to not take things for granted, to not to let your emotions run amok, and most importantly, to learn to deal with failure."

WHAT'S THE SECRET TO YOUR SUCCESS? "Hey, anything that I have used or have in our program — it's not me, I begged, borrowed or stole it from somebody else. And I think any good coach will tell you the same thing. We all use things from different people and that goes into our success both on and off the field. Other than that it is all about respect — respect for my players and respect for my peers."

WHAT WOULD YOU WANT TO SAY TO YOUR FANS, BOOSTERS, AND ALUMNI WHO HAVE SUPPORTED YOU ALL THESE YEARS? "The fans up here have been wonderful to me and I would just say thanks for your support. Thanks too for respecting what I am trying to do with my kids, whether it was at the American Legion level or at Concordia, I really appreciate it. This is more than just a game and we are trying to teach these kids a lot of good things that we think they can use later in life."

HOW DO YOU WANT YOUR COACHING EPITAPH TO READ — HOW DO YOU WANT TO BE REMEMBERED AS A COACH? "Bucky was a keeper of the game and he taught the game right. Whenever an opposing team stepped onto the field against my teams they had better have been ready to rock and roll, because we were going to give it our best effort. They might not always have won, but they played hard from the first pitch to the last."

GENE GLYNN: SAN FRANCISCO GIANTS

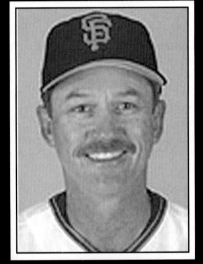

Gene Glynn grew up in Waseca and went on to be named as the very first "Mr. Basketball Minnesota" in 1975. From there, Glynn played basketball and baseball at Mankato State University before going on to play professional baseball. The second baseman was first signed by the Montreal Expos as a free agent in 1979 and would spend a total of seven seasons in the minor leagues. Glynn would have four stints at the triple-A level with Wichita in 1982-83 and Indianapolis in 1984-85, before retiring in 1985 as the player/coach with Indianapolis, under manager Felipe Alou.

From there, Glynn made his coaching debut in the Montreal system. Over the next 18 seasons Glynn would climb the coaching ladder, going from Jacksonville to West Palm Beach to Rockford to Spokane, where he was named Northwest League Manager of Year in 1990, to Waterloo to Colorado, where he served as the Rockies first base coach under manager Don Baylor. Glynn then went back to Montreal, serving as Alou's first base coach for a season, before moving on to spend the next three seasons as the Chicago Cubs third base coach under manager Don Baylor. In 2003 Glynn was hired to serve as the San Francisco Giants third base coach. Gene and his wife Julie have two sons, Gino and Christopher, and reside in the San Francisco Bay area.

MAX MOLOCK: ST. MARY'S BASEBALL

Max Molock was a baseball legend at Saint Mary's University in Winona. Molock, who was a multi-sport star for the Cardinals, graduated from Saint Mary's in 1936. In 1940 Molock took over as the head baseball coach at the school, while also serving as an assistant on the football and basketball teams. Also serving as the intramural director as well as an instructor in the physical education department, Molock would become a St. Mary's coaching legend. He would later even coach the hockey team from 1958-62 and later establish the school's wrestling program. On the baseball diamond is where he would make his biggest impact though. In all, Molock would guide his Cardinal baseball squads to 11 MIAC titles and achieve a conference record of 234-118 along the way.

Among his many coaching honors and accolades, Molock is a member of the NAIA Hall of Fame. In addition, Molock was later honored by St. Mary's when their baseball field was renamed as Max Molock Field in his honor. The MIAC also honored the legendary coach by naming their annual conference award after him as well — the Max Molock MIAC Most Valuable Player Award. Max Molock was a St. Mary's baseball icon and will forever be remembered as a coach who made a difference.

DENNIS DENNING
HIGH SCHOOL & COLLEGE BASEBALL: CRETIN & ST. THOMAS

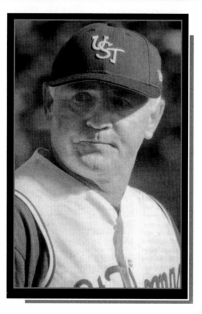

Dennis Denning grew up along West Seventh Street in St. Paul near the old brewery. Denning went on to attend Cretin High School, where, after failing to make the cut in his first three seasons, he finally made the varsity as a senior. Denning did have some success in the Summer months though, as his American Legion teams won three straight championships. From there Denning went on to play baseball at St. Thomas. After college Denning then signed with the Orioles as a catcher, but wound up playing infield in their minor league system. Denning made it to the Triple A level, but, after severely breaking his wrist, he called it a career. Denning then came home to teach at the elementary and junior high levels for 10 years before coming to Cretin-Derham Hall in 1977 to teach physical education, coach baseball and serve as the school's athletic director. Denning taught and coached baseball at Cretin for 17 years, creating a dynasty along the way. In all, he would post an amazing 378-76 (.833) record with the program. Denning's Raiders won their first two state titles in 1981 and 1982, and just kept on rolling from there, winning four more in 1986, 1989, 1990 and 1992 as well. Among the outstanding athletes Denning coached in baseball were NFL quarterbacks Steve Walsh and Chris Weinke, who also won the Heisman Trophy at Florida State in 2000. In addition, Denning also coached former Twins All-Star Paul Molitor in elementary school as well.

In 1994 Denning left Cretin to take over as the head coach at his alma mater, St. Thomas University. To no one's surprise, Denning wasted little time in putting St. Thomas baseball on the national map. In his nine seasons as the head coach, his Tommies have built the third-best won-loss record in all of Division III baseball at 314-80. Denning, who led the Tommies to NCAA runner-up finishes in 1999 and 2000, saw his 2001 team finish 10-2 in postseason play and win the first national baseball championship in school history. Despite graduating their top two pitchers from 2000, the 2001 Tommies won 27 of their first 31 games and held the No. 1 Division III ranking throughout April. An early-May slump dropped them to a third-place conference finish and nearly doused their NCAA play-off hopes, but the Toms went 3-0 to win the MIAC tournament and secured their seventh consecutive NCAA bid. From there they went 3-1 to win the NCAA Midwest Regional, and went on to win the Division III College World Series. Their 8-4 championship win over Marietta gave them a 39-10 overall record, and put them into the history books forever. Upon winning the title, Denning was named as the Division III National Baseball Coach of the Year. In addition, Denning's Tommies have won either the MIAC regular-season or post-season title in each of the last eight seasons, and reached the NCAA playoffs in eight of his nine seasons as well. Denning has also produced seven Division III All-Americans, with four of those honorees going on to be selected in the major-league baseball amateur draft. Simply put, Dennis Denning is a baseball coaching legend.

HOW WOULD YOU DESCRIBE YOUR COACHING STYLE? "You know, the key is just being a good person, working hard and being nice to everybody. Really, that's it. Beyond that I will say that I work real hard and I don't think there is anybody who out-works me. That brings some success. I also have very high expectations. I expect my kids to be good listeners, have a good work ethic and have a passion for the game. I would say that my teams are fundamentally sound too, and that we are pretty good with mechanics and with implementing our strategy. Beyond that it is all about a good, hard effort from my players. I also want our kids to have fun, that is very important too. I am lucky though, we have great kids here and that makes my job a lot easier."

HOW DO YOU MOTIVATE YOUR PLAYERS? "On the first day of practice every year I tell my kids what my expectations are and that I do play favorites. I tell them that if they want to tell their parents that I play favorites that it is OK, because I want to get it out of the way right away. Then, I tell them who my favorites are: guys who listen, guys that make good plays, guys who hustle, and guys who are nice to everybody on the team. You know, one of our goals is that I want every guy to try and be the best liked guy on the team — that is how you get good chemistry. I also try to get my kids to relax. I want them to have a high level of concentration, but I want them to be comfortable out there."

HOW HAS COACHING CHANGED THROUGH THE YEARS? "You know, 40 years ago it was so much different. Coaching has changed in that time so much that it is really unbelievable. The coaches were disciplinarians back then and would even hit guys to make a point. Nowadays, it is totally different and you have to be very sensitive as to whatever you say and do. I think I personally have changed in that I have mellowed and maybe become a little bit more understanding, but I still expect a lot from my kids. I expect my kids to be good human beings, to have a good presence on the baseball field, and to work hard."

IF YOU COULD MAGICALLY GO BACK IN TIME TO THE FIRST YEAR YOU WERE A HEAD COACH AND GIVE YOURSELF SOME ADVICE FOR THE FUTURE, KNOWING WHAT YOU KNOW NOW, BACK THEN, WHAT WOULD YOU SAY TO YOURSELF? "I would say don't make rash judgments and learn as much as you can about this game. If you try and learn as much as you can, then you can go out and teach it."

WHAT ARE THE CHARACTERISTICS OF LEADERS? "I tell my captains that none of their teammates are ever going to remember them because they hit .350 or because they hit 10 home runs. What they will remember is whether or not they were nice guys or whether or not they were jerks. So I tell them to be good guys, be nice to everybody and be good leaders."

LOOKING BACK WHAT ARE YOU MOST PROUD OF IN YOUR CAREER? "That I have never missed a day of work. I have been working for more than 30 years and I have never, ever missed a day. The bottom line is that as a coach, you can't miss out, because you have that commitment to your kids and to your team. I am also proud of all the kids that I got the opportunity to coach over the years, that is special. And you know, it is not all about the famous kids who went on to bigger and better things either. It is about a lot of different kids who were just fun to be around and who were good kids. I remember one kid back at Cretin in particular, Mark Wagner, who is actually a Major League umpire now. He got cut from our B-squad because he had a weak arm. So, one Summer he taught himself how to throw with the opposite arm. Well, he came back and made the team. He even went on to make captain of the varsity as a senior, and helped lead our team to a state championship as well. It is guys like that who made it all worth it."

HOW DO YOU BUILD TEAM UNITY & CHEMISTRY? "How come everybody mentions chemistry after a team wins the World Series? Because everything is easier when you are winning. A good coach builds good chemistry even when his teams are losing. Sometimes too, you have to do stuff as a team. Maybe it is running as a group, or taking a team outing or just having fun together. You need the kids to get to know each other outside of the game and to become friends, that is the key."

WHAT MOTIVATES YOU? "You know, winning our national championship was a great experience. But do you know what I remember most about it? The five and a half hour bus ride home from Appleton. The kids were just going crazy and it was wonderful. It is stuff like that really motivates me to be the best I can be."

WHAT ADVICE WOULD YOU HAVE FOR YOUNG COACHES STARTING OUT TODAY? "I would say learn as much as you can about your sport and then work as hard as you can. Then, try to get your kids to listen, to apply themselves, to be self motivated and to want to do well. Then, it is real important for coaches to not think that they are the key guy, because they are not. That important."

WHAT'S THE BIGGEST THING YOU'VE LEARNED FROM COACHING THAT YOU'VE BEEN ABLE TO APPLY TO YOUR EVERYDAY LIFE? "I would say patience, being a good listener and the fact that sometimes your kids do not hear the same thing you are saying."

WHAT'S THE SECRET TO YOUR SUCCESS? "First of all, you have to know the game and understand the fundamentals of your sport. Then, you have to have a passion for what you are doing. After that, you have to be able to communicate and motivate. I really want self motivators on my teams because I don't want to have to scream at guys to get them to do their jobs. Beyond that you have to lay out your goals for your players, encourage them to work hard and have high expectations. I want my kids to not only carry themselves well but to be good human beings. That's what makes good teams. You know, sometimes you can use sports to make kids really feel good about themselves, and that is very gratifying to see."

WHAT WOULD YOU WANT TO SAY TO YOUR FANS, BOOSTERS, AND ALUMNI WHO HAVE SUPPORTED YOU ALL THESE YEARS? "It has been a privilege to have made so many friends through the years. All of the volunteers, fans, assistants and supporters have been so great and I would just say thank you all very much, we couldn't do it without you."

HOW DO YOU WANT YOUR COACHING EPITAPH TO READ — HOW DO YOU WANT TO BE REMEMBERED AS A COACH? "I would just say that I was a good person. I have to laugh at questions like this because I just think there are way too many honors and awards these days in our society. It is all so overrated. We have like 50,000 All-State kids now. *Please!* I mean when we won the national championship I was named as the coach of the year. Come on. Are you telling me I was the best coach in baseball that year? We are honoring everybody all the time because we have to make everybody feel good about themselves. So, *my* epitaph, hmm. I told my wife that when I die I don't need a fancy funeral, just bury me, that's good enough!"

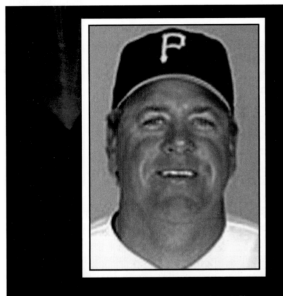

SPIN WILLIAMS: PIRATES PITCHING COACH

Spin Williams, a native of Davenport, Iowa, went on to play baseball at Winona State University, where he was an all-conference first baseman. Williams, who then played a couple of seasons as a pitcher in the Pittsburgh Pirates farm system, later went into coaching — and has been going strong ever since. Now entering his 25th season as a member of the Pirates organization, Williams has emerged as one of the game's top developers of young talent. Williams spent seven seasons, from 1994-2000, as the bullpen coach for the Pirates. That next year he was named as the club's pitching coach, and he has been there ever since. Today, Williams is regarded as one of the best in the business by his colleagues and peers.

LEW SHAVER: SOUTHWEST STATE UNIVERSITY WHEELCHAIR BASKETBALL

Lew Shaver began teaching and coaching at Southwest State in 1969 and spent 26 years as the head coach of the Southwest State wheelchair basketball team, compiling a record of 339-241 from 1969-95. During his tenure, the SSU wheelchair basketball team was one of the country's best, winning three National Intercollegiate Wheelchair Basketball championships in 1981, 1983 and 1986. SSU also finished as the NIWBT runner-up on six occasions and also won or shared the Central Intercollegiate Conference title from 1978 through 1986 — the league's first eight years of existence. Recognized nationally as a wheelchair basketball expert, Shaver has also written or co-authored three books on the sport. He was also the assistant coach on three international championship wheelchair basketball teams as well. In addition, Shaver coached football for four years at SSU, including the 1977 and 1978 seasons, when he served as head coach. One highlight came in 1977, when he snapped SSU's 22-game losing streak with a 29-25 win over Michigan Tech. Shaver also spent time as wheelchair track and field coach for many years and even spent one year as the assistant baseball coach as well. A real winner in every sense of the word, Lew Shaver is a true coaching inspiration.

JIM DIMMICK
COLLEGE BASEBALL: ST. OLAF

Jim Dimmick grew up in Wisconsin and graduated from Barron High School in 1946. After spending two years in the Marines, Dimmick went on to play first base for the St. Cloud State University Huskies, graduating in 1952 with a teaching degree. From there, Dimmick went on to teach and coach high school baseball for 15 years in both Wisconsin and Minnesota, developing 10 conference title teams along the way.

Dimmick's first teaching and coaching job was at Verona, Wis., High School, where he stayed for four years. From there he moved on to teach and coach at Luck, Wis., High School for a year, followed by four years at Cumberland, Wis., High School. Dimmick then moved to Minnesota in 1961 to coach high school baseball in West St. Paul, and also teach physical education and biology. He would stay for six years before finally getting his big break to coach at the collegiate level in 1967.

That year Dimmick came to St. Olaf to serve as the team's new baseball coach and teach in the school's physical education department. Over the next 27 years Dimmick's Oles would go on to make history, winning 14 MIAC championships, finishing second seven times, and appeared in the NCM Division III Regional Tournament on 13 different occasions. Coach Dimmick would eventually retire in 1994 with an amazing 589-259 career record. During his tenure in Northfield, nobody won more games in the MIAC than Jim Dimmick. Simply put, the man is a coaching legend.

The consummate teacher and coach, Dimmick also coached and taught the game he loved around the world. Among his many worldly baseball sabbaticals, Dimmick has conducted baseball clinics overseas in Colombia, Thailand, India, Sweden, Norway, Netherlands, Czechoslovakia, Italy and the Philippines. He even coached Solvesborg, Sweden, to a pair of National Championship Series' in both 1995 and 1998. He also served on the staff of the U.S. National Baseball Team in the summer of 1989 which toured the entire U.S. as well as Cuba and Puerto Rico. And, he coached a college all-star team which toured Alaska and Korea in summer of 1979. Dimmick served as a baseball clinician in several states too, including: Minnesota, Wisconsin, Iowa, Colorado, North Carolina and New York. Additionally, he even introduced baseball in Sri Lanka under the auspices of the U.S. Baseball Federation in 1984.

Among his many coaching accolades, Dimmick was inducted into the American Baseball Coaches Association Hall of Fame in 1995 and the St. Cloud State University Hall of Fame in 1999. He received Dick Siebert Award in 1978, and the Angelo Giuliani Award for contributions to baseball in Minnesota in 1993. In 1995 he was awarded the Minnesota Baseball Outstanding Achievement Award, presented jointly by the University of Minnesota and the Minnesota Twins. St. Olaf even retired his number in 1997. In addition, Dimmick also served as the president of the American Baseball Coaches Association, and presently sits on their Board of Directors as well. Finally, the MIAC Coach of the Year and the Minnesota High School Retired Coach of the Year Awards are both named in his honor — showing just how respected and appreciated he is in the world of coaching.

In addition to teaching and coaching, Dimmick was also very active in his church, where he served as a council member and Sunday school teacher for many, many years. The father of six, three boys and three girls, Jim Dimmick was the ultimate family man — something he is even more proud of than coaching baseball.

HOW WOULD YOU DESCRIBE YOUR COACHING STYLE? "I think I was a caring coach but also a competitive and intense coach. Our creed on a day of competition was that we played as hard as we could and we never quit. At the same time we always knew how to win and also how to lose. When we lost, we did it with grace and never made excuses. When we lost we also went back and analyzed it and the tried to get better. And, when we won we never rubbed it in and belittled our opponents. We also never looked at an opponent as an enemy either, rather as a worthy adversary. Of course, in the MIAC, it is a league of class people, from the coaches to the players, that have a mutual respect for each other and that it is why it is such a good conference."

HOW DID YOU MOTIVATE YOUR PLAYERS? "I have always believed in being positive. You can motivate an athlete much better with a pat on the back than you could with a kick in the rear end. Not that we didn't come down hard verbally on kids who made mistakes repeatedly and didn't come to play, but overall we felt that positive strokes were much better in getting kids to play their best."

WHO WERE YOUR COACHING MENTORS? "John Kasper was my mentor at St. Cloud State. He was a great, caring coach and I really respected him. I also admired Dick Siebert very much as well. I patterned much of my style after him too."

IF YOU COULD MAGICALLY GO BACK IN TIME TO THE FIRST YEAR YOU WERE A HEAD COACH AND GIVE YOURSELF SOME ADVICE FOR THE FUTURE, KNOWING WHAT YOU KNOW NOW, BACK THEN, WHAT WOULD YOU SAY TO YOURSELF? "I think I would say prepare extremely well for every contest realizing that while every contest is important, it is not too important. I think when I was younger I put too much pressure on myself and I took losses extremely hard. I used to look at my competition as enemies, and then I realized that they were just opponents. There is a big difference."

WHAT ARE YOU MOST PROUD OF IN YOUR CAREER? "I am most proud of the tremendous contributions that my players have made to society upon graduating from St. Olaf College. Once, at a coaches clinic, Joe Paterno (Penn State Football Coach) was asked what his best team ever was, and he said the greatest team at Penn State hadn't been determined yet. He said that they could make that determination until 25 years after the last graduating class was gone, then they could see which team had produced the most members which were contributing positively to society. That, in his opinion, was the best team. I guess I feel the same way about my kids. I have dozens and dozens of former players who have gone on to become successful businessmen, doctors, lawyers, teachers and coaches, all over the Midwest, and that makes me so proud. And I know that many of the things they learned in our program had a great impact on their success in life. That is special and something that I am very proud of."

WHAT ARE THE CHARACTERISTICS OF LEADERS? "The key to being a good leader is not caring about who gets the credit, they lead by example. They also know how to lose."

HOW DID YOU BUILD TEAM UNITY & CHEMISTRY?
"Chemistry is pulling for each other and realizing that the team comes before yourself. One thing we did was to take a Spring trip down south as a team every year to play some ballgames, and that helped us to bond a great deal. I mean we ate, slept and traveled together and it was just a wonderful way to build chemistry. We really got to know each other and it was great. Also, we did a lot of sharing together as a team. At the end of every practice and at the end of every game we used to have a fireside chat. That came from my days as a kid in the Great Depression when we listed to FDR on the radio. Our chats consisted of bearing our souls and telling each other good things about each other and why it meant something to be on that team. Every year, when the seniors played their last games, it was always a tearful event. So, belonging to a team that is really a team in every sense of the word, is a special thing. Just to hear those players sit around and talk about each other and tell each other what they meant to each other was chemistry in its purest form."

ON TEAMMATES: "I remember hearing Skip Bertman, the very successful coach at Louisiana State University, speak one time at a clinic about team building. He said that on a team you were all teammates and that one wasn't any more important than the other. Then, to demonstrate that, he asked everyone a hypothetical question. He said if you were dangling over a cliff on the end of a rope 1,000 feet above some rocks, who on your team would you like to have on the other end to pull you up? Well, some kids said their best friends, while others said they would want the strongest guy on the team. Burkman then said you won't have the team chemistry necessary to win until your kids realize that it doesn't matter who is on the other end of that rope. It could be anybody, regardless of how big and strong they were, and once they accepted that, then they would become a team."

ON CLUTCH PLAYERS: "A clutch player is just as happy if the person competing for his position had had a great day, while he was sitting on the bench. That's a special thing and is very rare."

ON AWARDS: "You know, if I had my way there wouldn't be any all-conference teams or most valuable players. Those are individual awards and they are fine, but when players have those as their goals, then they are thinking of themselves and not of their team."

WHAT'S THE BEST PIECE OF ADVICE YOU EVER GOT FROM ANOTHER COACH? "My father once told me that success is never determined by money, big houses, letters after your name, or trophies on your shelf. Success is determined by one thing and one thing only, and that could be answered with one simple question: 'When you leave the world, is it better because you were there?'
"

WHAT MOTIVATED YOU? "I loved the kids, I loved athletics, I loved the competition, I loved the camaraderie with the players and I just wanted to coach."

FAVORITE LOCKER ROOM SIGN? "Quitters never win and winners never quit."

WHAT ARE THE KEY INGREDIENTS TO CREATING A CHAMPIONSHIP TEAM? "The key in baseball is to find the best nine, not the nine best. That's an old cliché, but there is a lot of truth to it. If you can get a team of players that will live and die together, do anything to win, not be concerned about individual statistics, and just go out and play together, I think that is the ticket right there. I have seen many teams through the years that were just loaded with individual talent, but couldn't win as a team because they were playing for themselves. That is just not part of the team concept. In all the years that I was at St. Olaf, we preached that we were a family. So, when the younger guys came in every year, the older guys would look out for them and accept them as little brothers. That way, the younger guys never had to prove themselves as individuals, they were accepted from day one."

WHAT'S THE SECRET TO YOUR SUCCESS? "Loving my players, and then preparing and planning my practices so that we covered the game from A to Z."

WHAT WOULD YOU WANT TO SAY TO YOUR FANS, BOOSTERS, AND ALUMNI WHO HAVE SUPPORTED YOU ALL THESE YEARS? "Thanks for the memories and thanks for buying into our philosophy, which was to play and practice as hard as we could without ever quitting. Then, thanks too for accepting the results."

HOW DO YOU WANT YOUR COACHING EPITAPH TO READ — HOW DO YOU WANT TO BE REMEMBERED AS A COACH? "I would rather be remembered as a good father, a good churchman, and a caring coach who was more concerned about the contributions to a society of his athletes than by the trophies left standing on the shelves."

MIKE KELLEY: MILLERS & SAINTS

Mike Kelley was involved with the Millers and Saints, off and on, for more than four decades, between 1902-46. Kelley managed the Saints from 1902-1905, 1908-1912 and 1915-1923 and the Millers in 1906 and 1924-1931. In addition, Kelly owned the Millers from 1924-46 as well. Kelley first came to Minnesota in 1901, where, as the manager of the St. Paul Saints, he led the team to the American Association pennant in 1902. He would take over as the manager of the Millers in 1906, and over the next several years would also manage in Des Moines, Toronto and Indianapolis. In 1923 he ended his affiliation with the Saints. Five American Association championships and 12 first division finishes later, Kelley went on to purchase a controlling interest in the Millers, where he ultimately went on to serve as the team's president and manager. In 1932 he stepped down as the team's manager but continued to own the team until 1946, when he finally sold it to the New York Giants. When it was all said and done, Kelley had won 2,390 games — the third highest among all managers in minor league history. A shrewd judge of talent, Mike Kelley lived in Minneapolis until he died in 1955.

RON GARDENHIRE
PRO BASEBALL: MINNESOTA TWINS

Ron Gardenhire grew up in Oklahoma and went on to graduate from Okmulgee High School in 1975, where he was an All-State shortstop. From there, Gardenhire went on to earn All-Conference honors at Paris (Texas) Junior College. He would remain at Paris for two years before going on to earn All-Conference honors at the University of Texas. There, as a senior captain, Gardenhire led his Longhorns to a Southwest Conference championship and a fourth place finish in the College World Series.

After receiving his degree in physical education from Texas in 1979, Gardenhire was drafted by the New York Mets. His first stint in pro ball would come in the minors. Then, after earning All-Star honors in the Carolina League, Gardenhire got called up to the "show" in 1981. In his major league debut at St. Louis, Gardenhire singled off Bruce Sutter for his first big-league hit. Gardenhire would then spend the next several years playing up and down in the Mets farm system. Among the highlights of his professional career, Gardenhire hit the game-winning home run in the deciding game of the 1983 Class AAA World Series over Portland. Then, in 1986 Gardenhire was traded to the Minnesota Twins.

Two years later Gardenhire decided to retire from playing and got into managing. That same year he was named as the manager of Class A Kenosha. In 1989 Gardenhire was named as the league's Best Manager by Baseball America. In 1990 Gardenhire was named as the Southern League co-Manager of the Year and was also named as the league's Best Managerial Prospect by Baseball America. For his efforts, he was signed as the Twins' third base coach. For the next decade Gardy would be a fixture in the Twins dug-out. Two World Series titles and plenty of ups and downs along the way, Gardy would see it all.

In 2002, when Tom Kelly decided to finally retire, Gardenhire was named as the Twins new manager. That next season he then led the Twins to an improbable playoff run, beating the Oakland A's in the American League Divisional Series to advance to the American League Championship Series. There, the team eventually lost to the World Series Champion California Angels, but became the Cinderella story of baseball that year nonetheless. It was an amazing story for this team, which had narrowly escaped contraction earlier that year, to make it so far — and on such a low payroll as well. For his efforts, Gardy finished third in the American League Manager of the Year voting.

In 2003 Gardy had the Twins in the pennant race all season long and made Minnesota proud yet again. In just two seasons as a big-league skipper, Ron Gardenhire has established himself as one of the game's top managers. Gardy also dedicates his time in support of military veterans, is a spokesman for the Minnesota Department of Public Safety's "Buckle Up," "Drive at Safe Speeds," and "Don't Drink and Drive" PSA campaigns, and the "Minnesota Twins/3M Totally Awesome Coaches Award" program, which recognizes outstanding youth sports coaches in Minnesota. Ron and his wife Carol presently reside in the Twin Cities and have three children: Toby, Tiffany and Tara.

HOW WOULD YOU DESCRIBE YOUR COACHING STYLE? "I think I learned from a lot of different people a long time ago that the players are the ones who win the games. So, if you at least try to put them into the right situations, and just then let them play, then you will have a chance to be successful. From there I just try to stay out of their way and let them play the game because that is what they do best."

HOW DO YOU MOTIVATE YOUR PLAYERS? "When things are going good it is easy for the players to come to the park every day, but when they are going bad, that is when you, as a manager, earn your pay. So, you have to keep up a positive attitude as much as you can and make sure that your ballplayers are comfortable coming to the park even though things might not be going well for them. Sometimes you have to talk to them and other times you just need to give them a pat on the back. I think that once a player gets to the big leagues he shouldn't have to be that motivated to go out and play. It should pretty much be an everyday thing at this level because that is what they do for a living. So, self motivation is a big thing for these guys and then we just try and help out where we can."

WHO WERE YOUR COACHING MENTORS? "I always idolized my dad because he was an officer in the Army. I used to be in awe as a kid watching him march his men at the base down in Fort Ord. His men really liked him and they would laugh together and have a good time. He wasn't the prototypical screaming drill sergeant, sure he was tough, but he had a great relationship with his men too. When his guys would scream out 'Yes Sir, Mr. Gardenhire, Sir!' I used to think that was just the coolest. Then, as far as on the baseball side of things, I think I have had some great, great mentors. Joe Torre was my first manager in the big leagues and he was very calm. Davey Johnson was a players manager, and then of course there was Tom Kelly, who had a great impact on me both personally and professionally. So, I have been fortunate to have had some great role models in my life."

IF YOU COULD MAGICALLY GO BACK IN TIME TO THE FIRST YEAR YOU WERE A HEAD COACH AND GIVE YOURSELF SOME ADVICE FOR THE FUTURE, KNOWING WHAT YOU KNOW NOW, BACK THEN, WHAT WOULD YOU SAY TO YOURSELF? "Relax! You know when I first started coaching I was so gung-ho and I rushed a little bit. I lacked patience and I was a real screamer and yeller too. I wanted to go out and fix everybody. Now I can see that good things take time and you have to relax so that things can play themselves out. Players just have to do their thing and you have to let them grow as a person and as a player. You just can't rush that."

HOW DO YOU BUILD TEAM UNITY & CHEMISTRY? "It starts with our scouting department and when they go out and look at players. You have to not only look at great players, you also have to look at their background. You have to ask yourself what kind of kid he is and evaluate everything from their work ethic to their demeanor. A lot goes into that. So, we feel that it is important to draft the type of players that we feel will fit in here. We want guys who carry themselves well, respect the game, respect the fans, and respect the people around them. That all goes into building chemistry because we know the type of people who want to bring into our family."

WHAT'S THE BIGGEST THING YOU'VE LEARNED FROM COACHING THAT YOU'VE BEEN ABLE TO APPLY TO YOUR EVERYDAY LIFE? "Realizing that this is still just a game. Even though it is my life, it is something we all grew up as kids doing, playing baseball. I have also learned that even though I have a separate family life from my baseball life, there are parallels. You know, I want to treat my players the same way I treat my kids — with that much respect. I think my kids appreciate that at home, that I treat them with respect, and my players feel the same way. It is all about how you treat people, with respect."

WHAT'S THE SECRET TO YOUR SUCCESS? "Hard work and respect."

WHAT WOULD YOU WANT TO SAY TO YOUR FANS, BOOSTERS, AND ALUMNI WHO HAVE SUPPORTED YOU ALL THESE YEARS? "I would like to say thanks. Even though this is a small market team, we have big-time fans. They are just great and they are true fans. When you go out into the community they speak their mind to you but they are also very respectful of being a Twins

fan. Whether it is the Twins, Vikings, Wolves, Wild or Gophers, the fans here are very, very loyal and that is great. You know, this organization has built something here that is very special and that goes all the way back to guys like Harmon Killebrew and Tony Oliva. I think the contraction stuff last year really showed me how much people truly love this baseball team. More so now than ever, there is a lot of pride in this organization and the fans are the biggest part of that."

HOW DO YOU WANT YOUR COACHING EPITAPH TO READ — HOW DO YOU WANT TO BE REMEMBERED AS A COACH? "I hope that people would think that my players sure had a lot of fun playing for me because I really enjoyed managing them. I also hope that I will be remembered as someone who made sure that through a lot of preparation, hard work and respect, that the fans were able to have a great experience watching Minnesota Twins baseball."

TONY OLIVA: MINNESOTA TWINS

Pedro "Tony" Oliva grew up in the western province of Cuba, on his father's farm in Pinar del Rio, about 100 miles from Havana. There, he went to school through the 8th grade in a two-room wooden schoolhouse. He grew up as one of 10 kids — five boys and five girls. (He told his father he was a lucky man because he had hit .500!) Baseball consumed the boys life, and it would be his ticket to prosperity.

"When I was a boy, we would help my father with the work on the farm after school, and then play baseball," said Oliva. "We grew tobacco, oranges, mangos, potatoes, corn, and raised cows, pigs, chickens, and horses. My father loved the game and always found time for my brothers and me to play it. He helped all the kids play and enjoy the game by going to Havana to buy gloves, bats and balls for us. Once, he came back to the farm with nine gloves. We kept them in our house and when the kids came to our farm to play, they used them."

Tony got his big break when he was spotted by Cuban scout "Papa" Joe Cambria, who brought him to the United States for a tryout. His teammates on his Cuban team even chipped in to buy him some clothes for the big trip.

"Since I didn't have a passport, I had to use my brother, Antoine's. So, everyone started calling me Tony," said Oliva. "I found that I liked the name even better than Pedro, so I didn't ever tell anyone my real name."

The newly christened Tony was invited to camp with the Twins, and in 1961, he led the rookie league with a .410 average. After one-year stints in Class A and AAA, Oliva got called up to the majors in 1964. As a Twin, Oliva led the league with a .323 average, becoming the only rookie ever to win the batting title. He was even named Rookie of the Year, earning every penny of his lavish $7,500 salary.

Oliva would go on to become one of the greatest players in Twins history. In his second season, 1965, Oliva led the Twins to the World Series and won another batting crown en route to being named American League Player of the Year. Oliva also won a Gold Glove in 1966 and captured a third batting crown in 1971. In 15 seasons, six of which were affected by a knee injury, Oliva would finish with 1,917 hits, 220 home runs, 947 RBI's and had a career average of .304. His prowess as a hitter was demonstrated in the fact that he led the league in hits five times, and his 220 career home runs rank third all-time among Twins. An eight-time All-Star, Tony's No. 6 was officially retired on July 14, 1991.

From 1962-76 Tony-O was simply awesome. He could hit for power and average, as well as run, field, and throw. His versatility made him one of the most feared hitters of his day. If not for knee problems which cut short his career, Oliva would have been a certain choice for the Hall of Fame. After years of agonizing knee problems, Tony finally retired from the game in 1976 and began coaching for the Twins. It would be the beginning of a very long and successful tenure with his former club, as he went on to become one of the most successful hitting instructors in major league baseball. Tony would also work in the Twins' minor league system and scout for the club as well, providing much insight for the younger players on how to be a successful all-around ballplayer.

Tony-O will forever be remembered as one of the Twins all-time greats. From his infectious smile to that Cuban accent that is as strong today as it was 40 years ago, he is a real living legend and a true treasure for Minnesota baseball.

"I would like to be remembered as a ballplayer that gave 100 percent and also a person that was able to get along with everybody," said Oliva. "I think the fans here in Minnesota are great, and it was a pleasure to play here for them. I have lived here for over half of my life, so my family and I am grateful to the good people of Minnesota."

As far as the Hall of Fame goes, Oliva knows that had he not suffered through countless knee injuries in the latter stages of his career that he would be a shoe-in at Cooperstown. Let's just hope that the Veterans Committee comes to their senses in the coming years so that this outstanding ballplayer and person can be enshrined into his appropriate place in history. Tony, however, has his own views on baseball immortality and remains cautiously optimistic.

"Everybody thinks I should be in the Hall of Fame except for the people that vote," said Oliva. "I feel a little bit disappointed. I think I should be in the Hall because I achieved so much. It was too bad that I got hurt, but there were people that did less in the same amount of time than I did that got in. A lot of pitchers now in the Hall of Fame, who pitched against me, have told me over the years that when they were asked by baseball writers who they felt should be in the Hall that isn't, they said me. I had a lot of great accomplishments in my career, and I hope I can still make it in through the back door."

GARY GROB
COLLEGE BASEBALL: WINONA STATE UNIVERSITY

Gary Grob grew up in the southeastern Minnesota town of LaCrescent and went on to attend LaCrosse (Wis.) Central High School. From there, Grob served with the U.S. Marine Corps before coming to Winona State University in 1959. There, he played baseball for the Warriors and even helped to lead his team to the 1961 and 1962 NAIA World Series. In 1966, after earning his master's degree at WSU and serving as assistant coach under Luther McCown, he returned to the Winona baseball field as the team's new head coach. Since then, he has gone on to become a real Minnesota baseball coaching legend.

By the time Gary Grob finally retired after 35 seasons at Winona State, they had to completely rewrite the record books. In 1994 Grob surpassed legendary Gopher Coach Dick Siebert to become Minnesota's all-time leader in collegiate coaching victories. In fact, he is only the sixth NCAA Division II baseball coach to reach 1,000 career victories and just the 30th in all of NCAA baseball to reach the milestone. Grob's involvement and career at Winona State spans over four decades as a student, coach and instructor. During his illustrious career at WSU, Grob posted a 1,020-563-10 record, good for a gaudy .643 winning percentage. Over that span he won 15 conference championships, produced 161 All-Conference players, and saw 16 of his players sign professional baseball contracts. Three times his teams advanced to the NAIA World Series (1972 , 1988 and 1992 — where they finished 3rd), and when the school became an NCAA Division II member in 1995, Grob sent two teams on to the NCAA II regional tournaments as well. The first came in 1998, when the Warriors opened the NCAA Playoffs with a 5-1 loss to Northern Colorado but rebounded to beat Pittsburg State, 7-5, followed by Northern Colorado, 16-11, to advance on to the Region Finals — where they were beaten soundly by Central Missouri State, 15-3. They made it back in 2000, only to lose a pair to Rockhurst, Mo., 8-7, and Central Missouri State, 13-1.

Among Grob's many coaching accolades, he won 15 NAIA District 13 Coach of the Year awards and three NSIC Coach of the Year awards. Grob is a member of both the NAIA and American Baseball Coaches' Association Halls of Fame as well. Grob is retired and presently lives in Winona with his family.

HOW WOULD YOU DESCRIBE YOUR COACHING STYLE? "I wanted young men to come into our program with the knowledge of baseball and the willingness to learn. They needed to work hard and have fun doing it. More than anything else, I wanted to make my environment a fun environment. So, there had to be a focus because I never tolerated any nonsense. I grew up with the baseball bible in my hand, the rule book. That was number two to the bible in my family. My father was a very strict baseball man and by the time I was 15 years old I knew the rules of the game as well as anybody. That was my foundation. I also had some pretty good teachers along the way too with guys like Max Molock at St. Mary's, as well as Luther McCowan and Dick Siebert, who were just great too. I took bits and pieces from all of those people and that built the foundation for my understanding of the game. So, I guess my style might be described as one of playing hard, playing to win and playing fair. I enjoyed working with young men and helping them get to that next level. They were fun to work with because you could kid around with them, but they also came to the ballyard ready to play and perform. I worked my tail off to make sure that we did it right and we were fortunate to win a lot of ballgames in the process."

HOW DID YOU MOTIVATE YOUR PLAYERS? "I told them what we had to do, made sure it was done, and went from there. As far as disciplining went, I had a few simple rules but I expected them to be carried out and done correctly. Motivation to me was more of an expectation. So, I guess I wouldn't take no for an answer. I spent two years in the Marine Corps too, and that set a real foundation for discipline for me. I had a lot of pride in myself when I coached and I made my players dress and act accordingly. I wouldn't tolerate any bad publicity and really ran a tight ship. That motivated my kids to be good people and to stay focused on baseball. You know, I was a little bit out of the (Vince) Lombardi mold I think. To me I was more about expectations rather than a rah-rah. To get up on a band-stand and scream and holler was not my style. I did pull them aside and talk to them either as a group or as individuals and tell them what we had to do in order to win though. I also worked hard at preparing my guys for their next opponents so that they had a mindset for who was coming up on the schedule. I did a lot of research too, and that paid off for our teams in the long run."

WHO WERE YOUR COACHING MENTORS? "My dad was the guy who put a baseball in my hand when I was five years old. He played with me and pitched to me and taught me this great game. He was an old die-hard Yankees fan and just loved the game. He taught me to love this game and that is why he would have to be my No. 1 mentor. I also learned a great deal from Gopher Coach Dick Siebert, he was just an outstanding coach. I learned so much from his clinics over the years and passed a lot of that along to my kids as well. I had a lot of respect for him as a person and coach."

IF YOU COULD MAGICALLY GO BACK IN TIME TO THE FIRST YEAR YOU WERE A HEAD COACH AND GIVE YOURSELF SOME ADVICE FOR THE FUTURE, KNOWING WHAT YOU KNOW NOW, BACK THEN, WHAT WOULD YOU SAY TO YOURSELF? "I would just say stick with it and be patient."

LOOKING BACK WHAT ARE YOU MOST PROUD OF IN YOUR CAREER? "In over 35 years of coaching I would say that at least 90% of my players graduated. That means a great deal to me. I never missed a graduation ceremony and those were the proudest moments I had as a coach."

HOW DID YOU BUILD TEAM UNITY & CHEMISTRY? "I wouldn't hear anything else but... and that is how I created it. I wasn't a tyrant as a coach, but I had certain expectations and for me that was how I created team unity. One thing that I did specifically which I thought was pretty successful, was that I would talk to my kids on an individual basis. We didn't talk baseball all the time either, we just talked. That laid a foundation for unity and let me get to know my kids. They knew that I cared about them like a family member and that was very important to me. They all knew that I would be there for them whatever the situation might have been, but they also knew that if they needed a kick in the tail or an earful, then they were going to get that too. I really tried to create a family environment and that is how I have always operated."

WHAT MOTIVATED YOU? "You know, my three year old grandson goes to bed with his glove on and I just love stuff like that. It is so good to see the next generation of kids growing up and loving this great game, and things like that motivated me to be a great coach. You know, all four of my daughters served as bat girls for me at one point or another and that was very special too. My wife is great and my entire family was very supportive of me and my career and that always motivated me to be my best as well."

WHAT'S THE BIGGEST THING YOU'VE LEARNED FROM COACHING THAT YOU'VE BEEN ABLE TO APPLY TO YOUR EVERYDAY LIFE? "To just have fun and enjoy life."

WHAT'S THE SECRET TO YOUR SUCCESS? "I always felt that enthusiasm was so important. That, plus discipline were the ingredients to success I think."

WHAT WOULD YOU WANT TO SAY TO YOUR FANS, BOOSTERS, AND ALUMNI WHO HAVE SUPPORTED YOU ALL THESE YEARS? "Thanks for the memories and thanks for being a part of Winona State baseball for 35 years, it means the world to me. Thanks too for the good times and even for the bad times, because we learn from the hard times."

HOW DO YOU WANT YOUR COACHING EPITAPH TO READ — HOW DO YOU WANT TO BE REMEMBERED AS A COACH? "He cared, he showed interest and he always wanted to win."

BILLY MARTIN: MINNESOTA TWINS

Billy Martin was born in Berkeley, Calif., in 1928 as Alfred Manuel Martin. Billy's dad left the family before he was born, leaving him to be raised by his mother and his grandmother — both very strong-willed people. Billy grew up loving baseball and, despite being small, was determined to excel in the game. The speedy second baseman signed with the minor league Oakland Oaks right out of high school and learned the game under legendary manager Casey Stengel. Then, when Stengel left the Bay Area to manage the New York Yankees, Billy followed right behind him. Martin would go on to win six World Series titles with the Yankees from 1950-57. In fact, the only season between 1950 and 1957 that the Yanks failed to take the American League pennant was 1954, when Martin was called to serve in the military. He was eventually traded to the Kansas City A's, however, after getting caught up in a brawl outside the Copacabana — a famous Manhattan nightclub. Martin had earned a reputation for being a party animal and his "Billy the Kid" persona wasn't too far off. He loved to go late-night carousing, usually with Mickey Mantle, and it eventually caught up with him.

From there, Martin would end his playing career with the Minnesota Twins in 1961. He would remain with the Twins as a scout following his retirement though and eventually work his way up to become the third-base coach, where he was notorious for his ability to steal signs. He played a big part in the Twins' 1965 AL pennant and also had a lot to do with the development of shortstop Zoilo Versalles and second baseman Rod Carew as well. Then, in 1969, Martin was named as the team's manager. His fiery attitude was inspiring and the Twins, who had finished in seventh place the year before, went on to win the American League West championship under his tutelage. Harmon Killebrew was named as the league's MVP that season and things were looking good. The team eventually lost to Baltimore in the American League Championship Series, however, but Martin had established himself as a real fan-favorite. Attendance was way up and the team looked poised to become a power in the American League under Martin. Billy loved Minnesota and loved to hunt and fish as well. He drank a lot though, and that got him into trouble. The wheels would eventually fall off. Between another bar brawl with Twins pitcher Dave Boswell and the constant bickering with team owner Calvin Griffith, Martin, despite leading his team to a pennant, was fired after that season.

Martin would go on to manage in Detroit that next year, but battles with the Tigers general manager eventually got him fired again. So, he went to the last-place Texas Rangers, where he led them to an amazing second-place finish that next season. A change in team ownership ultimately cost Billy his job there, but in 1975 Billy returned to his beloved Yankees to serve as their new manager. It would be the first of many! Hired by owner George Steinbrenner, Billy led the Bronx Bombers to another World Series title in 1977. Martin would ultimately go on to become the most famous baseball manager in history. He would also become the most controversial manager in history, eventually getting fired and re-hired in the Big Apple a whopping five times. Booze, brawls and baseball became a common theme over the next decade for Martin, and the fans loved every minute of it. It was a soap opera like no other and that truly made Billy one of the game's all-time great characters.

Martin tragically died in a car accident on Christmas Day, 1989, at the age of 61. Although his life was plagued with trouble and controversy, both on and off the field, he would forever be remembered as a winner. Over his 16 year career as a major league baseball manager, Martin won five divisional titles, two AL Championships, and one World Series. He also earned a .553 winning percentage, a statistic that is among the all-time top 20 in history — and even more impressive when you consider some of the awful teams he was dealt along the way. Martin had earned a reputation for being a baseball genius who could turn almost any kind of team into a winner. But, because of his erratic and sometimes self-destructive behavior, Martin was also a train wreck waiting to happen — which made for some very interesting stories along the way. Sure, he had his faults, but Martin's players loved him and the managers and umpires respected him. He knew talent, could manage baseball and made history wherever he went. One thing is for certain, there will never be another Billy Martin — he was definitely a one of a kind.

JERRY HAUGEN
COLLEGE BASEBALL: ST. JOHN'S

Jerry Haugen grew up in the Twin Cities and graduated from Armstrong High School. From there, Haugen went on to play football and baseball at St. John's, graduating in 1976. After working as an assistant, Haugen took over as the head coach of the Johnnies in 1977 and has been going strong ever since.

Haugen currently has a career record of 494-413-4 (.544), which places him in the top 25 on the NCAA Division III winningest active coaches win list. In addition, the Johnnies have had 14 winning seasons in the last 16 years during his tenure. Since 1978, Haugen has coached over 63 All-MIAC performers and in 1993, he saw team MVP Jon Dold become the first SJU player in over 30 years to be drafted by the pros. Haugen currently ranks as the "dean" of MIAC coaches with 26 seasons of conference play under his belt. Among the highlights of his career, in 1994 Haugen was named as the MIAC Coach-of-the-Year. Then, in 1998, Haugen guided the Johnnies to a conference championship and advanced for only the second time in school history to the NCAA Division III Midwest Regional Tournament. In addition to coaching the baseball team, Haugen also serves as the defensive coordinator on John Gagliardi's nationally recognized Johnnie football team. Furthermore, Haugen has also worked as an assistant basketball coach and head hockey coach during his tenure at St. John's as well. Now in his 27th season as the Johnnies' head baseball coach, Jerry Haugen is still going strong.

HOW WOULD YOU DESCRIBE YOUR COACHING STYLE? "I guess when I was younger I coached with a little more emotion and spitfire. Now, I still have that emotion but I have toned it down a little bit. I think my football background as an assistant with John Gagliardi has helped a lot in shaping my ideas, he is just a great coach. I think overall I just try and prepare our kids the best I can and be the best teacher I can be. I want my guys to understand the game as best as possible so that they can help themselves. My dad was a teacher and as a result I am always teaching, in whatever I am doing. So, I just want our kids to be well taught and then they can go out and perform at their best."

HOW DO YOU MOTIVATE YOUR PLAYERS? "You know, at the division three level we are not dangling too many carrots in front of these kids. Basically, they are there for the love of the game. Obviously, we are all better coaches when we have great players. So if you can recruit great athletes who want to succeed and compete at a high level, then you have some motivation right there by getting kids who are self-motivated and can help lead the other guys. I have never been a real 'rah-rah' coach, I just try and go out there and teach my guys so that they understand the game and can play their best."

IF YOU COULD MAGICALLY GO BACK IN TIME TO THE FIRST YEAR YOU WERE A HEAD COACH AND GIVE YOURSELF SOME ADVICE FOR THE FUTURE, KNOWING WHAT YOU KNOW NOW, BACK THEN, WHAT WOULD YOU SAY TO YOURSELF? "I would look back and say trust yourself, trust what you believe and trust what you're teaching. You're the guy that's got to get up everyday and look at yourself in the mirror and ask if you're doing a good job. You just have to be true to yourself."

WHAT ARE THE CHARACTERISTICS OF WINNERS? "Consistency. A winner comes through in the clutch and is someone you can count on. Winners just overcome the odds and are there for their teammates on game day."

LOOKING BACK WHAT ARE YOU MOST PROUD OF IN YOUR CAREER? "I would say maintaining the level of competitiveness that I have had. You know, I think that at St. John's I have more sports seasons than anybody else there, even more than John (Gagliardi). I coached 13 years of three sports here and that translates into a lot of coaching. I am proud of that and of the lives I have touched along the way."

WHAT IS THE KEY TO RECRUITING? "First of all you need to have a good product. I am lucky, St. John's is a great place. Overall though, you are a salesman. You are selling yourself. You are selling your program. You're selling your school. We get good students here and that helps a lot too. As for the recruiting process itself, I am always honest with kids. I don't tell them what they want to hear, I tell them what's happening. The key is finding the great students and the great athletes, then coaching becomes a lot easier."

HOW DO YOU BUILD TEAM UNITY & CHEMISTRY? "Chemistry is really something that varies from team to team. Certainly with a young team you need to do more as a coach than if you have an older team, where the kids take care of that themselves. It all comes down to who your leaders are. You have to assess who those guys are on your team and then kind of bring them along to put them into the right situation. Sometimes you have to try and create more of it yourself so that things are kind of revolving around you as the focal point. Other times it is all on the kids and the good leaders will step up and create an environment where they all build unity together. Chemistry is a weird thing. Sometimes you get teams that are just close, whether the guys knew each other and were friends, or what have you. As a coach you are always looking for that bonding, whether it comes from you or from your top leaders. It's hard to define but it might just be the most important aspect of team sports though."

WHAT MOTIVATES YOU? "It surely isn't the money, I can tell you that! Seriously, it's a love for the game. I am very fortunate to be around a lot of goal oriented, motivated, positive people, and that motivates me to be my best."

WHAT ADVICE WOULD YOU HAVE FOR YOUNG COACHES STARTING OUT TODAY? "Take some communications courses so you can deal with parents. That is critical. You also need to have good social skills to handle anything that comes your way. I would say to find some role models too, that can be very helpful. You can take bits and pieces of them, but in the end your coaching style needs to be all your own. Then, just try and figure out what your philosophy is going to be. The sooner you figure that out the more successful you will become."

FAVORITE LOCKER ROOM SIGN? "What goes on in this locker room stays in this locker room."

WHAT'S THE BIGGEST THING YOU'VE LEARNED FROM COACHING THAT YOU'VE BEEN ABLE TO APPLY TO YOUR EVERYDAY LIFE? "I thought I became a better coach when I became a parent and started to raise my family. I have four children now and I deal with them in similar terms. I let them know I have expectations for them and make sure that things are understood. We just have a basic plan together and we execute that plan so it all works out."

WHAT IS THE KEY TO GOOD TIME MANAGEMENT? "Make sure you take care of the big rocks in your glass jar before you take care of the pebbles."

WHAT'S THE SECRET TO YOUR SUCCESS? "I think it is believing in yourself, being consistent, being fair and the bottom line is finding great guys that you can teach."

WHAT WOULD YOU WANT TO SAY TO YOUR FANS, BOOSTERS, AND ALUMNI WHO HAVE SUPPORTED YOU ALL THESE YEARS? "We have great, loyal fans at St. John's and they have been so appreciative through the years. I would just say thanks. Everywhere we go in the country to play, we always have fans there and that means a lot."

HOW DO YOU WANT YOUR COACHING EPITAPH TO READ — HOW DO YOU WANT TO BE REMEMBERED AS A COACH? "Wins and losses are not that important to me. I have been involved in baseball and football for a long time and I guess I would want to be known as a coach that taught the game well and made a difference. I would hope that I taught them some things that they will carry on in life past the baseball and football fields. It's all about educating them and becoming a teacher. I guess if someone said that not only you're a coach but you're a teacher of your sport, then that would be the best compliment I could get."

TERRY FLYNN: ST. THOMAS ACADEMY BASEBALL & BASKETBALL

Terry Flynn coached varsity baseball at St. Thomas Academy from 1960-72, earning a pair of State Catholic Baseball Championships in 1960 and 1969. Flynn also served as the varsity basketball coach at St. Thomas Academy from 1967-72 as well. On the hard court, Flynn was dominating, posting a six year record of 126-24, complete with a 35 game winning streak and a State Catholic Basketball Championship in 1970.

In addition, Flynn served as an assistant coach on the football team from 1960-70, and helped to lead the team to a pair of State Catholic Football Championships in 1968 and 1969 as well. During that time, the team also posted an impressive 28 game winning streak from 1968-70. Terry Flynn was among the best of the best and certainly was one of the top coaches of his era

WES WESTRUM: PRO BASEBALL

Wes Westrum was born and raised in Clearbrook. While Westrum hit a modest .217 lifetime batting average in the major leagues, it was his defensive skills as a catcher kept him in the major leagues from 1947-57 — all with the New York Giants. In 1950 the two-time All-Star led National League catchers with a .999 fielding average and led the league in assists and double plays as well. His best season came in 1951 when he hit .236 with 23 home runs and 71 RBI for the Giants. He also caught every game for the Giants in the 1951 and 1954 World Series as well. Prior to playing in the big leagues, Westrum played for the Minneapolis Millers, briefly, from 1941-42 and again in 1947, where he hit .294 with 22 home runs and 87 RBIs.

After his playing career, Westrum went into coaching and managing. After coaching for San Francisco from 1958-63, Westrum was involved in the only trade of coaches in major-league history, going to the Mets in exchange for Cookie Lavagetto. When legendary Mets manager Casey Stengel broke his hip during the 1965 season, Westrum was brought in to replace him. He managed the Mets for the next two years and finished with a combined record of 142-237. He would remain at the helm through 1967 until stepping down and being replaced that next season by Gil Hodges. In addition, he would also later manage the Giants from 1974-75, finishing with a record of 118-129 over his two seasons in the Bay Area.

Westrum's career managerial record would stand at 260-366. Following his term with the Giants, Westrum became a scout for the Atlanta Braves until he retired in 1992. Westrum, who returned to Clearbrook after he retired, died in 2002 at the age of 79. The pride of Clearbrook, Wes Westrum was one of the best.

TOM KELLY
PRO BASEBALL: MINNESOTA TWINS

Jay Thomas Kelly was born in Graceville, Minn. Baseball had always played a big role in his life because his father, Joe, was a Northern League pitcher during the 1940s and later played in the New York Giants system. His family ultimately moved east, where Tom grew up in New Jersey. Kelly went on to become an outstanding ballplayer at St. Mary's High School in South Amboy, N.J., and from there he went on to attend Mesa Community College, in Mesa, Ariz., and also Monmouth College, in West Long Branch, N.J. Baseball remained a big part of his life as he continued to get better and better at each level that he played at. During college Kelly was getting looked at by big league scouts and knew that he had a good shot at making it in the majors if he was just given the opportunity.

T.K. then fulfilled a boyhood dream in 1968 when the expansion Seattle Pilots selected him in the fifth round of the Major League Baseball free agent draft. So, he reported to Newark to play in the minor leagues. In his first year he hit an impressive .317, led the league in stolen bases and became an all-star. From there it was off to Clinton and then Jacksonville, until 1971, when he was signed as a free agent by the Minnesota Twins. After spending a year in Charlotte, he began a four-year stint in Tacoma, the Twins triple-A club. Then, in 1975, Kelly got the call he had been waiting for his entire career — he was going to the show. On May 19th, he got his first major league hit when he singled off Detroit's Joe Coleman. It wasn't a very long stint in the bigs, 127 at bats in 49 games to be exact. He ended up with 23 hits, while driving in 11 batters, scoring another 11 runs and batting a buck-eighty-one. Kelly's lone dinger of his career came off Tigers Pitcher Vern Ruhle. After a season at triple-A Rochester, Kelly caught another break. This time he found his calling as he would spend the next three years in Tacoma and Toledo as a player/manager. In 1979 and 1980, he managed a Twins' farm team in Visalia, where he led the club to two consecutive divisional titles. He was also named the California League Manager of the Year for two years in a row as well. Kelly was then promoted by the Twins to Orlando, where he was named as the Southern League Manager of the Year after guiding his team to the league championship.

In 1983, he got another call to the majors, this time as the new Twins' third base coach, becoming the first Minnesotan to ever become a member of the Twins' managerial staff. Then, in 1986, T.K. took over the Twins' managerial duties from Ray Miller. It would be the start of an historic ride. In 1987, Kelly became only the fifth manager in baseball history to win a pennant as a rookie when his Twins beat the Cardinals in the World Series. For his efforts the 37-year-old was named as the American League Manager of the Year. It was a tremendous victory for all of Minnesota and T.K. was given much of the credit. And deservedly so, for it was he who acted as the glue which held those players together. Kelly's heroes then won their second World Series over the Atlanta Braves just four years later. Kelly thus became the first Twins manager ever to lead his club to two divisional titles (and subsequent world championships), and the third manager ever in baseball history to have won two World Series while losing none. In 1991, Kelly again was again named as the American League Manager of the Year. And, in 1992, Kelly managed the American League All-Star team to a 13-6 victory in San Diego. Fittingly, Twins Centerfielder Kirby Puckett was named as the game's MVP.

In 2001 T.K. stepped down as the Twins manager and handed the reigns to long-time team coach, Ron Gardenhire. When the dust had finally settled, Kelly's career resume was simply amazing. Very quietly he became entrenched as baseball's longest-tenured manager, managing 2,385 games in his nearly 16 seasons behind the bench in Minnie. In addition, he also became the all-time winningest manager in Minnesota history, having won 1,140 games. TK also won a pair of World Series' in a span of five years. This may not sound impressive until one realizes that the Chicago Cubs have not won a single World Series since 1908, or the Red Sox since 1918. Kelly will no doubt go down in history as the greatest Twins manager of all time. Period.

On his longevity as Twins manager, T.K. was humble: "It just shows that I have had a lot of good players here over the years, and good players make managers look good. You have to remember that a manager is only as good as his players, and I've been very fortunate. I think it's the result of a good Twins minor league system, good scouting and good coaching. It's not just one person, and there are a lot of people involved."

Kelly's soft-spoken, 'lead-by-example' attitude filtered throughout the clubhouse and became infectious with all of his players. He was a stickler for the fundamentals, and it was no coincidence that his team committed very few errors, consistently posting a high fielding percentage. T.K. had a reputation of being a fan favorite, a media darling, and all-around good guy. Often referred to as the ultimate "player's manager," Tom Kelly was a Minnesota baseball coaching legend. Tom is presently retired from coaching and living in the Twin Cities, but still serves as a consultant to the Twins.

HOW WOULD YOU DESCRIBE YOUR COACHING STYLE? "I always felt that you had to adjust to the kind of team that you had. A lot of that depended on whether you had young players, old players or a combination of both. So, you had to make a lot of adjustments depending on what you had to work with. If you had young players, you had to not only figure out what they could do, but also remember to not put them into any kind of position where they wouldn't be successful and destroy their confidence as a result. If you had an older bunch, you could pretty much just write their names down on the lineup card and send them out there. With those guys it was really more of just not trying to get in the way. Young players today, in my eyes, have a much harder time handling any kind of failure. They tend to get very upset when they don't do well and have a hard time accepting some instruction in coaching because they have always done well and not failed in the past. That is why I think you see a lot of kids today get called up to the big leagues and then get sent back down. Other than that I guess there were a few things that I demanded or asked to be done, and that included things like being on time, being prepared, working hard, running balls out and trying to put on a good show to entertain the fans. So, I would say my style varied depending on the people that I had to work with. If you had more veterans then as a manager you could do more things, but it didn't always work out that way and that was all part of adjusting as a coach."

HOW DID YOU MOTIVATE YOUR PLAYERS? "I think this all comes down to pitching. If you pitch good then there is a lot of motivation. The best solution to motivation is to have solid pitching. That keeps the players involved in games and keeps the fans into it as well. The game flows well and everything looks good. So, if you don't pitch well and you get behind by four or five runs in two or three innings, then things go out the window. As a manager you want to jump up and down and stand on your head to do some things to try to motivate your players, but really it just comes down to getting somebody out there on the mound who can get somebody out. Again, camaraderie, leadership and all that stuff is all based around good pitching. If you have good pitching on that given day, you are going to do well and those other things will fall into place."

WHAT ARE THE CHARACTERISTICS OF WINNERS? "Winners are guys who come out and play the game at a high level during the good and the bad. If your team is doing good then a lot of people look good, but when your team is playing bad it is not so easy. Some player, however, are able to function in adverse conditions, represent themselves well on the field, can get clutch hits late in a ballgame, and continue to work hard regardless of the situation. These types of players are the ones that are the most important to a manager. Some guys can knock in runs when it is 5-0, but have a hard time when it is 2-2 in the eighth inning. A winning type player, hitter or pitcher, is able to come through late in a ballgame and just get the job done."

LOOKING BACK WHAT ARE YOU MOST PROUD OF IN YOUR CAREER? "For the most part our ball clubs always seemed to be respected by the other teams and they knew that when they played the Twins that they were going to have to play a real good game to beat us. We tried to play hard all the time and just played the game the right way, and I felt that we did that fairly well."

HOW DID YOU BUILD TEAM UNITY & CHEMISTRY? "Chemistry goes back to pitching. If you don't pitch good you are going to have a hard time building chemistry. I was lucky in Minnesota to have guys like Hrbek, Puckett and Molitor, who, despite making a lot of money, were just regular guys who came out every day to play the game. They set a pretty good tone in the clubhouse and if any problems would arise, they would take things into their own hands and get them under control. So, when you have your star players come in and conduct themselves very professionally, it makes it easy to have that chemistry in the clubhouse."

WHAT MOTIVATED YOU? "Competition was what motivated me. To prepare and compete against another team was always very enjoyable for me."

WHAT ADVICE WOULD YOU HAVE FOR YOUNG COACHES STARTING OUT TODAY? "You better like the game, you better like the hours and you better have a good work ethic. You also have to have some good people to work with around you so that you can get the job done. You can't do it all by yourself so you

need to surround yourself with good coaches who can help you set up a good program. Beyond that you need to be organized and prepared each and every day. Not having the answers for people or not having the work schedule prepared can create doubts amongst the players that you don't know what you are doing. Really, being organized might be the main priority."

WHAT ARE THE KEY INGREDIENTS TO CREATING A CHAMPIONSHIP TEAM? "Solid pitching, solid defense and a couple impact players that can generate some runs."

WHAT DOES THE TERM LOYALTY MEAN TO YOU? "This is a hard thing. I think that when most players hit the field they came ready to play, it didn't matter what uniform they had on. With regards to free agency and guys leaving, then I think players had to pretty much do what was best for them and their families. If and when that opportunity presented itself, then each player had to consider whether or not he could do better somewhere else. Again, there are a lot of circumstances involved in those situations and I always tried to stay out of that stuff because it could create a rift between the player and the manager. So, we just let the agents and general managers take care of those things. Really though, if a player felt like he wanted to move on, then we let him go. That was fine, because I always felt that we could find somebody else who wanted to play for us."

ON THE 1987 WORLD SERIES: "Being that it was my first full year as a manager, it was a very special thing. It was a new experience for me getting into the playoffs and into the World Series. Typically, we are somewhat afraid and apprehensive about new experiences, because we don't know what to expect. There was a lot of cautious optimism surrounding the whole experience. The playoffs were a little more nerve-racking than the Big Dance, but, all in all, it was an incredible experience."

ON THE 1991 WORLD SERIES: "By 1991, we knew what to expect, so I think I enjoyed that one a little bit more because I knew what was going on. I just wasn't as nervous this go around as I was in 1987. I frequently use the phrase 'storybook-like' to describe the games that series, because each game was like turning a page in a book to find out what was going to happen. Having the games come down to the ninth inning and the last at-bat was incredible. We were very fortunate to win, because either team could have easily won. What was really rewarding was the fact that we went from last place in 1990 to first place in 1991. It was also very special to me because we proved that smaller market teams could still win it all."

HOW DO YOU WANT YOUR COACHING EPITAPH TO READ — HOW DO YOU WANT TO BE REMEMBERED AS A COACH? "Somebody who tried to work hard, was prepared and had his players ready to play on any given day."

RON EKKER: COLLEGE & PRO BASKETBALL

After graduating from Winona State University in 1964, Ron Ekker went on to embark on a very prolific coaching career. After serving as an assistant coach out of college, Ekker went on to get his first big coaching gig at West Texas State in 1973. One of his first stars was Maurice Cheeks, who would go on to become an NBA All-Star and future head coach of the Portland Trail Blazers. Ekker would spend five seasons at West Texas, followed by a four year stint as head coach and athletic director at St. Louis University. In all, his college coaching record would stand at a very impressive 209-194 (.519). From there, Ekker spent 10 seasons, from 1982-93, coaching in the Continental Basketball Association (CBA) and the World Basketball League (WBL). In 1987 Ekker led the LaCrosse Catbirds of the CBA to a Western Division title with a 40-14 record. Ekker then joined the NBA's Dallas Mavericks, where, from 1991-2000, he served as an assistant coach and scout. In 2001 Ekker joined the Cleveland Cavaliers, where he is presently entering his third season as an assistant coach. And, with star rookie LeBron James about to hit the court in 2003-04, things are definitely going to be exciting for Ekker and the Cavs in the future. Ron and his wife Ginger presently live in Cleveland and have four children: Lisa, Brett, Carissa and Kelsey.

Jerry Kindall grew up in St. Paul, the oldest of three sons of a railroad working father, and graduated from St. Paul Washington High School in 1953. From there, Kindall went on to play baseball and basketball at the University of Minnesota. In 1956 Kindall, then a junior, was an All-American shortstop on the Gophers' NCAA Championship team that beat the University of Arizona in the College World Series title game. So good was Kindall that he opted to leave the Gophers after his junior year to play Major League Baseball. Kindall first signed with the Chicago Cubs and played in their organization for six years — two in the minors and four in the Bigs. He was then traded to Cleveland, where he played for two and a half seasons before being traded to the Twins in 1964, where he played on the 1965 American League Champion Twins."

In 1966 Kindall retired from baseball and came back to the University of Minnesota to get into coaching. He would spend one year working under John Kundla as a full-time basketball assistant and then one more working for Bill Fitch when Kundla stepped down that next season. (Prior to that Kindall had been coaching the freshman basketball team under Kundla for three years during his off-seasons.) By this time Kindall had already completed his English degree and was about to get his master's degree in physical education as well. In 1968, Kindall, who was also running the Williams Scholarship Fund for the U of M, took on the double duty of serving as an assistant baseball coach under Dick Siebert. Jerry was married at this point with four small children and was eager to take that next big step in the world of coaching. (Jerry met his wife, Georgia, a nursing student from Minneapolis, while he was a student at the U of M.) So, in 1972, when the University of Arizona's head coaching position became available, he jumped at it. Coach Siebert even helped him get the job and lobbied hard for him to get his big break.

Kindall wasted little time in making a name for himself in Arizona. Just three seasons after arriving in Tucson, Kindall led his Wildcats to the 1976 College World Series title. In so doing, Kindall became the first person ever to play on a national championship team as well as coach a national championship team. Kindall would guide the Wildcats for the next quarter century, leading them to two more NCAA National Championships in 1980 and 1986, as well as win six conference titles along the way. In addition, his Wildcats were either NCAA Regional finalists or champions 11 times and advanced to the NCAA College World Series in Omaha five times.

Kindall retired from coaching in the Summer of 1996 as the winningest baseball coach in the history of University of Arizona Baseball with 861 victories, good for a .620 winning percentage and an average of 36 wins per season. Among his many coaching accolades, Kindall was named College Baseball's Coach Of The Year in 1976, 1980 and 1986. He was also inducted into the College Baseball Coaches Hall of Fame in 1991, the University of Minnesota Sports Hall of Fame in 1995 and The University of Arizona Sports Hall of Fame in 1996. In addition, Kindall was very active on the national and international scene as well. He served as the head coach for the 1979 Team U.S.A. baseball team in the Pan American Games held in Puerto Rico, and was also an assistant coach for the 1991 and 1999 U.S. National Teams as well.

A tireless teacher of the game he loved, Kindall has coached and given clinics in Europe, Taiwan, South America, Aruba, China, Latin America, as well as in over 40 states in the U.S. He also authored the popular instructional book "Sports Illustrated Baseball"

along with numerous magazine articles on baseball coaching, and four instructional videos for coaches and players. Additionally, he served as the editor of "The Science of Baseball" and co-editor of the best seller, "The Baseball Coaching Bible."

Jerry, a widower, married Diane Sargent of Colorado Springs, in 1988, and presently resides in Tucson. Kindall has four married children: Betsy, Doug, Bruce and Martha. Diane, widowed in 1987, has two children: Rodney and Lisa.

HOW WOULD YOU DESCRIBE YOUR COACHING STYLE? "I think my style was a deliberate style, and that I had a good understanding of my players' abilities. It was a style that was also built on the experience of the players involved and how much I knew about their abilities and weaknesses. I did not play hunches in my coaching, and instead played by the book. I also always tried to coach my players in the fundamentals and prepared them in the basics: to run, throw, hit and field. I tried to do that constructively. Then, I taught them the strategies of the game and explained to them the reason why I was doing what I was doing. That was important. I also studied the statistical side of players, something I learned from Dick Siebert, whom I patterned much of my style after."

HOW DID YOU MOTIVATE YOUR PLAYERS? "I tried to motivate them with praise, support and encouragement. I feel that it is more important to encourage players than it is to criticize them. It is absolutely essential, however, to be constructively critical. There are always those teaching moments when you have to bring their faults and their failures to light. I just chose to do that constructively. In addition, my motivational talks were not based on hyperbole or hypothetical instances. They were based on past success involving real people and real occurrences — most of them from past Arizona baseball players. I wanted my players to visualize success and I gave them real life examples of others just like them who had already done it."

WHO WERE YOUR COACHING MENTORS? "I learned the game from Dick Siebert, both as a player and as an assistant coach. He was just great. He was also so well prepared. He had a tremendous knowledge of each players' abilities because he kept such careful statistics of them both in practice as well as in games. So, when he submitted a line-up, or inserted a pinch hitter, or brought in a relief pitcher, he had this resource of past successes and failures on that particular player that he had already chronicled. He was so good at explaining to his players why he was doing what he was doing. He was always coaching and enlightening us along the way. I learned a great deal from him."

IF YOU COULD MAGICALLY GO BACK IN TIME TO THE FIRST YEAR YOU WERE A HEAD COACH AND GIVE YOURSELF SOME ADVICE FOR THE FUTURE, KNOWING WHAT YOU KNOW NOW, BACK THEN, WHAT WOULD YOU SAY TO YOURSELF? "Don't try to do everything by yourself and don't assume all the responsibility of the program. Every coach will have assistants, at whatever level, and you need to use them wisely. We need to trust them with responsibility and rely on them for the program's overall success. Hire good assistants, train them, and then trust them to do the right thing. This will make you a much better coach in the long run."

WHAT ARE THE CHARACTERISTICS OF LEADERS?
"Leaders have to have a willingness to admit mistakes. Good leaders foster trust, both personally and professionally, in those that they are leading. They also are people of principle and integrity, which in turn grows trust."

HOW DID YOU BUILD TEAM UNITY & CHEMISTRY?
"Chemistry is created more by the players than by the coach. We allowed our players elect their own co-captains and it was simply not a popularity contest either. They considered leadership, consistency, integrity, honesty as well as performance on the field to pick their captains. We set high standards and when the players realized that we were setting those goals and standards for them, and not for ourselves as coaches, then they figured out why we were out there practicing, why we wanted to win games and why we wanted to represent our university honorably. We also had a list of team policies that the players had as much in put as the coaches. The players demanded more of themselves on those team policies then we might have otherwise without their input. That was fascinating to me."

WHAT MOTIVATED YOU?
"I always wanted to be a coach. My father, who was a hard working blue collar railroad man, loved sports and he taught me that although winning was important, winning with honor and integrity was what was most important. That was inbred from my family at an early age. My mom and dad literally raised us under Biblical principles. So, that has been a motivation for me too, to live up to those standards."

WHAT ADVICE WOULD YOU HAVE FOR YOUNG COACHES STARTING OUT TODAY?
"First, be organized and prepared. A fun, informative practice session is the responsibility of the coach and that takes time and energy. When your players realize that you are spending time to organize a good practice for them, then they will get on board much more quickly. I even went as far as listing each individual player's name on every practice plan to let them know that I was thinking of them specifically when I set up a drill. That allowed the players to feel that they were important and let them know that I was thinking of them to be involved as a valuable member of the team. Second, coaches need knowledge of the game. They need to know the rules and strategies, they need to go to clinics and they need to keep learning. Thirdly, do all you can to build trust in your players. I think the way you live your personal life is a factor here too. Now, I am not setting myself up as a great paragon of virtue and righteousness, but I believe that how I behaved and talked was a reflection to the team. So, if you don't want your players to use obscene language, tobacco, alcohol, or other harmful things, then don't do these things yourself. That is important".

WHAT'S THE BIGGEST THING YOU'VE LEARNED FROM COACHING THAT YOU'VE BEEN ABLE TO APPLY TO YOUR EVERYDAY LIFE?
"That hard work and perseverance pays off. We won a lot of games, but we lost a lot too, and you have to learn from those losses to get better."

WHAT ARE THE KEY INGREDIENTS TO CREATING A CHAMPIONSHIP TEAM?
"You must have good players to begin with. We had to recruit good kids, no question. Then, we changed some guys around in terms of their positions in order to get the most out of our line-up. You need a lot of things to come together with regards to chemistry, hard work and luck too. It just all has to come together for you."

HOW DO YOU WANT YOUR COACHING EPITAPH TO READ — HOW DO YOU WANT TO BE REMEMBERED AS A COACH?
"Coach Kindall had higher purposes for his players than merely teaching his players about winning baseball. He taught them what makes a good teammate, a good husband, a good father, a good man."

LLOYD STUSSY:
WELLS HIGH SCHOOL BASKETBALL

Lloyd Stussy was a Southern Minnesota coaching legend. After graduating from the University of Minnesota, Stussy spent his first four years out of college coaching at Tintah and Monticello. Then, in 1942, he went to Wells High School, where he would become a sports icon. In a career that spanned 36 seasons, Stussy's overall basketball record was 522-206 (.717). In 32 seasons at Wells, his Wildcats compiled a 465-196 record, won 10 District 5 championships and three Region 2 titles. Stussy also coached the Wells track team from 1942-67, and the school's baseball team from 1950-62 as well. His track teams won 20 consecutive conference titles, 10 district titles and three region titles, while his baseball squads won three district titles and one region title too. Stussy retired from coaching in 1974 to concentrate on his athletic director duties, ultimately retiring from that position in 1988. Stussy, who died in 2003 at the age of 85, was elected to the Minnesota State High School Coaches Association Hall of Fame in 1988. Perhaps Stussy's greatest legacy was the fact that at the time of his retirement, more than 50 of his former athletes were teaching and coaching throughout the Midwest.

BOBBY DILL:
MINOR LEAGUE BASEBALL & HOCKEY

Bobby Dill was born in St. Paul in 1920 and went on to star in baseball and hockey at Cretin High School. After graduating in 1939, Dill went on to play professional hockey for the next 12 years. Dill was a defenseman for the NHL's New York Rangers from 1943-45 and also played several years in the American Hockey League and the United States Hockey League. A nephew of Mike Gibbons, a former professional boxer, Dill was tough as nails, and earned his living the hard way. Dill wound down his professional career in the USHL, where he played five all star seasons for his hometown St. Paul Saints. In 1952 Dill was also player-coach with Springfield in the AHL. From there, Dill got into baseball, and went on to serve as a minor-league manager for affiliates of the New York Giants, New York Yankees and Cincinnati Reds. (He had also already played outfield with Minneapolis and Indianapolis several years earlier in the American Association.) Dill would later serve as a scout with the Minnesota North Stars and was inducted into the United States Hockey Hall of Fame in 1979.

TINK LARSON
HIGH SCHOOL BASEBALL: WASECA

Tink Larson grew up in southeastern Minnesota and went on to graduate from Kasson-Mantorville High School in 1960. Larson then went to attend Mankato State University, where he played baseball and earned his degree in teaching. From there, Larson went into professional baseball umpiring for a couple of years before getting into teaching. Larson's first teaching job was at Waseca High School, and, believe it or not, he has been there ever since. Larson started coaching town team baseball and American Legion baseball when he was only 19 years old, so he has been coaching for 42 years now. Incredibly, Larson has coached over 4,000 games at various levels during his career! He has estimated that he has around 2,500 wins and around 1,500 losses, give or take a few dozen here or there. Larson taught social studies, phys-ed and health for 33 years at Waseca High School, where he also coached the baseball team. In the process, he became a true coaching icon. In high school baseball in Minnesota, Larson is one of the winningest coaches of all time with more than 400 victories. He also won a state championship in 1990 as well.

A man of great integrity and honor, Larson even stepped down as the head coach to make sure that one of his sons best friends, Todd Mann, could get into the coaching ranks.

"I stepped down in order for him to get the job and that was very rewarding. Todd is now the athletic director too and that is great to see. And hey, I am an assistant with him and we are now great friends too."

Now retired from teaching, Larson still serves as an assistant coach with the football, baseball and basketball teams at Waseca High School. He also still coaches VFW and Legion baseball as well. Well known throughout Southern Minnesota as an outstanding teacher and coach, Tink Larson is among the best of the best in high school baseball.

HOW WOULD YOU DESCRIBE YOUR COACHING STYLE? "I believed strongly in the fundamentals and in discipline. We did things over and over again until we did them right because I always felt that it was the little things that made the difference between winning and losing. In a tight game, if you have a good team and you are playing against a good team, then anything you can do to pick up a run here or there or prevent a run here or there will make all the difference in winning or losing. So, we worked hard, focused on repetition and went out there and played baseball as best as we could."

HOW DO YOU MOTIVATE YOUR PLAYERS? "I really felt strongly that my players should be disciplined on the field and that they did things the way we felt that they should be done. So, we practiced hard to get better and we worked on execution. Whether it was bunting or stealing a base, we wanted our kids to be prepared so that their teammates could count on them in clutch situations. I just tried to treat everyone fairly and with respect."

WHO WERE YOUR COACHING MENTORS? "Dale Timm, my high school coach at Kasson Manterville, and Gene McCarthy, my coach at Mankato State. Dale knew how to handle kids and knew the game. Gene, on the other hand, emphasized pitching and defense — and I have followed suit as well. Both were solid on the fundamentals and I learned a lot from both of them."

IF YOU COULD MAGICALLY GO BACK IN TIME TO THE FIRST YEAR YOU WERE A HEAD COACH AND GIVE YOURSELF SOME ADVICE FOR THE FUTURE, KNOWING WHAT YOU KNOW NOW, BACK THEN, WHAT WOULD YOU SAY TO YOURSELF? "Be a little more patient. When you are young sometimes you do things too quickly. I think I was hard on my guys early on too, so maybe I would lighten up a bit and be a little nicer."

LOOKING BACK WHAT ARE YOU MOST PROUD OF IN YOUR CAREER? "It might sound a bit egotistical, but I would have to say our state championship that we finally got in 1990. I loved working with the kids, don't get me wrong, but that title was sweet."

HOW DO YOU BUILD TEAM UNITY & CHEMISTRY? "We were a little old fashioned and didn't like to put up with people with big egos. So, we tried to make everyone feel that they were just as equal as the next guy. That way we didn't have the superstar treatment and that sat well with our kids. We just encouraged our players to have respect for each other and play hard, that was how we built chemistry."

WHAT MOTIVATES YOU? "For me it was the challenge. I loved to take a team full of kids and see if I could make them better. From tee-ball to VFW to American Legion to high school ball, it was great to see kids develop and get better. Year by year it was great to see them come up through the ranks and then watch them turn into to solid ballplayers. There was a lot of satisfaction in that. Sure, wins are nice and we played to win, but to be able to work with these kids and watch them develop into as good of ballplayers as the could be was great. Then, if they went on and played at the next level, well that was great too. And, if down the road they come back after high school and thanked you for all the time that you spent with them, then that was also very rewarding — even more so than the numbers of wins you had over the course of your career."

WHAT ADVICE WOULD YOU HAVE FOR YOUNG COACHES STARTING OUT TODAY? "Give it some time and don't try to do it all at once. You have to be able to develop your programs underneath your varsity level and build a feeder system, and that takes time. Then, you need to develop a winning type attitude amongst your players and make it contagious."

WHAT'S THE BIGGEST THING YOU'VE LEARNED FROM COACHING THAT YOU'VE BEEN ABLE TO APPLY TO YOUR EVERYDAY LIFE? "That there are a lot of ups and downs, a lot of setbacks and you have to learn to deal with those setbacks, whether they are on the athletic field or in real life. Being able to handle success and failure in athletics carries over a lot into your everyday life."

WHAT IS THE KEY TO GOOD TIME MANAGEMENT? "Having a plan of what you are going to do. I never went into a practice, whether it was baseball or basketball or even in the classroom for that matter, where I didn't have written down what I wanted to do. That way I knew what I wanted to get done for the day and it was right there in black and white."

WHAT ARE THE KEY INGREDIENTS TO CREATING A CHAMPIONSHIP TEAM? "Good players. Hey, it's like (Twins Manager) Tom Kelly always says, 'What's chemistry? Winning.' You also need great pitching and outstanding defense. Beyond that, I think the better teams seemed to enjoy the game more, worked harder and had better unity."

WHAT IS THE BEST PIECE OF ADVICE YOU EVER GOT FROM ANOTHER COACH? "When I first came to Waseca the basketball coach here, Manny Beckman, told me: 'You will never please all of the people all of the time, so do it the way you want to do it so that you can please yourself.' That was great advice and I have never forgotten that."

WHAT'S THE SECRET TO YOUR SUCCESS? "Hard work is first. Then, I would say the development of our program, because when I came here we were just terrible. After that I would say it was being able to teach the game to the kids and getting the kids to respond to that teaching."

WHAT WOULD YOU WANT TO SAY TO YOUR FANS, BOOSTERS, AND ALUMNI WHO HAVE SUPPORTED YOU ALL THESE YEARS? "I would want to thank all of the people who have supported us over the years. We have come into contact with an awful lot of young people and the support that we have gotten from most of those parents has been outstanding. The community has been great here in Waseca and we wouldn't still be doing it if we didn't enjoy working with the kids."

HOW DO YOU WANT YOUR COACHING EPITAPH TO READ — HOW DO YOU WANT TO BE REMEMBERED AS A COACH? "He loved the game of baseball, he loved to play the game of baseball and he loved to coach the game of baseball".

"The one constant through all the years, Ray, has been baseball. America has rolled by like an army of steamrollers. It has been erased like a blackboard, rebuilt and erased again. But baseball has marked the time. This field, this game; it's a part of our past, Ray. It reminds us of all that once was good and it could be again." — Terence Mann (actor James Earl Jones) in the movie "Field of Dreams."

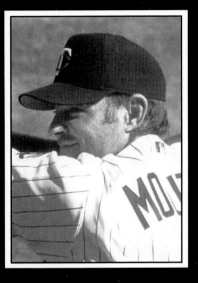

PAUL MOLITOR: MINNESOTA TWINS

Born and raised in St. Paul, Paul Molitor went on to star on the baseball diamond at Cretin High School. From there, Molitor earned All-American honors at the University of Minnesota, where he also led his Gophers to the 1977 College World Series. Molitor then went on to become a Major League All-Star, playing 21 big league seasons with the Milwaukee Brewers, Toronto Blue Jays and Minnesota Twins — where he came home to notch his historic 3,000th hit. Molly hung up his cleats in 1998 after posting a career batting average of .306. He will most certainly be a first ballot Hall of Famer in the Summer of 2004. Upon his retirement, Molly got into coaching with the Twins, serving as a hitting instructor. Will he become a big league manager someday? Stay tuned. This guy is a proven winner and if he does, he will most certainly become a winner in that aspect of the game as well.

GEORGE KEOGAN: NOTRE DAME BASKETBALL

George Keogan, a Detroit Lakes native, began his coaching career at St. Thomas College in 1915-16, and led the Tommies to a 13-2 record. From there, Keogan coached at Notre Dame, from 1927-43 and posted an amazing 327-96-1 record in South Bend without ever suffering a losing campaign. Recognized as one of the college game's more notable innovators of strategy and technique, Keogan's legacy might have even been greater than it was had he not tragically died in the middle of the 1943 season.

In one of his lighter career moments, Keogan once cut George Mikan, who came to South Bend to try out for his team. There, after a miserable try-out, Keogan mercilessly told the clumsy, uncoordinated kid, that he should *"Go back to DePaul, where he'd make a better scholar than a basketball player..."* Mikan, of course, would go on to be named as the greatest player of the first half of the century. (A guy named Michael Jordan was named best player of the second half...) Keogan was later enshrined into the Basketball Hall of Fame in 1995.

DENNY LORSUNG
COLLEGE BASEBALL: ST. CLOUD STATE UNIVERSITY

Denny Lorsung grew up in Alexandria and went on to graduate from Alexandria High School. From there, Lorsung played baseball at Austin Community College, and later transferred to St. Cloud State University, graduating in 1971 with a bachelor's degree in social studies. Lorsung was a catcher for the Husky baseball team under coach Jim Stanek and in 1969, was a member of the Husky team that finished third in the National Association of Intercollegiate Athletics (NAIA) National Tournament. Lorsung went on to captain the 1970 squad and earn the team's Most Valuable Player honors to boot — even winning the conference batting title that season with a .435 average.

Lorsung got his first big coaching gig in 1976 at St. John's University. In 1977 his Johnnies' won the MIAC title and he was honored as the MIAC Coach of the Year. That next year Lorsung came back to his alma mater, St. Cloud State University, to serve as an assistant coach for one year, before taking over as head coach in 1979. Since then he has been simply outstanding. Lorsung coached teams have appeared in North Central Conference post-season play 13 times, winning the NCC Championship in 1991. The Huskies were conference runner-ups in the 1986, 1989, and 1999 seasons, and he also led the Huskies to the 1980 Northern Intercollegiate Conference title as well. Now entering his 25th year at the Helm of St. Cloud State University Baseball, Lorsung has become the winningest coach in SCSU history with a 497-462-3 overall record. His overall collegiate coaching record stands at 534-486-3. As the Huskies went into the 2003 season, Lorsung ranks 27th in victories among active NCAA Division II coaches. Among his many coaching accolades, Lorsung has earned Coach of the Year honors in three leagues: the NCC (1991 and 2001), NSIC (1980) and the MIAC (1977). In addition, his vast knowledge of the game has also allowed him to direct baseball camps at such far away exotic locales as the University of Costa Rica.

With more than 500 wins Denny is still going strong and shows no signs of slowing down. He is one of Minnesota's very best.

HOW WOULD YOU DESCRIBE YOUR COACHING STYLE? "It changes each year and it changes with the players that you have. Basically, my feeling is that we need to give our kids an opportunity to improve and then give them the responsibility to make that happen. Then, I try and stay out of their way unless they need some help."

HOW DO YOU MOTIVATE YOUR PLAYERS? "I think that self-motivation is a more important thing. It's all about just talking to them and trying to get them to appreciate the skills that they have and what they possibly can do with that so that they can take that next step to be the best they can be."

WHO WERE YOUR COACHING MENTORS? "I would say the biggest influence that I had was Jim Stanek who was my coach at St. Cloud State and who was the coach before I got this job. He was an extremely organized man and I think that part of it really helped me when I was a young coach starting out. He was honest with his players and everybody that he dealt with, and that was a great quality that I learned from him as well."

LOOKING BACK WHAT ARE YOU MOST PROUD OF IN YOUR CAREER? "I don't think there is a kid who ever played for

me or tried out for my team that could say that I wasn't honest with him. I have always tried to be as honest as I could and I am proud of that."

WHAT WAS THE KEY TO RECRUITING? "The key to recruiting is just getting out there and seeing as many kids as you can. Then, once you meet them, it is so important to establish some kind of rapport with them so that they have a feel for what you and your program are all about. I would also say that there is no sense in recruiting kids who aren't going to enjoy playing for you, playing with the team that you have, or are not going to enjoy the atmosphere at your school or community."

HOW DO YOU BUILD TEAM UNITY & CHEMISTRY? "I don't think that you do. The only way that I can have an influence on that is by having the right people in my program. To give people the opportunity to practice and play and fulfill their abilities is what the coach can do. To build chemistry you have to have people who care about other people and who are leaders. One thing you will find at this level with coaches is that their biggest lament is not finding talent, it is finding good leadership. Once you have good leaders on your team, your team chemistry just happens."

WHAT MOTIVATES YOU? "I no longer have a fear of losing, unfortunately we have done it too much! Really though, winning games motivates me as does beating my opponent. I just love that."

WHAT ADVICE WOULD YOU HAVE FOR YOUNG COACHES STARTING OUT TODAY? "The most important thing is to do your best. Number two is to be as honest as you can. Number three is be able to look yourself in the mirror every night. Right now there are so many outside pressures on coaches, particularly at the high school levels and younger, with parents. So, unless you can be confident in what you are doing, it won't be any fun."

WHAT'S THE BIGGEST THING YOU'VE LEARNED FROM COACHING THAT YOU'VE BEEN ABLE TO APPLY TO YOUR EVERYDAY LIFE? "I am not sure it doesn't work the other way around, 'what are the things that I learned in my everyday life that I was ably to apply to coaching?' I would look at it that way."

WHAT'S THE SECRET TO YOUR SUCCESS? "Being straight forward and honest. Also, you need players. In addition, you need kids who want to win and will do whatever it take to win. Then, after all that, you have to have fun — this is still a game."

WHAT WOULD YOU WANT TO SAY TO YOUR FANS, BOOSTERS, AND ALUMNI WHO HAVE SUPPORTED YOU ALL THESE YEARS? "The support that the parents and former players give a team is the most important thing that the team has because it lasts for a long time. We have alumni who run our golf tournament, raise money and still talk to people about our program. Without that kind of support, it would be almost impossible to have any sort of success. So, thanks for sticking with us."

HOW DO YOU WANT YOUR COACHING EPITAPH TO READ — HOW DO YOU WANT TO BE REMEMBERED AS A COACH? "I would hope that people in my program would say that they had fun. That is what it is all about."

DICK SELTZ
HIGH SCHOOL BASEBALL: AUSTIN

Dick Seltz grew up in West St. Paul and graduated from St. Paul Humboldt High School in 1943. Seltz then went on to play college baseball at Hamline University with his brother Rollie, who later played major league baseball with the Brooklyn Dodgers. After college, Seltz played in the St. Louis Cardinals minor league system for a total of three years, while also spending three years in the Army during World War II. When he got out of the service, he returned to minor league baseball, where he was making $300 a month playing in the Northern League with the St. Cloud Rox. In 1948 he got an offer to teach and play baseball in the Southern Minnie League with Austin, for $500 a month. He agreed and the rest, they say, is history.

Seltz, whose roommate with Austin early on was future major leaguer, Moose Skowren, would play semi-pro ball and also coach and teach American History at Austin High School. In all, he would spend 36 years guiding the Packers and early on, his teams were amongst the best in the state — year in and year out. Seltz's teams won two state titles in 1954 and 1964, finished second five times, and also won 23 Big Nine Conference titles as well. Back in the day, Seltz was the winningest coach of them all, by far, winning 509 career ballgames. Seltz was also an assistant on the basketball team for 14 years as well. When it was all said and done, Dick Seltz had put Austin on the baseball map, and for that he should forever be remembered as a real high school baseball coaching legend.

HOW WOULD YOU DESCRIBE YOUR COACHING STYLE? "The only way to win ballgames was to have pretty good material. We worked a lot on defense and pitching too. In fact, I bet I spent at least 75% of my time working on defense, hitting ground balls and fly balls over and over again until my kids got it right. That was the key, to hold your opponents down and as long as you could get a little hitting, you had a chance to win. Another thing that I worked on with my kids was the take. You know, that is a lost art, to be able to stare down a pitcher and take him to a full count. I always felt that kids swung away too much. I wanted our guys to make them earn it, and if they didn't, I wanted them to get to first base on a walk. Then, we could and manufacture a run. I never believed in just sending a kid up there and then saying 'OK, swing…', I wanted them to be in that ballgame for every pitch. In high school baseball kids are such wild swingers and that never flew with me. On my teams if a player had a 3-1 count, it was an automatic take. The idea was to get somebody on base, because then something could happen."

HOW DID YOU MOTIVATE YOUR PLAYERS? "I motivated through discipline and hard work. I expected my players to come to practice every day and give it their best. I worked them hard and I treated them fairly, but I expected a good effort in return. I think that good ballplayers don't want to let their teammates down and that all went into it."

WHAT ARE THE CHARACTERISTICS OF LEADERS? "I think it is something you are born with. Some kids are just born leaders and they can get others to follow them."

LOOKING BACK WHAT ARE YOU MOST PROUD OF IN YOUR CAREER? "When kids come home and visit you and still call you coach, 30-40 years after the fact, that to me is about as good as it gets."

HOW DID YOU BUILD TEAM UNITY & CHEMISTRY? "I think you had to be very, very fair to everybody and make sure that they knew that too. Once you did that, and treated them all equally, then you could build trust and respect amongst one another. That was the key to creating team unity."

WHAT MOTIVATED YOU? "To coach high school baseball in Minnesota you have got to like what you are doing. I mean you freeze your tail off for one thing. Then, baseball is not nearly as popular as football or basketball, so you don't get the support from the administration that you would like. Really, you are out there a lot on your own so you have to just love it, plain and simple. Well, I did love it and that was why I stuck around so long. To teach those kids and make a difference in their lives was great. Then, the frosting on the cake was winning all those ballgames."

WHAT ADVICE WOULD YOU HAVE FOR YOUNG COACHES STARTING OUT TODAY? "I would go out and talk to some successful coaches and find out what helped them and made them winners. I tell you what, I have been out of coaching now for 15 years or so, but I bet I could give a younger coach a little advice where he could win another six or seven ballgames each season, and that's a fact."

WHAT'S THE BEST ADVICE YOU EVER GOT FROM ANOTHER COACH? "Keep it simple. That says it all."

WHAT'S THE BIGGEST THING YOU'VE LEARNED FROM COACHING THAT YOU'VE BEEN ABLE TO APPLY TO YOUR EVERYDAY LIFE? "I would say hard work and discipline. Coaching high school baseball is tough, tough work. I worked back in the '50s with no assistants to help out and that was tough. I mean hitting fly balls, ground balls, and pitching batting practice over and over again was hard work, let me tell you. I wanted to make sure that every infielder got at least 50-75 ground balls every day in practice, and the only way that was going to happen was if I did it myself. It was a big commitment, but my kids were worth it."

WHAT ARE THE KEY INGREDIENTS TO CREATING A CHAMPIONSHIP TEAM? "You have got to have good defense, good pitching and your kids have to be disciplined at the plate. We just focused on winning conference titles first, and if we did that, then we talked about state titles. I never wanted to put the cart before the horse."

WHAT'S THE SECRET TO YOUR SUCCESS? "Hard work and discipline. That was it."

HOW DO YOU WANT YOUR COACHING EPITAPH TO READ — HOW DO YOU WANT TO BE REMEMBERED AS A COACH? "He treated everybody fairly and was a hard worker. I enjoyed all 36 years, it was an honor and a privilege to coach all those fine young men."

Gene Mauch was born in Salina, Kan., in 1925 and at the age of 13 his family moved to Los Angeles. There, Gene grew up loving sports and went on to play football, baseball and basketball in high school. Mauch had the opportunity to attend USC or Stanford on football and baseball scholarships, but instead went into the Service, where he became an Air Cadet. After the Service, Mauch went back to his true love, baseball. From there, Mauch would go on to play a total of nine seasons in the major leagues, mostly as a second baseman. He first started out playing ball in Durham, in 1943, and from there the list of cities is long: Montreal, Brooklyn, St. Paul, Pittsburgh, Indianapolis, Chicago (AL & NL), Boston (AL & NL), St. Louis, Milwaukee, Atlanta, Los Angeles, and finally the Minneapolis Millers, where he retired as an active player/manager in 1959. He had a career .239 batting average — nothing to write home about, but solid nonetheless.

Mauch started managing at the young age of 27 with the Atlanta Crackers in the Southern Association. He continued to manage with the Millers and got his big break in 1960 when he took over for the Philadelphia Phillies. He stayed in Philly until 1968, when he left to guide the expansion Montreal Expos. Mauch then managed the Minnesota Twins from 1976-80, posting a career record of 378-394. He was a big fan-favorite with the people of Minnesota, and the players loved him too. From Minnesota Gene went on to guide the Angels, until finally hanging it up for good in 1987. He came out of retirement in 1995, to serve as a bench coach with the Kansas City Royals, but hung it up again that next year. He would retire as one of the most respected managers of all time. Mauch is among a select fraternity of big-league skippers on the all-time seniority list, having managed for more than three decades. He also holds the dubious distinction of managing the most years (26) without winning a pennant.

Mauch's no-nonsense attitude and tell-it-like-it-is mentality gave him instant respect and credibility. He was a player's coach and his players knew that he would always be there for them if they needed him. He was a throwback and a one of a kind baseball legend that America will never see the likes of again. Mauch was also an intense competitor and a great ambassador of baseball. He will be forever remembered as an integral thread in the fabric of Minnesota's baseball history.

ON BEING A MEMBER OF THE SAINTS, MILLERS AND TWINS: "You know, I loved Minnesota so much that I even considered moving up there at one point. I might have done so had somebody not told me that there were just two seasons there: July and Winter! There is nothing quite like Midwestern people though, they are great and I really loved the people up there. I can still remember playing with the Millers in Met Stadium and really enjoying myself, that might have been the most fun I ever had in baseball. Then, being with the Twins was wonderful. I worked with some great, great people: Calvin Griffith, Rod Carew, Tony Oliva, Larry Hisle, Lyman Bostock, Butch Wynegar, and my nephew, Roy Smalley. They were just outstanding people and such great ballplayers. I mean being able to have the opportunity to manage guys like Rod Carew and Tony Oliva, I felt like my time in Minnesota wasn't a job, it was a privilege."

HOW WOULD YOU DESCRIBE YOUR COACHING STYLE? "You know, I never even graduated from high school, and somebody asked me one time how the hell I got so smart. And I told him 'I'm not smart, it's just that everybody else thinks they're so damn smart if makes me look good!'"

HOW DID YOU MOTIVATE YOUR PLAYERS? "I always thought it was an insult to the players on your team if you claimed that you could motivate them. Baseball players don't need motivation. I always thought that was a slam and never did believe that. I just tried to be realistic with them, sure, but I thought it was an insult to their intelligence to say that they needed motivation. You know, if we ever got into a slump or were having a tough time I would gather a bunch of my players together in a little group and say 'Lookee here, we have one problem — you guys have forgotten how God damn good you are, now let's got out and play like we know how to play!'"

IF YOU COULD MAGICALLY GO BACK IN TIME TO THE FIRST YEAR YOU WERE A HEAD COACH AND GIVE YOURSELF SOME ADVICE FOR THE FUTURE, KNOWING WHAT YOU KNOW NOW, BACK THEN, WHAT WOULD YOU SAY TO YOURSELF? "All I knew how to do was to work as hard as I could every day, and I did that for my entire career. Then, you just had to hope that that was enough. I tell you what, if there was a hall of fame for hard work, I would have been in there a long time ago."

HOW HAS THE GAME CHANGED SINCE YOUR DAY? "I would say the lack of emphasis on winning each game. I came back after being retired for seven years and served as a bench coach for Bob Boone in 1995 with Kansas City, and I think we won seven out of our first nine games. Then, on the 10th game, we didn't get beat, we just lost it, threw it away, and nobody in that clubhouse gave a damn. So I said, 'My God, I have to put up with 152 more days of this?' It just seemed like nobody cared. They had done their little thing and tried as hard as they could. And, maybe that's the way it should be, but not for me. It was a sick feeling that hit my belly. It was at that point that I knew it was going to be my last go-around with them."

WHAT ARE THE CHARACTERISTICS OF LEADERS? "A good bullpen. You can't win without a bullpen. I repeat, you can not and will not win without a bullpen! The starting pitchers have been influenced too much by their agents and they will only go six innings or so these days, not a bad gig for $10, $12, $14 million a year, and then they will turn it over to their relievers. So, if you don't have other guys to turn it over to, you are in the sh--house and that aint going to change either."

HOW DID YOU BUILD TEAM UNITY & CHEMISTRY? "I always thought that the tempo for your team, the personality for your team, was established in Spring training. You know, we played little games amongst ourselves when we practiced and also simulating certain situations in our minds to get better. As a result, we established our attitude down there and that carried over into the season. I think that Spring training is the most important time of the year for a manager because that is when you get to know your players and see what you have to work with."

WHAT ADVICE WOULD YOU HAVE FOR YOUNG COACHES STARTING OUT TODAY? "I know you have to have enthusiasm because they know if you have it or not, and you simply must have it. You know they always talk about managers reading players, hell, the players read the managers just as much. They are evaluating him all the time and know if he is on the up-and-up or not. So, you have got to be sincere, caring and organized."

WHAT WAS THE BEST ADVICE YOU EVER GOT FROM ANOTHER COACH? "In 1950 I was 24 years old and played for Billy Southworth with the Boston Braves. Now, at the time, they were talking about me being a potential manager way down the road. So, Billy says to me 'Skipper, one of these days you are going to become a manager and I've got one piece of advice for you — don't fall in love with your ballplayers.' That was good advice and something I took with me throughout my career."

ON COACHING YOUR NEPHEW, ROY SMALLEY: "That was one of the greatest experiences of my life and I was never so proud of anybody in my years in baseball as I was Roy Smalley. There were a lot of people who told him that he never would have made the Twins had I not been the manager, but he ended up being an All-Star shortstop. I was never as proud of anybody in my life as I was my nephew. Never!"

WHAT'S THE BIGGEST THING YOU'VE LEARNED FROM COACHING THAT YOU'VE BEEN ABLE TO APPLY TO YOUR EVERYDAY LIFE? "I think it is in reverse, really. I think the kind of person you are dictates what kind of manager that you will be."

WHAT'S THE SECRET TO YOUR SUCCESS? "I would say it was because I knew the game and my players knew that I knew the game. If you were in the game as long as I was and didn't know it, then that would be criminal. I will say that I did know the game quite well and they were aware of that, so they trusted me to do the right thing. I would also say that the necessities for being a manager was having a bit of knowledge, a decent appearance and a lot of guts. Maybe I had those and maybe I didn't, but that was what I always thought was a prerequisite for being a successful manager."

HOW DO YOU WANT YOUR COACHING EPITAPH TO READ — HOW DO YOU WANT TO BE REMEMBERED AS A COACH? "I haven't got a hell of a lot to be proud of, but I know in my heart, and I get a warm feeling thinking about it, that for all the 30 or so years that I managed, that I worked my ass off every day and nobody ever got cheated when they hired me. Nobody."

DR. LOUIS COOKE: GOPHER BASKETBALL

Dr. Louis Cooke was a Gopher Basketball legend back in the day. In 1924, after 28 years of loyal service, Cooke decided to step down as the head coach of the Gophers. Cooke, who had had guided Minnesota to two national championships and five conference titles, called it quits with an astonishing 245-137-2 (.641%) career record. His legacy would include taking a mere fad sport no more popular than a gym class activity and helping to turn it into one of our nation's greatest national pastimes. Cooke Hall (gymnasium) was later renamed after him in his honor.

J.D. BARNETT: WINONA STATE BASKETBALL

J.D. Barnett was born in Chillicothe, Mo., and went on to earn four letters in baseball and basketball at Winona State University, graduating in 1966. Barnett, who led his Warrior baseball teams to a pair of conference championship in 1965 and 1966, would then go on to spend the next several years playing professional baseball in the Pittsburgh Pirates organization. From there, Barnett began his collegiate basketball coaching career, first as an assistant at Roanoke College from 1969-70, followed by a year at Richmond, and finally at West Texas State, from 1973-77. Barnett then had two quick head coaching stops at Lenoir Rhyne College and High Point College, respectively, in Hickory and High Point, North Carolina. Following a pair of assistant coaching stops, Barnett then landed the head coaching position at Louisiana Tech University, where he eventually earned Southland Coach of the Year honors. Barnett's coaching career catapulted from there as he later moved to Virginia Commonwealth University. There, he was twice named as the Sun Belt Conference Coach of the Year and brought VCU to national prominence with five appearances in the NCAA tournament from 1980-85. (In 1985 his team was ranked as high as No. 11 in the nation.) Barnett's success continued with another head coaching move, this time to the University of Tulsa, where, from 1985-91, he led the Golden Hurricane to a 107-73 record. He also led his teams to a pair of Missouri Valley Championships, two NCAA Tournament and two NIT Tournament appearances as well. Barnett would later serve as the head coach at Northwestern State University, in Louisiana, from 1994-99, leading the Demons to a second-place finish in the Southland Conference in 1998 — NSU's best ever finish. Today, after retiring with more than 300 wins in 20-plus years, Barnett is the Senior Associate Athletic Director at Tulane University. J.D. and his wife Susan have two daughters and presently live in Natchitoches, La.

JIM SENSKE
HIGH SCHOOL BASEBALL: NEW ULM

Jim Senske grew up in Humberd, Wis., and came to Minnesota when his family moved from Wisconsin to St. Paul when he was in the eighth grade. Senske went on to play baseball at St. Paul Wilson High School, and then played collegiately at Hamline University. Upon his graduation in 1960, Senske went to New Ulm to teach social studies and serve as an assistant on the baseball and basketball teams. In 1964 Senske was offered the head baseball coaching position. He took it, and the rest they say, is history.

Today Jim Senske is the winningest baseball coach in state history. For more than four decades Jim Senske coached baseball at Johnson Park in New Ulm. With his classic, old-school graveled voice, Senske could always be heard telling his boys to "Hit a rope!" or "Come on, hit a line drive!" Senske became the winningest coach in Minnesota high school baseball history in 1994, when his 510th career victory surpassed the previous mark held by Austin's Dick Seltz. Since then, Senske went on to win a state-record 707 games — nearly 200 more than his closest pursuer, truly putting him into a league of his own. Senske also led his teams to the Minnesota State High School Tournament a record 19 times and won 26 South Central Conference titles as well. Senske retired as a teacher in 1999, but kept coaching until 2003. In 2002, however, Senske's Eagles finally captured the Class AAA baseball crown, when they beat North St. Paul, 12-4, at Midway Stadium. It would be a fitting exclamation point to a truly extraordinary career. Senske also had two former players reach the major leagues: Terry Steinbach (1986-99; Oakland and Twins) and Brian Raabe (1995-97; Twins, Seattle and Colorado). (In addition, Senske guided the boys' basketball team for 18 years, leading them to a state tournament appearance in 1975, and also served briefly as an assistant football coach for the Eagles as well.)

Among Senske's many state and national coaching awards and accolades, in 2003 his No. 24 uniform was retired at Johnson Park — the first number to ever be retired at New Ulm High School. That day was also proclaimed as "Jim Senske Day" in New Ulm by Mayor Joel Albrecht. Senske is a baseball coaching legend. Period. He is the very best of the very best and has made Minnesota so proud. Today Jim and his wife Katie, who came to nearly every one of his games over the years, are retired and live in New Ulm as well as in the Rio Grande Valley of Texas. They have one daughter and two sons — who each played baseball at New Ulm for the old man as well.

HOW WOULD YOU DESCRIBE YOUR COACHING STYLE? "I was pretty aggressive, pushy and maybe even intimidating in my early years, but have mellowed considerably in my later years. I am still hard-nosed and old-school in my teachings I guess, but that has been my formula for success. I still am bothered by earrings and long hair and that sort of thing, but I have been able to bend — because if you don't, then you won't be able to stick around for as long as I have. I also told my kids to have a hard work ethic and to respond to drills by working to improve their weaknesses. I wanted to encourage them to have patience and to be dedicated to practicing in order to get better. For instance, I think every kid's weakness at the high school level is the inability to hit the curve ball. I always felt like we could teach a kid how to hit a curve, but I think on average it took about two years. Also, we worked a lot on having our kids learn how to take an outside pitch and drive it into right field. We worked a lot on that, and that was one of the reasons for our success. I also think

I started out treating everybody the same way, but I learned over the years in coaching that you don't get the best results that way. You have to treat each individual kid in the manner and style that he is going to react to. Each kid is different and each kid responds to criticism in a different way. Finding out what that balance is, is a big key to success. If you do it poorly, you may turn the kid off to the sport forever, but if you do it properly, then you've got a friend for life."

WHO WERE YOUR COACHING MENTORS? "I had two people who were great influences on me: Bill Fitzharris, who was my baseball and football coach at St. Paul Wilson, and the other was Paul Sokol, who was the basketball coach at St. Thomas College."

IF YOU COULD MAGICALLY GO BACK IN TIME TO THE FIRST YEAR YOU WERE A HEAD COACH AND GIVE YOURSELF SOME ADVICE FOR THE FUTURE, KNOWING WHAT YOU KNOW NOW, BACK THEN, WHAT WOULD YOU SAY TO YOURSELF? "I would tell myself to be more patient and be less confrontational. Baseball is a relaxed game and things are not learned in spurts — they take a lot of time."

HOW DID YOU BUILD TEAM UNITY & CHEMISTRY? "I asked everybody to do the best job that they could. Then, I always tried to be a role model in some sense as well. I also have a strong work ethic and I expect my players to share that same work ethic. I also think that there has to be time for fun. We used to play a lot of games where we competed in practice and played for treats and that sort of thing. Sometimes I would throw batting practice and we would make a fun game out of it, and that helped to keep the kids loose. Then, some nights we put our noses to the grindstone and took practices very, very seriously as well. You have to vary your practices and vary your expectations to build good team unity and build chemistry."

WHAT IS THE KEY TO GOOD TIME MANAGEMENT? "In over 40 years I never ever went to a practice without a practice plan. In fact, it was so detailed that it was usually scheduled down to the last five minutes. I honest to God would have felt useless and almost naked if I didn't have my practices organized. We worked short periods of time on certain drills, maybe 15 minutes or so, and then moved on to keep it fresh so the kids stayed focused. We did a lot of repetition of the same drills, however, and that reinforced what they were learning."

WHAT MOTIVATED YOU? "Certainly winning motivated me, but also keeping our tradition that we have established going strong was a big factor too. New Ulm is a baseball community and I took great pride in being a part of that. I took it personally to see to it that each year our teams were competitive and gave the community something to be proud of. I felt responsible to see to it that every new team was a little better than the one before it. We have a lot of pride in our community and our reputation is very important to us."

WHAT ADVICE WOULD YOU HAVE FOR YOUNG COACHES STARTING OUT TODAY? "Try to find a town that likes baseball and then spend some time in the trenches. You have to work on your summer program, and the younger the better I think.

That way you have a feeder system to work off of and can build a solid program from the bottom up. In New Ulm, for instance, we've had numerous clinics for our Babe Ruth and junior league programs where other coaches such as Dennis Denning (St. Thomas), Tink Larson (Waseca) and Dean Bowyer (Minnesota State Mankato) came in to teach. That helps a lot. You also have to not only really enjoy teaching and coaching the kids, but I also think you have to coach their coaches as well as their dads. That way you are all working towards the same goals. I would also recommend marrying a woman who likes baseball. My wife is our biggest fan and she truly enjoys it. She grew up going to ballgames with her father and that has been tremendous for me as well as for our program. Finally, I would say that you have to get good assistants. My B-Squad coach has been with me for 17 years and my varsity assistant has been here for 25. They teach fundamentals and are just invaluable. Consistency like that is incredible and really shows the kids that there is a real commitment from the top down."

WHAT'S THE BIGGEST THING YOU'VE LEARNED FROM COACHING THAT YOU'VE BEEN ABLE TO APPLY TO YOUR EVERYDAY LIFE? "If you work at something and stay with it, giving it your best effort, good things are going to happen for you. I just can't say enough about having a good, solid work ethic."

WHAT'S THE BEST PIECE OF ADVICE YOU EVER GOT FROM ANOTHER COACH? "Lighten up! I guess I was pretty serious in my earlier days, but I think I have mellowed since then quite a bit. I guess I just have great expectations from my players and demand success. I give a lot of time to coaching and I expect a lot of effort in return."

ON FINALLY WINNING A STATE CHAMPIONSHIP IN 2002: "We were elated. It felt so good to get that big monkey off our back. It was for our community and for all of those kids, and it really felt great. It wasn't just a win for that team, it was a win for all of my teams over the past 40 years. You know, it was always tough to see how quickly kids got over losing a ball game. I mean I always wanted them to brood over it a little longer. They could be laughing and having a good time just 10 minutes after the final out, whereas it took me a lot longer to get over it. That's just kids being kids I guess. I have gotten better at that, but it is still tough for me to lose. Losing can also be a learning experience and that is important to remember too. But, to finally win the big one, after all these years was very special."

ON THE FUNDAMENTALS: "I teach bunting relentlessly, I think it is that important. My teams practice it for 15 minutes a day, every day. You know, when you get into tournament play, and you start to see the better pitching, you have to take advantage of the scoring opportunities that you have. There sometimes aren't that many of them and if you don't bunt the runner up into scoring position or if you can't squeeze him home, then you are not going to win the tight ball games."

WHAT ARE THE KEY INGREDIENTS TO CREATING A CHAMPIONSHIP TEAM? "It is made up of a lot of things. Good kids. Good character. Kids who like the game. Supportive parents. A town that is willing to not only support your program, but also come out and watch the kids. You also need a school that embraces a philosophy where winning is important. All of those things go into creating a winner."

WHAT'S THE SECRET TO YOUR SUCCESS? "I think it is a combination of a lot of things. For starters I was lucky enough to land in a town where they liked their baseball way before I got here. Southern Minnesota was big into baseball at the amateur level going way, way back and I just piggybacked on that success. You know, one of my former athletic directors once called me the "Iron Marshmallow," because I have a deep, sharp voice and am a tough disciplinarian. But, I am also a softy who has a good heart, and I truly love the kids."

WHAT WOULD YOU WANT TO SAY TO YOUR FANS, BOOSTERS, AND ALUMNI WHO HAVE SUPPORTED YOU ALL THESE YEARS? "I would thank them for the opportunity that I have had to work with their kids. I would thank them for their time, for their effort, for their support and the for the sacrifices they have made so their sons could play this great game. I have just been so blessed over the years with so many good kids and really want to say thanks to all of them. It is so gratifying to see these kids later on in life, and to become friends with them as they start their own families is quite rewarding."

HOW DO YOU WANT YOUR COACHING EPITAPH TO READ — HOW DO YOU WANT TO BE REMEMBERED AS A COACH? "He led by example. He didn't expect more of his players than he did of himself. He was driven. He was a hard worker. He was very motivated. Baseball is a game of life and I am just so lucky that it has been such an integral part of mine."

HOWIE SCHULTZ:
ST. PAUL LIGHTS BASKETBALL

Howie Schultz graduated from Minneapolis Central High School in 1940 as a basketball and baseball star. From there, Schultz went on to play college baseball and basketball at Hamline. Regarded by many as Hamline's greatest all-time athlete, Shultz went on to play pro baseball with Grand Forks in the Northern League before signing with his hometown St. Paul Saints in 1942. That next summer Schultz was called up by the Brooklyn Dodgers, where he played for five seasons before losing his roster spot to a guy named Jackie Robinson. In 1947 Howie was dealt to the Phillies, where he played for two more seasons. He returned to Minnesota in 1951 and then began playing with the NBA's Minneapolis Lakers, where he would play for four more seasons. (Prior to that he had been playing pro basketball with the Anderson Packers and Fort Wayne Pistons.) In addition, Schultz also coached the St. Paul Lights, a short-lived professional basketball team which played during the 1950-51 season as members of the National Professional Basketball League. (Schultz would play pro basketball for three seasons, but during the summer would play townball. He first played for Willmar in the West Central League, before moving on to play with Faribault of the old Southern Minny. He finally hung up his spikes in the late 1950s, but not before becoming one of the state's all time top sports figures.) When Schultz completed his successful pro sports career, he began teaching and coaching (basketball and baseball) at Mechanic Arts High School until his retirement. Howie Schultz is truly a Hamline sports legend.

Wayne "Twig" Terwilliger was born in Clare, Mich., and went on to graduate from Charlotte (Mich.) High School. After serving with the Marines in Saipan, Tinian and Iwo Jima, Terwilliger went on to become a three sport star at Western Michigan University, graduating with a degree in social science. From there, Terwilliger played minor league baseball for a few years until making his pro baseball debut with the Chicago Cubs in 1949. In 1951 the second baseman and shortstop was dealt to the Brooklyn Dodgers, whose triple A minor league team was the American Association's St. Paul Saints. (Twig's Brooklyn teammates included the likes of Jackie Robinson, Peewee Reese and Gil Hodges.) So, Twig was up and down in the organization for the next couple of seasons, both in Brooklyn as well as at old Lexington Park in St. Paul. In 1953 Terwilliger moved on to play for two seasons with the Washington Senators and in 1955 he wound up with the Giants. There, Twig would also briefly play for the Minneapolis Millers, the Giants minor league affiliate, during this era as well. Terwilliger would remain with that organization for two more seasons before finishing his pro career with Kansas City in 1960. In all, Twig would spend parts of nine seasons in the major leagues and finish with a .240 career batting average.

From there, he got into managing, where he went on to become a legend. In 1961 Twig began his minor league managing career in Greensboro in the Carolina League with the Yankees organization. He then switched to the Senators organization, which later became the Texas Rangers. Managing through 1980, Twig compiled a lifetime record of 1,062 wins and 969 losses. Among the numerous minor league managerial gigs Twig had during his career were: Pensacola, Geneva, Asheville, Wisconsin Rapids, Burlington, Hawaii, Buffalo, Columbus, Lynchburg and Tulsa.

As a coach, Twig's coaching career began in 1969, when, as the manager of Washington's AAA team at Buffalo, Twig went to spring training with the Senators to help out new Manager Ted Williams. Teddy Ballgame and Twig hit if off and Williams would later pick Twig to serve as his third-base coach when he managed the Senators. That stint took them to Texas in 1972, when the franchise moved and the Senators became the new Texas Rangers. Twig would spend four years with the Splendid Splinter, becoming great friends along the way.

Twig's next big coaching gig came back in Minnesota, in 1986, when he joined Tom Kelly's Twins. There, Twig would serve as first-base coach of the Twins for nine seasons, and playing a big role in the team's two World Series Championships of 1987 and 1991. Following his sting with the Twins, Twig then went on to serve as the first-base coach for the independent minor league St. Paul Saints from 1995 through 2002. There, Twig became a celebrity of sorts with the fans at Midway Stadium. Just prior to his departure from the team in 2002, the Saints honored his legacy by retiring his number. In addition, St. Paul Mayor Randy Kelly signed a proclamation designating a day in late August as "Wayne Terwilliger Day" in St. Paul, honoring a true baseball pioneer.

In all, Twig has been in a baseball uniform for more than 5,000 professional games as a player, coach, and manager in the major and minor leagues. He is also one of just five men known to have been in pro ball for at least 50 consecutive seasons. (Don Zimmer, Connie Mack, Bill Fischer and Jimmie Reese are the others.) Twig is a real baseball icon and believe it or not, he is still going strong! That's right. Now in his late 70's, Twig, after leaving St. Paul,

became the manager of the Fort Worth Cats, an independent minor league club in Texas. Wayne, now in his 56th season of professional baseball, and his wife Lin, presently reside in the Dallas area. He has two children, Marcie and Steve, and two stepsons, Mike and Kevin.

HOW WOULD YOU DESCRIBE YOUR COACHING STYLE? "I think leading by example sums it up best. You know, I coached four years for Ted Williams with the Washington Senators and the one thing I heard Ted say over and over was, 'You have got to have enthusiasm to play this game!'. So, I think I have tried to follow that and to be as enthusiastic as I can. If you have 25 players seeing your enthusiasm, then that is contagious. I also believed in hard work and discipline. As far as on-the-field stuff, I guess one thing I believed strongly in was that I never worried about not running when we were ahead late in a game. I ran all the time and I think that business about 'showing the other team up' is a bunch of hooey. I don't care if another team runs up the score on us. I mean hey, if we can't stop them from running it up then that is our fault. So, things like that all went into my style."

HOW DO YOU MOTIVATE YOUR PLAYERS? "Again, it comes down to enthusiasm. Winning is so much fun for me and I think the players know that. They read that and it rubs off on them so that they want to please their manager."

IF YOU COULD MAGICALLY GO BACK IN TIME TO THE FIRST YEAR YOU WERE A HEAD COACH AND GIVE YOURSELF SOME ADVICE FOR THE FUTURE, KNOWING WHAT YOU KNOW NOW, BACK THEN, WHAT WOULD YOU SAY TO YOURSELF? "I was so intent on winning that I threw a lot of things aside early on. For instance, I probably overused some pitchers when I first started managing and I have since learned better. I know that winning is important but I also learned that there are a lot of ways to go about it."

LOOKING BACK WHAT ARE YOU MOST PROUD OF IN YOUR CAREER? "I think was most proud of the fact that I was able to make it to the big leagues. I was also very proud of my service in the Marine Corps, because that played a very big part of who I am today."

HOW HAS THE GAME CHANGED OVER THE PAST HALF CENTURY? "The biggest thing in my opinion is helmets. You know, baseball has pretty much stayed the same, but when players started wearing those big old heavy helmets, it changed everything. The hitters then started crowding the plate more and they didn't have any more fear. I mean there is a certain amount of fear in hitting that you are going to get plunked in the head, and when that fear is gone that changes everything."

WHAT ADVICE WOULD YOU HAVE FOR YOUNG COACHES STARTING OUT TODAY? "Don't get discouraged too easily. Just manage or coach the way you feel and learn from the experiences that you get along the way."

WHAT'S THE BIGGEST THING YOU'VE LEARNED FROM COACHING THAT YOU'VE BEEN ABLE TO APPLY TO

YOUR EVERYDAY LIFE? "I just appreciate people more. It took me a long time to grow up, it really did. I made a lot of mistakes along the way and now I can see the light. You really do learn something new everyday in this game and that just makes it more and more enjoyable for me."

WHAT'S THE SECRET TO YOUR SUCCESS? "I think I am a good listener and that goes a long way. Beyond that, I just tried to have fun out there and I think that was why the fans liked me as much as they did. For instance, when I was the first base coach with the Twins, after each inning that Kent Hrbek would make the last out he would throw his helmet up in the air as he ran past first base and I would run under it like a football player and catch it. Little stuff like that was real fun and I suppose that endeared me to the fans a bit. Then, when I was with the Saints, I used to go out to the parking lot and hang out with the tailgaters to talk baseball and that was a lot of fun too. I guess I just loved being around the people and that made the game very fun for me."

WHAT WOULD YOU WANT TO SAY TO YOUR FANS, BOOSTERS, AND ALUMNI WHO HAVE SUPPORTED YOU

ALL THESE YEARS? "The fans have just been great to me up there. They had so many nice things to say about me and I really appreciated that. You know, it is great to feel well liked and those fans made me feel so good all the time. It was just a great experience. From the old Saints to the Twins and back to the new Saints, it was really a great ride."

HOW DO YOU WANT YOUR COACHING EPITAPH TO READ — HOW DO YOU WANT TO BE REMEMBERED AS A COACH? "I am just so damn thankful to everybody who helped me stay in the game this long, it has been my life."

DALE RACE: UM-DULUTH BASKETBALL

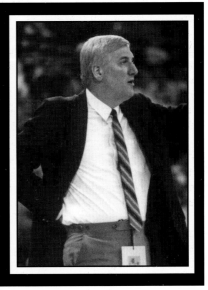

Dale Race would spend 18 years coaching basketball at the University of Minnesota-Duluth, where he became the winningest head coach in the 71-year history of the program. Race rolled up an overall record of 293-120 and guided the Bulldogs to nine 20-plus win seasons, eight Northern Sun Intercollegiate Conference championships (1986-92, 1997), eight appearances in the NAIA National Tournament (1985-92) and one NCAA Division II playoff berth (1997). (The seven straight conference crowns from 1986-92 was truly one of Minnesota basketball's greatest dynasties.) Race stepped down after 14 seasons as the head coach at UMD in 1998 to become the school's first Bulldog Club coordinator. Among his many coaching awards and accolades, Race is a member of NSIC, University of Wisconsin-Oshkosh, and Milton College (he served as the head coach at that now-defunct school from 1975-79) Hall of Fames. His career collegiate coaching record stands at 363-177 (.672). Race would later leave UMD to become an assistant at the University of Wisconsin-Green Bay under Tod Kolawcyk, a former player of his at UMD (1984-88), who is now the head coach of the Phoenix.

CHARLES "CHIEF" BENDER: MAJOR LEAGUE BASEBALL

Minnesota's first Hall of Famer, Charles Bender, was a man of Ojibwa Native American descent. The "Chief" as he was affectionately known, was born one of 13 children near Brainerd on the White Earth Reservation in 1883. In 1900 Bender enrolled in the Indian School at Carlisle, Penn., where he would go on to star on the school's football, basketball, track and baseball teams. Baseball quickly emerged as his sport of choice though, as he became a dominant pitcher. Bender began playing semi--pro baseball, under an assumed name of course (so he didn't lose his Carlisle eligibility), and found that he could do quite well against the big boys. It was there, against the Chicago Cubs that the legendary Connie Mack saw the youngster play and immediately signed him to a pro contract.

   The Chief would then go on to pitch for the Philadelphia Athletics, and later with Baltimore of the Federal League, and finally the Philadelphia Phillies, from 1903-17. He would compile a career record of 212 wins and 128 losses, and also win three American League Pitching Winning Percentage Titles in 1910, 1911 and 1914. Bender was one of the most dominant pitchers of his day, leading his Athletics to five World Series appearances along the way. (He still remains the only pitcher ever to have nine complete games in the big dance.) Bender would pitch until he was 42, and was still tough as nails until the very end. After his playing days he went on to manage the Athletics from 1951-53, and later served as either a coach or scout with the New York Yankees, Chicago White Sox, New York Giants and Philadelphia Athletics. An avid hunter, fisherman and even a champion clay pigeon shooter and pro golfer in his latter years, the Chief was later inducted into the Baseball Hall of Fame in Cooperstown in 1953.

DICK SIEBERT: GOPHER BASEBALL

A native of Fall River, Mass., Dick Siebert began his baseball days at St. Paul Concordia High School and went on to attend Concordia Junior College. From there he moved to the Concordia Seminary in St. Louis with full intentions of becoming a Lutheran minister. But the lure of baseball was too much for the calling of the pulpit, so Dick started his pro baseball career in 1932. Originally a pitcher, Siebert switched over to first base when he developed some arm problems.

Siebert went on to play for Ohio, Pennsylvania, and New York minor league teams, and, in 1935, he joined Buffalo in the International League. Siebert then became a member of the Brooklyn Dodgers system, and later the Chicago Cubs and St. Louis Cardinals systems until 1938, when he became a regular first baseman for the Philadelphia Athletics under the legendary Connie Mack.

Siebert played for the A's through 1945 and even appeared in the 1942 All Star game. He was chosen as an all-star again in 1945 only to see the game canceled due to wartime restrictions. Siebert later recalled his greatest day in the big leagues was when he broke up a no-hit attempt by Cleveland great Bob Feller. Siebert played in 1,035 games over his big league career and finished with a very respectable .282 lifetime batting average.

Siebert's pro career came to an abrupt end in 1946 due to some unfortunate contract problems with management. He simply traded in his first-baseman's mitt for a microphone when he accepted the position of sportscaster with WTCN radio in Minneapolis. But, only one year later, Siebert would get the baseball itch one more time. This time it was to take over as head coach of the Golden Gophers. (Later he would do radio and television work with WCCO as well.)

Dick took the reigns as the University of Minnesota head coach in 1947 from then-head coach David MacMillan. No one in the school's athletic department could've known it at the time, but they were creating a living legend when they hired him as head baseball coach. The "Chief," as he was affectionately known, would go on to become one of the greatest coaches in college baseball history.

Siebert helped develop baseball at all levels in Minnesota. He was a pioneer and was also credited with introducing the aluminum bat and designated hitter to college baseball as well. As a coach, he emulated many of the mannerisms of his long-time mentor, Connie Mack.

And, while he served as the president of the American College Baseball Coaches Association, twice was named as college baseball's Coach of the Year, and won three NCAA titles, Siebert considered the trouncing of Arizona in the 1956 College World Series and the amazing come-from-behind win over USC in the 1960 Series as his most memorable moments in baseball. He compiled one of the most incredible records in college baseball history. Until 2002, when John Anderson broke his record, Siebert was the winningest coach in Gopher history with a 754-361 record, and a .676 winning percentage.

He is one of only a few coaches at major universities to have coached a team to more than 700 wins. He sent five different teams to the College World Series and, of course, he brought home three titles. His teams also captured 11 Big Ten titles as well. Amazingly, he endured only three losing seasons. He is a member of the College Baseball Hall of Fame and was a recipient of college baseball's highest award, the Lefty Gomez Trophy, which recognizes the individual who has given the most outstanding contribution and service to the development of college baseball.

Siebert coached 31 seasons in Gold Country, and his last season was 1978. Sadly, on December 9, of that same year, the Chief died, succumbing to numerous respiratory and cardiac illnesses. Dick was survived by his wife Marie and their children: Marilyn, Beverly, Richard, Jr., and Paul — who went on to play ball in the major leagues with the Mets and Cardinals.

In his last year of life, Siebert was quoted as saying: "I actually expected my coaching job at the U to last a few years and then I would go into business. No one in the world could have convinced me then I would still be here 31 years later. But I loved it, working with great young men and staying active in the best form of baseball I knew, the college game."

On Saturday, April 21, 1979, the University of Minnesota Baseball Stadium was officially renamed "Siebert Field," in honor of their great coach and friend. The entire baseball world mourned his passing, and tributes to the coach poured in from every corner of the baseball world.

For more than three decades, the Chief brought honor and respect to the University of Minnesota baseball program. Dick was a true ballplayer and a real throwback to another era. A tireless worker, his life was consumed with Gopher baseball. The cold weather was no match for the Chief, because he worked at his craft all-year long. Whether it was from his old Cooke Hall office, or from the fieldhouse, he was always trying to improve and help his teams to win.

He was a man who learned virtually every aspect of the game of baseball throughout his life and chose to teach others what he had to learn mostly on his own. He was a teacher, a coach, a mentor and a friend. We appreciate coach Siebert for all these things, but also, and maybe especially, for the fact that he did so much of it with local home-grown talent. He will be forever thought of as the standard to which all other coaches will be measured against and will go down as one of the best. He was, in every sense, a true baseball coaching legend.

"He was a tremendous teacher," said former player Paul Molitor. "I think baseball at the University of Minnesota was successful under him because of the fact that he knew how to teach college players to be fundamentally sound. He taught us how to execute and gave us a chance to be competitive with any college team in the nation. When you played for the Chief, you were playing for a man with a national reputation. He felt he never had to go out of the state to get his players, and he competed on a national scale. The Chief put a lot of pride in that Minnesota uniform for us."

"Dick Siebert was a great coach, and I really enjoyed my playing days at the University of Minnesota working with him," added Dave Winfield. "I felt that I was as good a hitter as I was a pitcher in college, but they wouldn't let me hit, insisting instead that I become specialized. My friends would come to the games and yell at him, 'Put in Winfield and let him hit, because he's the best hitter you've got!' But it didn't matter how good or bad you were, you had to get out there and work when you played for the Chief. You could be a star on his team, but he played no favorites and treated everyone alike. I learned a lot playing for him."

"When you think about Dick, you don't just think about his record at Minnesota, which is distinction enough in itself," said Jerry Kindall. "But I don't think people realize what he did for college baseball in general. Dick was one of the leaders in restoring good relations with major league baseball. There was a time when there was an antagonistic, very tense, relationship between the colleges and the pros. He overcame that. And he was the biggest expert of all college baseball coaches on the rules of the game too. He served on virtually every committee that college baseball has instituted. I think it's safe to say — and I don't think I'm stretching it at all — that Dick was the most highly respected and honored coach in collegiate baseball."

MINNEAPOLIS MILLERS & ST. PAUL SAINTS WHO MANAGED IN THE BIG LEAGUES:

Felipe Alou played for the Millers in 1956. After playing in the big leagues for 17 seasons, Alou would go on to manage the Montreal Expos 1992-2001, and in 2003 he took over as the manager of the San Francisco Giants.

Walter Alston managed the Saints from 1948-49, winning an American Association regular season title and Junior World Series title in 1949. Alston would go on to manage the Brooklyn and Los Angeles Dodgers from 1954-76, winning seven pennants along the way. Alston would retire from baseball in 1976 after managing more than 2,000 games as the Dodger's skipper. He would later be inducted into the Hall of Fame in 1983.

Dave *"Beauty"* Bancroft, a former shortstop for the Phillies and Giants, managed the Millers in 1933 and went on to be inducted into the Hall of Fame in 1971.

Donie Bush, who had managed the Pittsburgh Pirates to the 1927 National League pennant, led the Millers to American Association titles in 1932, 1934 and 1935.

Charles Comiskey, who was an outstanding first baseman during his playing days of 1877-95, later went on to own and manage the St. Paul Saints from 1895-99. Comiskey moved the St. Paul franchise to Chicago in 1900, where as the White Sox they became one of the American League's pillar franchises. Comiskey was inducted into the Hall of Fame in 1939.

The Cantillon Brothers, Joe and Mike, managed the Millers, on and off, between 1907-23 — leading the Millers to three straight pennants from 1910-1912.

Jimmy Collins was the third baseman/manager of the 1909 Millers. With a .294 lifetime average in 14 major-league seasons prior to coming to Minneapolis, Collins, was inducted into the Hall of Fame in 1945.

Leo *"The Lip"* Durocher played for the Saints in 1927. The shortstop would go on to manage the New York Giants, Brooklyn Dodgers, Chicago Cubs and Houston Astros from 1939-55, and 1966-73. He was later inducted into the Hall of Fame in 1994.

Jimmie Foxx served as the first base coach of the Millers in 1957 under Manager Gene Mauch. (In 1957, when the Giants moved to San Francisco, the Millers were moved to Arizona, where they became the "Phoenix Giants." To fill the vacancy, however, the San Francisco Seals (a Boston Red Sox farm team) were moved to Minneapolis in their place.) Prior to coming to Minneapolis, Foxx was one of the top players in the game — earning MVP honors in 1932 and then following that up the next season by winning the Triple Crown. Foxx would later be inducted into the Hall of Fame in 1951.

Billy Herman managed the Millers in 1948. A 10-time National League All-Star, Herman had hit .304 in 15 seasons in the majors prior to coming to the Millers, and would be inducted into the Hall of Fame in 1975.

Miller Huggins was a scrappy second baseman for the Saints from 1901-03. Huggins would go on to achieve fame as the manager of the New York Yankees from 1918-1929, where he led the Yanks to six pennants and three World Series titles from 1921-28 — a stint which included guiding the infamous 1927 "Murderer's Row." He would later be inducted into the Baseball Hall of Fame in 1964.

Bill McKechnie, a shortstop and third baseman for the Millers in 1912 and for the Saints in 1913, was a .251 career hitter from 1907-20 in the major leagues. McKechnie would go on to win nearly 1,900 games as a manager with the Pirates, Cards, Braves and Reds from 1922-46. McKechnie remains the only manager to ever guide three different teams to the World Series, and he won championships in Pittsburgh and Cincinnati. He was inducted into the Hall of Fame in 1962.

Danny Ozark managed the Saints in 1960. Ozark would later go on to manage the Philadelphia Phillies from 1973-79 and in 1984 he managed the San Francisco Giants. He would retire from managing with a career record of 618-542.

Bill Rigney managed the Millers from 1954-55, winning a Junior World Series with the club in 1955. Rigney, who played with the Giants from 1946-53, went on to manage in the big leagues from 1956-76 with New York, Los Angeles, California, San Francisco and Minnesota — finishing with a career record of 1,239-1,321. Rigney managed the Twins from 1970-72 and led the club to a divisional pennant.

Chuck Tanner played for the Millers in 1959 and went on to manage four different clubs in the majors. In 1972 he was named American League Manager of the Year while with the White Sox and in 1979 he led the Pirates to a World Series title.

**Mike Kelley, Gene Mauch and Wes Westrum also had major league managing careers.
To read more about them, see their bios in the book.*

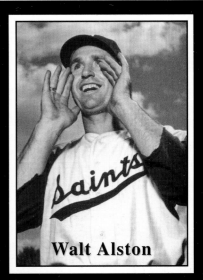

Walt Alston

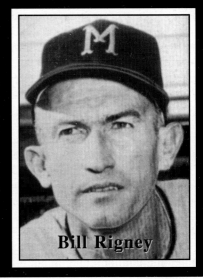

Bill Rigney

DUANE BAGLIEN
HIGH SCHOOL BASKETBALL: EDINA

Duane Baglien grew up in Fargo, N.D., and graduated from Fargo Central High School in 1943. From there, Baglien went into the armed services for a year before coming home to attend the University of Minnesota. There, he played baseball under Dick Siebert, basketball under Dave MacMillan and Ozzie Cowles, and even a little football under Bernie Bierman. His first coaching job came in 1951, at Winthrop, where he taught and coached for one season, followed by a two year stint at Slayton, and then another three years in Fergus Falls. There, he led his Fergus Falls boys basketball team to a third place finish at the state tournament in 1957 and then headed south that next season to take over at Edina High School. At Edina, Baglien taught health and history and coached the boys basketball team until 1969.

At Edina, Baglien took four teams to the state tournament, but he will forever be remembered for the "Edinasty," which saw his Hornets go undefeated and win three state titles from 1966-68. At the time the 69 consecutive wins was a national record and received much notoriety across the country. Among the stars of that era were Bob Zender, who went on to play for Cotton Fitzsimmons at Kansas State and Jeff Wright, who went on to star with the Minnesota Vikings. Baglien was also the Edina baseball coach and won a state title in 1968 as well. Two sports, two titles in one year — pretty impressive. In all Baglien coached baseball for 12 years and basketball for 18, but he decided to hang up his whistle just one year after his improbable winning streak in 1969. You see, he had a large family with six kids, and wanted to get into the administrative side of things. At that point he felt like he had done it all and wanted to give someone else a chance. He had several offers to coach at the collegiate level, but didn't want the instability with his large family. Baglien stayed on at Edina until 1986, when he retired as the assistant principal.

HOW WOULD YOU DESCRIBE YOUR COACHING STYLE? "I was a great believer in discipline and conditioning as far as my teams were concerned. Those two things were the most important for me. We worked pretty hard in practice and we put a lot of emphasis on defense and rebounding. My philosophy there was that offense was like going to the prom with your tux, and defense was like going to work with your overalls. We really worked hard on our defense and that was a big part of our success."

HOW DID YOU MOTIVATE YOUR PLAYERS? "Well, it's the old cliché, I just tried to get them to play as hard as they could, one game at a time. I have never seen anybody give 100% yet, so there is always something to give out there. I was always a firm believer that games were won and lost in the second half, so I made it a point to play my reserves in the first half so that they could get their feet wet early on. Then, in the clutch times we could go with our starters. But, if we needed to bring in a reserve, I knew that he would be ready to go because he had already been in the game in the first half."

LOOKING BACK WHAT ARE YOU MOST PROUD OF IN YOUR CAREER? "I had so much enjoyment working with kids. You get to meet and get to know so many great people along the way and that was so rewarding. They tried so hard for me and I really appreciated that. I was very proud of all my players and was fortunate to have had such good kids to be around. Then, as far as coaching was concerned, I am very proud of our 69 game winning streak

and three state titles."

HOW DID YOU BUILD TEAM UNITY & CHEMISTRY? "I gave every one of my players an honest chance to crack the lineup. If any of my reserves wanted to challenge a starter, we let them do that. They would play one-on-one and if he beat him I would start him that next game. That was very powerful and really worked. There was no favoritism that way and it kept everything on an even playing field."

WHAT MOTIVATED YOU? "I think we are all motivated to go out there and win, and as a coach you just want to do the best you can in order to give your kids the best opportunity to win. That is what it is all about in my opinion."

WHAT ADVICE WOULD YOU HAVE FOR YOUNG COACHES STARTING OUT TODAY? "I would tell them to learn as much as they could about their sport. They should go to as many clinics as they can, read up on it as much as they can and go to as many games as they can. That way they will be totally prepared and will have a great understanding of what is going on around them."

WHAT ARE THE KEY INGREDIENTS TO CREATING A CHAMPIONSHIP TEAM? "You have to have material and then you have to have kids who can work together. There can't be any animosity on your team and that goes back to chemistry. They have to be able to work together and have a good esprit de corps. Besides that, you have to establish the proper offense and defense for your personnel. That is very important too. So, you need all of that to come together, it is tough."

WHAT'S THE SECRET TO YOUR SUCCESS? "I had good material! You know, when I first came to Edina I don't think they had won a basketball game that previous year. I also knew that Edina was primarily a hockey and football school at the time, so when I came in I knew that there wasn't going to be a lot of pressure to win right away. Eventually the material caught up with me though, and we had some real good players on some real good teams along the way."

WHAT WOULD YOU WANT TO SAY TO YOUR FANS, BOOSTERS, AND ALUMNI WHO HAVE SUPPORTED YOU ALL THESE YEARS? "I would want to thank them for coming to all the games and showing us their support through the years. It is tough to get kids to play if you don't have people in the stands supporting them, so that meant a great deal to all of us."

HOW DO YOU WANT YOUR COACHING EPITAPH TO READ — HOW DO YOU WANT TO BE REMEMBERED AS A COACH? "I would like to be remembered as a coach who gave it his all and made a difference."

Mike Dreier grew up in Burnsville and went on graduate from Hamline University. And no, Dreier, unlike most coaches, did not play college basketball. Instead, he was a student of the game, learning, studying, watching and reading as much as he could about the sport. After graduating from Hamline, Dreier went on to get his first job teaching history at New London-Spicer High School. He also became the girls basketball coach there as well, and over the past 25 years he has very quietly become the winningest girls high school basketball coach in state history. Dreier's career amazing coaching record of 547-96 is No. 1 all-time, and he is still going strong. In addition, Dreier has led his Lady Wildcats to 12 state tournaments, won two state titles and finished second five times. A true student of the game, Mike Dreier is a real girls high school coaching legend.

HOW WOULD YOU DESCRIBE YOUR COACHING STYLE? "I would say I am very fundamentals oriented and I have very high expectations for my players. I just expect maximum effort at all times. I can get loud if my kids are not doing what they are supposed to be doing, but not very often. I think your players have to know that you care about them as people. Then they know that you are putting as much into it as they are. You spend a lot of time together with them and that helps you foster a relationship together."

IF YOU COULD MAGICALLY GO BACK IN TIME TO THE FIRST YEAR YOU WERE A HEAD COACH AND GIVE YOURSELF SOME ADVICE FOR THE FUTURE, KNOWING WHAT YOU KNOW NOW, BACK THEN, WHAT WOULD YOU SAY TO YOURSELF? "I would probably tell myself to just keep doing things the way I did it all along. I put my heart and soul into New London-Spicer Girls Basketball and I do everything I can to help these kids be everything they can be. So, I am not sure I would do anything different."

LOOKING BACK WHAT ARE YOU MOST PROUD OF IN YOUR CAREER? "I think what I am most proud of from a coaching standpoint is that we have been able to be as successful as we have been able to be over such a long a period of time. I also feel good about staying at the level we have been able to be at with our own kids from this rural area. Other coaches sometimes have the luxury of recruiting kids from surrounding areas, whereas here we only have so many girls to work with here. So, I feel awfully good about that too."

HOW DO YOU BUILD TEAM UNITY & CHEMISTRY? "You start by talking about it a lot and hope that people treat other people with respect. A lot of the time it is really just hoping that you are able to push the right buttons at the right time, whether it is getting on somebody or talking to them privately. You also have to have your leaders go out of their way to be good to other people and then make sure that everybody knows that their specific role is appreciated on the team."

WHAT'S THE BIGGEST THING YOU'VE LEARNED FROM COACHING THAT YOU'VE BEEN ABLE TO APPLY TO YOUR EVERYDAY LIFE? "Aside from having a good work ethic, I think that you need to be prepared for as many different things as possible and be able to deal with the lows as well as the highs."

WHAT ARE THE KEY INGREDIENTS TO CREATING A CHAMPIONSHIP TEAM? "It is really important to have team unity. You know, from what I have experienced, I think that the better girls feel about each other, the better they play together as a team The most successful teams that I have had obviously had talent, but at the same time they had kids who cared about each other and were able to put team goals ahead of individual goals. That is just so important."

WHAT WOULD YOU WANT TO SAY TO YOUR FANS, BOOSTERS, AND ALUMNI WHO HAVE SUPPORTED YOU ALL THESE YEARS? "I really appreciate everything that they have done for us. When I first got here girls basketball was a real afterthought and wasn't anything that anybody was really into. We won three games my first year, but we hung in there and built something that has become a real source of community pride. Since we got the program up and running we have since developed a real loyal following over the years, and that is great to see. Once you have success, then people will support you."

HOW DO YOU WANT YOUR COACHING EPITAPH TO READ — HOW DO YOU WANT TO BE REMEMBERED AS A COACH? "He cared about his players as people and he did everything that he could to allow them to be successful people."

JIM BREWER:
NBA BASKETBALL

Jim Brewer, a former All-American Center for the Gophers in 1973, went on to embark on a very successful NBA coaching career, most recently serving as an assistant with the Los Angeles Clippers. The Illinois native played for nine seasons in the NBA, with Detroit, Portland and LA, averaging nearly six points and six rebounds per game over his pro career. Brewer also served as a member of the 1972 US Olympic basketball team as well. In 1973 the three-time Gopher MVP's No. 52 jersey was retired at the old Barn.

PAM BORTON
COLLEGE BASKETBALL: UNIVERSITY OF MINNESOTA

Pam Borton grew up in Fayette, Ohio, and went on to graduate from Defiance College (Ohio) in 1987, where she got her degree in physical education. A four-year letter winner on the basketball team, Borton served as the team captain as a junior and senior, and was a third-team All-American both years. A three-time all-conference and all-district selection, Borton was also named as the conference and district player of the year as a senior. Borton scored more than 1,000 points during her collegiate career and was even voted Defiance College's Female Athlete of the Year in 1987.

After college Borton went on to serve as an assistant coach with the Bowling Green University women's basketball team for the 1988 season — also receiving her master's degree in sports management from the school as well. From there Borton served as an assistant at Vermont for five years before being named as the team's head coach in 1993. As an assistant, Borton helped lead the Catamounts to consecutive undefeated seasons in 1992 and 1993, including an NCAA record 53 consecutive regular-season victories. Then, in her first season as head coach, Borton led Vermont to a North Atlantic Conference title and an NCAA Tournament appearance. She would follow that up with a pair of runner-up finishes in both 1996 and 1997 as well. In all, Borton would guide the Catamounts to a 69-46 (.667) record in her four years as head coach.

In 1997 Borton joined the Boston College women's basketball staff as an assistant coach. There, Borton helped the Eagles to a 102-51 record over her five years with the program, including NCAA Tournament berths in 1999, 2000 and 2002. In 2001 Borton was promoted to associate head coach. She also served as the Eagles' recruiting coordinator and produced top 25 recruiting classes three different times.

In May of 2002, Borton was named as the new women's basketball coach at the University of Minnesota. She would inherit a program which had just posted a 22-8 overall record and advanced to the second round of the NCAA Tournament. Expectations were high for the new coach, however, but she answered the bell big time and hit the ground running. Borton came in and wasted little time in making some magic in Gold Country, leading her Gophers to an impressive 25-6 record and guiding them all the way to the Sweet 16 round of the NCAA Tournament. There, led by junior All-American guard Lindsay Whalen, from Hutchinson, the Gophers gave the Final Four-bound Texas Longhorns quite a battle, but fell in the end, 73-60. The Cinderella Gophers were the talk of college basketball in 2003 and Pam Borton was behind every bit of that success.

As the Gophers look to the future, it couldn't be brighter. With the team's nucleus still in tact, plus a top-ranked recruiting class coming in (including McDonald's All-American Center Liz Podominick from Lakeville), Minnesota is poised to advance even further into the post-season picture in 2004. Coach Borton is intent on maintaining and building upon that momentum and is well on her way to leading our Gophers towards a very bright future.

HOW WOULD YOU DESCRIBE YOUR COACHING STYLE? "I think I am a very determined and driven person in all aspects of my life. I really have high expectations for myself and that has a trickle down affect on my student athletes as well. I am definitely not a screamer and am definitely not stoic on the bench either, I am somewhere in the middle. I think I am a good motivator as far as the players knowing what to expect from me as a coach, and as far

as just working hard. I stress the fundamentals in practice and really just try to get my student athletes to work as hard as they can for the good of the team. I would also say that I am a players coach as far as being very open and relating well to my student athletes."

HOW DO YOU MOTIVATE YOUR PLAYERS? "I know my team and always have them very well prepared to play any opponent that we are playing. I am very focused on making sure that my team has all the tools necessary to go out onto the floor and be very successful. We work hard in practice on the X's and O's but we also work hard on working well together as a team. I try to stress a 'seize the moment' attitude for my student athletes and encourage them to play their best every time they hit the court. I reinforce the fact that how they do in practice is how they will play in games. So, I work a lot on repetition, on teaching and on preparation so that they have the tools to be successful in games."

IF YOU COULD MAGICALLY GO BACK IN TIME TO THE FIRST YEAR YOU WERE A HEAD COACH AND GIVE YOURSELF SOME ADVICE FOR THE FUTURE, KNOWING WHAT YOU KNOW NOW, BACK THEN, WHAT WOULD YOU SAY TO YOURSELF? "I would say to be more patient with the decisions that you make. Sometimes coaches make decisions too quickly, so I would say to make sure that you have all the facts and that you have done your homework before you make a big decision. You know, nothing can replace experience and I think the more years that you are in this business, the more you learn. You are constantly learning, so when you are done learning you should get out."

WHAT ARE THE CHARACTERISTICS OF LEADERS? "I think some kids are born with it and others can be taught. In my case I think I was a born leader and I try to lead by example with my players. That is just me. To be a leader it takes a lot of discipline and a lot of drive to be successful. Those are the things we look for in our captains."

LOOKING BACK WHAT ARE YOU MOST PROUD OF IN YOUR CAREER? "The decisions that I have made along the way thus far. I have been coaching for 16 years now, but I think I have taken the right steps in getting to where I am right now. This is the pinnacle of my career being here at the University of Minnesota. I mean I am only 37 years old and I am where I want to be, so that makes me very proud. To be able to take a team to the Sweet 16 in my first season was also very gratifying. We are getting there, but we are not there yet."

WHAT IS THE KEY TO RECRUITING? "Building relationships. You have to have student athletes and parents feel extremely comfortable with you as a person and as a coach."

HOW DO YOU BUILD TEAM UNITY & CHEMISTRY? "I think building team chemistry is on the players. It is what they do together off the floor with regards to becoming friends. It is about them spending time together, learning from each other, respecting each other and trusting each other. I mean you can't build chemistry by just showing up to practice and hanging out for two hours. So, they need to get together as a group and get to know each other, that is where team building starts."

WHAT IS THE KEY TO GOOD TIME MANAGEMENT? "You just have to be very organized not only for yourself but also for your student athletes, who are incredibly busy themselves, especially during the season. So, you have to be disciplined in what you do and remain very focused. You also have to have your priorities in line as far as what is important. Obviously, during the season your social life comes third if you are a student athlete. I mean you have to work on your academics, your basketball and you have to take care of your body. Then, add in homework, practice, training table, films, and travel time, and you can see that these people need to be extremely organized. So, as coaches we have to teach our student athletes the best time management skills that we can, for the good of the entire team."

WHAT MOTIVATES YOU? "For me it is seeing student athletes improve and seeing them succeed as quality people. To see them learn life skills through basketball is very rewarding. Sure, I love to win and I love the competition, but I am in this to be a great influence on my student athletes' lives."

WHAT ADVICE WOULD YOU HAVE FOR YOUNG COACHES STARTING OUT TODAY? "If this is really what they want to do then they have to work very, very hard. They have to be there for their student athletes too, and be able to open their doors to them to get to know them as people. There is more to this profession than winning basketball games and they have to remember that."

FAVORITE LOCKER ROOM SIGN? "Play Hard, Play Smart, Play Together and Have Fun."

WHAT'S THE BIGGEST THING YOU'VE LEARNED FROM COACHING THAT YOU'VE BEEN ABLE TO APPLY TO YOUR EVERYDAY LIFE? "Discipline, work ethic and being able to build relationships with people who you become involved with. At this level you become involved with student athletes, parents, boosters, donors, professors and fans, and I have learned to enjoy that part of the business as well."

WHAT ARE THE KEY INGREDIENTS TO CREATING A CHAMPIONSHIP TEAM? "You have to have everybody on the same page. You also have to surround yourself with good people who have the same goals that you do. You just have to work very hard.

You have to believe in your goals and dreams. You have to ask yourself if you are willing to do what it takes and pay the price to be a championship team. All of those things have to come together."

WHAT'S THE SECRET TO YOUR SUCCESS? "My work ethic and surrounding myself with good people. Those are the most important things. It isn't all about you as a head coach, it is about the people around you — your staff, your players and your program, and that is what matters most. From there you just need to work very hard to get it done."

WHAT WOULD YOU WANT TO SAY TO YOUR FANS, BOOSTERS, AND ALUMNI WHO HAVE SUPPORTED YOU ALL THESE YEARS? "I am very proud to be here at the University of Minnesota and love the community here. The fans have been so supportive and I really appreciate that. The fans and supporters here have made my feel at home in a very short amount of time and that means everything to me. I think we have the best fans in the country here and they are just great."

HOW DO YOU WANT YOUR COACHING EPITAPH TO READ — HOW DO YOU WANT TO BE REMEMBERED AS A COACH? "I would want to be known as someone who was very giving of herself to not just her players, but everybody that she came into contact with. I would also want to be remembered as someone was very sincere, very genuine, very down to earth, very approachable, very driven, very passionate and someone that people just wanted to be around all the time."

DON MONSON: COLLEGE BASKETBALL (UNIVERSITIES OF IDAHO & OREGON)

Don Monson, a native of Menahga, Minn., served as the head coach at the University's of Idaho and Oregon, as well as an assistant at Michigan State University under coach Jud Heathcote. His son, Dan, is presently the head basketball coach at the University of Minnesota.

ERNIE ANDERSON: AUGSBURG BASKETBALL

Ernie Anderson has been a member of the Augsburg community since the 1930s, when he attended Augsburg Academy as a prep student. Anderson played basketball and baseball at Augsburg, graduating from the college with a history degree in 1937. After receiving his master's degree from the University of Minnesota, he returned to his alma mater in 1947. Anderson would then go on to serve as men's basketball coach for 23 seasons and as athletic director for 34 years. He also taught in the health and physical education department for nearly four decades as well. During his 23-year basketball coaching career (1947-70), Anderson compiled a 266-239 overall record. The Auggies also won MIAC crowns in 1963, 1964, and 1965, advancing to NAIA district competition and the NAIA national tournament twice. Anderson earned MIAC Coach of the Year honors in each of those conference title seasons. Among his many coaching awards and accolades, Anderson was inducted into both the NAIA and Augsburg Athletic Halls of Fames in 1975. He also earned two Distinguished Service Awards from the Minneapolis Chamber of Commerce. In addition, Anderson served on several NAIA committees and on the U.S. Olympic Committee from 1969-73. For his lifetime of service to Augsburg, the college recently named their gymnasium floor after him in his honor. (The college had originally honored Anderson, along with fellow Auggie Football legend, Edor Nelson, in 1984, when the outdoor athletic field was christened as Anderson-Nelson Field. The field was rededicated in Nelson's honor in 2001, so that Anderson could also be honored on the basketball side.) An outstanding teacher and coach, Ernie Anderson is a true Auggie sports legend.

BOB BRINK
HIGH SCHOOL BASKETBALL: COLD SPRING ROCORI

Bob Brink grew up in Plankington, S.D., and graduated from Plankington High School in 1956. From there, Brink went on to play basketball at Yankton College for two years and then transferred and later graduated from Dakota Wesleyan University in Mitchell, S.D. He got his first teaching and basketball coaching job in 1960 in Plankington, followed by a brief stint in Tindel, S.D., before coming to Cold Spring-Rocori, Minn., where he taught physical education and biology and took over as the head basketball coach.

Now entering his 43rd year of coaching at Cold Spring-Rocori, Brink's career record stands at an astonishing 759-250. The second winningest coach in Minnesota history, Brink trails only Chisholm's Bob McDonald on the all-time wins list. Brink also has seven state high school tournament appearances over his illustrious career, including one state championship, which came in 1988. That year his squad went undefeated in Class AA, and even beat the likes of Bloomington Jefferson along with several other big Twin Cities schools, en route to bringing home the hardware. Brink has only had one losing season in the Central Lakes Conference during his tenure and is still going strong. In the world of boys high school basketball, Bob Brink is a living legend.

HOW WOULD YOU DESCRIBE YOUR COACHING STYLE? "I would have to say that I coach a lot on emotion and like to have a lot of heart to heart talks with my kids. I am also a pretty intense coach on the sidelines. I take pride in my kids being complete players in all phases of the game and I expect them to practice very hard every day. The only way to get better is to play hard and work on the fundamentals. We have had a lot of hard working blue-collar type kids on our teams here over the years and that is sort of indicative of our program. I also think my style changes from year to year depending on the material we have here. I used to be kind of a run and gun type coach where we would push it up the court and see how many shots we could get. My philosophy there was that the team which could control the tempo usually won the game. Recently though, I think we have been more of a ball control type team where we push it up as much as we can and then apply pressure on defense with the goal of forcing turn-overs. So, it has changed but we have always remained disciplined and worked hard. My teams always shoot free throws well too and really just try to make the most of their opportunities. That is all part of my style."

HOW DO YOU MOTIVATE YOUR PLAYERS? "I try to get them to be as self-motivated as possible. We set a lot of short term and long term goals both as a team and individually as well. I also encourage my players to dream big and then formulate a plan to reach those dreams. You know, it is really about simplifying everything. You still have to teach the basics and that starts with quick footwork. Basketball is a rhythm game and you work with your feet, hands and head. You just have to break the game down to the simplest points and then you can teach and motivate."

IF YOU COULD MAGICALLY GO BACK IN TIME TO THE FIRST YEAR YOU WERE A HEAD COACH AND GIVE YOURSELF SOME ADVICE FOR THE FUTURE, KNOWING WHAT YOU KNOW NOW, BACK THEN, WHAT WOULD YOU SAY TO YOURSELF? "First, I would tell myself to pick as many successful coaches brains as I could for advice.

Secondly, I would be more prepared. I came out of college thinking I knew it all, but looking back, I would have tried to learn much more sooner."

LOOKING BACK WHAT ARE YOU MOST PROUD OF IN YOUR CAREER? "I would say my commitment to making young people better people. I like to win and that is certainly part of it, but the respect I get from my kids is probably the most rewarding thing."

HOW DO YOU BUILD TEAM UNITY & CHEMISTRY? "I think chemistry comes from communication. I pride myself in developing complete players. I try to be a real positive person and I am always loud and enthusiastic, clapping my hands. Then, if I do see things that they need to improve on, I try to talk to them quietly on an individual basis after practice. Kids are sensitive, so I think you have to be positive with them. I let them know that I care about them as individuals and I try to tell them that I will always be there for them even when they are out of school. When you build that trust with each other, then I think that is where chemistry starts."

WHAT MOTIVATES YOU? "Winning more than anything. I love to win and I love to see kids get better. It is so much fun to watch them grow and get better. To see them take things that you give them and then have them put them in their repertoire is just very rewarding. We really stress team offense and team defense and in all our 700-plus wins we almost always have four or five kids in double figures. That is how we win, with complete players playing team basketball. I also have a no cut rule because I want my kids to be able to be in that peer group to be better people. There are a lot of coaches who don't do that, they just post a list and say good bye. I don't' do that to good kids. That is why I have stayed in coaching and that is why I have never had a lot of problems with parents. I take great pride in that."

WHAT ADVICE WOULD YOU HAVE FOR YOUNG COACHES STARTING OUT TODAY? "They have got to really love the game. You know for me, even after 43 years I still love to come in that gym and hear those balls bounce. You need to really have a passion for coaching and you need to have your heart in it, because the kids will pick up on that if you don't.

FAVORITE LOCKER ROOM SIGN? "Together we can make it happen."

WHAT'S THE BIGGEST THING YOU'VE LEARNED FROM COACHING THAT YOU'VE BEEN ABLE TO APPLY TO YOUR EVERYDAY LIFE? "I have four things that I really try to instill in my kids. First is your family, second is your spiritual commitment, third is academics, and fourth is extra curriculars, which includes basketball. So, if my guys have something to do with their families or with their church or with school, they can come talk to me and I will always let them out of a practice. I am big in priorities and the kids as well as the parents really appreciate that."

WHAT ARE THE KEY INGREDIENTS TO CREATING A CHAMPIONSHIP TEAM? "I would say not being afraid to lose. I used to think a lot about state titles, but now I tell my kids that it is not the end of the world when we lose, so they don't take it so hard. They know that there can only be one champion at the end of the year and once they know that, they don't play so tight. I don't want them to play not to lose, rather, I want them to play to win. You know there is a tremendous amount of pressure here in this community surrounding our basketball team, kind of like in the movie 'Hoosiers,' especially during that final game to get to the state tournament. So, I try to prepare my guys mentally for that and that seems to work out for us. Sure, you need good players, but you have to have mentally prepared and relaxed kids too."

WHAT'S THE SECRET TO YOUR SUCCESS? "I work hard. I also read a lot of books, I watch a lot of film and I just constantly keep trying to learn new things. I have listened to about every coach there is. I have heard so many great coaches from John Wooden to Hank Iba to Bobby Knight speak many, many times. I have always tried to go to at least two coaching clinics per year since I have been coaching, so that is more than 80 clinics in all. I usually take a lot of notes in hopes of picking up one or two things and that has really helped me stay on top of the game. Now, I watch Jim Smith's squad practice at nearby St. John's University and I also watch the Timberwolves practice when they come up here in the Fall too. I just always want to keep learning and keep being a student of the game."

WHAT WOULD YOU WANT TO SAY TO YOUR FANS, BOOSTERS, AND ALUMNI WHO HAVE SUPPORTED YOU ALL THESE YEARS? "I would like to tell them just how big a part they have played in our success. We pack our gym every night and our community is just wonderful. The 'Hoosier-type' feeling that we get in this small town is just great. So, thanks on down the line to the community, the booster club, our administration, the coaches, the players and to the fans for their support. To be a winner that many years in a row takes a lot of hard work and a lot of support, so thanks from the bottom of my heart. It all pays off on Tuesday and Friday nights when the band is playing and you look over at the scoreboard to see another victory. That is a great feeling."

HOW DO YOU WANT YOUR COACHING EPITAPH TO READ — HOW DO YOU WANT TO BE REMEMBERED AS A COACH? "I don't want my legacy to be so much for all the wins, but for the way I treated people and the difference I made with my kids."

ALFRED ROBERTSON: BRADLEY BASKETBALL

Alfred Robertson, a St. Cloud native, coached college basketball at Bradley University from 1921-43 and again from 1946-48, recording a career mark of 316-186.

STEVE FRITZ: ST. THOMAS BASKETBALL

Steve Fritz grew up loving sports in Blooming Prairie. It was there that Fritz led his team to its only trip to the state basketball tournament in 1966. Fritz, then a junior center, was the star of that team. That next year, however, he transferred Rochester Lourdes, where he would lead the team to the state Catholic title in 1967. (The move came about when Steve's father, who was also the basketball coach at Blooming Prairie, had died when he was just five years old. As a result, Steve's mother had five kids to raise. A nurse, she found a better job at the Mayo Clinic in Rochester.)

From there, Fritz went on to play basketball at the University of St. Thomas under legendary coach Tom Feely. There, the six-foot-five, 220 pound center started as a freshman in 1967. Fritz would go on to become a three-time all-MIAC performer, and helped lead the Tommies to a combined 84-24 record and two conference titles from 1967-71. Fritz led his team to the NAIA National Tournament in Kansas City, Mo., in 1970 and again in 1971. In his junior and senior years, the Tommies went 30-2 in league play, and Fritz won UST's coveted Mr. Tommy Award his final season as well. Fritz finished his playing career with 1,944 points, a school record at that time. He is still ranked second on St. Thomas' all-time career-scoring list and also ranks third in career rebounding with 915.

After graduating in 1971, Fritz joined Feely's staff as an assistant. He continued in that capacity until 1980, when he was named to replace the retiring Feely as head coach. It wouldn't be easy taking over for a legend, especially when that very legend would be at most of the upcoming games barking out advice from the bleachers! Fritz managed to do pretty well though, and has since gone on to become a legend of his own. In fact, the 2004 season will mark Steve Fritz' 24th as the Tommies' head coach. Here's a stat worth noticing: Since the 1904-05 season (the first year St. Thomas records were kept), the Tommies have won a total of 1,316 basketball games. As a player (1967-71), assistant coach (1971-80) and head coach (1980-present), Steve Fritz has been associated with 626 of those victories. In those 33 seasons, St. Thomas is 626-315 (.660) with 13 MIAC titles and 21 top-three conference finishes. (From 1988-95, St. Thomas won either the MIAC regular-season title or the league tournament championship seven consecutive years. During that seven-year span, the Toms were 119-21 in MIAC regular-season games.)

Fritz is an 11-time MIAC Coach of the Year, earning that honor in 1981, '86, '89, '90, '91, '93, '94, '95, 2000, 2002 and 2003. In addition, he was named NCAA West Region Coach of the Year in 1989, 1990 and 2002. In all, his teams have won nine conference championships and have advanced to the conference playoffs 15 of the last 16 seasons. His Toms have also earned six berths in the NCAA Tournament in the last 14 seasons, reaching the round of 16 in 1990 and 1993, and playing in the 1994 Final Four. Fritz's career record now stands at 414-198 (.676), including a 335-123 mark in MIAC regular-season games. His career winning percentage of .658 ranks him among the top 50 Division III coaches in the country. Incredibly, Fritz is now just three games shy of passing Tom Feely to become St. Thomas' all-time winningest coach.

Fritz, who has also served as the athletic director at UST since 1992, is now the winningest coach in any sport in St. Thomas history. His Tommie teams have never finished with a losing season, and he is still going strong. Steve and his wife Bev have three children: Joe, Peter and Maura, and presently reside in Mendota Heights.

Terry Culhane grew up in Marshall and graduated from Marshall High School as a two sport star in 1974. From there, Culhane attended Southwest State University in Marshall, where he played basketball and baseball. After receiving his teaching degree in 1978, Culhane got his first job filling in for a teacher on maternity leave in Marshall. One year later he moved 15 miles south to Milroy, where he went on to teach and coach girls volleyball and girls basketball for the next eight years. In 1987 Culhane took an elementary school teaching position in nearby Tracy. Meanwhile, the two schools combined athletically, so he continued to coach both sports for another 11 years. In 1997 Culhane moved back to Marshall, where he has continued to coach girls volleyball and girls basketball for the past seven seasons. During that time, Culhane has established himself as one of the best in the business.

Overall, Culhane has won five state titles in volleyball at Tracy-Milroy. In basketball, he has won three titles at Tracy-Milroy and another two at Marshall. Culhane also finished as the state runner-up in volleyball with Marshall in 2003, meaning he is well on his way to recreating another dynasty there. With more than 400 basketball victories and 500 volleyball victories, Terry Culhane is amongst the winningest coaches of all-time in state history in both sports, and is a true girls high school coaching legend. Terry, who continues to teach and coach, and his family presently reside in Marshall.

HOW WOULD YOU DESCRIBE YOUR COACHING STYLE? "I think I am a teacher first. I am also intense and have high expectations. I like to break things down and teach things, rather than just throwing out the balls and letting them play. I am fair, I respect the game and I don't get on officials very much because I don't think that is appropriate. I just work hard and try to get the most out of my kids."

HOW DO YOU MOTIVATE YOUR PLAYERS? "I just try to encourage them to do their best and to play hard. If they don't play hard then they don't get to play. We set goals and we try to achieve them, that is important too. We talk about what it is going to take for them to be state champions and about the price they are going to have to pay if they want to achieve that. Our kids make sacrifices and they work really hard, but it all pays off in the end. I don't measure our season by wins and losses. The only time I really worry about winning is when it comes down to state tournament time. I just believe that if you work hard and try to get better, then the winning will take care of itself."

LOOKING BACK WHAT ARE YOU MOST PROUD OF IN YOUR CAREER? "I am really proud of the kids who I have been able to coach. I have had some great kids over the years. I have gotten to know a lot of them and have built a mutual level of respect with many of them which is very special. I also feel very good about the coaches who I coach with. Everywhere I have been I have had great staffs with me and that makes all the difference in the world. I don't even like to call them assistants because I consider them to be co-coaches."

IF YOU COULD MAGICALLY GO BACK IN TIME TO THE FIRST YEAR YOU WERE A HEAD COACH AND GIVE YOURSELF SOME ADVICE FOR THE FUTURE, KNOW- ING WHAT YOU KNOW NOW, BACK THEN, WHAT WOULD YOU SAY TO YOURSELF? "There is nothing like experience. I think back to some of the dumb things that I said and did when I was a young coach and I have to just shake my head. And to think I thought I knew what I was doing back then! You know, I have never been afraid to ask for help and I have never thought that I knew it all. I am always willing to listen to people too. So, I would go out and talk to as many old-timers who had a lot of experience and find out as much as I could. That is the key."

HOW DO YOU BUILD TEAM UNITY & CHEMISTRY? "Chemistry is particularly important with girls. Having coached girls for a long time I have learned various techniques which have helped. In girls it is extremely important for them to be a part of the 'group.' You know, boys can me more interested in the individual stuff, but for the most part, girls are not that way at all I don't think. I don't believe in individual awards either. So, we don't give any MVP trophies or anything like that. We really stress the idea that this is a team and we are all in it together. I want everyone to know that the kid who doesn't play a lot is still just as valuable as the one who does. All of that comes into play when you talk about chemistry and motivation."

WHAT MOTIVATES YOU? "It is just fun for me. I enjoy coaching and I like working with kids. I like trying to do something well and that gives me great excitement. I get a great feeling out of being able to help kids accomplish things that they never thought they could, such as being a state champion. That is something that they will never forget and I am proud to be able to help them achieve that. It is a pride thing, and I guess that is just part of being an educator."

WHAT ADVICE WOULD YOU HAVE FOR YOUNG COACHES STARTING OUT TODAY? "It is so hard now. Parents want to become so involved and things are practically year round now, so it is tough. I would just tell them to be careful of all that, and then watch for hidden agendas from people who try to get too close to you. I have typically tried to keep a professional relationship with my players and their parents and that has helped to separate things. You just have to trust yourself and stay true to what you believe. You also need to have an administration that is supportive of athletics, because if you don't you won't get very far. I know a lot of good coaches who have ended up being replaced or have lost their jobs because of parents having issues with them and their administration not supporting them. The first time you get a parent that comes in and complains that his or her kid is not playing enough, that is when you will find out where you are at. Beyond that, get good assistants. That is important."

WHAT'S THE BIGGEST THING YOU'VE LEARNED FROM COACHING THAT YOU'VE BEEN ABLE TO APPLY TO YOUR EVERYDAY LIFE? "Things are never as good as you think they are and never as bad as you think they are."

WHAT ARE THE KEY INGREDIENTS TO CREATING A CHAMPIONSHIP TEAM? "Talent is first. You need to have talent. I don't care how good a coach you are, if you don't have good players then you will not be able to get it done. From there, I would say you need to have good players who believe in you and buy into what you are trying to sell. Then, you have to have them believe in each other and come together as a team together. You also need a good, hard working coaching staff to blend it all together."

WHAT'S THE SECRET TO YOUR SUCCESS? "If I had to say something, I suppose I would say that I have a value system and expectation level which I never waiver from. The stars on my team are not treated any differently from anybody else, and I am consistent with that. In fact, I am not afraid to lose a game in order to get a point across to a kid who may think they can just go through the motions. That is how you build respect I think."

HOW DO YOU WANT YOUR COACHING EPITAPH TO READ — HOW DO YOU WANT TO BE REMEMBERED AS

A COACH? "That I taught more than just the game. You know, it is so rewarding to have your kids come back and tell you that you taught them more than just X's and O's and that you taught them about life. That is very special. I am just an average Joe-blow fifth grade teacher who takes a lot of pride in teaching and happens to enjoy coaching. For whatever reason I have had a fair amount of success. Beyond that, I just want to be thought of as someone who is fair, respects the game and works very hard."

JOE HUTTON: HAMLINE BASKETBALL

It only makes sense that the "Birthplace of Intercollegiate Basketball," Hamline University, is also the home to Minnesota's greatest basketball coach of all time, Joe Hutton. Founded back in 1854, when Minnesota was still a territory, Hamline was the state's first university. Fittingly, it was also the first school in the entire nation to play a formal intercollegiate basketball game. That's right, the Pipers, right here in St. Paul, were the first to get it all started. According to Basketball Hall of Fame records the momentous game happened on February 9, 1895, when Hamline College, as it was then known, played the Minnesota School of Agriculture (now the Ag School on the U of M's St. Paul campus) on Hamline's campus in the Old Science Building. Hamline, which was guided by fellow-student and physical education director Ray Kaighn, was defeated by the Aggies by the score of 9-3, but it was a big deal in the world of sports nonetheless. (Kaighn was a former student of Dr. James Naismith, the inventor of basketball, back in Massachusetts.)

By the end of that year a local basketball league had been created consisting of several teams. Several teams, in addition to Hamline and the Ag School had joined including: the Minneapolis YMCA, Macalester College and Military Company A of Minneapolis. This was nine-man basketball, played in small rooms with low ceilings, complete with goalies and peach baskets for hoops. One month later the University of Chicago, led by future coaching legend Alonzo Stagg, played the University of Iowa. College basketball in America had officially arrived, with Hamline being given credit as its official birthplace.

The Pipers went on to become Minnesota's first national powerhouse thanks to the leadership of coaching legend Joe Hutton. Hutton, who took over at Hamline in 1930, following his stellar playing career at Carleton College, guided the Pipers to three National Association of Intercollegiate Athletics (NAIB) championships, which were held annually in Kansas City, in 1942, 1949 and 1951. Over the next 35 years Hutton racked up an incredible record of 588-186 (.760), en route to winning 19 MIAC titles and qualifying for 12 NAIA post-season tournaments. At the time of his retirement, Hutton was sixth all-time among the nation's top basketball coaches (from both large and small colleges and universities) in total wins. He was, in a word, awesome.

When the Lakers came to town in 1947 they begged him to be their coach, but he said no thanks. He was a Piper, and was going to stay a Piper. His two sons, Joe Jr. and Tom also played for him as well — Joe in the late 1940s and Tom in the late 1950s. In 1937 historic Norton Fieldhouse was christened with an exhibition game between mighty Stanford University and Hamline. That arena would later be renamed as Hutton Arena in his honor in 1986.

So good was Hamline back then, that they could've and should've represented the United States in the 1948 Summer Olympics in London. You see, back then the NCAA tournament champion was designated as Team USA. But Hutton, who was the Chairman of the NAIA, a rival tournament at the time, felt that he had to be loyal to his organization. So, Adolph Rupp's Kentucky Wildcats went instead and won the gold medal. Who knows what might have been?

Incredibly, eight of Hutton's former players went on to play pro basketball in an era when there just weren't that many pro jobs available. The most famous, of course, was Vern Mikkelsen, who, after starring for the Minneapolis Lakers, was later inducted into the Pro Basketball Hall of Fame. Other players included: Don Eliason (Class of '42), who played briefly with the Boston Celtics; St. Paul's Howie Schultz (Class of '45), who not only played with the Anderson Packers, Fort Wayne Pistons and Minneapolis Lakers, but also played pro baseball with the Brooklyn Dodgers from 1943-47 as well; Virginia, Minn., native Johnny Norlander (Class of '43), who played with the Washington Capitals from 1946-1951; Rollie Seltz (Class of '46), who played with the Anderson Packers and Waterloo Hawks from 1946-50; Joe Hutton, Jr. (Class of '50), who played for the Lakers from 1950-52; Hal Haskins (Class of '50), who played for the Saint Paul Lights and the Waterloo Hawks; and Humboldt High School's Jim Fritsche (Class of '53), who played for the Lakers, Baltimore Bullets and Fort Wayne Pistons from 1952-55.

The first coach ever selected to the Helms Foundation Hall of Basketball Immortals, in 1949, Hutton was later named as the president of the National Association of Intercollegiate Athletics. In addition, during the summer of 1945, he was one of four coaches selected by the Special Services Division of the Armed Forces to conduct basketball clinics for American occupation forces in Europe. Widely known as a modest, mild-mannered gentleman who was extremely popular with his players and students alike, Joe Hutton died in 1988 as a true Minnesota sports icon.

In 1995 Hamline recognized the 100th anniversary of the first inter-collegiate basketball game with a reenactment game and banquet held in Hutton Arena on February 4, 1995. Legendary UCLA coach John Wooden, whose teams won 10 NCAA championships, was the keynote speaker at the event as then-Governor Arne Carlson made a presentation declaring that day to be "Basketball Heritage Day in Minnesota." President Clinton even sent a note of congratulations, truly giving the Pipers the props they deserve.

MIKE DURBIN
WOMEN'S COLLEGE BASEBALL: ST. BEN'S

Mike Durbin grew up in Howard, OH, and went on to star on the football and basketball teams at East Knox High School. In 1981 Durbin received a degree in communications from Kent State University. From there, Durbin went on to teach and serve as an assistant coach at both Mt. Vernon Nazarene College, OH, and at his alma mater, East Knox High School. In 1985 Durbin took over as the Head Basketball Coach at Wittenberg University, in Springfield, OH. That next year, in addition to receiving his master's degree in sports administration from Ashland College, OH, Durbin was also named as the women's varsity basketball head coach at St. Ben's. Now, 18 years later, Mike Durbin holds the record for most MIAC wins by a women's basketball coach and also holds the record for most overall wins in the MIAC. His MIAC record of 303-55 (.846) is simply amazing, and his overall record of 386-106 (.785) is right there as well. In 1999 Durbin led CSB to the Division III National Championships as well.

Among Durbin's many coaching honors and accolades, he has twice been named NCAA Division III National Coach of the Year (1993 and 1998). In addition, he is a four-time MIAC Coach of the Year (1990, 1994, 1995 and 1998), and two-time West Region Coach of the Year (1994 and 1995). Durbin, who also serves as CSB's Sports Information Director, is a member of the College Sports Information Directors of America (CoSIDA) as well as the Women's Basketball Coaching Association (WBCA). The winningest coach in MIAC history, Durbin also travels extensively with his team to play around the world and he once even conducted a basketball camp in the Bahamas. Mike and his wife Teri, who is the Associate Director of Admissions at St. Ben's & St. John's, have one daughter and live in the St. Cloud area.

HOW WOULD YOU DESCRIBE YOUR COACHING STYLE? "I think my style is more of a cooperative one in which I use my staff but I also rely a great deal on the people who are involved in the arena of competition — in other words, my upper classmen and my captains. I rely on their feedback because they can bring insight to me and to our staff that I can use to make a decision for the entire group. I can be excitable and I can be emotional, but my style is more of someone who gathers information to make informed decisions. And I use all the sources that I possibly can before I make those decisions. Then, I think I have also become much more patient since I have had a family too. I would also say that my style is really a melting pot of experiences and philosophies from so many other wonderful coaches that I was able to work with and play for along the way."

HOW DO YOU MOTIVATE YOUR PLAYERS? "You know, if your philosophy is to be inclusive then you are going to have people take more responsibility for their own actions and the actions of the team, as opposed to putting it all on the shoulders of the head coach. So, I try to create a positive environment where people enjoy coming to practice and enjoy playing in a program that cares about them more than just because they can dribble or shoot a basketball. I stress to our players that they are truly ambassadors for their sport, so they need to act accordingly, with dignity and class. They are representing not only themselves, but their college as well, and that is important. Other than that, I just think that if you get good people with character, then they are easy to motivate because they want to learn and better themselves."

IF YOU COULD MAGICALLY GO BACK IN TIME TO THE FIRST YEAR YOU WERE A HEAD COACH AND GIVE YOURSELF SOME ADVICE FOR THE FUTURE, KNOWING WHAT YOU KNOW NOW, BACK THEN, WHAT WOULD YOU SAY TO YOURSELF? "I would tell myself to be more patient and let myself know that I don't know as much as I think I do. I thought I was ready to be a head coach when I first started out, but I wasn't even close to being really ready. I had a lot to learn."

HOW DO YOU BUILD TEAM UNITY & CHEMISTRY? "We spend a lot of time on team building within our program. I am a huge believer in the theory of you are only going to be as good as your senior class. We have done a variety of things along the way, including trying different exercises as a group to get to know one another better. We have done everything from doing challenging obstacle courses to having weekend retreats together. I think team chemistry starts with good people and people of character, so you have to recruit those kind of people for starters. You have to look hard at the kids you are recruiting, look at their families and make informed decisions about who you want to have in your program. None of those exercises will work if you don't have people with character doing them. People without character will let you down every time. Beyond that, we really try to get our upper class kids to mentor the younger players. We want those bonds to formulate and we don't allow hazing and that type of thing. I try to create a positive, welcoming environment for these kids and they respect that. I want them to have a very positive experience here and that is important to me."

WHAT MOTIVATES YOU? "I think it is the challenge. The winning is nice, don't get me wrong, but at this point the challenge is more about trying to stay on top. It is trying to see if you can get another entirely different group of kids to accomplish what the past group was able to accomplish. Can you get these kids to come together as a team to win 20-plus games year in and year out? That is a wonderful challenge and something that I really enjoy. I have always been the type of coach who judges success not necessarily on the wins and losses, but on how we played. Did we play to our potential? Sometimes leadership and chemistry are more powerful than talent."

WHAT ADVICE WOULD YOU HAVE FOR YOUNG COACHES STARTING OUT TODAY? "Be patient and give yourself some time to come into your own. I would also encourage a young coach to volunteer. Don't expect your first coaching job to be a paid one because mine certainly wasn't. Those years that I volunteered, however, were great because I learned so much about athletics and about myself."

FAVORITE LOCKER ROOM SIGN? "Success is a choice" & "Don't be Average"

WHAT'S THE BIGGEST THING YOU'VE LEARNED FROM COACHING THAT YOU'VE BEEN ABLE TO APPLY TO YOUR EVERYDAY LIFE? "I have learned that I have a choice if I want to be successful or not. I just always want to do my best and as of recently, I am trying to convey that very message to my seven year old daughter. We don't care if she gets an A, we just want her to try her hardest and do her best. That is how I feel about my teams too."

WHAT ARE THE KEY INGREDIENTS TO CREATING A CHAMPIONSHIP TEAM? "You have to have talent and you have to have people with character. Do you have gym rats? Do you have people who enjoy being around their teammates? Those are the keys. It all comes back to character though because if you are going to have people who will lie to you, or miss practice, or go to a bar on Friday night rather than prepare for their Saturday afternoon game, or if they just don't have their priorities in order, then you are not going to achieve success as a team."

WHAT'S THE SECRET TO YOUR SUCCESS? "For me it goes back to where I am at. The college that I work for is a tremendous institution for higher learning. I think the school itself attracts good families and that translates into good student-athletes. Typically, if a kid is a good student, and has made that commitment academically, then they know what it takes to be a good athlete. So, I have been lucky to get great kids with character and that makes a big difference. I also take pride in my ability to recruit and think that I can identify a person of character when I see them. I have also been blessed with good intuition skills and can spot a phony when I see one."

WHAT WOULD YOU WANT TO SAY TO YOUR FANS, BOOSTERS, AND ALUMNI WHO HAVE SUPPORTED YOU ALL THESE YEARS? "They have been an inspiration to the many athletes who have competed at St. Ben's and certainly to me as well. I have so many friends who have been supportive of both my vocation as well as my avocation, and that has been wonderful. With that has come encouragement to our players. I still get such a great deal of satisfaction when I hear that somebody has come to one of our games for the first time and walked away thinking it was fun and that they can't wait to come back to the next game. That happens year after year and that means the world to me. So, thanks to everyone who has supported our program."

HOW DO YOU WANT YOUR COACHING EPITAPH TO READ — HOW DO YOU WANT TO BE REMEMBERED AS A COACH? "I hope that people will recognize the opportunities and encouragement that I have given to our players as well as those girls who have come through our camps over the past 18 years."

GEORGE MIKAN: MINNEAPOLIS LAKERS

George Mikan, the legendary Hall of Fame Center with the NBA's Minneapolis Lakers, later served as the team's head coach in 1957-58. But, after posting a 9-30 record, Big George was relieved of his duties. Mikan would later go on to serve as the commissioner of the American Basketball Association as well.

MARSH DIEBOLD: CARLETON BASKETBALL

Marsh Diebold was a Carleton basketball coaching legend. The former All-Big 10 guard at the University of Wisconsin from 1924-25 went on to post a 126-75 record from 1930-42 as Carleton's head basketball coach. Diebold also posted a 63-28 conference mark, winning five MWC titles along the way. So good was Diebold that his teams were often refereed to as the "11th team in the Big 10," because his Knights would often times beat the likes of Iowa, Minnesota, Wisconsin and the University of Chicago.

DAVE GUNTHER: BEMIDJI BASKETBALL

Originally from LeMars, Iowa, Dave Gunther graduated from the University of Iowa in 1959 as an All-Big Ten Conference and honorable mention All-America selection. After coaching on the high school level for several seasons, Gunther accepted his first collegiate assignment in 1967 at Wayne State, Neb., where he compiled a 70-13 record in three seasons and guided the Wildcats to three consecutive national tournament appearances. In 1970 Gunther took over as the head coach at the University of North Dakota, where he remained on the bench for 18 years. During that span, he recorded a 342-177 record, led the Fighting Sioux to five conference championships, and earned four NCAA II Regional titles. In 1988 Gunther left coaching and was named the assistant athletic director at UND, working in fund raising, teaching and administering different facets of the program. Gunther then returned to the college coaching ranks in 1993 at Buena Vista, Iowa, where he was 25-25 in two seasons before moving to Bemidji State. There, Gunther guided the Beavers to four consecutive seasons with 10 or more wins, and racked up a record of 49-113. Then, in 2001, and after 38 years teaching, coaching and administering athletics, Gunther retired. He would leave the game as a coaching legend, complete with a career record of 476-328. During his career, Gunther garnered coach of the year honors seven times and he has been inducted into the Wayne State, University of North Dakota and Iowa State High School Halls of Fames.

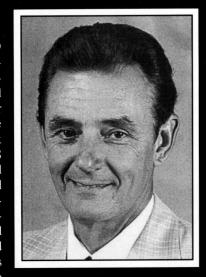

Jim Dutcher grew up in Alpena, Mich., and went on to graduate from Alpena High School in 1951 as an All-State football and basketball player. Dutcher then went on to attend the University of Michigan, where he played football and basketball, graduating in 1955. During his senior year Dutcher also served as an assistant varsity basketball coach at Ann Arbor High School as well. After college Dutcher served in the Army for two years, spending one year at Fort Knox, Ken., and another in Frankfort, Germany. There, he coached and played on the 3rd Armored Division Artillery basketball team.

Upon returning home to the States in 1957, Dutcher returned to Alpena, where he taught physical education and served as an assistant football and basketball coach at Alpena High School. That next year Dutcher took over as the Athletic Director and Head Basketball Coach at Alpena Community College, racking up a 105-70 record over the next eight years. In 1966 his team won the Michigan Junior College Conference Championship and advanced on to the National Junior College Tournament in Hutchinson, Kan. For his efforts, he received his second conference coach of the year award. During that time at Alpena Community College, Dutcher also received his masters degree from the University of Michigan as well.

In 1966 Dutcher was named as the Head Basketball Coach at Eastern Michigan University. There, he would guide EMU to a 126-50 (.723) record over the next six seasons. He also led the team to six straight post-season appearances, earning coach of the year honors in both 1971 and 1972 to boot. That next year Dutcher became an assistant at the University of Michigan, where his teams posted a 55-26 record over the next three years and made a pair of post-season appearances in 1974 and 1975.

Then, in 1975, Dutcher hit the big time when he became the head coach at the University of Minnesota. Dutcher would guide the Golden Gophers for the next 11 seasons, tallying a 190-112 (.629) record along the way. In 1980 he was named Big 10 Co-Coach of the Year and in 1982, after leading the Gophers to the Big 10 championship, he was named as both the Big 10 as well as the NCAA Coach of the Year. Under Dutcher the Gophers made several post-season appearances. In 1976 and 1977 his club qualified for the NCAA Tournament and in 1980 they lost to Georgetown in the N.I.T. Finals at Madison Square Garden. They also made post-season trips to the N.I.T. in 1981, 1982 and 1983 as well.

In 1986 Dutcher's tenure at the University of Minnesota ended. His legacy in Gold Country would include many outstanding players and many outstanding memories. Jim Dutcher was a teacher and a very respected and well liked coach. He gave back to the community and did what he could to grow the game he so dearly loved. Throughout his career he conducted clinics in as far away locales such as Uruguay and Brazil, and even worked with the Egyptian National Team in Egypt for a year in 1975 as well.

Upon his retirement from coaching, Dutcher took over as a Vice President at the Minneapolis brokerage form of Miller, Johnson & Kuehn. Then, in 1990, he joined the firm of RBC Dain Rauscher, where he is presently employed as a senior vice president. Dutcher has also served as a TV and radio analyst for Gopher Basketball games through the years as well. Jim still follows the Gophers, but now roots for San Diego State, where his son Brian, who had previously been a long-time assistant at Michigan, is now an assistant coach. Jim and his wife of 46 years, Marilyn, reside in Eden Prairie and have four children: Brian, Diane, Judith and Barbara.

HOW WOULD YOU DESCRIBE YOUR COACHING STYLE? "I think I was more laid back than a screamer. I believed in hard work and in the fundamentals. I think that if there was ever any criticism or corrections or screaming to be done it was done in practice. Then, during our games it was more of a control situation just to see if we were executing the things that had worked on in practice. So, we had two different environments, and each was unique in its own way. I liked to focus more on the execution side than on the emotion side. It was always my belief that the first five minutes of a ballgame are played on emotion but the majority of the game is played with execution. Sure, I wanted my players fired up and ready to play, but we wanted them to prepare and execute our game plan more than anything else."

HOW DID YOU MOTIVATE YOUR PLAYERS? "I think through pride more than anything. We tried to appeal to their sense of not wanting to disappoint themselves, their teammates, their parents, their coaches or their school. We let them know that they had a sense of responsibility to all of those things and that there was more than just themselves to be concerned about. We stressed the fact that it was a team game and that it took all of them working together to be successful. We wanted them to accept some responsibility for what happened out on the floor and to work their hardest for the good of the team. Pride was our big motivator though, and not fear or the fear of failure."

IF YOU COULD MAGICALLY GO BACK IN TIME TO THE FIRST YEAR YOU WERE A HEAD COACH AND GIVE YOURSELF SOME ADVICE FOR THE FUTURE, KNOWING WHAT YOU KNOW NOW, BACK THEN, WHAT WOULD YOU SAY TO YOURSELF? "Patience, more than anything. I would remind that guy that wins and losses are both temporary. There are long term lessons that come out of coaching and you just have to be patient."

LOOKING BACK WHAT ARE YOU MOST PROUD OF IN YOUR CAREER? "You always like to think that you reached some of your goals, and certainly we did that in winning the Big 10 championship. Then, seeing a lot of your players go on to have successful careers both on and off the court is also very gratifying. From Kevin McHale, Mychal Thompson, Flip Saunders and Ray Williams making it in the NBA, to Darryl Mitchell becoming a lawyer, it is wonderful to see. It is rewarding to think that you may have had some influence on these people and I am very proud of that."

WHAT WAS THE KEY TO RECRUITING? "Honesty was the most important thing. The parents wanted to know that you were somebody who was going to be a positive influence on their son's lives. You had to convey the message that their was a long term prospectus and that their were things more important than just beating Indiana. The players had to feel like they could trust you and that you would do your best for them."

HOW DID YOU BUILD TEAM UNITY & CHEMISTRY? "I think you have got to pick out the leaders on your squad and give them the opportunity to lead. Whether it was a Flip Saunders or a Darryl Mitchell or a Trent Tucker, there were guys who you could recognize which were natural leaders. Then, there were guys who were great players but were not necessarily great leaders, like Randy Breuer and Mychal Thompson. So, you have to identify the people with those characteristics and then give them a chance to develop that within your team. They are the ones who will ultimately create the team chemistry."

WHAT MOTIVATED YOU? "The fear of failure was what motivated me more than anything I think. You don't want to disappoint your players, you don't want to disappoint your fans and you don't want to disappoint yourself. So, you put in the extra time and the extra hours to make sure that you don't disappoint people."

WHAT ADVICE WOULD YOU HAVE FOR YOUNG COACHES STARTING OUT TODAY? "The key to coaching is to be true to yourself. There are many different kinds of coaching philosophies. I mean the differences between a Bud Grant and a Herb Brooks or a John Wooden and a Bobby Knight are very different approaches, but successful nonetheless. So, if you are not a screamer and try to become one, then that becomes very obvious to your players and they will think you are phony. So, you have to coach to your personality. Beyond that I would say just to keep their eye on the ball. They have to remember the wins and losses are temporary, it is what happens to the people who play for them and what happens to the program that they are working with that matter. There is nothing more useless than yesterday's win or yesterday's loss, they need to deal with the present, look to the future and not get too caught up in the past."

WHAT'S THE BIGGEST THING YOU'VE LEARNED FROM COACHING THAT YOU'VE BEEN ABLE TO APPLY TO YOUR EVERYDAY LIFE? "That you have to come to work every day and you can't rest on yesterday's laurels. Everybody has got their own problems and they don't particularly want to listen to yours. So, you have to just stick with it and do the best that you can in order to be successful."

WHAT ROLE DID YOUR FAMILY PLAY IN YOUR CAREER? "They were always very instrumental in my career. It was a family job in every sense. I always drove to our home games with my family and we drove home together afterwards too. I think that was unique. After I was done coaching a game I didn't meet with any outside groups or individuals, that to me was family time. I gave up enough of my time recruiting and coaching, so game time was family time in my opinion."

WHAT ARE THE KEY INGREDIENTS TO CREATING A CHAMPIONSHIP TEAM? "We had a stable staff and that was important. We had a good environment to play in, I mean Williams Arena was a great facility. We had a tremendous backing by our fans. We had good leadership at the top with Paul Giel, who gave me the

opportunity to run my own program. Then, we had talented players. It takes all of that to be successful in my opinion."

WHAT'S THE SECRET TO YOUR SUCCESS? "I would say it is surrounding yourself with good people. You have to be in a situation where you can get some support from the people you are working for and the people you are working with."

ON THE STATE-OF-THE-STATE OF MINNESOTA BASKETBALL: "I think the state-of-the-state of basketball in Minnesota is great, particularly at the high school level. That area has improved dramatically over the last several years. You know, back in our day if we got 'a' kid a year for the Gophers we were elated. Now, there are upwards of 10 division one players per year that come from Minnesota. So, certainly at the high school level it has improved a great deal. Beyond that the Gophers have always had good support and are doing well under Coach Monson. Then, having the two pro franchise in town helps, with the Wolves and Lynx. So, it is solid from top to bottom in my opinion."

HOW DO YOU WANT YOUR COACHING EPITAPH TO READ — HOW DO YOU WANT TO BE REMEMBERED AS A COACH? "That I was never a self promoter and any accomplishments that I ever had were not made at somebody else's expense."

GARY SENSKE: CROOKSTON BASKETBALL

Gary Senkse is a Crookston basketball coaching legend. The former Underwood and Eveleth High School Coach took over as the head basketball coach at the University of Minnesota-Crookston in 1981 and has been at the helm ever since. His NJCAA teams at UMC compiled a 176-117(.610) record that includes 12 consecutive winning seasons, a division championship, four division runners-up, a state championship, and a Region XIII runners-up title. The 1986 team recorded the most wins in a season with 21, and the 1992 squad recorded the fewest losses with six; both are school records. Over the past 29 years as a head coach Gary Senske has achieved a career record of 362 wins and 290 losses.

GUY KALLAND: CARLETON BASKETBALL

A 1974 graduate of Concordia College, Moorhead, Guy Kalland first got into coaching at the high school level, coaching for two years each at Eagle Bend and Cannon Falls High Schools. Kalland then went on to spend the next four years at Inver Hills Community College, leading the team to a 1982 state championship and runner-up honors in Region XIII. In 1979 Kalland was hired to serve as an assistant on the men's basketball team at the University of Minnesota. Then, in 1984, he was hired as the head coach at Carleton College. Since then, Kalland has led his team to the MIAC playoffs nine times in the past 13 years. He also reached a coaching milestone with his 200th win in 1998-99 and needs only 14 wins to surpass Jack Thurnblad as Carleton's all-time winningest coach. With an overall record of 246-232, Kalland is among the best in the business. In addition, Kalland also runs numerous basketball camps during the summer months, and is a professor of physical education at Carleton as well. Now entering his 20th year at the helm of the Carleton men's basketball program, Guy Kalland has established himself as one of the most successful coaches in the MIAC. Guy and his wife Linda have one daughter, Abby, who is also a member of Carleton's women's basketball and softball teams.

TOM FEELY
HIGH SCHOOL & COLLEGE BASKETBALL: ST. THOMAS

Tom Feely grew up in Farmington and went on to graduate from Farmington High School in 1937, where he played football, basketball and baseball. In 1936 Feely's football team went undefeated and unscored upon, without letting an opposing team get inside their 20 yard line, and was named as the mythical state champs. Feely then went on to play football, basketball, baseball and tennis at St. Thomas, graduating in 1941. From there, Feely got his first job at Loras Military Academy in Dubuque, IA, where he taught and coached football. When the war broke out Feely enlisted and later became a captain in the Air Force.

Four years later Feely came home to teach and coach at St. Thomas Academy. Feely coached eight years there, winning five state Catholic League championships in basketball and another in baseball. His overall basketball record at St. Thomas Academy was an amazing 154-32 from 1947-54. (From 1948-51 he was 95-5!) Feely was later a finalist for the Marquette University job, which ultimately went to Tex Winter. From the Academy, Feely went to St. Thomas University, where he taught and coached basketball for 26 years and baseball for 12. There, from 1954-80, Feely led his basketball Toms to an amazing record of 417-269, while also earning seven MIAC titles and six NAIA titles as well. In addition, Feely won nearly 200 games on the baseball diamond too.

An outstanding teacher and coach, Feely was even later hired to guide the Moroccan Olympic basketball team alongside Minneapolis Lakers Hall of Fame Coach, Johnny Kundla. Feely retired from coaching in 1981 but stayed on as a member of the faculty, teaching anatomy and physical education for another 10 years. He was replaced by former Tom, Steve Fritz, who, in 2003, became just the third men's basketball coach in MIAC history to reach 400 career wins. Among Feely's many coaching awards and accolades, he has been inducted into five halls of fames: the NAIA, St. Thomas (as a player and as a coach), Farmington High School and Mancini's. In addition, On Jan. 5, 1981 Senator Durenberger proclaimed "Tom Feely Day" in Minnesota, which was a fitting tribute to a true coaching legend.

Tom and his wife Toni had four sons. In addition, Tom is also very proud of his grandson, Jay Feely, who is presently the starting kicker for the Atlanta Falcons.

HOW WOULD YOU DESCRIBE YOUR COACHING STYLE? "My philosophy was always praise. I didn't ever want to run them down. Praise is a hell of a lot better than criticism. Oh, I used some criticism too, I don't want to act like I was some saint, because I did a lot of yelling and screaming too. But, in practice I would constantly try to praise my guys to build their confidence up. I worked hard to gain the respect of my players and that was real important to me. Also, I tried real hard to build chemistry on my teams, because that was very important in order for the team to be successful."

HOW DID YOU MOTIVATE YOUR PLAYERS? "I was a screamer out there in my early years but as I got older I became much more mild. One of the ways I motivated my players was by giving them days off and that worked better than working them to death in practice after a win or a loss. Another thing that I did which I thought was entirely different was that I had my guys scrimmage every day. We had the clock running every day as well, so that we could practice situations. That way we had an actual game going on every day and the kids were just used to that atmosphere when the real thing

happened. The kids loved it and looked forward to our practices. That was a big motivational tool and something that every coaching book in the world would advise against. I didn't care, that was how we did it and it worked."

WHO WERE YOUR COACHING MENTORS? "Oscar Lubeke was my high school coach at Farmington and he was someone who inspired me to get into coaching. I learned a lot from him and incorporated many of his teachings into my own coaching style. I knew early on that I was going to be a coach and that prepared me for my career."

LOOKING BACK WHAT ARE YOU MOST PROUD OF IN YOUR CAREER? "I am most proud of the fact that after all these years the kids still like me and still respect me. They still want to see me and talk to me and that makes me feel so wonderful."

WHAT WAS THE KEY TO GOOD TIME MANAGEMENT? "I had an alumni donate two big clocks for each end of our basketball court and we ran them every day. We stuck to those clocks like crazy to make sure that we were on schedule and that was how we had good time management."

HOW DID YOU BUILD TEAM UNITY & CHEMISTRY? "Chemistry and team spirit are more important than anything else and however you could achieve that is what you should do. On thing we did was we went to mass and communion on the day of each game, even when we were at an away game. That created some chemistry because we were all together and focused. Chemistry is important to your team. Too much jealously could ruin your team's chemistry, so I just tried to praise my guys and build them up so that they could gel as a unit."

WHAT MOTIVATED YOU? "I loved to coach. I knew early on that I wanted to be a coach, so for me I was motivated to come to work every day because I loved what I was doing. I also loved teaching kids too, that meant a lot to me to be able to make a difference in their lives."

WHAT ARE THE KEY INGREDIENTS TO CREATING A CHAMPIONSHIP TEAM? "First, you have to know your kids and know your starting lineup. I mean you really have to know their abilities. I wanted to know which kids were going to choke. Sometimes you had good kids who just choked and you had to be careful of that. I always went with my number one kid in the clutch and if he wasn't open we went to the number two guy. I went with my best players and that was how we won. The kid who wants the ball at the end of the game and is not afraid to take the shot is the one you want to give it to."

WHAT ADVICE WOULD YOU HAVE FOR YOUNG COACHES STARTING OUT TODAY? "Get to know your players and spend a lot of time with them so that you can find out who your best kids are. Then I would say play those kids, the best ones. Sometimes it is tough if you have a friend whose son is on the team and that kind of thing, but you can't do it. You can't play favorites, you need to play your best athletes."

WHAT'S THE BIGGEST THING YOU'VE LEARNED FROM COACHING THAT YOU'VE BEEN ABLE TO APPLY TO YOUR EVERYDAY LIFE? "To treat people right, to respect people, to not value them by how much money they make, and to judge each individual accordingly, with respect."

WHAT'S THE SECRET TO YOUR SUCCESS? "One thing was that I knew who the best kids were and always had them in my starting lineup. I didn't screw around. I also had a sixth man and a seventh man, etc., so that each player would know his role in our system. A lot of coaches nowadays don't know who their best players are and they are playing people out of position. I even used to post the starting lineup on our bulletin board and then list who they were going to guard as well. I also had a camera with a projector and we used to show our guys films of earlier games to identify their mistakes. That was revolutionary at the time I think."

WHAT WOULD YOU WANT TO SAY TO YOUR FANS, BOOSTERS, AND ALUMNI WHO HAVE SUPPORTED YOU ALL THESE YEARS? "Just being at St. Thomas meant the world to me and I am so proud to say that I was a part of that wonderful tradition. I was lucky enough to have so many great memories with so many great kids and it means the world to me to say that I was a part of that. So thanks to all the people who supported me over the years, it was a real honor. I deeply appreciate the fact that all those fans stuck with us through the years. Their spirit helped us win an awful lot of games."

HOW DO YOU WANT YOUR COACHING EPITAPH TO READ — HOW DO YOU WANT TO BE REMEMBERED AS A COACH? "I want to be remembered as somebody who cared for his players, somebody who was fair, somebody who treated his kids fair, and somebody who taught his kids well with a good, sound philosophy that they could use later in life to be a good person. Beyond that I would also have to say that winning or losing weren't the important things, it was how I raised my family and treated my kids — that is really how I want to be remembered most."

SONNY GULSVIG: CONCORDIA BASKETBALL

Edwin "Sonny" Gulsvig was one of the early stars of Concordia's basketball program. Gulsvig, who arrived on campus in 1946 as a freshman from Elbow Lake High School, earned nine varsity letters in football, basketball and baseball, before graduating in 1950 with degrees in economics, physical education and health. In 1955 Gulsvig took over as the team's basketball coach, and over the next 23 seasons he racked up 237 career wins. The 1976 NAIA District 13 Basketball Coach of the Year also served as an assistant football coach for 36 years and his duties as both a head and assistant baseball coach spanned 20 years as well. His commanding presence, booming friendly voice and warm humor made him virtually synonymous with Cobber sports both as a teacher and coach until he retired in 1991. A real coaching legend, he was also one of Concordia's most well-liked and respected teachers.

MOOSE KRAUSE: ST. MARY'S BASKETBALL

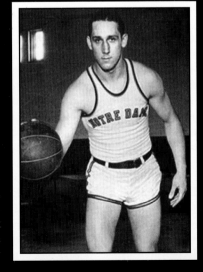

Edward "Moose" Krause grew up in Chicago and went on to earn All-American football and basketball honors at the University of Notre Dame in 1934. In fact, Krause followed Purdue's John Wooden as the second player in history to earn consensus All-America basketball honors for three straight years. At 6-foot-3 and 215-pounds, Krause was a giant. A star tackle for Knute Rockne's football team, Krause also starred on the hardwood for Hall of Fame coach George Keogan, a Detroit Lakes native. Krause was one of the first basketball players to average over 10 points a game, and established the all-time single-game, season and career scoring marks in South Bend. After college Krause came to St. Mary's University in Winona to teach and coach football, basketball and baseball. On the hardwood, Krause led the Redmen to their first MIAC basketball championship. In addition, Krause made history at St. Mary's in other ways too. For instance, in 1935, Krause's Redmen played in the first ever indoor college football game when they played St. Victor's College in the 124th Field Artillery Armory in Chicago. Then, in 1936, his Redmen became the first basketball team in U.S. history to fly to an intercollegiate contest, a basketball game at Notre Dame, piloted by his friend, Max Conrad. Credited with establishing the St. Mary's varsity basketball program, Krause was a one-man athletic department. In 1939 Krause left St. Mary's and organized the first basketball team at Holy Cross University. Then, in 1942, Krause returned to his alma mater to coach the Fighting Irish after the sudden death of his former coach, George Keogan. In six seasons, Krause guided the Irish to a 98-48 record, and later left coaching in 1948 to become Notre Dame's athletic director, a post he held for over 30 years. A true sports legend, Krause was later enshrined into the National Basketball Hall of Fame.

MYRON GLASS
GIRLS HIGH SCHOOL BASKETBALL: ROCHESTER LOURDES

Myron Glass grew up in North Dakota and then moved to Minneapolis when he was 12 years old. From there, all of the kids in Myron's family had to get jobs throughout high school in order to help support the family. As a result, Myron wasn't able to be involved in as many extracurricular activities as he would have liked to have been. Glass went on to graduate from Minneapolis South High School in 1962, where he played basketball until his junior year. From there, Glass went on to attend college at St. Cloud State, where he got his teaching degree.

Glass' first teaching and coaching job was at Rochester Lourdes High School, and, incredibly, he has been there ever since, teaching math and coaching various sports for some 35 years now. Glass began as a football coach and started the girls track and cross country programs at Lourdes as well. In 1983 Glass took over as the head girls basketball coach and he is now No. 3 all-time in career wins with nearly 500. Since 1987 Glass has won seven state championships in basketball and also has two state titles in girls cross country and two in track as well. One title in particular stands out though, in cross country, when, in 1981, his boys and girls cross country teams each won state with one of his girls winning the individual title and one of his boys taking second. (He would have won too, had he not hurt his knee.) Myron Glass is amongst the best of the best and a true Rochester sports institution. Glass presently lives in Rochester with his family and is still going strong, coaching his Eagles, and slowly working his way up the all-time wins list.

HOW WOULD YOU DESCRIBE YOUR COACHING STYLE? "The biggest thing I believed in was that each individual try their best, whether that was in practice, in a game or during the off-season. Then, from there the team takes care of itself. I am also very organized too and I want my kids to pay attention to the small details. One thing that I do with my kids is I always tell them to be on time at odd times, like starting practice at exactly 4:02, and not a minute later. I want them to focus on the little things and pay attention to the details, if they do that then they will pay attention to the big things. It also keeps them loose, which is important too. Beyond that, I just work very hard and believe in the fundamentals."

HOW DO YOU MOTIVATE YOUR PLAYERS? "I don't know if I am a great motivator, but I used the Bud Grant approach of one game at a time and I tried to prepare for each game in that specific time period. Then, hopefully my philosophy of everybody doing their best would be the motivation. I always felt that if they did that, then they would be fairly motivated and ready to go for each game. We tell our kids that success comes from playing up to the best of their abilities. I also run strict practices because I think that translates into playing well in games."

IF YOU COULD MAGICALLY GO BACK IN TIME TO THE FIRST YEAR YOU WERE A HEAD COACH AND GIVE YOURSELF SOME ADVICE FOR THE FUTURE, KNOWING WHAT YOU KNOW NOW, BACK THEN, WHAT WOULD YOU SAY TO YOURSELF? "I would tell myself to be prepared for a lot of hard work and for a big time commitment. And, you better do it to have fun, not for wins or self glory. Enjoy the kids and enjoy what you are doing. If you do those things, then you will have success and have fun along the way."

LOOKING BACK WHAT ARE YOU MOST PROUD OF IN

YOUR CAREER? "When I got to Lourdes a lot of the girls asked me why there weren't any sports for them to participate on, so I started a track team. We had 70 girls show up for our first practice and I think just two were able to make it around the track that first day without stopping for a breather. Then, I started writing letters to some of the other private schools in the area to see if they might want to start programs too. They agreed and that next year we had our very first track meet. A few years later we had the first ever state track tournament, an invitational, in Rochester. Before long other sports were joining in and it just snowballed from there. Eventually the Minnesota State High School League took it over in the early 1970s, but I was very proud to be able to say that I played a small part in starting all of that. So, we have come a long way since those days, and that is great to see."

HOW DO YOU BUILD TEAM UNITY & CHEMISTRY? "Chemistry is a very difficult thing, especially with high school girls. I just try to stress that out teams are not senior dominated teams or junior dominated teams or what have you. We go with a wide range of talent and that adds to our depth. So, if the kids can get along together from a wide range of ages, then that all goes into it. I think that the kids develop their chemistry with one another during the off-season when they are with their friends and are having fun. Then, when school starts you hope that they all come together as a team. It is a tricky thing, chemistry, but very important."

WHAT MOTIVATES YOU? "For me, I just enjoy working with kids. I have worked with young people my whole life and feel very lucky to be doing what I am doing. Being a coach and teacher becomes very rewarding when you see your kids working hard and having success."

WHAT ADVICE WOULD YOU HAVE FOR YOUNG COACHES STARTING OUT TODAY? "You will have to be able to ride the storm of criticism that will undoubtedly come from parents and from players. You will make mistakes along the way but you have to stick with it. Then, be organized and pay attention to the little things. You need to keep up with the game. Go to clinics, read things and keep up with the changes so that you can always be prepared."

WHAT'S THE BIGGEST THING YOU'VE LEARNED FROM COACHING THAT YOU'VE BEEN ABLE TO APPLY TO YOUR EVERYDAY LIFE? "Self discipline, paying attention to details and hard work. If you want to be successful at anything in life you have to work hard."

WHAT ARE THE KEY INGREDIENTS TO CREATING A CHAMPIONSHIP TEAM? "You have to have kids who are skilled and then you definitely need chemistry. It is important that your kids are also students both on and off the court. I mean in 2003 we had a 3.72 team GPA, which means we had some very smart student-athletes. So, as a coach, with kids like that, you are able to put things into your game plan the night before a game and know that they would understand it and be able to execute it. If you have kids who are mentally focused, as well as physically fit, then that is a big advantage too. It is all about balance."

WHAT'S THE SECRET TO YOUR SUCCESS? "Hard work and enjoying the kids. I have also surrounded myself with extraordinary assistant coaches too, and that has made a big difference in our teams' success over the years."

WHAT WOULD YOU WANT TO SAY TO YOUR FANS, BOOSTERS, AND ALUMNI WHO HAVE SUPPORTED YOU ALL THESE YEARS? "You never are able to thank the people enough and they never realize how much you appreciate their support. You know, the non-support people tend to drown out the support people, so you have to really thank the people who are there for you like

the parents and the administration. It has been a real pleasure to be associated with so many wonderful people through the years."

HOW DO YOU WANT YOUR COACHING EPITAPH TO READ — HOW DO YOU WANT TO BE REMEMBERED AS A COACH? "I have a plaque that reads something like 'a good coach coaches from the book, but a great coach coaches from the heart.' I like that. I cared about all my kids and I hope that I was able to make a positive difference in their lives."

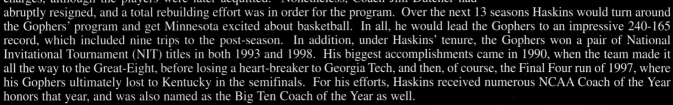

CLEM HASKINS: GOPHER BASKETBALL

Clem Haskins grew up playing basketball as one of 11 children on a farm in Campbellsville, Ky. Haskins then went on to a stellar prep career at Taylor County High School, where he led his team to the state tournament. From there, Haskins went on to star at Western Kentucky University, becoming one of the most dominant players ever to play in the Ohio Valley Conference. Twice leading the conference in scoring, the All-American was the only player in league history to be chosen Player of the Year for three consecutive seasons. He led the Hilltoppers to two conference titles and two consecutive appearances in the NCAA Tournament. Clem received his bachelor of science degree in 1967 and earned his master of arts degree in 1971.

In 1967, the Chicago Bulls selected Haskins with the third overall pick in the NBA draft. Haskins went on to play nine solid seasons in the league with the Bulls, Suns, and Bullets. He then returned to his alma mater; Western Kentucky, first as an assistant coach under Gene Keady and then as the head coach in 1980. After six stellar seasons with the Hilltoppers, which included 101 victories, several NCAA tournament bids, and a Rookie Coach of the Year honor, Haskins was named as the head coach of the Gophers in 1986.

Clem took over a U of M program which was in trouble. Before his arrival in Gold Country, three Gophers had been involved in an incident in Madison, Wis., that led to rape charges, although the players were later acquitted. Nonetheless, Coach Jim Dutcher had abruptly resigned, and a total rebuilding effort was in order for the program. Over the next 13 seasons Haskins would turn around the Gophers' program and get Minnesota excited about basketball. In all, he would lead the Gophers to an impressive 240-165 record, which included nine trips to the post-season. In addition, under Haskins' tenure, the Gophers won a pair of National Invitational Tournament (NIT) titles in both 1993 and 1998. His biggest accomplishments came in 1990, when the team made it all the way to the Great-Eight, before losing a heart-breaker to Georgia Tech, and then, of course, the Final Four run of 1997, where his Gophers ultimately lost to Kentucky in the semifinals. For his efforts, Haskins received numerous NCAA Coach of the Year honors that year, and was also named as the Big Ten Coach of the Year as well.

Haskins' list of accomplishments and achievements is long. He was an assistant coach for the 1996 U.S. Olympic Team (which he described as the "highlight" of his coaching career); he led the North squad to the gold medal at the 1991 U.S. Olympic Festival in Los Angeles; and he won another gold medal in 1994 when he led the U.S. Junior team in the Pan-Am games in Argentina.

Regrettably, Haskins left the Gopher program much the same way in which he arrived — in a whirlwind of controversy. In 1999, as the team was tipping off in the NCAA Tournament against Gonzaga, it was announced that four Gopher players, including three seniors, were not allowed to play that night on account of several alleged academic wrong-doings. It would be the beginning of what would become known as the "Gopher Cheating Scandal," a mess that would last for several years, ultimately casting an extremely dark shadow over the entire program and its players.

When the team came home to face the music, the media was swarming like buzzards. That off-season was the most turbulent in Gopher history. As the story grew, so did the allegations about who was involved in what. After a lengthy internal investigation by both the University of Minnesota and NCAA, it was discovered that systematic, widespread academic fraud and other rule violations had been committed throughout the men's basketball program. As a result of the probe, University President Mark Yudof announced that several top administrators in the men's athletics department, including McKinley Boston, the vice-president of student development and athletics, and Mark Dienhart, the men's athletic director, would not have their contracts renewed. — despite the fact that they knew nothing of the widespread academic misconduct which dated back to 1993.

The biggest blow, however, came when the University bought-out Coach Clem Haskins' contract for $1.5 million, shortly after the scandal was reported. (The school later sued to get most of the money back.) The investigation concluded that Haskins, who coached the basketball team during that time, knew that several members of the academic counseling staff (highlighted by the testimony of former tutor Jan Gangelhoff) had, on occasion, prepared various coursework that was turned in by at least 18 players. In addition, the investigation turned up evidence of mail fraud, wire fraud and even the misappropriation of federal funds (in the form of Pell Grants), as well. The report also alleged that Haskins broke rules by making cash payments to players and by telling players to mislead attorneys looking into academic fraud.

Haskins, who was one of Minnesota's most beloved sports figures, was allowed to operate his program in "an isolated fiefdom, virtually unchecked," thus making it possible for all of these alleged allegations to occur. The coach insisted he was unaware of any cheating and remained silent throughout the saga. The ultimate fall-out, however, was this: the NCAA Final Four run of 1997 was stricken from the books. That's right. Along with expense payments and prize money that was returned, somehow, the University and all of its fans are supposed to pretend that it all was just a dream. Well, it was a huge mess all right, but that Final Four run was something special that Minnesotans will never forget — regardless of what went down behind the scenes. The NCAA came down hard on the program, imposing future sanctions regarding scholarships and post-season play. The record books were also changed, taking stats away from players and reducing all-time records — but those are just numbers, the fans know better, and are still proud of the players that did play by the rules and made Minnesota proud.

Love him or hate him, Clem Haskins will forever be one of the most colorful and controversial coaching figures in Minnesota sports history. Despite what may or may not have happened off the court, on the court, Clem, whose legacy may be tarnished forever, could flat out coach — and his players loved him.

JIM HASTINGS
HIGH SCHOOL BASKETBALL: DULUTH CENTRAL

Jim Hastings grew up along the North Shore in Two Harbors and went on to graduate from Two Harbors High School in 1942. From there, Hastings went into the Air Force, and upon his return, enrolled at the University of Minnesota-Duluth, where he played basketball for the Bulldogs and graduated in 1950. Hastings' first teaching and coaching job came in Mandan, N.D., which lasted two years, followed by a three year stint in Jamestown, N.D. From there he wound up at Duluth Central, where he would become a coaching legend. Hastings spent 31 years as the head coach at Duluth Central, and in addition to his nine state tournament appearances and three state titles (1961, 1971 & 1979), he finished with a career record of 541-236 — good for 10th on the all-time career wins list. Among his many coaching awards and honors, Hastings was a five-time Minnesota state coach of the year. He was also a finalist for the National Basketball Coach of the Year in 1979. In addition, Governor Perpich proclaimed "Jim Hastings Day" on the day he retired, a first for a high school coach. Hastings retired from teaching and coaching in 1986 and presently lives along the Gunflint Trail near Grand Marais, as well as in Superior, Wis. He also still works for the Como Oil Company, where he has been employed part time for the past 41 years doing public relations work. An outstanding teacher and overall great guy, Jim Hastings is without question a Duluth high school basketball coaching legend.

HOW WOULD YOU DESCRIBE YOUR COACHING STYLE? "We were a disciplined team and we worked very hard on the fundamentals. We also tried to adjust to the material rather than the material adjusting to us, as the coaching staff. As far as style went, that varied from year to year depending on our talent level. Sometimes we were a pressure team, sometimes we were a set offense and sometimes we freelanced, depending on the quality of the kids we were working with. For instance, a kid like Greg Downing, we gave him a long leash and he was able to freelance out on the floor. That was very good for his teammates too, in that he set them up very beautifully and made them all look better because he was so good himself. So it varied from year to year, but the common thread through it all was hard work and focusing on the fundamentals, that is why we had such a good record for all those years."

HOW DID YOU MOTIVATE YOUR PLAYERS? "I was fortunate in that when I got to Central they had already had a pretty good basketball tradition. Consequently, we used that to motivate our kids. We told the kids that because the school had such a strong winning tradition that we didn't want to let the community down. So, they worked hard and were able to continue that winning tradition. The kids just felt that it was their responsibility to do well and not let anybody down."

WHO WERE YOUR COACHING MENTORS? "My high school coach at Two Harbors was Si Magnuson. He had had great success up there and he was really a fine man. He was my motivator and I really looked up to him. Even though I grew up in hockey country, basketball was king in Two Harbors. And even though Si never was able to lead a team to the state tournament, he had many, many teams which could've made it. He was just a great coach and I learned a great deal from him. I think he was the reason why I wanted to go into coaching."

IF YOU COULD MAGICALLY GO BACK IN TIME TO THE FIRST YEAR YOU WERE A HEAD COACH AND GIVE YOURSELF SOME ADVICE FOR THE FUTURE, KNOWING WHAT YOU KNOW NOW, BACK THEN, WHAT WOULD YOU SAY TO YOURSELF? "I think I would put a stronger emphasis on patience. As a young coach coming in and having already had some success as a high school and college player, patience was something I needed more of when I first started coaching. I wanted it all right then and I needed to learn to be patient and build my program from the bottom up. We got there, but it took a lot of hard work."

LOOKING BACK WHAT ARE YOU MOST PROUD OF IN YOUR CAREER? "I was very proud to have worked with such a great group of kids over the years. That is a cliché that I know is overused, but it is the truth. It was very satisfying for us as coaches and equally as satisfying for the kids that played for us to achieve success. We worked hard at it and were very determined. We set goals early on and tried to reach those goals, so that was very rewarding to me. You know, I would also add that I was particularly proud of my 1961 state championship team, which, at 27-0, was the first team sport in Duluth to go undefeated and win it all. That was quite a tribute to those kids. We had so many great players on that team, with Terry Kunze, Roger Hanson and Chet Anderson, those guys were great. Several of them went on to play division one ball and Anderson even went on to play tight end for the Pittsburgh Steelers. So, those were great kids on a great team. Those were great times and great memories."

HOW DID YOU BUILD TEAM UNITY & CHEMISTRY? "We were a neighborhood type of school, so most of our kids grew up with each other. When they all know each other and have already been playing with one another for years and years, that makes your job as the coach pretty easy with regards to building chemistry. The camaraderie was already there by the time the kids showed up for the first practice and that made it great. Overall though, we had that strong tradition and history, and that was always our guiding light to success."

WHAT MOTIVATED YOU? "Working with the kids really motivated me. I enjoyed watching them come in and learn and develop into young men and that was very rewarding to see. There were so many fine young men that came through our program over the years and to see them go on to become successful adults was just great."

WHAT ADVICE WOULD YOU HAVE FOR YOUNG COACHES STARTING OUT TODAY? "It is a different ballgame today, that is for sure. I would just tell them to stick with it. They should try to set goals early on and then try to reach those goals. That goes the same for rules and regulations, they should stick by them."

WHAT'S THE BIGGEST THING YOU'VE LEARNED FROM COACHING THAT YOU'VE BEEN ABLE TO APPLY TO YOUR EVERYDAY LIFE? "You have to take the bad with the good. You woke up in the morning and there were days when things did not go so well, but you had to fight through that and keep at it. Better days would come. You just can't give up, in whatever you are doing. My motivation from sports has given me what I have today."

WHAT ARE THE KEY INGREDIENTS TO CREATING A CHAMPIONSHIP TEAM? "Camaraderie is so very important I think. If you have kids who get along, then you are half way home. If you have kids who pull apart from one another, then you are in trouble. I was so lucky that we had kids from the neighborhood who got along and genuinely liked each other, and that made it a lot easier to win ballgames."

WHAT'S THE SECRET TO YOUR SUCCESS? "I just think that I had kids who wanted to achieve and working together we did achieve."

WHAT WOULD YOU WANT TO SAY TO YOUR FANS, BOOSTERS, AND ALUMNI WHO HAVE SUPPORTED YOU ALL THESE YEARS? "We had such great fans and supporters in Duluth. They were so supportive of our basketball program and that made it so wonderful for me and my family. I was lucky, that winning tradition was there long before I had gotten there, but we were able to continue with that success and the community really appreciated that. The loyalty to that part of town was something great and I was proud to be a part of that."

HOW DO YOU WANT YOUR COACHING EPITAPH TO READ — HOW DO YOU WANT TO BE REMEMBERED AS A COACH? "As someone who gave 100% in everything he did. You know, I had a great career and the older I get the more I cherish it. So many great memories and so many great people. Sometimes I will sit alone in my old leather chair up at my cabin in Grand Marais and just stare at my trophy wall which has clippings and photos from those days back at Central High School. I can sit there for an hour just reminiscing about those great, great memories. I think the older you get the more sentimental you get, but those were wonderful times. I miss it."

NIBS PRICE: CAL BASKETBALL

Clarence "Nibs" Price grew up in Duluth and went on to coaching notoreity. Price is just one of nine individuals ever to coach both the basketball and bowl-bound football programs for the same college. In 1929 Price led the Cal football squad to an 8-7 defeat over Georgia Tech in the Rose Bowl, a game that was famous for Roy Riegels' wrong-way run for the Bears. Then, in 1946, Price led his basketball Bears to a fourth place finish in the NCAA playoffs with a school record 30 victories. Price, who would coach basketball at the University of California from 1925-54, compiled a career record of 449-294 (.604). He coached football at Cal from 1926-30 as well.

JAY PIVEC: MINNEAPOLIS COMMUNITY & TECHNICAL COLLEGE BASKETBALL

Jay Pivec is a legend in the world of junior college basketball coaching. Pivec received an Associates degree at Normandale Community College before graduating from Mankato State University with a bachelors degree. He then went on to receive his masters degree at the University of Minnesota in 1982, where he was also an assistant under then head coach Jim Dutcher. The Gophers won the Big Ten conference title that year as well. From there, Pivec would serve as assistant coach for a total of four years between the University of Minnesota, Minnesota State Mankato, and Augsburg College, where his team's records were 91-26, good for a .778 winning percentage. Pivec then went on to become the head coach at both Jamestown College (1982-85), in North Dakota, and later at Montana State College-Northern (1985-90) — taking his teams to postseason play five of the eight years he was at the schools.

In 1990 Pivec took over as the head coach at Minneapolis Community and Technical College. Now entering his 14th year behind the Marauders bench, Pivec has guided MCTC to five National Junior College Athletic Association (NJCAA) regional tournament appearances, and two national tournament appearances — including a runner-up finish in 1992. With an overall record of 272-76 (.782), Pivec has also won the Minnesota Community College Conference tournament five times, and the Southern Division five times. In addition, he was named Coach of the Year in the MCCC in 1993, 1995, 2001 and 2003. More importantly, Pivec has helped over 40 players transfer to four-year colleges and universities after finishing at MCTC. Almost 95% of his players have gone on to four-year institutions, most on scholarship. In 21 seasons of coaching college basketball, Pivec has an overall record of 382-200 (.656). Among his many coaching accolades and honors, in 2003 he was inducted into the Minnesota Community College Athletic Hall of Fame. In the summers, Pivec also directs various youth basketball camps at the MCTC gymnasium. In addition, one of Pivec's top assistants at MCTC is former Gopher Melvin Newbern. Jay and his wife Mary have four children: Tyler, Katie, Zack, and Josie. Tyler also plays hoops for the Marauders as well.

"Our players are not here on athletic scholarships," said Pivec. "They are taking full loads. Most have jobs and are competing at the highest level they can. Our players are recruited to four-year institutions because of their hard work and the good reputation we have here, that is the real reward."

BONNIE HENRICKSON
COLLEGE BASKETBALL: VIRGINIA TECH UNIVERSITY

Bonnie Henrickson grew up in Willmar loving sports. She went on to become a prep star at Willmar High School before going on to play collegiately at St. Cloud State University from 1982-85. As a player, Henrickson helped SCSU win three Northern Sun Conference championships and advance to three NCAA Division II quarterfinals. In her four years as a player, Henrickson helped SCSU compile a 97-25 overall record and still ranks among the school leaders in several offensive categories. The three-time all-conference guard also served as the team captain during her junior and senior seasons. Henrickson graduated from St. Cloud State in 1986 and then went on to earn her master's degree in physical education from Western Illinois University in 1988, while serving as a graduate assistant coach with the women's basketball team.

From there, Bonnie headed east, to serve as an assistant coach at Virginia Tech from 1988-93. In 1993 she was then promoted to associate head coach under Carol Alfanso. The Hokies won two conference titles during that time and also made their first two NCAA Tournament appearances as well. In 1995 Bonnie left Tech and moved on to the University of Iowa, where she would serve as an assistant for two years. During that time her Hawkeyes made a pair of trips to the NCAA Tournament, including a Sweet 16 appearance in 1996, and won two Big 10 Conference titles along the way.

In 1997 Bonnie returned to Blacksburg to take over as the head coach at Virginia Tech. Her first season as head coach also brought the school's first Atlantic 10 Championship, its 300th win, and two All-Americans. The 22-10 Hokies also advanced on to the second round of the NCAAs in what would be the biggest turnaround in school history. That next year the Hokies posted a school-best 28-3 record, including a trip to the NCAA Sweet 16. For her efforts, Henrickson was named as the Atlantic 10 Coach of the Year. She also was a finalist for national coach of the year honors too. She was even selected to be an assistant coach on Team USA, which won the silver medal in Spain in the summer of 1999, competing in the World University games. In 1999 Henrickson's squad advanced to the second round of the WNIT with a 20-11 record overall, marking the third-straight 20-win season for Tech. In July of 2000, Bonnie was named as the head coach of the women's USA Basketball R. William Jones Cup team that traveled to Taiwan for the Jones Cup competition. The next season the Hokies finished with a 22-9 overall record, good for a fourth-place finish in Tech's inaugural season in the Big East Conference. The 2002 and 2003 Hokies each finished with 20-plus wins. Henrickson has now won at least 20 games and advanced to postseason play in all six years she has been Tech's head coach.

As one of Minnesota's greatest college coaches, Bonnie Henrickson continues to establish herself as one of the nation's brightest young coaches. With Bonnie steering the ship, it won't be long before her Hokies make it to the Final Four, and beyond.

HOW WOULD YOU DESCRIBE YOUR COACHING STYLE? "I have always felt that you just have to be yourself because if you are not, then your kids will see through that in a minute. Having said that, I would say I am a 'praise publicly — criticize privately' type of a coach. I don't embarrass our kids on the floor and that builds a lot of mutual respect. People have asked me how I stay so calm on the bench and I joke that I am just not smart enough to rant and rave and still try to think and make decisions. I think that if I can't maintain a level of poise and composure and can't control my emo-

tions, then I can't expect my players to do so either."

HOW DO YOU MOTIVATE YOUR PLAYERS? "A lot of it is individual one-on-one teaching, although we do motivate and challenge our kids a lot through group dynamics too. I think it starts with communication and understanding how competitive a young lady is and what motivates her. I always tell my players that if they need a 'win one for the Gipper' speech from me before every game, then they will struggle to have success at this level. We have had some great kids here through the years and that has helped a great deal too."

WHO WERE YOUR COACHING MENTORS? "I learned a lot from Gladys Ziemer, my coach back at St. Cloud State. She was not one to rant or rave and that definitely influenced my coaching style. She taught me to treat people right and to be respectful. I appreciate her so much because she fought for women's athletics long before it was ever popular to do that."

IF YOU COULD MAGICALLY GO BACK IN TIME TO THE FIRST YEAR YOU WERE A HEAD COACH AND GIVE YOURSELF SOME ADVICE FOR THE FUTURE, KNOWING WHAT YOU KNOW NOW, BACK THEN, WHAT WOULD YOU SAY TO YOURSELF? "It is never as good as you think it is and it is never as bad as you think it is. The other thing I would say is sometimes less is more. You need to work hard to get in shape but you also need rest, and that is important."

WHAT ARE THE CHARACTERISTICS OF LEADERS? "A leader can find a way to get people to do what they want them to do. Leaders can also make difficult decisions and handle the consequences."

LOOKING BACK WHAT ARE YOU MOST PROUD OF IN YOUR CAREER? "Just being able to get what I thought was a fantastic opportunity at Virginia Tech, and then make that work. We are all tremendously proud that we have been successful here, but I think ultimately how we have handled that success is the key. I mean we had the team GPA, our kids are great, they are role models in the community, our staff is well thought of and well respected, and we just have a great program. I am very proud of all that."

WHAT IS THE KEY TO GOOD TIME MANAGEMENT? "You have to be pretty efficient. I mean I know a lot of people who work long hours but don't get much done, and that applies for coaching, in business, in sales, or what have you. So, you have to stay on task, have a plan, be organized and be efficient with your time. My colleagues joke that I am anal, but I don't have time to search and dig and look for things, so I am pretty organized. I also don't micromanage my staff either, I give them a tremendous amount of responsibility and I let them work. I do hold them accountable, but I think most people prefer to work in that type of environment. I always have my pulse on everything but I don't always have to be in control of everything. It is a stressful job so you also have to take care of yourself and give yourself time to relax too. That is important, otherwise if you are tired and run down all the time, then you will be no good to your players either."

WHAT IS THE KEY TO RECRUITING? "It's relationships, identifying talent, communication and a tremendous amount of hard work. It's also making calls, writing letters spending time with people and just getting out there. Again, you have to be organized and follow up. This is a people business and the sooner you learn that the better."

HOW DO YOU BUILD TEAM UNITY & CHEMISTRY? "That is difficult but it is critical that you have good leadership to achieve this. Chemistry is communication, is doesn't just happen. It is a primary responsibility of mine because we have so many different egos coming into our program and that is tough to deal with at times. You have all of these young athletes who were all their leading scorers on their high school teams, and now we can only have one leading scorer, so everyone's role changes. We just stress unselfishness, honesty and hard work, and that all starts from day one and continues daily. I think my biggest task as the coach is to treat them all the same while treating them all differently, because they are all different people. I mean, what works for one might not work for the other. So, it is a process, but something that is definitely critical to your team's success."

WHAT DID IT MEAN FOR YOU TO BE A ST. CLOUD STATE HUSKY? "I say up to this day that if I had to do it all over again I would have made the exact same decision to go to St. Cloud State. I had opportunities at division one schools, but St. Cloud State was a great, great experience for me. I would have to also say that I sincerely appreciate what I have now in my career because of that experience. I made friends for life there and it was just a wonderful place to go to college. It was definitely the right place for me."

WHAT MOTIVATES YOU? "I think it is the fear of failure to be honest. With regards to our preparation, I watch a tremendous amount of film and really prepare for our practices. I just always want to be ready for our competition and that really motivates me. I am also extremely competitive and just hate to lose more than I like to win."

WHAT ADVICE WOULD YOU HAVE FOR YOUNG COACHES STARTING OUT TODAY? "Get involved in as many things as you can in your coaching profession. Volunteer, watch, learn, ask questions, stay involved and for heaven's sake don't be the last one to get there and the first one to leave in the morning. It is simple stuff. Be willing to sacrifice and work hard because there will be a lot of late nights and early mornings."

FAVORITE LOCKER ROOM SIGN? "Together, we are better."

WHAT'S THE BIGGEST THING YOU'VE LEARNED FROM COACHING THAT YOU'VE BEEN ABLE TO APPLY TO YOUR EVERYDAY LIFE? "I think just how important relationships with people are. I am very close with my family and have wonderful parents. They still live in Willmar and I love coming home to Minnesota as much as I can. So, staying close with my family has been very important to me and that has helped me stay grounded in my career."

WHAT ARE THE KEY INGREDIENTS TO CREATING A CHAMPIONSHIP TEAM? "If you are going to win it all, obviously you have got to be tremendously talented. You also have got to have kids who are tough, physically and mentally. Then, you need to be lucky. You also have to avoid injuries, you have to get the right seed in the NCAA tournament and everything just needs to come together for you at the right time. Believe me though, we are all better coaches with talent. Anyone who doesn't agree with that is fibbing!"

WHAT'S THE SECRET TO YOUR SUCCESS? "I have just been

very fortunate to have had great people around me. I have tremendous administrators, fantastic assistants and just great kids who want to be successful on and off the court. Also, I had great parents. They never told me how to work hard, they showed me and that all played a big part of who I am. It was a great blueprint for success."

WHAT WOULD YOU WANT TO SAY TO YOUR FANS, BOOSTERS, AND ALUMNI WHO HAVE SUPPORTED YOU ALL THESE YEARS? "I just appreciate the opportunity. I have a job that I love going to every day and feel very lucky, so thanks."

HOW DO YOU WANT YOUR COACHING EPITAPH TO READ — HOW DO YOU WANT TO BE REMEMBERED AS A COACH? "I hope that the young women who have been through our program and played for myself and my staff felt like they were better people because of their experience here. I hope that they were able to handle adversity in their own careers and in their family lives and persevere because of those experiences."

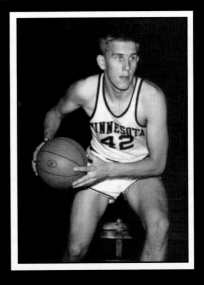

TERRY KUNZE: PRO BASKETBALL (MINNESOTA FILLIES)

Terry Kunze grew up in Duluth and went on to lead his Duluth Central High School team to the 1961 state championship. From there, Kunze played basketball at the University of Minnesota, averaging 11 points and 3.3 rebounds per game. Kunze then went on to play professionally for a short period of time with the St. Louis Hawks of the NBA, and later with the now defunct Minnesota Muskies of the ABA. He also played briefly in Europe as well. Then, after three years of serving as an assistant coach at the University of Minnesota and a year at East Carolina, Kunze came home again to coach the upstart Minnesota Fillies, a professional women's team, in 1979. In addition, Kunze's coaching career has also taken him to Europe and also as the head coach at Anoka-Ramsey Community College from 1990-96. One of the most recognized names in Minnesota basketball history, Terry Kunze presently serves as an assistant coach at Augsburg College. Kunze lives in Brooklyn Center.

RON HESTED
HIGH SCHOOL BASKETBALL: FAIRMONT

Ron Hested grew up in Lanesboro, Iowa, and went on to attend Luther College. There, Hested played basketball and ran track, graduating with a teaching degree. From there, Hested got his first job at Buffalo Lake, in 1961, where he taught social studies and served as an assistant coach on the basketball, baseball and football teams. Three years later Hested moved to Waukon, Iowa, where he stayed for two years before moving on to Kenyon, Minn., where he coached for six more. Then, in 1972, Hested moved to Fairmont High School, where he would teach and coach until retiring in 1997. With the Cardinals, Hested coached varsity basketball, and was an assistant in football, track and tennis. He was also the head girls tennis coach for five years as well. Hested would coach high school athletics for 36 years and when it was all said and done, he finished with a total of 16 conference titles, two state tournament appearances and 506 career wins. For his efforts, Ron was later inducted into the State High School Basketball Coaches Hall of Fame.

Upon retiring from teaching and coaching, Ron later joined two of his sons, Brad and Tim, in a new venture called the Minnesota Stars, which runs developmental camps for elite girls basketball players ranging in age from 15U to 17U. In addition, Ron runs several of the companies Hoops 101 Schools throughout the state as well. The goal of the Minnesota Stars is to provide opportunities for quality female athletes and to showcase their talents in front of hundreds of college coaches throughout the spring and summer. Highly respected by high school coaches, club coaches, recruiting services, and college coaches across the country, the Minnesota Stars play in high exposure tournaments and shootouts throughout the nation that are very well attended by college coaches.

A true Fairmont legend, Ron Hested is without question one of the best of the very best. An outstanding teacher and outstanding coach, Ron made Fairmont very, very proud. Ron and his wife Elaine presently reside in Fairmont and have three sons: Tim, Mike (AKA "Wheels") and Brad.

HOW WOULD YOU DESCRIBE YOUR COACHING STYLE? "I really believed in fundamentals and thought that you had to teach the game from the beginning. In order to be a success you had to do the little things well. Those are the things that I tried to emphasize throughout my career. When you teach the basics, the fundamentals, I really believe that helps your team to grow and improve consistently."

HOW DID YOU MOTIVATE YOUR PLAYERS? "I tried to motivate on an individual basis as much as possible. I tried to stress a 'pride in your performance' type of an attitude in my kids and I think that worked well. I wanted to encourage my kids to believe in themselves and want to do well. So I tried to build up their confidence so that they could play their best. We set a lot of goals with the kids and then worked with them on achieving them. We just tried to develop a team atmosphere so that we could play well together and try our hardest."

IF YOU COULD MAGICALLY GO BACK IN TIME TO THE FIRST YEAR YOU WERE A HEAD COACH AND GIVE YOURSELF SOME ADVICE FOR THE FUTURE, KNOWING WHAT YOU KNOW NOW, BACK THEN, WHAT WOULD YOU SAY TO YOURSELF? "Back then you could drive

kids pretty hard and put a lot of demands on them. The Vince Lombardis and Bobby Knights were in vogue at that time, but it is a different world today. So, I would probably treat my kids a little bit differently in that regard, maybe with a little softer touch, and that is probably for the better. You have to be more of a psychologist today than in those days and really be much more concerned with all the political correctness issues that we didn't concern ourselves too much with back then."

WHAT ARE THE CHARACTERISTICS OF LEADERS? "Talent and a desire to win. I think the best athletes are the best competitors. Nobody who gained great success was ever willing to lose easily, so to be a great champion you have to be a tremendous competitor. They have a great desire to succeed and are willing to make sacrifices for the good of the team."

LOOKING BACK WHAT ARE YOU MOST PROUD OF IN YOUR CAREER? "I am proud of the fact that I lasted 36 years. I am proud of the improvement that the kids made. I am proud of our success. I just enjoyed it all."

WHAT IS THE KEY TO GOOD TIME MANAGEMENT? "I tell you what, you are asking the wrong guy! I always taught five or six classes and coached two or three sports, so it was always a struggle for me to stay organized. The key for me was to do the things that you have to do when you have to do them. Beyond that it was about separating things. I mean when I left the practice field I went home to be a father. Sure, I had to prepare for my next day as a teacher and for my next practice, but it was about balance."

HOW DID YOU BUILD TEAM UNITY & CHEMISTRY? "I always tried to do that with an 'all for one' type of an attitude. We all worked together, we all won together and we all lost together. Everybody was in the same boat. We were not playing for one person and we were not trying to win individual medals, we were trying to win together as a team. When we all bought into that, then we had success, and I think that was a pretty good formula."

WHAT MOTIVATED YOU? "The thing that motivated me the most was seeing improvement. I loved to teach and I loved to see the kids as well as the team improve. Even when we didn't have very successful teams in terms of wins and losses, the improvement that the kids made was what it was all about. That was the most fun to me and really what motivated me to be my best."

WHAT ADVICE WOULD YOU HAVE FOR YOUNG COACHES STARTING OUT TODAY? "I would tell them that for starters they need to develop a program from the bottom up, and that means getting in to teach the little kids early. You need a feeder system that will funnel into your varsity level and that takes time to develop. You also have to coach your coaches at all those levels as well so that you are all on the same page. Then, you have to work with the various organizations that are associated with your sport. You also have to be a consensus builder and you have to get everybody to buy into your program. You just can't take it as it comes and say that you are going to coach them just during the season because those days are over. This is a full-time job today… and that is just with one sport. If a young coach just starting out can do all that, then

I think they can be successful."

WHAT'S THE BIGGEST THING YOU'VE LEARNED FROM COACHING THAT YOU'VE BEEN ABLE TO APPLY TO YOUR EVERYDAY LIFE? "Work hard, believe in what you can do and always give your best. Those things apply to whatever you are doing."

WHAT ARE THE KEY INGREDIENTS TO CREATING A CHAMPIONSHIP TEAM? "Talent of course, and also the blending of those talents. You can't have all guards and tackles in football and you can't have all forwards and centers in basketball, you have to have a good mix of people with talent. You also have to have people who are willing to work and sacrifice for the common good and then put aside their egos. It is very important too for the coach to get the kids to accept their roles on the team. That is extremely hard to do at times, but championship teams do that."

WHAT'S THE SECRET TO YOUR SUCCESS? "I didn't have any secrets, it was just a matter of working hard, having good assistant coaches and good people around me. I tried to get my kids to buy into what I was trying to accomplish and get them to make a commitment to our program. It all comes down to how well you work with people. If you don't work well with people, you probably won't have much success."

WHAT WOULD YOU WANT TO SAY TO YOUR FANS, BOOSTERS, AND ALUMNI WHO HAVE SUPPORTED YOU ALL THESE YEARS? "It was a real pleasure and I enjoyed every minute of it. The people were great and I appreciated all of their support. You know, I think that if you expect the best from the people, then you get a pretty good return. We had tremendous fans and tremendous support and that is all a coach can ask for."

HOW DO YOU WANT YOUR COACHING EPITAPH TO READ — HOW DO YOU WANT TO BE REMEMBERED AS A COACH? "I felt good about all the kids I had. I loved every one of them and I am just happy to have been associated with them. It was a pleasure, really, to have just been a part of the coaching profession. I was very lucky to teach and coach all of those great kids and to have a small impact on their lives."

DAVE MacMILLAN: GOPHER BASKETBALL

Dave MacMillan served two stints as Minnesota's Head Basketball Coach in the 1930s and '40s. After 18 seasons, the program's all-time winningest coach would retire with an impressive overall record of 197-157. The "Canny Scot" also won a co-Big Ten title in 1937, along with four conference runner-up finishes as well.

DON MEYER: HAMLINE BASKETBALL

A native of Wayne, Neb., Don Meyer attended the University of Northern Colorado and graduated in 1967. While at UNC, Meyer played baseball and basketball. On the baseball field, he posted a career pitching record of 22-2 and caught the attention of pro scouts. On the basketball court, Meyer led UNC to the 1966 NCAA college division playoffs and was named as an NCAA All-American. Meyer began his basketball coaching career at Western State (Colo.) where he was an assistant from 1968-70. From there he went to the University of Utah, where he served as an assistant from 1970-72 and also earned a Ph.D. From there, Meyer received his first head basketball coaching job in 1972 when he was hired by Hamline University. Meyer spent three seasons with the Pipers, registering a modest 37-41 record with a program that had a 30-177 record the six previous seasons. After a 5-20 record in his first season, Meyer turned things around, recording 16-10 and 16-11 records the next two years — even reaching the NCAA Division III Elite Eight in his last year with the program.

Since those days at Hamline, Meyer went on to become the fastest coach to reach 700 wins in the history of college basketball. Now into his fourth decade of coaching, Meyer is also among the top 10 winningest coaches in the history of men's collegiate basketball with a gaudy record of 769-264 and a winning percentage of .750. In addition, he has won one National Championship and has taken his teams to an amazing 14 national tournaments. Now entering his fourth year behind the bench at Northern State University, Meyer spent the previous 24 years coaching NAIA I David Lipscomb University in Nashville, Tenn. Meyer's Lipscomb teams spent a decade winning more games than any other team in the country, averaging more than 32 wins per season for 10 years before his move to Northern. Meyer's Bison teams made 13 national tournament appearances, winning the NAIA National Championship in 1986. Meyer was named NAIA National Coach of the Year in 1989 and 1990, and was selected to the NAIA Hall of Fame at the age of 47. He also assisted legendary Duke Coach Mike Krzyzewski with the Olympic Sports Festival South Team in 1983. An accomplished motivational speaker and writer, Meyer also produces instructional books and a 30-tape series entitled "Building a Championship Program," which is sold throughout the world. One of the very best in the business, Don Meyer is truly a basketball coaching legend.

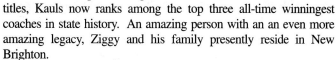

ZIGGY KAULS
HIGH SCHOOL BASKETBALL: MOUNDS VIEW

Ziggy Kauls was born in Latvia and lived in a German refuge camp as a young boy from the end of World War II until 1950. Kauls then moved to American when he was in the third grade with his family and wound up living in Forest Lake. There, he learned to love the game of basketball and played it whenever he could. After graduating from Forest Lake High School, Kauls went on to play basketball under legendary Coach Joe Hutton at Hamline, where he also got his teaching degree. Kauls then went on to teach math at Mounds View High School and later became the school's head basketball coach. In 1972 his team won the state AA title behind future NBA Center Mark Landsberger, and they won it again in 1999 behind Nick Horvath, who went on to play at Duke. Kauls retired from teaching in 1998, but still remains as the team's head coach as he heads into his 37th season behind the bench. With 575 career wins, 11 trips to the big dance and two state

titles, Kauls now ranks among the top three all-time winningest coaches in state history. An amazing person with an an even more amazing legacy, Ziggy and his family presently reside in New Brighton.

HOW WOULD YOU DESCRIBE YOUR COACHING STYLE? "It has evolved over the years as you learn more about the game. Initially you think you have all the answers and the longer you coach you see that there are different ways of getting things done. It is not as absolute as you once thought. I have always tried to have consistent discipline on our teams. I have just tried to enjoy the game for what it is — to play basketball and have fun. If you have some sense of purpose, then you have a better chance of winning than losing. Most people would probably say too that our kids have had a pretty strong commitment during the off-season. A lot of basketball can be developed on your own without an excess of structure. I have always felt that creative players become creative because they are doing it without somebody else telling them how to do it."

HOW DO YOU MOTIVATE YOUR PLAYERS? "I don't know if there is any one way of motivating your players. Good players don't have to be motivated, they just like to play basketball and they work hard. It helps as a coach to have some good, reachable individual goals as well as team goals for your kids, but mostly they are the ones who have to find motivation from within. We don't paste things on the wall or anything like that, we just talk about getting better each day and work hard throughout the season. One of my personal goals is to never put kids into situations where they look bad. What that means is that you might have to restrict what certain players do under certain circumstances. For instance, if a kid is not a good dribbler, then you don't put him in situations where he would be dribbling a lot. We just try to fit players into roles so that they function within the team and are successful. Outside of being outclassed in terms of talent, a lot of times when you see teams fail, or beat themselves, I think it has to do with kids trying to do things that are beyond their skill level, such as shooting from distances where they can't hit or dribbling into places where they can't get out of."

WHO WERE YOUR COACHING MENTORS? "I played basketball under Joe Hutton at Hamline, so he was certainly an influence on me. I was lucky, when I took this job all of my assistants were former head coaches, so that really helped too. I had just great support coming in here and that was just tremendous."

LOOKING BACK WHAT ARE YOU MOST PROUD OF IN YOUR CAREER? "If I look back over my 36 years of coaching I think that I have always kept trying and I have never stuck with just one style. My son recently pointed out to me that our Mustang record has gotten better every decade from the 1960s to now, and that means a lot to me. I am also very proud of the kids that we have had in our program and feel good about the kind of people that they have turned into."

HOW DO YOU BUILD TEAM UNITY & CHEMISTRY? "The biggest thing is that we always try to emphasize the team concept and that each kid has a big responsibility to his teammates. We always talk about what our strengths and weaknesses are and we try to get kids to understand that basketball can be fun if everybody is on the same page. I try to stress that you will go further as an individual if the team does well. Also, a lot of our kids are multiple-sport athletes who play different sports as well as basketball in the summertime, and that makes for very well rounded student athletes. Then, if they are friends, they tend to cheer for each other, and that builds chemistry."

WHAT ADVICE WOULD YOU HAVE FOR YOUNG COACHES STARTING OUT TODAY? "It'll be a big personal commitment. Just remember to keep trying and keep learning. Coach K (Duke's Mike Krzyzewski) once told me that I was an 'old young coach.' What he meant by that was that I was old in terms in age, but I was young in the sense that I was always looking at tapes, going to clinics and still learning. That was great advice. I have also learned a lot from my assistants, they are great recourses. Form your own philosophies based on what you like and dislike regarding your closes allies. Just create a style that fits your personality and what you believe in, and then stick to it."

WHAT'S THE BIGGEST THING YOU'VE LEARNED FROM COACHING THAT YOU'VE BEEN ABLE TO APPLY TO YOUR EVERYDAY LIFE? "Persistence. Persistence and consistency in coaching usually translates into pretty good results."

WHAT ARE THE KEY INGREDIENTS TO CREATING A CHAMPIONSHIP TEAM? "I think you have to be tough mentally, play well under pressure and you have to be consistent so that you don't beat yourself."

WHAT'S THE SECRET TO YOUR SUCCESS? "I don't think you can have good teams without good players. Good players make good teams, and that makes good coaches. I would say though that I think my commitment to the game has helped me stay grounded and that has also helped our teams be successful. I also think that watching my son grow up and develop and seeing the things that motivated or affected him positively or negatively had a big impact on me too. It helped me evolve as a coach and become a better person as a result."

WHAT WOULD YOU WANT TO SAY TO YOUR FANS, BOOSTERS, AND ALUMNI WHO HAVE SUPPORTED YOU ALL THESE YEARS? "I would want to thank all of our fans for their support over the years. We have great fans and they have never given up on us. They have always stayed faithful to the Mustangs and

I appreciate it. I would also want to thank all of my assistant coaches through the years, they have been fabulous too. From my son to Dave Leiser, a 1957 Mounds View grad who won the 2002 National Coaching Assistant of the Year award, I just really appreciate what they have done for me and for this program."

HOW DO YOU WANT YOUR COACHING EPITAPH TO READ — HOW DO YOU WANT TO BE REMEMBERED AS A COACH? "I just tried to do the best job I knew how."

400 WINS CLUB MEMBERS (GIRLS BASKETBALL)

1. Mike Dreier, New London-Spicer*
2. Carol Visness, Kittson Central*
3. Myron Glass, Rochester Lourdes*
4. Darrel Ulferts, SW Minn Christian
5. Mike Ciochetto, Chisholm*
6. Jim Lien, Walker-Hackensack-Akeley*
7. Randy Myhre, Barnum*
8. Dick Simpson, Brandon-Evansville*

* Active

HON NORDLY: NORTHERN IOWA BASKETBALL

Oliver "Hon" Nordly played college basketball at Carleton, graduating in 1927. From there, Nordly got into coaching, and went on to lead Rochester High School to nine conference titles in football, basketball and track. Nordly then went on to coach at the University of Northern Iowa, where he led his teams to 13 titles in basketball and golf.

JIM POLLARD: MINNEAPOLIS LAKERS BASKETBALL

Jim Pollard grew up in Oakland, where he starred on the Oakland Technical High School basketball team. Full of promise and potential, the young Pollard took his talents to Stanford University, where the All-American led the Indians to the 1942 NCAA championship. From there Pollard joined the U.S. Coast Guard and played on several service teams over the next three years, followed by a couple of semi-pro AAU squads as well.

Pollard's story of how he became a Minneapolis Laker is as interesting as the man himself. Just before the Lakers first season in 1947-48, General Manager Sid Hartman was assembling the pieces to put together a winning team. Specifically, they were trying hard to land a young six-foot-five jumping jack out of the California Industrial league named Jim Pollard, who was playing for the local AAU Oakland "Bittners." (On the East Coast, pro basketball was all the rage, but on the West Coast, there were only the AAU leagues, and they were every bit as good as the eastern pros.) In fact, a lot of pro teams had previously tried and failed to sign Pollard, who had been training for a spot on the coveted 1948 Olympic team. But somehow, someway, Sid was able to persuade the young star to forego his Olympic dreams and move to the tundra. The news spread quickly that somebody had finally talked him into signing. Oakland Mayor Joe Smith even called Pollard and pleaded with him not to go. But Jim liked the tenacious Hartman and agreed to sign a Laker contract. There was one catch though. In addition to his $12,000 a year, plus a $3,000 signing bonus, Pollard made Sid agree to bring along three of his Bittner teammates. He reluctantly agreed, and went on to become one of the game's all-time great ones. The rest, they say, is basketball history.

Pollard would lead the Lakers to six world championships alongside George Mikan, the game's first great center. Then, in 1955, Pollard announced his retirement from the Lakers to accept the head coaching position at LaSalle College in Philadelphia. There, he would post a modest 48-28 record over the next three seasons. Then, in 1960, after a three-year stint in Philly, Pollard rejoined his beloved Lakers, this time as their coach, taking over the reigns in midseason from John Castellani. He would have his work cut out for him though as the Lakers were 11-25 at that point, and things were not looking good. Minneapolis would finish the season at 25-50, and while they did upset Detroit in the first round of the playoffs, they ultimately lost to the St. Louis Hawks in the Divisional Finals. That season would be Pollard's last, as well as the last for the Lakers in Minneapolis. Pollard would later go on to coach the Chicago Packers, an NBA expansion team run by Max Winter in 1961-62, the ABA's Minnesota Muskies in 1967-68, as well as the Miami Floridians from 1968-70 — when the Muskies franchise was relocated to Miami. Pollard was a fabulous rebounder and all-around team player, he would finish his illustrious eight-year career with 6,522 points — good for a 13.1 points per game scoring average. He would later be inducted into the Pro Basketball Hall of Fame.

John Kundla was born in Star Junction, Pa., but moved to Minneapolis when he was five years old. Raised by his mother, Kundla went on to attend Minneapolis Central High School. After a great prep career, he went on to play basketball under coach Dave MacMillan at the University of Minnesota. Kundla also played baseball at Minnesota, but his main sport was hoops. In basketball, he earned three varsity letters and led the Gophers to the Big Ten co-championship in 1937. He captained the Gophers in 1939, and in addition to earning All-Big Ten Conference honors, was even selected as the winner of the prestigious Conference Medal of Honor for scholastic and athletic achievement.

Following graduation, Kundla went into the Service for a year. He then played one season of professional baseball with Paducah in the Class C Kitty League. Kundla also stayed active as a basketball player as well during this time, even leading his semi-pro Rock Spring Sparklers, of Shakopee, to the 1943 World Pro Tournament in Chicago. Kundla then took over as a basketball assistant to Coach MacMillan before accepting the head coaching job at De LaSalle High School in downtown Minneapolis. There, in addition to teaching history, Kundla coached the Islanders to a Minnesota State Catholic League basketball championship in 1944. From there, Kundla took over as the head basketball coach at St. Thomas University, where he coached the Tommies to a modest 11-11 record in 1947.

By this time, the Minneapolis Lakers had come to town. Originally, they had offered the head coaching position to Joe Hutton, who had been Hamline's coach since 1931 and had built the Pipers into a national small-college power. But, when Hutton declined, the Lakers decided to hire the 31-year-old Kundla as their first coach. Kundla left the security of St. Thomas and signed a three-year deal with Minnesota's upstart professional basketball franchise for a whopping $3,000 per year. It would be a very wise choice.

In 11-plus years as the Laker head coach, Kundla would go on to compile an impressive career record of 466-319. At the time of his retirement in 1959, only the legendary Red Auerbach of the Celtics had more pro coaching wins. Kundla also won 70 playoff games while losing just 35, a record that translated into an amazing six world championships for the state of Minnesota. In addition to coaching four NBA All-Star Games (1952-54), Kundla also became one of only three coaches in NBA history to have guided teams to three consecutive world titles.

"I've seen a lot of great teams, at least on paper, that won nothing," said Boston's legendary Coach, Red Auerbach. "Sure Kundla had great teams, but he did great things with them."

In 1958, tired of the stress and travel demands, Kundla stepped down as coach of the Lakers and became the teams' general manager. In his first move as G.M., he hired his recently retired star center, George Mikan, to be his coaching predecessor. It was a short-lived move which flopped though, as Kundla found himself back on the bench just a short while later.

In 1959, the day after the Lakers lost to the Celtics in the NBA Finals, Kundla announced his resignation, in order to return to his alma mater as the head basketball coach. After 11 seasons of coaching the Gophers, Ozzie Cowles had decided to step down, and Kundla jumped in to take over. Kundla coached the Gophers from 1959-68, earning 110 career wins against 105 losses in nine seasons. He also guided the U.S National Team into international competition in 1965, and served on the NCAA Rules Committee as well. In 1968,

University of North Dakota head coach Bill Fitch took over for the Gophers, and Kundla went over to the U's St. Paul campus, where he served as the University's Physical Education Director for several more years. Kundla was later inducted into the Pro Basketball Hall of Fame in 1995, alongside his former star power forward, Vern Mikkelsen, making it the first time that a coach and player were enshrined with one another.

"I can still remember Ray Meyer walking me down the aisle in Springfield, at the Hall of Fame, it was such a thrill," Kundla recalled. "My family was all there, and I don't think I will ever experience anything any better than that."

Kundla, a humble and quiet man, always kept an even demeanor on the court. Even as a young coach, he displayed sound judgment and always stuck to his beliefs that defense and discipline were the keys to success. A tremendous tactician, his greatest asset as a coach might have been in recognizing the strengths of his players, and then utilizing them. He somehow managed to keep three future Hall of Famers: George Mikan, Vern Mikkelsen and Jim Pollard, all happy and content — a feat nearly impossible by today's standards. He was a "players coach" and for that his men loved him. He will forever be remembered as one of the game's greatest.

"I was very lucky to be a Laker, and there is no greater thrill than winning a world championship," said Kundla. "The national recognition we got for the state of Minnesota was such a thrill for me to see. I was very proud of our Laker teams and I owe it all to my players. I'm grateful to Mikan, Mikkelsen, Martin, Pollard, Skoog, Grant, and all the others. We had players with such character, team spirit, and a will to win. I was just very lucky to be their head coach."

Johnny and his wife Marie later settled down in Robbinsdale, where they had six children and many grandchildren, who, by the way, all play basketball. Coach K is retired and enjoying watching the Timberwolves and Lakers. (He had a terrible dilemma in the 2003 NBA playoffs when the two teams squared off against one another!) In 2003 Kundla was also honored by the Los Angeles Lakers with a personalized NBA championship ring worth nearly $10,000 — three times more than his annual salary as the coach of the old Lakers!

"John Kundla is one of the greatest coaches of all time," said Vern Mikkelsen. "He's never been given the proper credit simply because everyone said that anyone could've coached our championship teams. I sort of look at John similarly today as I did with the Chicago Bulls head coach, Phil Jackson. Like Jackson, John was wonderful at coaching each of us at our own individual levels, and that really motivated us to play for him and win. I am just very grateful for the fact that he gave me the opportunity to play with the Lakers."

"John is just an excellent guy," added George Mikan. "He had a great way about him, and he could keep the players focused on the game. He also had the ability to help you when things weren't going your way. He could critique your game and correct any problems that you had to get you back out there. He was great at analyzing team defenses and he was a master at setting up plays to would help us excel. He is a wonderful person and a great coach."

HOW WOULD YOU DESCRIBE YOUR COACHING STYLE? "You know, we worked hard on defense and we tried to move the ball on the fast break in order to get good shots. Other than that we worked very hard in practice on the fundamentals and also on conditioning. We also were one of the first teams to have set-plays. We had different plays for each individual. For instance, Vern Mikkelsen's was the 'Askov,' Slater Martin's was 'Pensacola' and that helped quite a bit to keep guys involved throughout the entire game. Really though, when you had a starting line-up of George Mikan, Vern Mikkelsen and Jim Pollard, three hall of famers, I didn't need to do a lot of coaching! I just tried to get them all into the game so that there was balanced scoring and then stay out of the way. Believe me, these guys were so good that they didn't need me telling them anything. So my style was to give them the ball and just get out of the way!"

HOW DID YOU MOTIVATE YOUR PLAYERS? "It started with having guys with talent and character who were team players. They had to believe in winning and in playing team basketball. Once you have guys like that then you could do anything. Really though, I just tried to get my players to work hard and teach them the fundamentals. I also believed in the saying: 'praise loudly and blame softly.' I never yelled at a guy in public, that was just something I didn't do. Another thing was money. Back when we played, we got paid the further we went into the playoffs. So, guys really wanted to do well so that they could maybe make an extra thousand bucks. That was a big motivation back then."

COULD YOU STILL COACH TODAY? "The game has just changed so much. That was a different era and is really an entirely different game altogether. The dunking, the three point play, players taking steps (traveling), and it is just all one-on-one nowadays. The passing game is gone and with all the dunking you have it is just all showboating and individual play. The game is very exciting though. The players can shoot better, they can jump higher and they can dribble like crazy. But I still feel that passing is a lost art. Another thing now is that the players have all these long, guaranteed contracts. Back in the day you could really motivate a guy just from the fact that he could be traded or released in a heartbeat."

WHO WERE YOUR COACHING MENTORS? "Dave MacMillan was my coach at the University of Minnesota, and he was my mentor. I inherited his philosophy and I give him all the credit for my success in coaching. He later came in and served as an assistant for me with the Lakers and that was really quite a thrill."

WHAT ARE THE CHARACTERISTICS OF WINNERS? "They have to not only have talent, but they have to want to win championships. They also have to be team ballplayers and not worry about themselves. Being a team player and playing defense are the keys in my mind. Some guys just had that certain quality and you could just see that they were winners."

LOOKING BACK WHAT ARE YOU MOST PROUD OF IN YOUR CAREER? "The six championships with the Lakers, of course, that was very special. I was lucky to coach for as long as I did and at as many places that I did. The people I met and the relationships I made were also great. The only regret I have is that I never won in college."

HOW DID YOU BUILD TEAM UNITY & CHEMISTRY? "I was lucky that I had good players who were good people with talent and character. When you have players like that you don't need to do too much as a coach. The guys knew that if we won the world championship then they would get paid and really that was the big thing, money. Then, of course at the college level it was totally different. There, you just had to work with the players and build team unity by working hard and creating an environment where everyone could learn and grow as people and players."

WHAT MOTIVATED YOU? "I loved to win and I loved to coach. It was my job for many, many years and I took that very seriously. I would have to say that my family played a big part in motivating me as well. They all were very supportive and prayed for us whenever we took the court. I can still hear my wife yelling 'DEFENSE!' from out in the crowd to root us on. That was great and made me feel very good."

WHAT ADVICE WOULD YOU HAVE FOR YOUNG COACHES STARTING OUT TODAY? "There is a lot of psychology involved in coaching and you have to handle each player a little different. Some players you can ball out while others you have to be gentle with and just encourage them. Figuring out which ones to do which is the key."

WHAT'S THE BIGGEST THING YOU'VE LEARNED FROM COACHING THAT YOU'VE BEEN ABLE TO APPLY TO YOUR EVERYDAY LIFE? "I would say the ability to be able to get along with people."

WHAT WOULD YOU WANT TO SAY TO YOUR FANS, BOOSTERS, AND ALUMNI WHO HAVE SUPPORTED YOU ALL THESE YEARS? "Thanks so much to all the fans and supporters who came out and supported me and all of my teams, whether it was at the University or with the Lakers. It was a lot of fun and we couldn't have done it without you."

HOW DO YOU WANT YOUR COACHING EPITAPH TO READ — HOW DO YOU WANT TO BE REMEMBERED AS A COACH? "I got such a great satisfaction out of coaching. You know I think I enjoyed teaching in grade school, high school and college the most, because that was teaching the fundamentals. I took great pride in teaching the fundamentals, especially defense. It is amazing, I still see kids who I coached way back when they were in grade school and they remember things I said back then. It is such a great feeling to make a difference in young people's lives and to have made so many friends. Coaching and teaching were always my goal, and I feel very lucky to have achieved my goal in life."

NORM OLSON: UM-DULUTH BASKETBALL

Norm Olson coached basketball at the University of Minnesota-Duluth for 15 years, and led the Bulldogs to four MIAC titles, in 1958, 1959, 1961 and 1962.

JOEL MATURI
HIGH SCHOOL BASKETBALL: EDGEWOOD, WISCONSIN

Joel Maturi grew up in Chisholm and went on to earn nine letters in at Chisholm High School — four in football, three in baseball and two in basketball, under legendary coach Bob McDonald. A leader early on, Maturi also served as his senior class president before going on to graduate in 1963. From there, Maturi attended Notre Dame, where he walked on to the Fighting Irish football team as a defensive back. Why Notre Dame? You see, Joel's father was a tremendous Notre Dame football fan primarily because of a man named Joe Bach, a Chisholm native, who went on to become one of the "Seven Mules" linemen who blocked for the legendary "Four Horsemen." As a result, Joel's family made the trek to South Bend every year for a vacation to watch Notre Dame play football. So, when it came time for Joel to decide which college to attend, the choice was obvious. Joel got his degree in Government in 1967 and that same year he also served on the support staff of Ara Parseghian's first national championship team.

Maturi's first teaching job was at a small private school in Madison, Wis., called Edgewood High School, where he would remain for 19 years as a coach and administrator. There, he taught social studies, sociology, history, economics and religion, all while coaching football, baseball, basketball and track, at various times throughout his career. Maturi led his teams to a combined total of 10 state tournaments, with basketball emerging as his best sport. Maturi won about 70% of his games on the hardwood and led his basketball teams to a pair of state tournament runner-up's as well as one state consolation title. He later also served as the Athletic Director, Dean of Students and the Associate Principal as well. It is safe to say that this guy truly wore a lot of hats at Edgewood High! In 1992 Joel was inducted into the Wisconsin Basketball Coaches Hall of Fame.

After earning his master's degree in educational administration from the University of Wisconsin-Platteville, Maturi left the high school ranks in 1987 to get into college athletics. He would start out at the University of Wisconsin-Madison, where he would work his way up the ladder and ultimately achieve the title of associate senior director of athletics in 1992. There, he had direct responsibility for all aspects of football, hockey, wrestling, softball, men's and women's cross country, men's and women's crew, men's and women's indoor and outdoor track and field, and the office of academic affairs. For his efforts, Maturi was named Sports Person of the Year in 1993.

In 1996 Maturi left Wisconsin to take over as the director of athletics at the University of Denver. There, he oversaw budgeting and financial management, developed a gender-equity plan and a NCAA compliance manual. In 1998 Maturi left Denver to serve as the director of athletics at Miami University. There, he was responsible for budgets, policies and procedures for 19 men's and women's programs with more than 600 student athletes. During his tenure, Miami University teams did well academically and competitively, and in 2001 fully 12 teams earned grade point averages of 3.0 or better and the university finished third out of 13 teams in combined competition in the Mid-America Conference.

In 2002 Maturi got his big break when he was offered the director of athletics position at the University of Minnesota. It was a homecoming of sorts for the old Iron Ranger, who still has a lot of family here in the Land of 10,000 Lakes. Since then Maturi has had the daunting challenge of combining the men's and women's athletic departments into one, spearheading a fund-raising effort of mammoth proportions and overcoming many budget shortfalls as well. He has taken it all in stride though, and has made Minnesota proud. Seven

teams won conference titles in his first year and the Gopher Hockey team went back-to-back in winning their second national championship in a row too. The boss of all Gopher coaches, Maturi is a fixture at Gopher sporting events and is well known for the long hours that he puts in. A tireless worker and dedicated administrator, Joel Maturi might just be the best thing that has happened in Gold Country since the arrival of Goldy Gopher.

HOW WOULD YOU DESCRIBE YOUR COACHING STYLE? "My style was very repetitive with what I believed in. People might get tired of hearing me say the same things, but I have learned over time that repetition was the most important thing. I also believe you shouldn't get too fancy by getting way outside the box and doing too many things. You know most of us can only do so many things well and I try and pride myself on doing what I believe is important well, and hopefully the other things will fall into place as a result of that. Overall, I think I was pretty structured as a coach and tried to be very detailed and organized. I even posted every one of my practice plans from the first day I ever coached, so that the kids would know what they were going to do from the time they hit the field, court or track, to the time they hit the showers. Unlike some coaches, I also never used practice or extra running as a punishment, I just tried to stick to my values as best as possible. I would say I was pretty conservative too. I emphasized defense in every sport I coached. I also thought it was fun to do a lot of drills at the end of practices to simulate game situations. I wanted our kids to learn and be as best prepared as possible, and that certainly helped. Overall, I think I had very high expectations from my players, and we were successful as a result."

WHO WERE YOUR COACHING MENTORS? "I think that you learn a great deal from all the people that you have been mentored by and certainly for me to have learned basketball from Bob McDonald and football from Beck Brown at Chisholm was invaluable. They both had significant influences on my life and I would like to think that much of my coaching style came from them. Then, at Notre Dame, to play football under Ara Parseghian was also a wonderful experience. My first true coaching mentor when I got into coaching, however, was probably George Chryst. He was just great. I think you develop a style all your own, but you certainly emulate those that you had great respect for."

HOW DID YOU MOTIVATE YOUR PLAYERS? "I am a real emotional guy and I tried to use pep talks to get my kids fired up. I enjoyed that part of coaching immensely. I even tried to come up with a theme, or an angle, for every game and prepare that way. I also was a big believer in studying statistics, and then using those numbers to motivate my kids. I really tried to challenge them individually to be better than their last time out, and that worked well. One thing in particular that I did which I though was neat was I would oftentimes give kids index cards with notes written on them to inspire or encourage them. It was always something positive and it just gave the kids something to reflect on while we were on a long bus trip or something. For instance I might tell a kid I knew that he was going to have to guard the opposing team's best player that night, but I knew that he would do well because of his determination, hard work and preparation. Hey, that might have been a little corny, but I really enjoyed that and I think looking back that the kids did too. I also told my kids that if they made the team as freshmen, sophomores and juniors, then they automatically made the squad as seniors. I just felt that that was a message I wanted to send to those kids to reward their hard work. Looking back, it was definitely the right thing to do."

WHAT MOTIVATES YOU? "I don't want to admit it, but it is probably the fear of losing more than the high of winning. I am driven to succeed, it is who I am. I was that way as an athlete too. I worked harder than most other athletes because I didn't know if I was good enough and I worked harder than most coaches because I didn't know if I was talented enough. I don't think I have a lot of natural ability so I have to just work harder than everybody else. So, it's the drive to succeed and the fear of failure that really motivates me. I will say that in my old age I have learned to understand failures better because I truly believe in John Wooden's definition of success. He said that success is a piece of mind, a self satisfaction of you knowing that you have done your very best to become as good as you can be. So, I know that although sometimes I don't succeed on the scoreboard, I do believe that I have succeeded in other ways. Even though you can't win em' all, I can still put my head on my pillow at night. It's not always easy, but I know that if I stick to my plan, in the end we will be successful."

HOW DID YOU BUILD TEAM UNITY & CHEMISTRY? "It was easier to do at a private school I think. There was already chemistry within the building. You had something in common just because you were there and that certainly helped. We didn't have scholarships at our school so our kids had to pay their own way, and as a result, we had to do a lot of things together that built team unity. From parents helping to take tickets and ushering, to the players sweeping the basketball floor before games — everybody pitched in and that helped the kids become better friends as they got to know each other in different settings outside of school and sports."

WHAT ADVICE WOULD YOU HAVE FOR YOUNG COACHES STARTING OUT TODAY? "You learn from people who have been successful, but you need to not try and be those people. What I mean is, I believe certain people can succeed in certain environments — what I call 'fits.' A coach might fit better at a certain school or university because of various circumstances such as climate, proximity to family, etc. You just need to be happy wherever you go and find a good fit, regardless of things like money or recognition, and understanding that is very important. I have never taken a job where I haven't thought it was going to be my last job. I believe you should do that and give it everything you have got. Hey, if it leads to somewhere bigger and better, great, but that can't be your motivation I don't think. I don't think you can ever be happy always looking ahead to the next opportunity as a stepping stone. And if you are not happy, I am not sure you can succeed in this business. It's no different than what you tell your children: 'find a career doing what you enjoy doing.' The bottom line is that you need to enjoy and genuinely like what you are doing."

WHAT IS THE KEY TO GOOD TIME MANAGEMENT? "I don't think that I have good time management skills to be quite honest. I mean I wouldn't advocate the hours that I put in to anybody. I would like to think that I have given my family quality time through the years though, because it certainly hasn't been quantity. And I am not proud of that, that is for sure. But I am lucky, I have a wife and a family that has been very supportive of me and has understood my work ethic. They know that my drive comes from seeing other coaches being successful. From helping to raise money or just supporting an athlete when they are down are all things that take time and are all part of this job. It is a very demanding career and I am lucky that my family has understood that is who I am and that is what I have needed to do. I have become better at being organized and at delegating authority, but the external demands at the University of Minnesota are just immense."

WHAT'S THE BIGGEST THING YOU'VE LEARNED FROM COACHING THAT YOU'VE BEEN ABLE TO APPLY TO YOUR EVERYDAY LIFE? "We have a tremendous impact on the lives of young people and that was a bit overwhelming in some ways. That drove me to be a better person though because you do realize how much of a difference you can make in someone's life. I learned that it was important for me to make sure that I knew what I was saying and that the way I said it was positive and constructive. You just hope that in the end you were a good role model for them and taught them well."

WHAT'S THE BEST PIECE OF ADVICE YOU EVER GOT FROM ANOTHER COACH? "Don't flinch. A mentor and friend of mine once told me that and what he meant was this: He said 'Joel, you have worked very hard at your plan — your vision and mission.' It is OK to be flexible and make adjustments along the way, but don't compromise. The biggest mistake we make when we run into trouble or are not winning the big games that we want or need to be winning, and sometimes we abandon our plans. That is usually a mistake and is usually the wrong path to take. So, whenever I run into a trouble now, I always tell myself 'don't flinch Joel.' What I am telling myself is 'be true to yourself, be principled, stick with your plan and don't compromise.' That has been great advise and I would recommend it to anybody."

WHAT'S THE SECRET TO YOUR SUCCESS? "I don't know if there are any secrets. And really, that is not for me to judge. I just think that integrity, good values and hard work are the key to anyone's success. And also to surround yourself with good, honest people, that's very important too."

ON BEING THE ATHLETIC DIRECTOR AT THE UNIVERSITY OF MINNESOTA: "I think I have great insight into coaching because I was a coach for nearly 20 years. So I think that gives me a lot of credibility with the other coaches and they respect me for that. I understand the outside pressures of coaches with regards to the parents, the press, the boosters, and what have you. I also understand that sometimes kids don't do what coaches want them to do. I just want to listen and be as supportive as I can to all of our coaches and help them to be as successful as they can."

HOW DO YOU WANT YOUR COACHING EPITAPH TO READ — HOW DO YOU WANT TO BE REMEMBERED AS A COACH? "I hope that I am remembered as someone who cared and did his best. I don't need to be recognized as winning this many games or that sort of thing, I just hope that I am remembered as someone who worked hard to succeed for his teams as well as for himself. Even today, as an athletic director, I know if I make a lot of mistakes, but I hope in the end that people know that my heart is in the right place."

MEL TAUBE: CARLETON BASKETBALL

Mel Taube, reportedly fed up with big-time athletics, left his big-time coaching position at Purdue University for the cozy confines of Carleton College. There, Taube would coach basketball at Carleton from 1950-60, posting a 136-80 career record along the way.

DAN McCARRELL
COLLEGE BASKETBALL: MINNESOTA STATE MANKATO

Dan McCarrell grew up in Chicago and went on to graduate from the prestigious Wheaton Academy. After coaching high school basketball for six years in Illinois, McCarrell's first college basketball coaching job came in 1967 at Division III North Park College, where his Vikings' won three straight national titles in 1978, 1979 and 1980, and racked up a gaudy 296-160 record along the way. Incredibly, four players from those teams were drafted into the NBA, including future Chicago Bulls star, Michael Harper. McCarrell would stay at North Park College for 16 years before coming to Minnesota State Mankato in 1984.

McCarrell would coach at Mankato for 17 years, averaging 18 wins per season. In 1989-90, McCarrell led the Mavericks to a 20-10 record, marking only the fourth time in the program's 65 years that a Maverick team has achieved 20 wins in a season. In 1997, McCarrell became the 21st active coach in NCAA Division II to pass the 500-career win plateau, and in the last game of the 2000 season, he coached his 900th career game. McCarrell amassed an impressive 283-189 record along the way, becoming the school's all-time winningest men's basketball coach in the process. McCarrell finally retired from the game in 2001 with an overall career record of 579-349 (.603%) — which ranks him in the top 10 of all-time for Division II coaches. In fact, at the time of his retirement he was just a handful of wins behind such D-I college coaching legends as Duke's Mike Krzyzewski and Syracuse's Jim Boeheim. A noted teacher and strong strategist, Dan McCarrell is a Mankato coaching legend.

HOW WOULD YOU DESCRIBE YOUR COACHING STYLE? "I would say it is all about hard work, effort and trying to be well prepared with good intensity. I think you have to enjoy the game, understand the game and realize that you always have to work on improving and getting better because the game keeps changing. Then, you try to adapt and take advantage of the talent you get year to year from within that same philosophy. Different teams have different character, different strengths and weaknesses, so you just have to be flexible."

HOW DID YOU MOTIVATE YOUR PLAYERS? "I tried to insist on effort all the time. I also insisted on my players being on time because I think that is where everything starts. You show up to practice on time, you show up for shoot-arounds on time, you leave for games on time, and you get to class on time because it affects everybody. I think that discipline starts to erode if you don't insist on that. Then, I think you have to encourage your kids to work hard. I try to praise different things as a coach and try to compliment the team in various ways as well, always trying to get the best out of people. I just try and start with the little things, like a good screen, a nice

pass, a good rebound, or a solid effort like diving on the ground for a loose ball. Then, it builds from there."

LOOKING BACK WHAT ARE YOU MOST PROUD OF IN YOUR CAREER? "I think I am most proud of my ability to just hang in there. I have been a college head coach for 34 years and was a high school coach for six years before that, so to stand the test of time has been very gratifying. To coach different teams in different situations at different levels has been an amazing experience and I wouldn't trade it for the world. I think the relationships with my players has been wonderful too. I still hear from a lot of them and I take a lot of pride in the fact that I might have had something to do with their success in life. So, I am proud of that too."

HOW DID YOU BUILD TEAM UNITY & CHEMISTRY? "Each team is a little different. I think you have to demand the same from each player but you handle them differently. In other words, there are certain players that you have to stay on because if you don't then they will get lackadaisical. Then, there are other guys that you have to let up on otherwise they get too tight. Some guys, if you get on them too hard, they lose their confidence. So, I think the longer you coach and the more you deal with people, the more you realize that you have to be consistent in what you demand. You also have to handle your players differently because of different personalities, and that is important too."

WHAT IS THE KEY TO GOOD TIME MANAGEMENT? "I would say good organization. It is always a race against time during the season in whatever you are doing and you just have to use the time that you have wisely. So, you have to demand that your team is on time and that your players are respectful of that. Also, your players need to work hard and focus when they are there so that you get the most out of your time."

WHAT ADVICE WOULD YOU HAVE FOR YOUNG COACHES STARTING OUT TODAY? "You have to work hard, don't be afraid to make mistakes and don't be afraid to make unpopular decisions. Overall, you need to have thick skin in this business and that is something you should always remember."

WHAT'S THE SECRET TO YOUR SUCCESS? "I would say having good players and being able to motivate them. You also have to have a good staff of assistants that are prepared and work hard. You just really need to sell your entire system to your players and they have to believe in it in order to be successful."

WHAT WOULD YOU WANT TO SAY TO YOUR FANS, BOOSTERS, AND ALUMNI WHO HAVE SUPPORTED YOU ALL THESE YEARS? "I appreciate your support very much and want to thank you all very much. We had a lot of loyal backers and boosters and they are so important to our program."

HOW DO YOU WANT YOUR COACHING EPITAPH TO READ — HOW DO YOU WANT TO BE REMEMBERED AS A COACH? "I think as someone who worked hard, loved coaching, and cared about his players and assistants coaches."

KARL SALSCHEIDER: BEMIDJI BASKETBALL

Karl Salscheider served as the head basketball coach at Bemidji State for 13 seasons during the 1980s and 90s and became the program's all-time winningest coach with 147 victories.

RED SEVERSON
COLLEGE BASKETBALL: ST. CLOUD STATE UNIVERSITY

Marlowe "Red" Severson grew up in Summit, S.D., and played basketball, the only sport offered, at Summit High School. From there Severson went on to attend St. Cloud State, where he tried out for the junior varsity basketball team but did not make the cut. After receiving degrees in English literature and writing, Severson's first teaching and coaching jobs were in Browns Valley and Buffalo, where he stayed for a total of five years.

From there, at just 28 years old, Severson came back to his alma mater to take over as the head basketball coach at St. Cloud State in 1958. There, Severson led the Huskies to 10 NIC crowns in just 11 seasons and also guided his teams to the NAIA playoffs six times, including trips to the national Finals in 1962, 1964 and 1968. During his tenure at SCSU Severson posted an outstanding record of 207-66.

That next year Severson headed south, to Minnesota State-Mankato, where he coached the Mavericks for four seasons, posting a 43-61 record along the way. After 15 seasons of coaching, Severson then retired at the age of 43 with a 250-127 (.663) career coaching record.

At that point Severson got out of the game to focus on new teaching and business ventures. In addition, Severson would go on to write and produce nine basketball textbooks, a number of communication and motivational tapes, and many fundamentals films — all of which were well received at schools, colleges and libraries throughout the world. Severson also got into the real estate business and 20 years later his real estate company had brokered about 140 Dairy Queen Restaurant franchises throughout the Midwest. Severson later went on to serve as an assistant basketball coach under his son, Jim, at the University of Minnesota-Morris as well. Severson, who lives in both Minnesota and in Scottsdale, Ariz., is presently teaching, writing poetry and working on a new book.

HOW WOULD YOU DESCRIBE YOUR COACHING STYLE? "My style was based on teaching. I broke everything down into the fine elements necessary for one to understand and to be able to learn. Simplicity, sound teaching and fundamentals, backed up with discipline, that was my style."

HOW DID YOU MOTIVATE YOUR PLAYERS? "I motivated my players by turning them loose to do what they did best. I think my main motivation was our ability to articulate one with the other. Finally, the motivation came from working as hard or harder than they. With that in mind, I am sure that they had the same love for basketball as I did. I tried to teach them that the greatest teacher a player can have is himself."

ON HIS PHILOSOPHY OF COACHING AND TEACHING: "I don't use the word coach, I say teacher. I can spell coach, but I can't define it. From day one I have been a teacher, teaching basketball, teaching English, teaching composition and teaching teaching. I only coached for 11 seasons at St. Cloud State. I left early because I contracted a disease called 'ego-insanity,' a very insidious infectious disease which is caused by your own big ego. That manifested itself through that period of 11 years to my ego, which is nothing more than an illusion and is not real. It took more and more of my mind and my space and left very little room for God, my power source. So, you can imagine then the difficulty you would have in the real world that they were talking about, or in the materialistic world I should say, of win-

ning, and winning, and winning, and winning and not being reinfected, and reinfected and reinfected. Winning is one thing, but that is not the name of the game, so that is why I quit at just 43 years young."

HOW DID YOU BUILD TEAM UNITY & CHEMISTRY? "If your individual members are learning something each day, then unity can prevail. Because experiences in your heart and mind as a learner get you excited and energize you. It enhances and improves your life and others around you. Teaching individuals on your teams something new and rewarding each and every day built unity. They wanted to learn and not miss out on something that would improve their lives."

WHAT'S THE SECRET TO YOUR SUCCESS? "Total, total love and dedication to teaching. I am very, very proud to be a teacher."

HOW DO YOU WANT YOUR COACHING EPITAPH TO READ — HOW DO YOU WANT TO BE REMEMBERED AS A COACH? "Here is a teacher who foremost had learning in mind. Whether it be literary learning or basketball, here is a teacher."

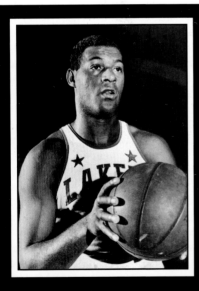

ELGIN BAYLOR:
NBA'S UTAH JAZZ

Elgin Baylor was the Rookie of the Year in 1959 with the Minneapolis Lakers. The high flying guard would go on to a Hall of Fame career with the L.A. Lakers before settling down to become a coach with the Utah Jazz, where he posted a modest 86-135 career record from 1976-79. Baylor went on to become the longtime GM of the L.A. Clippers as well.

SUZIE McCONNELL SERIO
PRO BASKETBALL: MINNESOTA LYNX

Suzie McConnell Serio grew up in Pittsburgh loving the sport of basketball. After a stellar prep career, McConnell Serio went on to play basketball at Penn State (1984-88), finishing her illustrious career in Happy Valley as the NCAA's all-time career assist leader with 1,307 — a record she still holds. A four-time All-Atlantic 10 Conference player, McConnell Serio averaged 14.9 ppg and 10.2 apg in 128 contests for the Nittany Lions, and as a senior, she was named as a First Team All-American after establishing a school single-season record of 682 points (20.7 ppg). McConnell Serio also set the Penn State all-time record for steals (507) and the single-game record for assists (21).

Prior to her professional playing career, McConnell Serio won two Olympic medals — a gold in 1988 in Seoul, South Korea, and a bronze in 1992 in Barcelona, Spain. Along with the Olympics, she also won a gold medal at the 1991 World University Games as well. From there, McConnell Serio moved back to Pittsburgh, where she began coaching at nearby Oakland Catholic High School. Then, after having four kids, the speedy point guard went on to play in the WNBA for three seasons with the Cleveland Rockers. As a rookie in 1998, McConnell Serio earned WNBA Newcomer of the Year and All-WNBA First Team honors after averaging 8.6 ppg and 6.4 apg (second in the league). Her 373 career assists ranks first on the Rockers' all-time list and 16th in WNBA history. McConnell Serio set the Rockers' single-game records for assists (12) and three-pointers (5) in 1998 as well. She was also a two-time winner of the Kim Perrot Sportsmanship Award (1998 and 2000), and finished her professional career with averages of 6.4 ppg and 4.6 apg in 81 contests.

While playing in the WNBA, McConnell Serio also continued to coach at Oakland Catholic High School. Then, when she retired, she continued to coach at the school, making history along the way. In 13 seasons she posted an all-time record of 321-86 (82.5%), including a 120-10 (92.3%) mark from 1999-2002, and five Class AAA state championships. With more than 300 victories, McConnell Serio established herself as a true high school coaching legend.

Then, on Jan. 21, 2003, McConnell Serio, at just 36 years of age, was named as the new head coach of the WNBA's Minnesota Lynx. She would waste little time in making a name for herself in the Land of 10,000 Lakes either, leading her squad to their first ever playoff appearance against the Los Angles Sparks in her rookie year behind the bench. An outstanding motivator and leader, Suzie McConnell Serio has been an influential figure in the world of women's basketball for nearly two decades.

Among her many coaching awards and accolades, in 1999 Sports Illustrated named McConnell Serio one of the Top 50 Athletes of the Century in the state of Pennsylvania, and in the same year she was honored as the Pittsburgh Athlete of the Year. McConnell Serio was also recognized as one of Cleveland's 50 Most Interesting People in 1998 by Cleveland Magazine, and as one of "The 10 Gutsiest Women of 1998" by Jane Magazine.

Suzie and her husband, Pete, have four children: Peter, Jordan, Mandy and Madison, and presently reside in the Twin Cities.

HOW WOULD YOU DESCRIBE YOUR COACHING STYLE? "I just try to be very positive with the team. I am also very encouraging yet demanding. I try to instill a winning attitude through a strong work ethic, through the tone of our practices and with hard work. Even my demeanor on the sideline is always very enthusias-

tic, positive and energetic, but I can still get on them when I need to. So, I don't know if there is any one specific style, but overall I would say that I coach in the moment."

HOW DO YOU MOTIVATE YOUR PLAYERS? "Vocally, I try to talk about what we need to do. It is always about opportunity, about challenging them and about expectations. I try to talk to them both as a group as well as individually. I am a big believer in building confidence and that is something I work very hard at instilling in my players."

LOOKING BACK WHAT ARE YOU MOST PROUD OF IN YOUR CAREER? "As a player I am very proud of winning a gold medal in the Olympics. To me that was the ultimate dream come true. Then, to play in the WNBA after having four kids was special too. To be able to play professional basketball here in the United States was also a dream come true for me. I also had some success in coaching too. Winning three state high school championships back in Pennsylvania was very special for me as well. To put those medals around their necks and to watch them cut down the nets was something that I will never forget. Those are moments as a coach that are the most rewarding I think. That is why you coach this game, to see that excitement from young people."

HOW DO YOU BUILD TEAM UNITY & CHEMISTRY? "I think that happens from the beginning during training camp and in the pre-season. You just try to come in with a positive, winning attitude and hopefully that becomes contagious among your team. You just have to get them working together and believing in the same things. A lot of it comes from gaining confidence and confidence comes from experiencing success. When you experience success that motivates you to want more and that is ultimately what we are all motivated by in this business. So, as a coach you look to get your team to work well together in order for them to build success together. It also has a lot to do with your players and their make-up together. You have to have your leaders bring the other players along to work together and instill that winning attitude."

WHAT MOTIVATES YOU? "I absolutely love the game of basketball. I just have a great deal of passion for this game, and for me to experience success in this game, whether that is as a player or coach, is what motivates me. I love winning too. I also understand that hard work and preparation is what allows you to experience that."

WHAT ADVICE WOULD YOU HAVE FOR YOUNG COACHES STARTING OUT TODAY? "I think it is important to let your passion for the game be known. You have to let that shine through to your players. You also have to be positive and encouraging. You are in a great position to instill confidence in players, and that is very important. Then, you need to talk about goals and expectations in order to get better and have success."

FAVORITE LOCKER ROOM SIGN? "Attitude determines altitude."

WHAT'S THE BIGGEST THING YOU'VE LEARNED FROM COACHING THAT YOU'VE BEEN ABLE TO APPLY TO YOUR EVERYDAY LIFE? "Well, having four children, I have learned to keep things in perspective as far as winning and losing. After a game when I come out of the locker room and I see my four kids waiting for me, it doesn't matter to them whether I won or lost. So, they help me keep things in perspective and let me remember that this is still just a game. The most important job in my life is my four children. Period."

WHAT ARE THE KEY INGREDIENTS TO CREATING A CHAMPIONSHIP TEAM? "Talent is the first thing. But, the ultimate is having your team believe in each other and share the common goal that winning is what they are all working to accomplish. To win a championship the players have to be unselfish and willing to do whatever it takes. They also have to accept their roles on the team in order for the entire unit to be successful."

WHAT IS THE KEY TO GOOD TIME MANAGEMENT? "I think it starts from an understanding of what you need to do. You need to have a purpose for everything that you do. When you get a day off, then you need to understand that you should use that day to rest and take care of your body. Then, you need to be organized so that you can manage it all."

WHAT'S THE SECRET TO YOUR SUCCESS? "It is no secret. It is hard work, confidence, believing in what I am doing and enjoying what I do."

WHAT WOULD YOU WANT TO SAY TO YOUR FANS, BOOSTERS, AND ALUMNI WHO HAVE SUPPORTED YOU ALL THESE YEARS? "Minnesota has been so great. I have loved being here and the fans have made me and my family feel very welcome. It was tough at first leaving my husband and kids back in Pittsburgh and moving here without them. But now that we are all here together, it has been great. The fans are wonderful here and so supportive of us."

HOW DO YOU WANT YOUR COACHING EPITAPH TO READ — HOW DO YOU WANT TO BE REMEMBERED AS A COACH? "As someone who worked hard, was very positive, very enthusiastic and had a positive impact on the players that she has coached."

JIM WITHAM:
MINNESOTA STATE MANKATO BASKETBALL

Jim Witham graduated from Bemidji State University, got his master's degree from the University of Minnesota and then got a doctoral degree from Indiana. Witham, who had coaching stints at Bemidji State and Iowa State prior to coming to Minnesota State Mankato, would coach the Maverick's men's basketball team from 1945-56 and built a record of 166-70 during that span. The 1947 Mankato team went 17-4 and advanced to the finals of the NAIA tournament in Kansas City, where they lost to Marshall in the national championship game. MSU also made an NAIA postseason appearance in 1948 as well. Witham, who owned a career collegiate coaching mark of 229-119, won outright conference titles in 1947, 1948, 1949, 1950, 1953 and tied in 1952, 1954 and 1956. Witham also coached the MSU baseball team for three seasons, from 1953-56, and was an assistant with the football team as well. A Mankato coaching icon, Jim Witham was inducted into the MSU Hall of Fame in 1966.

GUS YOUNG: GUSTAVUS BASKETBALL

Verl "Gus" Young graduated from Carleton College in 1932 and was the captain of the famous "Victory Five," a basketball team which lost only one game in three years. From there, Young would go on to teach and coach at Warroad, Buffalo, Hutchinson and Austin High Schools, as well as at Carleton and the U of M, where he was an assistant, before finally settling down at Gustavus — where he would emerge as a coaching legend. After finishing as the conference runners-up for three straight years, Young went on a three year championship run from 1954-56. Young would have a colorful eight year reign at Gustavus, finishing with an overall conference record of 82-34. It was during his reign that Joe Hutton's Hamline Pipers were dethroned as the perennial champions of the MIAC as well. Gustavus had many famed battles with Hamline during this era, as the two schools finished first and second eight times during the 1950s. Young's Gusties were also well traveled, playing colleges from 20 different states during his tenure in St. Peter. He also believed that sports had a great part to play in the development of a boy's character, so his teams always looked and acted the part of gentlemen. And Gus loved showmanship. In his typical fun-loving manner, he introduced fancy warm-up drills with multi-colored basketballs, a tuxedo-suited pep band, half-time variety shows that featured a 100-voice male chorus and spot-lighted flag ceremonies. Among his many coaching honors and accolades, the basketball court at Gustavus was re-named after him in his honor. After retiring from Gustavus, Young would later join the upstart Minnesota Pipers of the upstart American Basketball Association. First named as the team's Director of Special Promotions, Young would later serve as the team's head coach in 1968. Young later got into the bowling alley and restaurant business and was also active in the Fellowship of Christian Athletes. Young died on October 31, 1977.

BOB McDONALD
HIGH SCHOOL BASKETBALL: CHISHOLM

Bob McDonald has become synonymous with high school basketball in Minnesota and his story is as fascinating as he is. Born out of wedlock in New York in 1933, McDonald came to Chisholm when he was taken out of foster homes and raised by his grandmother and uncle. He grew up loving sports, especially basketball. He went on to play the game for legendary Chisholm High School Coach Harvey Roels, an old taskmaster whose career with the Bluestreaks spanned from 1921-54. McDonald graduated in 1951 and then accepted a scholarship to play basketball at the University of Michigan. He would stay just one semester, however, before transferring to Hibbing Community College, where he led the team to a national championship that next year. From there, McDonald briefly attended Macalester College before making his final stop at the University of Minnesota-Duluth, where he earned a teaching degree in social studies and physical education.

After graduating from UMD in 1955, McDonald coached for four years at McGregor High School and then two more at Barnum High School. In 1961 McDonald came home to teach history and coach basketball and track at his alma mater, even living at the same house he grew up in, about a block-and-a-half from Chisholm High School. McDonald's Streaks finished 12-9 that first season and were led by a kid named Joel Maturi, now the University of Minnesota's athletic director. McDonald worked his kids very hard and vowed that while his teams may not finish first in the state, they would be amongst the best shape in the state. While many of his kids would describe him as a disciplinarian, that is a term the coach doesn't care for, preferring instead to say he "simply has high expectations." No cussing, short haircuts and early curfews are all part of his regimented style. His kids wear suits and ties on the bus, and he expects them to act like adults — demanding that they be presentable to the community and behave themselves. Period.

Since his arrival back in 1961, McDonald has gone on to become the winningest coach in state history, with more than 800 victories over the past 48 years. (Only 40 boys' basketball coaches in the nation have won 800 games and only 11 of them are still coaching.) The numbers are simply amazing. He has coached in over 1,100 games and had winning seasons in 43 out of his 48 years. His teams have won 13 Range Conference titles, 15 district titles and eight section titles. He has also averaged 17 victories per year in a sport that for many years allowed only 18 regular-season games. He has also led his Streaks to eight state tournament appearances (1973, 1974, 1975, 1981, 1982, 1991, 1992 & 1995), as well as to three Class A state titles. His first came in 1973, when Chisholm defeated Melrose, which was led by superstar center, Mark Olberding, 53-52, for the school's first title since 1934. The second came two years later when Chisholm beat St. Paul Mechanic Arts, 44-33, to finish a perfect 27-0. McDonald's two oldest sons, Mike and Paul, were on both of those championship teams. The third came in 1991, when Chisholm outplayed Westbrook-Walnut Grove in the fourth quarter of the state championship game to win 77-61. Joel McDonald, Bob's youngest son, scored 86 points in the tournament and went on to become the leading boys' scorer in state history with 3,292 points.

In addition to being a basketball coaching legend, McDonald also spent 47 years as the track coach, where he finally won a state title in 2001 before retiring in 2003. He also retired from teaching several years ago as well, to focus solely on coaching basketball. He is having fun and taking it all in stride. In 1997 Darlene McDonald, Bob's wife of 43 years, died of cancer. In 2000 he married Carol Tiburzi, a widow who 48 years earlier had attended the Chisholm High School prom with that very Bob McDonald. He is now doing the unthinkable, "shacking up in Hibbing," Chisholm's biggest rival, and making the commute every morning. At just 70 years of age, this guy is not slowing down — so don't rule out 1,000 wins, he just may get there. Sure, he did have surgery on his prostate and colon, his shoulders were both replaced in recent years and there was that hernia operation too, but those were just nuisances — nothing this iron man can't handle. Fifty three years after graduating from Chisholm High, Bob McDonald, with that same patented crew cut, is still going strong. Death, taxes and snow on the Iron Range — all things you can count on. Bob McDonald coaching the Bluestreaks is another. The man is simply a legend. His legacy? How about six kids, all all-staters in basketball, and each going on to become high school basketball coaches. Not bad!

HOW WOULD YOU DESCRIBE YOUR COACHING STYLE? "A lot of people think I am a disciplinarian, but I prefer to say that I have great expectations of young people. So, if you have great expectations of young people then naturally your demands are a little greater. I am not a passive guy, there is no question about that. I do, however, have great feelings for the people who played for me. I appreciate what they have accomplished and what they have done for me in putting me where I am at with regards to my coaching career and my longevity."

HOW DO YOU MOTIVATE YOUR PLAYERS? "I used to be a fire and brimstone kind of a coach when I first started out, but I learned as I went along to ease up. One thing I did was to just leave the kids alone before the game and during the pre-game warm-up. I wanted them to just focus and relax. You know, I just tried to get my players to be self-motivated. I really banked on tradition heavily here and that was a motivational factor of the first class. When you have a tradition like we do in Chisholm with basketball, then there is a great pride that is associated with it. There is a pride in our community, a pride in our school and a pride in the program. Each player becomes a part of that tradition and that is what makes it grow and continue to be successful. That is what energized our players."

WHO WERE YOUR COACHING MENTORS? "My high school coach at Chisholm, Harvey Roels, he was a real coaching icon in Northern Minnesota. He coached for over 30 years up here and was a real fine person. Following him was O.J. Belluzzo, who helped me succeed Harvey. I learned a great deal from both of those men. So, since 1921 we have had only three coaches here, which speaks volumes for itself."

IF YOU COULD MAGICALLY GO BACK IN TIME TO THE FIRST YEAR YOU WERE A HEAD COACH AND GIVE YOURSELF SOME ADVICE FOR THE FUTURE, KNOWING WHAT YOU KNOW NOW, BACK THEN, WHAT WOULD YOU SAY TO YOURSELF? "That is tough because the times have changed so much nowadays. Back then you were able to do a lot more things vocally whereas now you have to be more resilient as a coach and be politically correct. Having said that, I would probably be less wound up and less intense if had it all to do over again. Intensity is good, but it sometimes diverts you from using common sense instead of just plain drive to accomplish your goals."

ON HIS SIX KIDS EACH BECOMING A TEACHER AND BASKETBALL COACH: (Paul, a former coach at Cotton and Tower-Soudan, has been coach at Vermilion Community College in Ely the past 13 years; Mike has coached at Cambridge-Isanti for 16 years; Tom has been at Ely for 15 years; Joel has been at Hibbing since 1999; Sue coached at Crosby-Ironton for 13 years; and Judy, a former varsity coach at Nashwauk-Keewatin and Fairmont, now coaches eighth-graders in Blue Earth.) "It is very rewarding to see, no question. You know, we never belabored the point of basketball at home. Home was home and basketball was basketball, but they got the passion for the game like I did and that is great to see. They have all paid their dues and each of them works very hard at what they do. Sure, I am proud of the fact that my kids all followed in my profession, but they have made their own names for themselves now. It is always fun to play them too. I guess it was easier coaching against my sons when they first started out because they were so tense and just wanted to win so badly. Then, after they finally beat me for that first time, they lightened up. It is very competitive, but don't get me wrong, I still want to win."

WHAT ARE THE CHARACTERISTICS OF LEADERS? "I think it comes back to values. I think good leaders are not only great athletes and communicators, they are also people who don't use drugs or alcohol, they are responsible and to are good students. It is all of that in my opinion."

LOOKING BACK WHAT ARE YOU MOST PROUD OF IN YOUR CAREER? "I am most proud of the athletes who have played for me. There are very few kids who I have had over this long period of time that have turned me off. That, I think is the essence of what keeps me going. I have had a lot of super players as well as super people. They are good athletes and gave everything they had to me and the program. As a coach, that makes me feel fulfilled."

HOW DO YOU BUILD TEAM UNITY & CHEMISTRY? "It is more difficult now because kids are more individualistic these days. But, you just have to get your kids into the gym, or what we call affectionately 'The Boys Club,' then they can develop a rapport with one another. If you can't get them into situations after hours or during the off-season, then they will have less respect for each other. So, you need to get them together so that they can become friends and from that the chemistry builds."

WHAT MOTIVATES YOU? "It wasn't about winning and losing for me. I always remembered that whenever I won, somebody else lost and they were probably just as miserable as I was happy. So, that doesn't factor into it for me. Sure, I am proud of my record, but the idea that I have won so many games is not of the essence to me at all, and I try to subdue that when people ask me about my record. Overall, I like to work with young people. Beyond that, very simply the basketball tradition at Chisholm High School propels me to the greatest degree. I grew up in this town and I feel that tradition towards the people I know in the community. That is what keeps me going."

WHAT ADVICE WOULD YOU HAVE FOR YOUNG COACHES STARTING OUT TODAY? "You have to be your own man, or woman, for starters. Then, you have to be moral, you have to be available to your kids, you have to tell them who you are and what you expect of them both on and off the court. You also can't be afraid to offend anybody. You have to be patient and you have to work hard too."

FAVORITE LOCKER ROOM SIGN? "What do you with yourself aside from the seven seconds that you are shooting the ball?"

WHAT'S THE BIGGEST THING YOU'VE LEARNED FROM

COACHING THAT YOU'VE BEEN ABLE TO APPLY TO YOUR EVERYDAY LIFE? "No matter how many times you fail, any success seems to level off the scales. If you can hang in there, good things do happen."

WHAT ARE THE KEY INGREDIENTS TO CREATING A CHAMPIONSHIP TEAM? "It is kind of a matter of chance, but you have to have kids who are in tight with one another. You have to have a bond there, chemistry. You know, I handle our pre-school kids all the way up to high school and have developed a great feeder program here. I mean I have seen it all from diapers to death here in Chisholm. So, having said that, the kids are used to me here. I meet them very young and by the time they get to high school I already know a lot about them. As a result, we don't have a lot of problems with our kids understanding our goals and expectations of them. That consistency is very important to the success of a program. Beyond that, sure you need some kids who can play, but chemistry and consistency are very important."

WHAT IS THE BEST PIECE OF ADVICE YOU EVER GOT FROM ANOTHER COACH? "To hold my ground. You are going to have a lot of people beating on you along the way because of self-centered interests and the like, or they don't feel you are doing a good job coaching. But most coaches know their kids a lot better than their own parents do. So, I keep a pretty good handle on what the kids are doing in school and I expect them to do their studies."

WHAT'S THE SECRET TO YOUR SUCCESS? "Consistency. We are doing the same things today that we did way back when we started nearly 50 years ago. We still wear our knee socks with the red and blue stripes, and I love that stuff. What it tells them is that the program has never really changed."

WHAT WOULD YOU WANT TO SAY TO YOUR FANS, BOOSTERS, AND ALUMNI WHO HAVE SUPPORTED YOU ALL THESE YEARS? "I would like to thank them all because if you last as long as I do you meet so many great people. It is always sad to see vacancies in the stands from where people who supported me over the years have passed away. Now we have the second and third generations coming through and it just keeps on going. So, thanks to our entire community which has supported me and our program so much through the years, that is what has kept me going."

HOW DO YOU WANT YOUR COACHING EPITAPH TO READ — HOW DO YOU WANT TO BE REMEMBERED AS A COACH? "That I was forthright to the end. That I thought about the relevance of the program to the community and myself and all the kids in town as being the essence of what I was and what I did. You know, if I think about my career in basketball, I remember the people, the players, the fans and the atmosphere, but I forget about the games. Really I do, unless it was something super important that happened that night. So, that is what it is all about to me."

JOHN WOODEN... the "MAGICIAN OF MINNEAPOLIS?"

Did you know that the *"Wizard of Westwood"* was almost the *"Magician of Minneapolis?"* That's right. Back in 1948, legendary basketball coach John Wooden agreed in principle to accept an offer to become the next head basketball coach at the University of Minnesota. But, due to a snowstorm, the Gophers couldn't get through to Wooden over the phone lines. When no call came, Wooden went ahead and accepted an offer to coach the UCLA Bruins. Wooden, of course, would build a dynasty at UCLA, leading his Bruins to a total of 10 NCAA basketball championships throughout the 1960s and '70s.

DAN MONSON
COLLEGE BASKETBALL: UNIVERSITY OF MINNESOTA

Dan Monson was born into basketball royalty. His father, Don, a native of Menahga, Minn., served as the head coach at the University's of Idaho and Oregon. As a result, Dan grew up loving sports. He would go on to attend Idaho's Moscow High School, where he emerged as a prep star. Monson later graduated from the University of Idaho in 1985 with a bachelor's degree in mathematics, and later obtained his master's degree in athletic administration from the University of Alabama-Birmingham in 1988. A football player for the Vandals, Monson turned his attention to coaching when a knee injury cut short his gridiron career. So, he coached the boys' basketball team at Oregon City High School in Oregon for one season in 1986 prior to taking a graduate assistant post under Coach Gene Bartow at the University of Alabama Birmingham.

In 1988 Monson became an assistant coach at Gonzaga University and in 1997, he took over as the program's head coach. Monson would invest nine years in helping to build the Gonzaga program into a perennial post-season contender. Monson then led the Bulldogs to a record of 52-17 during his head coaching tenure, and became known for his ability to recruit quality student-athletes to the private Spokane, Wash., institution. Then, after leading the Bulldogs to within a breath of the 1999 NCAA Final Four, the former West Coast Conference Coach of the Year was hired as the head coach at the University of Minnesota. That Summer Dan also expanded his coaching experience on an international level by helping lead the USA Basketball Men's World University Games Team to the gold medal in Palma de Mallorca, Spain. When he got back, it was off to Minnie for the adventure of a lifetime. Monson came to Minnesota under some pretty extraordinary circumstances, following the academic cheating scandal, but has done an amazing job since. Now entering his fourth season at the Old Barn, Monson has established himself as one of the best young coaches in the game and has thrust the Golden Gophers back onto the national scene. From 2000-03, Monson has led the Gophers to NIT post-season appearances, and in 2004 the Gophers appear ready to take the next step. Monson has recruited a solid nucleus of talent in the past few years, brought back home-grown transfers and convinced many of the state's top blue-chip players to wear the Maroon and Gold. Monson's Minnesota record is 67-55 and his overall five-year head coaching record stands at 119-72. He is among the very best and brightest in college basketball and has an extremely bright future. Dan and his wife Darci have two children, MicGuire and Mollie, and presently reside in the Twin Cities.

HOW WOULD YOU DESCRIBE YOUR COACHING STYLE? "In today's day and age I don't think you can be a very brimstone or a very passive coach. You have to be able to communicate with your players today on all levels and for me there is some of all that in there. With regards to my philosophy, I think finding the right time to be emotional and the right time to be passive is the challenge. I guess I would say my style is really a smorgasbord of different types of styles all wrapped up into one. I learned so much from so many different coaches and bits and pieces of their styles are intertwined into my own. Certainly, my father taught me what it means to be a coach. Then, learning from guys like Jud Heathcoate, who, my father was an assistant for at Michigan State, and Dan Fitzgerald, who I worked with for 10 years and really taught me how to coach, has meant a lot to me. That is what molds you, when you respect somebody else's style enough to use it to your own advantage."

HOW DO YOU MOTIVATE YOUR PLAYERS? "It is different from one day to the next and different from one situation to the next. The biggest way for me to motivate my players is by communicating with them and letting them know where they stand as well as where you stand as the coach."

IF YOU COULD MAGICALLY GO BACK IN TIME TO THE FIRST YEAR YOU WERE A HEAD COACH AND GIVE YOURSELF SOME ADVICE FOR THE FUTURE, KNOWING WHAT YOU KNOW NOW, BACK THEN, WHAT WOULD YOU SAY TO YOURSELF? "I would tell him that the future comes fast. As a young coach you think that your career will last forever, but it comes and goes almost with the blink of an eye. So, work hard and enjoy it along the way."

LOOKING BACK WHAT ARE YOU MOST PROUD OF IN YOUR CAREER? "That I have done it my way without compromising my own personal beliefs."

WHAT WAS THE KEY TO RECRUITING? " I think recruiting is all about selling. It comes down to personality and putting that product that you have in the best light. Our product here at the University of Minnesota is basketball, and we are very proud of that. Basketball in Minnesota has a lot of pride and tradition and that is something very, very special."

HOW DO YOU BUILD TEAM UNITY & CHEMISTRY? "To build chemistry it takes a lot of hard work, time and a commitment to do it together. We spend a lot of time off the court together and that certainly helps. Really though, you have to work at it and nurture it through different things."

WHAT MOTIVATES YOU? "I think it is the challenge of getting a lot of different people to get onto one page with one common goal."

WHAT ADVICE WOULD YOU HAVE FOR YOUNG COACHES STARTING OUT TODAY? "Get into it for the right reasons. If you set out to help people and have a real love for the game, then everything will all fall into place."

FAVORITE LOCKER ROOM SIGN? "TEAM: is an acronym for Together Everyone Achieves More."

WHAT ROLE HAS YOUR FAMILY PLAYED IN YOUR COACHING CAREER? "They have been so supportive. They have also de-emphasized the coaching part for me and given me perspective in life. The wins and losses aren't the most important thing in my life right now, whereas when I first got started in this business they were. I was young and naïve back then, but now I understand that there is more to live and that there are priorities. Since then, my priorities have changed."

WHAT'S THE BIGGEST THING YOU'VE LEARNED FROM COACHING THAT YOU'VE BEEN ABLE TO APPLY TO YOUR EVERYDAY LIFE? "Just the ups and downs. You are going to have good and you are going to have bad, so it comes down to how you are able to find a middle ground."

WHAT ARE THE KEY INGREDIENTS TO CREATING A CHAMPIONSHIP TEAM? "It is not just having good talent, it is not just having good coaching and it is not just having good chemistry — it is a combination of all those things. Sure, you have to have good basketball players, you have to have people who get along and you have to have people who trust each other. That is what is so challenging about coaching, there is no magic formula, it is a combination of a lot of ingredients."

WHAT'S THE SECRET TO YOUR SUCCESS? "I think it is the fact that I have stuck to my convictions and done it my way. I am proud of the fact that I have not gotten swallowed up in everybody's opinions, because in this job your head can spin from trying to please everybody."

WHAT WOULD YOU WANT TO SAY TO YOUR FANS, BOOSTERS, AND ALUMNI WHO HAVE SUPPORTED YOU ALL THESE YEARS? "I came to Minnesota during a situation which certainly wasn't a high point in the program's history. The people who supported Gopher basketball through those tough times were wonderful. I just really appreciate the support and patience that those people have given us and hopefully I can reward them along the way by getting the program back into a position that they are all proud of."

HOW DO YOU WANT YOUR COACHING EPITAPH TO READ — HOW DO YOU WANT TO BE REMEMBERED AS A COACH? "Number one would be that he was a person with morals; number two would be that he was a person of integrity; and being a good coach would be a distant third."

GLADYS ZIEMER:
ST. CLOUD STATE BASKETBALL

Gladys Ziemer coached women's basketball at St. Cloud State University from 1973-93, posting a career record of 321-212. For more than 20 years Ziemer guided the Huskies, leading them to five conference titles and seven NCAA tournament appearances. She is without question a Husky hoops legend.

RICH GLAS: COLLEGE BASKETBALL
UNIVERSITY OF MINNESOTA-MORRIS

Rich Glas was born in Bemidji. As a batboy, ballboy and waterboy, Rich had an all-access pass to every Bemidji State sport he wanted to attend, because his old man was the vice president of the university. He would go on to play basketball at Bemidji High School for legendary coach Bun Fortier, and then play ball at Bemidji State as well. After graduating from BSU in 1970, Glas moved on to Western Illinois, where he served as an assistant coach and also received his master's degree in 1971.

That next year he was hired as Jack Haddorff's assistant at Minnesota-Morris. Three seasons later Haddorff resigned, and Glas, at just 25 years of age, was named as the team's new head coach. After going 27-23 in his first two years, Glas and the Cougars broke through in 1977, going 21-6, winning the conference championship and advancing to the NAIA national tournament. In 1978 UM-Morris made the move to Division III, repeated as conference champions with a 22-6 mark and advanced to the Division III national tournament. Glas' 1979 team went 19-9, finished second in the NIC and again advanced to the postseason. With the program at UMM on solid footing, and with two NIC Coach of the Year awards and an NAIA District Coach of the Year honor to his name, Glas decided to move on to a new job and a new challenge.

Glas' next stop was at Willamette University, in Salem, Ore., where he would coach for five seasons and also serve as WU's athletic director for three of those years. The Bearcats went 66-64 under Glas, with the 1983 team going 19-8 and advancing to the NAIA national tournament. After the 1984 season Glas took a leave of absence from Willamette and spent a year on Lute Olson's staff at Arizona. Glas made such a favorable impression on Olson that when Hawaii coach Frank Arnold later called Olson looking for leads to fill an open assistant coaching position, Olson gave Arnold Glas' name and Arnold hired Glas. After three years of paradise, Glas came home to take over as the head coach at the University of North Dakota, where he has been ever since.

After going 3-15 in the NCC to finish last in 1989, Glas led UND on a worst-to-first charge. His 1990 team went 14-4 to win the NCC, then advanced on to the Elite Eight where they finished third and wound up with a 28-7 overall record. It was the first time in 65 years an NCC team had made such a dramatic improvement within the standings. Glas' 1991 team would fare even better, winning the NCC with a 17-1 mark (a league record for wins in a season that still stands), going 29-4 overall and advancing to the Elite Eight for the second consecutive year. Overall, Glas has led UND to seven NCAA appearances in his 13 years, with the Sioux, winning six straight NCC regular season or tournament championships between 1990 and 1995. He has also compiled a 13-year postseason record of 24-10 (.706), and his 249 overall victories at UND give him the second most wins in the program' storied history. Last season Glas won his 400th career game, becoming one of only 17 active Division II coaches to reach that level. He was named the Kodak/NABC North Central Region Coach of the Year in both 1990 and 1991 as well.

Now entering his 25th year of college coaching, Glas has more than 400 victories and is still going strong — making Minnesota very proud along the way. Glas and his wife Sandy have one daughter, Randi, and reside in Grand Forks. Randi's son, Jeff, is also a junior kicker on the Fighting Sioux football team.

Lute Olson was born on a farm just outside tiny Maryville, N.D., and went on to lead Grand Forks High School to the 1952 North Dakota State Championship, graduating in 1953. From there, Olson went on to play football, baseball and basketball at Augsburg College from 1953-56. At Augsburg Olson still had that small town atmosphere that he had grown up in, but nestled in the heart of a major metropolitan area. He also found a Lutheran school that meshed with his religious beliefs, and also really liked the close-knit athletic department fostered by Coaches Ernie Anderson and Edor Nelson — both father figure-type people. While at Augsburg, Olson's life was anything but traditional. He married his high school sweetheart, Bobbi, during his sophomore year, and because he received no financial aid, he sorted holiday mail and even worked the night shift at a local soft drink bottling plant driving trucks to support his family — which was about to get bigger that next year with the addition of his first child. (Olson even sang in a choir group called the "A-men," with three other teammates and sang at churches or wherever they were asked.) Olson was a six-foot-four forward in basketball, a tight end and defensive tackle in football and a first baseman in baseball. (On the hardwood, Olson was an All-MIAC selection in 1956 and finished his career as the Auggies' assists leader as well as the all-time steals leader. Olson loved learning the game under Auggie coaching legends Anderson and Nelson, and knew early on that coaching was to be his life's calling.

After graduating with degrees in history and physical education, Olson got his first teaching and coaching job at Mahnomen High School in 1956. He spent one season there before moving on to teach and coach basketball at Two Harbors High School, where he worked as an iron ore steamer in the winters to make extra money for his family. Olson would remain on the North Shore for two years before heading off to Loara High School (Anaheim, Cal.), in 1963. (Olson was offered the head coaching position back at Augsburg at that time, but he passed.) After one season at Loara, Olson spent a year at Marina-Huntington Beach High School, and then four more at nearby Marina High School, from 1965-69. (In all, he would compile a 157-86 record coaching high school basketball.)

That next year Olson got into college coaching, first with Long Beach City College, where, from 1969-73, he produced an amazing 103-22 record and won a JUCO State Championship. He then took over as the head coach at Long Beach State that next year, leading the club to a 24-2 record. Then, in 1975 he got his first big coaching gig at the University of Iowa, where he led the Hawkeyes to six 20-victory campaigns, a Big Ten title, and a trip to the NCAA Final Four in 1980. Olson would leave the Hawkeyes in 1983 as the winningest coach in school history with a 168-90 record, and head south, to the University of Arizona, where he has been ever since.

Now entering his 20th season with the Wildcats, Olson has emerged as one of college basketball's greatest all-time coaches. Olson's numbers are incredible. In 20 seasons at Arizona he has amassed an amazing 795-259 record. He has led Arizona to four NCAA Final Four appearances (1988, '94, '97 & 2001) and one NCAA Championship, which came in 1997 over Kentucky. (The 2001 Final Four was at the Metrodome, just a stone's throw away from his old stomping grounds at Augsburg.) In addition, he has won 10 PAC-10 Conference championships and advanced to the NCAA Tournament for the 19th consecutive season, which is the longest current streak in college basketball and is second longest in NCAA history (behind North Carolina's 27). One of only eight coaches in colle-

giate history to coach in five or more Final Fours, Olson is one of only 11 coaches who has taken two different teams to the Final Four and is one of only five head coaches in NCAA history to record 25 or more 20-win seasons. The seventh winningest active Division I coach of all-time, Olson also has nation's best winning percentage over the last 16 seasons at 429-101 (.809) as well. He has also produced nearly 50 NBA Draft picks along the way, showing his ability to recruit good talent.

Among Olson's numerous awards and accolades: he was the NCAA's National Coach of the Year (1988, '90), CBS-TV Coach of the Year (1989), PAC 10 Coach of the Year (1986, '88, '89, 93, '94, '98), NABC District 15 Coach of the Year (1989, '93, '94), USBWA District 8 Coach of the Year (1988, '93), Big Ten Coach of the Year (1979, '81), PCAA Coach of the Year (1974), Western Region Coach of the Year (1974), Basketball Times West Region Coach of the Year (1998), Naismith National Coach of the Year Finalist (1998). Additionally, Olson was the gold-medal-winning coach for the 1984 Jones Cup and 1986 World Championship team, the latter of which was the United State's last major international win with collegiate players making up the roster. Arizona even renamed their basketball arena after him as well. Last, but certainly not least, in 2002 Olson was enshrined into the Naismith Memorial Basketball Hall of Fame — an honor most deserving for one of the greatest coaches in modern history.

Lute and his wife Bobbi, who passed away in January of 2001, have five grown children: Vicki, Jodi, Christi, Greg and Steve, and 14 grandchildren. A true coaching legend, Lute Olson has truly made Minnesota proud.

HOW WOULD YOU DESCRIBE YOUR COACHING STYLE? "I believe that the young people you are working with should experience life's challenges. A lot of times we get so engrossed in what we are doing that we forget that basketball should be fun and that there should be great camaraderie that develops between the players and staff as a result of that. However, somebody has to be in charge and call the shots. So, when we get on the court it is very much of a dictatorship. When we get off the court though, it then becomes a family type atmosphere. Our philosophy is that you first have to start with good people. Good people will find a way to be successful and bad people will find a way to ruin whatever you are involved in, whether it is in business or coaching or whatever. Secondly, it is critical to lead by example. The players have to see that you are out front and that you are willing to put in every ounce of effort that you can put in to it in order to be successful. Thirdly, I think it is critical to keep the lines of communication open. Too often it is a case of where you assume you know what they are thinking and visa versa. So, I think everything needs to be talked out, regardless of the situation, because small problems become big problems if they are not dealt with accordingly. Another key is that you have to be organized so that the people you are working with see that there is not time being wasted and that everything you are doing is with a specific end in mind. Then, you need to make sure that your leadership is a positive type leadership. Negativity beats people down instead of building them up and I think confidence is so key in whether or not a person is going to be successful. I believe in the old statement: 'You will become what you think you can become.' Beyond that, you have to be ready to adjust on a constant basis and know that your best laid plans may not work out as you had hoped. So, you can't be hard nosed and say this is the way it is going to be, even if it is not working. You just need to remember to be flexible."

HOW DO YOU MOTIVATE YOUR PLAYERS? "The thing we stress with them all the time is that everyday they enter the practice court, if they don't leave the court as better players, then either they are not doing their job or we are not doing ours. Frankly, it is our job as coaches to motivate them to be the best that they can be and that is the central point with us at all times. You are going to come out and you are going to play as hard as you can and you are going to concentrate on becoming a better individual player as well as a team player."

HOW DO YOU EARN THE RESPECT OF YOUR PLAYERS? "I think that is a constant thing. If they feel like you are giving everything you have got to your job and that you know how to coach and that you know how to deal with people, then respect comes from the job that you are doing on a daily basis."

HOW DO YOU BUILD TEAM UNITY & CHEMISTRY? "We do evaluations like three times a year where the players evaluate one another and where they stand on the team. Then, the coaches and I will also evaluate them as well. After that I sit down with each kid individually and we go through everything as to where they are rated, their strengths and weaknesses and what they need to do to improve. I think one of the key things in coaching is having the players understand where they stand and what they need to do if they are going to improve their position on the team. Everything we do is based on a team situation and that is how we help to build unity amongst the players and coaches."

WHAT MOTIVATES YOU? "Whether you are in coaching or in business, I think your job is to be the best that you can be. That's what motivates me on a regular basis."

WHAT'S THE BIGGEST THING YOU'VE LEARNED FROM COACHING THAT YOU'VE BEEN ABLE TO APPLY TO YOUR EVERYDAY LIFE? "I think you have to feel good about what you are doing and you have to feel that you are giving it an all out effort. You have to recognize that you are a member of a team, whether you are talking about basketball, or being a member of the community, or with regards to your family. We emphasize a great deal to our players that we are all in this thing together and everybody has to give their best effort if we are going to be successful."

WHAT ARE THE KEY INGREDIENTS TO CREATING A CHAMPIONSHIP TEAM? "Good people, hard work and a focus on the team."

WHAT'S THE SECRET TO YOUR SUCCESS? "I tried to surround myself with good players who were good people. Then, I feel strongly that there is just no substitute for hard work and giving it an all out effort, in whatever you are doing. Also respecting people that you work with is very important, whether you are talking about your players, fans, members of the community, alums, administration, or what have you. That has been the key to my success."

HOW DO YOU WANT YOUR COACHING EPITAPH TO READ — HOW DO YOU WANT TO BE REMEMBERED AS A COACH? "That I worked hard and I did things the right way."

500 WINS CLUB MEMBERS (BOYS BASKETBALL)

1. Bob McDonald, Chisholm*
2. Bob Brink, Rocori*
3. John Nett, Winona Cotter
4. Jerry Snyder, Lake City
5. Lynn Peterson, Staples-Motley*
6. Ziggy Kauls, Mounds View*
7. Jack Evens, Bloomington Jefferson
8. Hugo Goehle, Hills-Beaver Creek
9. Len Horyza, Cretin-Derham Hall
10. Jim Hastings, Duluth Central
11. Darrell Kreun, Sibley East
12. Ron Ueland, Marshall Cty Central
13. Lloyd Holm, St. Louis Park
14. Lloyd Stussy, Wells-Easton
15. Al Andreotti, St. Cloud Tech
16. Red Pelzl, New Richland-HEG
17. Louie Mitteco, Totino-Grace*
18. Butzie Maetzold, Hopkins
19. Gary Shuler, Fergus Falls*
20. Ron Hested, Fairmont
21. Rick Decker, Rochester Lourdes*
* *active*

BILL FITCH: GOPHER BASKETBALL

A native of Cedar Rapids, Iowa, Bill Fitch went on to graduate from Coe College. He would later earn his master's degree in psychology from Creighton, where he also began his coaching career as an assistant baseball and basketball coach. Fitch would then go on to serve as the head basketball coach at the University of North Dakota from 1962-67, where he led the Fighting Sioux to an overall record of 94-45. Fitch also guided the Sioux to three straight North Central Conference titles (1965-67) and took those same three teams to the NCAA Tournament, finishing third in 1965 and fourth in 1966. (One of the stars of those teams was All-American Phil Jackson, who went on to become a pretty decent NBA coach in his day with the Chicago Bulls and Los Angeles Lakers!) Fitch left UND to serve as the head coach at Bowling Green, where he led his team to the Mid-American Conference title and a berth in the NCAA tournament.

In 1969 Fitch took over as the head coach at the University of Minnesota. There, Fitch's teams would ultimately show improvement, but, after posting a 25-23 record over two seasons, he would call it quits to pursue a career in the NBA. The Gophers did manage to finish fifth in both 1969 and 1970, thanks in large part to the efforts of Forwards Larry Mikan (the son of Laker great, George Mikan) and Larry Overskei, as well as Guards Eric Hill and Ollie Shannon. From Minnesota, Fitch headed to Cleveland, to begin his pro career with the expansion Cleveland Cavaliers in 1970. Fitch would spend a total of nine years in Cleveland before going on to coach the Boston Celtics for four years. He would spend five more with the Houston Rockets and then another three with the New Jersey Nets. The first coach to be named NBA Coach of the Year twice (Cleveland 1976 & Boston 1980), Fitch's overall career NBA record was a very solid 944-1,106, leaving him 5th on the all-time wins list.

BUTCH RAYMOND
COLLEGE BASKETBALL: MANKATO, ST. CLOUD & AUGSBURG

Butch Raymond grew up in the tiny town of Jasper and went on to play basketball at Augsburg College. He got degrees in both physical education and mathematics from Augsburg in 1963 and later received his master's degree in physical education from Mankato State in 1969. Raymond began his head coaching career in 1966 as the boy's basketball coach at Fairmont High School. From there, Raymond served briefly as an assistant at Minneapolis Southwest High School. In 1969 Raymond moved to the college ranks to serve as an assistant at Augsburg College, before taking over as the head coach in 1970. (Head Coach Ernie Anderson offered him the job but told him that he was his second choice, his first was Lute Olson, who went on to have a pretty decent career for himself at Arizona!) During Raymond's tenure at Augsburg his teams compiled an impressive record of 54-25 in three seasons. In 1973, Raymond moved another step up the coaching ladder, taking over the head coaching job at Division II Minnesota State-Mankato. While with the Mavericks, his teams went 161-133, winning two North Central Conference championships and making an appearance in the 1976 NCAA regional tournament. For his efforts, the program's all-time winningest coach received three Coach of the Year awards.

In 1984 Raymond left Mankato to take over at rival St. Cloud State University. Over the next 13 seasons Raymond would become that program's all-time winningest coach as well, racking up 231 wins, including three straight NCC championships along the way. For his efforts he was again named NCC and NCAA II Kodak Coach of the Year in 1986 and 1987. In 1997 Raymond went on to take over as the Athletic Director at Southwest State, where he has now been for the last six years. Under Raymond's leadership, the Mustang programs have enjoyed prosperity on and off the playing fields as well as in the classroom, where SSU student-athletes have excelled to new heights too.

Raymond spent 31 years coaching intercollegiate athletics and with a career record of 446-299, he is one of the most successful college basketball coaches in Division II history. He is a member of the Augsburg College and Minnesota State-Mankato Hall of Fames and has received a Distinguished Alumni Award from the Minnesota State High School Athletic Directors Association. Raymond and his wife, Linnea have three children, daughters Tracy and Suzy and son Brad, and live in Marshall.

HOW WOULD YOU DESCRIBE YOUR COACHING STYLE? "To me coaching was never a job it was always fun. That was my philosophy out on the floor with my players. I always wanted them to play up to their abilities and I wanted them to play as a team — because basketball is a team game. Having said that, I also wanted to make sure that they enjoyed whatever they were doing. My motto has always been 'The Run is Fun' which meant that our style of play was going to be very aggressive, very up tempo — both offensively as well as defensively. I also wanted my players to realize that they were doing this because it was a fun way to play the game. I mean when you watch a pick-up game out on the street the kids are not just standing around passing the ball 25 times, they are running up and down the court, being creative and having fun. You know, never once in my coaching career did I ever punish a player by making him run. Because to me that was not fun. Instead, the worst punishment that I felt I could ever give anybody was that they would have to miss practice. I was also a stickler for rules and one of the

things that was very important to me was that we were always on time. If anybody ever came even one second late, they would have to sit and watch practice that day. I am also old school in the sense that I didn't ever want to see our kids wear a hat in a restaurant or wear their shirts untucked out on the court. It was the little things and I wanted our kids to represent their university proudly. That was my style."

HOW DID YOU MOTIVATE YOUR PLAYERS? "I am a very positive person. Again, it comes down to fun, and motivating through having fun. I never wanted to motivate through negativity. Players understand when they do things wrong and you don't have to embarrass them or undress them in front of other people to make your point. I never did that in my coaching career and instead just tried to point out the positive things that were going on. If there was a problem, then I tried to address that in a one-on-one situation behind closed doors. I also tried to talk to the younger players through the older players and that worked well too."

WHO WERE YOUR COACHING MENTORS? "I played basketball at Augsburg for Ernie Anderson, who was probably as sound fundamentally as any coach there was. He treated people like men all the time and I took some things from him, he was great. Then, my first job was as an assistant at Minneapolis Southwest under Walt Williams, who really taught me about the up-tempo game. Both were great coaches and fine people. You know, I remember when Ernie (Anderson) asked me to become the head coach at Augsburg. I was coaching high school basketball in Fairmont at the time and he came down for a game and told me that I was his second choice for the job, and that he had already asked Lute Olson, himself an Auggie alumni, if he wanted it. Well, Lute declined it, so I agreed. But Ernie, being the great gentleman that he was, actually told me that he wanted me to be his assistant that first year. He said he did not want me to be the head coach that first year because the team was young and was going to have its share of losses, so he did not want me to start off that way. He told me to coach the freshman and teach them my philosophy, and observe the league for a year so I knew what I was getting into, and then I would take over from him in year two. That was very classy and really an amazing gesture."

IF YOU COULD MAGICALLY GO BACK IN TIME TO THE FIRST YEAR YOU WERE A HEAD COACH AND GIVE YOURSELF SOME ADVICE FOR THE FUTURE, KNOWING WHAT YOU KNOW NOW, BACK THEN, WHAT WOULD YOU SAY TO YOURSELF? "To keep it all in perspective and to remember that it is still just a game. I would also say to not judge yourself based on your team's wins and losses, rather on if your team is playing up to its ability. You know, early on defeats were very, very difficult on me. Very seldom did I ever eat before a game and if we lost I wouldn't eat afterwards. It just made me nauseous thinking about it and that wasn't healthy at all."

WHAT ARE THE CHARACTERISTICS OF WINNERS? "Winners are people who have a desire to improve and are never satisfied with how good they are. They also have a desire to win in the sense that they play the game to win and not to lose — there is a big difference there. Winners love competition too, whether that was a warm-up game in practice or in games, it doesn't matter."

WHAT WAS THE KEY TO GOOD TIME MANAGEMENT? "I think it comes back to organization and using your time efficiently. So, I really did my best to organize and plan my practices with time frames for everything. One thing that always bothered me was to see somebody just standing around in practice. When I saw that I thought they weren't having fun, so I worked hard to keep everybody doing something. As a result, we had very little down time during our practices. Then, because we were always on the go, our practices were much shorter than other coaches."

LOOKING BACK WHAT ARE YOU MOST PROUD OF IN YOUR CAREER? "I am most proud of the relationships that I had with my players. That means the most to me. Every time I get a chance to see my former players it just makes me feel great."

WHAT WAS THE KEY TO RECRUITING? "It was about relationships and communication. You know, I always told my players when I recruited them that what I hoped that they would do after four years of playing for me would be to ask me for two things: First would be if they asked me to be a reference for them when they get a job. Then, I knew that they had graduated, which was my first priority. Secondly, I hoped that they would invite me to their weddings, because that would mean that we were still friends through all the trials and tribulations of basketball."

HOW DID YOU BUILD TEAM UNITY & CHEMISTRY? "We tried to do a lot of things together. I was always a believer in having our team eat together, travel together, have movie nights together, bowling nights together, or whatever. I always had team meetings where everyone had input, and that got each player involved. We were like a family. We had Christmas parties and Thanksgiving dinners at my home as a team and that was great to have everyone get to know each other better. I have always felt that your team was only as good as your last player. So, I wanted our 12th man to feel just as important as my All-American. I treated them all the same and that was important to have good chemistry."

WHAT MOTIVATED YOU? "The challenge of the competition is what motivated me the most. I loved practices because that was like teaching in the classroom for me. That was always the most fun part of the day for me, I loved working with the kids. Then, during games I just enjoyed myself so much. The strategy and psychology and just seeing your players work hard as a team was just so much fun to be a part of. Coaching is not about winning and losing, it is about relationships. Now that I am an athletic director and no longer a coach I miss that aspect of the game."

WHAT ADVICE WOULD YOU HAVE FOR YOUNG COACHES STARTING OUT TODAY? "As a coach it is your job to fundamentally prepare your kids to play up to the maximum of their abilities. So, I would say for them to set realistic goals for each player and for the team and then try to reach those goals. Also, I would tell them to know themselves, know their abilities, and to know their strengths and weaknesses. Then, do the same for your players. Get to know them. And remember, coaching is not about winning and losing, it is about relationships."

FAVORITE LOCKER ROOM SIGN? "The Run is Fun."

WHAT'S THE BIGGEST THING YOU'VE LEARNED FROM COACHING THAT YOU'VE BEEN ABLE TO APPLY TO YOUR EVERYDAY LIFE? "That nothing gets done if you don't communicate. You can't assume that anybody knows anything or understands. So you have to make sure to communicate and also be a good listener."

WHAT ARE THE KEY INGREDIENTS TO CREATING A CHAMPIONSHIP TEAM? "You have to start with talent because you are not going to win without talent. Then you have to have leadership. You have to have someone on the floor who is your leader. After that it is about fitting your style of play into what the players have in terms of strengths and weaknesses. You also need chemistry so that your players get along and like each other. I think some guys coach with fear, others with fun, but for me, I always wanted my teams to play to win, I didn't want them to play not to lose."

WHAT WOULD YOU WANT TO SAY TO YOUR FANS, BOOSTERS, AND ALUMNI WHO HAVE SUPPORTED YOU ALL THESE YEARS? "I would want to thank them for being a part of our programs. My teams have always had tremendous home court advantages wherever I have been. We set all-time attendance records at Mankato and St. Cloud, and that was because of the great support that we had. We had great fans and I think that they knew our kids were going to play hard each night and give it their best."

HOW DO YOU WANT YOUR COACHING EPITAPH TO READ — HOW DO YOU WANT TO BE REMEMBERED AS A COACH? "I would like people to know that the reason I coached was for the player/coach relationships. That was the most important thing to me. I would also like people to know that it was always fun for me to coach and that I always wanted my players to have fun. That is what it is all about."

EVERETT DEAN: CARLETON BASKETBALL

Livonia, Ind., native Everett Dean is a Carleton Basketball coaching legend. An All-American guard at Indiana University back in 1920, Dean got into coaching right out of college. His first stop would be at Carleton, where, from 1921-23, Dean led the Knights to the conference's first three titles. Dean would guide the Knights to an amazing 45-4 record from 1921-24, before going on to coach at his alma mater, Indiana University. Dean led the Hoosiers to their first Big Ten Basketball Championship in school history in 1926, and overall he would coach the Hoosiers to three Big 10 titles over his 14 seasons in Bloomington, finishing with a record of 163-93. He also guided the Hoosier baseball team to three Big 10 baseball crowns as well. Then, in 1938, Dean decided to head west, and take over at Stanford, where he led the Cardinal for 11 seasons en route to a 167-120 career record. The highlight, however, came in 1942, when Dean led Stanford to its only Division I National Championship when they beat Dartmouth, 53-38, in the NCAA Finals. The star of that team was none other than Jim Pollard, a future Hall of Famer with our very own Minneapolis Lakers. Dean would retire from coaching in 1943 with a 375-217 career record. A true basketball coaching legend, he was later enshrined into the Basketball Hall of Fame in 1966.

FLIP SAUNDERS
PRO BASKETBALL: MINNESOTA TIMBERWOLVES

Flip Saunders grew up in Cleveland, Ohio, and went on to become an All-American guard at Cuyahoga Heights High School. In his senior season, 1973, Saunders was even named Ohio's Class A Player of the Year after averaging a state-high 32 points per game. From there, Flip continued his basketball career at the University of Minnesota, where he started 101 of his 103 career contests and became one of the program's all-time biggest fan-favorites. As a senior, he teamed up with Kevin McHale to lead the Gophers to a then all-time school-best 24-3 record.

Upon graduating in 1977 Saunders began his successful coaching career at Golden Valley Lutheran College. There, he compiled a 92-13 record, including a perfect 56-0 mark at home, over four seasons. In 1981, he joined the coaching staff at the University of Minnesota, as an assistant, and helped coach the Golden Gophers to the 1982 Big Ten championship. After five seasons in Gold Country, Flip moved on to become an assistant coach at the University of Tulsa, where he worked for two seasons before heading off to coach in the Continental Basketball Association. In the CBA Saunders achieved an amazing record of coaching success. In fact, he still ranks third all-time in the league with 253 victories.

Saunders began his pro career in the CBA in 1988 with the Rapid City Thrillers, then moved on to the La Crosse Catbirds for five seasons, before coaching the Sioux Falls Skyforce for one year. (From 1991-94 he also served as GM and team president of the Catbirds.) Saunders' impressive coaching resume includes seven consecutive seasons of 30-or-more victories, two CBA championships (1990 & 1992), two CBA Coach of the Year honors (1989 & 1992) and 23 CBA-to-NBA player promotions.

In May of 1995 Flip got his big break when he was hired by his old pal, Kevin McHale, to serve as the Assistant GM of the NBA's Minnesota Timberwolves. But his stay in the front-office would be short-lived though, because just six months later Flip replaced Bill Blair as the team's head coach. Since then, Saunders has been instrumental in developing young talent both on and off the court. In his first full season as the team's head coach, 1996-97, Saunders became the all-time winningest coach in franchise history, leading the team to a then all-time best record of 40-42 and its first-ever playoff appearance. He has since led the club to seven consecutive post-season appearances and is well on his way to leading the team to an NBA championship. Behind All-Star Forward Kevin Garnett's monster dunks and the leadership of Flip Saunders, the sky is the limit for the Timberwolves.

With an overall career NBA record of 328-276, Flip, who signed a five-year $20 million contract extension in the summer of 2001, is considered to be one of the very best and brightest young coaches in professional basketball. A true player's coach who has earned the respect of his colleagues, Saunders continues to make Minnesota proud. Flip and his wife Debbie have four children and reside in the Twin Cities.

HOW WOULD YOU DESCRIBE YOUR COACHING STYLE? "I think that I am someone who has taken a little bit from everybody. I would consider myself more of a teacher than a coach and just love the teaching, psychology and motivational side of the business. My style has always been to teach through repetition in practice, so that when players get into a game situation they have the ability to react and to play, and not think so much. I think that my players would describe me as a players-coach too, as far as being a communicator. Yet, they know that even though I am not a screamer , I am pretty demanding and believe in discipline. I mean I don't think that we would have teams that would be in the top three with regards to the fewest turnovers in the league every year if we weren't a disciplined team. Beyond that, I think it's really about understanding what players can and can't do. It's about getting players to maximize their potential and then giving them enough rope to hang themselves."

HOW DO YOU MOTIVATE YOUR PLAYERS? "The best way to motivate players is through playing time. I tell my players that I really don't determine how much they play. They determine that by how well they play. So, it is not always your five most talented players out on the court, but the five that play the best together. But, like every coach, I am always looking for something different, especially having been with this particular team for a long time. The players can only hear the same stories over and over so much, so you have to find different buttons to push. I have always said that every player has a motivational button and it is the coach's job to figure out what that button is. Some players need to be ridden, others need to have an arm put around them, and some need a little bit of both. I tell my players that they are not going to get a Knute Rockne speech for all 82 games, that just isn't going to happen. So, I encourage my players to motivate themselves too."

HOW DO YOU EARN THE RESPECT OF YOUR PLAYERS? "Your players can see right through you and they know the knowledge that you have. So, if you give them respect then they will give it back in return. I have always said to my players that when they are not at the top of their game that I have to be good enough as their coach to help them overcome that. And likewise, you want your players to be good enough so that they can overcome your deficiencies as well. That is really what a team is, where everyone is covering everyone else's back."

WHO WERE YOUR COACHING MENTORS? " I was very fortunate to play for Bill Musselman for two years and then Jim Dutcher for two years. They were very contrasting styles but I was able to pick out things from each one and put that into my own philosophy. Another guy that I really respect and learned a great deal from was Ed Prohofsky, who was a great coach at Marshall University High School in Minneapolis. He started out as an assistant with me at Golden Valley Lutheran College and has been with me for eight years now with the Timberwolves. To this day he has had as much influence on me as anybody I have been around. I am also an avid book reader. I have probably read every biography on coaches that there is from basketball to football to baseball. So, I try to take a little bit from that too. I have a lot of respect for Pat Riley, Phil Jackson and Rick Pitino, and also really enjoyed reading about guys like Red Auerbach and Vince Lombardi. I am a little bit of everybody and that is what makes me who I am. Another guy I really respect is Lou Holtz. When he was in Minnesota with the Gophers and I was an assistant there I got to know him a little bit. He is a an unbelievable motivator, has a wonderful perspective on life and a really has a great passion for what he does."

IF YOU COULD MAGICALLY GO BACK IN TIME TO THE

FIRST YEAR YOU WERE A HEAD COACH AND GIVE YOURSELF SOME ADVICE FOR THE FUTURE, KNOWING WHAT YOU KNOW NOW, BACK THEN, WHAT WOULD YOU SAY TO YOURSELF? "You know, I was really fortunate. I began coaching at Golden Valley Lutheran when I was just 21 years old and I was really in a situation where I didn't know any better. I had just finished playing 115 straight games with the Gophers, averaging almost 38 minutes per game, where I was basically the coach on the floor. So, it was just a carry over for me. But, as far as advice, I think like all young people, I was probably too emotional at times. Plus, at 21, I was probably playing the best basketball of my life, so I was still practicing and playing with the kids every day. I think looking back now, I would say 'hey, if you are going to coach, then coach, and if you are going to play, then play, but don't be a player/coach.' "

WHAT ARE THE CHARACTERISTICS OF LEADERS? "Leaders are communicators. Leaders are disciplined. Leaders are enthusiastic. Then, more than anything, leaders have a passion for what they do."

LOOKING BACK WHAT ARE YOU MOST PROUD OF IN YOUR CAREER? "I have been successful at every job I have ever taken as a head coach. At Golden Valley they were 10-17 the season before I got there and my first season we went 21-4. I was also proud of the fact that we went 56-0 at home and never lost a home game there. My first job in the CBA I took a team that was 18-36 and we went 36-18 during my first season for the league's best record. We probably would have won the championship but we had a bunch of guys called up to the NBA. Then, from there I went to LaCrosse and I think they were 15-37 and we ended up going 42-14 and won the CBA championship. Finally, coming to the Timberwolves, we had lost 60 games in four out of the last five years prior to me coming here and we turned that around to where we have made the playoffs seven straight years. So, I am proud of that too. Sure, we are not satisfied with that, and we want to advance on much further into the playoffs and win a championship, but we need to work harder."

WHAT IS THE KEY TO GOOD TIME MANAGEMENT? "Having a good wife! That is really the number one thing for me. It is extremely difficult to raise a family and be a coach, so I am very lucky to have a supportive wife who helps me tremendously. She keeps everything in perspective and that allows me to focus on my job."

HOW DO YOU BUILD TEAM UNITY & CHEMISTRY? "All chemistry is, is sacrifice. It is just convincing your players that everybody has to give up something for the good of the team. So, what you have to do is establish roles and communicate to the players that they understand what their role is. That way the team is bigger than the individual."

WHAT MOTIVATES YOU? "The number one thing that motivates me is helping people. You know, when I started out as a junior college coach my motivation was to help the players to go on and get scholarships so that they could get an education. When I became a CBA coach my motivation was to help the players reach their dreams by playing in the NBA. Over my seven years I had 25 players or so who were called up to play in the NBA nd I take as much pride in that as anything I have ever accomplished. Now, as an NBA coach I am motivated to win and to see my players play their best. If you can get your players to play up to their potential, then the wins will take care of themselves."

WHAT ADVICE WOULD YOU HAVE FOR YOUNG COACHES STARTING OUT TODAY? "I would say that they need to establish their own philosophy, and that will come from a combination of a lot of other people's philosophies all put together

into one. I think that all coaches steal ideas and concepts from everybody else, and this OK. Then, you have to coach with your heart and do what you believe is right. If you don't have a passion for what you are teaching and coaching, then you are not going to be successful. You also need to respect the job and know that the job can eat you up if you let it."

FAVORITE LOCKER ROOM SIGN? "Everything we have in our locker room relates to the team, like how a pack of wolves is stronger than any one individual."

WHAT'S THE BIGGEST THING YOU'VE LEARNED FROM COACHING THAT YOU'VE BEEN ABLE TO APPLY TO YOUR EVERYDAY LIFE? "You just have to roll with the punches. You can't get too emotionally high when things are going good or too low when they are going bad. You need to stay at a steady pace. Coaching teaches you what reality really is and just who and what is most important, like your family and religion. Sometimes coaching can be tough. When you are a public figure, one day you can be applauded and the next you can be booed, so you have to realize that it doesn't matter if you win or lose, it matters who you are as a person."

WHAT'S THE BEST PIECE OF ADVICE YOU EVER GOT FROM ANOTHER COACH? "Try to get to bed early. It is really important to get your rest. Having said that, I still find myself up until three in the morning trying to get stuff done, so it is a constant battle to get enough sleep, even now."

WHAT ARE THE KEY INGREDIENTS TO CREATING A CHAMPIONSHIP TEAM? "Number one is having good players. You also need players who are willing to sacrifice and who have a passion and enthusiasm for the game."

WHAT'S THE SECRET TO YOUR SUCCESS? "I believe you can accomplish anything you want through a lot of hard work, dedication and passion."

WHAT DID IT MEAN FOR YOU TO BE A GOPHER? "I take a lot of pride in being a Gopher. There is just nothing like Williams Arena, it is the greatest place in the world to play basketball. I can remember doing the pre-game warm-up to the music "Sweet Georgia Brown" and then coming up from the locker room to the sounds of '2001: A Space Odyssey.' It gives me goose bumps just thinking about it. That old barn was so great and I feel very lucky to have been a part of such a great program. It was very special and I am proud to say I was a Gopher."

WHAT WOULD YOU WANT TO SAY TO YOUR FANS, BOOSTERS, AND ALUMNI WHO HAVE SUPPORTED YOU ALL THESE YEARS? "You are always appreciative for the opportunity that is given to you. You know coaching is not a right, it is an opportunity. It makes me feel good that we can provide our fans with some great entertainment and to bring some happiness to their lives through basketball. So, I would thank the fans for supporting us and for sticking with us through the years. All I can say is that the best is yet to come."

HOW DO YOU WANT YOUR COACHING EPITAPH TO READ — HOW DO YOU WANT TO BE REMEMBERED AS A COACH? "I want to be remembered as someone who was respected by his players and someone who really cared about his players. I also want to be thought of as a coach who always went out there and got his teams to play up to the best of their potential, whether they had a lot of talent or not."

WHITEY SKOOG
COLLEGE BASKETBALL: GUSTAVUS

Myer "Whitey" Skoog grew up in Brainerd as the son of Norwegian immigrants. Sports were big in his life growing up, but not the obvious sports that we would associate him with today. In fact, prior to the 10th grade, Skoog's favorite sports were skiing, fighting and hunting — he didn't get into basketball until he was 16 years old. But when he did, it was magic. Skoog would go on to star on his Brainerd High School team, graduating in 1947.

From there, Skoog went on to play at the University of Minnesota. A guard for the Golden Gophers from 1947-51, Skoog earned All-Big Ten and All-America honors during his senior year. It was at the U of M where Skoog also made history for inventing what we now know as the jump shot — a technique that revolutionized the game of basketball. After his days in Gold Country, Skoog took his patented "jumper" to the Minneapolis Lakers of the National Basketball Association in 1951, where he became one of the premiere guards in the league. In 1957, after playing for several years in the NBA with the Lakers, Skoog suffered a back injury and was forced to retire.

Skoog then headed to St. Peter, where he was hired to serve as the head basketball coach at Gustavus. Over the next 24 years, Skoog would lead the Gusties to a 292-301 record, and five MIAC titles. There would be five second-place finishes along the way as well. Skoog's first three Gustie championship teams came from 1954-56 and included some of the programs biggest and most talented players: Jim Springer, Bill Patterson, Dick Kumlin, Duane Mullin, Cliff Straka, Jack Colvard, Johnny Patzwald and Bob Erdmann — who would later return to guide the program in the 1980s. Skoog added another MIAC crown in 1968 and a co-championship in 1975. That 1975 squad also made it to the NAIA national tournament in Kansas City. Standouts of this era included: Bill Laumaun, Carl Johnson, Dennis Wentworth, Jim Ellingson, Dan Hauck, Tom Carlson, Jim Chalin and Ron White. Of that group, Wentworth and Laumann were three-time all-MIAC players and both had professional tryouts.

Skoog stepped down from coaching basketball in 1981 to focus solely on teaching and coaching golf. You see, in addition to teaching health and phys ed at Gustavus, Skoog also coached the golf team from 1972-96 as well, leading the Gustie golfers to nine MIAC titles and just as many postseason national tournaments. Under Skoog, Gustavus earned a solid national reputation as one of the best golf programs at a school of any size.

Whitey Skoog is a Gustavus sports icon and a real Minnesota sports legend with an amazing legacy. Now retired, Whitey presently resides in the St. Peter area and has three children: David, Kristin and Amy.

HOW WOULD YOU DESCRIBE YOUR COACHING STYLE? "I would describe it as just using your mind. I believed in hard work and practicing the fundamentals. It's about values and the development of young people in athletics having the chance to succeed. So, it is coming up with the right ideas as a coach to put kids into successful situations. Sure, we tried to win every second we were on the floor, but there is a lot that went into developing young people and that was very important to me too."

HOW DID YOU MOTIVATE YOUR PLAYERS? "I always tried to work with young people as people and never put them down. I tried to get them to play better and compete as hard as they could by teaching them as best as I could. Honesty and integrity were very important to me and hopefully that came out in my ability to help motivate them as players."

WHO WERE YOUR COACHING MENTORS? "I learned a lot from my high school coach at Brainerd, Kermit Aase, as well as my college coach at the University of Minnesota, Ozzie Cowles. He said it like it was and really taught the fundamentals. I never had anyone analyze anything about me as a ballplayer and present it before me until I played for Ozzie. He showed me the stutter-step and how my quickness could be utilized out on the basketball court, and that changed everything for me. It was really a revolutionary thing."

WHAT ARE THE CHARACTERISTICS OF LEADERS? "I would say motivation, intelligent play, being able to adapt to changes to get better and having a broad perspective of the game. Leaders possess all of those qualities and are able to make their teammates around them better."

IF YOU COULD MAGICALLY GO BACK IN TIME TO THE FIRST YEAR YOU WERE A HEAD COACH AND GIVE YOURSELF SOME ADVICE FOR THE FUTURE, KNOWING WHAT YOU KNOW NOW, BACK THEN, WHAT WOULD YOU SAY TO YOURSELF? "I would remind him that this is a team game and that individuals make a contribution to the team."

LOOKING BACK WHAT ARE YOU MOST PROUD OF IN YOUR CAREER? "I would have to say the formation of the jump shot. That was something that I was very proud of and something that I think really helped to change the game."

WHAT'S THE BIGGEST THING YOU'VE LEARNED FROM COACHING THAT YOU'VE BEEN ABLE TO APPLY TO YOUR EVERYDAY LIFE? "You have to accept winning and losing. Losing doesn't make you a worse person and you can't let losing get you down. You have to keep it all in perspective and just work hard to get better in whatever it is."

WHAT WOULD YOU WANT TO SAY TO YOUR FANS, BOOSTERS, AND ALUMNI WHO HAVE SUPPORTED YOU ALL THESE YEARS? "I really appreciated the fans that came to our ballgames and supported us. We had some great fans at Gustavus and we still do. We didn't always win, but we competed hard and that was the most important thing."

HOW DO YOU WANT YOUR COACHING EPITAPH TO READ — HOW DO YOU WANT TO BE REMEMBERED AS A COACH? "As somebody who made a difference in the lives of young people."

BILL MUSSELMAN:
GOPHERS & TIMBERWOLVES BASKETBALL

Bill Musselman will be remembered in Minnesota sports history for a lot of reasons. Most importantly though, he will be remembered as a great coach and as a winner. A native of Wooster, Ohio, Bill Musselman went on to graduate from Wooster High School, where he was the captain of the basketball, football and baseball teams. He also lettered in those same three sports at Wittenberg University, in Ohio, and later earned his master's degree from Kent State. From there Musselman got into coaching, first as an assistant and then as the head coach at Ashland College. Then, in 1971, at a ripe old age of 32, Musselman became the youngest head basketball coach in University of Minnesota Gopher Basketball history. He would also become the architect of a re-building program that would be both exciting and memorable — for many different reasons.

Attendance nearly doubled at Williams Arena in his four-year career in Gold Country, and Musselman was the impetus, compiling a 69-32 record, for a .683 winning percentage, the best in school history. Musselman rescued the program and got people excited about basketball again. In 1972 he also made history, both on and off the court — here is what happened. The 1972 Gophers hit the court with one of the tallest and most talented lineups in the country. In addition to returning upperclassmen Center Jim Brewer, Forward Corky Taylor, and Guards Bob Murphy and Keith Young, Musselman added three junior college transfer players in six-foot-nine swingman Ron Behagen, six-foot-eight Forward Clyde Turner, and six-foot-three Guard Bob Nix.

Midway through the season the Gophers faced Ohio State at home, in the Barn. It was a big game, and everyone knew it. There were several sidebars going in as well — including how Buckeye Coach Fred Taylor didn't appreciate Musselman, a fellow Ohioan, recruiting JUCO kids. The media was all over it too. In fact, while the NHL All-Star Game was being played across town at the Met Center that same night, most of the media attention in the Twin Cities was focused on the basketball game. The Gophers had a chance to move into a first-place tie with a victory and the crowd was pumped. What the fans didn't know, however, was that this particular game would go down as one of the most significant games in Minnesota history. This was the game that would forever be remembered as "The Fight" and the beginning of the "Iron Five."

With the Buckeyes leading 50-44 and 36 seconds left in the game, OSU's, star Center Luke Witte broke toward the basket. As Minnesota pressed, Witte outran the field and caught the inbound pass. In the process, he was fouled hard by both Turner and Taylor. Turner was then called for a flagrant foul and was immediately ejected. Then, amazingly and nearly simultaneously, Taylor reached out to help Witte, who was down on the court, up to his feet. But instead of helping him up, he proceeded to knee him in the groin. The crowd was stunned, and subsequent mayhem broke out. OSU's, Dave Merchant rushed over to help Witte, pushing Taylor out of his way. Brewer and Taylor then ran down the court after Merchant, while Behagen, having already fouled out, came off the bench and attacked Witte.

For the next moments, complete pandemonium took over at Williams Arena. The nearly 18,000 fans in attendance were shocked, and many even jumped onto the court to partake in the festivities. Big Dave Winfield even got into the act and it got ugly in a hurry. Several Buckeye players were taken to the hospital, and a near riot ensued. Minnesota's Athletic Director, Paul Giel, then decided, after consulting with the game officials, to simply end the game and declare Ohio State as the winner. Outside, they started to throw rocks at the police cars as they took the players to the hospital. When it was all over, a huge black eye was left on the Gopher basketball program.

To better understand the entire "situation," you have to go back to the end of the first half where an incident took place that may have instigated it all. "Witte crossed in front of me," said Nix. "There's no question in my mind or anybody's that saw it. It was a deliberate elbow to my face. He just threw it, and he damn near decked me. It was seen by a lot of people, except the officials."

That night, following the incident, replays of the fight were played on virtually every newscast in the country. Every paper ran a story about it, and the next week, Sports Illustrated even featured the brawl as their cover story. Incredibly, all fingers pointed to Musselman as the instigator. They tried to paint a picture that his "win at any cost" attitude had animalized his players into a fit of rage. National media had concentrated only on the game-ending fight, and they never mentioned the half-time incident that precluded the retaliation. Attempts were made to dramatize and polarize Musselman and the Buckeyes' Fred Taylor, the two coaches with such different coaching philosophies. Taylor was a Big Ten coaching legend who built programs traditionally. Musselman, on the other hand, was a rookie who they said took short-cuts to success by obtaining junior college players. Taylor believed in recruiting kids and then developing them. Racism and even the Vietnam War were thrown into the stew. People were searching for a scapegoat, and the media had found one in Musselman.

"Obviously the fight was wrong, but I always felt that it was racially motivated," said Musselman several years later. "It was during the early 1970s, and there were a lot of racial overtones. The game got out of hand, and the officials let too much loose play go on. I took a lot of heat for it. It was ridiculous that people would insinuate that I wanted to have a fight. They tried to blame it on my pre-game warm-up routine, saying that it hyped the fans into a frenzy. It was too bad that it happened, but it was an intense heat of the battle thing."

Musselman, who said going in that he did not believe in "rebuilding years," kept his word and made his first year in Gold Country one of the program's most exciting, and dare we say "eventful" in history. His Gophers went on to win the Big Ten title that year and resurrected a program which had been on the downside. Not afraid to go outside the system and bring in junior college transfers, he left in 1975 under the shadow of allegations and investigations by the NCAA — most of which proved to be unfounded.

Musselman's amazing coaching career included posting a record of 233-84 as a college coach at Ashland, Minnesota and later at South Alabama. He was also a head coach in four pro leagues as well — the NBA (with the Cleveland Cavaliers and the Minnesota Timberwolves), CBA (including a stint with the Rochester Flyers), ABA and WBA, where his overall career record was 603-426. In addition, he was named as the CBA Coach of the Year in 1987 and 1988, winning four consecutive championships along the way.

"When I coached the Timberwolves they broke every NBA attendance record," said Musselman, who served as the franchise's first-ever coach. "There aren't many places where you are going to get 40,000 people to come to a basketball game! The fans there were just incredible, where else can you find fans like that?"

Musselman later served as an assistant with the NBA's Portland Trail Blazers until his tragic and untimely death in 2000, from bone marrow cancer, at the age of just 59. His son, Eric, also an assistant with the Wolves, is presently the head coach of the Golden State Warriors — making his father very proud indeed. "I think my teams always played hard and played together," said Musselman, on how he would like to be remembered as a coach. "I think that I have always had the ability as a coach to get the most out of my players, and my teams have always played as hard as they could. I always taught my players to get out of life what they put into it. I think it is important to teach an athlete to be able to face and handle adversity. Mental toughness is important to me, and I always wanted my players to be able to be prepared to handle the good times along with the bad."

JIM SMITH
COLLEGE BASKETBALL: ST. JOHN'S

Jim Smith grew up in Illinois and went on to earn all-conference honors in football, basketball and track at St. Edward's High School in Elgin, Ill. From there, Smith went on to play basketball at Marquette University. There, the four-year letter winner earned bachelor's degrees in English and history, graduating in 1956. After college, Smith got married and later took over as the coach of the Marquette freshman basketball team. He would remain at Marquette until 1961, earning his master's degree there as well. That same year Smith left Marquette to teach and coach at South Milwaukee High School. He stayed two years there and then went on to coach and teach at Brookfield East High School. That next year he got his big break when St. John's University called.

In 1964 Smith took over as the head basketball coach at St. John's University, and, believe it or not, he has been there ever since, making history along the way. In fact, with an amazing 618-411 career record in 39 seasons, Smith is the winningest coach in Minnesota collegiate basketball history. He passed legendary Hamline head coach Joe Hutton on March 3, 2001, when SJU defeated Gustavus Adolphus in the second round of the NCAA Division III basketball championship tournament. Besides ranking first among college coaches in Minnesota, Smith is also second among active NCAA Division III coaches for most victories and fifth all-time in Division III basketball history. His numbers are simply incredible. Smith has led his teams to seven MIAC titles, five MIAC playoff titles, nine trips to the NAIA tournament and seven trips to the NCAA Division III playoffs, including an appearance by the Johnnies in the 2000 and 2001 NCAA tournaments. In addition, Smith has won MIAC titles in each of the past five decades. In addition to his duties as basketball coach, Smith has also coached golf, cross country and track during his tenure on campus. He has even served as the school's athletic director, as well as an associate professor of physical education.

Among Coach Smith's many coaching honors and accolades, he is a six-time MIAC Coach of the Year, a three-time NAIA District Coach-of-the-Year, and earned NCAA Division III West Region Coach-of-the-Year honors in both 1993 and 2001 as well. In addition, Smith is a past president of the National Association of Basketball Coaches. In 1993, Smith was inducted into the St. Edward's Sports Hall of Fame and the City of Elgin Sports Hall of Fame.

Coach Smith has become a Johnny institution. As is Coach Gagliardi to the Johnny Football team, so too is Coach Smith to the Johnny hoops program. A living legend, Smith is as humble as he is respected by his peers. An extraordinary teacher and coach, Jim Smith has truly made Minnesota proud. Jim and his wife Adrienne have seven children, 12 grandchildren and reside in Sartell.

HOW WOULD YOU DESCRIBE YOUR COACHING STYLE? "I think I have mellowed through the years and am more understanding now than I used to be. My style is pretty basic. We don't do a lot of yelling, we don't tear people down and we don't criticize. Everything we attempt to do here is in a constructive manner with positive reinforcement. We try to deal with each individual during every practice and be as positive as possible with each person to help them meet their goals. I also rely a great deal on my assistant coaches to delegate responsibility. They are outstanding coaches and do a lot for our program."

HOW DO YOU MOTIVATE YOUR PLAYERS? "We rely on a lot of self-motivation here. So many of the players that we get here are self-motivated types of people anyway. I mean they come into our program as good students and they are usually highly motivated, whether it is in the classroom or on the athletic field. So, we encourage that and it works well for us. We don't do a lot of locker room signs, hand-outs or anything like that. We just have tough practices and let the kids compete, that's it.

ON PEP-TALKS: "I don't do pep-talks. In fact, the only pep-talk I ever did was at half-time during a game against Hamline years ago. I thought our guys needed to be inspired so I finished my impassioned Knute Rockne-like speech by hitting the chalk board to make a statement. Well, I broke my hand and that was the last pep-talk I ever gave!"

WHO WERE YOUR COACHING MENTORS? "While I had some great coaches at Marquette University, the coach that might have had the biggest influence on my style was Greg True, my coach at St. Edward's High School in Elgin Illinois. It was a very small school and he coached the only three sports that we had: football, basketball and track. I participated in all three and learned a great deal from him. He was a no nonsense kind of guy and I respected him a great deal."

IF YOU COULD MAGICALLY GO BACK IN TIME TO THE FIRST YEAR YOU WERE A HEAD COACH AND GIVE YOURSELF SOME ADVICE FOR THE FUTURE, KNOWING WHAT YOU KNOW NOW, BACK THEN, WHAT WOULD YOU SAY TO YOURSELF? "I would tell myself what I usually tell our players now and that is that athletics here at St. John's are an extremely important part of their education and it is more than just winning and losing, it is preparation for life. The competition, sportsmanship, the will to win, and the hard work, all go into the experience of playing basketball at St. John's and that is something we take very seriously here."

WHAT ARE THE CHARACTERISTICS OF LEADERS? "Some leaders are very vocal and others lead by example. Some are great leaders on the court while others are great off the court. Leadership, I think you are born with it. We do, however, have all our seniors serve as captains during their senior year. So, we anticipate by the time that they are seniors that they are going to develop into good leaders."

LOOKING BACK WHAT ARE YOU MOST PROUD OF IN YOUR CAREER? "In 39 years we have had only one person who didn't graduate. That in itself tells parents and student athletes alike that we care. I am very proud of that. I am also very proud of the kids who have come through here and have gone onto success in their own lives. When your alumni get together and reflect on their positive experiences here, that really makes you feel good."

WHAT IS THE KEY TO RECRUITING? "Being honest, being fair and being sincere. You need to show them what they want, both academically as well as athletically. You have to make contacts at all levels and then work hard every year. You know, we don't promise our recruits anything when they come in. We just tell them that they will be given full consideration and every opportunity to compete with everybody else. Beyond that it is up to them. Other schools promise kids different things but we have never done that. Beyond that, we just look for kids who just love the game and are gym rats. We want guys with a real passion for the game, that is what it is all about."

HOW DO YOU BUILD TEAM UNITY & CHEMISTRY? "You create chemistry by dealing with everybody fairly and honestly and with an even hand. It is hard, but if you can do that then the players respect what you are doing. We also do team building, which starts each year with a two or three day retreat. We try to bond there and it helps us get to know each other better as teammates. We also take trips together overseas after the season and that is a wonderful experience, living and traveling together."

WHAT MOTIVATES YOU? "I think every coach has a great desire to win. The competition keeps me going and it is really what drives me. You know, coaching basketball is a really creative experience. It gives me the opportunity to utilize my creative juices and that makes it fun. I look at every practice and every game as a challenge. I even look at recruiting as a challenge. You get to build all of this year in and year out and it is very exciting. I also enjoy dealing with these kids, they are great student athletes, have good families and good values, so to make a difference in their lives is very special."

WHAT ADVICE WOULD YOU HAVE FOR YOUNG COACHES STARTING OUT TODAY? "Be prepared to work extremely hard and be prepared to put in a tremendous amount of time. And, if you are going to get married, make sure you marry somebody who is going to be realistic with regards to what your hours are going to be. Seven day, 15 hour days are not uncommon and that is just the reality of it. Also, if you are a young guy just starting out, be sure to network. If you want to move up the ladder you need to make contacts along the way."

WHAT'S THE BIGGEST THING YOU'VE LEARNED FROM COACHING THAT YOU'VE BEEN ABLE TO APPLY TO YOUR EVERYDAY LIFE? "Hard work has always carried over into everything I have done. Also, you have to keep a level head. When people are panicking around you, you need to be calm and think your way through things."

WHAT'S THE SECRET TO YOUR SUCCESS? "Surrounding yourself with good people is tremendously important. Having good assistant coaches is the key. You have to let them do their own thing and not micro-manage them. We also listen to our players and try to learn from them constantly. If you are surrounded by good people, the wins will come... guaranteed."

WHAT WOULD YOU WANT TO SAY TO YOUR FANS, BOOSTERS, AND ALUMNI WHO HAVE SUPPORTED YOU ALL THESE YEARS? "I would want to thank everybody from the bottom of my heart, especially my family. I have a wonderful wife and seven great children who have always been there for me. There were many, many times that I was not around when they were growing up because of my coaching and I appreciate their support so much. I would also like to thank our alumni, they have been very supportive through the years both financially as well as emotionally and that has been great too."

ON MAKING NCAA HISTORY BY BECOMING THE FIRST GRANDPA/COACH TO HAVE HIS GRANDSON PLAY FOR HIM: "It was not always easy, that was for sure. I did not want to show him any favoritism, so I was very, very tough on him and that was sometimes difficult. He was a good player though and a great kid. I was very proud to have had him as a player. It was a lot of fun to be out there together."

HOW DO YOU WANT YOUR COACHING EPITAPH TO READ — HOW DO YOU WANT TO BE REMEMBERED AS A COACH? "I would like to remembered as a person who was fair, ethical, moral and dealt with people in a very honest way."

DENISE DOVE-IANELLO: COLLEGE BASKETBALL

Denise Dove-Ianello, a former Armstrong High School girls basketball star who went on to become the leading scorer in Northern Illinois University history, was recently named as an assistant women's basketball coach at the University of Wisconsin. Dove-Ianello had previously served as the associate head women's basketball coach at the University of Arizona from 1992-2003.

JIMMY WILLIAMS: GOPHER BASKETBALL

Jimmy Williams has been an assistant coach in the Land of 10,000 Lakes for more than three decades. A native of Havana, Fla., Williams, who originally played for Bill Musselman at Ashland College (Ohio), followed Musselman to the University of Minnesota upon his graduation in 1970. Williams was an All-American basketball player for the Eagles and helped the school to the 1969 college-division national title. Williams began his assistant coaching career at Minnesota in the 1971-72 season under Musselman, and continued there during Jim Dutcher's tenure. While he was at Minnesota, the Gophers won a pair of Big Ten titles, finished in the upper division of the conference nine times, made eight postseason appearances and had a .500 or better record 12 times. With the Gophers, Williams recruited and coached 21 players who went on to play in the NBA, and Basketball Times rated him as one of the nation's top 15 recruiters. Williams would stay 15 years in Gold Country before moving on to coach at San Diego State (1989-92), Tulsa (1988-89), University of Nebraska (1990-99) and at Oklahoma State (2000). In 2001 Williams joined the Timberwolves' coaching staff after 27 years as a Division I college assistant. Williams, who coached both Kevin McHale and Flip Saunders at the University of Minnesota, was happy to be back home again.

Karen Stromme wound up in Duluth when her father, Graden "Soup" Stromme, was named as the general manager of the Duluth Dukes baseball team back in 1959. Karen, who was six feet tall by the time she was a seventh grader, was an outstanding prep athlete. She would go on to graduate from Duluth Central High School in 1978 as a three-time All-Lake Superior Conference center on the basketball team and was also chosen as the Trojans' Most Valuable Senior Athlete that year as well.

From there, Stromme followed in her old man's footsteps by attending St. Olaf. (Graden played basketball at St. Olaf before going on to become a football, baseball and basketball coach for nearly 40 years at Morgan Park High School.) There, Stromme had a brilliant basketball career, tallying 1,423 points as a four-year starting center with the Oles. A two-time team captain, Stromme was also a four-time All-MAIAW Tournament team selection. Also a three-time letter winner in golf, she graduated from St. Olaf in the spring of 1982 with a degree in sociology and American studies. (In 1994 Stromme was inducted into the St. Olaf Athletic Hall of Fame.)

That next year Stromme joined the University of Minnesota-Duluth as an assistant women's basketball coach. Then, in 1984, she took over as the Bulldog's head coach. She wasted little time in making a name for herself either, leading the Bulldogs to a share of the school's first-ever Northern Sun Intercollegiate Conference championship during her rookie season. Since then, Stromme has made basketball history. Now entering her 20th season as the head coach at Minnesota-Duluth, Stromme has racked up an amazing 400-164 overall record. In addition, Stromme's Bulldogs have captured the NSIC crown 10 of the last 15 years (11 times overall), while also earning six trips to the NCAA Division II North Central Regionals (1995, 1996, 1999, 2000, 2001 and 2003). Stromme also guided the Bulldogs to seven successive appearances in the NAIA National Tournament (1988-94), and has earned 20 or more victories in 14 of the past 16 seasons.

In addition to her basketball responsibilities, Stromme also served as Minnesota-Duluth's first (and only) women's varsity golf coach for four seasons before the sport was discontinued in 1993. Stromme is also active on the international scene. The past president of the NAIA Women's Basketball Coaches Association, Stromme was also the chairperson of the USA Basketball Team Selection Committee which picked the U.S. entry for the 1996 and 2000 Olympic Games. Additionally, she served as an assistant coach for Team East at the 1995 U.S. Olympic Festival.

In the world of women's college basketball, Karen Stromme is amongst the best of the best. She has put the University of Minnesota-Duluth women's basketball program on the national map and is just getting started. An amazing motivator and teacher, Karen is a player's coach to the core. Her vitality and enthusiasm are infectious and that is why she is so well liked and respected by her players and peers alike.

HOW WOULD YOU DESCRIBE YOUR COACHING STYLE? "I think my philosophy is to be as positive and optimistic as possible. I believe that so much more can be accomplished from thinking positively and expecting good things from people. I think that I have had that influence on our teams over the years and that is something that I am proud of. Our practices are full of energy and are just about being positive and having a great attitude. My dad always told me to be true to yourself, and I have lived by that. I never try to emulate any other coaches, I just try to be me because that is who I am. Players pick up on that too, so it is important to be consistent and to be a good leader. It is about finding life lessons that compliment your core values, that is my style."

WHO WERE YOUR COACHING MENTORS? "My dad, Soup Stromme, was first and foremost. We moved to Duluth in 1959 when he was named as the general manager of the Duluth Dukes. He is a wonderful man and I learned so much from him. Then, I grew up two doors away from (UMD Football Coach) Jim Malosky, and used to love going to UMD Football games. Our families were good friends and growing up it seemed like everything we did evolved around athletics. So, he certainly he was a mentor as well. He stressed hard work and honesty and those were great values that I adopted into my own coaching philosophies. The life lessons I learned from being around those two was invaluable. I mean we went to state tournaments for family vacations where other kids were going somewhere sunny and warm. That was the environment I grew up in though and I loved it. It really shaped who I am today."

IF YOU COULD MAGICALLY GO BACK IN TIME TO THE FIRST YEAR YOU WERE A HEAD COACH AND GIVE YOURSELF SOME ADVICE FOR THE FUTURE, KNOWING WHAT YOU KNOW NOW, BACK THEN, WHAT WOULD YOU SAY TO YOURSELF? "You know, I don't think I would say a thing. I think back to that naïve, energetic 23-year-old and I wouldn't tell her a thing. I think everybody has to find their way by making their own mistakes. I would, however, say that maybe my competitive nature got the best of me at times. I can remember losing games early on in my career and being so mad at my players that I couldn't even look at them. I wouldn't let them talk on the bus ride home and it was ridiculous. Luckily, I have gotten a lot better in that department!"

WHAT ARE THE CHARACTERISTICS OF WINNERS? "You know, after every practice our team huddles up and collectively says the word 'winners!'. So, I talk about winners a lot. So many people in our society think that winning is about a score or who won. Instead, what we try to say is that being a winner is about the choices you make and the values you have. If you make enough right choices in your everyday life, then pretty soon you automatically just do the right thing, and it is a lifestyle. We have goals for our team such as work ethic, having a team attitude, valuing your teammates, trusting your coaches and teammates, and by achieving those goals we do win. So, winning is not the goal, it is the result of achieving those goals. Winning is about your daily life and the decisions you make every day. All of those things affect way more than just one individual when you are on a team."

LOOKING BACK WHAT ARE YOU MOST PROUD OF IN YOUR CAREER? "I think that I have done things the way that they should be done. I think that I have treated my players fairly and with respect. I worked very hard and followed the rules. I tried to keep my players in mind first. Finally, I had a passion for the game and a respect for the game. I have really enjoyed everything."

WHAT IS THE BEST PIECE OF ADVICE YOU EVER GOT FROM ANOTHER COACH? "Pick your battles. In other words, put your energy towards things that you can make a difference with and don't waste your energy fighting those things that you can't make a difference with."

HOW DO YOU BUILD TEAM UNITY & CHEMISTRY? "It starts by doing your homework when you are recruiting. You have to search out and target good people first and foremost. I would imagine that you can fall into the trap of only going after great players, like at the division one level, but I just believe it is about recruiting good people with good values. That is what we have found has made a difference in our program. Once you get those people, then you can come together as a team."

WHAT MOTIVATES YOU? "If you are not competitive then you better not be in coaching. Sure, I love the competition and I love winning, but for me it is the day to day exposure with young, motivated, passionate players. That is what motivates me."

WHAT ADVICE WOULD YOU HAVE FOR YOUNG COACHES STARTING OUT TODAY? "Work hard and have a good work ethic. You just have to have a lot of energy, a lot of passion and a love for your job. Then, don't forget that the number one reason that you are out there is for your players. If you get caught up in the wins and losses then you will struggle because that can swallow you up. If you can go home after each day and say to yourself that you did the right things, and you have a passion for those things, then you will be OK. It is such a wonderful profession, but you have to have a daily check and balance about why you are doing it. Otherwise it can consume you. As coaches we are in the spotlight, we are role models and we can have a huge effect on a lot of people's lives."

WHAT IS THE KEY TO GOOD TIME MANAGEMENT? "You know, it is like they say, it takes 30 days to form a good habit. So, it is having priorities and sticking to them. For me, I put fitness way up there on my priorities and that is something I really value, so I make a profound effort to be able to work out every day. You just have to make yourself do it and be very self disciplined to get things done. Then, you also have to be able to de-program and have down time too. That is very important to be able to recharge your batteries and come back refreshed. I mean as coaches we don't want to teach our kids to be obsessed with our jobs and not worry about our families because we are gone all of the time. So, it is about balance."

FAVORITE LOCKER ROOM SIGN? "Go Hard or Go Home."

WHAT'S THE BIGGEST THING YOU'VE LEARNED FROM COACHING THAT YOU'VE BEEN ABLE TO APPLY TO YOUR EVERYDAY LIFE? "If you will expect good things from people you will find it and if you expect bad things, you will find that too."

WHAT ARE THE KEY INGREDIENTS TO CREATING A CHAMPIONSHIP TEAM? "Start with your foundation and that begins with your core values. You have to instill those things early on and keep reinforcing them, things like fundamentals and defense. From there you have to focus on attitude and work ethic. If you get all of those things, then you have the basis for building a championship team."

WHAT'S THE SECRET TO YOUR SUCCESS? "I just try to be happy and have a positive attitude. I am the eternal optimist and just always try to be true to who I am. It is being energetic, loving to work hard and having a great family that supports you."

WHAT WOULD YOU WANT TO SAY TO YOUR FANS, BOOSTERS, AND ALUMNI WHO HAVE SUPPORTED YOU ALL THESE YEARS? "I would just give them all a huge resounding thank you. They are my life. You know, I have so many great friends who I have made through basketball, from my former players on down the line and it has been so wonderful. I just appreciate everyone's support so much."

HOW DO YOU WANT YOUR COACHING EPITAPH TO READ — HOW DO YOU WANT TO BE REMEMBERED AS A COACH? "She did it for the love of the game and for the love of her players with all her heart."

OZZIE COWLES:GOPHER BASKETBALL

Osborne "Ozzie" Cowles grew up in Browns Valley and went on to earn all-state honors in football and basketball. From there, Cowles went on to star at Carleton College, where he earned 11 letters in football, basketball, and baseball. Upon graduating in 1922, the three-time all-conference guard came back to Carleton in 1924 to serve as the school's head basketball and baseball coach. There, he led the Knights to an impressive 67-26 record. In 1930, Cowles left Carleton to coach at River Falls State Teachers College in Wisconsin, where from 1932-36 he posted a 32-18 record. From there, Cowles headed to Dartmouth, where he would lead the Big Green to seven Eastern Intercollegiate Conference (now Ivy League) championships and a trip to the 1942 NCAA Tournament finals against Stanford. (There, ironically, he would lose in the Finals to fellow Carleton alum Everett Dean, who was the head coach at Stanford.) In all, Cowles would spend 11 seasons in Hanover, NH, posting a career record of 142-38. In 1946 Cowles came back to the Midwest to take over as the head coach at the University of Michigan. There, he would post a 28-14 record and win a conference championship in 1948. That Spring, however, Cowles came home, to take over as the new head coach of the Golden Gophers. Ozzie would coach at the University of Minnesota for 11 years, leading the Gophers to a pair of Big Ten runner-up finishes en route to a career record of 148-93. A true coaching legend, Cowles was later enshrined into the College Coaches Hall of Fame.

CAROL VISNESS
GIRLS HIGH SCHOOL BASKETBALL: KITTSON CENTRAL

Carol Visness grew up in Rugby, N.D., and went on to graduate from North Dakota State University, in Fargo, with a teaching degree. From there, Carol went on to teach physical education and health at Kittson Central High School, where she also coached girls basketball. Now entering her 29th season as the program's head coach, Carol is the second winningest girls high school basketball coach in state history with 525 wins. She won her first state title in 2002 and has had numerous trips to the tourney over the years. Among her many coaching accolades, Carol is most proud of the fact that two of her daughters played basketball for her and then went on to play collegiately at Concordia Moorhead.

HOW WOULD YOU DESCRIBE YOUR COACHING STYLE? "I don't say a lot, but I do expect a lot. I am a pretty quiet person, but am also pretty demanding of my kids. I expect a lot of their time both during the season as well as in the off-season. I don't look for perfection but I do look for excellence and a commitment to hard work. If someone is going to play in our program they are going to have to be committed to playing basketball year round and be willing to put in a lot of extra time. We don't demand that, but it is an expectation we started years ago. The kids who come through the program and are committed to it are very successful. That, in turn, has brought our program a lot of success along the way."

HOW DO YOU MOTIVATE YOUR PLAYERS? "Well, it is isn't so difficult to motivate our kids anymore, because they pretty much want to be there and be a part of what we have built. I think we have built a really good, winning atmosphere here and after our kids see that, they become very self-motivated. We have rewards for different things, but overall I think our kids want to be a part of this tradition and are motivated by winning."

WHO WERE YOUR COACHING MENTORS? "That's tough because they're weren't hardly any women's coaches back when I was a kid playing sports. Now, with Title IX, there are a lot more women at all levels of the game, but back then it was tough. Now, I would have to say it would be Pat Summitt, at Tennessee, she is just a great coach. And, of course, anybody that is in coaching would have to respect John Wooden (UCLA's basketball coach) and really pay attention to the things that he has done."

IF YOU COULD MAGICALLY GO BACK IN TIME TO THE FIRST YEAR YOU WERE A HEAD COACH AND GIVE YOURSELF SOME ADVICE FOR THE FUTURE, KNOWING WHAT YOU KNOW NOW, BACK THEN, WHAT WOULD YOU SAY TO YOURSELF? "Maybe to be a little more understanding and a little more compassionate."

WHAT ARE THE CHARACTERISTICS OF LEADERS? "I think you are either born with it or develop it at a really young age, not in high school. I see those qualities in kids as early as elementary school and in junior high, so I think it is already developed and already there at that point. I also don't think you can make people into leaders either. You just see those people and know who they are. It is really nothing you can do as a coach to make a kid into a leader. So, I would say that the qualities a leader possesses are something he or she is born with."

HOW DO YOU BUILD TEAM UNITY & CHEMISTRY? "I think that is created from the kids themselves. You need the right combination of kids that get along well with each other and the right leaders as well. There also has to be a lack of jealously and you need a group that truly wants everyone to do well. It is a unique situation to create that environment, but overall I think you need to get lucky with your group of kids who feel that way towards one another. As a coach you can help by trying to treat all of the kids the same and that kind of thing, but overall good chemistry happens when you get the right combination of kids at the right time, whose personalities just mesh well."

LOOKING BACK WHAT ARE YOU MOST PROUD OF IN YOUR CAREER? "I think I am most proud of the fact that I had three daughters play together. They were pretty close in age and on one occasion, a sub-section championship game, I got to watch them all play together in the same game. That was pretty special. The fact that they all played and enjoyed the game was very rewarding to me."

WHAT ADVICE WOULD YOU HAVE FOR YOUNG COACHES STARTING OUT TODAY? "Find out early what you believe in and what your philosophy is in coaching. Then, implement it and stick with it. Just stick to your style and you will end up getting what you want."

WHAT MOTIVATES YOU? "I think watching my kids succeed is the biggest thing for me. But, I also get a lot of satisfaction out of watching my kids work hard and then having it pay off for them. And that doesn't necessarily mean winning, but more on seeing them improve as athletes and as people. I mean when you see little girls come to our camps as second graders, and then see them progress to become starters on the high school team is pretty special. You know, we have been lucky in that most every season is a winning one here for us. So, I guess you could say success is measured by wins and losses, but I think it's more about how hard your kids work and how much they improve."

WHAT'S THE BIGGEST THING YOU'VE LEARNED FROM COACHING THAT YOU'VE BEEN ABLE TO APPLY TO YOUR EVERYDAY LIFE? "Not everyone is going to agree with what you do, but if you stick to what you believe is right and you have been fair, then you will be OK. I mean that happens in life too. You just have to follow your own conscience I guess and just believe in yourself."

WHAT'S THE BEST PIECE OF ADVICE YOU EVER GOT FROM ANOTHER COACH? "Don't substitute too early. It is a pretty simple thing, but it has been a valuable lesson for me."

WHAT ARE THE KEY INGREDIENTS TO CREATING A CHAMPIONSHIP TEAM? "You have to have a group of kids with a common goal that are willing to put in extra time, hard work and are not concerned with individual egos, and are committed to the end result."

WHAT'S THE SECRET TO YOUR SUCCESS? "I would say perseverance and not being afraid to go the extra mile. We have been committed for a long time to winning here and that says a lot about the people in this community. So many people believe in our system and have helped out with camps and leagues and that has really paid off for our kids. You know, I will keep coaching until it becomes a job to go to the gym. When it is no longer fun, that is when I will retire. Until then, I am having a ball."

WHAT WOULD YOU WANT TO SAY TO YOUR FANS, BOOSTERS, AND ALUMNI WHO HAVE SUPPORTED YOU ALL THESE YEARS? "Thanks for being there. We have some really good support here and that is just wonderful for our program. They have always stood by our team and by myself and that has been great. I would thank them for the opportunity to be here for all these years and I really appreciate it."

FAVORITE LOCKER ROOM SIGN: "My favorite might be 'Plant your feet and stand firm in what you believe.' Overall, most of my signs deal with hard work and commitment. Things like 'The harder you work the luckier you get,' always stand out to me. Recently, rather than having a particular one up in our locker room, we have each player find something that fits themselves and they put that up on their own lockers."

HOW DO YOU WANT YOUR COACHING EPITAPH TO READ — HOW DO YOU WANT TO BE REMEMBERED AS A COACH? "We worked hard, we played hard, we played fair and it was a great time."

DAVE SCHELLHASE: UM-MOORHEAD BASKETBALL

Dave Schellhase, a two-time All-American at Purdue and a national scoring champion, was brought in to serves as the new head coach at Minnesota State Moorhead in 1975. Schellhase wasted little time in making a name for himself, leading the team to a pair of NIC titles and trips to the NAIA National Championships in 1980 and 1982. After 18 years with the Dragons, Schellhase left Moorhead to take over as the head coach at Indiana State University.

ERV INNIGER: AUGSBURG BASKETBALL

Erv Inniger grew up Berne, Ind., and was a standout performer in high school, where his teams went 67-0 over three regular seasons. Inniger then went on to play basketball for Indiana University during the mid-1960s, where he was captain of the Hoosier team that won the 1967 Big 10 championship and finished third in the NCAA Regional. Inniger played baseball as well in college, where he was a standout pitcher. He then went on to play two years of pro basketball in the American Basketball Association with the Minnesota Muskies and the Miami Floridians. After retiring from pro ball, Inniger went on to coach four seasons at Golden Valley Lutheran Junior College (66-32) and then five seasons at Augsburg College, where his teams were 99-42. From there, Inniger went on to become the winningest men's basketball coach in North Dakota State history, guiding the Bison to a 244-150 record over 14 seasons including one North Central Conference title in 1981. His teams won 20 or more games twice and had 19 wins on four other occasions. In addition, his teams racked up 13 consecutive winning seasons from 1978 to 1991 and finished in the first division of the NCC 11 times, including runner-up finishes three times. The 1981 team advanced to the NCAA Division II regional where they finished third, and his 1983 team made it to the NCAA regional title game, falling by two points to Morningside. Since leaving his coaching duties at NDSU in 1992, Inniger has served as an associate athletic director at NDSU for the past 10 years. Among his many coaching honors and accolades, Inniger is a member of the 1988 Indiana silver anniversary all-star team as selected by the Indiana Basketball Hall of Fame, and in 2001 he was inducted into the NDSU Athletics Hall of Fame as well. Irv and his wife Linda have two sons, Bart, who captained the 1992 Bison basketball team, and Brett, who played college basketball at Concordia.

LES WOTHKE
COLLEGE BASKETBALL: WINONA STATE UNIVERSITY

Les Wothke grew up in LaPort County, In., and went on to play basketball at Greenville College, Il., graduating in 1961. From there, Wothke coached at two high schools in Illinois before going on to serve as an assistant coach for several years at Eastern Illinois University, where he also earned his master's degree in 1964. Wothke's first head coaching position came in 1970, when he was offered the job at Winona State University. He would stay in Winona for five seasons, leading the Warriors to four straight Northern Intercollegiate Conference championships, as well as NAIA District 13 Championships in 1973 and 1975 as well. Twice WSU advanced to play in the NAIA national tournament under Wothke. Wothke's Warriors earned winning streaks of 26 straight NIC games and 42 straight at home, and even established 103 Winona State and NIC records. Wothke posted an incredible 51-8 conference record at Winona and for his efforts, he earned NSIC Coach of the Year honors on three different occasions.

From there, Wothke went on to serve as an assistant at the University of Illinois under Lou Henson from 1975-79. In 1980 he took over as the head coach of Western Michigan University, where he led the team from worst to first that next season, earning Mid American Conference Coach of the Year honors to boot. Over the next three seasons he would post a 42-41 overall record before leaving in 1984 to take over as the head coach of the U. S. Military Academy (Army). Wothke would guide the Cadets for eight seasons, garnering Metro Atlantic Athletic Conference Coach of the Year honors in 1985 and finishing his tenure at West Point in 1990 with a modest 92-135 record.

Then, in 1992, Wothke came back to Winona State for a second go-around. This time it would be for keeps. Wothke's objective this time was to "transition the program from NAIA to the NCAA Division II level and to establish a successful, competitive program." He would do just that, and more, leading the Warriors to a 85-79 record from 1992-98. In his second stint in Winona, Wothke produced a 100% graduation rate — something he was very proud of. On the court, his Warriors also snapped a 26-game losing streak to the University of Minnesota-Duluth that had covered 16 years — sweeping the Bulldogs in the process, which was the first time that had happened in 51 years. Wothke finally retired from coaching in 1998, becoming the school's winningest coach along the way with an impressive 183-110 (.625) overall record in 11 seasons. In addition, his NSIC record was even better, at 91-43.

Overall, in his three collegiate head coaching assignments, Wothke compiled a 317-286 (.526) career record over 22 years. The consummate teacher and player's coach, Wothke also gave back to the game he so dearly loved. In fact, he lectured at more than 150 clinics and campus' throughout the nation, and was also the head clinician at foreign clinics in such far away exotic locales as Syria, Turkey and China. Wothke is presently retired and living in Winona.

TRIVIA QUESTION: *Who is the only college basketball coach in the nation to have three of his assistants go on to become head coaches in the Big Ten?*

ANSWER: Les Wothke: Steve Fisher at Michigan (an assistant at Western Michigan), Ricky Byrdsong at Northwestern (an assistant at Western Michigan) and Randy Ayers at Ohio State (an assistant at U.S. Military Academy).

HOW WOULD YOU DESCRIBE YOUR COACHING STYLE? "My teams were very disciplined, but it was an aggressive discipline where we tried to emphasize a very strong man-to-man defense. Then, on offense we were also very aggressive where we always tried to take the ball to the basket. As far as practice went, I just loved it. I was an organization freak. Our practices were detailed to the minute on virtually every practice plan I ever made going back more than 25 years. I was so detailed that I would end drills in the middle of whatever was going on in order to move on to the next drill. I wanted to always follow my plan and make sure that we covered everything that I wanted to cover. I stayed on schedule to the minute. If there was something that we weren't doing well that we had to stop on in the middle of, we would come back to that after the practice was over. That was my style."

HOW DID YOU MOTIVATE YOUR PLAYERS? "Most of it was pride. There was one stretch at Winona State where we won 42 in a row at home and that was special. That was all about pride. We just felt that we were going to outwork people and were going to be totally prepared for every situation. That in itself was a very motivating thing I think. We talked a lot about patience, pride and poise and those were the motivating factors. We always felt that we weren't going to beat ourselves. So, I think the key word was pride, and everything fell into place from there."

ON THE LEAP FROM DIVISION III TO DIVISION I: "When I left Winona State in 1975 I went to the University of Illinois and worked under Lou Hensen. That was a real eye opener. I think the biggest thing was being able to determine and project talent. You know, it was tough to see a high school senior and then project two or three years down the road when he would be able to contribute to your program. Then, the details were just extraordinary. Hensen was just one of those guys who was not going to be outworked and he was just a stickler for the details. At that level it is a 12 month a year job and it requires total dedication to be successful. The scope of all of it was a big change, from the public speaking to the booster groups to the clinics to the golf outings to the alumni functions, it was a total involvement.

IF YOU COULD MAGICALLY GO BACK IN TIME TO THE FIRST YEAR YOU WERE A HEAD COACH AND GIVE YOURSELF SOME ADVICE FOR THE FUTURE, KNOWING WHAT YOU KNOW NOW, BACK THEN, WHAT WOULD YOU SAY TO YOURSELF? "To remember that you win with character. The key to any successful program is recruiting quality people. You have to realize, however, that you can't save the world. What I mean by that is that you simply can't take that person with a questionable work ethic or character, and think that you can change them. You are much further ahead of the game if you can recruit young athletes with those qualities coming in. The other thing is that you have to realize that it is the players who win. It's like the old saying: 'If you ain't got no animals, you ain't got no zoo.' So, sure, coaches play a role, but it is the players who make it happen out on the court."

WHAT WAS THE KEY TO RECRUITING? "The key for me has always been having outstanding assistants. On the division one level they are your eyes and ears, because they are out there seeing the kids. Their ability to judge character and talent is so important. Once the assistants have laid the groundwork and have gotten the players in, it is then your job as the head coach to close the deal and make the sale. I have always encouraged my assistants to help evaluate the talent and make honest suggestions throughout the entire process. Beyond that it is very important to do a lot of research. I remember going into a high school in Chicago with Lou Henson and seeing Lou find the janitors and asking them about the kids. They have a different perspective on the players than the coaches do and it is important to get as much objective feedback about the kids that you can."

HOW DID YOU BUILD TEAM UNITY & CHEMISTRY? "If you are recruiting young men with character, there is a common bond with them immediately — they are already dedicated to their sport. So, as a coach and recruiter, you try to bring in people who are comfortable with one another. I can say this, I never recruited a player who, after his on-campus visit, I didn't meet with my current players to see how he fit it. And we rejected some people as a result. That is where your first loyalty is in your recruiting, to the people that you already have. It is your job to recruit people who fit in with them, both socially, morally, academically and athletically. Another thing is something I learned at the military academy at West Point with Army, and that was the question 'Would you want your teammate to be in a fox hole with you when it got ugly?'. In other words, are they going to cover your back? I also asked my kids if they would want to be their own teammate, meaning would they want to play alongside someone with their own work habits, moral standards, ethics, desires, dedications, and overall willingness to work. In my opinion, that really says a lot about them."

WHAT MOTIVATED YOU? "I loved the competition. The things that I enjoyed most about coaching were recruiting and practice. Recruiting to me was a competition because it allowed me to go in and sell myself, my program and our university to a young man and his family. Then, the coaching and the practice brought it all together and I just loved that aspect of the game."

WHAT IS THE KEY TO GOOD TIME MANAGEMENT? "I think organization and discipline are the keys. I spent more time creating my practice schedules than I did on the actual practice. I wanted to make sure that we were covering everything that needed to be covered and not letting anything slip through the cracks. I wanted to make sure that we remembered to do the sideline-out-of-bounds-drill, or the spread-offense, or the 30-second-drill. So, as a coach you have to be totally disciplined to that and then demand excellence from your players and assistants to achieve success."

WHAT'S THE BIGGEST THING YOU'VE LEARNED FROM COACHING THAT YOU'VE BEEN ABLE TO APPLY TO YOUR EVERYDAY LIFE? "There is an old saying: 'Easy wrong, hard right.' What that means is that it is so easy to make wrong decisions and so difficult to make right decisions. But you have to set standards that you can live with. You need to teach those standards to the young men who play for you and let them know that this is what is expected and these are the reasons why. You just have to have the ability to make that tough right decision when you need to in life. So, I think I have taken that philosophy into my own life and tried to always remember it."

WHAT ARE THE KEY INGREDIENTS TO CREATING A CHAMPIONSHIP TEAM? "You need chemistry at all levels, not just between the players, but also the chemistry that you create as a coach with your players. I always think too that when kids walk out of the locker room, they need to leave their ego at the door. They can pick it up when they come back in, but don't bring it out on the court. True champions put the team first and themselves second. If kids learn that in athletics, then they will be successful in life."

WHAT'S THE SECRET TO YOUR SUCCESS? "I would say having outstanding assistants and the ability to recruit quality people. The other thing that really stands out here in my opinion is honesty. There is no way that you can be successful and not be dedicated to the young men that you are coaching. The rewards all come after they have graduated. That is when you really appreciate the people that you have worked with. To watch them grow in their lives and succeed is so rewarding. You just hope that maybe you played a small part in that."

ON COMING BACK TO WINONA STATE AFTER BEING IN THE BIG-TIME: "You know, when I coached at Profitstown High School in Illinois our biggest rival was Erie. To beat them was the biggest thing in the world at the time. Then, when I coached at Illinois, we beat Michigan State, when they had Magic Johnson. Then, at Army we beat Navy. Now, do you know what? The win at Erie was just as fulfilling as the win at Michigan State or at Navy. You adjust to the level that you are coaching at and you just try to be the very best that you can be at that level. Really, the difference between a really good division one player and a really good division two player is a couple of inches and a half a step. That's it. And believe me, I had a lot of kids at Winona State who were division one quality, but wound up slipping through the cracks."

WHAT WOULD YOU WANT TO SAY TO YOUR FANS, BOOSTERS, AND ALUMNI WHO HAVE SUPPORTED YOU ALL THESE YEARS? "I hope they realize how important their role has been in the success of my programs. Their support and loyalty just can't be measured, so thank you very much. You also get to know a lot of these people as friends and that is special too."

HOW DO YOU WANT YOUR COACHING EPITAPH TO READ — HOW DO YOU WANT TO BE REMEMBERED AS A COACH? "I think the goals for his players were much higher than 10 feet. You know, I was concerned for the young men who played for me. I wanted them to have a great college athletics experience and I really wanted to prepare them for their futures as best I could."

FRED ENKE: UNIVERSITY OF ARIZONA BASKETBALL

Fred Enke was born in Rochester in 1897 and went on to play football for the Gophers from 1918-20. From there, Enke went into coaching football, first at the University of Louisville and later at the University of Arizona. Enke then got into coaching basketball, where, from 1925-1961, he won 497 basketball games at the University of Arizona. In all, he would coach for 38 seasons, posting a career record of 522-344. Enke died in 1985 at the age of 88.

Ken Baumann grew up in Lamberton and graduated from Lamberton High School. From there Baumann attended Bemidji State, where he got his teaching degree. Baumann's first teaching and coaching job was in Mahnomen, near the White Earth Indian Reservation in Northwestern Minnesota, and he would remain there ever since, coaching football and teaching social studies and physical education. Baumann would later serve as the school's athletic director before retiring in 2003. In all Baumann coached at Mahnomen High School for 32 years and when it was all said and done, he had won six championships (1980, 90, 91, 92, 93, 98), the most ever by a high school football coach. With an amazing 287-65-2 career record, Baumann ranks second on the all-time career coaching wins list. In addition, his son was the quarterback on the 1998 state championship team as well. In the world of high school football, Ken Baumann is amongst the best of the very best and is a true Mahnomen legend. Ken is retired and lives with his family in Mahnomen.

HOW WOULD YOU DESCRIBE YOUR COACHING STYLE? "I would say that I was a perfectionist and I expected things to be done properly. I was very simple in my approach over the years and didn't change a lot of things. I think what we did, however, as little as it was, we did pretty well."

HOW DID YOU MOTIVATE YOUR PLAYERS? "Enthusiasm, encouragement and a lot of positives. Sure, I got on them ever now and then, but there were a lot more of the positives than negatives in how I motivated them. I also challenged my kids to be their best. I wanted them to work hard as a team, that is why we were successful."

IF YOU COULD MAGICALLY GO BACK IN TIME TO THE FIRST YEAR YOU WERE A HEAD COACH AND GIVE YOURSELF SOME ADVICE FOR THE FUTURE, KNOWING WHAT YOU KNOW NOW, BACK THEN, WHAT WOULD YOU SAY TO YOURSELF? "We only won one game my first year, so it was a rough start. But I learned to be patient with my kids and I learned how to communicate with them. I also learned then that I had to get to know my kids in order to better understand them. Then I could motivate them and build them up as a team."

HOW DID YOU BUILD TEAM UNITY & CHEMISTRY? "Part of the reason for our success was that we had a staff which was together for a very long period of time. My main assistants were with me for 25-30 years, and that gave our program a lot of continuity. As coaches we knew what each other was going to do before we even did it a lot of times, and that just made coaching a lot easier. Then, I think the kids picked up on that and that rubbed off on them. I think all of my assistants were great motivators too, and they were great with kids. We had something pretty unique for a small school, but that all went into building chemistry with our kids."

WHAT MOTIVATED YOU? "The competition. Obviously the wins are great and you are always trying to win, but I loved the competition. The preparation before the game and then the strategy during the game were all part of it too. The competition was just so exciting and I loved it."

WHAT'S THE BIGGEST THING YOU'VE LEARNED FROM COACHING THAT YOU'VE BEEN ABLE TO APPLY TO YOUR EVERYDAY LIFE? "Keep working at what you are doing and don't quit. I also learned that you have to be yourself because you can't fool your kids."

WHAT ARE THE KEY INGREDIENTS TO CREATING A CHAMPIONSHIP TEAM? "Obviously you have got to have talent. That is first and foremost. I mean let's face it, you can't make chicken salad out of chicken crap! Beyond that it is getting your kids to work together to accept their roles on the team. The teamwork that you develop on your staff is also extremely important. All of those things need to come together in order to have a championship team."

WHAT WOULD YOU WANT TO SAY TO YOUR FANS, BOOSTERS, AND ALUMNI WHO HAVE SUPPORTED YOU ALL THESE YEARS? "We had something very special here and I was very fortunate to be a part of that. We had tremendous community support from our fans and Friday nights were very special to all of them. So, I would say thanks for their support. We gave them something to be very proud of and to be able to say that I helped to put Mahnoman on the map was very rewarding."

HOW DO YOU WANT YOUR COACHING EPITAPH TO READ — HOW DO YOU WANT TO BE REMEMBERED AS A COACH? "As somebody who worked hard at what he was doing and as somebody who gave kids a chance to succeed."

JOE KAPP: CAL FOOTBALL

Joe Kapp led the Minnesota Vikings to their first-ever divisional title and playoff game in 1968 and the following year guided the Vikings to Super Bowl IV against the Kansas City Chiefs. Kapp was a gritty quarterback who played more like a linebacker, and that is why his teammates loved him. After his playing career, Kapp went on to serve as the head coach of the Cal Bears from 1982-86, earning PAC-10 Coach of the Year honors in 1982. Kapp later got into acting and even appeared in several Hollywood movies.

study, constantly evaluate and constantly assess yourself and find out what works and what doesn't and why."

FAVORITE LOCKER ROOM SIGN? "We always ridiculed the teams that were 'Rah-Rah!' and did the Knute Rockne yelling and screaming stuff during their warm-ups and from the sidelines. That kind of false bravado didn't appeal to me so we never did any of that. In fact, we just laughed at those who did."

WHAT'S THE BIGGEST THING YOU'VE LEARNED FROM COACHING THAT YOU'VE BEEN ABLE TO APPLY TO YOUR EVERYDAY LIFE? "Planning and executing a plan and then evaluating it afterwards. It is all very structured and all very businesslike to me. There is not a lot of emotion involved with hysteria and frenzy for me. It is cold and analytical. You can apply a lot of things that you learn both as a coach and as a player to future situations in your life. I can also look back at a lot of big decisions that I have made in my life and know that they were made because of skills I learned as a player and coach."

WHAT ARE THE KEY INGREDIENTS TO CREATING A CHAMPIONSHIP TEAM? "You have to have serene, self-confident players who are strong in the fundamentals and physically very fit. I think psychologically that serenity is the key. They also have to be self confident, know what their task is, know what they are supposed to do, they know how to do it, and then get it done. Some can and some can't. So, when you face a team that does what they are supposed to do better than your kids are supposed to be doing it, then you are going to lose. But, if your kids are self confident, knowledgeable about what their task is and know how to do it, then you have every chance to win."

WHAT'S THE SECRET TO YOUR SUCCESS? "Hard work, preparation, studying, not leaving anything to chance and lots, and lots and lots of luck! Any coach who doesn't tell you that luck enters into it is crazy."

WHAT WOULD YOU WANT TO SAY TO YOUR FANS, BOOSTERS, AND ALUMNI WHO HAVE SUPPORTED YOU ALL THESE YEARS? "I would want to thank them for their efforts, their support and for their understanding. They have taken the thorns with the roses and we appreciate that. I am just very lucky to be a part of such a great tradition at St. Thomas. There have been so many great coaches that have come out of the Catholic schools and I am honored to be just be a part of that. Aside from Tom Feely at St. Thomas Academy, there was Dick Rinehart, who was a coaching legend in basketball and football at De La Salle, Tom Warner was a football and baseball legend at Cretin, Joe Mayer was a football legend at Rochester Lourdes, John Nett was a basketball legend at Winona Cotter, and that is just to name a few. Before the schools all combined, there was a wonderfully rich history in the Catholic and private leagues. A lot of those schools were much, much better than the public schools. It was a different time, but it was great to be a part of all that."

HOW DO YOU WANT YOUR COACHING EPITAPH TO READ — HOW DO YOU WANT TO BE REMEMBERED AS A COACH? "That I was honest and that I was fair. That was the most important thing."

TED COX: TULANE & OKLAHOMA STATE FOOTBALL

Ted Cox, a former Gopher from 1922-24, went on to coach at the University of Wisconsin River Falls, where he posted a record of 11-1-1 from 1926-27. He then went 26-10 at Tulane from 1932-35, followed by a 7-23 mark at Oklahoma State University from 1936-38.

JAKE CHRISTIANSEN: CONCORDIA FOOTBALL

Jake Christiansen grew up in Northfield and went on to become a five-sport star at St. Olaf. After earning his master's degree in education from North Dakota State University, Christiansen got into teaching and coaching. His first job was at Deer River High School. From there he became assistant coach at Flint, Mich., and in 1929 he was named head football coach at Valparaiso University in Indiana. In each case he transformed losing teams into winners. At Valparaiso, Christiansen would spend 11 years teaching and coaching football. In 1941 Christiansen came to Concordia and made history. From 1941 until his retirement in 1969, Christiansen won 145 games and lost only 66. Jake wasted little time in making a name for himself at Concordia, leading his Cobbers to an undefeated season in 1942, just his second year on staff. One of the highlights of his tenure came in 1964, when his squad won an NAIA national championship. After winning the conference crown that year, the Cobbers represented the MIAC in the ninth annual Small College Playoffs (NAIA) by defeating Linfield, Ore., 28-6, in the semifinals and tying Sam Houston of Texas 7-7 in the NAIA title game to earn NAIA co-champion honors. For his efforts, Jake was named NAIA Coach of the Year.

In all, Christiansen would finish his illustrious football coaching career with a 197-112-12 overall record. When he retired in 1969, his 197 wins made him the winningest active collegiate football coach in the nation at the time. His 28-year history with the Cobbers had only one losing season. As those who played for him have said, though, "You never lose when you play for Jake." Additionally, for 20 years his coaching clinics attracted the biggest names in athletics to the campus. Christiansen also served as the school's Athletic Director and even coached basketball at Concordia, earning a career record of 223-233 on the hardwood as well. Jake retired in 1969 and died in 1992 at the age of 92. An outstanding teacher and coach, Jake "The Sly Fox" Christiansen was a true Concordia legend. Concordia's football stadium was later renamed in his honor. Jake and his wife Bertha had six children: Karl, Winifield, Sonja, Elsa, Judith and Susan.

JERRY BURNS
PRO FOOTBALL: MINNESOTA VIKINGS

Jerry Burns grew up loving sports and went on to graduate from the University of Michigan, where he was a quarterback on the 1950 Rose Bowl team. Burns began his coaching career in 1951 as an assistant at the University of Hawaii. His first big coaching break came in 1961, when he took over as the head coach at the University of Iowa. In 1965 Burns left Iowa to get into the NFL. His first gig was with the Green Bay Packers, where, as an assistant, he coached in Super Bowls I and II.

In 1968 Burns came to Minnesota, where he was hired by Bud Grant to serve as his offensive coordinator. Burnsie would finish out the rest of his professional career in Minnesota, making a lot of history over the next 28 years along the way. From 1968-85 Burns played a huge role in guiding the Vikings to four Super Bowl berths and 11 Central Division titles. Burns was also very instrumental in developing what is now known as the "West Coast Offense," which he implemented into his single-back style offense in order to take advantage of Running Back Chuck Foreman's amazing running and pass catching abilities. A real innovator, Burns would change the face of the game over his illustrious coaching career.

On January 7, 1986, the longtime assistant finally got his big break when he was named as the head coach of the Vikings. He would replace a legend in Bud Grant, but was up to the challenge. Burns would serve as the team's head coach for the next six seasons, going 52-43 along the way. In addition to winning one NFC Conference title in 1989, Burns led the purple to the playoffs on three different occasions. The first came in 1987, when, after beating New Orleans and San Francisco, the Vikes lost a heart-breaker to the Redskins, 17-10, in the NFC Championship Game. With just seconds left on the clock, Minnesota was trailing 17-10 and were fourth-and-goal from the three yard line. Quarterback Wade Wilson then dropped back to pass, looked right and then threw left to a wide open Anthony Carter. But Running Back Darrin Nelson, who thought the ball was for him, dove in front of Carter at the goal line and had the ball bounce off his hands to the horror of the Minnesota fans back home. The Vikes were done.

The next two playoff appearances came against the 49ers in both 1988 and 1989, when the Vikes lost in the second and first rounds, respectively. In the latter, Quarterback Steve Young, replacing an injured Joe Montana, somehow scrambled like a chicken with his head cut off around 10 would-be Viking tacklers to score an unbelievable 45-yard touchdown run to clinch the game. It was a painful ending to an outstanding season. Overall, Burns' career playoff coaching record was a modest 3-3, but each time his teams got knocked off, it was to the eventual Super Bowl champion.

Burnsie was a player's coach to the core, and that is why his players loved him. His hard-nosed style and no-nonsense approach was contagious and his players would run through a wall for him. They knew that he would go to bat for them, no matter what, and that gave him a lot of credibility. Long known for his now infamous foul-mouthed language, Burnsie wasn't afraid to get out there and mix it up either. He also assembled a tremendous coaching staff which included the likes of then-newcomers Pete Carroll, Marc Trestman and Tom Batta, as well veterans Bob Schnelker and Floyd Peters.

Burns retired at the end of the 1991 season, leaving the game he loved on his own terms. He presently lives in Eden Prairie where he is enjoying his retirement and playing plenty of golf.

HOW WOULD YOU DESCRIBE YOUR COACHING STYLE? "I really just tried to be my own man and do things the way I saw them. I worked under Forest Evashevski at Iowa and Vince Lombardi at Green Bay, both were tough, demanding, vocal coaches and that rubbed off on me. Then, I worked with Bud (Grant), who was more quiet and passive, and also with George Allen, at Whittier College, and he was just an agitated and excited type of a guy who was so hard working. So, I learned a lot of different things from some great coaches, but I just tried to be my own guy and that worked for me. Anytime you try to personify somebody else there is a phony element that shows through and it is soon recognized by your players. So, I was always aware of that."

HOW DID YOU MOTIVATE YOUR PLAYERS? "I tried to have fun with my guys, but they also knew that I expected them to work very hard. I tried to respect my players and I think my players respected me in return."

IF YOU COULD MAGICALLY GO BACK IN TIME TO THE FIRST YEAR YOU WERE A HEAD COACH AND GIVE YOURSELF SOME ADVICE FOR THE FUTURE, KNOWING WHAT YOU KNOW NOW, BACK THEN, WHAT WOULD YOU SAY TO YOURSELF? "You can't not recognize the importance of organization. You just have to know where you are going so that your assistants know where they are going, and then your players will know where they are going. You can't confuse them or confuse issues. You also can't one day stress the importance of a certain factor of the game and then maybe a week later minimize the importance of that as you parallel it to something else you are trying to do. So, successful coaches have good organizational ability."

WHAT ARE THE CHARACTERISTICS OF LEADERS? "The number one thing in my opinion is intelligence. Everybody just thinks it is ability but leaders have to be smart. They also has to have desire, have a determination to succeed, have to be able to get along with their teammates and coaches, and be good overall team players."

HOW DID YOU BUILD TEAM UNITY & CHEMISTRY? "Sometimes it is just there and you don't have to create it. Sometimes the players themselves come together as a team and you can just feel it. Other times you can recognize the divisiveness that surrounds your team and when you see that there is some separation between the offense or defense or between players, you try to meld them together by talking to them. You tell them that they are a team and that they have to learn to play together. You have to get them to recognize their strengths and weaknesses and then get them to work with each other. You also have to reinforce what each players' responsibility and role is within the team. Chemistry is really an up and down thing that goes throughout the season. Obviously, anytime you are winning it is a hell of a lot easier to keep your team unity together than when you are losing."

WHAT ADVICE WOULD YOU HAVE FOR YOUNG COACHES STARTING OUT TODAY? "The number one thing in my opinion is organization. They have to be organized. Beyond that they have to have thick skin and not be too concerned about the criticism that will come. If they believe in what they are doing, then they should stay with it and work hard. It is a tough job, but rewarding."

WHAT'S THE BIGGEST THING YOU'VE LEARNED FROM COACHING THAT YOU'VE BEEN ABLE TO APPLY TO YOUR EVERYDAY LIFE? "Getting along with people and just understanding that another guy's opinion is just as important to him as yours is to you. And, that his opinion might not necessarily be right, or that yours might not necessarily be right either, but that you have to work together and compromise."

WHAT'S THE SECRET TO YOUR SUCCESS? "Hard work. There are no shortcuts."

WHAT WOULD YOU WANT TO SAY TO YOUR FANS, BOOSTERS, AND ALUMNI WHO HAVE SUPPORTED YOU ALL THESE YEARS? "I would want to thank them and tell them that I appreciate their support. I enjoyed being a coach and couldn't have had the success I did without them. Their support was very instrumental in any success that I may or may not have had and I appreciate that.

HOW DO YOU WANT YOUR COACHING EPITAPH TO READ — HOW DO YOU WANT TO BE REMEMBERED AS A COACH? "Everybody is important to the success of your team, and I hope that I was able to treat the little guy with the same respect as I treated the big guy."

PAT BOLAND: NFL's CHICAGO CARDINALS

Pat Boland was born in Duluth in 1906 and went on to play football at the University of Minnesota from 1930-31. He would later go on to play pro football and even wound up coaching in the NFL with Chicago in 1946, where his career coaching record would stand at a modest 2-3-1. Boland died in 1971 in Duluth.

ED ROGERS: ST. THOMAS FOOTBALL

Ed Rogers was a Native American of Chippewa descent who was from Walker, Minn. Rogers played six years of football at the Carlisle School, where he was also the team captain. From there, Rogers came to the University of Minnesota, where he played End from 1902-03. After his playing days, Rogers coached at St. Thomas University and then at Carlisle. He was later enshrined into the football Hall of Fame.

DENNIS GREEN: VIKINGS FOOTBALL

Dennis Green was born in Harrisburg, Pa., the youngest of five brothers, and went on to earn all-state honors as a running back at John Harris High School. Green also served as class president in high school. Green then went on to play as a flanker and running back at the University of Iowa, where, in 1968, he posted one of the best rushing days in school history with 175 yards and two touchdowns against Texas Christian. Green, who graduated with a degree in recreation education, earned honorable mention All-Big Ten honors in 1969 and 1970. Following his collegiate career, Green went on to briefly play defensive back for British Columbia of the Canadian Football League in 1971.

From there Green got into coaching. In 1972 Green began his coaching career as a graduate assistant at Iowa. He then spent a season as running backs/receivers coach at Dayton before returning to handle the same role at Iowa from 1974-76. In 1977, Green moved on to oversee the running backs at Stanford. After serving for seven seasons as a collegiate assistant, Green's first NFL coaching stint came in San Francisco as wide receivers/special teams coach in 1979. He then returned to Stanford as offensive coordinator in 1980, when Cardinal quarterback John Elway set a PAC 10 record for touchdown passes in a season with 27.

Green's first head coaching opportunity came at Northwestern University from 1981-85, when he was named Big Ten Coach of the Year. Green's next stop would be back at San Francisco, where he served as an assistant with the 49ers. Then, in 1989, Green got a big break when he was named as the head coach at the University of Stanford. Green would spend the next three seasons reviving Stanford's football program. In 1988, the season before his arrival, the Cardinal posted a 3-6-2 record. In 1990 Stanford upset then No. 1 ranked Notre Dame in South Bend. During Green's final season at Stanford in 1991, he led the Cardinal to the school's longest winning streak (7) since 1951; their most PAC 10 victories (6) since 1970; and their first bowl appearance since 1986 — where they barely lost to Georgia Tech in the Aloha Bowl.

On January 10, 1992, Green was named as the head coach of the Minnesota Vikings. He would stay in the Twin Cities for 10 seasons, ultimately leaving the franchise in 2002 with a career record of 101-70 (.591). Green would lead the Purple to four Central Division titles and two NFC Championship games in 1998 and 2000. In addition, Green's Vikings made the playoffs in eight out of Green's 10 seasons and the 1998 club set the NFL single-season scoring record at 556 points, averaging 34.8 points per game.

Upon his departure from the Vikings in 2002, Green embarked on a very successful business career. In addition to serving as a television and radio football analyst, Green also formed a relationship to host PAX TV's "FLW Outdoors," a TV show which features his analysis of fishing competitions. Green is also the first African-American to own a NASCAR Winston Cup Team, Denny Green Racing, LLC., through a partnership with Galaxy Motorsports.

Among Green's many coaching honors and accolades, he was named NFL Coach of the Year in 1992 by the Washington Touchdown Club and in 1998 by Sports Illustrated and the Maxwell Club. Green was also selected Community Coach of the Year by the World Sport Humanitarian Hall of Fame in 2001. In 1993, Green received Pop Warner's Golden Football Award for his distinguished record of service to youth, community, country and humanity. A strong advocate of community involvement, Green initiated "Community Tuesdays," which had players active in the Twin Cities on their day off, a concept that spread to the entire National Football League. Green was also involved with the Minneapolis Boys & Girls Clubs Outdoor Programs, as well as the "Meals on Wheels" program, delivering meals to senior citizens. Additionally, Green started the "Bus Green Music Team" in his late father's name to provide music education and instruments to inner-city youth. Dennis and his wife Marie presently reside in San Diego and have two children. Dennis also has two adult children from a previous marriage. Will he get back into coaching in the future? Only time will tell, but don't count him out — he's a winner.

JIM CHRISTOPHERSON
COLLEGE FOOTBALL: CONCORDIA UNIVERSITY

Jim Christopherson grew up loving sports in tiny Henning and went on to play football under legendary coach Jake Christiansen at Concordia from 1957-60. In 1959 Christopherson was named captain of the Cobbers and went on to earn MIAC Most Valuable Player honors that season as well. After graduating in 1960, Christopherson played professional football for the Minnesota Vikings for two seasons, even leading them in scoring in 1962 as a tight end. Christopherson would then go on to play one more year of pro ball for Toronto in the Canadian Football League before hanging it up in 1964.

From there, Christopherson came back to Concordia, where he served as an assistant under Christiansen for six years. Then, in 1969, Christopherson got his big break, succeeding Christiansen as the team's new head coach. Christopherson wasted little time in making a name for himself too, leading his Cobbers to a national runner-up finish in his first season. That would be the beginning of an illustrious 32-year career which would include two National Championships, 11 MIAC titles, seven postseason appearances and an overall career coaching record of 218-101-7. The national titles came in 1978, when the Cobbers defeated Findlay College (Ohio), 7-0, and in 1981, when they shared the title with Austin College (Texas). During a span from 1976 until 1990 the Cobbers finished in the top two in the conference 13 out of 15 times, and won four straight from 1978-81. In addition, Concordia also produced 17 All-American players and 121 All-MIAC athletes under Christopherson's tutelage.

At the time of his retirement Coach Christopherson, who only had four losing seasons in his tenure, was ranked third in wins among active NCAA Division III coaches. He was also 5th in winning percentage (70%) among active Division III coaches with more than 15 years of experience and 16th in winning percentage among all active Division III coaches.

Among Christopherson's many coaching accolades, he was named MIAC Coach of the Year six times and in 1981 he was named as the NAIA National Coach of the Year. In 1995 Christopherson was inducted into the Minnesota Coaches Hall of Fame. He is also a past president of the NAIA Football Coaches Association. Christopherson retired on Dec. 31, 2000, to spend more time with his family. Jim and his wife Sandy presently reside in Moorhead.

HOW WOULD YOU DESCRIBE YOUR COACHING STYLE? "Obviously, we prepared and worked hard all week so that when we showed up on Saturdays we were ready to go. I guess I took the position that if I was going to coach as a career and last for 32 years that I was not going to burn myself out. I was going to enjoy it, and I delegated a lot of responsibility to my assistant coaches, who were just outstanding. Our goal was always to just be in contention for the conference championship during the last two weeks of the season. We knew that if we stayed close to the pack then we always had a shot. We were either first or second in the MIAC 18 out of the 32 years I was the head coach, so that strategy worked out pretty well. You know you borrow ideas here and there from other coaches along the way and you just try to always get better. No matter how old you are, you are never done learning in the game of football."

HOW DID YOU MOTIVATE YOUR PLAYERS? "I would say I was pretty low-key. I was not a yeller, I just tried to prepare my players and then turn it over to them come game time."

WHO WERE YOUR COACHING MENTORS? "I played for Jake Christiansen, who was a coaching legend for nearly 30 years here at Concordia. I also served as an assistant under him for six years and we won a national championship together in 1964. Then, when he retired in 1968, I took over. So, he was a real mentor to me and really influenced my coaching philosophy. I also learned a great deal from Harry Gilmer, who was the defensive coordinator for the Vikings when I played for them back in the early 1960s."

IF YOU COULD MAGICALLY GO BACK IN TIME TO THE FIRST YEAR YOU WERE A HEAD COACH AND GIVE YOURSELF SOME ADVICE FOR THE FUTURE, KNOWING WHAT YOU KNOW NOW, BACK THEN, WHAT WOULD YOU SAY TO YOURSELF? "I guess I would've smelled the roses a little more as I went along, but overall I don't think I would've changed too much. Sure, I was pretty intense my first 10 or 15 years, so maybe I would've delegated a little more responsibility too. I have been asked a lot throughout the years why I didn't want to try my luck at the division one level or even in the pros, and I guess I was always happy at Concordia. I didn't want to move around a lot and I really enjoyed the stability of being in a good community with my family, that was very important to me."

WHAT ARE THE CHARACTERISTICS OF WINNERS? "Certain coaches are just winners. They have the philosophy, the intensity and can just communicate their message. They can come in and turn an entire program around in no time and that is incredible. I mean wherever Herb Brooks went he won. If John Gagliardi had gone on to coach in division one he would've been a winner. Look at guys like Jim Tressel (Ohio State) or Lou Holtz (University of South Carolina), they are winners wherever they go."

LOOKING BACK WHAT ARE YOU MOST PROUD OF IN YOUR CAREER? "You know, if you looked purely at wins and losses I am satisfied, I was one of only 35 or so coaches have ever won more than 200 games in college football. I was proud to be in a conference like the MIAC too, where you get such good kids and we have around a 98% graduation rate. That doesn't happen at the division one level. I guess if I had to pick a couple of certain things that I was proud of, it would be our two NAIA national championships in 1978 and 1981. We were able to do that with two entirely different teams and that was special as a coach. To rebuild like that was very satisfying."

HOW DID YOU BUILD TEAM UNITY & CHEMISTRY? "First of all you have to recruit good, quality players. I have always said that we won championships with people and not with players. You recruit guys that love the game of football and the rest takes care of itself. We just tried to make the game as much fun as possible for our players. If that meant taking a day off here or there to recover, or what have you, then that really helped. We tried to celebrate game day on those 10 Saturdays during the Fall because that was what we were preparing and practicing so hard for all season."

WHAT MOTIVATED YOU? "The challenge was what motivated me. To mold them from the start of training camp into the post-season was what it was all about for me. Every Summer around August

I would get the football itch and by the 10th of August I would pull the dock out and get ready for the season. I just loved it and loved teaching those kids from start to finish. To have that opportunity, to work with those young men and help to make something out of them, was very special."

WHAT ADVICE WOULD YOU HAVE FOR YOUNG COACHES STARTING OUT TODAY? "To be patient and just hang in there. Also, be sure to delegate a lot of responsibility to your coaching staff and then you can enjoy the game a little bit more."

FAVORITE LOCKER ROOM SIGN? "Learn from your defeats but cherish your victories," and "Things are never as bad as they seem…Things are never as good as they seem… Reality is somewhere in between."

WHAT ARE THE KEY INGREDIENTS TO CREATING A CHAMPIONSHIP TEAM? "You have to have talented players, but you also have to have quality, high achieving men who are very motivated. You know a coach can motivate a player to a certain extent, but sometimes young men just need to be told what to do in order to be successful. That's what a coach does. Show a young man how he can succeed and he will take it and run with it. That is the key, not to stand up in front of a group and preach to them, but to take individual players and tell them how they can be better. Once you integrate all of those individuals into a team, then you've got something."

WHAT'S THE SECRET TO YOUR SUCCESS? "Passion. I wanted to recruit players that had a love for the game because that was what I had. I have always said this is the greatest game ever

DEWEY SCANLON: NFL's CHICAGO CARDINALS

Dewey Scanlon was a native of West Duluth. After graduating from Valparaiso University, Scanlon went on to coach the NFL's Duluth Kelly's and Eskimos from 1924-26, and then the Chicago Cardinals in 1929. His overall coaching record was 17-15-4.

invented and I just love it. It was the time of the year when it is just great to be outside — it was cooling off and the leaves were turning, and that was just football season. Period. I spent 50 consecutive years, from the time I was a seventh grader until I the time I retired, in the game of football. That is a lifetime of football and I never lost my passion for the game. I still love it as much now than when I was playing eight-man football in high school. Passion was the secret to my success."

WHAT WOULD YOU WANT TO SAY TO YOUR FANS, BOOSTERS, AND ALUMNI WHO HAVE SUPPORTED YOU ALL THESE YEARS? "They were all a part of the team and we appreciated their support. Concordia Cobber football, even though it is a small-time division three program, is a very valuable part of the constituency of this college."

HOW DO YOU WANT YOUR COACHING EPITAPH TO READ — HOW DO YOU WANT TO BE REMEMBERED AS A COACH? "I had a passion to see my players succeed, my teams succeed and to enjoy all of the relationships that the great game of football has given to me."

SID GILLMAN: NFL FOOTBALL

Sid Gillman was a legend in the world of football. Recognized as one of the game's great innovators, Gillman reshaped the landscape of the game as one of the most forward thinking coaches in gridiron history. Gillman was born in Minneapolis in 1911 and went on to graduate from Minneapolis North High School in 1931. From there, Gillman would go on to star as an end at Ohio State University, where he was chosen to play in the first ever College All-Star game in 1934. From there, Gillman went on to play for the NFL's Cleveland Rams in 1936, but hang it up a short time later to get into coaching. After serving as an assistant, Gillman was named head coach at Miami University, Ohio, in 1944 and compiled a 31-6-1 record in four seasons. He then spent a year as an assistant at Army, before taking over as the head coach at the University of Cincinnati in 1949. Cincinnati won three Mid-American Conference titles and two bowl games under Gillman, posting a 50-13-1 record along the way. However, the school was put on probation for recruiting violations in 1955, and with that, Gillman moved on to take over as the head coach of the NFL's Los Angeles Rams.

Under Gillman, the Rams won the Western Conference crown in his first season, losing to the Cleveland Browns, 38-14, in the league championship game. Gillman then became the first coach of the Los Angeles Chargers in the new American Football League in 1960. The Chargers, who moved to San Diego in 1961, won five Western Conference championships in six years and beat the Boston Patriots 51-10 for the 1963 AFL title. Ulcers ultimately forced Gillman to leave coaching in 1969, but he would return for the 1971 campaign. Then, in 1973, he took over as the general manager of the Houston Oilers. He would replace Bill Peterson as the team's coach midway through the season, however, and was named American Football Conference coach of the year in 1974 after leading the team to a 7-7 record. Gillman would retire that following season with an overall professional record of 123-104-7. (His college record at Miami and Cincinnati was a combined 81-19-2.)

As a coach, Gillman truly changed the game. A strong proponent of the passing game, Gillman designed pass patterns that almost always featured five receivers, with at least one of them going deep. He loved the deep threat because it stretched defenses, making it easier to complete short passes or to run the ball. Gillman is really the original mastermind behind what is now known as the "West Coast Offense." Gillman is also considered the first coach to study film of his opponents. (Maybe this is because his father owned several movie theaters back in Minneapolis, where he watched countless silent movies as a kid!) Gillman would have film developed, splice it together and then run it through the projector to evaluate his opponents. Fifty years ago this was revolutionary. Squinting through his projector, Gillman scrutinized the movies until he could anticipate their mistakes and manipulate their vulnerabilities. Gillman insisted the cameras roll at every practice and he even graded his players based on their development. He loved to watch and break down film, and that, more than anything, may be his lasting legacy.

Innovative and dynamic, Sid Gillman was a winner. The" professor," as he was affectionately known, Gillman is also one of the only coaches ever to be enshrined into both College and Pro Football Halls of Fame. Gillman died on January 3, 2003, at the age of 91. Sid and his wife Esther had four children.

MIKE DALY
COLLEGE FOOTBALL: SOUTH DAKOTA STATE UNIVERSITY

Mike Daly grew up in Fairmont and played quarterback and safety under legendary football coach Tom Mahoney. Daly went on to play college football at Augustana under future Gopher Coach Jim Wacker. Daly graduated from Augustana in 1971 and then served as a student assistant coach at Auggie for a year. Daly then went on to the University of Minnesota to serve as a graduate assistant under Cal Stoll. Daly got his masters degree at the U of M and then headed back to Augustana for two more years serve as an assistant. From there, Daly went to South Dakota State, where he served as the defensive coordinator for four years. Daly then became the defensive coordinator at North Dakota State, where he would serve for five years. NDSU won a national championship in 1983 and finished second in 1984 under his tutelage. Daly then went to Idaho State and served as a coordinator for one year, followed by a two year stint at Tulsa as a defensive coordinator. From there, Daly became the defensive coordinator at the University of Wisconsin, where he would spend the next three years working for the Badgers.

Daly then spent a season in the Canadian Football League, coaching the special teams units for the Saskatchewan Roughriders. From there, Daly headed to Western Michigan to serve as an assistant for one year. (There, he would coach alongside fellow Fairmont native Jerry Rosburg, now the Cleveland Browns Special Teams coach.) Daly then finished his illustrious coaching career at South Dakota State, where he served as the head coach from 1991-1996. That next year he retired and said good bye to the game he loved. He wanted to coach his 13 year-old son at the youth level and had simply had enough. Mike and his family presently reside in Sioux Falls, S.D., where he has a very successful career in the financial services industry with American Express.

HOW WOULD YOU DESCRIBE YOUR COACHING STYLE? "I was pretty firm with people and expected a lot in return. I certainly wasn't their buddy but I felt that I was fair and was always there for my players. I had a low tolerance for mistakes and a high regard for those who did things right both on and off the field."

HOW DID YOU MOTIVATE YOUR PLAYERS? "In general, it was through a disciplined practice setting. I tried to create motivation through a rewards system. If they practiced well, good things were going to happen, and if they practice poorly, then they were not going to see Saturdays. That was tough but it seemed to work."

WHO WERE YOUR COACHING MENTORS? "Certainly my high school football coach Tom Mahoney would be right up there. He was a great person and a great coach. I just learned a great deal from him."

IF YOU COULD MAGICALLY GO BACK IN TIME TO THE FIRST YEAR YOU WERE A HEAD COACH AND GIVE YOURSELF SOME ADVICE FOR THE FUTURE, KNOWING WHAT YOU KNOW NOW, BACK THEN, WHAT WOULD YOU SAY TO YOURSELF? "I wish I would have been a little bit more understanding of kids' weaknesses. I sometimes think I expected too much and wasn't able to totally put up with kids that didn't meet my expectations. I just think I could've been a little bit more laid back, at times I was probably too tough on people."

HOW DID YOU BUILD TEAM UNITY & CHEMISTRY? "I tried to create chemistry by making sure that everybody understood and respected the fact that everybody had a role on the team. And no matter what the role was, it was important and it mattered. I emphasized to them that we were only as good as how well each person played that role."

WHAT ADVICE WOULD YOU HAVE FOR YOUNG COACHES STARTING OUT TODAY? "Hang on! Kids are the same today than they were when I got into the business. They all want to succeed and they all want to make the most of their abilities. So, it is our job as coaches to help them make it. We just need to find each kids' hot button and push it regarding whatever it is that makes them tick. That is the key. The cookie-cutter approach doesn't work, you have to identify each kids' button and motivate him individually."

FAVORITE LOCKER ROOM SIGN: "Play like a champion today."

WHAT'S THE BIGGEST THING YOU'VE LEARNED FROM COACHING THAT YOU'VE BEEN ABLE TO APPLY TO YOUR EVERYDAY LIFE? "It was obvious as soon as I left coaching and got into the financial services industry that I could see my leadership, strategic and organizational abilities come to life."

HOW DO YOU WANT YOUR COACHING EPITAPH TO READ — HOW DO YOU WANT TO BE REMEMBERED AS A COACH? "I tried to surround myself with good people and I tried to help my players be the best they could be."

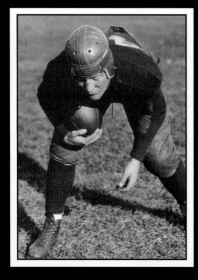

HERB JOESTING: NFL's MINNEAPOLIS REDJACKETS

Herb Joesting, who became known as the "Owatonna Thunderbolt" as an All-American running back at the University of Minnesota from 1925-27. Joesting ;ater served as the player/coach of the 1929 Minneapolis Redjackets, one of Minnesota's early NFL teams.

BERNIE BIERMAN: GOPHER FOOTBALL

Born in 1894 to German parents on a farm near Springfield, Minn., Bernie Bierman's boyhood home was in Litchfield. As a youngster, Bierman had to overcome a bone infection in his leg that kept him bed-ridden and on crutches. But, after going through several operations to correct the problem, he quickly emerged as a prep star in football, baseball, basketball and track at Litchfield High School. *(His family later moved to Detroit Lakes, and as evidence of his stature as a local legend, all three communities: Springfield, Litchfield and Detroit Lakes have claimed him as their own home-town hero!)*

From there, Bierman decided to follow in his big brother Alfred's footsteps and play football at the University of Minnesota. There, as an All-Conference halfback, Bernie captained the undefeated 1915 Big Ten title team. Bierman was a three-sport letterman at the U of M, also starring on the basketball team and running track as well. After graduating, Bierman went on to become a successful high school coach in Billings, Montana, before going off to fight in World War I as a Captain in the Marines. "The Marine Corps taught me discipline, organization and to love life," Bierman would later say. Returning from the Service in 1919, Bierman took over as the head coach at Montana University, where he remained until 1922. Bierman left coaching after that season to work for a Minneapolis bond house, but came back that next year to become an assistant under former Gopher teammate, Clark Shaughnessy, at Tulane University. After a couple of seasons in New Orleans, Bierman took over as the head coach at Mississippi A&M. Two years later, he returned to serve as the head coach of Tulane. He guided the Green Wave from 1927-32, posting a 39-10-1 record and even leading the squad to a 1931 Rose Bowl appearance.

In 1932 Bierman came home to be named as the head coach the University of Minnesota, where he became a living legend. Known as the "Grey Eagle," for his prematurely gray hair, Bierman could flat-out coach. He could also recruit, which he did like no other in the program's history. His rosters were loaded with big Minnesota farm kids and leather-tough kids from the neighborhoods of Minneapolis and St. Paul. Bierman trained them mercilessly, sometimes six days a week, for as long as he felt necessary. His boys were going to be in shape come game day. Period.

During Bierman's first 10 years as Minnesota's head coach (1932-41), better known as the "Golden Era," the Gophers not only won seven Big Ten titles, they also won five national championships as well (1934, 1935, 1936, 1940 and 1941). During one amazing span, the Maroon and Gold went three straight seasons and half way through a fourth without a defeat, and lost just eight conference games during the entire Golden Era. With five undefeated teams in all, there was no other team in the country that could match Minnesota's dominance in that 10-year span. Under Bernie, Minnesota ruled the college football world, much like Miami and Florida State do today.

"Bernie was a task master and you had to survive to play for him," said former player Bud Grant. "You were tested all the time and the people who survived, played. It was like the Marines. A lot of people went by the wayside. If you could survive the practices and scrimmages and not get hurt, then you could play. Bernie was from a different era of football back then."

Bierman's players were schooled in practice and on timing to such a degree that Bierman would inspect their footsteps in the grass to see if they went where they were supposed to go as blockers, tacklers or runners. They also got a good dose of Bierman's philosophy, whether they wanted it or not: "There's only one thing worse than going into a game convinced you can't win," said Bierman. "That's going into a game convinced you can't lose."

In 1942, Bierman rejoined the military for a three-year stint to serve in W.W.II. He returned to coaching in 1945 but never adapted to two-platoon football which had become the norm following the war. He would coach the Gophers for six more seasons before finally retiring from coaching in 1950. With a 93-35-6 coaching record at Minnesota, Bernie was without question the greatest college football coach in Gopher history. He would ultimately retire with a 146-62-13 career record in his 25 years of coaching. A recipient of numerous Coach of the Year awards, he was later inducted into the College Football Hall of Fame.

Asked about the secret to his success, the Gray Eagle said this: "There's nothing secret about blocking, tackling and hard charging. That's fundamental. Given a reasonable share of material that has speed, brains, some brawn and a burning desire to give — and school it as thoroughly as possible in these fundamentals — then, with a few good breaks, you're bound to win once in a while."

Upon his retirement, Bierman spent some time as a color commentator on Gopher radio broadcasts. Bernie later moved to California, where, in 1977, he died at the age of 82.

BOB OTTO:
MINNESOTA STATE MANKATO FOOTBALL

Bob Otto grew up in Fort Dodge, Iowa, and went on to star a member of the famous "Iron Men" football teams at the University of Iowa from 1939-41. After serving in the armed services, Otto came home to graduate from Iowa in 1947, also earning a master's degree from Iowa in 1948. Following graduation he served as the athletic director and head football coach at Buena Vista College from 1948-53. That next year he came to Minnesota State Mankato, where he would become a football coaching legend. Otto would served MSU for 30 years, coaching Maverick football teams from 1953 until 1969. Otto's teams built a 74-70-4 record during that time, captured five Northern Intercollegiate Conference titles (1958, '59, '60, '61 and '68) and placed in the league's first division every season. Otto also served as the school's men's basketball coach for one season, leading the 1955 team to an 18-4 mark. Otto was named MSU's Men's Athletic Director in 1970 and served in that capacity until his retirement in 1983. Otto later went on to become enshrined into the MSU, the Northern Intercollegiate Conference and North Central Conference Halls of Fame. In addition, MSU's Highland Arena was renamed as Otto Arena in his honor in 1991.

TONY DUNGY
PRO FOOTBALL: MINNESOTA VIKINGS

Tony Dungy was born in Jackson, Mich., and went on to graduate from Parkside High School in Jackson. From there, Dungy went on to play football and basketball at the University of Minnesota. On the gridiron, Dungy quarterbacked the Golden Gophers from 1973-76, finishing as the school's career leader in pass attempts (576), completions (274), passing yards (3,577) and touchdown passes (25). In addition, Dungy rushed 413 times for 1,345 yards and 16 touchdowns, earning the team's MVP Award two times. As a senior, Dungy played in the East-West Shrine Game, the Hula Bowl and the Japan Bowl and upon completion of his career, he ranked fourth in Big Ten history in total offense behind Mike Phipps, Archie Griffin and Bob Griese. On the hardwood, Dungy played only during his freshman year in Gold Country, averaging 2.6 points per game. Dungy graduated with a bachelor's degree in business administration in 1976. And, in addition to his incredible on-field performance, Dungy was also a two-time Academic All-Big Ten selection.

"The University of Minnesota is really where I got my start," said Dungy of his alma mater. "I owe a lot to Head Coach Cal Stoll. He helped shape some of my values and some of the things I wanted to do in my life. The 'U' is where I developed a lot of the values that I carry with me today."

Following his college career, Dungy signed as a free agent with the Pittsburgh Steelers, where he was converted from quarterback to wide receiver to safety. In 1978 Dungy ranked second in the AFC with six interceptions and played in the Steelers' 35-31 victory over the Dallas Cowboys in Super Bowl XIII. That next year he was traded to the San Francisco 49ers, where he played in 15 games before being traded to the New York Giants. He would retire that next season, however, and in 1980 came back to serve as the defensive backs coach at his alma mater, the University of Minnesota.

That next season Dungy got his first NFL coaching job with the Steelers, where he worked from 1981-88. He was promoted to defensive backs coach in 1982 and held that job for two seasons until he became the NFL's youngest coordinator in 1984, when the Steelers named him defensive coordinator. In 1989 he moved to Kansas City and from 1989-91, Dungy served as defensive backs coach of the Chiefs under Marty Schottenheimer, helping to guide the team to the playoffs in 1990 and 1991. In 1992 Dungy returned to Minnesota, this time to serve as the defensive coordinator of the Vikings. In his first year with Minnesota, Dungy's defense led the NFL with 28 interceptions and ranked first in the NFC and second in the NFL with 42 takeaways. Dungy would continue to have a great deal of success in Minnesota, where he further developed a reputation as one of the game's top young assistants and brightest defensive minds. In four seasons with the Vikings, his defenses intercepted an NFL-high 95 passes as Minnesota made three playoff appearances.

In 1996 Dungy got his big break when he was named as the head coach of the Tampa Bay Buccaneers. There, Dungy would perform one of the greatest turn-arounds in pro football history. In 1997, after guiding the Buccaneers to a 10-6 record and a wild-card playoff victory over Detroit, Dungy was named Professional Coach of the Year by the Maxwell Football Club. Then, in 1999, the Buccaneers won the NFC Central, their first division championship in 18 seasons, and made it all the way to the conference finals. During Dungy's tenure in Tampa, the Bucs quickly developed a reputation as one of the NFL's stingiest defenses. Dungy coached the Buccaneers from 1996-2001, compiling a 54-42 regular season record with the fran-

chise and leading them to the playoffs in four of his six seasons. In 2002 Dungy left Tampa Bay to take over as the new head coach of the Indianapolis Colts, where he is presently employed.

Dungy's defenses, beginning during his Steelers tenure, have had a reputation for being among the NFL's most aggressive. In 20 seasons as an NFL head coach or assistant, his defenses have scored more than 60 touchdowns. To put that into perspective, since the 1970 AFL-NFL Merger, only 10 teams have scored as many as seven defensive touchdowns in a season. Four of those have come under Dungy's guidance.

Widely considered one of the most respected and popular coaches in the NFL, Tony Dungy is a player's coach to the core. He is very soft-spoken, modest and chooses to lead by example, always conducting himself with dignity and class. He has always been very involved in the communities that he has coached in as well and has become an outstanding role model for kids everywhere. Whether he is donating his time for Fellowship of Christian Athletes, or Athletes in Action, or Mentors for Life, or Big Brothers/Big Sisters or the Boys & Girls Clubs, Tony Dungy has always been there when asked upon.

Tony and his wife Lauren presently reside in Indianapolis and have five children: daughters Tiara and Jade and sons James, Eric and Jordan.

HOW WOULD YOU DESCRIBE YOUR COACHING STYLE? "I think I got my style from the coaches I worked for, specifically Chuck Noll and Denny Green. I guess I try to emphasize fundamentals and what I think is important to win. But I also want to create an atmosphere where the players can do their best. I think players naturally want to win, so you just have to create that environment where they can grow and learn and be free to improve."

HOW DO YOU MOTIVATE YOUR PLAYERS? "I think you have to look for self-motivated guys first and foremost. But you motivate the guys that you have by the end product and the achievements, and in our case that is a Super Bowl. From there, you just have to show them the ways that you are going to win and tell them that this is what we have to do as a team to win."

WHAT DID IT MEAN FOR YOU TO BE A GOPHER? "When you are playing for your school, representing them in the Big 10 Conference, playing against the best players in college football, it was a great thrill. Now, looking back as an alum, you see all the people who have come through the program and you realize that you were a part of it. That gives me a great feeling because I really enjoyed my time there at Minnesota. The school pride and school spirit was tremendous there and it was an honor to represent such a great university. I remember being recruited by both Cal Stoll and Bill Musselman and that was an exciting time. The atmosphere at the school was very positive at that time and I really liked the fact that it was a good academic school with a good business community nearby.

WHAT IS THE KEY TO GOOD TIME MANAGEMENT? "You have to be able to delegate, you just can't do everything. You have to have good people around you and then trust that they can do certain things. Then, you can focus on the things that you really need to do and not have to worry about the other things."

WHAT ARE THE CHARACTERISTICS OF WINNERS?
"Winners are driven. They are very goal oriented. They learn from adversity and from their mistakes. They have an attitude that doesn't allow them to give up, no matter what the situation. Guys who have those characteristics are going to end up winning a whole bunch more than they lose."

HOW DO YOU EARN THE RESPECT OF YOUR PLAYERS?
"By proving to them that you know what you are talking about and by being consistent and by being fair. The first thing that they want is someone who can help them, and then they want someone who they can trust and that they can count on."

LOOKING BACK WHAT ARE YOU MOST PROUD OF IN YOUR CAREER?
"I have been involved with some real good programs and been involved with some people who have won. In Tampa the fact that we brought some excitement to the city and brought some high character guys in there was great. To see the city get passionate about our players not only because they were good athletes but because they were good people was very rewarding."

HOW DO YOU BUILD TEAM UNITY & CHEMISTRY?
"You have to talk constantly about team goals and about the end result with regards to where you are trying to go as a team. You just have to keep emphasizing that. Everyone wants to do well individually, and you have to talk about how individual performances will help you win, but it is all about the team win and you just constantly have to keep pointing out team, team, team, and winning, winning, winning. That is where we all have to derive our success from."

WHAT MOTIVATES YOU?
"I think the biggest motivation is trying to get your players to play the best they can every single time out. You feel like if you do that as a coach then you are going to be successful and that you are going to have good enough players on good enough teams. I know that if we play the best that we can, then that is going to hold us in good stead. So you are disappointed even if you win ballgames but you don't play up to the level that you feel your team can play at. That's worse than playing an absolute great game and losing. Sure, you are disappointed, but you know you played as well as you could play. So, it is taking stock in what you do and how your team plays, then the scoreboard will take care of itself."

WHAT ADVICE WOULD YOU HAVE FOR YOUNG COACHES STARTING OUT TODAY?
"Get into situations where you can learn as much as you can. Observe real good coaches in real good programs. Spend the time and the extra effort it takes to watch other people work. Also, don't be motivated by money in the very beginning. Don't be afraid to take a job that might not be high paying if you can be with someone that you can learn from."

FAVORITE LOCKER ROOM SIGN?
"Expectations and Execution — No Excuses No Explanations" That basically sums up everything. Expectations are what you think, and execution is what you do. Then, excuses and explanations are what you say. So, a lot of positive thoughts, a lot of positive action and very little talk is what that is all about."

WHAT'S THE BIGGEST THING YOU'VE LEARNED FROM COACHING THAT YOU'VE BEEN ABLE TO APPLY TO YOUR EVERYDAY LIFE?
"That no one goes undefeated in anything that you do. There are always going to be setbacks and you have to be prepared for them. You have to respond to setbacks and that is eventually going to determine how well you do. I mean everyone can keep it going in the good times but when you have a setback, how do you respond? That is they key."

WHAT ROLE HAS YOUR FAMILY PLAYED IN YOUR COACHING CAREER?
"Your family is very important because they have to be supportive in order for you to experience any type of success. But you also have to stay abreast of them and keep focused on them as much as possible. Because to have a successful team and not have a successful family is not what you want in life."

WHAT ARE THE KEY INGREDIENTS TO CREATING A CHAMPIONSHIP TEAM?
"I would say chemistry, team unity, and getting players who all want to focus in on winning. That is much more important than talent. Sure, you have to have talent to some extent, but most people have pretty good eyes for talent. I think somehow creating that atmosphere where everybody is pushing in the same direction is what you want to strive for."

WHAT'S THE SECRET TO YOUR SUCCESS?
"I think I have the ability to stick to a philosophy that I believe in. I have been trained by some really good people and I have had the chance to watch some good people, so I have built a philosophy based on what I have learned. Then, you have to be stubborn and just stick to that no matter how things go."

WHAT WOULD YOU WANT TO SAY TO YOUR FANS, BOOSTERS, AND ALUMNI WHO HAVE SUPPORTED YOU ALL THESE YEARS?
"I would probably just say that I gave 100% all the time, I did my best and I did it with the right intentions and motivations. I appreciate all the support from everybody from Minnesota to Indianapolis, where I am now, and just want to say thanks, I have enjoyed every minute of it."

HOW DO YOU WANT YOUR COACHING EPITAPH TO READ — HOW DO YOU WANT TO BE REMEMBERED AS A COACH?
"I would like to be remembered by the people that I was around, by my players and by the other assistant coaches as somebody that they could count on and trust. That would probably be the most important thing."

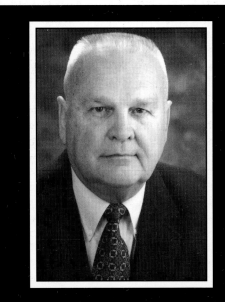

DAVE SKRIEN: PRO FOOTBALL BRITISH COLUMBIA LIONS (CFL)

Dave Skrien played football for the Gophers from 1948-50. From there, Skrien would get into coaching, first as an assistant with Ball State and then with the Gophers. Skrien later took over as the head coach with the British Columbia Lions of the Canadian Football League. Skrien coached the Lions from 1961-67 and reached the Grey Cup twice during his tenure — winning the championship in 1964 over Hamilton. In addition, Skrien also coached the Saskatchewan Roughriders from 1969-73 as well. Skrien, who also coached high school football at Minneapolis Washburn, later came back to coach as an assistant yet again with his Golden Gophers from 1992-95.

Ross Fortier grew up in Bemidji and went on to graduate from Bemidji High School. There, he played for his dad, Bun, who was a legendary head basketball coach and assistant football coach at Bemidji for many, many years. An outstanding athlete, Ross then went on to become a four-sport letter winner at North Dakota State University, graduating in 1960 with a teaching degree. Fortier then became a student assistant for a year, followed by a stint in the Army. When he got out of the Army that next year he returned to NDSU as a full-time assistant. Two years later he took over as the head coach at Melrose High School. From there, he came to MS-Moorhead to work on his masters degree, and later he became a full-time assistant there as well. In 1967 Fortier went back to NDSU as an assistant under Ron Erhardt, who went on to coach in the NFL. Fortier stayed three years and went 29-1 over that stretch, winning two national titles along the way.

Fortier then returned to MS-Moorhead in 1970 as the head football coach and remained there for 23 years, until retiring in 1993. (Fortier would stay on for another six years, however, as a physical education teacher.) Fortier would leave the game with a 152-80-4 career record, which included 16 consecutive non-losing seasons. He also led MSU to nine NSIC championships and seven trips to post-season play. His Dragons were nationally-ranked from 1979 through 1991, including the number one spot on the final 1981 NAIA poll. His 1982 club built the nation's longest win streak of 20 games that ended with a 31-28 road loss to NCAA I-AA Illinois State. Thirteen of Fortier's players signed professional contracts, and under Fortier the Dragons brought home 10 national statistical titles. Fortier also developed 52 All-Americans, six national statistical champions and 106 All-NSIC selections. In addition, Fortier served as men's athletic director, NAIA District 13 chairman, and created both the NSIC Metrodome Classic and the Snow Bowl. He is a member of the Minnesota High School Football Coaches Hall of Fame and both the NAIA and NDSU Halls of Fame.

During his professional career, Fortier also spent 35 years in the Minnesota Army National Guard and that is actually why he retired in 1993, because he got promoted to brigadier general and had to step down. Fortier retired from the military in 1996 and is presently living in Detroit Lakes and in Florida. An outstanding teacher and coach, Ross Fortier is without question a MS-Moorhead football legend.

HOW WOULD YOU DESCRIBE YOUR COACHING STYLE? "I think you have to understand the philosophy of the school you are at for starters. Then, you have to blend in and adjust to that. Our philosophy at Moorhead State was that we were going to build the school through academics and through the arts, and that athletics was important, but not of a primary importance. So, we didn't have that many assets and resources to go along with it. As a result, we had to understand where we stood in the chain and then work from there. I understood that. So, my philosophy was to build the best program that we could with what we had available within the philosophy of the school. My philosophy was that we would bring in a lot of freshman and junior college kids every year, set our standards high, work them hard and then look for the cream to rise to the top. We had some good success based on that, and that was a big part of our plan. We were basically a running team to start with but as we got better quarterbacks and receivers we evolved into the passing game a little more, which gave us a more balanced offense later on. Then, on

defense we ran a lot of man-to-man coverage and that worked well for us. You know, I spent 35 years in the Minnesota Army National Guard, and I learned a lot about motivating people, about leadership and about discipline. As a result, I was able to apply a lot of that insight into my coaching style.

HOW DID YOU MOTIVATE YOUR PLAYERS? "I motivated through good preparation. We worked hard to organize practice and prepare the players. If they felt that they were prepared, then that is a big part of motivation. All of that preparation during the week, the film study, the scouting reports, and training on and off the field, goes into their confidence. Once they have confidence, then you can do anything. I always thought that the pre-game pep-talk was overrated. If they weren't ready to go at that point, nothing was going to matter. It was all about preparation."

WHO WERE YOUR COACHING MENTORS? "I would say my dad, Bun. You know, Bun was a football coach at heart, but never got that chance because of Red Wilson, who was a great football coach for many, many years at Bemidji High School. He started coaching the basketball team in 1950 and in 20 years I think he took 18 teams to the state tournament, it was an amazing run. I think his winning percentage is something like 83%, he was a great, great coach and his players really liked him. He was a real innovator as well. He adapted to his personnel well too. I remember when I played for him we were small, so we played a full-court press for entire games. Then, later on when he got bigger kids, he slowed it down and ran a pattern offense. So, he was a smart guy and was a real good coach. He was also a great motivator and teacher too."

LOOKING BACK WHAT ARE YOU MOST PROUD OF IN YOUR CAREER? "I would say my family. I have a wonderful wife and three wonderful daughters. I was able to find a balance in all of that with teaching, coaching and the military, so I am proud of all of that. I got my doctoral degree when I was still coaching and was able to do a lot of things in my life which I am very proud of."

WHAT WAS THE KEY TO RECRUITING? "You are recruiting for your school first and foremost. Now, we didn't have a very good scholarship program and I think we were fifth in the conference for scholarship dollars, which was like $20-$30 thousand per year. So, we had to go back to selling the fine points of our school and on getting a good education. We also sold the Fargo Moorhead area to go to school in and to live in afterwards too. Then, we sold them on being a part of a winning program which had a lot of success both locally as well as nationally. All of those things factored into it. We didn't have a lot of money, so I tried to sell the bricks and the grass. There was a lot of competition between the MIAC, NCC and NSIC schools in going for the best talent. But, their were a lot of kids to choose from and you just had to try your best to sell them on your program. Beyond that, it just meant getting out to see and meet as many kids as you could in order to see what was in their heads and hearts. I can't stress that enough."

HOW DID YOU BUILD TEAM UNITY & CHEMISTRY? "When you bring in 100 football players during the preseason and start working together and living together, it develops naturally. If you make progress and the kids feel like they are making progress and

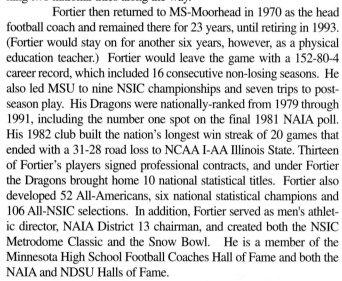

you are doing something worthwhile, then it just comes together naturally. Each team has its own personality based on the individual personalities of that season. I was always pretty level-headed and when I did get excited it was usually for a purpose, so we were always pretty even keeled as a team. When we had players with great leadership, we had better teams. Coaches are certainly important, but you have to have good players with the right attitude and work ethic. If you do things right from day to day then it will all fall together for you."

WHAT MOTIVATED YOU? "I always saw myself as a teacher first and a coach second. Our athletic department was an educational tool for our kids to learn in. My motivation was to teach the kids and to be a good teacher. I wanted to prepare them for later in life because not many of these guys were going to go on and make a career in pro football. So, we tried to prepare them to be good citizens in life. That was very enjoyable to me. Sure, winning football games was a lot of fun, but in the long run it was very satisfying to see my kids grow and develop into good young men."

WHAT ADVICE WOULD YOU HAVE FOR YOUNG COACHES STARTING OUT TODAY? "I taught a coaching class in college, so I have to think back to what I was saying all those years! I guess I would say that they need a philosophy. I see a lot of coaches who don't have a philosophy for their lives as well as for their coaching careers, and they struggle. You need a philosophy on every aspect of your life and then stick to it and work at it."

FAVORITE LOCKER ROOM SIGN? "Do not enter this room if you are not willing to pay the price"

ON TRAINING: "Coaches need to be careful how they condition athletes and to not develop an adversarial relationship with them. I didn't want to over condition them, otherwise they would get mad at you and that might hurt your chemistry. So, we developed a timing standard for running certain distances, like a 350 yard route around the field, and then had them measure their heart rates afterwards. What this did was let the kids see how well they were doing and how much they were improving running the same distances. This took my judgment out of it too, as far as making them work harder, it was black and white as to whether the guys would meet certain standards or not. That put the pressure back on them to be successful and off of me.

But, as a result it made the players come together to try harder and gel as a unit."

WHAT ARE THE KEY INGREDIENTS TO CREATING A CHAMPIONSHIP TEAM? "First you have to have players and then you need good coaches with good philosophies. It is a blend of talent, leadership and hard work. You know, our main goal every year was to win a conference championship. We knew that we never really had a good chance to win a national championship because we didn't have a scholarship program which would allow us to compete. Even in the playoffs we would compete against teams which gave out 50 full-rides, while we were sitting there with maybe five full-rides, split up between dozens and dozens of partial scholarships. We hung in there though and had a lot more success than a lot of other programs with even more resources, and I was proud of that."

WHAT'S THE SECRET TO YOUR SUCCESS? "You have to have good players, and I was lucky there. You also have to have good assistant coaches, which I was lucky to have as well. I only had two full-time assistants, so I had eight or nine student coaches, which helped out tremendously."

WHAT WOULD YOU WANT TO SAY TO YOUR FANS, BOOSTERS, AND ALUMNI WHO HAVE SUPPORTED YOU ALL THESE YEARS? "We certainly appreciate their support. Being a small school we didn't have a huge fan base, but our fans were very loyal. The parents, especially, traveled around with us and they were just fantastic. So thanks to all of them for all of their support."

HOW DO YOU WANT YOUR COACHING EPITAPH TO READ — HOW DO YOU WANT TO BE REMEMBERED AS A COACH? "As a teacher, an innovator, a hard worker and as a person who was fair to people."

DAVE KRAGTHORPE:
OREGON STATE FOOTBALL

Dave Kragthorpe grew up in Mound and went on to star as a three sport athlete at Mound High School, graduating in 1950. On the gridiron, however, Kragthorpe was an all-state two-way tackle. Kragthorpe's coach at Mound was future Gopher Coach Cal Stoll. In 1951, Stoll left Mound to serve as an assistant at Utah State University and Kragthorpe would be his first recruit. With that, Kragthorpe went on to play football at Utah State, where he earned all-conference honors in his junior and senior seasons. Kragthorpe, who also played baseball at USU, graduated with a degree in physical education in 1955. From there, Kragthorpe signed with the NFL's New York Giants, but had what would prove to be his only season of pro ball cut short when he was called upon to serve in the Navy. Two years later Kragthorpe got into coaching, with his first job coming as the freshman coach at Utah State University. In 1958 he took over as an assistant at Idaho Falls High School, where he also taught phys ed. In 1960 Kragthorpe took over as the head football coach at Roosevelt High School, in Wyandotte, Mich., where he would teach and coach for five seasons.

In 1964 Kragthorpe got his first college gig at the University of Montana, where he served as an assistant for three seasons. Then, in 1967, he became a coordinator at South Dakota State University, and eventually took over as the team's head coach in 1969. That next season, however, Kragthorpe left SDSU to become an assistant at BYU, where he would remain for the next 10 years, eventually becoming the team's assistant head coach. Kragthorpe finally got his big break in 1980, when he was named as the head coach at Idaho State University. There, Kragthorpe took a team that had lost 15 straight games and led them to a Big Sky Conference title as well as an NCAA Division I-AA championship in just his second season. In 1983 Kragthorpe left ISU and became the athletic director at his old alma mater, Utah State University. That next year though, he left to serve as the head coach at Oregon State University, where he would remain for the next six years before retiring in 1990. In all, Kragthorpe's career collegiate coaching record was 40-59-2. Dave and his wife Barbara have two children, Kurt and Steve — who became the head foot-

JOHN GAGLIARDI
COLLEGE FOOTBALL: ST. JOHN'S UNIVERSITY

John Gagliardi was born on Nov. 1, 1926, in Trinidad, Colo., a small coal-mining town just miles from the New Mexico border. John's father, Ventura Gagliardi, came to America at 16 in search of a better life. He found his way to Trinidad, where he worked in the coal mines, learning the language as he went along. A very religious man, Ventura worked hard and after becoming a blacksmith, later owned an auto-body shop. He would get married along the way to a woman named Antoinette, and John would be the fifth of their nine children. John grew up in the midst of the Great Depression, but found sports to be a great outlet for having fun.

John eventually went on to star for Trinidad Catholic High School. And, ironically, it would be there where his storied coaching career would begin as well. It all started when his high school football coach, Dutch Clark, was called to service in World War II. You see, without a coach, the school was just going to drop the football program. Most of the young men in the area had been called into action overseas, and there was no one available to take over. So, Gagliardi talked the administration into letting him serve as the team's coach. They agreed and John took over the reins at the age of just 16, serving as the player-coach for his senior year.

Gagliardi agreed to coach the team again that next year after he had graduated. He worked at his father's body shop and enrolled in Trinidad Junior College on the side. Even at that young age people could see the man had a gift for teaching, working with young people, and instilling in them a winning attitude. That next year John enrolled at Colorado College, where he continued to coach at nearby St. Mary's High School. His teams would win a total of three conference titles, and in 1946 he even led his Tigers to the Colorado Parochial School state title game.

After graduating from Colorado College in 1949, the 22-year-old Gagliardi accepted his first college coaching position at Carroll College, a small Catholic liberal arts school in Helena, Mont. The college, which was thinking about dropping football because of losing seasons and lack of interest, took a gamble on Gagliardi which would pay off big-time. He coached not only the football program at Carroll, but also the basketball and baseball programs as well. Inheriting an athletic program in utter disarray, John turned things around in a hurry. On the gridiron he led the football team to a 24-6-1 record, claiming three straight conference titles along the way. On the hardwood, Gagliardi's basketball teams claimed two conference titles and even upset national power Gonzaga, 68-66, in 1953.

Before long Gagliardi's success drew the attention of another small Catholic college — St. John's University of Collegeville, Minn. St. John's needed a coach to succeed the mythical Johnny "Blood" McNally, a former Green Bay Packer and Duluth Eskimo great and a charter member of the Pro Football Hall of Fame. SJU had not won a conference title in 15 years, and needed to get it turned around. So, the monks at St. John's made him an offer he couldn't refuse — raising his salary from $2,400 to $4,200. Meanwhile, Blood offered Gagliardi his own gloomy prediction: "Nobody could ever win at St. John's." Despite Blood's less than encouraging words, Gagliardi accepted the job and headed east to Collegeville to begin the next journey of his life in the shadows of beautiful Lake Sagatagan.

John immediately quieted the skeptics by winning the Minnesota Intercollegiate Athletic Conference (MIAC) title that fall with the help of his first great halfback, Jim Lehman. Lehman, the father of Minnesota golfing great Tom Lehman, went on to lead the

country in scoring that year as well. Gagliardi would later go on to turn around the Johnnies' track and hockey teams as well, proving his unique coaching methods and motivational skills could make any team a winner. The rest, they say, is history.

Now, some five and a half decades later, John is about to make history again when he surpasses Grambling State University Coach Eddie Robinson on the all-time career wins list. Going into the 2003 season, John was just nine wins away from breaking Robinson's record and becoming the winningest coach ever in the history of college football — at any division. So, with the eyes of the sports world focused on him, John is set to make Minnesota very proud.

Coach Gagliardi has built one of the nation's top NCAA Division III programs at St. John's. The attitude and winning tradition he instills in his players is simply unprecedented. Among this seven-time national coach of the year's many achievements are his three small college national championships. The first came in 1963, when his Johnnies edged Prairie View A&M of Texas, 33-27, at the Camellia Bowl in Sacramento, Calif. Gagliardi's second title came two years later, when his Johnnies crushed Linfield College of Oregon, 35-0. (Amazingly the Johnnies' defense allowed just 27 points to be scored against them that entire season!) St. John's then added their third title in 1976, when they beat Towson State of Maryland, 31-28.

As a collegiate coach Gagliardi's teams have won 24 conference titles and have appeared in 41 post-season games. In the past 39 years, SJU has been nationally ranked 37 times and they own a 28-13 post-season record as well. From 1962-64 SJU owned the nation's longest winning streak, with 20 wins. Then, in 1993, SJU averaged 61.5 points per game, setting a record that may never be broken.

Among his numerous awards and achievements, Gagliardi has been inducted into the Minnesota and Montana Halls of Fame and is a member of the College Football Hall of Fame as well. He has been the subject of a Sports Illustrated cover story and was awarded the Football Writers of America Citation of Honor. Perhaps his greatest honor will live on forever though. In 1993 the NCAA honored the coach by naming the Division III equivalent of the Heisman Trophy after him. The Gagliardi Trophy is now given annually to the nation's top NCAA Division III football player.

In addition, he has been featured nationally on: ESPN, CNN, CNN/SI, The Today Show, CBS News Sunday Morning, Sports Illustrated, The Wall Street Journal, USA Today, New York Times, Boston Globe, Los Angeles Times, Washington Post, and Chicago Tribune. There have even been several books written about him, including: "No-How Coaching: Strategies for Winning in Sports and Business from the Coach Who Says 'No!', by Jim Collison, "Gagliardi of Saint John's: The Man, The Coach, The Legend," by Don Riley and "The Sweet Season," by Austin Murphy.

The winningest active coach in college football history, Gagliardi currently owns a 400-114-11 career record. And Gagliardi's teams are still setting the standard for MIAC competitors. In 1993, SJU became the first NCAA team since the 1904 Gophers to score more than 700 points in a season. Then, in 2000, St. John's made the national title game, followed by a pair of national semifinal appearances in both 2001 and 2002. In 2001, Gagliardi became only the third coach in NCAA college football history to coach 500 career games. And the guy is still going strong! It is amazing!

Now entering his 55th season on the sidelines, Gagliardi's success is attributable to more than mere football strategy and tactics. He is an astute judge of talent. He creates a fun environment filled with high expectations, and he concentrates on methods and practices that truly focus on winning. John Gagliardi has built a legacy that is unrivaled in college football, and what's frightening for all the other MIAC schools is that he may just be getting his second wind as he prepares for his incredible saga of passing Coach Robinson on the all-time wins list. With so many records and so many success stories, John Gagliardi has built a legacy that is unrivaled in all of football. Here is a man who has touched so many lives and truly made a difference in this world, and for that he should be thanked.

John and his wife Peggy live in Collegeville and have four children. It's business as usual for the coach though as he entered his 55th season of coaching and prepared for his emotional journey to instant football immortality — hopefully late in the Fall of 2003. We'll see you all at the festivities, but remember… please, NO Gatorade shower!

HOW WOULD YOU DESCRIBE YOUR COACHING STYLE? "We dare to be different up here and that has been a big part of our success, no question. I guess my style is all my own and I really don't know how I would describe it. It is unique that is for sure. We were pretty successful from the get-go and we just stuck with what we were doing and it has worked for us ever since. But you know, I have never really coached on anybody else's coaching staff, so I think that is why my style is so unique. I know that most coaches have styles which are a blend of other coaching influences, whether it was from when they played in high school or college, or from serving as an assistant coach under someone else after that. Well, for me, I actually coached my high school team when our coach got called off to serve in the war, and I never played in college after that, so maybe that is why my approach to coaching is so different and unique from the other guys."

HOW DO YOU MOTIVATE YOUR PLAYERS? "You know, I don't do a lot of Knute Rockne-like speeches up here, that is for sure. I think the best thing we can do for our players is to thoroughly prepare them for life on and off the field. I think being brilliant in the basics, and just teaching the fundamentals so that players are ready to play is the key. I have always agreed with the slogan 'success breeds success,' and that I think it is easy to be motivated if you know what you are doing."

DID YOU HAVE A MENTOR? "The one coach I truly look up to is Bud Grant. He is the greatest coach of all time. He is so even keeled and humble and that to me is what it is all about. He also has such a high degree of common sense too. I mean I think common sense these days is not so common, if you know what I mean! It is just profound how smart he is. He is just a rare guy and a real throwback. It was a real honor to coach his two sons too, I was flattered that he would send them here to play in my program."

IF YOU COULD MAGICALLY GO BACK IN TIME TO THE FIRST YEAR YOU WERE A HEAD COACH AND GIVE YOURSELF SOME ADVICE FOR THE FUTURE, KNOWING WHAT YOU KNOW NOW, BACK THEN, WHAT WOULD YOU SAY TO YOURSELF? "Well, I would sure know what stocks to pick! But really, I would probably tell myself, 'Hey it's going to be a great ride, hang on!' You know, sure I would say try a be a bit more patient and maybe don't get so bent out of shape over the little things. Just hang in there, somehow it will all work out."

WHAT ADVICE WOULD YOU HAVE FOR YOUNG COACHES STARTING OUT TODAY? "I think that young teachers and coaches just starting out are in a great field. To be able to work with young people and give them some direction is so admirable. I would just say that I hope they love what they are doing, because there will be a lot of ups and a lot of downs along the way. I guess I would

tell them to work hard and enjoy themselves, that is what it is all about."

HOW DO YOU BUILD TEAM UNITY & CHEMISTRY? "We just go about our days working hard to get ready. There is no secret, really. You just hope you get a group of good kids who can play well together and hopefully it all fits together. As for building team unity, we just practice and play together and go from there. When the season is over we tell them to go and enjoy their student life. We don't want to interfere with their college experience, we just want them to be well rounded people and have fun while they are getting their educations. We feel that they should not only be able to bond with their teammates, but with their classmates at school as well. If that translates into chemistry on the field, then so be it."

WHAT IS THE KEY TO GOOD TIME MANAGEMENT? "I don't know if I am the best guy to talk to about this or not. You know, for me, I just say we are going to practice for an hour and a half today and that is that. We start at a certain time and we end at a certain time. Period. You know, if we haven't got it done by then we are just not going to get it done. Sure, being organized is great, but sometimes you just have to go with the flow too."

WHAT MOTIVATES YOU? "Football is just a great game, and to be a part of this great game is motivation enough for me. Beyond that it is nice to have a good job and a place to go to work. I don't require a lot of motivation, I just do what I have to do to get it done. I don't live in the past or in the future, I just try to do my best today. You know, football is complex enough without trying to make it even more difficult. I just keep it simple and treat people the same way I like to be treated."

WHAT'S THE BIGGEST THING YOU'VE LEARNED FROM COACHING THAT YOU'VE BEEN ABLE TO APPLY TO YOUR EVERYDAY LIFE? "To tell you the truth, I think it is the other way around. You try and live your life right and treat your family and kids well — that is the biggest thing. They are the most important thing and that should never be forgotten I think. Then, if those values carry over to your coaching, you will be just fine. I just have never put coaching in front of my family and I am a better person and coach for it. Too many coaches neglect their families and that is no way to live in my opinion. Looking back, I am sure grateful that I married the right gal, that has been the key. Don't get me wrong, I think you have to throw everything you have into your profession, but at the same time you have to find a happy balance. I have tried to maintain that in my life and maybe that is why I have been successful."

WHAT ARE THE KEY INGREDIENTS TO CREATING A CHAMPIONSHIP TEAM? "Well, you obviously have got to have some players who can play ball. You need talent first and foremost. Then, as a coach, you need to give these players a plan that they can follow. You know, you can't do everything, but you just have to work with what you have got and you will be successful. The players have got to know what to do and as a coach it is your responsibility to prepare them the best you can. You just have to work hard and try like heck to get it done. But hey, sometimes that is easier said than done. Remember, those guys on the other side of the line are trying to do the same exact thing!"

WHAT ARE THE CHARACTERISTICS OF WINNERS? "There are a lot of ways to get a job done, and I just think that winners succeed with whatever cards they are dealt. Successful coaches just seem to have a unique way of making the most out of whatever talent they have. Whatever situation they are in, the successful coaches find a way to adapt and succeed. Whether it is the quality of players they get that year or what have you, the good ones get the most out of their players and find a way to win. That's the key."

WHAT'S THE SECRET TO YOUR SUCCESS? "You know, I hate to say it, but I am not a big guy on advice or motivation or any of that stuff. Sorry, but it is the truth, it is just not me. I get asked these questions a lot and all I can say is that there is no magic wand for success. You just have to work hard and get the most out of whatever cards you are dealt. I think the secret is, there is no secret. You know, I never set out to set a goal of becoming the winningest all-time coach, but it is now approaching a reality. One of the things I have lived by is 'No Goals, Just High Expectations.' That is the way I have functioned all of my life and it has worked out for me. I always had high expectations for myself and always worked hard to be successful, but I really tried to stay away from setting specific goals. I always tell my guys 'You cannot be undefeated unless you win this game, this week.' I also think that I have never really looked too far ahead or too far behind, I just live for the day."

HOW DO YOU WANT YOUR COACHING EPITAPH TO READ — HOW DO YOU WANT TO BE REMEMBERED AS A COACH? "I have got so many things to be thankful for. Maybe one thing in particular that I am most proud of is that because of the way we practice, I think I have saved a lot of guys from getting hurt and specifically from suffering bad knee injuries. We've never gone 'full-go' in practice and that has saved a lot of guys, no doubt. I think that concept has been accepted by a lot of other coaches around the country now too, and that is just great for the players, who are still working hard but are suffering fewer injuries as a result. Overall, there are a lot of things I would hope to be remembered for, but overall I just worked hard and had fun."

TOM SKEMP: ST. MARY'S FOOTBALL

Thomas Skemp was a coaching legend at St. Mary's back in the 1920s. Skemp, who coached football, baseball, basketball, track and tennis for the Redmen, also introduced an organized intramural athletics program at the school as well. Skemp was even responsible for starting inter-high school tournament competition for basketball in southeastern Minnesota. The man who coined the term "Redmen," and got St. Mary's into the MIAC, Skemp's football teams went undefeated in 1924, 1925, 1927 and 1929. In addition, in 1924 and 1925, St. Mary's was recognized as the State and Northwest Football Champions. Skemp wasn't afraid to schedule tough competition for his boys either. In 1928, for SMC's Homecoming, the Redmen even defeated Notre Dame's "B" squad, 19-7. In all, Skemp would post a career record of 52-28-6 on the gridiron, outscoring his opponents 1,477 to 731 along the way. A real innovator, Skemp was inducted into the St. Mary's Hall of Fame in 1973.

GAGLIARDI'S "WINNING WITH NO's"

The Overall Program
* No athletic scholarships
* No big staff, just four assistant coaches
* No coordinators
* No freshmen or junior-varsity program
* No discipline problems
* No insisting on being called "Coach," players call him John
* No players cut
* No pampering athletes
* No one persuaded to come out or stay out
* No hazing tolerated

The Season
* No staff meetings
* No player meetings
* No film sessions after Monday
* No special diet
* No training table - team eats with other students
* No special dormitory
* No signs in dressing rooms
* No slogans
* No superstitions
* No play-books
* No statistics posted
* No newspaper clippings posted

The Practices
* No practice pants - shorts or sweats worn at practice
* No agility drills
* No lengthy calisthenics (about three minutes)
* No pre-practice drills
* No practice apparatus or gadgets
* No blocking sleds or tackling dummies
* No tackling
* No laps
* No wind sprints
* No special coaching clothes worn
* No use of the words "hit," "kill," etc...
* No clip boards
* No whistles
* No practice on Sundays
* No practice on Mondays
* No drills
* No spring practice
* No practice in rain, extreme heat or cold
* No practice if mosquitoes, gnats, etc... are bad
* No long practices - varies from 30 to 90 minutes
* No practice under the lights
* No water or rest denied when players want it
* No practice modules
* No underclassmen carry equipment other than their own

The Games
* No big deal when we score - we expect to score
* No trying to "kill" opponent
* No trash talk tolerated
* No tendency charts
* No use of headphones
* No coaches in press-box
* No player NOT played in rout (143 players once played in a game)
* No spearing allowed
* No cheap-shots or foul play tolerated
* No counting tackles
* No precision pre-game drills
* No big games pointed to
* No special pre-game or post-game meals
* No computer analysis
* No cheerleaders
* No Gatorade showers!

The Off-Season
* No meetings
* No between season practices or conditioning
* No captains' practice
* No study or tutoring program necessary
* No weightlifting program

The Results
* No player has not graduated
* No discipline problems
* No player lost through ineligibility
* No class has NOT had at least one prospective pro player
* No small college has larger crowd support
* No wider point margin in national playoff history
* No team has fewer injuries
* No team has fewer penalties
* No small college coach has won more games

ERNIE NEVERS: NFL's DULUTH ESKIMOS

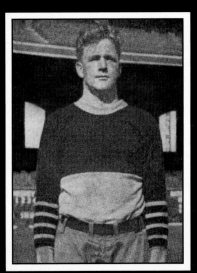

Ernie Nevers was one of the greatest football heroes our country has ever known. The speedy blonde-haired fullback could do it all. He ran, passed, kicked, punted, returned kicks and punts, called signals, and played a mean cornerback on defense. He revolutionized the game, and even saved the once fledgling NFL from going broke way back in 1926, when he came home to play in one of the most storied football seasons of all time, with the upstart Duluth Eskimos.

Born in 1903, in Willow River, Minn., Ernie later moved to Superior, Wis. It was at Superior Central High School where he blossomed into a three-sport star in football, baseball and basketball. At the age of 16 his folks moved to California, where Ernie graduated from Santa Rosa High School. After graduation he attended Stanford, and soon became a featured triple-threat fullback in Pop Warner's explosive double wing offense. The once timid teenager was now a household name throughout America.

"As a youngster I was very shy," confessed Nevers. "I was scared to death of people. But football gave me an outlet for my emotions. You get the chance to go man-to-man and see if you can stand up against the best they can throw at you. On a football field I was just a different person."

Nevers, a two-time All-American selection, had been a headliner all through his collegiate career, but he reached superhuman status during the 1925 Rose Bowl against Notre Dame and the vaunted Four Horsemen. There, against the better wishes of his doctor, he played through one sprained and one broken ankle. With a pair of tin-snips and a hammer, Coach Warner concocted a crude artificial ankle brace out of sheet aluminum and rubber inner tubing, and taped it to Nevers' lower legs. Amazingly, Ernie played the entire 60 minutes, rushed for 114 yards on his two bum-hoofs, and even registered half of the team's tackles on defense. He played valiantly, but came up short though, as the Irish won, 27-10. That next year, against California, in his final college game, the workhorse handled the ball on every offensive play but three.

Pop Warner, who coached both Nevers and the legendary Jim Thorpe, was once asked who was the better player of the two. "Nevers," Warner quickly replied. "He could do everything Thorpe could do and he tried harder. No man ever gave more of himself than Ernie Nevers."

By the time the football season was over with during his senior year, Ernie was in big demand. So, with a semester of school remaining, he decided to turn pro. His first gig was for $25,000 to play in a series of all-star games against the New York Giants in Florida. Shortly thereafter, he signed a pro basketball deal for a Chicago team in a league that was a forerunner to the NBA. Then, that Spring he signed a $10,000 pro baseball contract as a pitcher with the St. Louis Browns. But after a year, he decided to get back to the gridiron and suit up for his old grade school pal, Ole Haugsrud, and his upstart NFL Duluth Eskimos. There, he got a $15,000 contract plus 10% of the gate, to serve as the team's player/coach. Haugsrud even renamed his team as the "Ernie Nevers' Eskimos" in his honor. More importantly though, his presence, credibility and star-power single-handedly saved the NFL from going broke.

Ernie's two-year stint in Duluth was epic. In 1926 alone, the Eskimos played 29 games, 28 of them on the road, and traveled nearly 20,000 miles. Nevers played all but 29 of the total minutes for that season, with those idle minutes coming after he ruptured his appendix. Nevers set five league marks for rushing, passing, and scoring that year, as the team barnstormed throughout the country. The Eskimos folded in 1928 (they later became the Washington Redskins) and Ernie headed back to coach for a year under Pop Warner at Stanford. He came back in 1929 though, this time with the Chicago Cardinals.

Nevers played for the Cardinals from 1929-1931, also serving as player/coach for the latter two years. His most memorable moment in the Windy City came on Thanksgiving Day, 1929, when the Cards played the cross-town Bears, and their star running back, Red Grange, at Comiskey Park for the City Championship. Nevers came out, smashed over the Bear's goal-line six times, and kicked four extra points. The final score: Nevers 40, Bears 6. That's right, he set an NFL record by scoring all 40 points by himself! And, to prove it was no fluke, he scored all of his team's points again in a 19-0 win over Dayton that next Sunday.

"Ernie was probably the first of the triple-threat backs," said Grange. "He could run, kick and pass. He was a star through and through. Guys like Nevers and Bronko Nagurski would have played the game for nothing."

In 1931, after suffering too many nagging injuries, the five-time All-NFL star hung up the cleats for good. He stayed on as a coach though, through the 1937 season, and again in 1939. His final numbers were awesome. In his five NFL seasons, he passed for 25 touchdowns, rushed for 38 touchdowns, kicked seven field goals, nailed 52 extra points, and tallied 301 career points. Not bad for just 54 games of work.

He made one final coaching stint in 1946, when he led the ill-starred Chicago Rockets in the All American Football League. He later moved to California, where among other business interests, he became the director of the California Clippers, Oakland's pro soccer team.

Once referred to as "America's all-time one-man team," Ernie Nevers was, in a word, amazing. He was to the NFL back then, what Gale Sayers, Walter Payton and Emmitt Smith all later exemplified. In 1963 Nevers was inducted as a charter member of the Pro Football Hall of Fame. Many years later Sports Illustrated called Nevers the "best college player of all time." He died on May 3, 1976, in San Rafael, Calif., at the age of 73, ironically, just six weeks after his old friend, Ole Haugsrud, had passed away. Legendary — that was Ernie.

DWIGHT REED:
LINCOLN UNIVERSITY FOOTBALL

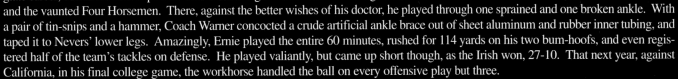

Dwight Reed, a former Gopher from 1935-37, went on to become a coaching legend at Lincoln University (MO). There, Reed became the winningest football coach of all time for the Blue Tigers and later even had the campus football stadium renamed after him in his honor.

GEORGE GIBSON
PRO FOOTBALL: MINNEAPOLIS REDJACKETS

George Gibson was born in New York and raised in Medford, Okla. There, Gibson went on to become a star lineman on his high school football team, graduating in 1923. He then came to the University of Minnesota to play football. Why Minnesota? You see, Gibson's father was a railroad man and George followed him around the country, working for him in the Summers as a high schooler. George and his brother Francis followed the wheat harvest north, riding the rails from Oklahoma, up to Portal, North Dakota, a little town on the Canadian border. There, they shucked wheat 11 hours a day for 60 cents an hour, plus room and board. When they came through the Twin Cities, he fell in love with Minneapolis, so he decided to come to school here. His older brother William had played football at the University of Michigan and he too wanted to play big-time football up north.

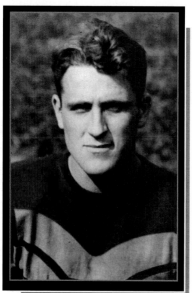

George and Francis were in great shape from working the wheat fields all Summer, so they both decided to try out for the Gopher freshman football team. The next fall, George made the varsity — the only sophomore to do so. Francis, however, transferred to North Dakota because they promised him a good job after graduation. George would emerge as a two-way starting guard with the Gophers over the next couple of years, later becoming team captain in 1928. Back then, it was the captain, who, along with the quarterback, called the plays. On offense Gibson played running guard on the single wing and would ultimately earn All-American honors alongside the great Bronko Nagurski — who was also his best friend and roommate.

George graduated in 1929 with an degree in geology. But he wasn't done with football just quite yet. After graduation, he accepted a job as the player/coach with the Minneapolis Red Jackets, one of Minnesota's first NFL teams. Gibson received a total salary of $3,900 as player-coach of the Red Jackets, which was big money back in the day. Times were tough because of the Great Depression, however, and the team went broke after just a season and a half. When the club folded, the Red Jackets actually combined forces with the Frankford Yellow Jackets, the professional team in suburban Philadelphia, for the remainder of the 1931 season. Gibson would serve as their player-coach as well. The combined squad, which played a double schedule, proved to be a logistical nightmare though. Many of the players were cut, while others simply lost interest. As a result, the team lost its remaining four games in a big way to the Chicago Bears, Brooklyn Dodgers, Providence Steam Rollers and Portsmouth Spartans, by the ugly combined total of 106-7. While Gibson was accorded All-Pro honors that season, the team's disappointing 1-7-1 record did not bode well. Unfortunately, the Frankford franchise went belly-up following that season. Both Green Bay and Chicago tried to recruit Gibson to play for them, but he had already set his sights on becoming a geologist.

"I tell everybody I was the only player-coach who worked for two teams that both went bankrupt in the same year," Gibson recalled jokingly. His career pro coaching record was a meager 3-10-1, and he had simply had enough.

"The player limit was only 20," recalled former Gopher and Red Jacket Herb Joesting, "and it was rugged after we combined with Frankford. A few times we played in Philadelphia on Saturday and hopped a train to play again on Sunday. It's too bad we couldn't have carried on here," he added. "We had the start of a good team and it could have been built into something, but we didn't have the money. The Depression was on. It was a rugged way to make a living, but it

was a job, and they were scarce in those days. And, hey it was fun."

In 1934 George moved back to Minnesota, where he earned his doctorate in geology at the U of M. From there, he went on to teach geology and coach football at Carleton College until 1938. One of the highlights of his Carleton coaching career came in 1936 when his boys barely lost to a tough Iowa team which they had held scoreless through three quarters. Gibson would stay for just five years in Northfield, but did manage to lead his team to an undefeated co-championship of the Midwest Conference in 1936.

In the late 1930s Gibson went to work for the Socony Vacuum Oil Company, looking for oil in the Egyptian desert. George recalled that one evening when he was out in the desert "about 100 miles from nowhere," he turned on his short-wave radio and much to his surprise, he picked up the Nebraska-Minnesota football game. To make it even better, the voice he heard broadcasting the game was that of his older brother William, who had become the editor of the U of M Alumni Weekly newspaper and also served as a football analyst on the side.

By 1940 World War II was heating up and all Americans were ordered out of the Egypt. During his last days in Cairo, George witnessed daily air raids from his hotel window. He knew it was time to go. His trip home took two months though. Because of the war in Europe, he had to go the long way home by train, plane, and ship via Jerusalem, the Persian Gulf, Bombay, Capetown and Trinidad. That entire time, his wife, who had already returned home with their two sons, had no idea where he was. When he finally got home Gibson decided to move to Midland, Tex., where geologists were needed to map the Permian Basin and find oil for the war effort. Nearly a dozen years later he became an independent geological consultant, and made a fortune.

Since then George went on to become one of the most respected and successful geologists in the world. He has also given back to the University of Minnesota in a huge way. His generosity was most evident in 1985, when the $5.5 million "Gibson-Nagurski Football Complex" was opened adjacent to the Bierman Field Athletic Building in his honor. Dedicated to education and football, the facility set the standard to which many others around the nation were compared. Then, in 2000, another $5 million facelift of the building was completed, all thanks to George. He also gave a good sum of money to the Geology Department at the University as well.

"I still think back on my time in college," George would recall. "What I remember most is how well I was treated by both the athletic and geology departments. They went overboard to help me and push me along. Over the years, I've tried to repay that help by giving something back. That's why I endowed, with my late wife, the George and Orpha Gibson Chair in Hydrogeology, and have also supported men's athletics. I've never forgotten that my success started at the University of Minnesota."

Believe it or not, at 98 years young, George Gibson still goes to the office every day in Midland. He loves what he does and is still sharp as a tack. He even still follows the Gophers and feels strongly that "Coach Mason is close, real close to bringing a championship back to Minnesota." The oldest ever living NFL alumni, George Gibson is a Minnesota sports treasure.

HOW WOULD YOU DESCRIBE YOUR COACHING STYLE? "We ran the ball a lot back then. I was mild I suppose and just tried to get my boys to play their best out there. I never berated my players, I just tried to encourage them to give them more confidence. We had a lot of different plays and what not, but we just tried to beat our opponents fair and square and show good sportsmanship."

HOW DID YOU MOTIVATE YOUR PLAYERS? "I tried to imitate Doc Spears, he was a heck of a football coach. I didn't like to get them too excited before games but I just encouraged them to give it their best effort. I knew that if we worked harder than our opponents then we would win more games than we lost. I also liked Knute Rockne's approach to coaching. We played against his Notre Dame teams several times and after each game he would come over and pat you on your back and tell you that you played a fine ballgame. He was quite a yeller to his boys, but they respected him. He was very popular with the newsmen and I could see why, he was a darn good football coach. When he came over and talked to our boys that got their confidence up and that was something special. I was later named to Knute's All American team and that was a real honor."

WHO WERE YOUR COACHING MENTORS? "I learned a lot from my coach at the University of Minnesota, Doc Spears. I also admired Bernie Bierman. We were similar I think in that we both were mild mannered. I remember that his teams never really came running out on to the field before the game, they just walked. He was not real excitable, he just worked on the fundamentals and had his boys play hard during the game."

WHAT DID IT MEAN FOR YOU TO BE A GOPHER? "It meant nearly everything to me to be a Gopher. It was such a thrill to play for such a great program and it was something I will never forget. To play with Bronko Nagurski was also a thrill. We were roommates one year and boy was he one whale of a player. He was so modest and really such a decent person. The Gophers were a fine ballclub back then and it was a real privilege to play for them. I have since donated some money to their program to build the Gibson/Nagurski indoor practice facility and that meant a lot to me to be able to do that. I love the Gophers."

WHAT WOULD YOU WANT TO SAY TO YOUR FANS, BOOSTERS, AND ALUMNI WHO HAVE SUPPORTED YOU

ALL THESE YEARS? "You know, I think back to what the great comedian George Burns said when he too was in his 90's. When a reporter asked him if he still drank, still smoked cigars and still went to night clubs with women, Burns said 'yes' he did. The reporter then asked him what his doctors had to say about that and Burns replied, 'They're all dead!'." Really though, I would say thanks from the bottom of my heart to all those fine people up there in Minnesota. Those were some great memories and some great people. I still have a great regard and great hope for the Gophers. I think Coach Mason is a sensational coach. He took on a big job there in that tough Big 10 Conference, but he is a fine man and I think that one of these days he will come through for us."

MILT BRUHN: WISCONSIN FOOTBALL

Milt Bruhn, who played Gopher Football from 1932-34, went on to coach at the University of Wisconsin from 1956-66, posting a career record of 52-45-6 with the Badgers.

GEORGE MYRUM: GUSTAVUS FOOTBALL

George Myrum was a coaching legend at Gustavus. From 1924-38, old George did it all. As the head football coach, Myrum would rack up a 63-20-6 record from 1926-38, including three undefeated seasons and six conference titles. The undefeated 1926 team won the school's first MIAC title, allowing only three points all season. It would be the first of many more to come. The 1920s and 30s were a period of dominance under Myrum, who led the team to six titles in all during this era (1926, 1927, 1933, 1935, 1936 and 1937). One of the stars of the mid-1930s was Wendell Butcher, the "Worthington Walloper." Butcher led the Gusties to three straight crowns and played every minute of every game in that same span. He was leading scorer in the conference his junior and senior years and was also leading rusher and leading passer as well. Butcher was elected to three All State teams and was named Little All -American in 1937, before going on to play professionally with the Brooklyn Dodgers of the old AFL for six years.

As a tactition, Myrum perfected the double-wing attack at Gustavus, which featured among other things: using the quarterback and fullback to handle the ball, full spins and half spins, a man-in-motion, balanced and unbalanced lines, positioning of backs as to depth and width, and even quick-kicks — with one man holding the ball and another man punting it. In addition, as the varsity baseball coach Myrum won several state championships and in 1938 his basketball team shared the conference championship. Myrum had a dream at Gustavus and that was to have the best facilities as possible. He planned and supervised the construction of a new stadium in 1929 and the present fieldhouse in 1938, and though he never lived to see the completed structure, his dream was fulfilled. Coach Myrum was tragically killed on November 12, 1938, when the bus carrying the team home from the season's final game at St. Norbert's College, in Wisconsin, crashed into a stalled truck. Myrum was the "Knute Rockne" of Gustavus football. Their similarities were eerie. Both were contemporaries in the coaching field, both were Norwegians and both were short in stature. They also had tremendous coaching savvy and both were great inspirational leaders. Ironically, both died in tragic accidents, Rockne in a plane crash in 1931, and Myrum in the bus accident in 1938. George Myrum was a Gustie football coaching legend, plain and simple.

BUD GRANT
PRO FOOTBALL: MINNESOTA VIKINGS

Harry "Bud" Grant was born and raised in Superior, Wis. His father, Harry, Sr., was the Superior Fire Chief. Bud grew up playing sports and became a tremendous prep athlete. After playing football, baseball and basketball at Superior's Central High School, Bud joined the Navy in 1945 and was stationed at the Great Lakes Naval Station outside of Chicago. Bud continued his athletic prowess at Great Lakes, where his team played Big Ten clubs under football Coach Paul Brown and basketball Coach Weeb Ewbank, both hall of famers. In 1946, Bud was discharged and enrolled at the U of M.

There, even without a scholarship (because he was in the service, the G.I. bill paid for his tuition), he would excel in three sports, earning nine letters from 1946-1949. He was a two-time All-Big Ten End on the gridiron, starred as a forward and was the team MVP on the basketball team, and also played centerfield and pitched for the baseball team — where he even led the team in hitting as a freshman. Under Bernie Bierman, Bud played with Gopher greats such as Leo Nomellini, Clayton Tonnemaker, Gordie Soltau, Billy Bye, Jim Malosky and Vern Gagne. To earn spending money in the Summers throughout college, Grant became creative. Since he could pitch three days a week and bat clean-up, he played baseball as a "ringer" for several small town-teams around Minnesota and Wisconsin, where he could mop up as much as $250 bucks in a good week.

"Being a Gopher kind of grows on you a little bit," said Bud. "It wasn't anything that I felt particularly strong about when I got there, but now it means a lot. Back then, the Gophers were the only game in town, and we always played before a packed house. It was a tough time, with no scholarships and little money, but we had a lot of fun."

By 1950, Bud had finished his tenure at the U of M, and was considered by most to have been the most versatile athlete ever to compete there. (That was affirmed when he later beat out Bronko Nagurski and Bruce Smith to be named as the "Top Athlete at the University of Minnesota for the First 50 Years of the Century.") From there he joined George Mikan and Jim Pollard as the newest member of the mighty Minneapolis Lakers dynasty. As a Laker, Grant averaged 2.6 points per game in each of the two years he played for the club, both of which were NBA championship teams.

Anxious to try something different, Bud then joined the NFL's Philadelphia Eagles, who had made him their No. 1 draft pick that year. So talented was Grant, that in 1952, after switching from linebacker, where he led the team in sacks, to wide receiver, he finished second in the league in receiving and was voted to the Pro Bowl. After two years in Philly, Grant decided to take a 30% payraise and head north of the border to play for the Winnipeg Blue Bombers of the Canadian Football League. In so doing, Bud became the first player in NFL history to play out the option on his contract. He dearly missed hunting and fishing, something he figured he could readily do in up in Winnipeg.

There, Grant played both ways, starting at corner and at wide receiver. He led the league in receiving for three straight years and also set a record by intercepting five passes during a single game. Then, in 1957, after only four years in the league, and at the prime of his career, the front-office offered the 29-year-old the teams' headcoaching position. He accepted and proceeded to lead the Blue Bombers to six Grey Cups over the next 10 years, winning four of them.

On March 11th, 1967, Grant came home again, this time to take over as the head coach of the Minnesota Vikings. It was a position that former Lakers owner, Max Winter, who now ran the Vikings, had originally offered to him, but had declined, back in 1960. Bud took over from Norm Van Brocklin, and although he only won three games in his first season, that next year he led the Purple to the division title. The year after that, in 1969, they made it to the Super Bowl, and Bud was named the league's Coach of the Year. It would be his first of four.

That was the beginning of one of the greatest coaching sagas in all of sports. Bud could flat out coach, and his players not only respected him, they also liked him. Bud treated them like men, didn't work them too hard in practice, and his players always knew they could count on that post-season playoff check.

Grant, who went on to coach for 28 years, won a total of 290 regular season and post-season games, 122 as coach of the Winnipeg Blue Bombers of the CFL from 1957-66 and 168 as coach of the Vikings from 1967-83 and 1985. At Minnesota, his teams made the playoffs 12 times, and won 15 championships: 11 Central Division (1968-71, 1973-78, and 1980), one NFL (1969) and three NFC (1973, 1974 and 1976). In 1994 Bud was inducted into the Pro Football Hall of Fame in Canton, OH. With it, he became the first person ever to be elected to both the NFL and the Canadian Football League Halls of Fames.

"It's something that they can't take away from you," said Bud, who's presenter at the event was his old friend, Sid Hartman. "Usually in sports there is a new champion crowned every year, but this is forever."

Today, Bud and his wife Pat live in Bloomington. They have six children and many grandchildren. And, although he is officially retired from football, he still has an office at the Vikings headquarters and still consults with the team from time to time. Now, when he is not spending time either with his family or in the great outdoors, hunting or fishing, he has championed many causes that are near and dear to his heart. Among them is the fight against commercial fishing with nets and spears on Minnesota lakes. Bud is a zealous activist when it comes to preserving our natural resources and does all that he can to help conserve them for future generations. Bud is a true Minnesota treasure and a legend in every sense of the word.

HOW WOULD YOU DESCRIBE YOUR COACHING STYLE? "I would say I was fair, honest and worked hard. Coaching isn't X's and O's, it's management. Another thing, I always wore a headset because I wanted to know every defense that was ever called, every offensive play that was ever called, every part of the kicking game as it was unfolding, and each substitution as it happened. That was my style. I wanted to know what was going on with all aspects of our team. Now, I let my assistants do their thing. I delegated a lot of responsibility to my assistants, but the buck stopped with me."

HOW DID YOU MOTIVATE YOUR PLAYERS? "I don't like the word motivate. I would instead say 'make the players realize what they have to do in order go get better, to make their career longer, to make more money, to stay healthy, or to do all the things that they have to do on a daily basis to enhance their careers.' Motivate might be what you are doing, but it is in a different context in my eyes. Now, professionally, you 'motivated' your players with money. It is a good job, and if they don't perform well, then they won't have that job and they will be out of money. Now, as a coach you don't talk about that, but that is what athletes think about. They most certainly want to keep their jobs. Most of them, at least in the era that I coached, liked to play football. I know that I did because I could have made a lot more money doing things other than playing football when I came out of college. In those days the money wasn't as important as it is today. Now players worry about contracts, free agency, injuries and keeping their jobs. So, money motives athletes subconsciously to do well. Beyond that, motivation was about figuring out how to deal with each individual on an individual basis. You have to talk to each player in a different vain. For instance, I have a dog that when I holler at her, she doesn't do very well. But if I love her and tell her what a good job she is doing, she does great. You can apply that to players too. Some players you could holler at and they were used to being hollered at and they probably figured 'hey, at least the coach is watching me.' Other guys, you had to back off and try something else. You can't treat everyone the same, but in order to get their attention sometimes you had to approach them differently. I believe you could treat players differently under a team concept. Other than that, I always dealt in facts and tried to leave the emotions out of it. Sure, you might have to raise your voice to be heard, but as far as giving 'Win one for the Gipper' speeches, that was not me. You have to have something that your players will listen to. I also never used clichés because your players can see through that, especially if you use them more than once in a speech. So, you lose credibility motivating like that I think. In order to get your players attention, you have got to have something that pertains to what you are doing. Then, it comes down to preparation. Really, everything is done before you even get to the game. Big speeches are not going to do much on game day. These are professional athletes and they owe it to their teammates to be ready to play when the whistle blows."

WHO WERE YOUR COACHING MENTORS? "When I was at Great Lakes Naval Academy I learned the game under both Paul Brown and Blanton Collier. Paul Brown, in particular was a real innovator and someone I admired. I mean we had things like playbooks, practice schedules and detailed scouting reports, which today are commonplace, but back then it was revolutionary. Then, at the University of Minnesota I learned a lot from Bernie Bierman. He had a lot of success with the Gophers and his players respected him."

IF YOU COULD MAGICALLY GO BACK IN TIME TO THE FIRST YEAR YOU WERE A HEAD COACH AND GIVE YOURSELF SOME ADVICE FOR THE FUTURE, KNOWING WHAT YOU KNOW NOW, BACK THEN, WHAT WOULD YOU SAY TO YOURSELF? "I started coaching at just 29 years of age and really had no mental preparation to handle the job when I got it. I mean I had just come off of being an All-Star receiver and got right into coaching that next season. Heck, I figured at that time that I was going to play for another five years, not get into coaching. But, that was how I got into it and it was a real transition. I was so fortunate first starting out in Winnipeg and luckily had success pretty quickly. So, I am not sure what I would have done differently to tell you the truth other than to maybe have a few balls bounce different ways every now and then."

ON THE PARALLELS BETWEEN SPORTS AND HUNTING: "I love the outdoors and I have a real passion for hunting. When I go out hunting I am out there not only to shoot a gun, but also to observe and get a feel for the lay of the land. If I shoot a deer, duck, or pheasant, then sure, that is part of it, but hunting to me is about the entire experience of being outdoors. In my opinion, if you are an outdoors person, then you enjoy it all from a garter snake to a butterfly to a tree to a stream. You observe, you enjoy what you see and that makes you a true outdoors person. Now, in football, from a head coaches standpoint, you also have to be an observer because you have to see everything. So, my whole life I have been an observer and having played every position on the football field, except the interior line, I think I

can observe things that are happening and recognize where changes or developments, or whatever has to take place. Being an observer rather than a yeller and a screamer out on the sidelines was more my style."

ON RETIREMENT: "I enjoyed going to work every day and coaching. I didn't retire because I was tired of coaching, or because I was burned out, or because I had enough money. I was just ready. I had other things I wanted to do and had had enough. I still wanted to hunt and fish and spend time with my family. I left on my own terms and that was something I always said I would do."

WHAT MOTIVATED YOU? "Everybody has a different concept of competition. For me, personally, I felt that I was more competitive than almost anybody I ever played against. They might have had more ability than I did, but I always felt that I was a better competitor. I worked at that and as a player I could compete longer, be in better shape so I could outlast you and beat you at the end, you couldn't intimidate me and to me, that was all part of being competitive."

WHAT ARE THE KEY INGREDIENTS TO CREATING A CHAMPIONSHIP TEAM? "You need a lot of things to go right to win a championship, especially injuries. I remember one time when I was coaching in Winnipeg, we had won the Grey Cup the year before and then that next year we had nine injuries. Well, we won the first game, tied the second and then proceeded to lose the next 14 in a row. Seven of those nine players who were injured from that season came back the following year and we won another championship as a result. I never coached as hard in my life when we were 1-1-14. And, most of those injuries were on defense so we were losing games by scores of like 41-38 and 35-28, and what have you. So, we could score points, but we couldn't stop anybody. The point was, I coached as well as I could, but to no avail. We still couldn't win. Those players came back and we won it all, that is when you realize that it is the players who win ballgames, and not the coaches."

IF A MOVIE ABOUT YOUR LIFE WAS MADE, WHO WOULD YOU WANT TO PLAY YOU? "How about Charlton Heston? But at the peak of his career, not now!"

WHAT ADVICE WOULD YOU HAVE FOR YOUNG COACHES STARTING OUT TODAY? "It seems like the world is just full of coaches now, from little league to high school and from assistants to volunteers, and many of those coaches have aspirations of getting to the next level. I guess I would say that you have to be patient because it is hard to get instant results in coaching. You have to remember that you are not so much a motivator, as you are a teacher. I would also say that there are not a lot of rewards in coaching. I mean you see the glamorous side of it every Sunday afternoon on TV in the Fall with the pro game, but that is just the tip of the iceberg. The rest of the time it is a whole lot of work. It is seven days a week, three nights a week, 26 weekends in a row and not a day off for six months. So there is not a lot of glamour in it, that is for sure. Even at the high school and college level it is a full time job, what with spring training and weight lifting programs and what have you. So, if you want to get into coaching it is really not something I would advise. That's just me!"

HOW DID YOU BUILD TEAM UNITY & CHEMISTRY? "Chemistry comes with winning, I mean they always talk about chemistry when teams win, but when was the last time you heard a guy say 'Yeah, we're 0-12 but we've got great chemistry…'? You know, a football team is made up of anywhere from 30-60 players, depending on the level you are coaching, and they are all different personalities. Chemistry is important because it benefits in the enjoyment and satisfaction you get from doing a job well. Football is not just winning and losing, you have to have some fun and have a good time. That means you have to have a good time working hard

RED DAWSON: NFL's BUFFALO BILLS

Red Dawson was born in Minneapolis in 1906 and went on to attend Wisconsin River Falls and later Tulane. Dawson would then go into coaching and eventually wound up as the head coach of the NFL's Buffalo Bills from 1946-49, posting a career record of 19-25-4. Dawson led his Bills to the 1948 title game, but wound up losing to legendary coach Paul Brown's Cleveland Browns, 49-7. Dawson died in 1983 at the age of 1977.

in practice, in games, after the games, on the bus, and everywhere that you are as a team. That way guys want to come to practice because they enjoy playing and enjoy getting compliments from the coaching staff and from their teammates. Then they play well and have a great experience. If everyone shares in that great experience, and if everyone gets along as teammates, then you have chemistry."

FAVORITE LOCKER ROOM SIGN? "We never had any fancy slogans or anything like that. You know what we had? We had pictures of guys like Jim Marshall out there in the cold, soaking wet and muddy out in the snow and you could see his sweat and his breath in the cold. I mean here was one of our greatest players ever playing in the worst kind of weather and just laying it out on the line. To me that was better than some silly slogan."

WHAT'S THE BIGGEST THING YOU'VE LEARNED FROM COACHING THAT YOU'VE BEEN ABLE TO APPLY TO YOUR EVERYDAY LIFE? "If you want to be a coach you have to realize that is hard to have regular hours. You figure out pretty quick that whatever time it takes, whatever effort it takes and whatever thought process it takes, there are no time elements that you can adhere to. You just have to develop a work ethic to put in the time to get the job done. You know, over the years I probably had to release thousands of players. So, I would tell them that if they took the same work ethic that they put into playing football, and apply it to another endeavor or career, they would be successful. And I truly believe that."

WHAT'S THE SECRET TO YOUR SUCCESS? "There aren't any secrets. It was pretty obvious in that if you got the best players you generally could win. If you don't have the best players, no coach in the world is going to be a winner. College coaches know that, that is why they recruit so hard to get the best players. Most coaches will

win with the best players. In professional football you are drafting and you have free agency, and it is the same thing. Now, there are a lot of winners, but you have to remember, there is only one champion. That is something different. So, you have to work hard and keep winning, even though you might not win the championship every year."

WHAT WOULD YOU WANT TO SAY TO YOUR FANS, BOOSTERS, AND ALUMNI WHO HAVE SUPPORTED YOU ALL THESE YEARS? "The thing you have to remember about football at any level is that it is entertainment. It might be life and death down on the field, but it really has no residuals. Football is entertainment and you have to keep that in perspective. We tried to provide as much entertainment as possible and winning, of course, was the driving force to create that entertainment. So, you appreciate the support you get and the enthusiasm that is generated, but what you are doing is just providing entertainment. It is not like we were going out and building a new product or you were selling a new service or that you were a brain surgeon. I mean come on. We were in the entertainment business and you have to remember that. So, as bad as you may feel or as bad as the fans who may support you might feel, you have to keep it all in perspective. It was just entertainment and some people forget that. Now, you appreciate all the support you get and the more the better, but you have got to be able to recognize what it is — entertainment."

HOW DO YOU WANT YOUR COACHING EPITAPH TO READ — HOW DO YOU WANT TO BE REMEMBERED AS A COACH? "There were people who could run faster, jump higher, throw harder and shoot better than me, but I don't think anybody competed any harder than I did. I felt that I always had an advantage over my opponents because I never got tired. The longer we played, the stronger I got. Then I could beat you. And I applied that same theory to coaching. That was the type of player who I was always looking to get to play for me. Also, one thing that most coaches can't say, is that I've never been fired. I've always left whatever I was doing on my own accord, and I am proud of that. Every dollar I have ever made was from professional sports. I've had no other business or profession, and the only investments that I've got are six kids with college educations. Other than that, I don't have much."

JOHN RONING: UTAH STATE FOOTBALL

John Roning starred as an end on the University of Minnesota's 1934 national championship team. Roning would go on to serve as the football, basketball and track coach, as well as the director of athletics at Gustavus from 1939-42. His 1940 football team was conference champ and his overall record was 17-5-1. Roning's 1942 basketball team defeated four different conference champions, but, because Gustavus was not in a conference that year, the team could not be recognized nationally. His overall basketball record would stand at 47-20.

After leaving Gustavus in 1942, Roning went on to serve as an assistant coach for the Gophers, before joining the Navy that next year. In 1946, he returned to Minnesota as an assistant under Bernie Bierman until 1950. In 1951 Roning became the head football coach and director of athletics at Utah State. Roning would go on to be elected Coach of the Year of the Skyline Conference in both 1951 and 1954. In 1955 he became the head football coach at the University of Denver and was elected Coach of the Year in 1956 and Come-back Coach of the Year in 1958 as well. In 1960, when DU gave up football, Roning became the athletics director at the University of South Dakota, a position he would hold until 1971. Among his many coaching honors and accolades, in 1956 Roning was elected to the Board of Trustees of the American Football Coaches Association, and in 1957 he was elected to the NCAA's College Football Rules Committee. In addition, Roning was elected to the North Central Conference Hall of Fame in 1971. That same year Roning became Commissioner of the Big Sky Conference, with its headquarters in Boise, Idaho. Roning retired in 1977.

JOE MAYER
HIGH SCHOOL FOOTBALL: ROCHESTER LOURDES

Joe Mayer grew up in Waterloo, Iowa, and went on to attend Loras College in Dubuque, where he played football. Mayer's first teaching and coaching job was at Rochester Lourdes and, incredibly, he remained there for 27 years until retiring in 1983. Mayer taught phys ed and business at Lourdes and coached football for 27 years, posting a 164-71-4 career record along the way. In addition to winning five state mythical championships, and nearly a dozen conference titles, Mayer also won a MSHSL state championship in 1979 when his boys beat Apple Valley for the Class A title. (Lourdes played in two Catholic league conferences, the Central Catholic Conference, which included Cretin, St. Thomas Academy, De La Salle, Benilde and Hill Murray; and also the Don Bosco Conference which included Fridley Grace, Benilde, De La Salle, Holy Angels, St. Agnes, St. Bernard's, Winona Cotter, Austin Pacelli and Brady.) Over the years Mayer also served as the head basketball coach, track coach and tennis coach at Lourdes as well. Joe is retired and presently lives in Rochester.

HOW WOULD YOU DESCRIBE YOUR COACHING STYLE? "The kids who played for me would tell you that I was a pretty tough task master. But at the same time football was a sport and was supposed to be played for the fun of it. So, even though we had a lot of hard work to do, we tried to make it as fun as possible. We tried different things offensively and defensively over the years and that kept things interesting. I always felt that it was one thing to be a professional coach, where you decided that you were going to run a certain offense and defense and then went out and got the players you needed to do it, as opposed to being a high school coach, where you took whoever came through the door and tried to mold them together into a team. So, we worked hard and were disciplined, and that translated into success out on the field for us."

HOW DID YOU MOTIVATE YOUR PLAYERS? "We set goals for them and I was also an advocate for positive thinking in trying to get them to believe in themselves. I wanted them to believe in them-

selves both individually and also as a team so that they would have the ability to win."

LOOKING BACK WHAT ARE YOU MOST PROUD OF IN YOUR CAREER? "I am most proud of the success that our kids achieved after high school. Hopefully, sports gave them the confidence to go out and move ahead in life."

HOW DID YOU BUILD TEAM UNITY & CHEMISTRY? "Besides the hard work and toughness, we tried to have a good time at practice. We joked with the kids a lot and had fun. Prior to every game the last words I always said before my players came out of the locker room was 'let's go have fun!'. Really it was stressing the positives from the weakest player to the strongest. We also always tried to play as many kids as we could even though we had a small roster and some of our kids were of limited ability. Still, we tried to get those kids into the game on special teams so that they could feel like they were a part of the team. That all went into building chemistry."

WHAT MOTIVATES YOU? "Winning was great, but seeing my kids do well was what motivated me. I wanted them to be the best they could be and that made me very proud as a coach and teacher."

WHAT'S THE SECRET TO YOUR SUCCESS? "I think it goes back to positive thinking, which helped me a lot. Also, we did not do everything in a traditional way. By that I mean we probably would on-side kick anywhere from 10-20 times a year and we expected to get half of those back. We even on-sided the opening kick-off from time to time, and that stirred things up out there. We were also one of the few teams that I knew of that would even punt on third down if we were in a bad situation. That is almost unheard of today but we would do things like that if we believed in our defense."

HOW DO YOU WANT YOUR COACHING EPITAPH TO READ — HOW DO YOU WANT TO BE REMEMBERED AS A COACH? "He expected much and he gave much."

WALT KIESLING: NFL's PITTSBURGH STEELERS

Born in St. Paul in 1903, Walt Kiesling first starred on the gridiron as a guard at Cretin High School. Kiesling then went on to play at St. Thomas College in the early 1920s, and from there jumped right into playing pro football with the Duluth Eskimos in 1926. "Big Keys," as he was affectionately known, stayed in Duluth for two seasons before moving on to the Pottsville Maroons. Kiesling bounced around for several more years in the NFL after that, eventually playing with the Chicago Cardinals and Chicago Bears from 1929 to 1934 — even earning All-NFL honors in 1932. From there, Kiesling went on to play with the Green Bay Packers from 1935 to 1936, where he won an NFL Championship in 1936, and finally with the Pittsburgh Steelers from 1937 to 1938. "He was big like Babe Ruth, and a left-hander, too," said former teammate Johnny "Blood" McNally. "Like Ruth, he played his best when he had some belly on him." Despite his size, however, Kiesling had remarkable speed, and was one of the first great pulling guards to play the game.

The 12-year veteran later served as the head coach of the Steelers on four different occasions throughout the 1940s and 1950s, and also worked as an assistant with the Green Bay Packers during that time as well. Kiesling finally resigned his post with the Steelers in 1957 because of failing health. After 34 seasons of pro football, he died in 1962. Kiesling was later inducted into the Pro Football Hall of Fame in 1966.

Dick McCann, the former director of the Hall of Fame, once said of Kiesling: "He didn't just watch pro football grow from the rocky sandlots. He shoved it along the way. He gave almost half a century to the game he loved."

MIKE GRANT
HIGH SCHOOL FOOTBALL: EDEN PRAIRIE

Mike Grant grew up in Bloomington as the son of football coaching royalty and went on to graduate from Bloomington Lincoln High School in 1975 — the same year his father's Vikings lost a heart-breaker in the playoffs on a certain Hail Mary prayer which was answered by the Dallas Cowboys. From there, Grant went on to play football at St. John's University under legendary coach John Gagliardi. There, the tight end helped lead his Johnnies to the national championship in 1976. After graduating in 1979, Grant went on to serve as an assistant football coach at Minnetonka High School for two years. Then, at age 24 he became the head coach at Forest Lake High School, where he taught and coached for six years — winning his first conference title in 1986. Two years later, Grant took a one-year leave from Forest Lake to work as an assistant under both John Gagliardi and also Jim Smith, coaching football and basketball at St. John's. He then returned to Forest Lake for three more years, taking the team to a top five state ranking along the way.

Finally, in 1992, Grant took over as the head football coach at Eden Prairie High School, where he has remained ever since. When Grant took over the program, the Eagles had won just five games in the previous three years. Since then, he has created a dynasty. With more than 300 kids trying out for his team every year, Grant has created a winning atmosphere in Eden Prairie that has not been seen before. In his first year at E.P., Grant jumped in and won the conference title. Since then, the guy has been unstoppable. In fact, over the last seven years his teams are 86-3 and overall he is 115-12 in his 11 seasons as head coach. (Overall his career high school record is 160-54.) In addition, he has four undefeated seasons, four state championships (1996, 1997, 2000 and 2002), and his teams have not lost a conference game since 1995. The numbers are simply astonishing. Grant, who taught history and economics at E.P., now serves as the full-time athletic director and football coach.

Perhaps not quite the gridiron legend the old man was, Mike Grant is getting closer and closer every year. In the ranks of high school football, no one is better these days the he is. And who knows, John Gagliardi is getting up there in years and is poised to break the all-time wins record in 2003, maybe Grant will take over the reigns in Collegeville? Stay tuned!

HOW WOULD YOU DESCRIBE YOUR COACHING STYLE? "You know, I learned so much from being around my dad and then to play for John Gagliardi at St. John's, that really shaped my style. I think I learned from my dad how to deal with people and about all the things that surround the game, like the reporters, the practicing and dealing with your coaching staff. Then, from John I learned so much both as a player and as a coach. He taught me how the game should be played, about winning and losing and what the basics are. He is really one of the smartest people I know. Overall, coaching is just about hard work and building relationships, and my style is right in line with that. The common thread with coaching is common sense. It is about with dealing with people and about simplifying the game so players can be successful."

ON BEING BUD GRANT'S SON: "You know, for 46 years my life has revolved around the Fall football season. That is just how I grew up and it remains the same for me today. Living that lifestyle has been great and I am so lucky to have been brought up in it. My dad was a great coach and father and he taught me so much. You know, there is

a great beginning and a great end to every season, and you really wind up looking forward to rebuilding for the next football season every year. It is a great job and a great lifestyle. I have had so many great opportunities to meet so many great people with the Vikings and it has really helped shape me as a person."

HOW DO YOU MOTIVATE YOUR PLAYERS? "You know, I have always felt like you can't peak for a game because for every peak there is going to be a valley. So, you just have to continually preach to your kids at a high level on a continuous basis."

IF YOU COULD MAGICALLY GO BACK IN TIME TO THE FIRST YEAR YOU WERE A HEAD COACH AND GIVE YOURSELF SOME ADVICE FOR THE FUTURE, KNOWING WHAT YOU KNOW NOW, BACK THEN, WHAT WOULD YOU SAY TO YOURSELF? "I think the one word answer would be simplify. I think too many coaches over coach when they are younger and we need to realize that the game is actually simpler than you think. So, you have to just get to the core things, the really important things in winning, and forget about the little stuff which can sometimes wind up consuming most of your time. You have to be able to simplify the game by visualizing, that is the key. You have to remember that there are things that just don't matter."

WHAT ARE THE CHARACTERISTICS OF LEADERS? "I think a lot of leadership comes from how you were raised. I also think a lot of how you deal with stress comes from how your parents dealt with stress. Being a coach is all about dealing with stress, and leadership has to do with the ability to be the calm in the center of the storm. It's also about trust and honesty, that is at the core of leadership as well. You have to ask yourself if you trust your players to go out and do what they need to do, and visa versa, do your players trust you to be honest and lead them. When you have that, then you get the best athletes to come and try out for your team."

LOOKING BACK WHAT ARE YOU MOST PROUD OF IN YOUR CAREER? "While I am proud of the fact that I was able to build two good programs, Forest Lake and Eden Prairie, the biggest thing is when my former players come back to visit me. To sit around, reminisce and tell stories is just great and that means more than any championship to me."

WHAT IS THE KEY TO GOOD TIME MANAGEMENT? "You know, it might be overrated. So many coaches get too bent out of shape in running their practices down to the minute. To me it is not so much about time management, but to have a feel for things. You may say that you are going to have a half hour meeting, but some meetings need to go 20 minutes while others might go 40. It just depends on the situation of what you have going on at that time. It is just about getting the job done. I mean look at Gagliardi, he is doing 45 minute practices now. That to me is simply amazing, but he does it and he just keeps on winning. So, for me I think it is important to have a feel, a touch and a sense of when you are ready, rather than having a nice typed itinerary everyday for yourself."

HOW DO YOU BUILD TEAM UNITY & CHEMISTRY? "I think a lot of chemistry starts with your seniors. They lead by example and set the stage for everyone else, and it all sort of falls in line from there. I will say too that it's not the easiest thing to do, to build team unity, with a new program. So, you have to work hard at it as a coach during the beginning of your program. But, now that we are into it, there is such a tradition of understanding about what has to happen and what has to be done that our players can carry a lot of that out themselves. I just try to convey to the kids that it is all about learning and about what we do to prepare our team. I tell them all the time that this is their team and it is not about me. I remind them that we have won state championships and we are going to win more in the future, so this is about their time, right now. I want them to take ownership in the team and to do the right thing. If we do that, then we will have a lot of fun and we are going to win a lot of ballgames. Working hard is fun and winning is fun, and that is the formula. You just sort of have to preach the gospel about what your program is all about and that is how tradition and chemistry is built. We continuously show the kids video of great players making great plays and convince them that we are going to be great. We really don't have a bunch of division one athletes on our team either, so it is not about having great players, it is about having good players who play great."

ON LEARNING THE GAME FROM THE GREAT JOHN GAGLIARDI: "I know John as well as anybody in the world. He is the most competitive, dynamic, outspoken and demonstrative person you will ever meet. You see, the thing about John is that he likes to play that role where all these other coaches look at him and say 'Well, John wins because he's got this guy and that guy and they are so lucky…' and they don't realize that they are getting out-coached every darn week They just don't get it. They don't follow the game and realize that they are literally getting out-coached every week. Let me tell you, you don't go 50 years and win that many football games without knowing what is going on. And I have been behind closed doors with him as he breaks the game down and evaluates what transpired. He is smarter than any of them, I guarantee you that."

WHAT MOTIVATES YOU? "At the high school level I really don't worry about winning at all. I won't say that I don't want to win, but it really isn't the most important thing to me. For my dad, or for Gagliardi, that was the basis of their jobs. I mean if they didn't win they might get fired. But here, at this level, my concern is more about figuring out how these kids are going to have a great experience. If we create great experiences for kids, then the best athletes are going to want to come out for your squad. Then, when you have the best athletes working hard for you and playing well, then you have a chance to win. That is our formula and it just works for us."

WHAT ADVICE WOULD YOU HAVE FOR YOUNG COACHES STARTING OUT TODAY? "I think in order to be successful, you have to be lucky enough to learn from a veteran. I was fortunate enough to have some old grizzled veteran assistants with me at Forest Lake when I first started out and that was great for me. So, if you can have a mentor, that will really help I think. Otherwise coaches become what I call 'textbook coaches' in that they have to rely on books to learn about coaching, rather than learning from someone first hand. I would say watch and listen, that is the key."

WHAT'S THE BIGGEST THING YOU'VE LEARNED FROM COACHING THAT YOU'VE BEEN ABLE TO APPLY TO YOUR EVERYDAY LIFE? "Coaching is a way of life for me. It is all about relationships and that has really gone way beyond the football field for me. I mean it is about managing relationships with your co-workers, your students, your players, your friends, or your family. That is life and for me coaching is a way of life."

WHAT ARE THE KEY INGREDIENTS TO CREATING A CHAMPIONSHIP TEAM? "I think you have got to be real consistent. To be a champion you just need to be very consistent in your play. For me, to be honest with you, my greatest thrill in coaching is

not the four state championships, it is the nine out of 11 Lake Conference championships and seven in a row. Because you can get an injury or get a bad bounce in the state tournament and get beat or visa versa. But, if you can win your conference title seven years in a row, that is consistency, and that is how you go on to win state championships."

WHAT'S THE SECRET TO YOUR SUCCESS? "If I knew I would can it and sell it! Really though, I think it is all about honesty and trust. Your kids have to know that you are going to do what is best for the team. I think too that having great assistant coaches who have believed in the philosophy of treating the kids well and making it fun has been very important. (Grant's defensive coordinator is Gene Wise, his old high school coach at Bloomington Lincoln.) Beyond that we have created an atmosphere where the best athletes in our school want to be on our team and that has been huge. From there, we have built a program that the entire community has embraced, making Friday nights in the Fall great for everybody."

WHAT WOULD YOU WANT TO SAY TO YOUR FANS, BOOSTERS, AND ALUMNI WHO HAVE SUPPORTED YOU ALL THESE YEARS? "My first thanks would go to my assistant coaches, who have really bought into my vision of what high school football is all about. Secondly, I would thank all of our players who have given so much. Thirdly, and maybe most importantly, would be the kids who hung in there and maybe didn't get a chance to play very much on Friday nights. I am always amazed at the kid willing to be the fifth string senior and play on the scout team. Those kids are absolutely as important to us as any of our stars, and I might even respect those kids even more because they are all about the team."

HOW DO YOU WANT YOUR COACHING EPITAPH TO READ — HOW DO YOU WANT TO BE REMEMBERED AS A COACH? "It wasn't just about winning and losing, more than anything it was that he cared about his kids as people."

PHIL BENGSTON: NFL'S GREEN BAY PACKERS

Phil Bengston was born in 1913 in Roseau and went on to become an All-Big Ten Tackle at University of Minnesota in 1934. From there, Bengston went into coaching. In 1968 Bengston, then an assistant with Green Bay, would replace the legendary Vince Lombardi as the Packers head coach and go on to lead the Pack to a 20-21-4 record from 1968-70. In 1972 Bengston took over as the head coach of the New England Patriots, but posted just a 1-4 record before hanging it up. His career NFL coaching record was 21-25-1. Bengston died in 1994 in San Diego.

JOHN GUTEKUNST
COLLEGE FOOTBALL: UNIVERSITY OF MINNESOTA

John Gutekunst was born in Sellersville, Pa., and went on to graduate from Pennridge, Pa., High School. From there, Gutekunst went on to serve as the captain of both the football and baseball teams at Duke University from 1963-66. That next year Gutekunst started his collegiate coaching career at Duke, where he was an assistant from 1967-78. He later coached at Virginia Tech from 1979-83, before going to the University of Minnesota to serve as the defensive coordinator and secondary coach under Lou Holtz. Then, when Holtz left the Gophers for Notre Dame in 1985, Gutekunst was named as the team's new head coach. Gutie would guide the Golden Gophers from 1985-92, coaching the team to a pair of bowl games. The first was a 20-13 win over Clemson in the 1985 Independence Bowl and the other was the 1986 Liberty Bowl, which they lost to Tennessee. One of the highlights of that season, however, was his team's 20-17 upset win at No. 2 ranked and previously undefeated Michigan. Minnesota posted winning records in four of the six seasons Gutekunst was the head coach and his defenses were among the best in the Big Ten Conference during his tenure in Gold Country.

Gutekunst left Minnesota in 1992 with a modest 29-36-2 record and went on to serve as an assistant in the Arena Football League with the Tampa Bay Storm. That next season he landed as an assistant at Wake Forest. In 1993 he moved on to serve as an assistant at South Carolina, and from 1994-95 he did the same at Rutgers. Then, following a three-year gig as the defensive coordinator at Rhode Island, Gutekunst wound up back in South Carolina working yet again with Lou Holtz. Gutie has been at USC since 1999 and seems to have found a home with the Gamecocks. There, he has been a part of one of college football's biggest turn-arounds, and has watched his squads play in three straight bowl games. For his efforts, he was named as the Assistant Coach of the Year by the American Football Coaches Association in 2000 and has done an outstanding job handling USC's defensive secondary.

Gutekunst, who has more than 30 years of coaching experience at the college level, has earned the reputation of being one of the top defensive coaches in the college game. He has made a lot of stops along the way, but Gutie will always be known for his hard work and positive attitude. The fans appreciated his effort in Minnesota and respect what he did for Gopher Football. John and his wife Leah have three children: Brian, Michael and Jon, and presently reside in Columbia, S.C.

HOW WOULD YOU DESCRIBE YOUR COACHING STYLE? "They can name you head coach but they can't name you leader — you have to earn that on your own. Without being a leader you can't be a successful head coach. That is where you start. Then, you have to do it within the framework of your personality because although you might be able to fool the press, you can't fool the players. So, you have to be your own man, and from there it comes down to hard work and leadership."

HOW DO YOU MOTIVATE YOUR PLAYERS? "I think it is hard to motivate people who don't have a sense of responsibility because everything turns to an 'I.' So, I think if you have a sense of responsibility then the group effort becomes what is important. Plus, I think playing the game changes. Playing the game gets harder and harder to play well, the higher the level of competition you go and if you don't really enjoy the game and thrive on that competition, it's

almost like a false sense of motivation that lasts until the first crisis in the game — and every game is going to have one. So, I think the kids have to have confidence and that confidence comes from learning the fundamentals. That means as a coach you have to teach the fundamentals and let them see how that works within the framework of whatever offense of defense you are using. Beyond that there is just a passion that you have where you can't let your teammates down. I think you have to motivate groups as a head coach and I think you have to motivate individuals as an assistant coach."

IF YOU COULD MAGICALLY GO BACK IN TIME TO THE FIRST YEAR YOU WERE A HEAD COACH AND GIVE YOURSELF SOME ADVICE FOR THE FUTURE, KNOWING WHAT YOU KNOW NOW, BACK THEN, WHAT WOULD YOU SAY TO YOURSELF? "Do it your way. I think I would still come back to what got me here and just believe in myself. There can only be one leader in a direction that a team is going to go and you have to do it your way."

WHAT IS THE KEY TO GOOD TIME MANAGEMENT? "I think humor. When you talk about time management everybody talks about schedules and this and that, but for assistants it is different. I think for them it is always about a series of projects — summer football camp, notebook, game plan, recruiting, etc. When you finish those you are basically done, but when you are the head coach you have to learn to walk away knowing that there are things on your desk that need to be and should be done. So, if you don't have that ability to walk away, which I think comes from having a sense of humor, then you won't last in this business. Having a sense of humor is the ability to laugh when things are funny or things are getting crazy, and if you lose that then you lose your drive. If you lose your drive, then your management falls apart around you. So, for me, that is how I approach it."

LOOKING BACK WHAT ARE YOU MOST PROUD OF IN YOUR CAREER? "I would say it is an amalgam of several things, from great games to great individuals to my family to my career. I am proud of all of that."

WHAT IS THE KEY TO RECRUITING? "You just have to work hard and be able to sell your program. I think young people want the opportunity to play at a place that believes it can win and be successful. The harder it is for the young man to say no to you, the greater chance you have as a coach for him to say yes to you. So, you have to try to develop a personal relationship with him under the context of the NCAA rules. You need to get to know him and you also need to really know your own program so that you can sell it. I also tell kids that if they are not serious about their academics, then they don't want to play for Coach Holtz. That is very important to us and to our program. We challenge kids to make sure that not only we are the right fit for them, but also that they are the right fit for us."

HOW DO YOU BUILD TEAM UNITY & CHEMISTRY? "I think unity, chemistry, morale or whatever you want to call it comes from everybody getting better. So, if an individual sees that he is becoming better, then that is where it starts. You know, you can only have 11 starters in football, so it is obvious that not everyone is going to be a starter. I think if you look back at great teams, their were always certain individuals who had the ability to pull people together. From there, the chemistry just developed from the players caring for one another."

WHAT MOTIVATES YOU? "For me it is the constant pursuit of trying to play the perfect game. Sure, there is a passion and drive to win, but it is more about getting myself and my players to play the best they can play. You know, I am most relaxed on game day, those 60 minutes are as good as it gets as a coach. All of your hard work and preparation are brought to the table and the challenge begins. If you say it is only about winning then you are a fool, because you know somebody is going to win and somebody is going to lose. So, in my opinion it is about striving to be the best you can be on every play, every series, every quarter and every game. For me it is the pursuit of that elusive perfect game."

WHAT ADVICE WOULD YOU HAVE FOR YOUNG COACH-ES STARTING OUT TODAY? "There is no coaching without play-ers. I think that when you are in the educational environment, regard-less of the level, we have to recruit and develop good players. But, we also have to be conscious of their academic pursuits. There are only so many professional jobs available every year, so I can't say enough about how important it is for these kids to get their educations. Sometimes that is tough, especially with the money out there in pro football, but as coaches we have the responsibility of doing our best to emphasize the value of a college degree. We can never forget that."

WHAT'S THE BIGGEST THING YOU'VE LEARNED FROM COACHING THAT YOU'VE BEEN ABLE TO APPLY TO YOUR EVERYDAY LIFE? "I have never forgotten that every play-er is someone's son. So, as that applies to football I would just say 'never give up' and never stop working hard for those young people."

WHAT ARE THE KEY INGREDIENTS TO CREATING A CHAMPIONSHIP TEAM? "Good players, desire, confidence, teaching and a passion to want to succeed as a group."

WHAT'S THE SECRET TO YOUR SUCCESS? "Aside from having really good friends, which is so important to me both person-ally and professionally, I remember back to something my mom always told me: 'whatever job they ever give you, just do it to the best of your ability.' I have always lived by that in whatever I do, big or small, and that has worked well for me. Aside from that, I love what I am doing. I think about in baseball when the umpire starts a game he doesn't yell 'Work Ball!', he yells 'Play Ball!.' This is still a game and it should be fun."

WHAT WOULD YOU WANT TO SAY TO YOUR FANS, BOOSTERS, AND ALUMNI WHO HAVE SUPPORTED YOU ALL THESE YEARS? "Minnesota had such a great football tradi-tion in the early 1960s, when I was a kid, so for me to come there and be the head coach was just a real privilege and honor. The people there were so knowledgeable and the fans were just so supportive of me and of our program and I really appreciated that."

HOW DO YOU WANT YOUR COACHING EPITAPH TO READ — HOW DO YOU WANT TO BE REMEMBERED AS A COACH? "I would say: there is a man who didn't waste his life nor let me entirely waste mine."

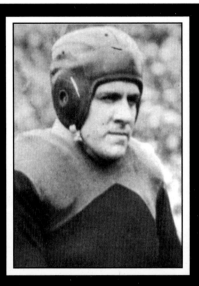

BIGGIE MUNN: MICHIGAN STATE FOOTBALL

Clarence "Biggie" Munn, a Minneapolis native and All-American guard and punter on the Golden Gopher Football team in 1931, went on to win a pair of back-to-back national champi-onships in 1951 and 1952 as the head coach of the Michigan State Spartans. Munn, who also amassed a 28-game winning streak during that time at MSU, is also credited with developing the "multiple offense" scheme, which revolutionized college football. With a 54-9-2 career record in East Lansing, Munn was later enshrined into the College Football Hall of Fame. Biggie stepped down from coaching in 1953, after leading his Spartans past UCLA in the Rose Bowl. Munn, who was later honored when the hockey arena at Michigan State was renamed after him in his honor, died in 1975. He was a Gopher and Spartan legend.

JOHN MADDEN: NFL's OAKLAND RAIDERS

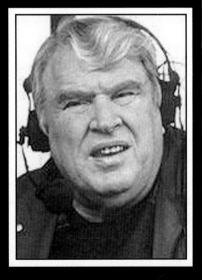

Did you know that John Madden is one of us? That's right, Madden was born in 1936 in Austin. He moved from Spamville as a kid though, and was raised in Daly City, Calif. Madden went on to play college football at California Polytechnic College at San Luis Obispo in the late 1950s. There, he was an All-Conference lineman and also a catcher on the school's baseball team. He would then go on to serve as an assistant coach with San Diego and Oakland for several years. Before becom-ing one of the most famous football broadcasters on the planet, Madden first made his mark as the coach of the Oakland Raiders. From 1969-79 Madden guided the Raiders to an overall record of 103-32-7, leading the team to seven AFC Western Division titles and a victory over our Minnesota Vikings in Super Bowl XI. Madden's winning percentage (.750) is the best of any head coach in NFL history. Through the years he has become synonymous with NFL football and has endeared himself to millions of fans nationwide for his ability to explain the game's finer points with a unique sense of humor. After more than two decades as a game analyst for CBS and Fox, this legendary broadcaster presently serves as an expert analyst on Monday Night Football. His video games and television endorsement deals have made him a household name and a very wealthy man. From his "Madden Cruiser" bus, to his numerous books, to his horse trailer, to his six-legged turkey award on Thanksgiving day — this 15-time Emmy Award nominee wreaks of football... and that is why we love him. John and his wife Virginia presently reside in Pleasanton, Calif., and have two sons.

DICK HANSON
HIGH SCHOOL FOOTBALL: BURNSVILLE

Dick Hanson grew up in Grand Forks, N.D., and went on to graduate from Grand Forks Central High School. There, he was a member of the 1952 state high school basketball championship team which also included future University of Arizona coach, Lute Olson. Hanson then went on to attend the University of North Dakota, where he played on the golf team. Hanson got into coaching during his freshman year at UND, where he coached several sports at St. Mary's parochial school in Grand Forks. His first job was at Grand Forks-St. James High School, where he was an assistant in football and basketball and as well as the school's first golf coach. It was there, however, that he realized that football was his passion.

Hanson moved to Burnsville in 1960, and began teaching math and coaching the golf team. He also served as an assistant under Bob Pates on the football team until 1968. That next year he resigned as the golf coach and took over as the head football coach. He went 8-1 that first year and would go on to become a football coaching legend. He coached the Blaze from 1969-93 and his teams won five state titles along the way (1972, 1980, 1985, 1989 & 1991). Hanson's overall record was an impressive 192-56-2 over his 25 year tenure, and many of his kids went on to play collegiately as well. In addition to his numerous coaching honors, Hanson also has several teaching accolades, including being named Minnesota Teacher of the Year in 1964. In addition, in 1965 he was runner-up for national Teacher of the Year. Then, in 1984 the White House gave him the Presidential Award for Mathematics.

Dick presently resides near Brainerd, where he still continues to teach at several local colleges and also gives workshops on using the internet. In recent years he's given workshops for teachers on locating and using interactive math Web sites — "Grandpa Dick Surfs for You" is his handle.

Hanson also still watches football very closely, taping and analyzing games from all levels — and still getting that coaching fix that he loves. In addition, his contributions to education continue through the "Dick Hanson Scholarship Fund," which has raised more than $70,000 since 1994. The fund awards six $1,000 scholarships to two to Burnsville High School students, two to Lakeville High School students and one to an Eagan High School student, all of whom express an interest in teaching. In addition, one scholarship will go to an area teacher for professional advancement. "Our children and grandchildren are going to be in good hands," Hanson said. "There are some marvelous people who are attracted to teaching."

HOW WOULD YOU DESCRIBE YOUR COACHING STYLE? "I think we are really blessed to be entrusted with some of the best people that God has made on this planet. So, when the parents give you those people who they have molded for many years and you get to work with them, you are really lucky. I liked the complexity of the game, the chess aspect of it, and that played into my philosophy quite a bit. I studied the game constantly, and really got into watching film. I had 12 VCR's going nonstop in my basement when I was coaching, to try to keep on top of what was going on."

HOW DID YOU MOTIVATE YOUR PLAYERS? "I always felt that if you had 80 players on your team then you better have 80 different ways to motivate them. Because what turns this guy on might turn that guy off, so you better try it all. So, I tried everything. One thing we did was have spirit sessions on Thursdays, where the only rule was you couldn't talk football. There, I gave them everything

from Vladimir Horowitz's last concert in Moscow to Mother Theresa. We tried it all. I wanted them to be well rounded individuals, that was important to me. It just came down to figuring out what motivated each kid and then doing that to get the best out of him."

LOOKING BACK WHAT ARE YOU MOST PROUD OF IN YOUR CAREER? "I think that we related to kids of all abilities. We never had to cut kids either. I mean if we had a slow, heavy kid we played him on the field goal team or if we had a fast, tiny guy, he could play on the punt coverage team. Our main goal every year, and I think we achieved it, was that the kids had to feel better when they came off the field than they did when they stepped on to the field for a practice or for a game. We also kept our door open for the kids to come in and talk anytime they wanted. We were very open with one another and that helped us to communicate and build trust and respect with one another."

IF YOU COULD MAGICALLY GO BACK IN TIME TO THE FIRST YEAR YOU WERE A HEAD COACH AND GIVE YOURSELF SOME ADVICE FOR THE FUTURE, KNOWING WHAT YOU KNOW NOW, BACK THEN, WHAT WOULD YOU SAY TO YOURSELF? "Listen to the kids more. We used to spend an enormous amount of time trying to sort things out among the coaches and later, when I was more experienced, we spent an enormous amount of time listening to the kids as to what was going on right in front of their faces."

HOW DID YOU BUILD TEAM UNITY & CHEMISTRY? "I had a great staff, my assistant coaches were just outstanding men. In addition to that, we leaned on our seniors heavily."

WHAT MOTIVATED YOU? "The kids. It was like Christmas every Fall, opening that new package. To see how hard they worked to get ready for the season and to see how much they wanted to commit to it was just great."

WHAT ADVICE WOULD YOU HAVE FOR YOUNG COACHES STARTING OUT TODAY? "Videotape everything that moves. Also, follow the coaches that you admire. One thing we tried to do was to take our staff to Spring meetings every year. Then, whenever we could we would go to a team that had won a national championship and spend some time with them. We would film their early practices and sit in with the coaches on their coaches meetings in the morning and then sit in with their players during their position meetings in the afternoon. Then, we would film the practice session. That was extremely beneficial for us. We learned so much from that. When you study the game like that it really becomes a lot like chess."

FAVORITE LOCKER ROOM SIGN? "I got a saying from Michigan's great coach Bo Schembechler one time that read: 'Those who stay will be champions.' I really liked that. We always wanted to emphasize that championships are not always in the trophies, but in the memories."

WHAT'S THE BIGGEST THING YOU'VE LEARNED FROM COACHING THAT YOU'VE BEEN ABLE TO APPLY TO

YOUR EVERYDAY LIFE? "I think just giving it your best shot and you can often be better than you know how to be."

WHAT ARE THE KEY INGREDIENTS TO CREATING A CHAMPIONSHIP TEAM? "You have got to have the family, the community, the staff and the commitment from the kids. We stuck to the clock down to the minute during practices and we gave the kids consistency in everything we did. That helped them focus a lot. I think some of our practices were tougher than our games. We worked very hard and that got the kids prepared to play on Fridays."

WHAT'S THE SECRET TO YOUR SUCCESS? "I surrounded myself with great people, kept my eyes open for innovation and never forgot that it was a 365 day a year job. Beyond that, I think one of the biggest things that I did was to tape everything that moved with regards to football. Videotaping was huge for me. I was an offensive guy, so to try to sell my defensive coordinator on what we were doing, there was no way I could do it unless I had an example on tape. He was a Michigan fan, so I even went as far as to tape Wolverine games to show him how a particular stunt worked that I wanted to incorporate into our playbook. He bought it every time. Visualization is such a big thing and really made a huge difference for us. So, I taped everything I could on Saturdays and Sundays to get new ideas and to see how the big boys were doing it. That is how we constantly got better. My basement had 12 VCRs going non-stop with tapes all over the place, and there were kids coming in and out watching film day and night. It was just great. And it was addicting. I miss it terribly. And even though I am retired, I still find myself taping games."

WHAT WOULD YOU WANT TO SAY TO YOUR FANS, BOOSTERS, AND ALUMNI WHO HAVE SUPPORTED YOU ALL THESE YEARS? "They were incredibly loyal to us, in the good years and the bad, and we really appreciated that."

HOW DO YOU WANT YOUR COACHING EPITAPH TO READ — HOW DO YOU WANT TO BE REMEMBERED AS A COACH? "He gave it his best shot. You know, the bonds that you make in football are really lasting in life and that is something that I tried to pass on to my kids."

BUD WILKINSON: OKLAHOMA FOOTBALL

Born in 1916, in Minneapolis, Bud Wilkinson attended the Shattuck School in Faribault. There, he quickly emerged as a brilliant student-athlete both on the gridiron, as a quarterback & guard, and on the ice, as a hockey goaltender. So good was Wilkinson as a goalie, that in 1932, he led Shattuck to an undefeated record and in the process, he went unscored upon over the entire season. He graduated in 1933 Cum Laude with the rank of First Lieutenant, and headed north, to the U of M, where he would emerge once again as one of his school's all-time greats.

Wilkinson distinguished himself in football and hockey in Gold Country, even finding time to also letter in golf. As a guard on the 1934 and '35 undefeated national championship teams, he was termed by the famous writer Grantland Rice as "The best offensive guard in college football." Due to injuries, Bernie Bierman asked Wilkinson if he would switch from guard to quarterback that next year. He did, and in 1936, Bud directed Minnesota to their third straight undefeated national championship. When it was all said and done, Wilkinson had done it all. Not only was he an All-American goalie on the Gopher Hockey team, but he had also garnered back-to-back All-American honors on the gridiron. In addition, he also won the school's highest honor for scholastics and sports — the Big Ten Medal of Honor.

Following graduation, Wilkinson played in the college All-Star game, quarterbacking the collegeiates to a 7-0 victory over the Green Bay Packers, the first time in history the All-Stars had beaten the pros. He also played on the Galloping Gophers, an all-star basketball team that traveled around the Midwest playing independent teams, including the Harlem Globetrotters — whom they defeated. From there, Wilkinson went on to Syracuse University, where, in addition to serving as an assistant football coach under Ossie Solem, he earned his Masters Degree in English. He then briefly returned to Minnesota as an assistant to Bernie Bierman before being commissioned in the US Navy.

After the war, Wilkinson was considered for the Gopher coaching job, but he turned it down and instead went to the University of Oklahoma, where he would become the team's head coach in 1947. At OU Wilkinson would forever change the game, and in the process become one of college football's greatest ever coaches. After tying for the 1947 championship, the Sooners won 12 straight conference crowns. Additionally, in between 1953 and 1957, his teams won 47 consecutive games over five straight undefeated seasons — an all-time national record. His teams also appeared in eight Sugar & Orange Bowl games, and he was named as the Coach of the Year on numerous occasions as well. His record at OU was an astounding 145-29-4, with three national titles to boot. At the time of his retirement, in 1963, Bud had become the winningest coach in college football.

Wilkinson was also an innovator. He is credited for creating the "swinging gate" formation and a 1950s version of the "no-huddle" offense which he called the "go-go offense" He also didn't believe in red-shirting but still managed to graduate an incredible 90% of his student-athletes. Although his national coaching honors and accolades are too many to mention, among his major ones include being inducted into the College Football and National Football Coaches Hall of Fames; being elected president of the American Football Coaches Association; and receiving the Sports Illustrated Silver Anniversary All-American Award in 1962.

After retiring, Wilkinson even ran for senate in 1964, where, despite winning the Republican primary, he lost in the general election. Then, after a career in TV broadcasting, among other business interests, Wilkinson later coached in the NFL with the St. Louis Cardinals in 1978 and 1979. He hung em' up after just two sub-par seasons though (9-20), and returned to the TV booth, where he served as an analyst for both ESPN and ABC.

In addition to later becoming OU's Athletic Director, Wilkinson led quite a celebrated life after football. He was a consultant to President Nixon and a member of the White House Staff from 1969-71. He was also a special consultant to President Kennedy on physical fitness from 1961-64, and he later served as the Republican National Committeeman for Oklahoma during the late 1960s.

Sadly, Wilkinson died in 1994 at the of 77 after battling heart problems. He will always be regarded as one of Minnesota's greatest all-time athletes, coaches and humanitarians. He is arguably America's greatest ever college football coach.

LOU HOLTZ
COLLEGE FOOTBALL: UNIVERSITY OF MINNESOTA

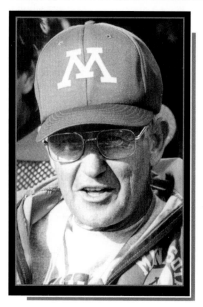

Lou Holtz was born in Follansbee, W. Va., and grew up in nearby East Liverpool, Ohio. After graduating from East Liverpool High School, Holtz went on to play linebacker at Kent State for two seasons before an injury ended his career. He would earn his bachelor's degree in history from Kent State in 1959 and then head to Iowa, where he would serve as an assistant coach and also earn his master's degree in arts and education in 1961. From there, Holtz went on to serve as an assistant at several schools, including: William & Mary (1961-63), Connecticut (1964-65), South Carolina (1966-67), and Ohio State (1968), where the Buckeyes won the national championship.

Holtz's head coaching career began in 1969 at William & Mary at the age of 32. In just his second season at William & Mary, Holtz won the Southern Conference title and advanced on to play in the Tangerine Bowl —the only postseason appearance in the history of the school. From there, Holtz headed to North Carolina State, where he produced the best four-year won-loss record (33-12-3) in the history of the school. In 1973 his Wolfpack won the ACC championship and then went on to win the Liberty Bowl, it would be the first of four straight bowl appearances for Holtz at NCSU. He took over a NCSU program that had won only three games in each of the previous three seasons before he arrived, and when he left he was named as the Atlantic Coast Conference Coach of the Year.

In 1976 Holtz left North Carolina State and made the jump to the NFL, taking over as the head coach of the New York Jets. It would be a short-lived trip, however, as his squad did not play well and he was forced to return to the college ranks that next season. In 1977 Holtz took over as the head coach at Arkansas. He quickly made a name for himself at Arkansas by taking his first Razorback team to an 11-1 record, highlighted by a stunning 31-6 upset of second-ranked and once-beaten Oklahoma in the Orange Bowl. For his efforts, Holtz was named National Coach of the Year. By the time he was finished coaching the Razorbacks seven seasons later, he had produced an amazing 60-21-2 (.735) record and six straight bowl appearances.

From there, Holtz came to Minnesota, where he took over from Smokey Joe Salem and resuscitated a Gopher program that had combined for a 4-18 record in its previous two seasons. In 1984, Holtz took over a 1-10 team that gave up 518 points the previous year and produced a respectable 4-7 record. "Sweet Lou," who came to Gold Country amidst the hype and fan-fair of a rock star, took the campus by storm. Holtz fever was everywhere and with it came a renewed sense of pride the Gopher football program hadn't seen in decades. Holtz could recruit, coach and preach to the masses better than anyone. He could sell ice in the North Pole and sand in the desert, and before it was all said and done, thousands upon thousands of fans would follow him like the Pied Piper into that big teflon tent otherwise known as the Metrodome to watch their Gophers make an about face.

In 1985, Holtz took his rebuilding process a step further, by coaching Minnesota to a 5-1 start, with the only loss being a 13-7 decision to eventual national champion Oklahoma. The Golden Gophers were ranked in the top 20 at midseason and eventually finished 6-5, marking the program's first winning season since 1981. Season ticket sales doubled under his tenure, fundraising grew by leaps and bounds, recruiting took on a whole new meaning and football was king again in the Land of 10,000 Lakes — all thanks to one man, Lou Holtz. Minnesota then went on to defeat the Clemson

Tigers in the Independence Bowl — a game which was played after Holtz had departed to take the Notre Dame job. (His assistant, John Gutekunst, would replace him behind the bench.) A devout Catholic, Notre Dame was Lou's ultimate prize.

After leaving Minnesota, Holtz made history with the Fighting Irish. In just his third season at Notre Dame, Holtz led the Fighting Irish to the 1988 national championship with a perfect 12-0 record, a season in which he earned National Coach of the Year honors. From 1986-90, Holtz's record was an astonishing 100-30-2 at Notre Dame. He led the Fighting Irish to nine consecutive New Year's Day Bowl games and his five postseason bowl victories are more than any other Irish coach. In addition, three times during his stay at South Bend, his Fighting Irish squads achieved the highest graduation rates in the country. Academics were always important to Holtz, and the fans and players alike appreciated it.

Holtz stepped down from Notre Dame in 1996, citing the fact that he did not want to surpass the legendary Knute Rockne on the all-time wins list as one of his reasons for leaving. From there, he served as a college football analyst for CBS Sports for two years. Then, in 1998, Holtz was named as the head coach at the University of South Carolina, where he has been ever since. Once again, Holtz performed his magic, this time turning around a USC program which had been on life-support. From a winless record in 1999 to consecutive Outback Bowl victories and two straight years of top 20 status, Coach Holtz has resuscitated the life back into Gamecock football. The Gamecocks entered the new millennium riding a 21-game losing streak — the nation's longest, and have not looked back since Lou came to town. In 2000 Holtz was named as both the National Coach of the Year and SEC Coach of the Year.

As he begins his fifth season at USC and his 32nd season overall as a head coach, Lou Holtz is still going strong. He entered the 2003 season as the third winningest active coach and tied for eighth place all-time with 238 victories, while his 12 bowl game victories rank fifth on the all-time list. The numbers are simply amazing. Holtz has taken four different programs to top 20 finishes, won a national championship, won multiple national coach of the year honors, and guided teams to 23 postseason bowl games. Incredibly, 23 of his 31 collegiate teams have earned post-season bowl bids and 18 have finished in the final AP top 25 rankings. In addition, Holtz has become the only coach in NCAA history to ever lead six different programs to bowl games.

Among his many, many coaching accolades and honors, Holtz has authored two best-selling books: "The Fighting Spirit," that chronicles Notre Dame's 1988 championship season, and "Winning Every Day," that focuses on 10 strategies which can assist an individual in achieving success in his or her professional and personal life. A world-renown speaker and student of motivation, Holtz has also championed countless charitable and educational causes. Most recently, he was named the 1998 Man of the Year by the Walter Camp Football Foundation for his exemplary service to the game of football and to his fellow man.

Lou and his wife of 42 years, Beth, have four children: Luanne, Kevin, Elizabeth and Skip — who presently serves as the assistant head coach and offensive coordinator under his old man at USC. Simply put, Lou Holtz is a legend among legends and is truly the very, very best of the very, very best. Period.

ON YOUR TIME WITH THE GOPHERS IN MINNESOTA: "When I came to the University of Minnesota I didn't know much about the state other than the fact that it was really cold! But really, it was a wonderful experience and I thoroughly enjoyed the people up there. Number one, it was such a great place to live. I mean you had culture, you had a tremendous business community, and it was just a beautiful place to live. I remember when my family went camping up in the Boundary Waters one Summer, that was something I will never forget. You also had such great people there too. I mean I became like brothers with Sid Hartman and Harvey Mackay, and then you had Paul Giel, who was such a legend up there too. When I got there, I quickly learned to appreciate the values that the people of Minnesota espouse. Then, as far as football went, it was actually easier to turn around the Gopher program than most people would think because of the character and integrity of the athletes who we had on our team. Being the only Division One program up there too, it gave you a real advantage when it came to recruiting. I mean the people really got behind us when I was there and that meant a lot to me. You know, the fans up there were just great, and really some of the best in the country. They supported us so much and were really a big part of our success during that time."

HOW WOULD YOU DESCRIBE YOUR COACHING STYLE? "Basically, it is good fundamentals; it is discipline; it is unselfishness; it is togetherness; it is focusing on what you have to do; and it is nothing real fancy. You just have to give your players something to do and then demand that they do it. As a coach, you try to take whatever situation you are in and figure out the best way to win with the personnel you've got. You know, at Minnesota, I knew we could get big offensive and defensive linemen from the area, but we had to recruit elsewhere for speed. But, to win in the Big 10 at that time, I just didn't feel that we could throw the ball on a consistent basis because we didn't have our indoor facility built yet, and the players couldn't throw year round — which you really have to be able to do. So, I felt that the option would give us the best chance to win, and that it was we did. We recruited Rickey Foggie and some other great players, and that gave us a chance to really be competitive by having a fast, mobile quarterback. We stuck to our plan and we had good success with it."

HOW DO YOU MOTIVATE YOUR PLAYERS? "Number one, you eliminate those who aren't motivated. I think motivation is nothing more than having a goal, or having something that you really, truly wish to accomplish as a team. We always talk about core values too. That is what holds this country together; that is what holds a family together; and that is what holds a team together. If you don't have core values, then anything goes. Core values are things you will not compromise on, period. Everybody on the team must believe in those same values and that comes back to trust, commitment and a genuine caring for one other. These are all absolute necessitates that you have to believe in or you cannot be successful as a team. I also believe that your discipline program has to be done through academics. Kids need to go to class; they need to study; and they need to be accountable. If they do those things, then that carries over onto the football field. You can't have discipline on the field unless you have discipline off the field, and the best way to achieve that is through academics."

HOW DO YOU BUILD TEAM UNITY & CHEMISTRY? "Team chemistry is getting a group of people together who share the same common goals. Then, you have to get them to get to know one another. Too many times we pass judgment on people based on how they look; the way they dress; the music they listen to; or on their ethnic or religious backgrounds. When you really get to know people and understand them, then you can have chemistry. People have to learn to understand and appreciate each other, and realize that we all have the same purpose. If one kid hurts, we all hurt, and that is what it is all about. It is just showing people that you care. You know, it comes down to attitude. It is either 'here I am,' or 'there you are.' If your attitude is 'here I am,' then that means you are selfish, insecure and want attention. We don't have a place on our team for 'here I am.' We want kids whose attitudes are 'there you are,' which means they are concerned and care about others. Then, we make sure that people understand that every time they achieve something it is because somebody else enabled them to do it. Nobody accomplishes anything by themselves and we should always be appreciative of those who made our lives possible."

WHAT ADVICE WOULD YOU HAVE FOR YOUNG COACHES STARTING OUT TODAY? "You have to start with a philosophy that you really and truly believe in. Then, they have to realize that the only reason that they have a job is because of the players. They also have to realize that their obligation is to those players — to help them grow as people and to help them succeed both on the field and in the classroom. Then, most importantly, they have to be able to handle adversity in life. You just can't succeed if you don't believe in yourself. I also think there are too many coaches who want to be geniuses and want to out-smart other people, and that is not their purpose — their purpose is to help their kids succeed on and off the field. And, the only way to do that is to teach your kids how to succeed. You have to teach them the value of hard work; the value of appreciation; the value of being a competitor; and most importantly, the value of believing in yourself."

WHAT MOTIVATES YOU? "There isn't anything that I am out to prove or anything else. I am motivated by the obligation that I have with my players and to see to it that they grow as people both on and off the field. If they come to play for you and put their faith and confidence in you, then that is a big responsibility. You can't look them in the eye if you haven't done everything you possibly could to prepare them to be successful. That is what motivates me. I just don't want to let other people down who are counting on me. I feel very strongly about the obligations that an individual has. When you join a team, or bring a child into the world, or become a member of a business, you have obligations and responsibilities — and you cannot take those lightly. I have obligations to our coaches, our players, our fans, our faculty and our university, so how could I possibly not be motivated. If I was obligated just to myself, and not to all those other people, then shoot... I am old, I am tired, I am worn out, I would like to play more golf — but I have obligations and couldn't live if I didn't do everything I could to honor those obligations."

WHAT'S THE SECRET TO YOUR SUCCESS? "I don't have any secrets. I go back to my core values, which is you can trust me and you know that I am going to do everything I can to make our program the very best. Then, I am going to care about the players, the people and about the school. I coach the fundamentals and try to make players better. Players become good when you teach them the basic fundamentals. There just aren't enough coaches who emphasize that I don't think. You know, there isn't anything fancy about me, just good, sound fundamentals and core values — that's it."

ON THE INFAMOUS "NOTRE DAME CLAUSE": "I went to the University of Minnesota and did everything I could to turn that program around. When I got there, I seriously planned on coaching there the rest of my life. I never went there thinking that it was going to be temporary or anything else. So, everything we tried to do, we tried to do it on a foundation that would last a lifetime. We never tried to cut corners, or play tricks, we just tried to build a good, solid program. You know, what people don't understand is that when I went to Minnesota, there were five other coaches who had already turned the job down. I mean they had lost 17 straight conference games by an average score of 47-13. So, I was hesitant to take the job at first, but finally decided to do it after praying on it. Then, I decided to put the Notre Dame clause in my contract. For me, being a Catholic, and following Notre Dame all my life, that was a very appealing job to me. What people do not understand about the clause, however, is that in it, it said that if we (Minnesota) had accepted a bowl bid, and Notre Dame had contacted me after that, then I was free to talk to them. I was not free to contact them, and I was not free to talk to them if we had not accepted a bowl bid. The logic was this. If we took a Minnesota program that was down and took it to a level where it was able to go to a bowl game, then I would be free to leave if I so desired. Because, by that time, the program would have gained respectability and wouldn't have any difficulty in recruiting and in bringing in a good, competent coach to take it to the next level.

Now, Gene Corrigan was just hired as the new athletic director at Notre Dame at that time, and he had tried to hire me three different times when he was at the University of Virginia. So, I figured that if we were successful at Minnesota, then I would take the Notre Dame job if all of that played out. I wasn't sure if all of that would happen initially when I got to Minnesota, but I wanted to make sure that I had the chance to evaluate my options should it all play out. When it did, that is when I made my decision. I remember too that University of Minnesota President, Ken Keller, tried to get rid of that clause on several occasions. He came to me and wanted me to sign a lifetime contract. I initially agreed to what he had proposed, but he later withdrew the offer and said he couldn't do it. The two guys who can verify all of this are Sid Hartman and Harvey Mackay. That is what I want people to understand, is that I didn't go to Minnesota with the idea that I was going to leave. I came there thinking I was going to spend the rest of my life there. It didn't work out, but my time there was wonderful and I wouldn't trade it for anything."

HOW DO YOU WANT YOUR COACHING EPITAPH TO READ — HOW DO YOU WANT TO BE REMEMBERED AS A COACH? "I always tried to be honest and forthright. I am not very smart, but I always tried to do what was in the best interest of the players and in the best interest of the school."

GEORGE LARSON
HIGH SCHOOL FOOTBALL: CAMBRIDGE

George Larson grew up in the small town of Bryant, S.D., where he played six man high school football. He then went on to play college football at Northern State University under legendary coach Clark Swisher, losing just two games in his four year playing career. Larson received his teaching degree at Northern State and then went on to get his first job in Jeffers, Minn., where he coached and taught everything from science to health to physical education. On the gridiron Larson wasted little time in making a name for himself, leading Jeffers to their first Red Rock Conference football championship in 30 years.

From there, he came to Cambridge, to teach and serve as an assistant football coach under Jim Foley. Larson served as an assistant for two years and then took over as the head coach in 1960. He would go on to become a football coaching legend. Larson taught physical education at Cambridge High School from 1960-91, and retired from teaching in 1991. Larson stayed on to keep coaching football until 1993, and then retired after that. He also served stints as the athletic director and also coached baseball and track too.

Larson got that itch a few years later though, and came out of retirement in 1999 to scratch it, returning as Cambridge's coach once again. Larson finally retired for good in 2000, even going out on top with his third state championship — the Class AAAA title. When it was all said and done some 38 years later, Larson had finished his illustrious career as the winningest coach in Minnesota high school football history with a career record of 307-66-6 (83%). He also won three state titles (1986, 87, 2000), 25 conference championships, two state runner-up's and numerous section championships.

Among his many coaching accolades, Larson is the only coach to be named the Minnesota Football Coach of the Year twice, and is a member of both the Minnesota Football Coaches Association Hall of Fame as well as the Minnesota State High School League Hall of Fame. A tireless worker for the game he loved, Larson served on the MSHSL board of directors for two years, and he was also president of the Minnesota Football Coaches Association in 1993. His biggest honor came after he retired, however, when the Cambridge-Isanti High School football field was renamed as "George Larson Field" in his honor. Presently, Larson lives in the Cambridge area where he is an Isanti County Commissioner and an avid outdoorsman.

HOW WOULD YOU DESCRIBE YOUR COACHING STYLE? "I guess I was a holler-type guy I suppose, I mean there were times when I would get really fired up. But, my kids understood that and that I only wanted to get the best out of them. Fundamentals win football games but if you are animated then your kids were going to be animated, and that was the way I felt."

HOW DID YOU MOTIVATE YOUR PLAYERS? "This came down to preparation I think. We always tried to instill in our kids that they had to work hard in practice and really prepare themselves. Then, after seeing this enough, they eventually become believers. So, I just tried to fire them up so that they could play their best. I always felt that if we worked hard on the fundamentals, and believe me, we worked long, hard practices, then our kids were prepared. I always felt that family, church and their studies should come first, but on game day I wanted them to be focused. In the end our kids took a lot of pride in being a Blue Jacket football player."

WHO WERE YOUR COACHING MENTORS? "I learned a great deal from so many people. I think back to my college days at Northern State under legendary coach Clark Swisher. He was a fantastic coach, a great motivator and he had his teams well prepared. Then when I came to Cambridge I learned so much from Jim Foley. He was an old single-wing coach and had some great ideas on the fundamentals. You know, the fraternity of high school football coaches is probably the most fantastic fraternity in the world. I mean you share everything with everyone, including your arch-rivals. I think about Bob Roy at St. Louis Park, or Tom Mahoney at Fairmont, or George Thole at Stillwater, they were just great men and great coaches."

IF YOU COULD MAGICALLY GO BACK IN TIME TO THE FIRST YEAR YOU WERE A HEAD COACH AND GIVE YOURSELF SOME ADVICE FOR THE FUTURE, KNOWING WHAT YOU KNOW NOW, BACK THEN, WHAT WOULD YOU SAY TO YOURSELF? "I would probably say lighten up a little bit and relax. I don't know. I just enjoyed coaching from day one and had a real fun career. I mellowed as I got older, but I really don't know if I would change a lot."

WHAT ARE THE CHARACTERISTICS OF LEADERS? "If you expect people to do things, you have to lead by example. Leaders are people who go by doing. They just have to work harder than the next guy. I also think leaders know if they are going to win before they even hit the field."

LOOKING BACK WHAT ARE YOU MOST PROUD OF IN YOUR CAREER? "I am probably most proud of the relationships that I had with my kids and the feelings and pride that they got from playing football at Cambridge High School."

HOW DID YOU BUILD TEAM UNITY & CHEMISTRY? "I treated everyone the same, from the star quarterback to the little guy on the end of the bench. In fact, I was probably harder on my stars than I was on anybody else. You also had to make everyone feel important. I tried to get as many kids into our ballgames as possible, whether it was on special teams or what have you, because I always felt that was important too. I particularly took care of my seniors who stuck with me. They earned their time and I made sure to get them out there as much as possible. Overall though, we just built that 'esprit du corps' or togetherness, and tried to create a winning atmosphere."

WHAT MOTIVATED YOU? "You know towards the end it wasn't so much winning, but the disgust of losing. I hated to lose so I worked harder in order for us not to lose. Then, I used to tell the kids 'hey, you worked hard all week in practice and if you want to have fun on the weekend, the only way you are going to do that is by winning on Friday.' Winning is important, but not at all costs. I always said that if we have to cheat to win, then I would rather lose. When you played a Cambridge football team, you walked off the field knowing you played a team that had good sportsmanship and that they played clean. That was what we stressed and that motivated me to be my very best."

WHAT ADVICE WOULD YOU HAVE FOR YOUNG COACHES STARTING OUT TODAY? "Get a gal who is going to support you all the way. If you are going to be a successful coach you really need a supportive wife. She is the most important part of this element because if you have to worry about how much time you are putting in to your career, then you might as well not go into coaching. I was really fortunate to have a wife who supported me 100% during the football season and handled a lot of the responsibilities around the house and with the kids during that time. That was just great to have that support so that I could focus on football, and that was one of the big reasons that I was so successful I believe. Also, surround yourself with good people who are willing to put in their time. My assistants were both with me for over 30 years each and that made a big difference in our success too."

FAVORITE LOCKER ROOM SIGN? "We had a sign above the locker room door that each kid touched as he left which read: "101%.""

WHAT'S THE BIGGEST THING YOU'VE LEARNED FROM COACHING THAT YOU'VE BEEN ABLE TO APPLY TO YOUR EVERYDAY LIFE? "I really believe that the harder you work at something, the more you are going to get out of it. I have found that to be true in my everyday life as well. Even now after I am retired, I apply that same logic to my job as a county commissioner. People feel that I am there for them and that makes me feel very good."

WHAT ARE THE KEY INGREDIENTS TO CREATING A CHAMPIONSHIP TEAM? "First of all you have got to have at least a few good athletes. But, I think that if you make your average kids better, then that is what's going to make you a champion. The good ones will always be good, but taking the average ones and making them a little better, that is what will get you over the top. You know, Cambridge used to play against a lot of much bigger schools, and we went with some kids sometimes who weren't the best athletes, but they played above their abilities and that was the key."

WHAT'S THE SECRET TO YOUR SUCCESS? "Number one, I had a very supportive wife who let me be the best coach I could be. Number two, I had great assistant coaches who were very loyal.

Number three, I coached in a great community that was very supportive of me. Beyond that, I worked really hard. The kids though are really what it was all about. They believed in me and bought into my system, and that was great."

WHAT WOULD YOU WANT TO SAY TO YOUR FANS, BOOSTERS, AND ALUMNI WHO HAVE SUPPORTED YOU ALL THESE YEARS? "It was a great run and I really enjoyed it. It was just a wonderful experience. I just hope that the fans, coaches, parents, boosters and players had as much fun as I did."

HOW DO YOU WANT YOUR COACHING EPITAPH TO READ — HOW DO YOU WANT TO BE REMEMBERED AS A COACH? "He was a fired up type guy who really wanted to win and do the best that he could for his kids. I just hope that my kids will always take that Blue Jacket pride with them in life, that is what's most important."

MIKE SHANAHAN: NFL'S DENVER BRONCOS

Mike Shanahan served as an assistant coach with the Gophers in 1979. Shanahan, who also coached the Raiders in 1988, would go on to lead the Denver Broncos to back-to-back Super Bowl championships in 1997 and 1998. He is presently the coach of the Broncos.

MIKE MARTZ: NFL'S ST. LOUIS RAMS

Mike Martz served as an assistant coach with the Gophers in 1982. Martz, a Sioux Falls, S.D., native, would go on to lead the St. Louis Rams to a Super Bowl title in 2001. He is presently the coach of the Rams.

DR. HENRY WILLIAMS: GOPHER FOOTBALL

Something, or rather someone, big happened to Minnesota in 1900. That was the year that University officials, after a string of one-year coaching stints from a variety of former players, hired Dr. Henry L. Williams on a part-time basis to serve as their football and track coach. Williams, a former star player and teammate of All-American Pudge Heffelfinger (a Minnesota native) at Yale University, who then attended medical school at the University of Pennsylvania, accepted a three-year, $2,500 contract, with the understanding that he also be able to carry on his medical practice. Williams, whose three-year commitment ultimately turned into the University's first full-time coaching job, would last for more than 22 years. It also marked the beginning of a new football era in Minnesota during which the Gophers would win or share eight conference titles over the next 16-seasons. Additionally, Williams was the creator of several football innovations that would place him among the immortals of the game. Among his contributions to the sport included: the advent of the Forward Pass (which became legal in 1905); Criss-Cross Plays, which halfbacks and ends passed the ball back and forth to each other while going in opposite directions; Revolving Wedges; Tackle-Back formations, On-Side Quarterback Kicks; and perhaps most importantly was the now infamous "Minnesota Shift," which was the forerunner of all quick shifts since implemented in the game and long considered as the most devastating offensive weapon introduced into modern football. After Williams posted just average teams in both 1920 and 1921, the University Athletic Board, which had a lot of power in those days, fired him as the team's head coach. One of the final straws came in 1921 when Williams finally gave in to demands that he put numbers on his players' uniforms. Instead of using the one and two digit variety, however, he instead put four digits on each player so that the fans were just as confused as the team's opposition. It was a bitter ending for one of Minnesota's greatest coaches. Many didn't realize it, but Williams never had more than one assistant through all his years behind the bench, and through it all continued to practice medicine full-time. Sadly, he died only 10 years later, in 1931.

TOM MAHONEY
HIGH SCHOOL FOOTBALL: FAIRMONT

Tom Mahoney grew up in Proctor and went on to graduate from Minneapolis Edison High School in 1945. From there, Mahoney went into the Navy for one year and then went on to graduate from the University of Minnesota in 1950, where he also played football under Bernie Bierman. Mahoney then worked as an assistant under Snapper Stein for one year with the Gophers before going on to Lake City, where he taught social studies and coached football and baseball for five seasons. In 1956 Mahoney moved on to Fairmont, where he would become a high school football coaching legend.

When Tom Mahoney retired from coaching in 1990 he stood alone as the state's all-time winningest head coach. In 39 seasons at Lake City and Fairmont, Mahoney had complied a record of 256-94-8, which, at the time, was No. 1. Mahoney's record 213th win came on Friday, Sept. 23, 1981, when his Fairmont Cardinals beat St. Peter. The big win moved him past the previous leader, Red Wilson, who had coached most of his career at Bemidji High School. Aside from being an outstanding teacher and coach, Mahoney, who also served as the athletic director for many years at Fairmont, should also be recognized for his many contributions off the field as well. For decades he was a member of nearly every committee of the MHSFCA and his commitment has continued since his retirement. Mahoney has long been considered the "thinker" of the association, and many of the programs developed through the years have been from his brain-storming. Among them are the All Star Game, the playoff system, the "Butch Nash" Award, the Distinguished Service Award, and so much more. Fittingly, in 1990 Mahoney was inducted into the Minnesota State High School League Coaches Hall of Fame. Mahoney is also a member of the State Athletic Directors Hall of Fame as well as the Edison High School Hall of Fame.

Since he hung up the whistle for good, Mahoney has also stayed active as the MSHSL Region 2A Secretary. Tom, who is now playing plenty of golf in his retirement, and his wife of nearly 50 years, Pat, live in Fairmont. They have seven children and many grandchildren. A living legend with a truly amazing legacy, Tom Mahoney has, arguably, done more for high school football in the state of Minnesota than anybody. A man of great character and class, Tom was a giant in the world of high school football. And, he was just a great guy who was very well liked and respected by his peers as well as his players.

HOW WOULD YOU DESCRIBE YOUR COACHING STYLE? "You know, I knew that I wanted to be a coach from the time I was in the ninth grade, so when that finally happened it was a dream come true. I loved working with young people and being a teacher. I think my style was to be fair and to give everybody a chance. I had an empathy for anybody who came out and tried out for the team, because they loved the game and really wanted to play. So, I tried to get the best out of them by helping them out as best as I could and by being fair. Beyond that I went to every coaching clinic I could go to so that I could always get better. I learned a lot from my playing days at the University of Minnesota too, and that all went into my philosophy of coaching. You know, the offense that we ran was a combination of the single wing, split-T, wing-T and a whole bunch of other things that were unique and different at the high school level at that time. I also think that we stuck with the unbalanced line longer than anybody else. We just tried to stick with what worked and then worked hard to get better. We were fortunate to have a lot of success

over the years and it was really a great, great ride."

HOW DID YOU MOTIVATE YOUR PLAYERS? "I think that I motivated my guys by having them work hard and by having a good work ethic. Our practices were organized and we knew the direction that we wanted to go. We also tried to know the abilities of our kids and we worked from there. I don't think that I was a big rah-hah guy, I just tried to work with each player and get the best out of him. That was how our teams achieved success."

WHO WERE YOUR COACHING MENTORS? "Without a doubt my coaching mentor was (longtime Gopher Assistant Coach) Butch Nash. Much of my coaching style was learned through being around him. We later worked together when I was the freshmen trainer and he really took care of me. He was there whenever I needed him and he has been a good friend through the years. Of course, I learned a great deal about the game of football and about dealing with kids from Bernie Bierman as well. He was very organized and taught me a lot about the value of assistant coaches too."

IF YOU COULD MAGICALLY GO BACK IN TIME TO THE FIRST YEAR YOU WERE A HEAD COACH AND GIVE YOURSELF SOME ADVICE FOR THE FUTURE, KNOWING WHAT YOU KNOW NOW, BACK THEN, WHAT WOULD YOU SAY TO YOURSELF? "I have a grandson who wants to become a football coach and I just told him these very things. I told him that I think he has to be loyal, fair and to understand that every kid is out there because he wants to be."

WHAT ARE THE CHARACTERISTICS OF WINNERS? "Winners are people who are dedicated, they work hard, they fight and they don't let adversity get the better of them."

LOOKING BACK WHAT ARE YOU MOST PROUD OF IN YOUR CAREER? "I am proud of my players. So many of them have gone on to do such wonderful things in their lives and I am proud of the fact that I may have played a very small part in their success. Beyond that there are a few other things that I was proud of, like my work with the state coaches association and developing and implementing a high school football playoff plan. We have come a long way since that has come to life and that has been great to see. Then, on the field I am proud of our 31 game winning streak that we had at one point. That was quite an accomplishment and would be pretty tough to achieve today because only team in each class is going to wind up undefeated. But mostly it was the kids, that what this job is all about."

HOW DID YOU BUILD TEAM UNITY & CHEMISTRY? "I think our kids knew where they stood because we had a lot of one on one and group challenges and competitions doing different activities. Kids earned their spots that way. It wasn't by favoritism or by names or by who they were. They earned it by their performance on the field. The chemistry just developed from there. I also tried to mix up our rosters by getting some younger guys into the lineup. We didn't just have senior-oriented teams and then wait for our sophomores and juniors to come along. The best kids played and I think my kids respected that."

WHAT MOTIVATED YOU? "I just liked my job. I don't think I ever went to work thinking about whether or not I liked what I was doing. I was lucky. It was easy for me to get up and go to work and my motivation was always there. I never feared losing, but I sure liked winning. Although, winning wasn't everything. It was performing well and working hard. If we won, great, and if we got beat, then we had to work harder and move on."

WHAT ADVICE WOULD YOU HAVE FOR YOUNG COACHES STARTING OUT TODAY? "Work hard, listen, observe, be fair to your kids, and show them respect. Kids will respect discipline if you have a reason for it and if you are fair across the board. Also, particularly if you are an assistant coach, be loyal. That is very important."

FAVORITE LOCKER ROOM SIGN? "Just do it!"

WHAT'S THE BIGGEST THING YOU'VE LEARNED FROM COACHING THAT YOU'VE BEEN ABLE TO APPLY TO YOUR EVERYDAY LIFE? "That there are ups and downs in everything and that you have to work hard to learn from your downs. That way there will be a lot more ups."

WHAT ARE THE KEY INGREDIENTS TO CREATING A CHAMPIONSHIP TEAM? "Talent, without a doubt. You have got to have the horses, without them you are not going to win."

WHAT'S THE SECRET TO YOUR SUCCESS? "I just worked hard at it. I had very loyal assistants, a great program, a great community, great fans who were very supportive, a great booster club, and great administrators. As a result, I had a great time being a coach. I loved teaching and coaching and that was my secret."

WHAT WOULD YOU WANT TO SAY TO YOUR FANS, BOOSTERS, AND ALUMNI WHO HAVE SUPPORTED YOU ALL THESE YEARS? "Gosh, where would I start? I mean just thanks, the support was wonderful. From the players to the parents to the boosters to the fans, thank you from the bottom of my heart. I was lucky to have the opportunity to do something good for kids and I appreciated that. It was a great ride."

HOW DO YOU WANT YOUR COACHING EPITAPH TO READ — HOW DO YOU WANT TO BE REMEMBERED AS A COACH? "That he did the best he could."

JOCKO NELSON: GUSTAVUS FOOTBALL

Jack "Jocko" Nelson was a prep star at Hibbing, where he played basketball, football, track and baseball. After a stint in the U.S. Navy, Nelson attended Gustavus in 1946, lettering in football, basketball, hockey, track and baseball. Nelson even squeezed in a season of pro baseball between his sophomore and junior years as well. Following his graduation, Nelson taught and coached football and basketball at Grand Marais and Mora High Schools for four years. From there, he went on to serve as an assistant football coach at Utah State (1955-58), the University of Colorado (1958-59), and the University of Michigan (1959-66), before returning to Gustavus in 1966. There, he would take over as the head coach and lead the Gusties from 1966-71. His 1967 and 1968 Gusty teams were MIAC Champions and his overall record was 32-11-4. In 1971 Nelson headed north, to assume the position of linebacker and special teams coach for the Minnesota Vikings, under Head Coach Bud Grant. Nelson remained with the Vikings until his untimely death on November 19, 1978. During that time Nelson also owned and operated a family business, Jocko's Clearwater Lodge, on the Gunflint Trail. Jocko and his wife Lee had four children. A Gusty legend, Jocko will always be remembered as a real winner with a passion for sports.

CLARK SHAUGHNESSY: STANFORD FOOTBALL

Clark Shaughnessy grew up in St. Cloud and went on to earn All-American honors as a Gopher fullback and tackle in 1913. From there, Shaughnessy would go on to become one of the most prolific coaches in Minnesota sports history. Shaughnessy coached college football at Tulane University from 1915-20 and again from 1922-25. He then went on to coach at Loyola from 1926-32, and then at the University of Chicago from 1933-39. In 1940, Shaughnessy went to Stanford where, as head coach, he created his version of the T-formation. During his first year at Stanford, Shaughnessy's team went undefeated and won the national championship, defeating Nebraska by a score of 21 to 13 in the Rose Bowl. Shaughnessy then went on to coach football at the University of Maryland in 1942 and 1946, while also coaching basketball at Pittsburgh from 1943 to 1945 as well. From there, Shaughnessy got into the pro game. After serving as an assistant coach with the NFL's Washington Redskins in 1947, Shaughnessy became head coach of the Los Angeles Rams in 1948. There, his Rams won the Western Division title in 1949, before losing to Philadelphia, 14-0, in the NFL Championship game. Shaughnessy would post a 14-7-3 record with the Rams before moving on to become a consultant for the Chicago Bears from 1950-62. Shaughnessy gave college coaching one more try from there, and he ended his career as coach of the University of Hawaii in 1965. Shaughnessy would retire with a career college coaching record of 149-106-14. Shaughnessy, who studied military tactics to learn new strategies, was truly a student of the game. He is also credited with inventing the "Man in Motion T—Formation," a version of the T-formation used today by almost all high school, college, and professional football teams. A true innovator of the game, Clark Shaughnessy died in 1970 at the age of 78.

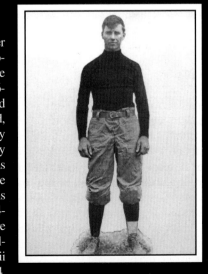

JIM MALOSKY
COLLEGE FOOTBALL: UM-DULUTH

Jim Malosky grew up in northern Minnesota and went on to graduate from Crosby-Ironton High School, where he played football and basketball. From there, Malosky headed south, to play quarterback under Bernie Bierman at the University of Minnesota. The late 1940s were some of the most glorious in Golden Gopher gridiron history, and Malosky was a big part of that. Names like Bud Grant, Gordy Saltau, Leo Nomellini, Billy Bye, Verne Gagne and Clayton Tonnemaker were just some of the reasons why the Gophers were the real deal back in the day. Malosky would play for the Gophers from 1947-49, graduating with a degree in teaching.

Following his days at the University of Minnesota, Malosky went into the Army. There, he coached a military football team and once even came into a game when his quarterback went down and threw a 97 yard touchdown pass. When Malosky got out of the service he began teaching and coaching high school football, first at Morris High School for five years and then at Edina Morningside High School, in 1957.

In 1958, Malosky got his big break when he was asked to serve as an assistant football coach at the University of Minnesota Duluth under Lloyd Peterson. (Peterson, who had been at UMD since 1931, retired in 1969 after serving as the football coach, basketball coach, wrestling coach and athletic director.) After spending five seasons learning the ropes, Malosky took over as the program's head coach in 1963. Malosky would make the most of his opportunity, and over the next 34 years he would go on to become a Minnesota coaching legend.

Malosky wasted little time in turning the UMD football program around, and within three years, his Bulldogs had earned an MIAC championship. When it was all said and done, Malosky had rewritten the record books. In fact, he rolled up more victories than any coach in the history of NCAA Division II history, amassing a 255-125-13 (.665) career record along the way — good for 11th on college football's all-time coaching win list, right up there with the likes of Pop Warner, Bear Bryant, Joe Paterno and Bobby Bowden. Malosky guided the Bulldogs to three MIAC titles (1960, 1961 and 1973) and six Northern Sun Intercollegiate Conference championships (1979, 1980, 1985, 1990, 1995 and 1996) as well. In addition, no less than 20 of his Bulldogs attained various All-American honors during his tenure and five went on to play in the National Football League.

Among his many coaching accolades, Malosky was named Coach of the Year by the MIAC, NSIC and NAIA on 10 occasions. In 1994 he was inducted into the Minnesota High School Football Coaches Association Hall of Fame and in 1996 he was inducted into the University of Minnesota's Hall of Fame. In addition, he is the namesake of the Jim Malosky Award which is presented annually by USA Football to the NCAA II Coach of the Year. Malosky coached the Bulldogs until 1997, when, after suffering a stroke and going through a knee replacement, he decided to finally retire. He had also served as an associate professor in UMD's Departments of Health, Physical Education and Recreation before retiring as well.

For nearly four decades Jim Malosky was a fixture along the University of Minnesota-Duluth sidelines. He was an outstanding leader, motivator and truly earned the respect of his players and peers alike. Jim and his wife Lilah have four children: Lisa, Linda, Tamme and Jim Jr. — who went on to become a UMD assistant football coach as well.

HOW WOULD YOU DESCRIBE YOUR COACHING STYLE? "I played for Bernie Bierman at the University of Minnesota and learned a great deal from him. I was a single-wing quarterback at the U of M and in my three years there Bernie only called one play. That's right, I called every play that our team ran and I was very proud of that. I learned a lot from that experience and that gave me great insight into coaching. Our styles, however, were much different. He was very quiet and steady on the sidelines and just didn't get too excited about anything. I never sat still for a minute and used to jump up and down on the sidelines to get my kids fired up. I was never more than 10 yards away from my team at all times, I wanted to be right in the action. I was a hands-on coach and was very critical of my players. I was an Army guy so I liked discipline. I demanded excellence from them and wanted them to work very hard. I pointed out a lot of the negative things that my players did so that I could work with them on improving every aspect of their games. One thing I am proud of though, is that in all my 40 years I never swore on the football field. As for my philosophy, however, we ran the ball. Period."

HOW DID YOU MOTIVATE YOUR PLAYERS? "I prefer to think of it more in terms of preparation rather than motivation. We worked hard during the week to be prepared and then we just played on game days."

HOW DID YOU BUILD TEAM UNITY & CHEMISTRY? "You know, when we won games the players took all the credit and when we lost I took all the blame. That built team unity."

WHAT MOTIVATED YOU? "I enjoyed the preparation and the practices and then seeing that come to life in our games. I also loved the challenge of beating my opponent because it was a great feeling when we won."

WHAT'S THE BIGGEST THING YOU'VE LEARNED FROM COACHING THAT YOU'VE BEEN ABLE TO APPLY TO YOUR EVERYDAY LIFE? "Discipline, the willingness to stick with something for a long time and to do the best that you can."

WHAT'S THE SECRET TO YOUR SUCCESS? "Hard work and discipline. Sometimes I worked until 11 or 12 at night preparing for our next game, but that was what you had to do to be successful. You know, I won 255 ballgames, but I didn't score one touchdown and I didn't throw one block. It was my ballplayers who won the games and I was very proud of them. It wasn't about me, it was about them. If you have good players and good people with you, then you can have success."

WHAT WOULD YOU WANT TO SAY TO YOUR FANS, BOOSTERS, AND ALUMNI WHO HAVE SUPPORTED YOU ALL THESE YEARS? "You know, I had other offers to coach elsewhere, but I loved UMD and that is why I spent 40 years there. I enjoyed every day there and was very proud to be their coach. I always felt like Duluth was a big little town. The fans there were very loyal and I appreciated their support. People sometimes complained that we didn't pass enough because it seemed like we only ran the ball left and ran the ball right. But you know, we won 255 games, so maybe that wasn't a bad idea after all!"

HOW DO YOU WANT YOUR COACHING EPITAPH TO READ — HOW DO YOU WANT TO BE REMEMBERED AS A COACH? "I knew the game of football and worked very hard at it. I just enjoyed going to work every day. I was honest and fair to all my ballplayers and hope that I made a difference in their lives. I respected them and hope that they respected me."

RUSSELL TOLLEFSON: NFL's MINNEAPOLIS MARINES

Russell Tollefson was born in Minneapolis in 1891, and went on to play football at the University of Minnesota from 1912-13. Tollefson would later coach the Minneapolis Marines, Minnesota's first NFL team, in 1922, where he posted a record of 1-3.

JIM SIMS: UM-CROOKSTON FOOTBALL

Jim Sims is a Mahnomen native and a graduate of Minnesota State University-Moorhead. After graduating, Sims coached high school football for several years. Then, in 1976, Sims got the job as the head football coach at the University of Minnesota-Crookston. From 1976-95 his teams compiled an impressive overall record of 93-66-1 during his 19-year tenure and won three division team championships, finishing with three Minnesota State runner-up titles. In addition, Sims' teams were ranked in the top 15 teams in the nation on three separate occasions. Other accomplishments include his 1982 football team, which went on to play in the Midwest Bowl in Illinois.

Among his many coaching honors and accolades, Sims received Northern Division Coach of the Year honors on two occasions, and seven of his former players went on to be named as NJCAA All-Americans. Sims was also the head track coach for seven years at Crookston, winning two division championships there as well. Sims is currently Director of Student Activities at Thief River Falls Lincoln High School and was inducted into the "Prowler" Hall of Fame in 1996.

DAN DEVINE: NOTRE DAME & GREEN BAY PACKER FOOTBALL

Dan Devine is a Duluth coaching legend. A native of Augusta, Wis., Devine would go on to graduate from Proctor High School in 1942. Devine then went on to star on both the University of Minnesota-Duluth football and basketball teams. The quarterback and guard also served as his senior class president. Devine would graduate from UMD in 1948 with a degree in history.

From there, Devine would go on to coaching stardom. Dan Devine started coaching at East Jordan high school in Michigan. He then went on to become an assistant at Michigan State under former Gopher Biggie Munn, and also earned his master's degree there as well. Devine would then go on to assume the head coaching job at Arizona State from 1955-57. At ASU, Devine brought with him a multiple offense concept which combined the theories of the Wing-T, the Single Wing, the Double Wing and the new 'Flanker' offenses. In 1957, his third and final season with the Devils, he led them to a 10-0 record with the NCAA's top scoring offense. As head coach at ASU, Devine, who took over the program at just 31 years of age, accumulated a 27-3-1 record. Devine then left ASU in 1957 to take over at the University of Missouri, where he would remain until 1970. Devine led his Tigers to a 93-37-7 (.700) mark and among his achievements at Missouri were victories in the 1961 Orange Bowl, '63 Bluebonnet Bowl, '66 Sugar Bowl and '69 Gator Bowl. Devine also brought the first black players to Arizona State and to Missouri, but never considered himself a pioneer in integration.

In 1971 Devine took over as the head coach and general manager of the NFL's Green Bay Packers. He would spend three years behind the Packer bench, posting a 25-28-4 overall record along the way. In addition, he also received NFC coach-of the-year honors in 1972 — the same year he led the Pack to a 10-4 record and a Central Division title. From there, Devine headed east, to South Bend, Ind., where he became the head coach at Notre Dame in 1975. Having to fill the shoes of Hall of Fame Coach Ara Parseghian, Devine would do all right, leading the Fighting Irish to victories in the 1976 Gator Bowl, '77 Cotton Bowl and '78 Cotton Bowl. At the 1977 Cotton Bowl, Devine won the NCAA National Championship with an 11-1 record. Perhaps Devine's greatest moment at Notre Dame, however, came at the 1979 Cotton Bowl, when quarterback Joe Montana made history. The Irish trailed Houston 34-12 with 7:25 left to play before an unforgettable comeback was engineered and the Irish pulled off a 35-34 last-second victory. Devine resigned from Notre Dame in 1980 with a 53-6-1 (.890) record. Overall, Devine's career collegiate coaching record was a very impressive 173-46-9 (.778).

Devine would later go on to become the executive director of the Arizona State Sun Angel Foundation in Phoenix, where he remained for seven years. In 1987 he left the Sun Angels, but not the university, accepting a position to direct an upstart ASU program designed to combat substance abuse. Then, in 1992, Devine returned to Missouri to serve as the school's athletic director, retiring two years later in 1994.

Devine died in 2002 in Tempe, Ariz., at the age of 77. Dan and Joanne, (who he met when she was the homecoming queen back at UMD) had seven children: Dan, Jennifer, Mary Jo, Diana, Sarah, Lisa and Jill. Devine, who was elected into the National Football Foundation Hall of Fame in 1985, was viewed as a soft-spoken individual, lacking the fiery personality of many high profile coaches — but his results were anything but average. Dan Devine was a Minnesota football coaching legend.

GLEN MASON
COLLEGE FOOTBALL: UNIVERSITY OF MINNESOTA

Glen Mason grew up loving sports and went on to play football at Colonia High School in New Jersey. From there, Mason went on to attend Ohio State University, where he played linebacker on Ohio State's 1970 Big Ten championship football team. Mason graduated in 1972 and that next year he began his coaching career as a graduate assistant at Ball State University. His first full-time position was as the offensive coordinator at Allegheny College in 1973. Mason then returned to Ball State for one season in 1974 as the defensive line coach, and also received his master's degree there as well. He then worked the next two seasons as the offensive line coach at Iowa State before taking over as the offensive line coach at Illinois in 1977.

In 1978, Mason returned to his alma mater and spent the next eight years working as an assistant under legendary Ohio State Head Coaches Woody Hayes and Earle Bruce. In each of those seasons, the Buckeyes appeared in a postseason bowl games. Mason was promoted to offensive coordinator in 1980, where he served until 1986. During his tenure as offensive coordinator, the Buckeyes led the Big Ten in scoring offense four times and total offense twice. In 1986 Mason got his big break, taking over as the head coach at Kent State University. There, he had two successful seasons and even led the Golden Flash to their first winning season in more than a decade. For his efforts he was named as the 1986 Mid-American Conference Coach of the Year.

In 1988 Mason was hired to turn around a struggling University of Kansas football program. Prior to his arrival, the Jayhawks had gone winless in 15 consecutive Big Eight games, and had won a total of four games in the previous two seasons. In 1991 Mason won Big Eight Coach of the Year honors after he produced the school's first winning season since 1981. From 1992-95, he guided the Jayhawks to 29 wins, the most in any four-year period at Kansas in the previous 85 years. In 1992, Mason was a finalist for National Coach of the Year honors when he led the Jayhawks over Brigham Young in the Aloha Bowl, the program's first bowl win since 1961. Mason was also honored as the 1995 Big Eight Conference Coach of the Year when he led Kansas to a win over UCLA in the Aloha Bowl, and a No. 9 ranking in the final Associated Press poll.

In 1997 Mason was again hired to take over a struggling program, and this time it was at the University of Minnesota. Mason wasted little time in making a name for himself in Gold Country as his Gophers broke or tied a total of 28 school records during his first season. In 1999, Mason's Gophers posted an 8-3 regular season record and a fourth-place conference finish at 5-3. They missed an invitation to the Rose Bowl by just a field goal, but still went on to play in the Wells Fargo Sun Bowl in San Antonio. Ranked No. 12 in the national polls, the Gophers were back on top. For his efforts, Mason was named the National Coach of the Year and was a finalist for the Football Writers Association Eddie Robinson and Paul "Bear" Bryant National Coach of the Year awards. In 2000 Minnesota earned a bid to the Micronpc.com Bowl in Ft. Lauderdale. It was the first time since 1985-86 that a coach had led his team to back-to-back bowl berths. The Gophers lost for the second straight season, but were thrilled to be playing football in December nonetheless. Then, in 2002 the Gophers finally got it done when they went 7-5 and beat Arkansas in the Music City Bowl in Memphis.

Now in his seventh year as Minnesota's head coach, Mason has changed a struggling program that hadn't posted a winning season since 1990 into one of the top Big Ten programs. His Gophers

have reached bowl games in three of the past four seasons and are playing great. Mason is a proven winner and is poised to bring the Gophers back to their glory days of old. He is also a very well liked and respected coach as well. Among his many coaching accolades, Mason is one of only three coaches in NCAA history to be named the conference coach of the year in three different conferences: Big Ten (1999), Big Eight (1991 & 1995) and Mid-American (1986). A past president of the American Football Coaches Association, Mason's career head coaching record stands at 88-94-1. Combine that tally with his assistant coaching record, and the coach stands at 201-149-4 over the past 30 years.

Glen and his wife Kate live in the Twin Cities and have five children — sons, Pat and Brian, and daughters, Chris, Alissa and Mallory.

HOW WOULD YOU DESCRIBE YOUR COACHING STYLE? "When I look at my job as a coach I don't think it is very complicated, but that is not to say it is not difficult. It is difficult in the sense that you have to get a large number of very different people to do things that they don't normally want to do in order to achieve the goals that you want to achieve. So, however good you are at getting those people to do that is determinant on how successful you are going to be in your job. My style changes as situations change, so you try to evaluate and calculate that in order to go forward with what you think the best approach is. At times, depending on what day it is, you might find me with completely different coaching styles, it just depends on the situation."

HOW DO YOU MOTIVATE YOUR PLAYERS? "I think that the best motivated team is comprised of individuals who are self-motivated. Those are the types of players who have a burning desire to be successful. So, I like to surround myself with as many of those types of players as possible, and certainly from a recruiting standpoint we look for self-motivated players. Then, you need to help them by clearly defining what their goals are and what they have to do to get where they want to go. I believe much more in a cerebral approach to motivation rather than a 30 second pre-game pep-talk which everybody on the outside thinks is what really fires a team up. I don't really believe that."

IF YOU COULD MAGICALLY GO BACK IN TIME TO THE FIRST YEAR YOU WERE A HEAD COACH AND GIVE YOURSELF SOME ADVICE FOR THE FUTURE, KNOWING WHAT YOU KNOW NOW, BACK THEN, WHAT WOULD YOU SAY TO YOURSELF? "I'd probably tell him to hang in there and that good things happen to people who hang in there and do the right thing. It might not come as fast as you want, but eventually you will probably get to where you want to go. Starting out as a graduate assistant coach and hoping to get a job is tough, but you have to pay your dues and work hard, it will come eventually if you just stick with it."

WHAT ARE THE CHARACTERISTICS OF LEADERS? "I think certain people have an innate desire to be leaders, and to be in a position where they want to make decisions under pressure. Others don't. Then, the actual experience that they have as well as what they do with that experience with regards to how they develop, is probably what determines who are the good leaders and who aren't the good leaders."

LOOKING BACK WHAT ARE YOU MOST PROUD OF IN YOUR CAREER? "I am proud of the fact that I have been able to have gone into some places to coach which weren't very good and I was able to survive, so to speak, and make those teams better. We have taken losing programs and have turned them into competitive, winning programs that have gone onto bowl games, and I am very proud of that."

WHAT IS THE KEY TO RECRUITING? "Recruiting is all about sales. You have to sell your product and you have to sell yourself. You have to know your product extremely well and you have to know what your buyer, or perspective student athlete, is interested in buying, then convince him that your product is it."

HOW DO YOU BUILD TEAM UNITY & CHEMISTRY? "Molding our team is the most important thing we do. In football you have to take a large group of people, some white kids, some black kids, some city kids, some farm kids, some rich kids, some poor kids, some fast kids, some slow kids, some strong kids and some weak kids, and then put them all together to make a team. So, I don't know if there is any one definitive answer other than that when you go to put a team together you have to develop an atmosphere where there are no tourists, or anyone just along for the ride and not pulling their weight. Then, you have to set the tone by putting your strongest, smartest people — the guys who epitomize what you are trying to accomplish, right out in front and up on a pedestal and have everybody try to emulate them. Those are your leaders. Everybody wants to excel and wants to work towards excellence, so that helps them to define their goals. Finally, you have to get everybody to make a big investment. That brings people together. The more they invest, the more return they are going to demand. So, if you massage those three factors all together and eliminate the people who are not going to adhere to your philosophy, and make a conscious effort while you are recruiting to add the right people in there, then sooner or later you will come up with a pretty strong team."

WHAT MOTIVATES YOU? "There is a high level of accountability in my sport. Let's face it, when you talk about fear, we all know in the back of our minds that if we don't win enough games then we will get fired. But, I don't think you work and drive yourself out of that fear. It is tough because even though you prepare for 365 days, you only have 11 games in the Fall to showcase your success. And, even though most will look at the scoreboard to judge how we are doing, there are other factors that play into your team's success. There are also a lot of hidden battles that you have to play in college athletics because not only are you trying to win games, but you are also trying to graduate kids and have them act in a responsible manner."

WHAT IS THE KEY TO GOOD TIME MANAGEMENT? "You can't waste time worrying and spending time on things that you don't have any control over. Figure out what you have a chance to control and then put your time and effort into that ."

WHAT ADVICE WOULD YOU HAVE FOR YOUNG COACHES STARTING OUT TODAY? "Coaches today make more money than they ever did when I was coming up in the ranks. When I first got into this business you didn't make any money and there was never any hope that you would. You were in it for the right reasons. You know, this job can be very draining emotionally on you and your family because of all the scrutiny and all of the public attention that is given to you. So, you still better make sure you are in it for the right reasons. Do you really like to coach? Do you like being called coach, or do you really like to coach, because there is a big difference. Do you like working with that 17 year old kid out of high school kid on an athletic, academic and social standpoint to help him be the best student athlete that he can be? You have to ask yourself those tough questions and then make sure that you are doing it for the

right reasons. Then, you need to develop some thick skin because this can be a very, very tough business."

FAVORITE LOCKER ROOM SIGN? "We have two signs that read: 'Attitude' & 'Team,' and I can't think of two more important things in our sport."

WHAT'S THE BIGGEST THING YOU'VE LEARNED FROM COACHING THAT YOU'VE BEEN ABLE TO APPLY TO YOUR EVERYDAY LIFE? "Be yourself, never jeopardize your principles and guard your honesty and integrity at all costs. I have also learned that in coaching, when times are good they are great, and when times are bad they are really bad."

WHAT ARE THE KEY INGREDIENTS TO CREATING A CHAMPIONSHIP TEAM? "I don't think there is a difference in preparing a team or a championship team, it is all degrees of success that a team is going to achieve. There is a talent factor in that equation, however, that once you start putting a team together as a coach you should negate. I mean you can have a great team and not have much talent. Then, sometimes you can have a pretty successful group of guys but not have a great team because you have great talent. So, you can be misled on those factors and I think that is the misleading thing that the general public doesn't quite understand. Obviously, the more talent you put into a group of guys, and you mold that together as a team, then the more success that team is probably going to have."

WHAT'S THE SECRET TO YOUR SUCCESS? "I would say the biggest thing is 'stick-to-it-ive-ness,' if that is even a word. When you go into situations where the roads are bumpy, and if you don't hold on, if you question yourself, if you lose faith, then you are not going to make it. So, I am stubborn and I have the ability to hold on. I have the firm belief that at the end of the day, whenever that is, that we will be successful."

WHAT WOULD YOU WANT TO SAY TO YOUR FANS, BOOSTERS, AND ALUMNI WHO HAVE SUPPORTED YOU ALL THESE YEARS? "There are fans and then there are supporters. A lot of times the fans are with you only when the things are good. The true supporter is with you every step of the way. So, for those people in each place that I have been, thank you. You never forget them and you are always very, very appreciative of their commitment to you and your program."

HOW DO YOU WANT YOUR COACHING EPITAPH TO READ — HOW DO YOU WANT TO BE REMEMBERED AS A COACH? "I have a favorite saying: 'Some people were born on third base and think that they hit a triple.' I mean some guys go into coaching situations where everybody has won and they in turn win, and then they think that they are great coaches. Well, that has not been the case for where I have been. So, I would turn that saying around I suppose and say: 'He wasn't born on third base, but he did hit a triple.' You know, I want this program to be successful like any other Minnesotan and not just in the short term, not just during my tenure, but forever. Hopefully we have made a lot of progress that will continue to build on that foundation. That way Gopher Football will be successful for a long, long time — even when I am just sitting up there in the stands as a supporter."

OSSIE SOLEM: IOWA FOOTBALL

Ossie Solem, a standout end on Doc Williams' 1912 Gopher squad, first went on to coach professionally with the (then) semi-pro Minneapolis Marines (later an NFL franchise) from 1912-15. Solem would then go on to become the head coach at the University of Iowa, from 1932-36, and then at Syracuse, from 1937-45.

AL MOLDE
COLLEGE FOOTBALL: WESTERN MICHIGAN UNIVERSITY

Al Molde grew up in Montevideo and went on to graduate from Montevideo High School in 1962. After graduating with majors in biology and physical education from Gustavus in 1966, Molde, who played football and wrestled for the Gusties, went on to coach and teach at Luverne High School from 1966-68. That next year Molde moved on to the college ranks as a graduate assistant football coach at South Dakota State University, where he also received a master's degree in physical education in 1970. From there, Molde served as an assistant at the University of Utah, where he also received a doctorate in exercise physiology. In 1971 Molde returned to the Midwest to take over as the head football coach at Sioux Falls College. He would stay for two seasons before the moving on to the University of Minnesota-Morris, where he accepted the position of head football coach and athletics director.

Seven years later, Molde moved up the ranks from Division III to Division II, taking over as the head football coach and athletics director at Central Missouri State University in 1980. Molde just kept on climbing the coaching ladder from there, with his next head football coaching stop coming at Division I-AA Eastern Illinois University in 1983. Four years later Molde made it to the big-time when he got the call to take over at Division I-A Western Michigan University. He would serve as the head football coach at Western Michigan for 10 years, turning the program around in the process. Overall, Molde's career coaching record would stand at 168-104-8 (.614), which ranked him 10th among active Division I coaches in both victories and winning percentage at the end of the 1996 season. That year Molde had a homecoming of sorts when he stepped down as the head coach and came back to his alma mater, Gustavus Adolphus College, to serve as the school's new director of athletics. He replaced former football coach, turned A.D., Jim "Moose" Malmquist, who had held the post for nearly a quarter century. Al and his wife, Ingrid, who had met at Gustavus and were married in the College's Christ Chapel, have four sons: Michael, Brian, Matthew, and Evan.

HOW WOULD YOU DESCRIBE YOUR COACHING STYLE? "I always believed in positive reinforcement. I felt that we had to maintain our focus on building up the confidence of our athletes. So, while we corrected technique and that sort of thing, we were always trying to build our players up. I always instructed my assistant coaches to make sure that the players understood that when you were upset with them for making a mistake that they were upset with their behavior, and not at them as a person. I didn't ever want my coaches to tear people down, that was not acceptable to me. That philosophy worked pretty well for us over the years and most of my coaches were with me for 20-25 years too, so that says a lot. I really considered my coaches to be my partners and not so much as assistants. I just felt strongly that players can only win when they feel confident, so that is what we tried to do. We emphasized what they did well and when they made mistakes we pulled them aside and talked to them about it to correct it, without humiliating them. We just always let them know that we valued them as human beings and we treated them as adults. That positive atmosphere then led to a mutual level of respect between the coaches and players."

HOW DID YOU MOTIVATE YOUR PLAYERS? "I always felt that motivation was a process and not just some switch you flipped on. I mean it was too late if a player expected to be motivated two

hours before a game. It involved a lot of things and not the least of which was a commitment to a great work ethic. That meant working very hard in the off-season too. I viewed that as preparation for motivation. If a player didn't prepare himself to be in a motivated state, then it was very hard for a coach to come in and just throw out a speech or something to get them going. So, we talked about our games with the players and we talked about our objectives from a long range perspective. I really believed in communicating with the players, so I talked to them every day before and after practice. We had a good long practice and talk on Thursdays and then Fridays were an off day for us, which was somewhat unusual. I just didn't believe in hitting the field at all on Fridays, instead we would do a walk through at the hotel or in a parking lot somewhere. I felt like building their legs and building their energy was more important than any physical exertion. So, I motivated them continually. My pre-game speech was more about reminders and of the continuation of our bigger message."

IF YOU COULD MAGICALLY GO BACK IN TIME TO THE FIRST YEAR YOU WERE A HEAD COACH AND GIVE YOURSELF SOME ADVICE FOR THE FUTURE, KNOWING WHAT YOU KNOW NOW, BACK THEN, WHAT WOULD YOU SAY TO YOURSELF? "It took me a long time in my coaching career to open up and become more open to ideas and suggestions. I had a blinders on early in my career so I probably would have changed that. The further along I got in my career and the higher I climbed on the coaching ladder, the more I realized that I needed to delegate and learn how to manage people. I mean when I started out I had no assistants and I did it all, then, by the time I was at the division one level I had 15 people reporting to me, so it was a process to learn how to communicate with people and to delegate responsibility. So, if I were to start over I would want to have a more open approach to other ideas and input."

LOOKING BACK WHAT ARE YOU MOST PROUD OF IN YOUR CAREER? "The fact that wherever I coached we built winning programs and we won. I can say that unequivocally. Every place I came into was also a place which had not had a winning program, and we turned it around. So I am very proud of that."

WHAT WAS THE KEY TO RECRUITING? "Recruiting is selling. More than anything it is selling yourself to your prospects. It is selling your institution, as well as your program, but mostly it is you — as the coach that you are selling. It is convincing a young man that his best opportunity lies with you and your program. Once you understand that it becomes a lot easier. You also need to have good assistants who are also good at developing relationships with these young men and can convince them that your program is the best for them."

HOW DID YOU BUILD TEAM UNITY & CHEMISTRY? "Chemistry is tough and I don't know if coaches can create it. I do, however, think that there are some ways to enhance your chance to have chemistry on your team. One way is to get players on your team that fit the program you are trying to develop. That way you know something about the players which are coming in. You know if they are team players, if they will buy into your system, or if they will sacrifice individual goals for team goals, and that kind of thing. Then, personalities are a big part of chemistry too. If you recruit football players who would tend to gravitate towards one another in high school, then that will build chemistry at the collegiate level. If they are friends off the field, then they will be friends on the field, and that too is a big part of team chemistry. If they have similar personalities and similar thoughts about goals and dreams, then that is also a big part of it. Sometimes chemistry was there and other times it wasn't. Chemistry is a strange thing, but it is a wonderful thing if you can get it."

WHAT MOTIVATED YOU? "I am a very competitive person and I just hate losing. I really despise losing. So, that motivates me more than anything, the thought of not winning."

WHAT IS THE KEY TO GOOD TIME MANAGEMENT? "You have to have a good laid out plan that is done in advance. We planned in segments and broke things down into pieces and that helped us as a coaching staff. So, you have to have good organization and develop a good plan."

WHAT ADVICE WOULD YOU HAVE FOR YOUNG COACHES STARTING OUT TODAY? "Persistence is the key. It is like the old cliché, if at first you don't succeed, try, try again. Be persistent and usually you will find success. Then, remember that there is no substitute for hard work. Also, I would say be committed and pursue your goals."

WHAT ARE THE KEY INGREDIENTS TO CREATING A CHAMPIONSHIP TEAM? "Talent is the first ingredient. No coach wins without good talent. Period. Secondly, you need to have excellent coaches. Then, there is a certain amount of luck that is involved. You have to catch some breaks along the way and you have to stay healthy. If you have those three things, then your chances of winning it all are much better. Then, besides all of that, in football I would also add that you have to have a great quarterback. I think it is hard for a team to win it all with just an average quarterback."

WHAT'S THE SECRET TO YOUR SUCCESS? "One, I think I had good organizational skills. Two, I think I was a good people person who could get along well with others. Three, I worked very hard. Four, I understood the formula for how to put a program together. Five, I was very persistent and stayed after my goals. Six, I loved winning and was a very competitive person."

HOW DO YOU WANT YOUR COACHING EPITAPH TO READ — HOW DO YOU WANT TO BE REMEMBERED AS A COACH? "I would like to be remembered as an excellent coach. I would also like to be remembered as someone who achieved his objectives and did so while not just being given all the tools. I mean I was never handed the Notre Dame job! I have worked in programs where there was a significant amount of work to do to build them back up and that required a lot of hard work. So, I would like to be viewed as a coach who not only built successful programs, but also as a coach who had a positive influence on his players."

GIL DOBIE: COLLEGE FOOTBALL

Gilmore Dobie played for the Gophers from 1899-1901. From there, he would go on to become a college football coaching legend. Dobie started out at North Dakota State, where he posted two consecutive undefeated seasons. He then came to the University of Washington, where, incredibly, he kept that unbeaten streak in tact for the next nine seasons. That's right, from 1908-16, he never lost a game. In Dobie's nine years with the Huskies, his teams outscored opponents 1,930 to 118, and recorded 26 shutouts. He had compiled a astounding record of 58-0-3, which transpired into a streak of 61 consecutive games without a defeat when he left Washington for the University of Maryland that next year — an NCAA record which still stands to this day.

Dobie coached through 1935, moving from Navy to Cornell, where he won a pair of National Championships in 1921 and 1922. Ironically, his only two losing seasons in coaching would come at Cornell, where, upon his firing he made the legendary quip "You can't win with Phi Beta Kappas." Dobie rounded out his 33-year career at Boston College, where he retired with an amazing 180-45-15 career record. A true coaching legend, in 1951 Dobie was inducted into the College Football Hall of Fame.

SIG HARRIS: GOPHER FOOTBALL

Sigmund Harris played quarterback for the University of Minnesota from 1901-04 and then went on to become an assistant coach with the Gophers from 1905-20, and again from 1929-41. Despite being just five-foot-five and 140 pounds, Harris, a native of Dubuque, Iowa, was one of the greatest players in the early 1900s. The speedy quarterback was also Minnesota's punter, punt returner and defensive safety. Except for a 6-6 tie with Michigan in 1903, the Gophers won every game during the 1903 and 1904 seasons. In 1903, Sig was named first team Fielding Yost All-American as he led Minnesota to a record of 14-0-1, outscoring their opponents 656-12 along the way. The 6-6 tie with Michigan, incidentally, was also the game which inaugurated "The Little Brown Jug" rivalry that continues to this day. Then, in 1904, Minnesota went undefeated and outscored its opponents 725-12 (all 12 of those points were scored by Nebraska), even beating up on Grinnell, 146-0. After graduating in 1905, Harris became an assistant coach at Minnesota, a position he would hold for 28 years in all. Harris would later be inducted into the International Jewish Sports Hall of Fame, and was also selected as the quarterback on Knute Rockne's All-Time Jewish Team. Harris died in 1964 at the age of 81. "He was a dynamic little man who literally breathed Minnesota spirit, and was known and admired by thousands of alumni," said George Barton of Harris, the former sports editor of the Minneapolis Tribune.

BUTCH NASH
COLLEGE FOOTBALL: UNIVERSITY OF MINNESOTA

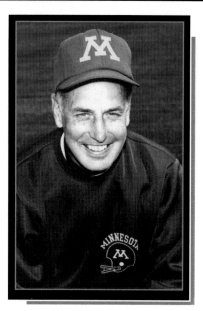

Butch Nash grew up in Minneapolis and graduated from Edison High School in 1935. In high school Butch played basketball and football, and was originally going to walk on to the Gopher basketball team, but tried out for football instead because he loved it so much. He would go on to play football at the University of Minnesota from 1936-38, lining up as a defensive end opposite hockey legend John Mariucci. As a student, Nash worked in the Memorial Stadium ticket office between classes to earn a living back then, as there were no special scholarship programs for athletes at the time. He made most of his money, however, from scalping the free tickets players received for more than triple their face value. That was a cool 10 bucks for a $3 ticket. Not bad!

After graduating, Butch got his first teaching and coaching job at Anoka High School in 1939. He stayed for two years and then went to Winona High School, where he remained for one year before going into the service for World War II. Butch returned to Winona for another year after the War and was then hired as an assistant by Bernie Bierman in 1947. Nash remained as an assistant at the U of M for 37 years until finally hanging it up in 1984. He would stick around as a volunteer coach, however, until 1991. Over his illustrious career in Minnesota, Nash lived through the hiring and firing of seven different head coaches. He saw history being made first hand and watched the evolution of the game — from a national championship to a Rose Bowl, Butch saw it all. Butch Nash is among the most respected people in the world of college football. The man simply bleeds maroon and gold and that is why he is so beloved.

HOW WOULD YOU DESCRIBE YOUR COACHING STYLE? "I was very low key. I was not one to rant and rave, I just tried to be a teacher. I would get down at a grass roots level and really talk to the kids. I would explain to them what we had to do and why we had to do it a certain way. That was my way of coaching."

HOW DID YOU MOTIVATE YOUR PLAYERS? "I used to tell my guys that they should be able to hold their heads high, win or lose, and be able to say that they did their very best on every play. Then no one could criticize you for how the game may have turned out. I also told them that they are here in college for a very short time, and that they have just so many games to play, so make them count. It goes by fast and then they have the rest of their lives ahead of them."

WHO WERE YOUR COACHING MENTORS? "To play and coach under Bernie Bierman was a real thrill. He was a great man, a good teacher and a good friend."

IF YOU COULD MAGICALLY GO BACK IN TIME TO THE FIRST YEAR YOU WERE A HEAD COACH AND GIVE YOURSELF SOME ADVICE FOR THE FUTURE, KNOWING WHAT YOU KNOW NOW, BACK THEN, WHAT WOULD YOU SAY TO YOURSELF? "I would just tell myself to keep on doing what I did, but maybe do it a little harder. I missed my dream of becoming a head coach at the University of Minnesota, but that was just the way it was. So, I did the best that I could. I worked with the kids as best I knew how to make them better football players. Maybe, hopefully, somewhere along the way I helped them to become better people too. That was a great reward for me."

LOOKING BACK WHAT ARE YOU MOST PROUD OF IN YOUR CAREER? "It was just the feeling that I had knowing that I was doing something for the men I coached, and that the men I coached admired me. They respected me as a coach and that meant a great deal to me. I just loved my kids and really had a great relationship with them."

HOW DID YOU BUILD TEAM UNITY & CHEMISTRY? "For me, as an assistant, I just tried not to be critical of them all the time. I tried to teach them as best as I could. I also never berated them, instead I tried to build them up as much as possible. I tried to never lose my temper too, that was important."

WHAT ADVICE WOULD YOU HAVE FOR YOUNG COACHES STARTING OUT TODAY? "I would say you have to work hard. There is no substitute for that. You have to be willing to put in the time and effort. Then, you have to be patient with your players and make sure they understand what it is that you want and demand. Then, work with them on always getting better. And remember, they are human beings. Sometimes we forget that."

WHAT'S THE BIGGEST THING YOU'VE LEARNED FROM COACHING THAT YOU'VE BEEN ABLE TO APPLY TO YOUR EVERYDAY LIFE? "I think it would have to be not letting a disappointment or defeat ruin your life. You have to come back from adversity, keep your head up, and you fight, fight, fight until things get better. You just can't ever give up. The same is true for kids. You can't give up on them. You have to just keep working with them and working with them until they get better."

WHAT ARE THE KEY INGREDIENTS TO CREATING A CHAMPIONSHIP TEAM? "First, you have got to have the people who are capable of winning a championship. Then, you have to have team unity and loyalty. They have to be able to play as one, and the coaching staff has to contribute to that. I also think you have to have great morale because a lot of games are won on spirit."

WHAT'S THE SECRET TO YOUR SUCCESS? "I tried to do my best all the time and tried to represent the University of Minnesota as best as I could. I just did whatever I could to help my ballplayers, they meant everything to me."

WHAT WOULD YOU WANT TO SAY TO YOUR FANS, BOOSTERS, AND ALUMNI WHO HAVE SUPPORTED YOU ALL THESE YEARS? "First I would want to thank the University for giving me the opportunity to coach. It was the greatest honor in the world to coach for Bernie Bierman at the University of Minnesota and I will never forget that. Then, I can't thank enough all of those great football players that played for me, it was a privilege to coach them. Beyond that, thanks to all the people who supported me through the years, that means a great deal. I have nothing but the best in my heart for the University of Minnesota and its football program. I would do anything for that program, it means everything to me."

HOW DO YOU WANT YOUR COACHING EPITAPH TO READ — HOW DO YOU WANT TO BE REMEMBERED AS A COACH? "I would like to be remembered as a coach that cared greatly for the people that he coached. I just tried to give my best and do what was best for the team."

GEORGE O'LEARY
PRO FOOTBALL: MINNESOTA VIKINGS

George O'Leary was born in Central Islip, N.Y., and went on to graduate from Central Islip High School. He then went on to play football at the University of New Hampshire, where he earned his degree in physical education. From there, O'Leary came back to coach at his alma mater. From 1968-76 he taught physical education and later served as the head football at Central Islip High School. (One of his players at Central Islip was a six-foot-eight quarterback by the name of Mike Tice, who just happens to be his boss as of 2002!) In 1977 O'Leary took over as the head coach at Liverpool High School (N.Y.), where he posted a 37-8-1 record in five seasons. Then, in 1980, O'Leary moved on to become an assistant at Syracuse University. He would stay for six years with the Orangemen until leaving for Georgia Tech, where he would serve as an assistant with the Yellow Jackets from 1987-91. The team finished 11-0-1 in 1990 and won the National Championship that year to boot.

That next year O'Leary made the jump to the NFL, serving as the defensive line coach for the San Diego Chargers for two years. In 1994 O'Leary went back to Georgia Tech to become the head coach. He would stay at Tech until 2001, emerging as one of the game's best young coaches. O'Leary amassed a 52-33 record while leading the Yellow Jackets to Bowl appearances his last five seasons. For his efforts he was given the 2000 Bobby Dodd Award as the National Coach of the Year, and he was also named as the Atlantic Coast Conference's top coach in both 1998 and 2000. O'Leary then left Georgia Tech to became the head coach at Notre Dame in December of 2001. When that didn't work out, however, he instead joined his old student, Mike Tice, as an assistant with the Vikings in 2002.

With the Vikings, O'Leary was brought in to serve as the assistant head coach & defensive line coach. Under his direction the Viking's rushing defense moved up to 10th in the NFL in 2002 from 30th in 2001. In addition, Tackle Chris Hovan emerged as one of the top players in the game, finishing the season with a team-high 36 quarterback hurries and was even selected to the Sports Illustrated All-Pro team. In 2003 O'Leary was promoted to defensive coordinator, where his squad looks poised to make it back to the playoffs. George and his wife Sharon reside in Eden Prairie and have two daughters, Chris and Trish, and two sons, Tim and Marty.

HOW WOULD YOU DESCRIBE YOUR COACHING STYLE? "I am the kind of guy who will correct something right then and there if I don't like what I see. I have always emphasized the importance of players learning from their mistakes and working hard to improve themselves. I want my players to do things the right way and I lean on them sometimes because I want them to play the best that they can play. I study a lot of tape and I just try to learn as much as I can about my players. I also stress hard work and really just encourage my guys to communicate and play tough football."

HOW DID YOU MOTIVATE YOUR PLAYERS? "I think that coaches need to know their players' hot buttons. You have to understand what turns one player on might turn another player off. I think to be successful you have to be somewhat self motivated. I also think that motivation and competitiveness go hand in hand. You know, in practices I always coach from the sideline and not out on the field, because those guys are out there on their own on Sundays and I can't be there to tell them what to do or motivate them. In order for play-

ers to be successful they have to have a lot of acquired traits, and it is my job as a coach to make sure that they acquire those traits. I also use a lot of trigger words to help communicate with my guys. For instance, I might yell 'M.Y.F.' which stands for 'Move Your Feet.' This way the kids get to know that you are not carrying on a conversation with them during the game, you are just trying to help them out and get them to quickly associate trigger words with certain things. You need trigger words so that your players understand what it is that you want and then how to get it done quickly. Sometimes young coaches will take M.Y.F. and make two or three paragraphs out of it, and that wastes time. And in a game, you don't have that time."

HOW DID YOU BUILD TEAM UNITY & CHEMISTRY? "I think chemistry comes from the coaching staff. If everybody in the room that you are working with has one goal in mind, to win, then egos never get in the way. The best way to destroy chemistry is to let some people do certain things their way, and then have everybody else abide by a different set of rules. Rules are made for everybody and they should be followed by everybody. I have always been big on that, whether it is someone on the first string or someone on the third. I don't buy the fact that you have to treat certain players differently because all that does is lead to other problems in your locker room. If you have team rules, then you have rules for everybody. You know, I have sat first stringers down for missing classes. Those are my rules, period. You have to be fair to everybody, otherwise your players won't respect you and you won't have chemistry amongst the team."

WHAT ADVICE WOULD YOU HAVE FOR YOUNG COACHES STARTING OUT TODAY? "Young coaches sometimes talk too much and explain things too much. I am a big believer in the strategy of 'tell them, show them and then do it.'"

WHAT IS THE BEST ADVICE YOU EVER GOT FROM ANOTHER COACH? "You got two ears and one mouth for a reason... to listen twice as much as you talk."

WHAT'S THE BIGGEST THING YOU'VE LEARNED FROM COACHING THAT YOU'VE BEEN ABLE TO APPLY TO YOUR EVERYDAY LIFE? "It would say it is a never quit attitude, which I try to apply to everything in my life. Whether it is football, golf or even reading a book, I like to do it well."

WHAT'S THE SECRET TO YOUR SUCCESS? "The secret is having good people around you. You just have to get your coaches involved. I don't think that there is any secret to football, and I don't think that anybody has come up with any new ideas — it is all begged, borrowed or stolen for the most part. So, the two key words that I have used in everything that I have done are accountability and responsibility. That is the key."

HOW DO YOU WANT YOUR COACHING EPITAPH TO READ — HOW DO YOU WANT TO BE REMEMBERED AS A COACH? "He worked hard and he was fair. That is how I would like to be remembered."

EDOR NELSON
COLLEGE FOOTBALL: AUGSBURG

Edor Nelson was born and raised in Dawson and graduated from Dawson High School in 1933, where he played football, baseball, basketball and track. Nelson went to Augsburg that next year and played football, basketball and baseball, graduating with honors in 1938. From there, Nelson got his first teaching and coaching job in Lamberton, where he stayed for three years. After that he went into the armed services for five and a half years during World War II, later working under General Patton, and even serving as a prisoner of war for six months in a German prison camp. When he returned home in 1946 he went back to Augsburg and began teaching and coaching several sports, including football, basketball and baseball, as well as wrestling and hockey — both of which he is credited with starting at the school. (He also got his master's degree from the University of Minnesota in 1947 as well.)

Nelson would go on to become a fixture at Augsburg. In all, he coached football at the school for 23 years (1947-69), finishing with a 58-118-10 record, the most wins in school history. He also coached baseball for 33 seasons (1946-79), earning MIAC titles seven times (1947, 48, 59, 61, 63, 73 and 75). Nelson was an associate professor in Augsburg's health and physical education department for 32 years as well, retiring in 1978. Among Nelson's many coaching accolades, he was inducted into the Minnesota Football Hall of Fame in 1973 and was also named MIAC Baseball Coach of the Year in 1975 as well. Then, in 2001, Augsburg honored Edor by re-dedicating their outdoor athletic field in his name as the "Edor Nelson Field." Today Edor is retired and living in Minneapolis. He still goes to the YMCA everyday to work out and stay in shape. He still follows Auggie athletics, and also roots for his son, who coaches high school football in Eagan as well.

HOW WOULD YOU DESCRIBE YOUR COACHING STYLE? "I believed that the kids came first and I based all of my coaching on that philosophy. I adapted my style to the players I had and just got them to work as hard as they could. We had some good years at Augsburg and we had some great kids along the way. I also believed that education came first and sports were secondary. We liked to win of course, but we had our priorities straight."

HOW DID YOU MOTIVATE YOUR PLAYERS? "I always told them that what they were doing was preparation for life. I reinforced to them that sports was a stepping stone for their careers. I told them that they were not going to play sports all their life and that they were going to have to get a job and work later on. So, they should learn as much as they could and try as hard as they could so that they could better be prepared for life after college. I would ask them what they wanted to do with their lives and then we would sit down and set goals together. Then, we would analyze those goals periodically to see how they were doing."

WHO WERE YOUR COACHING MENTORS? "My high school coach, Art Agge. He was a St. Olaf graduate and a great basketball player. He took me under his wing and I learned a lot from him. He was a great guy and I wanted to be like him."

IF YOU COULD MAGICALLY GO BACK IN TIME TO THE FIRST YEAR YOU WERE A HEAD COACH AND GIVE YOURSELF SOME ADVICE FOR THE FUTURE, KNOWING WHAT YOU KNOW NOW, BACK THEN, WHAT

WOULD YOU SAY TO YOURSELF? "I just feel that I have lived a very complete life and I don't know if I would do much differently to tell you the truth. Maybe I would have been a little bit more aggressive early on in my demands with the college for the development of other sports, for example, but other than that I was pretty satisfied."

LOOKING BACK WHAT ARE YOU MOST PROUD OF IN YOUR CAREER? "I would say the results that came about later in life with many of my players is what I am most proud of. The success that they had was just wonderful to see. I think almost every one of them turned out to be a good citizen and that makes me very proud."

WHAT WAS THE KEY TO RECRUITING? "Sell them on a good education. I used to tell them that they were coming to college for a purpose and Augsburg offered a very fine education. The parents always went along with that too."

HOW DID YOU BUILD TEAM UNITY & CHEMISTRY? "I used to set a lot of team goals as well as individual goals for my kids. I think most of my kids got along for the most part and that carried over to the athletic field. We spent a lot of time together off the field and that helped to build unity together too. I used to tell my kids to make every minute count and that would translate into success both on and off the field."

WHAT MOTIVATED YOU? "My interest in kids. I was interested in developing good citizens, that was my biggest motivation. I wanted them to be successful in life."

WHAT ADVICE WOULD YOU HAVE FOR YOUNG COACHES STARTING OUT TODAY? "Remember that the kids are the most important thing. Treat them all fairly and remember that you are working with the development of youth. Beyond that, keep it all in perspective and don't get carried away with things. Life is too short for that."

WHAT'S THE BIGGEST THING YOU'VE LEARNED FROM COACHING THAT YOU'VE BEEN ABLE TO APPLY TO YOUR EVERYDAY LIFE? "I think it has given me an interest and perspective in many other things. I have a great interest in being patriotic, I have a great interest in the community as a whole and I have a great interest in just living a good life."

WHAT ARE THE KEY INGREDIENTS TO CREATING A CHAMPIONSHIP TEAM? "Loyalty, teamwork and cooperation are the biggest things. Sure, you need to have some talent, but you can't get very far without the other things."

ON HOW THE GAME HAS CHANGED: "You know, sometimes I think some of the parents have gotten too carried away. Too often they care only about their own kids and they forget about why the kids are there. Some of them need to be more realistic in what sports really means. I think sports have kind of gotten out hand a little bit. It used to be more down to earth. I think that sports are just a part of life and they are not as important as everyone wants to make them out to be. Sometimes the fans are out of hand and that is sad to see too.

I think back to my days in the armed services, that was life and death and really important. Sports is just supposed to be fun while you get your education. We need to remember that I think."

WHAT'S THE SECRET TO YOUR SUCCESS? "I suppose my family. They encouraged me a great deal and that meant a lot to me. Also, I was genuinely interested in the development of young people and I cared about the kids I worked with."

WHAT WOULD YOU WANT TO SAY TO YOUR FANS, BOOSTERS, AND ALUMNI WHO HAVE SUPPORTED YOU ALL THESE YEARS? "I think they should all be very proud of what these kids have done for the University, the community and for our country. Thanks to everyone who helped make that possible and for their support."

HOW DO YOU WANT YOUR COACHING EPITAPH TO READ — HOW DO YOU WANT TO BE REMEMBERED AS A COACH? "I would like to be remembered as someone who had his players best interests at heart. I wanted my kids to go on and become successful in life. I also did something to help make this a better country and a better community, and that is how I would like to be thought of."

RAY ECKLUND: KENTUCKY FOOTBALL

Ray Ecklund played football for the Gophers from 1922-23 and then went on to coach at the University of Kentucky from 1925-26, posting a record of 15-3.

PUDGE HEFFELFINGER: GOPHER FOOTBALL

Walter "Pudge" Heffelfinger was so big and so strong that he actually played for the Gophers while he was a senior at Minneapolis Central High School. (The eligibility rules were quite a bit more relaxed back in the late 1880s than they are today!) After Pudge played for Minnesota for one season, he then headed east to Yale, where he played under legendary coach Walter Camp. There, Pudge led his teams to a 54-2 record, a national championship and became a three-time All-American guard. Recognized as the first "pulling guard," Pudge was regarded by most football pundits as the nation's best college football player. After his playing days in Yale, Heffelfinger decided to turn pro. In fact, Heffelfinger would have the distinction of becoming America's first-ever professional football player. That's right, on November 12, 1892, Heffelfinger played a game for the Duquesne Athletic Club of Pittsburgh, and was paid $500, the first time a player was known to be given money for his playing services. In the game, Heffelfinger forced a fumble, picked up the ball, and ran 35 yards for the only touchdown as Duquesne beat the arch-rival Allegheny Athletic Association. Heffelfinger would then go on to coach Lehigh University to a 6-8-0 record in 1894 and had a 7-3-0 record at the University of Minnesota in 1895. He then became a stockbroker, but occasionally helped out with the coaching at Minnesota as well. Pudge, who would continue to play semi-pro and charity games, played all the way until he was 65 years old. A real football pioneer and legend, Heffelfinger was later enshrined into the College Football Hall of Fame. He died in 1954 at the age of 87.

FRITZ CRISLER: GOPHER FOOTBALL

Herbert Orrin "Fritz" Crisler was hired to serve as the Gopher's new coach and athletic director in 1930. The Earlville, Il., native would remain in Gold Country for just two seasons, finishing with a record of 10-7-1 (.588). Crisler, who was an All-American end at the University of Chicago in 1921 and later served as an assistant for eight seasons under legendary coach Amos Alonzo Stagg after graduating, hired former Gophers Bert Baston, Sig Harris and Frank McCormick as his assistant coaches at Minnesota. Crisler's first season was a trying one though, as he remained under the intense media pressure that went along with having the top sports coaching position in the Midwest. The players were having a hard time adjusting from (previous coach) Doc Spears' military-like practices, to Crisler's quiet and subtle style, which included no profanity. Crisler, after just two years at the helm, was replaced by one of Minnesota's most famous sons, Bernie Bierman. Crisler would, however, go on to coach at Princeton and then at Michigan, where, from 1938-47, he became one of the conference's most successful all-time coaches with a 71-16-3 record. Crisler retired as a coach in 1947 after beating USC, 49-0, in the Rose Bowl. He remained at Michigan as the school's athletic director until 1968. Crisler's overall career record was 116-32-9 (.768).

TOM PORTER
COLLEGE FOOTBALL: ST. OLAF

Tom Porter grew up in Bayport and went on to graduate from Stillwater High School in 1947. From there, Porter attended St. Olaf, where he played football, hockey and baseball, graduating in 1951 with a teaching degree. The all-conference guard and linebacker on the football team then went into the Service for two years. Then, upon his return home from Korea, Porter got his first job in Neenah, Wis., where he taught physical education and coached football and track for four years. Porter then came back to St. Olaf in 1958 to teach anatomy, kineseology and physical education. He also took over for Ade Christensen as the head football coach and coached hockey and track as well. (It is interesting to note that in 1959 the Dallas Cowboys held their training camp at St. Olaf and were led that year by a rookie quarterback named Don Meredith.) Porter would go on to coach football at St. Olaf for 32 years, claiming six conference titles and winning 171 games along the way. A real Ole football legend, Tom Porter retired from coaching in 1991 and today lives near Northfield in Dundas.

HOW WOULD YOU DESCRIBE YOUR COACHING STYLE? "I was not a highly emotional or vocal coach, my technique was more low-key. I stressed execution and performance and tried to challenge my athletes to develop and play at their highest level. I also felt that if they were in the right cooperative mood, then that would carry over into the team concept."

HOW DID YOU MOTIVATE YOUR PLAYERS? "In football, because you only played once a week, your players had a build-up of performance with regards to strategy and skill development that you tried to employ for that game. There was also a build-up in the competitive level too that you could prepare for mentally as opposed to some other sports which were played daily or several times a week, like baseball or hockey. So, we built on that and tried to motivate our kids to be the best we could, all while keeping everything in perspective. We stressed the fundamentals, but also encouraged our guys to have fun and play hard."

ON DIVISION III ATHLETICS: "Because we were a division III college with no scholarships, we had a lot of students who were in our program not because they were football players, but rather because football was an extension of the overall education that they were seeking. So, during any given week, there were probably times when football was definitely not the most important thing in their lives. But, come Saturday afternoon, football was it. Then, they put other things aside and focused on winning. I think that division three athletics have their sports programs in the proper perspective where it is a part of the education, but not the whole ball of wax like it is at bigger schools. For those who take advantage of that, it can have tremendous lasting values. I am just a firm believer that there are many educational advantages to be gained through playing intercollegiate athletics that you could never get in a classroom."

WHO WERE YOUR COACHING MENTORS? "I played for Ade Christenson at St. Olaf. He was a tremendous builder of our football program and was the pioneer and mentor for all of us. If you were to mention one name with St. Olaf Football, it would have to be Ade Christensen. He was a real legend and a helluva coach. He established a great program and great philosophy here at St. Olaf and

I was honored to be his successor when he stepped down to become the athletic director. He was a very strong mentor of mine."

IF YOU COULD MAGICALLY GO BACK IN TIME TO THE FIRST YEAR YOU WERE A HEAD COACH AND GIVE YOURSELF SOME ADVICE FOR THE FUTURE, KNOWING WHAT YOU KNOW NOW, BACK THEN, WHAT WOULD YOU SAY TO YOURSELF? "I would say to be yourself. Coaches come in many shapes and sizes, there is no one mold for successful coaches. Some are emotional, volatile people like Lou Holtz, while others are more low-key, like Bud Wilkinson. Both are winners. I would also say that a coach doesn't have to be a cheerleader. And what I mean is that there are other things that a coach can do not only during the course of preparation for any given week, but also during a ballgame as far as making decisions or teaching kids certain things. That is important."

WHAT ARE THE CHARACTERISTICS OF WINNERS? "Someone who can challenge himself and someone who can lead by example both on and off the field."

HOW DID YOU BUILD TEAM UNITY & CHEMISTRY? "I really enjoyed working with young college men because you could put a lot of responsibility on their shoulders. So, to build unity, I liked to bring the people involved in on decision making. The players respected that and appreciated having a voice. I would meet formally with my co-captains every week, and then informally with them when they felt necessary. We didn't coach by committee, I was the head coach, but I wanted my players to understand my decisions and keep them well informed. I think that helped to keep everyone involved and helped to build chemistry."

WHAT'S THE BIGGEST THING YOU'VE LEARNED FROM COACHING THAT YOU'VE BEEN ABLE TO APPLY TO YOUR EVERYDAY LIFE? "Perspective would be an important term to use here from the standpoint that it is so easy for a coach to feel that his program is so important to him that it has to be of utmost importance to everybody else. So, to learn to appreciate that other people might have a different set of values and that you have to come to appreciate those is also important."

WHAT ARE THE KEY INGREDIENTS TO CREATING A CHAMPIONSHIP TEAM? "Good players. But, you also have to have a certain camaraderie amongst your players too. There is a great dependency amongst teammates in the game of football, and that is important too. Those teams that can draw the best out of each other, are will find a way to be successful. There is just a certain type of leadership that has to come from within the squad itself. The coach certainly has to be a leader, but he can't exert all the leadership. This is probably not true at the high school level, but it is most definitely the case at the college level where you have more mature men. You just need strong individuals who can lead their teammates."

WHAT'S THE SECRET TO YOUR SUCCESS? "Certainly, you have to start with quality players. If you have good players then you will have good teams. So, I hoped that my coaching would enable them to improve and develop within their potential, but overall you have to have good players because you aren't going to perform any miracles from the coaching standpoint."

WHAT WOULD YOU WANT TO SAY TO YOUR FANS, BOOSTERS, AND ALUMNI WHO HAVE SUPPORTED YOU ALL THESE YEARS? "Ade Christensen established a great program and philosophy here at St. Olaf and I felt that my job was to perpetuate that success. So, it would be my hope that as people look back over the years, that I did not diminish those great things that he established. As for the fans, I really appreciate their support, no question. But the support shouldn't be for me, it is for the program that I was running and the players who were involved with it. They are what is most important."

HOW DO YOU WANT YOUR COACHING EPITAPH TO READ — HOW DO YOU WANT TO BE REMEMBERED AS A COACH? "As a coach I guess I would like to think that my players felt that they got a fair shake and that I attempted to bring out the best in their abilities. I also hope that their time involved in intercollegiate athletics at St. Olaf was a valuable part of their formative years."

CAP McEWAN: NFL's BROOKLYN DODGERS

Cap McEwan was born in Alexandria in 1893 and went on to play football at the University of Minnesota and also at Army. McEwan would later go on to coach for two years in the NFL with the Brooklyn Dodgers from 1933-34, posting a career coaching record of 9-11-1. McEwan died in 1970 at the age of 77 in New York.

ROGER FRENCH: BYU FOOTBALL

Roger French, a Minneapolis Central graduate who went on to play End at the University of Minnesota from 1950-52, later served as the offensive coordinator at Brigham Young University for more than 20 years.

DAN RUNKLE: MINNESOTA STATE MANKATO FOOTBALL

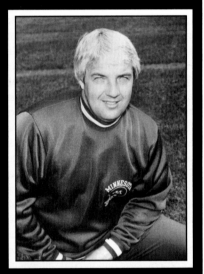

Dan Runkle spent 21 years as the head football coach at Minnesota State University, Mankato. With a career record of 108-124-2, Runkle is the all-time winningest football coach at MSU, along with being the 14th winningest coach in NCAA Division II history. Runkle, who earned ten letters in football, basketball, and baseball at Illinois College, had previously coached as an assistant at the University of Utah, the University of South Dakota, Northern Arizona University, and the University of Minnesota, under Head Coach Joe Salem, before taking over at MSU. An innovator, Runkle was also very flexible in his coaching style. While his option-oriented rushing teams of the late 1980's established most of the school rushing and total offense records, his "high-tech" offensive teams of the 1990's established school and conference marks for passing and total offense. Among his many honors and accolades, Runkle was the 1987 North Central Conference Coach of the Year, 1991 Football Gazette Division II National Coach of the Year, and in 1993 he was inducted into the Illinois College Hall of Fame. During his tenure at MSU, Runkle also worked hard with his student athletes to help them achieve an impressive graduation rate of 93%. Runkle stepped down as the head football coach at Minnesota State in 2002. That same year he was hired to serve as the Athletic Director at the University of Dubuque, in Iowa. Runkle is the proud father of two MSU graduates, Tad and Sara. Dan was also married in the summer of 1992, and his wife, Deb, was a member of the MSU family working in the Sports Medicine Department. One of the most respected men in college football, Dan Runkle was a Minnesota State University, Mankato coaching legend.

JIM LIND: UM-MORRIS FOOTBALL

Jim Lind grew up in Isle, Minn., and went on to play college football, first at Bethel College and then at Bemidji State, where he played defensive back, before graduating in 1974. Lind entered coaching that next season as head football coach at Underwood (Minn.) High School. Two years later he became a graduate assistant at St. Cloud State, before earning the offensive coordinator job there in 1978. He then moved to nearby St. John's University for one season, before serving as the Defensive Coordinator at BYU in 1981. (Lind earned his master's degree at St. Cloud State and Doctorate in Professional Leadership in Physical Education and Athletics at BYU.) From there, Lind went on to become the head coach at the University of Minnesota-Morris, where he directed the Cougars to two Northern Intercollegiate Conference championships and earned NIC Coach of the Year honors in 1984 and NAIA District 13 Coach of the Year honors in 1986. In 1987 Lind took over as the head coach at the University of Wisconsin-Eau Claire, where he would remain until 1991. Lind then broke into the professional ranks, first with the Green Bay Packers, where he served as an assistant. He would remain with the Pack for seven years before moving on to become an assistant with the Seattle Seahawks in 1999. Since then, Lind has served as the Linebackers and Tight Ends Coach with the Seahawks, which is his current position as we head into the 2003-04 season. Jim and his wife Cindy presently reside in Seattle and have two sons, Erik and Bryan.

JERRY ROSBURG
PRO FOOTBALL: CLEVELAND BROWNS

Jerry Rosburg grew up in Fairmont and played high school football under legendary coach Tom Mahoney. Rosburg then went on to play linebacker at North Dakota State University, where he graduated in 1978. From there, Rosburg embarked on a 20 year college coaching journey which would ultimately lead him to the NFL, where he currently is in his third season as the Cleveland Browns special teams coordinator.

Rosburg's coaching career first started as an assistant coach and teacher at Fargo Shanley High School in 1979. From there, he began his college coaching career at Northern Michigan University as a two-year graduate assistant in 1981 and helped the school earn a Division II playoff appearance. He was then appointed to a full-time assistant at NMU the following season and coached the Wildcats' linebackers for three years before being elevated to defensive coordinator and secondary coach in 1986. In addition, Rosburg also received his master's degree from Northern Michigan in 1983. Rosburg's next stop took him to Western Michigan University in 1987, where, as the linebackers and special teams coach, his Broncos made it to the California Bowl in 1988. Three years later Rosburg wound up at the University of Cincinnati. There, he coached the secondary, linebackers and helped the Bearcats to an 8-3 record in 1993 and a 6-5 record in 1995. In 1996 Jerry came home for one season to serve as the secondary coach at the University of Minnesota. That next year he headed east, to serve as an assistant at Boston College. In 1999 Rosburg served as cornerbacks/special teams coach at Notre Dame, helping the Fighting Irish to a 9-3 finish in 2000 and an appearance in the Fiesta Bowl.

Finally, in 2001, Rosburg made it to the "show," where he took over as the special teams coordinator for the Cleveland Browns. His special teams units finished second in the NFL in field goal percentage that year as Kicker Phil Dawson connected on 22-of-25 attempts (88%). In addition, the Browns possessed the third ranked kickoff coverage unit in 2001, allowing just 18.7 yards per return. As we head into the 2003-2004 season, Rosburg is continuing to climb the coaching ladder and is enjoying success on a team that is clearly on it's way up. With Head Coach Butch Davis steering the ship, Rosburg is keeping some good company. Is there a head coaching position in Jerry's future? We can only hope so. He is certainly making Minnesota very proud. Jerry and his wife Sherry presently live in

the Cleveland area with their three children, Megan, Margaret and Jerad.

HOW WOULD YOU DESCRIBE YOUR COACHING STYLE? "My philosophy is to try to put players in the best possible position to be successful, and that comes through good teaching, good preparation and having good players. That's really what it comes down to. I am a teacher at heart and that has shaped my coaching style a great deal. Being a high school teacher forces you to be organized and to have a plan. You have to seek methods for motivating kids, to evaluate people and to make the subject matter interesting. Being a coach and teacher at that level is a great training ground for being an NFL coach and that certainly played a role in who I am today."

HOW DO YOU MOTIVATE YOUR PLAYERS? "Everybody is different. You know dealing with professional athletes it is a whole different deal. As long as players see that you are trying to help them to make themselves better, and are trying to help the team win, then usually they will listen to what you have to say. In my position, however, as a special teams coach, it is unique in that you have the opportunity to work with virtually every player on the team. At times, you are coaching them all and that is a great opportunity to get to know them and work with them. As a coach you are measured by the performance of your players and that is why you have to do a good job. It is a slippery slope for all of us though, coaches and players, because we are in the same boat together trying to get better and trying to win. That in itself is great motivation."

WHAT ARE THE CHARACTERISTICS OF WINNERS? "In my opinion the characteristics of winners are players who are willing to work very hard to prepare and who also have a passion for the game."

LOOKING BACK WHAT ARE YOU MOST PROUD OF IN YOUR CAREER? "You know, getting to where I am has been a step-by-step process and every job that I have gotten has seemed to be a little bit better than the last. So, I have been blessed by being around good people in a lot of good programs and have had a lot of good players. It has been a great ride and I hope that this journey into coaching is just getting started."

WHAT ADVICE WOULD YOU HAVE FOR YOUNG COACHES STARTING OUT TODAY? "Learn as much as you can from as many people as you can. Young coaches will ask me way too often 'How do I get to the NFL?' and my answer is by doing a good job at the job you are at. So, don't look ahead. You have to do well where you are at and if you are good enough then good things will happen for you."

HOW DO YOU WANT YOUR COACHING EPITAPH TO READ — HOW DO YOU WANT TO BE REMEMBERED AS A COACH? "I would hope that I have had a positive influence on other players lives. That is one of the things that I have really relished about my profession is that I have made some great relationships with both coaches and players over the years. I have just tried to do the best that I can and have tried to help players both on and off the field to better themselves. That is what coaching is really all about in my opinion."

WILLIAM SPAULDING: GOPHER FOOTBALL

William Spaulding coached at the University of Minnesota from 1922-24, leading the Gophers to an overall record of 11-7-4. Spaulding's shining moment at Minnesota came in 1924 against Illinois in a game dedicating the new Memorial Stadium. Illinois' legendary running back Red Grange had been dominating the Big Ten that year, but the Gophers pounded him and eventually knocked him out of the game. The Gophers were then led by Clarence Schutte, who stole Grange's thunder by running for 282 yards in a 20-7 Gopher victory. Spaulding would later go on to serve as the head coach at UCLA from 1925-38 and eventually became the school's athletic director from 1938-47. UCLA's practice field is named Spaulding Field in his honor.

ADE CHRISTENSON: ST. OLAF FOOTBALL

Ade Christenson was born in Soldier's Grove, Wis., but grew up in Northfield. Christenson went on to graduate from nearby St. Olaf in 1922, where he also starred in three sports. Christenson had originally planned on going to medical school, but as a favor to a friend he agreed to coach for a year at Story City (Iowa) High School. Once there, he was hooked, and never left the coaching profession. Christenson would go on to coach four high school teams to conference championship seasons. His first two came in Story City, followed by one each at both Greenway-Coleraine and Minneapolis Roosevelt.

Christenson joined the St. Olaf physical education faculty in 1927 and was named head football coach in 1929. During World War II Christenson earned his master's degree at the University of Southern California and then coached the Ely High School team to an undefeated season before returning to St. Olaf in 1945. When he retired from active coaching in 1958, his St. Olaf football teams had won six conference championships. (The 1953 team even led the nation in several offensive categories.) He also coached track for 31 of his 38 years at the college and was basketball coach for nine years as well. Upon his retirement, Christenson devoted his attention to his duties as St. Olaf's athletic director.

Christenson's style was summed up like this: "A highly inventive and creative coach, Christenson usually had plays, formations, and strategies that surprised and confused the opponents, such as the fullback spinner series from the double wing and the shovel pass. Offensive football was his forte. To him defense was the period of time between offensive thrusts, and he assigned defensive strategies to assistant coaches. By today's standards, Ade's team's employed a "wide open" style of play. They relied on quick movements and deception, finesse rather than physical force."

In addition, Christenson also started St. Olaf's intramural program, which was nationally recognized for involving 85 percent of the men on campus, and it was emulated by many colleges and high schools throughout the nation. The years following World War II were tough. Coaches had to somehow blend 17-year-old high school graduates with worldly 25-year-old combat veterans. Christenson's intramural clubs, with their emphasis on teamwork, participation and companionship, helped to do that.

Among his many coaching awards and accolades, Christenson was inducted into the Minnesota Coaches Hall of Fame in 1970. Additionally, St. Olaf College paid tribute to their former coach of 38 years by renaming their athletics complex in his honor of his contributions. With a philosophy strong on discipline, principle, and faith, Ade Christenson was a true Ole legend in every sense of the word.

Christenson insisted that his coaches be teachers first and that they resist the temptation to bend the rules to win. He was a firm believer in the personal value of athletic competition, but he never viewed sports as an end in itself. It was said that he taught and coached through athletics. Football, basketball, and track were but media through which he conveyed the meanings and lasting qualities of a Christian life. In 1958, Ade published a book, "Verdict of the Scoreboard," in which he attacked professionalism in college athletics and called for colleges to "restore dignity and honor to competitive sports." College athletics "will never reach its quality of greatness outside the framework of amateurism," he said. "Our pledge to athletics must be written in a deep faith and a selfless love. Throwing touchdown passes is important in the final outcome of a football game, but touchdowns are not a justifiable reason for the establishment of scholarships, grants, free rides, and convertibles as living testimony to what is considered important in American education."

"Though his players knew him as a superb teacher, and opposing coaches respected him as a brilliant gridiron tactician, it was the force of his own life and personal example that made the deepest impact on those who knew him," said former Ole coaching legend Tom Porter in his book entitled "Called to Serve." "When I meet men who played under him, I sense always that note of respect and affection that men reserve for another man whose influence has strengthened the fiber of discipline and integrity in their own lives."

JOE BENDA: ST. JOHN'S FOOTBALL

Joe Benda attended Duluth Cathedral High School from 1918-23 and played football and basketball, even leading his team to a mythical state football championship in 1922. From there, Benda went on to play football at Notre Dame under legendary coach Knute Rockne. Benda also played basketball for the Fighting Irish for two years under coach George Keogan — a Detroit Lakes native. Benda graduated in the spring 1928 and was named head football coach at Duluth Cathedral in the fall of 1929. There, in addition to playing for the Duluth Kelly's pro football team, he guided his team to a tie for the Head of the Lakes championship with a 7-1 record that season.

Benda then took over as the head coach at St. John's in 1930. There, he turned the program around, winning the school's first conference title in 1932 with a team that did not give up a point all season. Titles followed in 1935 and 1936 before Benda departed for an assistant coaching job back at Notre Dame. Benda returned from 1941-42 and again from 1945-49, but he couldn't get the Johnnies back to their old form. In 1948 Benda developed Hodgkin's disease and became progressively weaker. By the end of the 1949 season he became so weak that he was unable to stand for any length of time and finally had to drive his car to the practice field and coach from the front seat. Tragically, he died from the disease in the summer of 1950 at the age of just 45. Benda was head football coach for 14 seasons at SJU (1930-36, 1941-42 and 1945-49) and finished with an overall career record of 47-32-8 as well as a 35-25-7 tally in the MIAC. In addition, Benda also served as the head basketball coach in Collegeville for 14 seasons (1931-37 and 1942-49) and finished with a career record of 68-152 as well as a 44-103 mark in the MIAC. Benda was also the head baseball coach for one season in 1945 during WWII. Joe Benda died way too young, and will forever be remembered as a St. John's icon who spent his entire life helping others.

GRADY ROSTBERG
HIGH SCHOOL FOOTBALL: HUTCHINSON

Grady Rostberg grew up in Gilby, N.D., and went on play six-man football at Gilby High School. From there, Rostberg attended Mayville State University, where he served as the captain of his football and basketball teams, while also playing baseball as well. Rostberg started out his coaching career as a basketball coach at Hatton, N.D., High School, before going on to get his masters degree at UND. From there, Rostberg got his first coaching and teaching job, coaching football and teaching Math, at Brownton, Minn., High School in 1963. In 1969 Rostberg came to Hutchinson, where he has remained ever since and become a legend along the way.

Rostberg retired in 1998 after 28 years of coaching football at Hutch, going out in style with a state title that year to boot. In all, Rostberg won three state championships (1983, 1984 & 1998), and finished his illustrious 34 year coaching career with a record of 277-89-2, good for fifth on the all-time wins list in state history. In addition, his legacy includes the fact that his two daughters and son are all coaches and his two daughters both married coaches. His son, Andy, who led the Tigers to the 1983 & 1984 state titles as the team's quarterback, is now the head football and head basketball coach at Hutch, carrying on the old man's legacy. Grady is a true Minnesota coaching icon, and one of the most respected men in the business. Grady is retired and presently resides in Hutchinson with his family.

HOW WOULD YOU DESCRIBE YOUR COACHING STYLE? "I have my kids work hard and we practice the fundamentals. We have built a winning tradition here in Hutchinson and I am very proud of that. Once you have that, then it is easy to coach. You know, football is a numbers game and you need to get a lot of kids coming out to your program in order to be successful. You also need to get kids to feel good about the game of football at a young age. So, we built a feeder program here for our junior high aged kids and that has been great. You can't alienate young kids at that age because they might develop later on and turn out to be super athletes. You can also scare them away by having too much conditioning and too much hitting early on. So, we didn't do any of that stuff, we just scrimmaged intramurally and had fun. Then the kids had a good experience, just like they were out in the back yard. Once they get that love of the game, then they can move on and get serious.

HOW DID YOU MOTIVATE YOUR PLAYERS? "Everybody says that you should treat kids the same, but I am not so sure that is true. I think you have to treat kids depending on their own personalities and the type of individuals that they are. I think you should treat them not necessarily the same, but try to do what is best for each individual. One kid might be motivated by you being tough on him, and another might be motivated by something entirely different. So, as a coach you have to be able to read kids and try to deal with them as individuals. You know, until you have kids of your own, you can't really understand what is going through their minds. After you have kids, you have a better feeling for what is important for them and for how you should treat them."

ON GRANDPARENTS: "You know, we had a lot of grandparents working as coaches with our kids at our youth levels and that worked out fabulously. They are just the greatest people because they have all lost their egos and are just interested in the kids and in seeing them have fun. That is how it should be, but some of the other sports have really gotten away from that. Some of them are so organized that sometimes kids just get burned out a young age and then you've lost them. That's too bad."

WHO WERE YOUR COACHING MENTORS? "You know, Tom Mahoney from down in Fairmont was a real mentor to me. When I was a young guy starting out in the South Central Conference he really took me under his wing and showed me some things. I really liked the things that he did as a coach. He was so organized and just really taught me some valuable lessons that I have carried with me to this day. I still remember playing in Fairmont one time and can recall as we were heading on to the field I saw the band come marching over from the high school to the field. I just thought 'man, that is really neat!'. You know, us football coaches, we are all copycats, so I went ahead and had our band start doing the same thing shortly thereafter. I got a lot of help from Tom over the years, as did my son, and I appreciate his friendship to this day."

IF YOU COULD MAGICALLY GO BACK IN TIME TO THE FIRST YEAR YOU WERE A HEAD COACH AND GIVE YOURSELF SOME ADVICE FOR THE FUTURE, KNOWING WHAT YOU KNOW NOW, BACK THEN, WHAT WOULD YOU SAY TO YOURSELF? "You know at that time you have an ego and are trying to prove yourself. Your self worth at that point is sometimes based on whether or not you can win a football game or not. So, I guess I would tell myself to not be so concerned with winning. Just go out and do the best that you can and try to get the kids to do the same. I was such a competitor when I played and that definitely carried over to my coaching style."

WHAT IS THE KEY TO GOOD TIME MANAGEMENT? "As a coach and a teacher it was tough. You taught five classes a day and then coached the team after school, so it got to be tough at times. You just had to be organized and plan well to be successful. I was lucky, I had a supportive wife and family and that made a big difference too."

LOOKING BACK WHAT ARE YOU MOST PROUD OF IN YOUR CAREER? "I suppose the three state championships are right up there, but really it is when former players come back and say nice things about you and your program. To be able to think that you affected some people in a positive way is very gratifying."

HOW DID YOU BUILD TEAM UNITY & CHEMISTRY? "You have to get them all pointed in the same direction. I just think that success breeds success and failure breeds failure. Football is a hard sport to turn around because unlike say, basketball, where a couple of good kids can change everything, you need a lot of good kids at some key positions. So to develop team unity we used to try to have our kids do things together. Whether that was hanging out during the summer or going hunting or what have you. That kind of stuff really gets the kids to know one another, and that builds chemistry. As coaches we also tried to support them not only as football players but as people, so we tried to go to their games in other sports too. It takes time to build unity and it starts from having a good tradition with your program because then you have kids that see the success at a young age and want to come out for your team. They see the kids having fun and winning and naturally, they want to be a part of that. It is really a process, but once you get it, it is very valuable."

WHAT MOTIVATED YOU? "As a kid growing up with my dad and uncles I can still remember talking about sports all the time. They used to always talk about never, ever giving up and that stuck with me. So, I learned to love the game and respect the game at a very early age and have just always been motivated to succeed in whatever I do."

WHAT ADVICE WOULD YOU HAVE FOR YOUNG COACHES STARTING OUT TODAY? "I would tell them to find a guy like Tom Mahoney when they are young, like I did. Look for a successful mentor that you can embrace and learn as much as you can from him. Now, I am at the point where other coaches, even from other sports, want to talk to me about success and that means the world to me."

HOW DID YOU EARN THE RESPECT OF YOUR PLAYERS? "You know, when I was younger, I put the pads on with the kids. Sometimes if they can see that you did this yourself and walked in their shoes, they will listen to you a little bit more. Beyond that it is the golden rule: treat people like you like to be treated."

FAVORITE LOCKER ROOM SIGN? "It was 'BIG-A,' because we used to stress the 'big attitude.' That was always important to our program and really it applies to everything in life in that attitude is everything."

WHAT'S THE BIGGEST THING YOU'VE LEARNED FROM COACHING THAT YOU'VE BEEN ABLE TO APPLY TO YOUR EVERYDAY LIFE? "Coaching is hard work and hard work pays off. Coaching is also a microcosm of life, I mean you are deal-ing with people and have to learn how to treat them. I also think that most successful coaches are probably successful teachers as well. They know how to connect with kids and that is all part of it."

WHAT ARE THE KEY INGREDIENTS TO CREATING A CHAMPIONSHIP TEAM? "You can't win a lot of football games without good players. You can lose with good players, but you can't win without them."

WHAT'S THE SECRET TO YOUR SUCCESS? "We had great players, great backing from our administration and community, and we just had fun. You teach what you know, you keep it simple, have a good attitude and you work hard. That is it."

WHAT WOULD YOU WANT TO SAY TO YOUR FANS, BOOSTERS, AND ALUMNI WHO HAVE SUPPORTED YOU ALL THESE YEARS? "I would just thank everybody for all their support over the years and for coming to the all those games to see our kids. It has been a great ride and it has gone way too fast, but it was all worth it. There are too many people to thank individually, but I would have to thank my wife because I don't think she missed more than one game in all 28 years here in Hutchinson. She just loves foot-ball so I am a lucky man. You know, I loved my job and think that teaching and coaching is the greatest profession in the world. You don't get rich but I wouldn't trade it for all the world."

HOW DO YOU WANT YOUR COACHING EPITAPH TO READ — HOW DO YOU WANT TO BE REMEMBERED AS A COACH? "I would like to be remembered as someone who loved the game and loved his players."

LLOYD HOLLINGSWORTH: GUSTAVUS FOOTBALL

Lloyd Hollingsworth was a Gusty coaching legend. After winning 11 letters if football, baseball and gymnastics at Gustavus, Hollingsworth went on to serve as both the athletic director and foot-ball coach of the Gusties for 15 years, compiling a record of 94-33-5, and garnering nine MIAC titles from 1942-1961. (He would later earn a master's degree from the University of Minnesota and his doctorate from New York University.) Holly's 1946 team was undefeated and two of his teams were invited to bowl games. His record of leading the Gusties to five conference titles in succes-sion broke the previous record by two and he would go on to own the best record in the history of the conference as well.

Hollingsworth was an innovator. He bought new plastic helmets, getting rid of the old leather ones and thought they should be dressed up a little bit. So he called then-Michigan athletic director Fritz Crisler and asked if they could use their winged logo that the Wolverines used. He agreed and the rest is history. Hollingsworth would take the Gusties on an incredible ride during the 1950s, leading them to an amazing eight conference championships throughout the decade.

An early star of Hollingsworth's era was Running Back Harold "Swen" Swanson, who was selected as a member of a college all-star team and played in the Little Olympic Bowl in Gilmore Stadium, LA. One of the more storied squads was the 1950 group, which finished the regular season with a 9-0 record before losing NAIA Playoff games to UW-LaCrosse, 20-13, and Texas Abilene Christian, 13-7, in what was billed as the "Refrigerator Bowl," a promotion for the Evansville, Ind., appliance indus-try. The game was played in a muddy downpour, where the Gusties got... "iced." Stars of that team included Quarterback Tom Zweiner, End Haldo Norma, Center Kenny Quist, Halfback Gene Payne and Little All-American Tackle Cal Roberts.

In 1953 the NFL's New York Giants held their preseason camp at the Gustavus campus, which was really quite a big deal at the time. Thousands of dignitaries from the world of Minnesota football came to watch the team, which was led by Tom Landry, Frank Gifford and Emlin Tunnell. They often times scrimmaged the Packers at Minneapolis' Parade Stadium and also played intersquad games in front of near-ly 10,000 fans in both St. Peter, in what was called the "Green Giant Bowl," and also in Austin, to play the "Spam Bowl."

The Gusties dominated the 1950s, even making several post-season runs as well. One of the better ones came in 1958, when the 8-1 squad went on to lose to Arizona State, 41-12, in the NAIA Playoffs. One of the stars of the late '50s was Little All-American Defensive Lineman Bill Beck, who went on to play briefly for both the New York Giants and the Dallas Texans of the AFL.

In addition, Hollingsworth coached baseball, hockey, tennis, basketball and gymnastics at Gustavus over the years. (In fact, in 1935 he coached the Gustie gymnastics team to its sixth consecutive Northwest Gymnastics Meet title.) Holly gave up his head coaching duties in 1961 to concentrate on his duties as athletic director and chairman of the department, but did return to the football field as an assistant coach from 1966-69. Hollingsworth's coaching and athletic career at Gustavus, interrupted twice for military tours of duty during WW II and the Korean conflict, spanned from 1942-78. Hollingsworth, was later inducted into both the NAIA and Minnesota Coaches Hall of Fames. In addition, on September 24, 1983, Gustavus Field was renamed Hollingsworth Field in his honor. Holly is a true Gusty legend.

RON STOLSKI
HIGH SCHOOL FOOTBALL: BRAINERD

Ron Stolski grew up in North Minneapolis and went on to graduate from Patrick Henry High School in 1957, where he played football, basketball and baseball. From there, Stolski played quarterback at Macalester College, where he also served as the team captain. In 1960 Stolski graduated with a teaching degree and wound up getting his first job in tiny Kensington. There, he taught English and coached eight man football, among other sports, from 1962-63. In 1964 Stolski moved to Slayton and in 1965 he found his way to Princeton. In 1970 Stolski moved on to Park Center and in 1975 he wound up in Brainerd. There, he took over as the athletic director and head football coach, and he has since become a coaching legend.

At one point, prior to the state playoff system taking affect in the early 1970s, Stolski had an 18-game winning streak over a two and a half year span. Over his storied career, Coach Stolski has won 13 conference titles, three section titles and was a semifinalist at one state tournament. He is a member of four halls of fames, and is the past president of the Minnesota Football Coaches Association. In addition, Stolski was also a past board member of the National Interscholastic Administrators Association, the high school equivalent of the NCAA. Now entering his 42nd year as a head coach, Stolski's record on the gridiron is 283-132-5. Presently, he is the winningest active coach in Minnesota and should break George Larson's all-time wins record of 307 in a few years, if all goes as planned.

HOW WOULD YOU DESCRIBE YOUR COACHING STYLE? "I think I am a sound fundamentalist. I also make great use of my staff and together we really care about our kids. I have also been told that I am a great motivator and that is certainly something I take great pride in. We are a rushing team and have been for four decades now. We try to control the tempo of the game by running the ball and by playing sound defense. From there, we just try to have our kids ready to play on Friday nights."

HOW DO YOU MOTIVATE YOUR PLAYERS? "There are so many ways to motivate. One of the best ways, however, goes like this: 'Create and maintain an environment that people want to be a part of.' You know, as an athletic director I have had over 150 coaches under me over the years. From time to time I will get a young coach who will come into my office and tell me that he or she is concerned about winning and losing. I always told them that their job was to create and maintain an environment that people want to be a part of. Period. If they do that, then kids will be taught well and they will play. Eventually the wins will follow. So, that is what we try to do with our staff and with our kids and it has been a very successful model for us."

IF YOU COULD MAGICALLY GO BACK IN TIME TO THE FIRST YEAR YOU WERE A HEAD COACH AND GIVE YOURSELF SOME ADVICE FOR THE FUTURE, KNOWING WHAT YOU KNOW NOW, BACK THEN, WHAT WOULD YOU SAY TO YOURSELF? "I don't know how much I would change to tell you the truth. As I have grown I better understand the value of working smart instead of working long. I think I have always been big into the fundamentals and that hasn't changed much. I will say this though, that when you are young you tend to think that you can do it all through motivation and you can just kick

doors down and go out and play. It doesn't help though if you are not fundamentally sound. It's like the old story of the two boxers in the ring right before the fight and one fighter makes the sign of the cross. Just then two guys in the crowd look at each other and one says to the other 'wow, he made the sign of the cross, do you suppose that will help?' The other guy answers, 'it does... if he can fight!' I think that as coaches, if we understand that we are just a part of a bigger picture and are not the actual picture, then we will be OK. Football is not the big picture, it is just a part of the school's mission statement regarding academics and athletics."

LOOKING BACK WHAT ARE YOU MOST PROUD OF IN YOUR CAREER? "That we have been able to have players who have come back over the decades and say 'coach, you cared about me...'."

WHAT ARE THE CHARACTERISTICS OF LEADERS? "Leaders have a vision, leaders can accept change, leaders work harder than anybody else, leaders have compassion and leaders never look at a clock."

HOW DO YOU BUILD TEAM UNITY & CHEMISTRY? "You know, chemistry is not that difficult and it is probably much more simple than a lot of people make it out to be. Chemistry is built through trust, loyalty and the occasional chance to be a part of something greater than ourselves. It begins with the belief that we can, and that has been a guiding philosophy of mine for many, many years. After all, this is only a game... but this is such a marvelous game! In this game, we can learn lessons in life and that makes us better people."

WHAT MOTIVATES YOU? "I think the love of the game and the love of the kids. I think football is the greatest game we play on this earth. Just being with the kids and trying to do them a bit of good is very rewarding. One of the greatest lessons I have learned along the way is that it is not about me as the coach, it is about the kids you work with. So, what motivates me everyday is that I still believe that I have something to offer kids. The day I don't feel that way will be the day I clean my locker out."

WHAT ADVICE WOULD YOU HAVE FOR YOUNG COACHES STARTING OUT TODAY? "Be willing to do all the little things. Then, the big things will take care of themselves. You be the guy who pours the coffee. You be the guy who gets the ice. Do the little things and you will have success both on and off the field. Then, make sure that your wife and family is on board, that is very important to your success as well."

FAVORITE LOCKER ROOM SIGN? "We operate by a philosophy called the 'Warrior Way,' which is our style, the way we do things, the way we play and the way we aspire to be. It's foundation is based on respect."

WHAT IS THE KEY TO GOOD TIME MANAGEMENT? "Preparation with passion is success, preparation without passion is foolishness, and passion without preparation is disastrous."

WHAT'S THE BIGGEST THING YOU'VE LEARNED FROM

COACHING THAT YOU'VE BEEN ABLE TO APPLY TO YOUR EVERYDAY LIFE? "The value of keeping your shoulder to the wheel, the value of seeing the big picture, and the value of understanding the benefits of putting a group of people together for a short time on this earth and becoming one heart beat."

WHAT ARE THE KEY INGREDIENTS TO CREATING A CHAMPIONSHIP TEAM? "First of all you have to have talent. I think you have to have kids who know how to play this game. Then, you have to have a good sound philosophy on both sides of the ball, as well as on special teams. Then, you have to have a staff that works well together and shares that common bond of caring about kids. As a coach you most certainly need to have a knowledge of the game as well. You just have to know what you are talking about in order for your kids to listen to you and respect you."

WHAT'S THE SECRET TO YOUR SUCCESS? "First would be keeping up with the game. I have a thirst for knowledge and am always trying to learn more about this game. Second, I just love this game and third, I have been able to surround myself with great people. You know, you never set out to coach for 50 years, but as long as there is fire in my belly, as well as in my wife's belly, I am still going strong. We are 70-17 in the last eight years here, and I am still having fun."

WHAT WOULD YOU WANT TO SAY TO YOUR FANS, BOOSTERS, AND ALUMNI WHO HAVE SUPPORTED YOU ALL THESE YEARS? "It has been a great ride. Thank you for helping create what we call in Brainerd the 'Warrior Way.' I learned a lot more from the kids I coached and from the people I met through coaching than I ever taught them."

HOW DO YOU WANT YOUR COACHING EPITAPH TO READ — HOW DO YOU WANT TO BE REMEMBERED AS A COACH? "He cared about his kids, he challenged them and he taught them how to work hard."

MARK MAUER: COLLEGE FOOTBALL

Mark Mauer, a former Nebraska quarterback and St. Paul Harding High School graduate, went on to serve as an assistant football coach at Wisconsin, Ball State, Nebraska, North Dakota State and New Mexico State. He continues to climb the coaching ladder and is making Minnesota proud along the way.

WES FESLER: GOPHER FOOTBALL

Wes Fesler only coached in Minnesota for three seasons, but definitely left his mark in Gold Country. Fesler was hired by the Gophers in 1951 and would remain until 1953, posting a modest 10-13-4 record along the way. He did have one thing going for him, however, the Winona Phantom — Paul Giel, who tore up the gridiron during Fesler's era and finished second in the 1953 Heisman race. Fesler, who was a three-time All-American End at Ohio State from 1928-30, also earned All-American honors with the Buckeye basketball team in 1931 as well.

The Youngstown, Ohio, native coached football at Wesleyan in 1942, at Pittsburgh in 1946, and at Ohio State, from 1947-50, where his football teams went 21-13-3. The 1949 Buckeye squad won the Big Ten championship and beat California, 17-14, in the Rose Bowl. In addition, Fesler also coached basketball at Harvard from 1933-41 and at Princeton in 1945. Fesler's overall record was 118-36-8 in football and 39-55 in basketball. Fesler was later inducted into the College Football Hall of Fame.

DENNIS RAARUP: GUSTAVUS FOOTBALL

Dennis Raarup's collegiate playing career was spent at Gustavus, where he was a defensive back and kicker played for three MIAC Championship football teams under Lloyd Hollingsworth from 1950-52. Raarup was also an outfielder on the baseball team as well. Graduating with majors in math and physical education in 1953, Raarup went on to earn a master's degree from the University of Minnesota and a doctorate from Northern Colorado University. After coaching and teaching at several high schools in Wisconsin in the early and mid-1960's, Raarup returned to Gustavus as an assistant coach under Jocko Nelson in 1968 and was named head coach in 1971. Raarup would guide the Gusties until 1987, becoming the winningest coach in Gustavus football history along the way. During his 17-year tenure in St. Peter, Raarup's squads won three conference titles, finished second four times and third twice. And, his 1987 team finished with a perfect 10-0 regular season record.

Among his many coaching honors, Raarup was named MIAC Coach of the Year in 1971, 1972, 1977 and 1987, NAIA District 14 Coach of the Year in 1972, and the American Football Coaches Association's Area 6 Coach of the Year in 1987. Raarup is the winningest coach in Gustavus football history with a record of 99-68-1. In addition to coaching football, Raarup was also an assistant football coach and later even served as the head wrestling and head baseball coach — even leading the team to a conference title in 1971. Raarup has also served as a member of the physical education faculty at Gustavus for the past 28 years including the past 11 as chair of the department. Additionally, Raarup currently serves as an assistant on the Gusty football team. Dennis and his wife Sharon live in St. Peter and have three children, Todd, Tammy and Troy.

MIKE TICE
PRO FOOTBALL: MINNESOTA VIKINGS

Mike Tice was born in Bayshore, N.Y., and went on to graduate from Central Islip High School in 1977. There, he played quarterback at Central Islip High School under head coach George O'Leary — who now works for Tice as the Vikings defensive coordinator. Tice, who also lettered in basketball and lacrosse, then went on to play quarterback at the University of Maryland. There, he threw for 1,824 yards and 10 touchdowns during his junior and senior seasons. As a two-year starter at Maryland, Tice's back-up was future NFL All-Pro Boomer Esiason.

Upon graduating in 1980, Tice went on to play in the NFL for 14 years as a tight end. The 6-foot-8-inch Tice originally signed with Seattle and played with the Seahawks from 1981-88. He spent the 1989 season with the Washington Redskins and then returned to Seattle to play from 1990-91. (In 2002, Tice would be named as the tight end on Seattle's all-time team by Football News.) In 1992 Tice signed on with the Vikings and played three seasons with the Purple before hanging up his cleats in 1995 to become an assistant coach with the team. Over his 14-year NFL career, Tice caught 107 passes for 894 yards and 11 touchdowns and blocked for running backs that rushed for over 1,000 yards in a season five times — including 1992, when Terry Allen set a then Vikings season record with 1,201 yards.

Tice's coaching career began in 1996 as the Vikings tight ends coach. In 1997 Tice took over as the coach of an offensive line that sent two starters to the 1998 Pro Bowl, Randall McDaniel and Todd Steussie. In 1998 the Vikings made history, advancing all the way to the NFC Championship Game before losing a heart-breaker to the Atlanta Falcons. That team set a league record for points scored in a season (556), and also set an NFL record for touchdown passes (41). The '98 team also set Vikings records for total yards (6,264) and fewest sacks allowed in a 16-game season (25). Three of the five starting offensive linemen in the 1999 Pro Bowl were Vikings (McDaniel, Steussie and Jeff Christy), and Mike Tice had a big hand in that. In 1999 the Vikings offense ranked third in the NFL in total offense and in 2000 the Purple made it back to the conference finals. In addition, the Vikings established an NFL record by recording 30 straight games from 1999-2000 with over 300 yards of total offense, snapping a record held by the 1949-51 Rams.

In 2001 Tice was named as the interim head coach for the team's regular season finale. It was a fitting promotion. After all, in five seasons coaching the Vikings offensive line, Tice guided five different players (Matt Birk, Jeff Christy, Randall McDaniel, Todd Steussie and Korey Stringer) to 10 Pro Bowl appearances. Then, in 2002, Mike Tice took over for Denny Green to become the sixth head coach in the Minnesota Vikings history. The Vikings led the NFL in rushing (2,507 yards) for the first time ever in 2002 and behind Quarterback Daunte Culpepper, set team records for rushing touchdowns (26), yards per carry (5.3) and first downs (350). Randy Moss also had a career high 106 catches while Michael Bennett rushed for 1,296 yards — the second highest total in team history. The Vikings offense was second in the NFL that year as well, trailing only the Super Bowl runner-up Raiders (6,237 to 6,192) in total yards.

In his last 19 years of being associated with the NFL, Tice has only had three losing seasons. In his seven seasons as an assistant and head coach with the Vikings, the team has compiled a 65-47 (.580) record, has made the playoffs five times and has played in two NFC Championship Games. The bottom line is this: Mike Tice is a winner. Sure, his teams have struggled in his first two seasons as head

coach, but just watch this team in 2003 and beyond. With Tice steering this ship, the sky is the limit for this club.

In addition to being named as the recipient of the Byron "Whizzer" White Humanitarian Award in 1987, Tice is also extremely involved in the local community and with numerous charities. Tice presently serves as Honorary Head Coach for Special Olympics Minnesota, and through the Viking Children's Fund, Tice also heads up the Tice Academic Team, which provides post-secondary scholarships for area youth who demonstrate strong leadership skills. Tice also initiated player fine fund program "Fine Money for Fine Causes" which distributes the proceeds to area charities. Mike has also joined his wife, Diane, and the Vikings Coaches Wives in supporting the Ronald McDonald House during the 2003 season.

Tice continues his commitment to youth coaching through his own summer football camp, Mike Tice/United Way Youth Football Day and his annual National Football Foundation Youth Coaches Clinic at Winter Park. Among the organizations Mike has volunteered with include: American Cancer Society, Boy Scouts of American, Children's Miracle Network, African American Adoption Agency, St. Joseph's Home for Children, Gridiron Geography, St. Paul Public Schools--Principal for a Day, Play it Smart, The HIKE Foundation, Salvation Army/Nordstrom Holiday Giving Tree, Edina Football Youth Foundation, Susan G. Komen Race for the Cure and Mentoring Partnerships of Minnesota.

In addition, Tice's brother, John, a former a tight end with the New Orleans Saints from 1983-92, is currently the Vikings' tight end/assistant offensive line coach, making Mike and John the first brothers tandem to ever coach with the team. Mike, who has a real passion for horse racing and even used to breed horses, and has wife Diane presently reside in Edina with their two children, Adrienne and Nathan.

HOW WOULD YOU DESCRIBE YOUR COACHING STYLE? "My style has been formulated by some of the great coaches that I have been blessed to play for, starting with George O'Leary, my high school football coach who is now my defensive coordinator here with the Vikings. From there, I had Jerry Clayborn, a Hall of Famer at the University of Maryland. Then at the pro level I was fortunate enough to play for three legends in Chuck Knox, Joe Gibbs and Dennis Green. So, I played for some great, great coaches. Having said that, I would say that my style is kind of my personality with a lot of their philosophies. And the interesting thing about all of those men was that they were all sticklers for detail and they were all sticklers for doing things the right way, not just getting things done. They stressed practicing the right way, practicing perfectly. My philosophy is really about paying attention to the small details because then the big details take care of themselves. Another part of my philosophy that I think is very important is respect. Respect is a big word. I am talking about respecting the game, respecting the coaches, respecting the building, respecting the people that work in the building, and on down the line. What helps me is the fact that I played in the NFL, and I am a big guy with a deep voice. So, I gain a little bit of instant respect for that, because they know I was one of them. But that only gets you so far. You have to lead by example in this business. I always say don't waste your time, the guy next to you's time or my time by being out here and just going through the motions. Do it the right way and you will take your game to the highest level that you can take it. My style is nothing more than trying to be real. You know, I make a lot of mistakes, but I own up to those mistakes and people appreciate honesty. Sometimes I have to tell my players things that they don't really want to hear, like 'maybe you are not as good as you think you are…', and that is tough but sometimes necessary. So, that is my style. It is not like I am a pioneer in how to do this or do that, I think my style is taken from these men that I have been fortunate enough to play for and the one common bond that they all had was that they were, A) all winners, B) they demanded excellence, C) they all paid attention to the small details, and D) they all knew how to motivate.

My philosophy is an amalgam of many great minds combined with my personality. Andy what is my personality? Well, I am a New Yorker, I like to cook, I love people, I like to talk, I like sharing knowledge with people, and I can't help myself sometimes with what my wife calls 'TMI' or Too Much Information, where you might ask me a little question and it might take me five minutes to answer, like right now! You know, my wife says I drive people crazy because I am always correcting them. Well, you know what? I am coaching from the time I wake up in the morning until the time I go to sleep at night and I coach anything and everything. If we go golfing, I will be coaching you. I am sorry, but I just can't help myself. I also fashion myself as a teacher and have had some relative success in developing offensive linemen. I think too that I am a perfectionist and perfectionists tend to wear on people because they are never satisfied with their results and are always trying to do better. So, hey, that's me and I like what is happening here in Minnesota. We are building something really good here and we are going to have some success, trust me."

HOW DO YOU MOTIVATE YOUR PLAYERS? "The biggest thing that has helped me is being a player. I try to put myself into their shoes and I have credibility with them because I was one of them. I ask myself what they need — love, discipline, what is it? You need to let them know that you know that they are doing well, but at the same time you need to constantly throw little teaching tools in there for them to work on. I compliment them, but I also want to teach them at the same time so that they can always step up their games and be the best that they can be. You know, I don't really have a coaching style that is filled with X's and O's. I am not a football mastermind or a football genius. What I try to do is figure out the way that each player responds to my teachings and figure out the way that each player can be motivated. Some players are motivated by you yelling at them and that makes them angry, and they play better angry. Some players are motivated by you telling them how good they are. Some players are motivated by just telling them the right way to do things and they get it done, like Matt Birk — one of the smartest kids I have ever coached. Then, you can also motivate by giving a guy a day off, or by rewarding the team by letting them out of a run or something. Beyond that, everybody likes to be stroked and to be told that they are doing well, so I think you need to remain positive, but firm. Beyond that it is about being real and just having fun. I love to bust balls and have fun. We have to step back and chill out every now and then or else we would go crazy. One thing I love to do is to dig up old pictures of guys from high school with big afros or whatever, and then put them up for the whole team to see at our Friday meetings. Man, do we laugh! We laugh with each other and we laugh at each other. To me that is a motivating tool, because we are keeping loose and having fun. You know, this is a tough, stressful business and do you know why? Because this is America and everybody likes a winner and they don't like a loser. That is reality. That is how I motivate."

HOW DO YOU BUILD TEAM UNITY & CHEMISTRY? "It starts with bringing in players with good character. From there it requires me, as the head coach, to be consistent and to be real. If Randy (Moss) is messing up, then Randy needs to be talked to. Consistency is what the players are looking for from me and they want to see how I deal with situations. If I am fair to everybody, equally, then they will respect that. That is where chemistry starts. I have a saying that is very, very important to me which is 'if we can't laugh at each other, we won't win a championship together.' And what that means is if you can't laugh at yourself, then you have gotten too big for your britches. When that happens you have problems in your locker room. Beyond that, you just need players. I mean you can't win a thoroughbred horse race with a mule. You can have the greatest coaching staff in the world, but if you don't have talent, then you are fooling yourself. So, chemistry is a unique thing that is necessary to win, but difficult to achieve."

WHAT MOTIVATES YOU? "It makes me feel good that the goals that I set for myself way back when have been realized to this point. I was able to play in the NFL for 13 years, however I did not win a championship nor did I make the big money. But, I was able to become a head coach. So, I am on track with my professional goals, and that makes me feel good, but I am not yet satisfied with what I have accomplished — I want very badly to win a Super Bowl and that is what drives me. I want to be able to win that championship for our players, coaches, support staff, organization and for the fans. That might sound corny, but I really mean that and it is really important to me. I think about that every day. I think about what we need to do to be better every single day and I won't be satisfied until we get there. My passion for winning a championship is overwhelming and mark my words, we will win a championship, without a doubt, there is no question in my mind."

WHAT'S THE SECRET TO YOUR SUCCESS? "Success goes to the people that you surround yourself with. I have great assistant coaches in the trenches with me and they are the ones passing on the message, teaching it the way you want it taught. They deserve a lot of credit. I also have an organization and management team here with the Vikings that is on my side, and that means a lot. You can't do it by yourself, it is truly a team game in every way. So, if you can get all those people on the same page and can get them all pointed towards that one goal of winning a championship, then that is how you achieve success."

WHAT WOULD YOU WANT TO SAY TO YOUR FANS, BOOSTERS, AND ALUMNI WHO HAVE SUPPORTED YOU ALL THESE YEARS? "I want to thank the fans for being so loyal to the Vikings. You know, I answer all my own fan mail and I get letters from all over the country. We have a lot of Vikings fans everywhere. So, the one thing I want to tell them is this: We want to win a championship as much as you do, so please remain positive for us. We will win a championship. And we will win it because the passion is there."

HOW DO YOU WANT YOUR COACHING EPITAPH TO READ — HOW DO YOU WANT TO BE REMEMBERED AS A COACH? "I want to be known and remembered for being a straight forward teacher; a guy who knew how to develop young talent; and a guy who helped mold and develop young men. He knew his players and he developed good players with character."

C.P. BLAKESLEE: MINNESOTA STATE MANKATO FOOTBALL

C.P. Blakeslee was a Minnesota State Mankato coaching institution. Blakeslee coached the Maverick football team from 1923-34 and won back-to-back Little Ten Conference championships in 1931 and 1932. In addition, Blakeslee also coached the Maverick basketball team from 1921-39, posting a 121-87 career record on the hardwood. In 1962 the school paid tribute to their former coach by naming the newly constructed 7,200-seat football stadium as Blakeslee Stadium, in his honor.

GEORGE THOLE
HIGH SCHOOL FOOTBALL: STILLWATER

George Thole grew up in Petaluma, Calif., and went on to play football at Utah State for one year before transferring to North Dakota State University on a football scholarship. Thole played guard for the Bison from 1959 to 1961, where he was a two-year starter for the Herd. From there, Thole went on to get his master's degree from Moorhead State University. His first teaching and coaching job came in 1965 at Central Cass High School in Casselton, N.D. There, he coached football, basketball and track. It was on the grid-iron, however, where Thole made his mark, going undefeated in three straight seasons. Thole then moved on to the University of Minnesota in 1968 to serve as a graduate assistant for Murray Warmath's Gophers for one year before serving two years as an assistant coach at Richfield High School under Dick Walker.

Then, in 1971, Thole moved on to Stillwater High School, to teach physical education and serve as the head football coach. His time there would turn out to be one of the most storied coaching careers in upper Midwest history. In all, Thole would spend 29 years at Stillwater, posting an amazing 285-69-2 (80.5%) record along the way. In addition, his Ponies won four state championships (1975, 1982, 1984, and 1995) and twice finished as state runner-ups (1977 and 1989). In all, their were 18 state tournament appearances, 14 final fours, 17 conference championships and 12 sectional titles. With 285 career wins, Thole ranks third on Minnesota's all-time winningest coaches list and that doesn't include his three years in North Dakota — which would put him over the top.

A past president of the Minnesota State Football Coaches Association, Thole has coached All-Star football teams in Minnesota and Ireland and has received over 100 coaching awards. Among them are inductions into the Minnesota State Coaches Association Hall of Fame as well as the NDSU Hall of Fame. Thole has been named as the Large School Coach of the Year on three occasions (1974, 1982, and 1995) and was the State Coach of the Year in 1982 as well. Thole and his wife Karen live in Stillwater and have one daughter and one son, Eric, who quarterbacked that 1982 Stillwater state championship team. George is retired and recently completed an instructional book with his former offensive coordinator, Jerry Foley, titled "From Veer to Eternity — or How to Build a High School Dynasty." When it comes to high school football in Minnesota, George Thole is simply the best of the very best and a true legend in every sense of the word.

HOW WOULD YOU DESCRIBE YOUR COACHING STYLE? "I think my style is somewhere between Woody Hayes and Woody Allen… No, but really, I was a disciplinarian and at the same time I would always make sure I found something good to say about each player before they got out of each practice. I was heavy into discipline though as far as being tardy or any of that stuff. We convinced our players that this was the only way to go and they bought into it. I also think humor was a big part of my style as well, to keep it loose. I mean sometimes I would tell jokes before a big game, especially if I thought they were real tense. That was just my personality and I tried to always keep it fun. I just did whatever was necessary. If they needed a big Knute Rockne half-time speech, I would give them that. Or, if they were playing too well then I would have to talk them down to bring them back to earth. It just depended on the situation."

HOW DID YOU MOTIVATE YOUR PLAYERS? "I was called the 'great motivator' but it is hard for me to explain that. I think I just

tried to get my players to improve on more of a day to day basis. Then, we absolutely sold our seniors on the concept of 'give us your greatest football during your senior year,' basically. I used every gimmick there was as far as stars on the helmets and performance awards for victories and that sort of thing. The performance awards, however, were only given to the players if we won that particular ballgame. So, I guess I gave them a lot of positive strokes and tried to encourage them to give their absolute very best. We convinced them that they could hustle 100% of the time and that is what we asked of them. You know, maybe you won't be all-conference or all-state, but you certainly can hustle. Everybody can do that."

WHO WERE YOUR COACHING MENTORS? "I learned a lot from Dick Walker at Richfield and Murray Warmath at the University of Minnesota. Then of course I was very interested in whatever Lou Holtz was doing, he is a great coach too."

IF YOU COULD MAGICALLY GO BACK IN TIME TO THE FIRST YEAR YOU WERE A HEAD COACH AND GIVE YOURSELF SOME ADVICE FOR THE FUTURE, KNOWING WHAT YOU KNOW NOW, BACK THEN, WHAT WOULD YOU SAY TO YOURSELF? "Over the next three decades the kids are not going to change, but you are going to change. The kids were still 17 years old 30 years later, I just went from 26 to 60, that is what changed. We change and our perceptions of them change, but the kids are the same today as they were back then."

WHAT ARE THE CHARACTERISTICS OF LEADERS? "There are just certain people who can lead and certain people who can't. I know a lot of great football minds but they just can't get it done coaching. So, it is a special thing."

LOOKING BACK WHAT ARE YOU MOST PROUD OF IN YOUR CAREER? "I am real proud when my former players introduce me to their kids. You can see that the dad is real proud and that he wants his kid to meet his old coach. That makes me feel pretty good. I love living in Stillwater because I get a positive stroke every day here. That is a wonderful thing."

WHAT WAS THE BEST PIECE OF ADVICE YOU EVER GOT FROM ANOTHER COACH? "The best advice I ever got was to never forget about how import special teams are. I mean I always made sure we could punt well. It's a small thing, but you have to cover it well and place it to the right spot and that kind of thing. A lot of people don't realize it but special teams play a bigger role in games than they might imagine."

HOW DID YOU BUILD TEAM UNITY & CHEMISTRY? "Chemistry is an interesting thing. It is very important to have but very difficult to create. You know, I have always said that there are three types of kids. The first is the smart kid, who does whatever it is that you tell him and you have no problems with. Then there is the kid that is smarter than he thinks he is, and you have to build his confidence up. Lastly there is the kid who is not as smart as he thinks he is. This is the kid you have to tweak a little bit and get to line up straight. Overall, you just have to know how to handle all of these kids. Some kids you can scream at and others need a pat on the back.

Figuring out which ones need which is the key."

WHAT MOTIVATED YOU? "Once we got to the point where we had something like 27 consecutive winning seasons, you get to the point where you don't want anybody to take that away from you. We set our sites very high at Stillwater and we had to work hard to achieve that. You know, some schools talk about winning a state championship, but the kids really didn't believe it. Well, at Stillwater we said that every year and honest to God we believed it. So, when we didn't win it, I was devastated. It was a great tradition and I was proud of that."

WHAT ADVICE WOULD YOU HAVE FOR YOUNG COACHES STARTING OUT TODAY? "First of all, I would say make friends with the custodians and the grounds crew at your field. Then, get out and see as many other sporting events at your school as possible. I got so much praise from the people in this community because they saw me at every sporting and fine arts event that you could possibly go to. That made an impression on people."

FAVORITE LOCKER ROOM SIGN? "We don't meet competition, we destroy it."

WHAT'S THE BIGGEST THING YOU'VE LEARNED FROM COACHING THAT YOU'VE BEEN ABLE TO APPLY TO YOUR EVERYDAY LIFE? "Coaching forces you to live with a beginning and an ending, a start and a finish. I think that helps in your everyday life because otherwise you would never get anything done."

WHAT ARE THE KEY INGREDIENTS TO CREATING A CHAMPIONSHIP TEAM? "Perspiration and inspiration for starters. Then you not only have to have good players, but you have to have the players in the right positions. You also have to have opportunities and you have to stay healthy."

WHAT'S THE SECRET TO YOUR SUCCESS? "Success breeds success. I think the secret of coaching is to get people to do things that they didn't think they could do. That's it in a nutshell. I had good players with talent and my opponents had good players with talent, the difference is what you did with them and what kind of a program you had. You just had to get them to play at a peak level. I also think that I had the ability to see something and then break it down and simpli

fy it. That is really a valuable tool when you are coaching. Another thing was that my personality allowed me to go right after problems and mend fences right away before they became major problems. I also kept my staff together for a long time with very few changes, that helped a lot too."

WHAT WOULD YOU WANT TO SAY TO YOUR FANS, BOOSTERS, AND ALUMNI WHO HAVE SUPPORTED YOU ALL THESE YEARS? "It was one heck of a 29 year run. Without the fans, coaches and players I would be just another pretty face!"

HOW DO YOU WANT YOUR COACHING EPITAPH TO READ — HOW DO YOU WANT TO BE REMEMBERED AS A COACH? "He was an innovator and not an imitator."

EARL MARTINEAU: WESTERN MICHIGAN FOOTBALL

Earl Martineau, a former All-American halfback for the Gophers in 1923, coached at Western Michigan University from 1924-28, posting a 26-10-2 career record.

JIM WACKER: GOPHER FOOTBALL

Jim Wacker was born the son of a Lutheran minister in Detroit and would go on to an illustrious coaching career. Wacker's first college coaching job was as an assistant at Concordia College (Nebraska) for five years. During that time he also served as the head wrestling and tennis coach. Wacker's resume since that time is covered with success stories. His Texas Lutheran teams won the NAIA national championships in 1974 and 1975 and his Southwest Texas State teams won NCAA Division II national championships in 1981 and 1982. Twice during his coaching career he has been recognized as the National Coach of the Year. Wacker completed his 37-year coaching career with a 160-130-3 record. Other coaching jobs included Concordia High School (Portland), Augustana College (S.D.), North Dakota State, Texas Christian and the University of Minnesota.

Wacker came to Gold Country in 1992 after spending eight seasons at Texas Christian University. Known for his ability to rebuild and run clean programs, Wacker would be an instant fan-favorite. Also known for his upbeat attitude, over-the-top enthusiasm and fun-loving demeanor, Wacker coached the Gophers from 1992-96, compiling a modest 16-39 record. While the Gophers did develop some explosive passing attacks under Wacker, they struggled in most other facets of the game. There were some bright moments along the way though, such as their upset victories over Wisconsin in 1993 and 1994, and an exciting win over Syracuse in 1996. Then, there was the 59-56 win over Purdue in 1993, which would stand as the "signature game" of the Wacker era. Wacker also demanded academic excellence of his teams and took Minnesota to the top of the Academic All-Big Ten Team selections for three straight years. Wacker went on to do television and radio work after he was let go from Minnesota in 1996. Then, in 1998, he took over as the athletic director at Southwest Texas, a position he would hold until 2001. Tragically, Wacker died on August 26, 2003, at his home in San Marcos, Texas, after a long battle with cancer. He was 66. Jim was survived by his wife, Lil, three sons and six grandchildren. Jim Wacker was a true friend to the game of football and will dearly be missed.

DICK TRESSEL
COLLEGE FOOTBALL: HAMLINE

Dick Tressel was a product of some pretty good thoroughbred football lineage in his family. Dick, who played his college football for his late father, Lee Tressel, at Baldwin-Wallace College in Berea, Ohio, earned four letters both as a defensive back and as a baseball player. (Lee Tressel was a coaching legend in Ohio, compiling a career record of 155-52-6 at Baldwin Wallace and even won the 1978 Division III National Championship.) In 1970 Tressel earned a bachelor's degree in physical education from Baldwin-Wallace and in 1976 he was awarded a master's degree in physical education from Florida State University. In 1978, after serving as an assistant for several years, Dick's illustrious football coaching career began at Hamline University. In all Tressel would spend 23 years at Hamline, where he was both head football coach and director of athletics. He compiled an overall record of 124-102-2 with the Pipers and turned the program into a winning tradition. In addition, he was the NCAA Division III National Coach of the Year in 1984, leading Hamline to the MIAC championship. They would add another crown in 1988, recording an equally impressive 8-1 mark that year as well.

In 2000 Dick retired after 32 years of coaching. He had received a doctorate degree from the University of Minnesota in 1996 and wanted to move on. Two years later he joined the coaching staff at Ohio State University, where his younger brother Jim, who had formerly been at Youngstown State University, had been named as OSU's new head coach. Dick assumed the role of associate director of football operations at OSU, assisting in the day-to-day operations of the football program. He also monitors the academic progress of the student-athletes, coordinates community outreach and service programs and serves as a liaison between the football office and other support services. His hard work paid off in 2003 as the Buckeye's won the NCAA College Football National Championship over Miami.

(When his brother won the national title, it marked the first time in history that a father-and-son combination had ever both won national championships in college football. In fact, the Tressel trio holds every college coaching record for father-son and father-sons that are kept, including each having more than 100 victories and being named National Coach of the Year.)

"Growing up in a close family football atmosphere kind of made my decision to go into coaching an easy one," said Dick. Presently, Dick and his wife Connie reside in Columbus, Ohio. They have three sons: Mike, Ben and Luke, who all played collegiately as well — Mike as a cornerback at Cornell, Ben as a quarterback at Hamline and Luke also as a cornerback at Hamline.

HOW WOULD YOU DESCRIBE YOUR COACHING STYLE? "I think that we felt like we needed to be very consistent in the division III world. I mean at that level the kids were playing because they simply wanted to and just loved the game. So, at that level my coaching style sort of fell in line in the sense that I was never a real big yeller or threatened to take things away. I just tried to be very positive and make sure the kids realized what benefits they were receiving from football and then go from there."

HOW DO YOU MOTIVATE YOUR PLAYERS? "We tried to motivate them through the process of just being the best they could be and by doing things right all the time. We just encouraged them to consistently be a quality person and to be a person who did everything

as hard as they could and as well as they could. That was in their control and we tried to motivate the things that were in their control. We also tried to convince our kids that by doing the things that they had control of well, then they could be successful both on the football field and in life."

WHO WERE YOUR COACHING MENTORS? "I would have to say my father, Lee. Growing up with him was a wonderful experience and he was just a great coach. I learned a great deal from him and he really shaped a lot of my coaching style."

IF YOU COULD MAGICALLY GO BACK IN TIME TO THE FIRST YEAR YOU WERE A HEAD COACH AND GIVE YOURSELF SOME ADVICE FOR THE FUTURE, KNOWING WHAT YOU KNOW NOW, BACK THEN, WHAT WOULD YOU SAY TO YOURSELF? "I think I would tell myself to just be who you are and realize that you represent yourself, your family and your program in everything that you do, Then I would say don't ever forget that and remind yourself of that every day."

LOOKING BACK WHAT ARE YOU MOST PROUD OF IN YOUR CAREER? "I am probably most proud of the fact that I have three sons who are all football coaches. (Mike is at Ohio State as a graduate assistant, Luke is at the University of Minnesota as a graduate assistant and Ben was at Hamline.) They all felt good enough about what I was doing to pursue coaching as a career and that makes me feel great both as a father and as a coach. So, I guess looking back I realize that coaching was good for my family in a lot of different ways."

HOW DO YOU BUILD TEAM UNITY & CHEMISTRY? "We tried to do it by having as much interaction outside of the football world as we could. We worked hard at trying to make sure guys knew each others names and that they had social times together to become friends. I also think that we tried to create an environment where everybody felt like they were on the same level. We always wanted to avoid castes by age or by position. We just went out of our way to take the time to create interactions among the players so that they really knew each other as people, that's how chemistry is built."

WHAT MOTIVATES YOU? "For me it is the challenge, because the challenge has to do with what goes on off the field as well as what goes on, on the field. I would also say that to be able to make a difference in kids' lives is a great feeling and certainly something that motivates me to be the best coach and person that I can be."

ON WINNING A NATIONAL CHAMPIONSHIP WITH YOUR BROTHER AT OHIO STATE UNIVERSITY: "When it was all said and done we kind of looked at each other and said 'You know what, the plan worked!' All these things that we said we believed in and planned for actually worked and we did it. That was an exciting place to be and something I will certainly never forget. I was very, very proud of my brother and I know that my dad would have been very proud as well. You know, after we won the title a cartoon appeared in the Cleveland newspaper which had a picture of Woody Hayes and our dad high fiving up in heaven. That just said it all."

WHAT ADVICE WOULD YOU HAVE FOR YOUNG

COACHES STARTING OUT TODAY? "I would say just to realize what a tough profession it is and how hard it is to feel like you control your own destiny. I would also say that without real hard work you can't get anywhere in life. You just have to hang in there and your chance will come, but it may not be as quick as you want it. There is a lot of good competition out there and you just need to be patient."

WHAT'S THE BEST PIECE OF ADVICE YOU EVER GOT FROM ANOTHER COACH? "I think the best piece of advice I ever got was from my principal, who was a former coach, when I was a high school coach. It came after a Friday afternoon pep rally when I gave a speech to the student body telling them that if these guys (my football players) had any courage at all then they would go out and play a great game that night. Afterwards, he told me that after I say something like that I had better stop and think about the after affects. He said that I needed to realize what I was saying if things didn't work out and we didn't win, then I was telling everyone that these kids had no courage if they didn't win that night. So, I learned to basically not get caught up in the moment and to be smart about what I say. Once you say something, it is out there forever. You just can't take it back."

WHAT IS THE KEY TO GOOD TIME MANAGEMENT? "I think it is a willingness to stop long enough and make good plans. You have to make time to effectively plan and then take time to evaluate whether or not your plan is achieving the goals you set out for it. People who don't take time to plan, and sort of just make plans on the run, they eventually get caught and fail."

FAVORITE LOCKER ROOM SIGN? "My favorite was 'PMA: Positive Mental Attitude.' We just tried to look at the positive side of things and build on those."

WHAT'S THE BIGGEST THING YOU'VE LEARNED FROM COACHING THAT YOU'VE BEEN ABLE TO APPLY TO YOUR EVERYDAY LIFE? "I think that it's the process of consistency and repetition in doing things that you believe in over and over, and you will be successful."

WHAT ARE THE KEY INGREDIENTS TO CREATING A CHAMPIONSHIP TEAM? "You need good players, that's where you have to start. Then, add in a little luck and pretty soon those good players start to believe in themselves. Once they believe they can reach their goals, then they are more likely to be successful."

WHAT'S THE SECRET TO YOUR SUCCESS? "I would say the pursuit of quality and class in everything I did as well as a willingness to do whatever it took to try and help my football program at Hamline to be a quality program."

WHAT WOULD YOU WANT TO SAY TO YOUR FANS, BOOSTERS, AND ALUMNI WHO HAVE SUPPORTED YOU ALL THESE YEARS? "Once a Piper Always a Piper! We had some great fans, alumni, boosters, supporters, coaches and players through the years and I would just say thanks to all of them for their support. It was great!"

HOW DO YOU WANT YOUR COACHING EPITAPH TO READ — HOW DO YOU WANT TO BE REMEMBERED AS A COACH? "I would like to be remembered as a football coach who cared about people, both as individuals and as football players. I hope that I was able to help them become as good a football player as they could be. I also was very concerned about their social and academic well being too. I always hoped that my players would go on to become well rounded individuals and citizens long after college. That was very important to me as a coach and as a person."

250 WINS CLUB MEMBERS: (HIGH SCHOOL FOOTBALL)

	Coach	School
1.	George Larson-r	Cambridge
2.	Ken Baumann-r	Mahnomen
3.	George Thole-r	Stillwater
4.	Ron Stolski	Brainerd
5.	Grady Rostberg-r	Hutchinson
6.	Jim Roforth-r	Osakis
7.	George Smith-r	Mahtomedi
8.	Mike Mahlen	Verndale
9.	Neal Hofland	Chokio-Alberta
10.	Les Dreschel-r	Red Lake Falls/Crookston
11.	John Hansen-r	Osseo
12.	Tom Mahoney-r	Fairmont

r = retired

CAL STOLL: GOPHER FOOTBALL

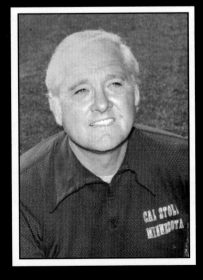

Cal Stoll first learned the game playing six-man football up in tiny Tower City, North Dakota. He would then go on to play defensive end at the University of Minnesota, graduating in 1949. Stoll, who also served his country in World War II, went on to coach at Mound High School before moving on to take over as an assistant at Utah State University in 1951. After several other coaching stops, Stoll would later take over as the head coach at Wake Forest, where he would lead his Demon Deacons to back-to-back conference championships in 1970 and 1971. Stoll then got the call to come home to his alma mater, where he would take over the head coaching duties from Murray Warmath. To his new post Stoll brought more than 20 years of coaching experience, and from the looks of his squad, he was going to need every bit of it. He had the support of the fans though. After all, he was the first "M" man since Bernie Bierman to come back as the school's head coach. In his seven seasons on campus Cal Stoll's teams won 39 games and lost 39 games. His .500 record had its share of ups and downs, but was not impressive enough to earn him an eighth campaign behind the Gopher bench. Making matters even more difficult for Stoll was what was later referred to as the "Big Two" and the "Little Eight." The "Big Two" were Ohio State and Michigan, who won every football title in that 70s decade, while the "Little Eight" was simply everyone else — including Minnesota. With Woody Hayes at Ohio State and Bo Schembechler at Michigan, it gave teams little hope of ever getting over the hump. Incredibly, during the Stoll years, only Minnesota, Purdue and Michigan State managed to win even one game from the "Big Two." To his credit though, Stoll outlasted all the other "Little Eight" coaches from the time he came into the conference back in 1972. Minnesota was 27-29 against Big Ten teams from 1972-78. However, if you were to exclude the Ohio State and Michigan games, they were a respectable 26-16. That translates to paltry 1-13 against the "Big Two," with the Michigan upset in 1977 being the only exception. Stoll would go on to become a very successful businessman until his untimely death in 2002.

MARC TRESTMAN
PRO FOOTBALL: OAKLAND RAIDERS

Marc Trestman grew up in St. Louis Park and went on to graduate from St. Louis Park High School. From there, Trestman played football at the University of Minnesota from 1974-75, serving as a back-up to quarterback Tony Dungy. In 1977 Trestman was unhappy about the playing time he wasn't getting, so he transferred to Minnesota State Moorhead, where he played quarterback for the Dragons under legendary coach Ross Fortier. Trestman would stay for just one season, however, before heading back to Gold Country to graduate in 1978.

Following college, Trestman signed as a free agent defensive back with the Vikings and spent the 1978 and '79 training camps with Minnesota. From there, he hung up his spikes and decided to go to law school at the University of Miami. There, he became a volunteer coach with the Hurricanes and then wound up as a full-time assistant as the team's quarterbacks coach. The next season the Canes won a national championship by beating Nebraska in the Orange Bowl. With no formal coaching training, Trestman trained himself on how to approach the game. Two years later, in 1985, Trestman came home when Bud Grant hired him to serve as an offensive backfield assistant with the Vikings. He learned a ton under Grant, and has been moving up the coaching ranks ever since.

Trestman then went on to join the Tampa Bay staff as quarterbacks coach in 1987 before moving to Cleveland, where he served first as quarterbacks coach and then, at just 31 years of age, was promoted to offensive coordinator during the 1989 season in which the Browns reached the AFC Championship game. Trestman came home again in 1990 to serve as an assistant under new Vikings Coach Jerry Burns. He would stay for two seasons, working with Vikings quarterback Rich Gannon, who he would later be reunited with in Oakland. Then, when Denny Green was hired as the Vikings new coach, Trestman found himself out of work. So, he decided to take a breather from football and took a job with a brokerage firm in Florida selling municipal bonds. The San Francisco 49ers persuaded him to return to the field a few years later in 1995 as their offensive coordinator, and he responded by producing an offense which led the league in scoring and passing and ranked second in total offense. But the pressure of replacing Mike Holmgren loomed large in San Fran, and Trestman was let go following the 1996 season. He then caught on with the Detroit Lions for one year before going to the Arizona Cardinals, where he would spend the next three seasons working as the team's offensive coordinator.

In 2000, Trestman hooked up with his old friend John Gruden as an assistant with the Oakland Raiders. Then, when Gruden left Oakland in 2002 to take over as the new coach of the Tampa Bay Buccaneers, he wanted to take Trestman with him to be his offensive coordinator. But Oakland wouldn't release him, and named him offensive coordinator under Bill Callahan instead. Under Trestman, the Raiders offense finished No. 1 in the NFL in total offense and No. 1 in the league in passing in 2002. In addition, Quarterback Rich Gannon passed for 4,689 yards, and the Raiders made it all the way to the Super Bowl, before losing a heart-breaker to Gruden's Buc's.

At just 45, Marc Trestman is already a 15-year coaching veteran, yet he is still considered to be among the very brightest young minds in the game. In 2003-04 Trestman enters his third year with the Raiders, his second as the team's offensive coordinator. Marc and his wife Cindy have two daughters, Sarahanne and Chloe, and reside in the Oakland Bay area. Marc still gets home quite a bit too, to see his

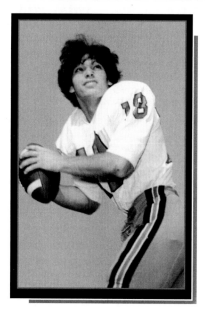

family, which now lives in Minnetonka. In addition, he also gets to see his quarterback, Rich Gannon, who lives in nearby Victoria with his wife Shelly — the daughter of former Vikings running back Bill "Boom-Boom" Brown.

HOW WOULD YOU DESCRIBE YOUR COACHING STYLE? "You have to be yourself first and foremost. From there I would say at times it is a very straight forward clinical approach where we emphasize 'this is what we are going to do and this is why we are going to do it.' I think my players know that when they come through the door every day they know what to expect. It is not going to be a system where one day a guy is going to be real high and the next day he is going to be real low. It is pretty level headed and even keeled emotionally. On the other side of it I think I am very direct with my players and the people that I work with. Sometimes you have to make strong statements or statements that can be difficult, but as long as you are putting the team first and the organization first, then there is a place for that as well."

HOW DO YOU MOTIVATE YOUR PLAYERS? "As the offensive coordinator and quarterbacks coach I have a lot of work to do each and every day to make sure that our players are all working together as a team. Because our offense is so complex, I just have to work that much harder with my players to make sure that everyone is on the same page. We have a number of different packages in our offense and that all takes time to teach and learn. I think at this level most players are pretty self motivated, so I just try to teach my players as best as I can and encourage them to give it their best effort. I like to work with my players on an individual basis as much as possible in order to really understand what that individual's strengths and weaknesses are. That takes a lot of time, but it is worth it. We try to manage our time as best as we can so that we are at full strength emotionally as well as physically. You know, a player's time in this league is very short, so I want to do as much as I can, as quickly as I can to help him achieve his goals. You have to motivate each player individually and you really have to get to know your players too because every player not only has a unique personality, but he also comes from a different background and upbringing. That is what is so unique about this game. So, to be able to mold them into a team by getting them to love each other, care for each other, play for each other and succeed with each other is just amazing."

WHO WERE YOUR COACHING MENTORS? "Bud Grant was a tremendous influence on me because he hired me into the league and the time I spent with him was significant. He just had a big influence on my growth as a coach and my opportunity to coach in the National Football League. You know, growing up in Minnesota and going to a lot of Vikings games as a young person, it was a real thrill to be able to learn the game from somebody like him who I admired so much. To watch the way he handled himself and the way he operated was invaluable."

IF YOU COULD MAGICALLY GO BACK IN TIME TO THE FIRST YEAR YOU WERE A HEAD COACH AND GIVE YOURSELF SOME ADVICE FOR THE FUTURE, KNOWING WHAT YOU KNOW NOW, BACK THEN, WHAT WOULD YOU SAY TO YOURSELF? "I would tell him to find a guy who he could work under and who could train him to be a coach.

Then, go to work and just don't stop working because everybody in this business has a tremendous passion for the game and to be successful. From there, you have to keep working hard and hope you get lucky."

WHAT ROLE HAS YOUR FAMILY PLAYED IN YOUR CAREER? "They have been incredible. My wife has been my number one supporter and I wouldn't even know where to begin to thank her for what she has done for me. We have two daughters who have been very supportive as well. I am sure it is tough on them at times moving around so much. I mean my 11 year old daughter has lived in nine different places so far and that is difficult. But they are both very social and have enjoyed the adventure along the way and I think they will be stronger, more independent women because of it."

HOW DO YOU BUILD TEAM UNITY & CHEMISTRY? "The work ethic is the most important thing. You don't achieve success in this business unless you really, really work at it. You have to show the players that you are exceptionally prepared for your job and you have to show them how to prepare. If you can get your players to believe that working hard at what they do is the key to the team's success, then you will be successful as a coach. Team unity starts with hard work and an incredible work ethic. From there you have to have leaders and guys who believe in what you are doing, and then they can carry it from there. You know, it is not the coaches, but the leadership of the players that really carries the team. There also has to be a clarity of mission and a consistency of how you operate, because the players are trained under that. Once they have a sense that you are operating and dealing with people on a consistent level, then they start to buy in. Of course you have to have some success along the way too, so that the players can believe in what you are doing."

WHAT MOTIVATES YOU? "I have had an unbelievable passion for the game for as long as I can remember and I really don't know why. I was never a great player but there was something in my mind that just made me want to play football. You know, I never thought I would ever coach. I mean, I went to law school and was all set to be a litigator, but my passion for this game got the best of me. What can I say, the stars aligned and I fell into coaching. It has been a wonderful thing. Then, after I got into coaching and then got out for three years to work in the private sector, I was hired back by the San Francisco 49ers to be their offensive coordinator following their Super Bowl championship season. I knew then that it was destiny and that this should be my profession. It has been a great adventure to be in this business and I am very lucky and honored to be a part of it. Aside from that, I love the challenge of this game and I love to win. It is different being a coach than it was being a player, but the thrill of victory is what drives all of us in one way or another. You know, as a coach you just want to help guys to become as successful as they can be. I really don't think about winning or losing a game or winning a Super Bowl, I just want to do everything I can to help them be the best that they can be."

ON HIS 2003 RAIDERS SUPER BOWL RUN: "Certainly playing in the Super Bowl was an amazing experience for us, but it really wasn't so much about being in the Super Bowl as much as it was the journey in getting to the Super Bowl. It was tough too to take over an offense in a transition year with a new head coach. You know John (Gruden) ran the offense when he was the head coach here, so when that was turned over to me after he left for Tampa, it was tough for me to develop credibility with the quarterbacks and the players. We expanded our offense so dramatically this last year and our approach to football changed so dramatically too. So, to get them to buy into that was tough, but we worked hard and kept at it. The journey to the Super Bowl last year was so unbelievable. To watch the guys grow together, believe in each other and believe in what we were doing was very gratifying."

WHAT ADVICE WOULD YOU HAVE FOR YOUNG COACHES STARTING OUT TODAY? "If you don't have a passion for what you do and are not willing to pay the price, then you won't be successful."

WHAT'S THE BIGGEST THING YOU'VE LEARNED FROM COACHING THAT YOU'VE BEEN ABLE TO APPLY TO YOUR EVERYDAY LIFE? "Coaching has taught me a lot about life. I know that hard work and a passion are the keys. My number one and two priorities in this world are being the best dad I can be and the best husband I can be. Then, I want to be the best coach I can be. If it is in my destiny, and I hope it is, to be a head coach in this league then that is the direction that I would like to go"

WHAT'S THE SECRET TO YOUR SUCCESS? "I have a real passion for what I do and I work very, very hard. I work very long hours throughout the entire year and I just love what I do. It is not so much about wins and losses for me, it is about the preparation and the everyday work. Then, to be able to make a difference in your players lives, that is the real reward."

WHAT WOULD YOU WANT TO SAY TO YOUR FANS, BOOSTERS, AND ALUMNI WHO HAVE SUPPORTED YOU ALL THESE YEARS? "Thank you for your support in the bad times even more than in the good times because that is when you need it the most. For those people who have called or written a note when I was down, I can't thank you enough because in this business you don't get patted on the back very often. It seems like you are always under scrutiny in this business, especially by the media, even when you are successful, so I appreciate the support I have gotten from people who have helped me to follow my dreams."

HOW DO YOU WANT YOUR COACHING EPITAPH TO READ — HOW DO YOU WANT TO BE REMEMBERED AS A COACH? "That through his hard work and passion he was able to give the guys who played for him every chance to be as successful as they could be, because that is why you coach this game."

STUB ALLISON: CAL FOOTBALL

Leonard "Stub" Allison played football at Carleton in the early 1920s, where he earned All-state honors on three occasions. From there, Allison went on to become the head football coach at the University of South Dakota from 1922-27. Allison then went on to coach at the University of California from 1935-45, even leading his Bears to a Rose Bowl victory over Alabama in 1938.

MURRAY WARMATH
COLLEGE FOOTBALL: UNIVERSITY OF MINNESOTA

Murray Warmath grew up in the tiny western Tennessee town of Humboldt and graduated from a nearby military prep school in 1930. From there, Warmath went on to play college football at the University of Tennessee under General Bob Neyland, where he lined up as a tight end and guard, graduating in 1934. Warmath's illustrious coaching career would span many, many years, starting as an assistant at Mississippi State from 1939-45. From there, Warmath went on to coach at Army and in 1952 he took over as the head coach back at Mississippi State, posting a 10-6-3 record from 1952-53.

In 1954 Warmath took over as the new head coach at the University of Minnesota. With the resignation of Wes Fesler as the Gopher's football coach, rumors ran wild about reports that former Gopher All American Bud Wilkinson, who was coaching at Oklahoma at the time, was going to be named as the team's new skipper. It never happened, however, and in late January of 1954, Gopher athletics director Ike Armstrong announced that Warmath had been selected to fill the vacant the post. The choice of Warmath, a virtual unknown, was unacceptable to many Gopher fans, who, in addition to being upset about hiring a coach who was not a member of the Big Ten family, were reeling about the University's inability to lure their native son, Wilkinson, back to campus.

Warmath brought four "Dixie" assistants with him, but opted to keep Butch Nash on staff, a popular move on his part with the fans and alums. A student of the split "T" offense, complete with a plethora of flankers spread out behind the line, Warmath did pretty darn good in his first year, even quieting a few of his critics. Warmath also showed his military roots by announcing that the team would have practice every morning at 6:30 a.m., something that went over about as good as a warm beer on a hot day with his players.

In addition to All-American Running Back Bob McNamara, there were several other standouts from the Fesler era on the squad including: Gino Cappelletti, John Baumgartner, Don Swanson and Jimmy Soltau. There were also a couple of promising young sophomores in Dick "Pinky" McNamara — Bob's younger brother, Center Dean Maas and future All-American Tackle Bob Hobert. The team rallied behind their new coach and finished with a very surprising 7-2 record that year, with wins over Nebraska, Pittsburgh, Northwestern, Illinois, Michigan State, Oregon State and Iowa, and just a pair of losses to both Michigan and Wisconsin. Chants of "Mac and Cappy" (McNamara and Cappelletti) were everywhere at Memorial Stadium that year, as the Gopher faithful liked what they saw. Under Warmath, the program had a chance.

Warmath would go on to make history in Gold Country, and he did it on his own terms. Through the 1950s most of the players on the Gophers' roster were Minnesota-born and raised. That was beginning to change, though, as Warmath started recruiting high school athletes from out of state. At that time, a number of universities around the country refused to recruit African-American players, but Warmath was more than ready to recruit the best kids to Minnesota for a chance to earn a degree and play Big Ten football. Among the early African-American players that Warmath recruited were Pennsylvanians Judge Dickson, a star running back, and Sandy Stephens, who became the first black quarterback to earn All-American honors. In addition, he found a couple of future All-Americans in the Carolinas in Bobby Bell and Carl Eller, who would both go on to star in the NFL as Pro Bowl Tackles as well.

Everything came together in 1960, when the Gophers,

despite losing to the University of Washington, 17-7, in the Rose Bowl, went on to stun the college football world by winning the national championship. (In those days the national champion was crowned at the conclusion of the regular season, so Minnesota won the title before going to the Rose Bowl.) The highlight of the season came when the No. 2 Gophers beat the No. 1 ranked Iowa Hawkeyes, 27-10. Fans will never forget watching All-American Tackle Tom Brown riding on his teammates' shoulders carrying Floyd of Rosedale around Memorial Stadium after the game. Fittingly, for his perseverance and courage, Warmath received full vindication by being named as the NCAA Coach of the Year. Bud Wilkinson would later comment on Warmath's achievement: "What he did under that pressure was one of the greatest things to happen to college coaching in a long, long time."

The Gophers, behind Big Ten MVP, Sandy Stephens, went on to win the Rose Bowl that next season, 21-3, over UCLA. They would come close again that next season, but were robbed of another run for the roses after a very controversial game in Wisconsin. The run was over. For three glorious seasons in the early 1960s, Minnesota had produced a very respectable 22-6-1 record, entitling them to a National Championship, a Big Ten title, and a Rose Bowl victory. The next few years would take a toll on Warmath, however, as his team began the dreaded rebuilding process. They went through some ups and downs over the next couple of seasons and then put it all together in 1967 when they shared co-Big Ten honors with Indiana and Purdue. From there, the team slid into mediocrity over the next couple of seasons. Times were tough in Gold Country, and Warmath knew it. The numbers were down in the stands, and it didn't take a rocket scientist to figure out that there was a direct correlation between the dwindling fan base at old Memorial and a very good "other" football team which was now tearing up the National Football League down in Bloomington's Metropolitan Stadium. With that, Warmath, after 18 seasons in Gold Country, resigned. A man of dignity, toughness and pride, the Autumn Warrior took a program in shambles and built it into a national champion, and for that he will always be remembered as one of the great ones.

After coaching the Gophers, Warmath served as an assistant with the Minnesota Vikings for two years and then spent another 10 years as a scout for the team. In all Warmath would spend 65 years in the game of football, playing, coaching and scouting. A true football coaching legend, Murray Warmath, now in his 90s, lives in the Twin Cities.

HOW WOULD YOU DESCRIBE YOUR COACHING STYLE? "I would say that I was a strict disciplinarian, first and foremost. I learned the game from General Bob Neyland at the University of Tennessee, and he was one tough coach. I was also very conservative. Beyond that I tried to work a lot harder than most other coaches and a lot of times luck goes with hard work. I sincerely loved the game and I liked being associated with all the young men. I felt it was a great education for them. You know, during the 1960s, the hippy era, there were a lot of kids who just lacked discipline in the home and I think that football gave a lot of those kids direction in life."

HOW DID YOU MOTIVATE YOUR PLAYERS? "I just went after them and told them how I wanted certain things to be done. I had a lot of rules for my players and I think that motivated them to stay in line with the program. I worked my players hard and always felt that if we were in better physical condition then we would have a big advantage. I also planned well for all our practices and games and then we tried to go out and execute that plan on Saturdays. Discipline was the key to motivation and that was something I believed in strongly."

ON RECRUITING YOUNG AFRICAN AMERICAN FOOTBALL PLAYERS TO MINNESOTA IN THE 1950s: "You know (laughing), I think I did more to advance the cause of integration than Hubert Humphrey did! At the time, during the 1950s, I wasn't having a lot of luck recruiting out of Ohio and Michigan. Meanwhile, Notre Dame was coming in here and getting some of our best boys. So, I began recruiting in the South, in the Carolinas, as well as in Pennsylvania, and was fortunate to get some great kids from down there. It was tough at times though. I mean a lot of people in Minnesota just weren't ready for that change (recruiting young African American players) and I really don't know why. I was just looking for good football players, and I found them. We were real lucky to get some great ballplayers like Bobby Bell, Carl Eller and Sandy Stephens. They sure made a big difference on our teams though and played a big part in our success during that era. But it was tough on them at times, I'm sure."

WHAT ARE THE CHARACTERISTICS OF WINNERS? "It is a will to excel. You also have got to have pride in what you are doing and really like what you are doing to give it that effort. It is about loving your work and then having a game plan that can be carried out. That's what winners do, they have a passion and they have a plan."

LOOKING BACK WHAT ARE YOU MOST PROUD OF IN YOUR CAREER? "I had a wonderful group of young men here in Minnesota and I never had a real problem with any of them. I know that I tried to be honest, forthright and stern when I had to be with my players, and I felt like they were the same to me."

HOW DID YOU BUILD TEAM UNITY & CHEMISTRY? "You just preach it to them every day and then go out and work like heck to make sure that your kids are in the best physical shape of their lives."

WHAT MOTIVATED YOU? "I liked the game of football and liked the spirit of competition. I was taught to win and I tried to win every time I hit the field. Hard work and commitment motivated me and that was how I motivated my players. Then to see them do well was very satisfying too."

WHAT ADVICE WOULD YOU HAVE FOR YOUNG COACHES STARTING OUT TODAY? "Prepare yourself mentally and physically. Just get in there and work hard and do the best you can, then you don't ever have to look back. Beyond that, have a plan and stick to it."

FAVORITE LOCKER ROOM SIGN? "The team with the fewest mistakes wins."

WHAT'S THE BIGGEST THING YOU'VE LEARNED FROM COACHING THAT YOU'VE BEEN ABLE TO APPLY TO YOUR EVERYDAY LIFE? "Hard work and discipline. It takes a lot of hard work, discipline and commitment to be successful in whatever you do. Success also requires some luck, but I have always felt that people that work the hardest are always the luckiest."

WHAT ARE THE KEY INGREDIENTS TO CREATING A CHAMPIONSHIP TEAM? "You have to have good players. Period. If you are going to win a horse race, then you have got to have a good race horse. Because the best horse usually wins. Sure, the jockey steers him, but the jockey doesn't win the race."

WHAT'S THE SECRET TO YOUR SUCCESS? "I liked what I did, I worked hard at it and I was committed. Then, people who work hard get the lucky breaks. I was lucky a lot too."

WHAT WOULD YOU WANT TO SAY TO YOUR FANS, BOOSTERS, AND ALUMNI WHO HAVE SUPPORTED YOU ALL THESE YEARS? "I love everything about Minnesota except for the horrible cold. I have been here for almost 50 years now, but being from Tennessee I have never been able to get used to the weather. If it weren't for the caliber of all the great people that I have met, I would have headed south decades ago. So, thanks for the support, I have really appreciated it. I have spent the majority of my life here and it is home to me now. When my wife died after 63 years of marriage I thought about going back to Tennessee, but this is home now and I am very happy to be here."

HOW DO YOU WANT YOUR COACHING EPITAPH TO READ — HOW DO YOU WANT TO BE REMEMBERED AS A COACH? "I have never been anything other than a football coach in my life and I am a lucky man for that. I think that I had a good influence on a lot of people and that was important to me too. I just hope that my players had the same amount or respect and regard for me as I did for them."

GERHARD MEIDT:
MINNEOTA HIGH SCHOOL FOOTBALL

Gerhard Meidt won four state championships in his 32 seasons of coaching high school football. The first came in 1972 at Rothsay High School, with three more coming from 1986-88 at Minneota High School. Meidt would finish his illustrious coaching career with a 236-79 career record. In addition to taking his teams to numerous state playoff appearances, Meidt's Minneota teams also accumulated a 48-game consecutive winning streak at one point. After coaching at Minneota and Big Lake High Schools, Meidt moved into the college ranks to serve as an assistant coach with his son, Chris, first at Bethel College, where Chris was named the 2001 National Assistant Coach of the Year by the American Football Coaches Association. Then, when Chris was named as the head coach at St. Olaf, Gerhard followed and presently serves as his offensive line coach there too. Chris, a 1988 graduate of Minneota High School, played quarterback for his father and was a member of the 1986 and '87 state championship teams. A two-time all-state quarterback, Chris was named as the Associated Press Minnesota Player of the Year in 1987. While in high school, Chris set national passing records for career attempts (1,122), completions (646) and touchdown passes (101). At just 33 years of age and already a head college football coach, Chris, who received a degree in mathematics from Bethel College in 1992 and earned an MBA from the the University of Minnesota in 1996, is well on his way to surpassing his old man's coaching legacy. The Meidts are among the best of the best when it comes to coaching football, and continue to make Minnesota proud.

JOHN MARIUCCI: GOPHER HOCKEY

John Mariucci is the godfather of American amateur hockey and the patriarch of the sport in our state. In fact, what John did for the sport was immeasurable. With his passion for competing, teaching, and spreading the gospel about the sport he loved, Mariucci went on to become the country's most important figure in the development of amateur hockey. Here is the story of a true Minnesota legend.

John Mariucci was born the son of Italian immigrants on May 8, 1916, on the great Mesabi Iron Range in Eveleth — the birthplace of hockey in the United States. He grew up on Hay Street, also referred to by locals as "Incubator Street" because it was said that there were so many nationalities living there, and every house had eight or nine kids inside. Many of the kids of the immigrants would play hockey to stay out of trouble. Some kids didn't even have skates, so they wore overshoes, while others used tree branches for sticks. John found his first pair of skates in a garbage can and, because he didn't have money to buy equipment, wrapped old magazines around his shins for pads.

Even though it was a mid-sized Minnesota Iron Range town, Eveleth was as sophisticated as New York City when it came to hockey. Eveleth even had a team, the "Reds" which played big-time pro hockey against cities such as Toronto, Philadelphia and Chicago. Eveleth kids would try to emulate the many Canadians who were imported to the city to play hockey as one of the forms of entertainment provided for the iron-ore miners. John learned the game from legendary hall of fame coach Cliff Thompson, whose tenure as the Eveleth High School hockey coach lasted nearly 40 years.

In 1936, Maroosh left the Range and headed south to the University of Minnesota. There he starred as a defenseman for Larry Armstrong's Gopher hockey team and also played offensive and defensive end alongside of Butch Nash under legendary football coach Bernie Bierman. In 1940, led by Goalie Bud Wilkinson, the future football coaching legend at the University of Oklahoma, Mariucci captained the National AAU Championship team. (At the time that was the only championship available in college hockey.) After the season, Maroosh, who was named as an All-American, was offered the head coaching position at the U of M, but turned it down to play in the pros.

After a brief stint with Providence in the American Hockey League, Maroosh joined the Chicago Blackhawks to finish out the 1940 season. At that time the NHL employed few Americans and not many college-bred players. (To put this into perspective, by 1968, only six Americans and five collegians had ever played in the NHL!) Johnny played there until 1942, when he was summoned to join the U.S. Coast Guard in New York. There, he played for the Coast Guard team in the Eastern Amateur League during the second world war. After turning down another offer to coach at the U of M, he returned to the Hawks for the 1945 season. Then, in 1947, Maroosh became the first American-developed player ever to captain an NHL team.

The rugged Maroosh was one of the biggest celebrities in Chicago during his playing days there. He became famous among Windy City hockey fans for his brawls. One in particular, with Detroit's Black Jack Stewart, remains the NHL's longest ever — lasting more than 20 minutes. In 1948, Maroosh left the Hawks. For his career in the NHL he scored 11 goals and 34 assists for 45 points over 223 games. He also played in two Stanley Cup playoffs. More importantly though, he led the team in penalty minutes, racking up more than 300 over his career. A goal-scorer he wasn't. This guy was a role-playing hatchet-man who protected and defended his teammates. That's why they loved and appreciated him.

"You know, when I was playing with New York I got to know the Bentley brothers, who played for years with John in Chicago," recalled Glen Sonmor, one of Mariucci's best friends. "Now John, as you know, was the ultimate warrior out on the ice. He knew his role and he loved it. He knew that he wasn't there to score 50 goals, he was there to play solid hockey and to protect his teammates. So, one time I asked those Bentley brothers about what it was like to play hockey with that big Dago, John Mariucci. They said that playing with John made hockey fun for them again. Before John got there (Chicago) other players used to intimidate them and make runs at them because they were the stars of the Blackhawks. Well, when John got there it took just one trip around the league for every team to learn not to even look funny at the Bentley brothers. They left them alone after that because anybody from that point on knew that if tried anything with those guys, that John was coming to get them. And back then you didn't have any of the penalties or rules about coming off the bench to mix it up. I remember Max (Bentley) saying, 'Anybody who tried to intimidate us had to have some pretty big balls because as soon as they went after us they would have to turn around and get ready for big John, who would come flying off the bench in a hurry. And there wasn't any doubt as to why he was coming either because he left his stick and gloves back on the bench!' John used to love beating the crap out of guys and he was pretty darn good at it. Those Bentleys told me that after that no one would mess with them with the exception of one guy, Black Jack Stewart. They said that Black Jack would get bored out there sometimes and decide to make it interesting so he would take a shot at one of the Bentley's just so John would come after him. Those two used to love brawling with each other, and then they would go out and have beers together after the game. It was crazy, but that was the kind of guy John was, he would knock you down and then pick you back up."

"One time Maroosh was playing in a game against a Kansas City farm team," recalled Willard Ikola, a fellow Evelethian and friend of Maroosh. "A rookie gave Maroosh some stitches in that big honker he had with a cheap shot. Maroosh tried to run him down, but the kid, realizing who he had whacked, jumped right over the boards and ran up the stairs. Maroosh jumped up and followed him right outside. Sparks were flying from the stairs as Maroosh was yelling at him from behind. He chased him right out into the street in front of the arena, and then calmly walked back down the stairs to the ice. He was even talking to the ladies in the stands on his way back down. He went on the ice and finished his shift like nothing had happened. The next night Maroosh was still mad, but the front office wanted the kid who hit him to get some playing time, because he was going to get called up shortly from the farm team in Kansas City. John agreed, but only if the kid came up to him and apologized in person. That night the kid came to John's room and apologized in fear, and Maroosh laughed it off telling him to keep his damn stick down next time. Big John, the captain, took the kid under his wing after that, and helped him out. That's the kind of guy John Mariucci was."

Mariucci went on to play for St. Louis of the American League, St. Paul and Minneapolis of the U.S. League, and again with a Coast Guard team before hanging up his skates for good as an active player in 1951. He then turned to coaching, when he was named the head coach of Minneapolis Millers hockey team of the A.A.L.

After a year with the Millers, Maroosh finally elected to coach the Gophers, replacing former Blackhawk and Gopher, Doc Romnes. It was only a part-time job for him though, as he continued to also work as a salesman for the Falk Paper Company as well. In his first season in Gold Country he was awarded Coach of the Year honors. It would be his first of many. Maroosh got Minneapolis residents excited about college hockey, and they responded by coming out in droves to see his Gophers. The U even had to add an upper tier of seats to the Williams Arena rink to accommodate them all. Always a joker, Maroosh was always trying new things to keep the fans interested and was always on the lookout for new recruits. One time while watching the giant Bill Simonovich, from Gilbert, Minn., play with the varsity basketball team, John said: "Man, what a goalie he'd make! Give him a couple of mattresses and a pair of skis and nobody would ever score on him."

In a sport dominated by Canadians, Maroosh championed the Americans and in particular, Minnesotans. After watching an NCAA Final one time, he said: "It's asinine that the only two Americans on the ice for the NCAA championship game were the referees." Maroosh was a visionary and saw the potential growth of the sport.

"College could be a developmental program for our own country, for the Olympics and for the pros," he said. "College hockey is a state institution and should be represented by Minnesota boys. If they're not quite as good as some Canadians, we'll just have to work harder, that's all."

It became political for him as he battled to stop the importation of the older Canadians and give the American kids an equal playing field. In the late 1950s, the U's Athletic Director, Marsh Ryman, refused to play Denver's Canadian-filled teams. This ultimately led to the end of the WIHL and the creation of the WCHA in 1959.

"What I was against was the junior player who played in Canada until he was 21, then, if the pros didn't sign him, he would come to this country to play college hockey as a 22-year-old freshman against our 18-year-olds," said Mariucci. "It wasn't fair to our kids, who were finishing college at the same age Canadians were freshmen."

Although Maroosh never won the NCAA championship during his 14-year tenure at the U of M, he came pretty darn close in 1954 with the best line ever to play college hockey. When the 1953-54 collegiate hockey season started, the U of M was on a mission to avenge their NCAA Finals loss to Michigan the season before. After losing the first two games of the new season, the Gophers got back on track and lost only one of the next dozen games. After splitting with Michigan, Minnesota then swept Michigan State twice, Michigan Tech, North Dakota, and Denver, only to get beat twice by Michigan at season's end. The Gophers finished the year with a 24-6-1 record, the best in the nation, and won their second straight WIHL Conference crown.

Hockey fans were anticipating a rematch in the NCAA Finals in Colorado Springs between Minnesota and Michigan. But the maroon and gold had to first get by Boston College in the semifinals. Minnesota pummeled an out-manned BC club, 14-1, behind an amazing effort from the best line in college hockey: John Mayasich scored three goals and added four assists, Dick Dougherty scored four goals and added two assists, while Gene Campbell added three goals and two assists. Then, to the Gophers' disappointment, they found out that the Michigan Wolverines had been knocked off by unheralded Rennselaer Polytechnic Institute (RPI) in the semifinals.

Minnesota was clearly favored to win it all, (by five goals) in most spreads. Down 3-0 in the second, however, the Gophers rallied behind a Kenny Yackel blast, followed by a Dougherty one-timer from Campbell that made it 3-2. Then, after peppering the Engineer goalie, Mayasich put in a back-hander to even it up at three-apiece in the third. Four minutes later Mayasich set up Dougherty on a pretty "five-hole" goal to finally take the lead. But, at 16:10 the men from Troy, N.Y., evened things up to send the game into overtime.

At 1:54 of the extra session, after a mix-up out in front of the net, RPI's Gordie Peterson, grabbed a loose puck on the doorstep and promptly drilled it home to win the game by the final of 5-4. It was a devastating defeat and a big blow to Mariucci, who wanted so badly to win the big one for Minnesota. After the game, the players huddled around their coach to shield him from the press and their cameras. It was the first and only time Minnesota hockey players would ever see this giant of a man shed a tear. Despite the loss, Yackel, Mattson, Dougherty, and Mayasich were all named to the All-American team.

The Noble Roman left the University in 1966 with a record of 207-142-15, including conference championships in 1953 and 1954, as well as three NCAA playoff appearances (including another Final Four appearance in 1961). Included in his tenure was an Italian homecoming of sorts, when he was led the Americans to a silver medal in the 1956 Olympics in Cortina. There were 11 Minnesota natives on the team that stunned heavily favored Canada before falling to the Soviet Union. Mariucci's successor at the U of M was Glen Sonmor, a former teammate with the Minneapolis Millers.

In 1966, another chapter of Mariucci's storied life unfolded as he became chief scout and special assistant to Wren Blair, GM of the NHL's expansion North Stars. There, Maroosh applied his vast knowledge of recruiting, coaching, and scouting. In 1977 Mariucci coached the U.S. National team and a year later he rejoined the North Stars, this time as the Assistant G.M. under his former player, Lou Nanne. "One word of advice to all you coaches," said Maroosh. "Be good to your players — you never know which one might someday be your boss..."

John's accomplishments and honors are far too great to list here. Some of his more notable ones, however, include: Being inducted as a charter member of the U.S. Hockey Hall of Fame in his hometown of Eveleth; being inducted into the NHL Hockey Hall of Fame in Toronto; and receiving the NHL's coveted Lester Patrick Award for his contributions to U.S. hockey. He also made a difference by giving to others. In fact, he devoted much of his life to Brainerd's Camp Confidence, for the mentally-retarded, a cause he dearly loved.

On March 2, 1985, in an emotional ceremony to give thanks and immortalize the man forever, the U of M renamed the hockey half of Williams Arena as Mariucci Arena, in his honor. It was also declared as "John Mariucci Day" in Minnesota by Governor Perpich. During the ceremony, long-time friend Robert Ridder said: "During the 1980 Olympics, a U.S. Destroyer passed a Russian ship and signaled to it: 'U.S.A. 4, Russia 3.' Probably nobody on that boat ever heard of John Mariucci, but it wouldn't have been possible without John Mariucci." In 1987 Maroosh died at the age of 70 after a long bout with cancer. He had seven children and several grandchildren.

This gentleman brawler was a legend, on and off the ice. Although he was tough as nails, his wit, intelligence, and personality were one-of-a-kind. John was one of the toughest Italians who ever lived. His face has often been referred to as a "blocked punt," because it was so beat up. But what separated him from the goons was that he wouldn't just knock his opponents down, he'd pick them up and then make them laugh. Perhaps Herb Brooks said it best: "In all social causes to better an institution, there's always got to be a rallying force, a catalyst, a glue, and a magnet, and that's what John was, for American hockey. The rest of us just filled in after him."

Full of wit, he was described as a newspaperman's dream-come-true. From his famous brawls, which included once breaking thumb-wrestling champion Murray Warmath's thumb, Mariucci gained a lot of mileage. Local reporters found themselves having a lot of dinners that turned into breakfasts while listening to his endless stories. The sports community was in awe of him, and he made journalists who hated the sport of hockey want to start covering it.

He was also the pioneer in the development of hockey in Minnesota. Because of that, his legacy will live on forever. Every kid that laces up his or her skates needs to give thanks to the man that started it all. He started grassroots youth programs, put on coaching clinics, attended new arena openings in countless cities across the state, helped former players find coaching positions, and even encouraged hockey moms to write to city councils to build rinks and develop recreation programs. Because of him, hockey in Minnesota carries the same pedigree as basketball in Indiana or football in Texas. Described best by his friends and players as "father-like, magical, and even super-human," he was simply the greatest. *Thanks, Maroosh.*

DEAN BLAIS
COLLEGE HOCKEY: UNIVERSITY OF NORTH DAKOTA

Dean Blais grew up in International Falls and went on to play hockey at International Falls High School under legendary coach Larry Ross. From there, Blais headed south, to the University of Minnesota, where he was named the Gophers' Rookie of the Year in 1970 and an NCAA All-Tournament selection in 1971. Blais went on to play for the U.S. National Team in 1973 before beginning a three-year professional career in the Chicago Blackhawk's minor league system. Blais' coaching career began at the University of Minnesota, where he got his bachelor's degree in physical education and also served as an assistant coach during the 1976-77 season under Herbie Brooks. Blais then became head hockey coach at Minot, N.D., High School in 1977, where he led his team to a conference championship and a pair of state tournament appearances in 1979 and 1980.

In 1980 Blais went to the University of North Dakota, where he became an assistant coach in a program that had just won its first of three national titles of the 1980s. During Blais' nine seasons at UND, the Sioux won two more NCAA titles, in 1982 and 1987, and claimed a third-place finish at the NCAA Championships in 1984. The Fighting Sioux would post a 239-130-11 (.643) record during his tenure as an assistant coach from 1980-89. Blais would also earn his master's degree in education from UND during that time as well.

In 1989 Blais came back to Minnesota to take over as the head hockey coach at Roseau High School. That next year he guided the Rams to the 1990 state title, earning Minnesota High School Hockey Coach of the Year honors along the way. He then coached Roseau to conference and regional championships in 1991 before being named an assistant coach under Dave Peterson for the 1992 U.S. Olympic Team which took fourth-place at the Olympic Games in Albertville, France. Following the Olympics, Blais signed on as the athletic director and hockey coach back at International Falls High School. He would lead his alma mater to a conference title in 1993 before going on to become the head coach at UND in 1994.

Since then, Blais has set the hockey world on fire. In the past eight years UND has won four WCHA regular season titles: 1997, 1998, 1999, and 2001. In 1997 Blais led the Sioux to their first NCAA title in 10 seasons and just three years later, in 2000, repeated the feat to win the seventh NCAA Division I hockey championship for the University of North Dakota. In addition to adding a 2001 NCAA second-place trophy, Blais was named the WCHA Coach of the Year for the third time in 2001.

On the national level, the American Hockey Coaches Association named Blais as the recipient of the Spencer Penrose Award as the nation's top collegiate coach on two separate occasions. Under Blais, the Sioux have posted winning seasons in seven of the last eight years and reached the 30-win plateau in four of the past six seasons. In his career at UND, Blais has posted an impressive 206-95-25 (.670) record. Active with USA Hockey, Blais also coached the west team at the 1999 Women's Ice Hockey Summer Festival in Lake Placid, and was also an assistant coach for the U.S. National Team which competed in the 2000 International Ice Hockey Federation Pool A World Championship in 2000.

Today, Blais continues to lead one of the top programs in the nation at the $100 million state-of-the-art Ralph Engelstad Arena, which opened in 2001. During his tenure behind the UND bench, Dean Blais has consistently produced Fighting Sioux hockey teams which are among the elite in the WCHA and the nation. His teams

have also stepped it up in the classroom too, earning a cumulative GPA above 3.0 for seven consecutive semesters over the past couple of seasons. A true hockey coaching legend in both Minnesota and in North Dakota, Blais is still going strong and truly making a difference in the world of hockey. Dean and his wife Wendy live in Grand Forks and have three children: Sarah, Ben and Mary Beth.

HOW WOULD YOU DESCRIBE YOUR COACHING STYLE? "It has changed over the years. I think 20 years ago I was more of a 'It's my way or the highway' type of a coach, but I have had to adjust because the players have adjusted. Now, I think that I am more of a 'player's coach' and I would hope that my players described me that way as well."

HOW DO YOU MOTIVATE YOUR PLAYERS? "I think the best way is self motivation. It's up to the players to get motivated for every practice and every game. I want them to get into a routine so that they are mentally and physically prepared come game day. I also think motivation starts at the top. If you are an intense coach, then that will rub off on your players. So, the teams that you coach are a direct reflection of the coaches personality. I am intense and I expect my players to play intense. I always want to win, so I would say that my motivation is probably the fear of losing."

WHO WERE YOUR COACHING MENTORS? "I have been fortunate enough to learn the game from some great coaches: Larry Ross, Herb Brooks, Bob Johnson, Dave Peterson and Glen Sonmor, and each of them has rubbed off on me in a certain way."

IF YOU COULD MAGICALLY GO BACK IN TIME TO THE FIRST YEAR YOU WERE A HEAD COACH AND GIVE YOURSELF SOME ADVICE FOR THE FUTURE, KNOWING WHAT YOU KNOW NOW, BACK THEN, WHAT WOULD YOU SAY TO YOURSELF? "I would say just stay with what you have been doing. It has worked and will continue to work."

WHAT IS THE KEY TO GOOD TIME MANAGEMENT? "Practice makes perfect and perfect practices make perfect games. Practices should be hard work, challenging, and a learning experience, while games should be the fun part of it."

HOW DO YOU EARN THE RESPECT OF YOUR PLAYERS? "I think by being intense and by being fair. If you are phony or not knowledgeable, the players see right through that. You have to treat them like you want to be treated."

WHAT ARE THE CHARACTERISTICS OF WINNERS? "I think winners hate to lose. It comes down to tradition and doing everything they can to be better. I look at a guy like Zach Parise. He is a rink rat who goes out and practices on his own; he is dedicated in the weight room; he is not a big partyer; and he is focused on being the best player he can be. That is why he was a first round draft pick. He is a winner."

LOOKING BACK WHAT ARE YOU MOST PROUD OF IN YOUR CAREER? "There are a few things. Obviously winning a state high school championship with Roseau was big. Then, winning a national championship here at North Dakota was very special too.

Then, being in the Olympics was also something I will always remember. More than anything though, I am just proud of the people who I have met and have had an opportunity to be around in the game of hockey."

WHAT IS THE KEY TO RECRUITING? "You have to have a good plan and there are definite steps to creating a recruiting plan. The first one is talent recognition. You have got to be able to go out and pick out the best players. Some people have that knack and others just don't. I think it is God-given. Then, you look at certain things like hockey sense, skating ability, size, strength, and attitude, and then determine if that is the type of player who will fit into your type of system. The second part is getting to know the kids' parents and coach and then bringing him in to see if he fits in with your team. Do your players like him? Do they think he will fit it? Then, will he fit in here academically as a student-athlete? All of that, along with your staff, your facilities and your history go into recruiting, and it all comes back to having a good plan."

HOW DO YOU BUILD TEAM UNITY & CHEMISTRY? "I think it starts with your captains, who are your leaders. You either have it or you don't. It has a lot to do with recruiting. You can't make leaders, you either have them or you don't. All it takes are a couple of bad apples to ruin the whole barrel. Sometimes as a coach you know that you have a championship caliber team, but without that chemistry and winning attitude, you won't win. The same is true the other way too, where you might have a team that is not that talented, but has chemistry and will win. It is very important."

WHAT MOTIVATES YOU? "When a player is recruited to come here to North Dakota they know that they were brought here to win. Likewise, I was hired to win and to make them winners. Winning is an attitude and it carries over to the community. Our community expects our teams to win and that puts a little pressure on the coaches and on the players. It is good pressure though and that is healthy. This is a tough league, the WCHA, and you have to perform at the highest level to be successful."

WHAT ADVICE WOULD YOU HAVE FOR YOUNG COACH-ES STARTING OUT TODAY? "Be patient with your team and be organized. Beyond that, get the parents tuned in to your philosophy and to what you are trying to do. I think that is the biggest thing, at any level. They can really help you or they can really hurt you. Everyone has to be on the same page and that is very important."

WHAT'S THE BEST PIECE OF ADVICE YOU EVER GOT FROM ANOTHER COACH? "To stay in college and not go to the National Hockey League. You want to be in a position where it is hockey 24 hours a day, 365 days a year, and it is fun. Coaching in col-

lege is about teaching, not just managing egos and spoiled million-aires."

FAVORITE LOCKER ROOM SIGN? "The Harder you Work the Luckier you Get," and "It's Amazing What Can Be Accomplished When No One Cares Who Gets The Credit."

ON THE GOPHERS WINNING BACK-TO-BACK TITLES: "I am very proud of them. I was a part of that 'Pride on Ice' tradition. It is great for hockey up here and that makes us all proud. I mean Minnesota and North Dakota have won four of the last seven national championships. That is awesome. I played at the University of Minnesota and then coached there as an assistant under Herbie Brooks too, so it is great to see them do well. I feel that if we can't win it here, at UND, in any given year, then it is good to see them do it. They have had a nice run. They have good coaching and good players and we should all be proud of them."

WHAT ARE THE KEY INGREDIENTS TO CREATING A CHAMPIONSHIP TEAM? "Talent, leadership, unselfishness and depth. You also need players who will buy into your system and will be willing to play a lesser role on your team."

WHAT'S THE SECRET TO YOUR SUCCESS? "I think being prepared has always been a big part of my style, as well as working hard on the technical side too. You have to be a student of the game and you also have to be very organized, those are the keys."

WHAT WOULD YOU WANT TO SAY TO YOUR FANS, BOOSTERS, AND ALUMNI WHO HAVE SUPPORTED YOU ALL THESE YEARS? "I would say thanks. Hockey is a fun and exciting game, especially if you have had kids that played the game. Parents know, you have to haul them all over the dog-gone country and you spend a fortune on everything from equipment to ice time so that you can see them have fun. And you know, even if they don't get a scholarship, it is still all worth it. Just from the enjoyment of playing the game and meeting people. Hockey people are the best people in the world. College hockey is just very special. So, we try to help develop players both on and off the ice. It is our job to make sure that they are doing a good job in the classroom as well as on the ice, and our fans appreciate that."

HOW DO YOU WANT YOUR COACHING EPITAPH TO READ — HOW DO YOU WANT TO BE REMEMBERED AS A COACH? "I would like to be considered as one of the top coaches in college hockey. You know, I was meant to be a hockey coach. I just love it and that passion started at a very young age. I remember in the fifth grade wanting to be a coach, and then I got to be that. So for me it is a dream come true to be doing what I love."

LOU VAIRO: JUNIOR & OLYMPIC HOCKEY

Lou Vairo has become one of America's most senior international coaches. In 2003 Vairo served as the head coach of the U.S. National Team for the fourth consecutive year. Vairo also served as the head coach of the 1984 U.S. Olympic team in Yugoslavia, as well as an assistant for the 2002 U.S. team in Salt Lake City. In addition to coaching internationally, Vairo has also been involved with professional hockey in the United States, having spent two years as an assistant coach with the National Hockey League's New Jersey Devils. Vairo's ties to Minnesota take him back to his junior hockey days, when he spent three seasons during the mid-1970s as the coach of the Austin Mavericks in the United States Hockey League, leading the team to a Junior A National Championship in 1976. Vairo, who has served as the Director of Special Projects for USA Hockey since 1992, is one of the most experienced hockey coaches in America, having directed national and professional teams in both the United States and Europe for more than two decades. Vairo was honored twice in 1994 for his lifetime commitment to hockey, receiving both the John "Snooks" Kelley Founders Award from the American Hockey Coaches Association, and the Walter Yaciuk Award from USA Hockey's Coaching Education Program. Vairo also has authored many books and articles on hockey which are used by coaches throughout the world.

HERB BROOKS
COLLEGE, OLYMPIC & PRO HOCKEY

Herbert Paul Brooks was born in St. Paul on August 5, 1937 and grew up in a hockey-crazy family. His father was a well known amateur player in the 1920s, while his kid brother, David, played for the Gophers in the early 1960s and also on the 1964 U.S. Olympic team as well. As a boy growing up on St. Paul's tough East Side, a training ground for many future Minnesota hockey stars, Herb was a typical hockey playing rink-rat. He would go on to star at St. Paul Johnson High School from 1952-1955. As a senior, the forward led Johnson to a 26-1-2 record en route to winning the state championship. In the title game, Brooks scored two goals in the 3-1 victory over their Mill City rivals, Minneapolis Southwest.

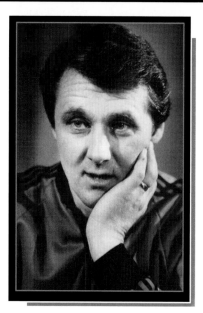

"Winning the state championship, that represented your neighborhood," said Brooks. "I would have to say that it was my biggest thrill ever. It was just the guys in the neighborhood and that was special."

An outstanding athlete, Herb also earned three varsity letters as a first baseman on the baseball team as well. Before long, the colleges were calling.

"I had an interview with the Air Force Academy, because I really wanted to be a fighter pilot," said Brooks. "Unfortunately, because I was slightly color blind, I washed out of the Academy. I also had a scholarship at Michigan, but my dad encouraged me to walk on at the U of M and try to play for John Mariucci, so that was the route I took."

At Minnesota, Brooks became known for his blinding speed. "He was one of the fastest, if not the fastest, player in college hockey in that era," Mariucci would later recall. Brooks would learn a lot from "Maroosh," saying that he had more to do with shaping his ideas in hockey than any other individual. Brooks wore a Golden Gopher sweater from 1957-59, scoring 45 points over his three-year career. He graduated from the U in 1961 with a B.A. in Psychology.

The next phase of Brooks' life involved his lifelong dream, the Olympics. After graduation, he began to build a successful career in the insurance business, but never fully got away from the game that continued to dominate his life. Herb tried out for the 1960 Olympic team which played in Squaw Valley, Calif. He played well, eluding every cut except the final one, when he was literally the last player to be released from the team's final roster.

Herb then sat at home with his father and watched his buddies from the neighborhood, the same kids who he used to play hockey with out on the frozen ponds, bring home the gold. Herb was torn. On one hand he was genuinely happy for his old pals. On the other he was jealous as hell, because they were living out his dream. At that very moment Herb's father, Herb Sr., looked at him and said: "Looks like Coach cut the right guy…" It was right then and there that Herbie knew his destiny. He was going to make the 1964 team, and one day, he was going to coach an Olympic team. Period.

Brooks worked like a dog, and for his efforts spent nearly a decade playing for either U.S. Olympic or National teams. From 1961 to 1970, he played on two Olympic teams and five National teams — more than any player in the history of United States hockey — captaining many teams.

"To me the Olympics are not about 'Dream Teams,' they're more about dreamers. They're not about medals, but the pursuit of medals. The Olympics are not about being No. 1, they're about sacrificing and trying to be No. 1. That's why the Olympics will always be special to me."

Herb went into coaching after that, becoming an assistant under Coach Glen Sonmor at the U of M. At the same time, he pioneered Junior Hockey in the state as the first coach of the Minnesota Junior Stars in the Minnesota/Ontario Junior-A League. Then, in 1971, Sonmor left to become the coach of the WHA's Fighting Saints. That next season Brooks was named as the Gopher's new coach. The youngest college hockey coach in the country, Brooks would inherit a program that had just finished in last place. The challenge of turning it all around was just what Herb was looking for.

The chant "Her-bee!, Her-bee!" would become an all too familiar sound at the "Old Barn" throughout the tenure of the man who would become Minnesota's greatest hockey coach. Brooks instilled a new brand of pride and tradition that next season, starting with his newly designed jerseys which proudly featured the Minnesota "M" on the front. Brooks promised he would bring, "exciting, dynamic people into the program," and he kept his word. In only seven years, he would build a dynasty at Minnesota. More importantly, he did it all with Minnesota kids.

With his extensive knowledge and experience in European hockey, Herb became an advocate of the Russian style of play and in particular, the coaching style of Anatoli Tarasov. He would instill this philosophy in motivating his own players. From 1972-1979, Brooks was simply dominant. With his no-nonsense attitude, he went on to win the first three NCAA championships in University of Minnesota hockey history, in 1973, 1976 and 1979.

While at Minnesota, Brooks won 175 games, lost only 100, and tied 20 for a .636 winning percentage. Herb guided five All-Americans: Les Auge, Mike Polich, Tim Harrer, Neal Broten and Steve Ulseth, while 23 of his protégés went on to play in the NHL as well.

"We went to the finals four of my seven years there, and we made a great run of it," said Brooks. "I think I put a lot of pressure on the players, and I had a lot of expectations of them. I didn't give them an 'out,' and I think I was always able to find the kids who were really competitive. The common denominator of all the guys who played throughout my seven years was that they were really competitive, very hungry, very focused, and mentally tough — to go along with whatever talent they had. I think that really carried us."

"Do you believe in miracles?" The next chapter of Brooks' life is the one that would make him a household name, the "Miracle on Ice." After coaching the 1979 U.S. National team in the World Games in Moscow, Herb was then named as the coach of the fabled 1980 U.S. Olympic team. Brooks guided the squad to their incredible upset of the heavily-favored Soviet Union team, setting the stage for the huge win against Finland in the gold medal game. A grateful nation, saddened by the unfolding events of the Iranian hostage crisis, hailed the team as heroes. The victory would go down as one of the most memorable moments in U.S. history and will forever remain etched in our memories as one of the greatest sporting events of all-time.

When Herb took over as the team's coach he set out to assemble a roster of kids of whom he could trust. He researched countless candidates, made thousands of phone calls, and tried to find out which players he could count on come crunch time. When it was all said and done, 12 Minnesotans had made the cut. In addition, nine were players that Brooks had coached as Gophers: Roseau's Neal Broten, Grand Rapids' Bill Baker, White Bear Lake's Steve Janaszak, Rochester's Eric Strobel, Duluth's Phil Verchota, Minneapolis' Mike

Ramsey, Babbitt's Buzz Schneider, St. Paul's Rob McClanahan and Richfield's Steve Christoff. The three other Minnesotans were: Warroad's Dave Christian, who played at North Dakota, and Virginia's John Harrington and Eveleth's Mark Pavelich — both of whom played at Minnesota-Duluth.

"They were really mentally tough and goal-oriented," said Brooks of his squad. "They came from all different walks of life, many having competed against one-another, but they came together and grew to be a real close team. I pushed this team really hard, I mean I really pushed them! But they had the ability to answer the bell. Our style of play was probably different than anything in North America. We adopted more of a hybrid style of play — a bit of the Canadian school and a little bit of the European School. The players took to it like ducks to water, and they really had a lot of fun playing it. We were a fast, creative team that played extremely disciplined without the puck. Throughout the Olympics, they had a great resiliency about them. I mean they came from behind six or seven times to win. They just kept on moving and working and digging. I think we were as good a conditioned team as there was in the world, outside of maybe the Soviet Union. We got hot and lucky at the right times, and it was just an incredible experience for all of us."

After a brief coaching stint in Davos, Switzerland, Herb's coaching success continued in the National Hockey League with the New York Rangers, where he gained 100 victories quicker than any other coach before him. For his efforts, he was named NHL Coach of the Year in 1982. His Broadway stint with the Rangers lasted until 1985.

Then, in an amazing move, Brooks came home and accepted the head coaching position at St. Cloud State University in 1987. He would be revered as the school's savior, leading the Huskies to a third place finish in the national small-college tournament, and more importantly, getting them elevated to NCAA Division I status. He stayed for only a year, but with his clout, got the school a beautiful new arena and really got the Huskies' program turned around.

"I've never met Herb Brooks, but I feel like I owe him everything," said Bret Hedican, former Husky and current NHL All-Star. "He's done so much for St. Cloud Hockey, it's incredible."

The next stop in Brooks' hockey resume was Bloomington, to coach the Minnesota North Stars. This was another homecoming of sorts, as Herb took over the reigns from Lorne Henning and became the first Minnesota native to coach the NHL team. The season, however, didn't go well for Brooks. Unable to overcome an enormous number of injuries, the Stars finished in the Norris Division cellar. Then, citing philosophical differences with management, Brooks resigned that next season.

Brooks took some well deserved time away from coaching for a few years after that to embark on a successful business career which included motivational speaking, TV analysis, NHL scouting and occasional coaching. Then, in 1991, he took over the New Jersey Devils minor league team in Utica, NY, and was later promoted to be the head coach of the NHL team in 1992. He got the coaching bug again a few years later, when he guided the French Olympic team in 1998. Following that he became a scout with the Pittsburgh Penguins, ultimately taking over as the teams' head coach in 1999. He then came full circle in 2002 when he guided the U.S. Olympic team to a dramatic silver medal at the Winter Games in Salt Lake City. Once again, Herbie had made America proud.

Throughout his career Herb Brooks has earned great recognition both individually and for his country. As a player he was selected as the Associated Press Athlete of the Year and ABC Sports Athlete of the Year. As a coach he was named as the NHL Coach of the Year in 1982. He was also named as Sports Illustrated's Sportsman of the Year, and his 1980 U.S. Olympic team was named as the Sports Achievement of the 21st Century. In addition he has been inducted into many Halls of Fames including the United States Hockey Hall of Fame, The International Ice Hockey Hall of Fame, the University of Minnesota and the State of Minnesota Halls of Fames, while also receiving the coveted Lester Patrick Award for his contributions to

American hockey. Several movies and documentaries have also been made about him, including a new Disney movie entitled "Miracle," which will be released in early 2004 starring Kurt Russell as Herb.

Tragically, on August 11, 2003, Herb was killed in a one car accident just north of Minneapolis on Interstate 35. Ironically, he was returning home from the U.S. Hockey Hall of Fame Golf Tournament in Northern Minnesota, where he was once again doing his part to promote the growth of American hockey. His funeral was a veritable who's who of the hockey world, with dignitaries, politicians, coaches and fans alike, all coming out to pay their respects to one of the true patriarchs of the game. One of our nation's most charismatic and innovative coaches, "Herbie" was a true American hero and a real Minnesota treasure. His legacy will live on forever in the youth of America as they continue to enjoy the fruits of his hard work. In the world of coaching, no one was larger than Herb Brooks. A legend in every sense of the word, Herbie was simply the best of the absolute best, and will dearly be missed.

HOW WOULD YOU DESCRIBE YOUR COACHING STYLE? "As far as X's and O's are concerned, I tried to blend the European style of hockey with the North American style —a hybrid system that was unique and different. I basically wanted to create an environment to give this game back to the players as much as possible. At the same time, bringing out their creativity and ability to react at the highest possible tempo. As far as my psychological/motivational style, I believe in setting high standards for players, being open and honest with the players, and respecting an honest effort. I am always looking at an athlete and a team and addressing the psycho/physiological being."

HOW DID YOU MOTIVATE YOUR PLAYERS? "Motivation is really a combination of things. Obviously communication is very important. It is the ability to sell a concept. Sometimes it's the all important four words: 'ask questions and listen.' Coaching is selling. You're just selling X's and O's and you're selling team building. So, to be a good coach you have to be a good salesman. You have to get your players to somehow buy into your system and your philosophies. That is the key. Players must know that you care about them. I am not a touchy-feely type of a person but I try to show my respect and caring for them in other ways."

WHO WERE YOUR COACHING MENTORS? "Certainly John Mariucci was first and foremost. I will always remember when I first started coaching with the Gophers and he told me that this job is not just being the coach at the University of Minnesota. He said it was much bigger than that and told me it was about doing whatever you possibly could to help make hockey better in the state of Minnesota. That is why I went to St. Cloud State to coach, because it was that important to John Mariucci. He said it was not about what you accomplish, but what you really contribute towards. John gave countless hours of his time to youth hockey associations through whatever means he could to promote the game. I have tried to follow his lead. I learned a great deal from Glen Sonmor as well. He always talked about the importance of not only looking at the qualifications of players but also at the qualities of players. He reinforced to me that while skills are important, you need people with character. I also learned a lot from Murray Williamson while playing for him in the Olympics. He was very organized all the time and had a good time-line for the season. He was always trying to think outside the box. Most recently I have learned a lot about physiology as it applies to hockey from Jack Blatherwick — a brilliant man."

IF YOU COULD MAGICALLY GO BACK IN TIME TO THE FIRST YEAR YOU WERE A HEAD COACH AND GIVE YOURSELF SOME ADVICE FOR THE FUTURE, KNOWING WHAT YOU KNOW NOW, BACK THEN, WHAT WOULD YOU SAY TO YOURSELF? "When I started coaching at the University of Minnesota it was a stressful time. After Glen

Sonmor left the program to coach professionally in the World Hockey Association, the team slid into last place in the WCHA, and the crowds at Williams Arena were only around 2,500 per game. We had to do a lot of things fast. Even though Glen left a core of good players, I didn't have the luxury of being as patient and understanding as I probably would have liked to have been. I was just in overdrive trying to get so much done with very little resources. I wish I had a little more patience and was a little more understanding."

WHAT ARE THE CHARACTERISTICS OF WINNERS? "I don't know if there is any one real definition of a winner. Winners in my opinion are those who are willing to make sacrifices for the unknown, both for themselves and for the team. Once you have that, then the results take care of themselves."

WHAT ARE THE CHARACTERISTICS OF LEADERS? "Again, I don't know if there is any one real definition of a leader. Leadership is not a function of titles but of relationships. You have to wear a lot of different hats as a leader. There is a time to talk and a time to listen, and a good leader knows this. Leadership is a much debated topic. Leaders are visionaries. Leaders are not managers. Leaders give people something to believe in, then they've got something to belong to and then they have something to follow. That is a real key component of a good leader. Most importantly, leadership is the battle for the hearts and minds of others. It is not a spectator sport. It is not necessarily a popularity contest. Leaders have to show good habits. They have to display a sincere purpose and have passion for what they are doing."

WHAT WAS THE KEY TO RECRUITING? "Playing, hard work and communication — a never ending battle in your scouting trying to find quality people. You win with people, not with talent. So the quality of the people is very important in building your team. I always looked for people with a solid value system. I recruited kids from a cross-section of different personalities, talents and styles of play. Recruiting is basically work, more work and it is never ending."

HOW DID YOU BUILD TEAM UNITY & CHEMISTRY? "It's up to the coach to create an environment which has a high level of comradeship, at all times reinforcing team concepts stressing strength of association and the power that can be attained when working together. The team reflects your value system, your instincts, your philosophies, and it is just matter of how well you can articulate it and sell it to your players."

WHAT MOTIVATED YOU? "As a player it was the goals that I set for myself. If you don't have goals you are going to be used by people who do have them. When I started coaching at the University of Minnesota I wanted to coach an NCAA championship team. And, I wanted to coach an Olympic team. While at the University, I also wanted to create a positive environment for our players so that they could grow as people, grow as athletes, and receive a good education. But the overriding motivation for me while at the University of Minnesota was to coach an Olympic team. To do that, I knew that we had to be very successful in order to be considered. The entire time I was there though, I was thinking about coaching the Olympic team. I am very proud of winning three NCAA national titles, but to go on to become the coach of Team USA was what it was all about for me. After the Olympics I had to re-evaluate what I wanted, and decided the next challenge would be in the National Hockey League. My motivation there was to win a Stanley Cup. That is a very elusive thing though that requires a lot of variables to fall into place."

ON PRACTICE: "I believe my practices were demanding and hopefully challenging. I tried to make our practices almost atypical situations so that games were easier — easier to adjust to the play, easier to read plays, easier to function on the ice. I was always striving to bring them out of their psycho-physiological comfort zones so that they were always improving their quickness, their execution of plays and the sharpness of their minds. I just always felt that the pace and the ability to execute at a high tempo was crucial. That way we were prepared for any set of circumstances that might have been thrown at us. I was always trying to lift the floor of their comfort zones during practice all the time."

WHAT ARE THE KEY INGREDIENTS TO CREATING A CHAMPIONSHIP TEAM? "You've got to have talent. Period. Then, you have to have people who, in some way shape or form, understand that the name on the front of the jersey is more important than the one on the back."

WHAT WOULD YOU WANT TO SAY TO YOUR FANS, BOOSTERS, AND ALUMNI WHO HAVE SUPPORTED YOU ALL THESE YEARS? "Thank you for your support. (long pause and a chuckle…) I hope you got your money's worth!"

WHAT DID IT MEAN FOR YOU TO BE A GOPHER? "An awful lot. At the time there were very few alternatives for us coming out of high school because of the heavy influence on Canadian athletes in college hockey. It was really tough. Luckily, John Mariucci kept the door open for us. We had a few other alternatives, but not many — certainly not all the options that kids have today. So, for me to be able to play at the University of Minnesota was a real honor and it meant a lot. Then, to come back as a coach was also very special."

ON BEING THE COACH OF THE "TEAM OF THE CENTURY," THE 1980 "MIRACLE ON ICE": "It was a great thrill to represent your country on the Olympic stage with some great athletes. Without a doubt it was a dream come true for me."

ON COACHING AT ST. CLOUD STATE: "It was a wonderful experience. The President of St. Cloud State, Dr. McDonald, along with Bill Radovich, a St. Cloud State Vice President, Morris Kurtz, the Athletic Director, various members of the administration, and many people in the St. Cloud community, wanted to have a Division One hockey program. We sold the concept to the state legislature, the governor, and the people of Central Minnesota, raised $10 million dollars, built the arena and somehow got it done. Look at them now, it's a great, great story."

ON THE TRANSITION TO THE PROS FROM COLLEGE: "You really have to be able to function on the fly at that level due to the fact that there is not a lot of preparation and practice time. With players on individual contracts, building team goals can be a challenge and at times difficult. It is a lot more challenging than being a college coach."

ON MAKING YOUTH AND HIGH SCHOOL HOCKEY BETTER: "We have to broaden the base of the pyramid, recognize the late talent of individuals, and value and understand the need for preparation of skill development. Competition without preparation is anti-development and we are on a slippery slope in youth hockey today with the 'Triple A' and 'Showcase' concepts. I think in high school they must play at least 30 games in a season and with 20 minute periods. We have the coaches, players and the infrastructure to do this and hopefully that can get done."

HOW DO YOU WANT YOUR COACHING EPITAPH TO READ — HOW DO YOU WANT TO BE REMEMBERED AS A COACH? "He sacrificed for the unknown and had truly peace of mind. You know, I have always felt strongly about the name on the front of the sweater being much more important than the name on the back. They'll forget about individuals in this world, but they'll always remember the teams. That is how I want to be remembered."

RUBE BJORKMAN
COLLEGE HOCKEY: UNIVERSITY OF NORTH DAKOTA

Rube Bjorkman grew up in Roseau loving hockey. He would go on to lead his Roseau Rams to a state high school hockey tournament title in 1946 and a second place finish in 1947, his senior year. Bjorkman, who was nicknamed the "Masked Marvel" at Roseau High School because he wore rubber goggles over his eyeglasses out on the ice, went on to attend the University of Minnesota from 1947-51, playing hockey under Coach Doc Romnes. Bjorkman then played on the 1948 U.S. Olympic team as well as on a pair of U.S. National teams in 1952 and 1955. He also briefly played professionally with the St. Paul Saints in the early 1950s as well. From there, Bjorkman went on to teach math and coach hockey at Greenway High School from 1955-63. That next year Bjorkman got the head coaching job at RPI, where he led his squad to a third place finish in the NCAA tournament. Bjorkman coached at RPI for just one season before moving on to take over at the University of New Hampshire. Bjorkman had great success at UNH, earning Coach of the Year honors en route to taking the program from division two to division one status. He would stay at UNH from 1964-68, before going on to take over as the head hockey coach at the University of North Dakota. There, Bjorkman led the Fighting Sioux from 1968-78, producing several outstanding teams along the way. A past president of both the Minnesota State High School Hockey Coaches Association and the American College Hockey Coaches Association, Rube Bjorkman truly made a difference in the world of hockey. Upon his retirement from the game, Bjorkman's career coaching record was a very solid 224-223-11. After retiring Bjorkman moved to Warroad, where he spent the next 20 years working for Marvin Windows. Rube presently resides in Warroad.

HOW WOULD YOU DESCRIBE YOUR COACHING STYLE? "I always felt that playing hockey was a privilege, so I expected my players to work and respect the game. I was also disciplined and focused on the fundamentals. I tried not to leave much to chance. Back then it was more of an offensive oriented type of a game, because we didn't have all of this dominant defensive philosophy going on with the trapping systems and what have you. So, I stressed more of the finesse game rather than the physical, smashing type of hockey. That was my style."

HOW DID YOU MOTIVATE YOUR PLAYERS? "By setting a good example for them and working hard myself. I wasn't a screamer or anything like that, I just expected my players to work hard and play hard. Once again, I always felt that playing hockey was a privilege. That should be motivation enough."

WHO WERE YOUR COACHING MENTORS? "My high school coach at Roseau, Oscar Almquist, was my mentor. I grew up and learned the game of hockey under Oscar, he was just such a fine coach. He was probably the greatest coach that I ever knew. He was fair, he made you work and he knew hockey. He taught me to respect the game of hockey and I tried to pass that on to my players."

LOOKING BACK WHAT ARE YOU MOST PROUD OF IN YOUR CAREER? "I enjoyed all of it. I enjoyed working with the people all the way up the line. The thing that sticks out the most in my mind is our success in the state high school hockey tournament because that was the thing that opened the hockey doors, so to speak, for me. It was also something very important and special to our community, which was great to be a part of."

WHAT WAS THE KEY TO RECRUITING? "Hard work. You just had to have the wherewithal to get out there and do it. We recruited a lot of Northern Minnesota kids up in North Dakota, so we would watch as many high school games as we could. That was where the talent was."

WHAT WAS THE KEY TO GOOD TIME MANAGEMENT? "You know, maybe it was my mathematical background, but I just felt that there was just one answer to things and one way to get there. So, I was disciplined with how I approached things. I did not want to waste a lot of time on things, so I just jumped in and got right to them in a hurry."

HOW DID YOU BUILD TEAM UNITY & CHEMISTRY? "By trying to recruit good character people. Sometimes the best leaders aren't the prettiest looking hockey players. You just had to have people who had a lot of desire and determination. I think that my teams through the years were always a cohesive unit. They stuck together, they hung out together, they roomed together and they got along. They weren't always the best of friends, but they all had a common goal. They were a unit off the ice as well as on the ice, and that was important."

WHAT MOTIVATED YOU? "Winning motivated me and just being around hockey motivated me. Hockey was a way of life for me and I grew up with the game. Back in Roseau, where I grew up, people talked about hockey year round. Sure, there was a time for baseball and a time for football, but hockey was always on our minds."

WHAT ADVICE WOULD YOU HAVE FOR YOUNG COACHES STARTING OUT TODAY? "First of all they need to know the game, totally. They need to know how to communicate not only with the kids but also with the parents. Then, they need to have some pretty thick skin."

WHAT'S THE BIGGEST THING YOU'VE LEARNED FROM COACHING THAT YOU'VE BEEN ABLE TO APPLY TO YOUR EVERYDAY LIFE? "You better not look for somebody else to do it for you, you better do it yourself. You just have to work hard and stick to it."

WHAT ARE THE KEY INGREDIENTS TO CREATING A CHAMPIONSHIP TEAM? "First would be having good players, then you have to be lucky."

WHAT'S THE SECRET TO YOUR SUCCESS? "Hard work. I worked hard for hockey all my life. I also tried to stay involved with the game and give back to it as much as I could."

WHAT WOULD YOU WANT TO SAY TO YOUR FANS, BOOSTERS, AND ALUMNI WHO HAVE SUPPORTED YOU ALL THESE YEARS? "I can't say enough for those people who stuck with me all those years. I never will forget those good people."

HOW DO YOU WANT YOUR COACHING EPITAPH TO READ — HOW DO YOU WANT TO BE REMEMBERED AS A COACH? "He worked hard and tried his best."

DON BROSE
COLLEGE HOCKEY: MINNESOTA STATE MANKATO

Born and raised in St. Louis Park, Don Brose received his bachelor's degree in 1962 from Concordia College in Moorhead, where he earned 12 varsity letters in hockey, baseball and football. Brose then went on to earn his master's degree in physical education from the University of Maryland in 1964, while coaching freshman baseball for the Terps as well. Brose later returned to Minnesota and assumed the football and baseball coaching duties at Heron Lake High School before joining the Minnesota State Mankato coaching staff in 1965. Brose, who was serving at the time as a baseball assistant to Jean McCarthy, was asked to start Mankato's hockey program in 1969. He agreed, and the rest they say, is hockey history.

From 1969-2000 Brose accumulated a 536-335-79 record with the Mavericks and posted winning records in 26 of his 30 years at the helm. In addition, nearly three dozen of his best players went on to earn All-American honors, with countless others going on to play in the professional ranks. Brose's Mavericks made it to the NCAA national tourney on 11 different occasions, with the pinnacle coming in 1980, when they won an NCAA Division II national title. In addition, the 1979 and 1991 squads finished as the national runners up, the 1978 and 1981 teams took third, while the 1986 club placed fourth. For his efforts, Brose was named as the American Hockey Coaches Association Coach of the Year in 1980 and the Northern Collegiate Hockey Association Coach of the Year in 1987 as well.

Brose was also very active in the promotion of hockey. He was a member and chairman of the NCAA Ice Hockey Committee; was selected to the coaching staff of the national Midget Camp (1981, 1982 and 1985) in Colorado Springs; and was a member of the coaching staff of the 1992 US Olympic Trials. Brose was also selected to a four-year term on the Board of Governors of the AHCA and was the AHCA's president from 1992-94. In addition, Brose served as the president of the WIHA and was also the chairman of the NCAA rules committee for seven years. A true student of the game, Brose even spent the 1984 season studying and learning European hockey techniques in Sweden, and also studied in Russia for three weeks in 1976 as well.

With a rock-solid work ethic and a firm commitment to his kids, Brose, a tenacious taskmaster, was the driving force behind getting the Mankato program to where it is today. "This is a dream come true," he said of finally getting his program elevated to division one status. "The progress has been long, but amazing. It is hard to believe we started as a club team with no indoor or outdoor hockey rink in Mankato. Thanks to the tremendous support of the Mankato community and leadership from several individuals, MSU and Mankato can be very proud of the new heights reached by MSU Hockey."

Minnesota State hockey and Don Brose have become synonymous with one another. Starting from scratch back in the late 1960s, Brose built Mankato hockey from nothing into one of the nation's top small-college programs through a lot of hard work and dedication. His teams earned a "lunch bucket" reputation for their spirit and desire, both direct reflections of their tireless leader. Now standing 11th on the NCAA's all-time win list with 536, Don Brose is a Minnesota hockey institution. Don is presently retired and lives in the Mankato area with his family.

HOW WOULD YOU DESCRIBE YOUR COACHING STYLE? "I always tried to teach life and hockey was my median for teaching that. It was all about honesty, integrity and morality, that

was my style. And it was all about the little things. Like table manners when we went out to eat, or how to treat people — I just wanted to try and teach things that would carry on later in life with my players. That was important to me."

HOW DID YOU MOTIVATE YOUR PLAYERS? "I always tried to encourage them to be the best that they could be and if they settled for anything less than that then they were cheating themselves. And, I wanted them to know that they were not only cheating themselves, they were also cheating their teammates, their coaches, and their school."

WHO WERE YOUR COACHING MENTORS? "I would say Jake Christiansen, my football coach at Concordia. He taught me so much about coaching and about life."

WHAT IS THE KEY TO TIME MANAGEMENT? "You just have to be organized. Period. I even took care of all of the small piddly things so that my assistants could be involved in more of the recruiting. That was important because as a head coach you don't get a chance to get out as much and identify talent. I always had good assistants and I wanted them to get out there and see as many kids as possible."

WHAT ROLE DID YOU FAMILY PLAY WHILE YOU WERE COACHING? "The were very supportive. It was very difficult during the first part of my coaching career because we had three young kids and my wife was terminally ill. So, that was a very tough struggle for me. Then I remarried and she has been very supportive. She was a school teacher so she understood what it took to be a teacher and coach, and she has just always been there for me."

WHAT ARE THE CHARACTERISTICS OF WINNERS? "Winners want to get to the next level. They want to identify how to be successful. They respect the integrity of the game. They want to always get better and they will work at it. They don't count on their skill, but rather they count on how to get the best out of that skill."

LOOKING BACK WHAT ARE YOU MOST PROUD OF IN YOUR CAREER? "I think trying to teach individuals that hockey was a medium for life. You know, we always wanted to win, but it was a method for teaching other things. I would hope that my players would say that I was always trying to teach lessons through hockey. I have had some great kids here through the years too, and I am proud of all of that."

WHAT WAS THE KEY TO RECRUITING? "I would say it is a combination of identification, communication and being able to determine the potential from players that might not have reached their full potential at that time."

ON MANKATO HOCKEY GOING DIVISION ONE: "It's really been a thrill of a lifetime to see how far this program has come. When I first came to Mankato I was hired to serve as the assistant baseball coach. Shortly thereafter they asked me if I wanted to start a hockey program. I remember asking where the arena was. The athletic director then told me that they didn't have an arena. So I asked where the outdoor rink was, and he said that they didn't have one of those either. So, I went to the recreation director and he wound up calling Gustavus and they ended up loaning us a set of goalie pads. We then scrounged up another pair of pads and put together a four team intramural league. Then, from the best players of those four teams we put together a club team. We then went around and played the local colleges and even some high schools, and just tried to get better. That next year we rounded up enough money to build a new outdoor rink. So, from 1965-73 we were an outdoor program. It was tough just to get to that point. We were playing our games all over the place and the administration really wanted to kill the program. I think we had like two home games scheduled one season because we kept getting rained out or the ice would melt. Then, in 1974 we got All Seasons Arena built on campus and we have been chugging along ever since. So, to see that go from Division III to Division II, where we won a national championship, to now Division One, is just amazing. Now, we have such a beautiful new arena and the entire community has just embraced us. We are playing some great hockey now too, and that is very gratifying to see. It has been a real journey, but one that I am very proud to have been a part of. You just couldn't draw it up any better in my opinion."

HOW DID YOU BUILD TEAM UNITY & CHEMISTRY? "We just tried to create an environment where there would be good interaction and communication between the players and the coaches. We also tried to get the captains involved as much as possible too. I always tried to make sure that the captains were elected on a leadership basis and not on a popularity basis. I also explained to the captains that I was going to be very hard on them and that they would have to be on a different wave length because they would be the go-betweens between the players and coaches."

WHAT MOTIVATED YOU? "Pride and really trying to be the best that I could be."

WHAT'S THE BIGGEST THING YOU'VE LEARNED FROM COACHING THAT YOU'VE BEEN ABLE TO APPLY TO YOUR EVERYDAY LIFE? "Integrity, honesty and always trying to be the best you can be — whether it is in society, in school or on the ice."

WHAT ARE THE KEY INGREDIENTS TO CREATING A CHAMPIONSHIP TEAM? "I would say it is a combination of communication, goal setting and solid player interaction with the coaches."

WHAT'S THE SECRET TO YOUR SUCCESS? "I am just so proud of what this program has become and so proud of all of our kids and what they have brought to this university and to this community. I feel that the program continually steps to a new level and I am so excited about Maverick Hockey, it really is a great success story."

WHAT WOULD YOU WANT TO SAY TO YOUR FANS, BOOSTERS, AND ALUMNI WHO HAVE SUPPORTED YOU ALL THESE YEARS? "Hey! Thanks for a great ride! The fans were just awesome, the players were great and I am very pleased that they gave me an opportunity to reach some of my goals and dreams and I hope that they got a lot in return too."

HOW DO YOU WANT YOUR COACHING EPITAPH TO READ — HOW DO YOU WANT TO BE REMEMBERED AS A COACH? "That he brought a program from being non-existent to a division one model for success. Twice his program was nearly eliminated, once from the university and the other from the state university board, but that never stopped him from continually trying to strive to get to that next level."

ANDY MURRAY: SHATTUCK ST. MARY'S HOCKEY

Andy Murray, originally from Gladstone, Manitoba, served as the head coach of the Shattuck-St. Mary's prep school team in Faribault in 1998, posting a 70-9-2 record that year en route to winning the U.S. Midget Triple-A title. Murray would leave Shattuck that next year, however, to take over as the head coach of the NHL's Los Angeles Kings, where he has been ever since. Murray, who also served as an assistant to North Stars head coach Glen Sonmor during the team's Cinderella Stanley Cup run of 1991, has spent nearly 25 years coaching the game of hockey.

MIKE KEMP: UNIVERSITY OF NEBRASKA-OMAHA HOCKEY

Mike Kemp grew up in Duluth and went on to graduate from Duluth East High School. Kemp then went on to play hockey at Gustavus, graduating in 1975. From there, Kemp's coaching career came full circle, starting and stopping in Omaha. You see, Kemp first came to the University of Nebraska-Omaha in the mid-1970s to serve as the head coach of the club hockey program. Hopes for club hockey to grow into a varsity program were slashed after one year, however, and Kemp returned to his alma mater, where he began a 20-year career as an assistant coach. Kemp spent five years as an assistant at Gustavus and then went to the University of Wisconsin in 1981, where he spent one year as an assistant under Bob Johnson. After a year as an assistant at the University of Illinois-Chicago, Kemp returned to the Badgers in 1983 under new head coach Jeff Sauer. As the head recruiter, Kemp secured some of the most talented players in Wisconsin history. Twelve went on to play in the Olympic Games, 16 earned first or second-team all-American honors, 44 were Western Collegiate Hockey Association all-academic team selections, and four were named player of the year in the WCHA. In addition, the Badgers won one WCHA regular season championship, four WCHA playoff titles, appeared in nine NCAA tournaments, finished runners up twice and won one national championship. Not bad! Then, in 1996, Kemp got the call to come back to the University of Nebraska-Omaha to serve as the program's first NCAA Division I varsity head hockey coach. Since then, Kemp has built the program into an emerging CCHA power. In 2000 UNO defeated 10 of 11 different CCHA opponents while ending the season with a runner up finish at the conference tournament. For his efforts, Kemp was a finalist for both the CCHA Coach of the Year Award and the Spensor Penrose Trophy for National Coach of the Year honors. The Mavericks continued their success in 2001 by posting a school-record 24 wins and Kemp was again a finalist for national coach of the year honors. Then, in 2002 UNO posted 21 wins and was ranked as high as No. 5 in the national polls. Now entering his seventh season with UNO, Kemp has posted a career record of 97-114-23. Kemp, an active member of the American Hockey Coaches Association, is also an avid runner and has competed in the Boston Marathon. Mike and his wife Julie presently reside in Omaha and have two children: Emily and Sarah.

BRAD BUETOW
COLLEGE HOCKEY: UNIVERSITY OF MINNESOTA

Brad Buetow grew up in Mounds View and went on to become one of the school's best all-around athletes, earning all-state honors in football, track and hockey. On the ice, Brad and his twin brother Bart led their No. 1 ranked Mounds View High School team to the 1968 state high school hockey tournament, where they were upset by Coleraine in a double-overtime semifinal thriller. From there, Brad went on to play hockey, football and even competed as a high jumper on the track team at the University of Minnesota. He could do it all, and his grades didn't suffer either, as evidenced by the fact that he graduated summa cum laude in physical education from the U of M and later received his master's degree in psychology.

On the ice Brad was a scrappy, hard working forward who became a fan favorite at Williams Arena. After college he tried to make a go of it in the professional ranks with the Cleveland Crusaders of the World Hockey Association, but a knee injury cut short his career. Brad came home after that to teach at Breck High School before joining up with Herb Brooks' Gopher Hockey coaching staff in 1975. From 1975-79, Buetow served as Herbie's assistant, winning a pair of national championships along the way. Then, in 1980, when Herbie was named as the coach of the 1980 U.S. Olympic Hockey team, Buetow was named as Minnesota's interim coach. One year later, in his first full season as head coach, Buetow's Gophers won the WCHA and finished second in the nation. Buetow took them back to the NCAA Finals again that next year as well. He won another WCHA title again in 1983, but after that the Gophers took a back seat to the University of Minnesota-Duluth. UMD was tough in that stretch during the early 1980s, and the Gophers couldn't catch them. Many felt that Brad's "militaristic training methods and mandatory study sessions" were too tough. For whatever the reason, after seven very productive seasons he was let go. At the time of his firing Buetow had a 175-100-20 (.689) record, the winningest record of any active coach in college hockey.

Disappointed, Brad chose to take the high road, and went on to coach for three years at U.S. International University in San Diego. From there, he took over at Colorado College, where, over the next five years, he continued to recruit Minnesota kids and give them the opportunity to play hockey at the next level. In 1995, Buetow got into professional coaching, starting with the Quad City Mallards of the Colonial Hockey League, and spent the next several years working with various minor league teams.

In all, Buetow would coach for 20 years at the college level, posting a 296-235-20 career record, and earning coach of the year honors on three occasions. Buetow even served as the President of the American University Hockey Coaches Association at one point. Later, Brad started the Brad Buetow School of Hockey, which he has served as the director of now for nearly a quarter century.

Today Brad and his family live in Colorado Springs, where, in addition to scouting for the Detroit Red Wings, he runs hockey schools all across the nation as well as a Triple A elite youth program in Denver. One of America's premier college hockey coaches, Brad Buetow was truly one of the best of the best.

HOW WOULD YOU DESCRIBE YOUR COACHING STYLE? "I would like to think I did my homework on players and on teams so we were always well prepared. I think we really developed kids skill-wise and fundamentally-wise and mentally tried to make them a little more resilient and flexible for any situation. I think

it was an aggressive and ambitious style. We played real fast and also played real physical, that was key."

HOW DID YOU MOTIVATE YOUR PLAYERS? "I think at the collegiate level most kids are self motivated. They are educated kids who want to achieve goals and succeed. So, for me it was really about being positive and encouraging them to be their best. I also pushed them a lot too. I really think that the best athletes like to be pushed and challenged."

WHAT DID IT MEAN FOR YOU TO BE A GOPHER? "It meant a great deal. Glen Sonmor gave my brother Bart and I the opportunity to be Gophers back when they only had three scholarships a year at the U of M and that was a dream come true. My roots are still very deep there, I mean I played there for five years and coached there for 12. Now, to see them have this success, with the two national championships, it is just great to see. I am very proud of what they have done."

IF YOU COULD MAGICALLY GO BACK IN TIME TO THE FIRST YEAR YOU WERE A HEAD COACH AND GIVE YOURSELF SOME ADVICE FOR THE FUTURE, KNOWING WHAT YOU KNOW NOW, BACK THEN, WHAT WOULD YOU SAY TO YOURSELF? "I would tell myself to enjoy it a little more. I was very hard driven and was a work-aholic. Sure, we had great success, but I would say looking back it would have been nice to just enjoy the journey a little bit more."

WHAT ARE THE CHARACTERISTICS OF WINNERS? "They are confident, not cocky, and not intimidated by other people or other situations."

WHAT DOES LOYALTY MEAN TO YOU? "That is the number one thing in my mind. Loyalty is first and work ethic is number two. People can learn X's and O's but loyalty is special."

LOOKING BACK WHAT ARE YOU MOST PROUD OF IN YOUR CAREER? "I really worked hard for kids and tried to help them have good experiences so that they could be successful both on and off the ice.

WHAT WAS THE KEY TO RECRUITING? "It is just doing your homework and getting out and seeing a lot of games. I remember when I was a head coach I used to see close to 200 hockey games a year. Every day after practice I would race around town to see two or three games a night. It was tough, but that was what you had to do in order to be successful at that level."

HOW DID YOU BUILD TEAM UNITY & CHEMISTRY? "You try to put kids into the best light with each other so that they have an opportunity to shine. If you do that then the kids will gain a lot of self respect as well as respect from their teammates. It is important to remember though that having a lot of different personalities is good for the team. That is what makes a team diverse and successful. It is just bringing them all together as one to be successful, that is the key."

WHAT IS THE KEY TO GOOD TIME MANAGEMENT? "I think you have to allow your assistants to be directly involved. For me that was Mike Foley, he was my top assistant for years and I learned a great deal from him. He was a fantastic coach. So, you have to just utilize those people so that you can focus on whatever it is that you need to be focusing on."

WHAT MOTIVATED YOU? "I would say the challenge. That is why I loved coaching at the collegiate level. You had all week to formalize a game plan and then you could go out and execute it on the weekends. In the pros it was much different. I worked six years in the pros and there it was all about keeping your guys rested. So, to see your kids at the college level respond to your different tactics was very gratifying."

WHAT ADVICE WOULD YOU HAVE FOR YOUNG COACHES STARTING OUT TODAY? "To just be all ears. Young coaches are impatient because they want to become head coaches. They just have to be patient. There is a lot to learn and not just on paper. You have to pay your dues. I mean I was an assistant for six years and got paid about $3,000 a year. I certainly wasn't doing it for the money but I needed to learn as much as possible in order to advance my career."

WHAT'S THE BIGGEST THING YOU'VE LEARNED FROM COACHING THAT YOU'VE BEEN ABLE TO APPLY TO YOUR EVERYDAY LIFE? "Be persistent and don't give up. You are going to have your peaks and valleys along the way, but if you stay with it then good things will happen. Just don't get down, and if you do, don't get down too far. You will get back up with time."

WHAT ARE THE KEY INGREDIENTS TO CREATING A CHAMPIONSHIP TEAM? "You have to have some leaders who are good in the locker room and who can motivate your kids in practice. Beyond that you really need solid goaltending that peaks at the right time."

WHAT'S THE SECRET TO YOUR SUCCESS? "I think you just have to believe in yourself. I took over from Herb Brooks, but I never tried to be Herb Brooks. I just tried to be Brad Buetow and I thought I did a pretty good job. I just had a passion for the game, worked hard and loved being around it."

WHAT WOULD YOU WANT TO SAY TO YOUR FANS, BOOSTERS, AND ALUMNI WHO HAVE SUPPORTED YOU ALL THESE YEARS? "Thanks for everything, I enjoyed every minute of it. The fans in Minnesota are the best. I mean to walk up those old wooden steps from the locker room at old Mariucci Arena with the band playing the rouser and the fans going crazy, it was amazing. My heart used to pump 100 mph and I would get goose bumps. I mean that says it all right there! It was a great atmosphere and the people there were great to me."

HOW DO YOU WANT YOUR COACHING EPITAPH TO READ — HOW DO YOU WANT TO BE REMEMBERED AS A COACH? "He was a hard working, fair person."

COONEY WEILAND: NHL's BOSTON BRUINS

Ralph "Cooney" Weiland, who starred for the Minneapolis Millers for four seasons from 1925-29, would go on to play for 11 seasons in the NHL as a member of the Boston Bruins' famous "Dynamite Line." After his playing career, the Ontario native went into coaching. As coach of the Bruins, Weiland led his boys to a Stanley Cup title in 1941. Weiland would later spend four seasons as coach of the American Hockey League's Hershey Bears before going on to take over as the head coach at Harvard University in 1950. Weiland would guide the Crimson for the next 21 years before retiring in 1971. That same year, Weiland was inducted into the Hockey Hall of Fame.

BILL BUTTERS: GOPHER HOCKEY

Bill Butters grew up in White Bear Lake and went on to graduate from White Bear Lake High School. From there, Butters played hockey at the University of Minnesota under legendary coaches Glen Sonmor and Herb Brooks from 1971-73. Butters immediately made an impression on Brooks for being a tremendous team player. As a result, Butters would be named captain of the team during his senior year.

The sturdy defenseman then turned pro at the age of 22 in 1973, signing with the Oklahoma City Blazers of the CHL. During his rookie season he scored 25 points while racking up 174 penalty minutes in a league known for its toughness. Butters began the following year back in Oklahoma City, but went on to sign a contract with the Minnesota Fighting Saints of the WHA later that season. Butters played for the Saints during that next 1975-76 season as well, but was traded to the Houston Aeros for the last 14 games of the year. He would sign with the Fighting Saints as a free agent following that season, only to be shipped off again, this time to the Edmonton Oilers, followed by the New England Whalers just seven games later. Butters remained with the Whalers until midway through the 1977-78 season, when he jumped to the NHL and signed a contract with the Minnesota North Stars. Butters returned to the North Stars in 1979, before retiring with the Oklahoma City Stars of the CHL that next year, ending his pro career in the city where it all began seven years earlier. As a player, Butters was known for his ability to clear away opposing forwards from in front of his net. He was tough, he was loyal and his teammates loved him.

"You can find a good many defenseman who command greater skills than Billy, but I don't think you'll find anyone, anywhere who plays the game with more intensity," said Butters' former coach, Glen Sonmor.

Butters then came home, where he spent the next five years as an assistant at Breck High School. Then, in 1985, Butters came back to Gold Country to serve as an assistant under Doug Woog. He would work as an assistant with the Gophers from 1985-88 and then again from 1991-94, specializing in scouting, recruiting and working with the team's defenseman. Butters would later go on to coach at Bethel College from 1995-98, where his son, Ben, earned All-American honors as a defenseman.

Several years ago Butters got out of coaching to get into teaching. Butters now spends his time working for Hockey Ministries International, which, among other things, runs Christian hockey camps throughout North America. More recently, Butters was honored when he was asked to give the eulogy at Herb Brooks' funeral in August of 2003. "Herbie was a father figure to me," said Bill. "I love the guy like a lot of us did. It's humbling and an honor to be able to honor the man. He did so much for guys like me." A man of great faith and character, Bill and his wife Debby presently reside in the Twin Cities and have three children: Ben, Anne and Rebecca.

KEVIN CONSTANTINE
PRO HOCKEY: SAN JOSE, PITTSBURGH & NEW JERSEY

Kevin Constantine grew up in International Falls loving the game of hockey and would go on to play goalie under legendary International Falls High School hockey coach Larry Ross. From there, Constantine went on to play between the pipes at Rensselaer Polytechnic Institute from 1977-80 and was later a ninth-round draft pick of the Montreal Canadiens. Constantine failed in his effort to make it with the Canadiens, however, and moved to Reno, Nev., where he finished his business degree at the University of Nevada-Reno. There, Constantine got the coaching bug and wound up taking over the local Junior C team. It would be the beginning of a very successful coaching career.

In 1985 Constantine was hired to serve as the new head coach of the United States Hockey League's North Iowa franchise. The team went 17-31 in Constantine's only season, but two years later he was offered another job coaching the USHL's Rochester team. This time Constantine made it count, leading led the Mustangs to a 39-7-2 record and the 1988 USHL championship. Constantine, who was just 29 years old at that point, then took his players one step further by winning the National U.S. Junior A championship. That success in turn helped him earn an assistant coaching job with the Kalamazoo Wings of the International Hockey League. He would spend the next three seasons with the Wings, which won the IHL East Division crown in 1991.

That same year Constantine was hired to coach the San Jose Sharks' top IHL affiliate in Kansas City. There, Constantine led the Blades to a 56-22-4 record and the IHL championship in 1992. For his efforts, Constantine was named as the IHL Coach of the Year. That next year the Blades dominated, giving Constantine a two-year IHL record of 102-48-14. As a result, Constantine got the call he had been waiting for — he was headed to the "show." At just 34 years of age, Kevin Constantine became the youngest coach in the NHL when he took over as the new head coach of the San Jose Sharks in 1993. Considered by many to be one of hockey's hottest coaching prospects, Constantine didn't disappoint. During his rookie year as an NHL head coach, Constantine led the Sharks to their first ever playoff berth after an incredible 58-point improvement in the standings. Constantine's '94 Sharks then shocked Detroit in seven games to reach the second round of the playoffs, where they took Toronto to another seven games before their dramatic run ended. After the playoffs, he finished as the runner-up for NHL coach of the year honors.

Proving the 1994 playoffs were no fluke, the Sharks went back to the postseason in 1995. This time San Jose stunned Calgary in another seven-game series, before bowing out in the next round. When the Sharks' run of success finally ended with a dismal 1996 season, however, Kevin was the team's first casualty. He found work pretty quickly though, as an assistant coach with the Calgary Flames in 1997. Constantine wasn't there long though, as that Summer he was hired as the new head coach of the Pittsburgh Penguins.

Pittsburgh would not be an easy fix. Constantine inherited a Penguins squad that had just said goodbye to one of NHL's all-time greats in Mario Lemieux and could not come to contract terms with their star forward, Petr Nedved. Just when it seemed like it was all going to fall apart, their new coach led them to an amazing 40-24-18 season and a Northeast Division Championship — it was the fourth best showing in franchise history. It got tougher from there though, and Kevin was ultimately let go in 2000. That next year Constantine was hired in mid-season to take over as the head coach of the New Jersey Devils. Despite the fact that he led the Devils to a 20-8-3 record during the final 31 games of the 2001-02 season, he was let go

at year's end.

From there Kevin went back to the Steel City, where he founded the Pittsburgh Forge Junior A hockey team, competing in the North American Hockey League. As the team's general manager and coach, Kevin helped build the Forge into a national power, winning the national junior championship in 2003. In his two seasons with the Forge, Kevin's clubs amassed an overall record of 80-24-8 and advanced 18 players onto scholarships with Division I college hockey programs. Then, in the Summer of 2003, in addition to serving as a hockey color analyst on TV and running a $20 million sports complex in Pittsburgh, Kevin was hired to serve as the first ever head coach of the expansion Everett, Wa., Silvertips Major Junior team.

In all, Kevin Constantine has spent 378 games at the top of his profession, accumulating an overall record of 159-153-66 with the San Jose Sharks (1993-96), the Pittsburgh Penguins (1997-00) and the New Jersey Devils (2001-02). He remains the only coach in NHL history to take two eighth-seeded teams to first-round Stanley Cup Playoff upsets (San Jose over Detroit in 1994 and Pittsburgh over New Jersey in 1999). In addition to his many coaching accolades, Kevin has also been honored by USA Hockey, which serves as the governing body over all amateur hockey in the United States, with their Distinguished Achievement Award. The award is given annually to a United States citizen judged to have made the most outstanding contribution as a professional to the sport of ice hockey in the U.S.

Presently, Kevin and his family are residing in Everett, Wa., but since he still has a lot of family back in International Falls, he spends his Summers back home and on Gull Lake in Brainerd.

HOW WOULD YOU DESCRIBE YOUR COACHING STYLE? "I would say that for starters that I hate to lose and some of my players might even say that I hate to tie. I think I am passionate, detailed, thorough, organized, prepared and intensely dedicated towards the process of winning."

HOW DO YOU MOTIVATE YOUR PLAYERS? "You know, it goes back to the sign that I always hang in my locker rooms: 'WIN is an acronym for what's important next.' And what that means is we always need to be thinking about what comes next in whatever it is that we are doing. I mean, if we win a game, great. We can celebrate. But what's important next? We need to refocus for the next game. Or if we score a goal, great. But what's important next? We need to try even harder to score again on that next shift and focus so that we can win the game. So, I try to motivate my players by continuously preparing them for the future, whether that is in five minutes or five days. Beyond that I also try to get my players to buy into the process of winning where we find things that we can do better than our opponents and just focusing on those things. We will concede things that we are not better at, but when we focus and work on the numerous little things that we are better at, then we can beat anybody."

LOOKING BACK WHAT ARE YOU MOST PROUD OF IN YOUR CAREER? "I am proud of the positive influence that I have had on the players which I have coached. I hope that I have had an impact on their lives through giving them a foundation to believe in. I have also been able to turn teams around in a hurry through a lot of hard work and by getting my players to buy into my philosophy. In addition to two national championships at the junior A level, and one IHL championship, I was also very proud of my accomplishments with the San Jose Sharks. When I first came to San Jose they had the worst record in the National Hockey League. After my first year we finished 58 points better, which is still an NHL record, and beat Detroit in the first round of the playoffs. That meant a lot to me."

HOW DO YOU BUILD TEAM UNITY & CHEMISTRY? "I have always believed the best way to build chemistry is to have a common set of rules to guide behavior. What that does is it puts everybody on an equal footing. If you don't have that then you are creating different rules for different people. Then there is a fairness, and within that everyone understands that the team and its set of rules is more important than any individual player and their wishes. That then creates of sense of 'we are in this together' amongst your players. I have always felt that the team goal and the behavior that the players show towards that goal will bring a team together. So, if that goal is strong enough that everybody believes in it, and if the plan is good enough where everyone is working towards it, and if discipline and behavior are administered based on those goals, then everybody is going to feel like they are a part of something bigger than themselves. Through that you will have chemistry, guaranteed."

WHAT MOTIVATES YOU? "I think the fear of losing is a much more powerful motivator than winning. I also really enjoy the process of having a group that doesn't necessarily believe that when you walk into the room for the very first time that they are capable of accomplishing incredible things. Then, to start that long day by day process of getting better, and to see your players start to believe in themselves, that really motivates me."

WHAT ADVICE WOULD YOU HAVE FOR YOUNG COACHES STARTING OUT TODAY? "The first thing I would tell them is that this had better be something that they love. Then, until they reach the pro level they are probably not going to get paid a lot. And, they are not going to have a lot of time on their hands because this is very time consuming. So, if those things don't bother them during their formative years of coaching, then go for it because the rewards of working with people and watching them grow and develop is amazing. After that I would just say be yourself and don't be afraid to show the things that they are great at. As for the things they are not great at, watch and learn and study from others, but don't change who you are. Just remember, there are a million different ways to coach and be successful. Finally, you have to stick with it. You know, one third of all NHL coaches get fired every year. So, you are going to have failures along the way, but you have to just hang in there."

WHAT'S THE BIGGEST THING YOU'VE LEARNED FROM COACHING THAT YOU'VE BEEN ABLE TO APPLY TO YOUR EVERYDAY LIFE? "I am a strong believer in the thinking of anything you want bad enough you can go out and get it, and I am living proof of that. I certainly had neither history, pedigree or player accomplishments to warrant me being in the NHL, let alone becoming a coach in the NHL. But I was willing to pay the price to work hard and dedicate myself. So, I look at myself in the mirror and say 'hey, if I can get to the NHL, then any athlete willing to dedicate himself towards his goals, can certainly have a good shot at getting their too.' I guess I think desire is more powerful than athletic ability."

WHAT ARE THE KEY INGREDIENTS TO CREATING A CHAMPIONSHIP TEAM? "Well, as much as us coaches want to think that we are a major factor in the outcome in teams, it is still the personnel that gets it done out on the ice. As coaches we are very dependent upon the players that we are given by the GMs and scouts. Within that, a coach can have a great influence on how that talent performs. Certainly a great example of that would be the Minnesota Wild of 2003. On paper that team was very average but Jacques Lemaire did a masterful job with those guys and got them to buy into his sys-

tem. That was a great story. But, in hockey I would say without a doubt the main ingredient to creating a championship team would be your goaltender. Goaltenders and defense win championships. History has proven that a good defense beats a good offense, so you have to have a solid structure of defense to compliment your offense. So, that is where it starts."

WHAT'S THE SECRET TO YOUR SUCCESS? "You have to instantly set a goal and it has got to be something greater than people on an individual basis thought was ever possible. Then, you have to lay out a game plan. Now, the players have something to buy into. From there you have to work extremely hard. Once you start having success, it is contagious."

WHAT WOULD YOU WANT TO SAY TO YOUR FANS, BOOSTERS, AND ALUMNI WHO HAVE SUPPORTED YOU ALL THESE YEARS? "You know, I am so fortunate to have the opportunity to make my living through the sport of hockey. The fans to me are my lifeline because they support what I do, so I will always be very appreciate and grateful to them."

HOW DO YOU WANT YOUR COACHING EPITAPH TO READ — HOW DO YOU WANT TO BE REMEMBERED AS A COACH? "I would want to be remembered as someone who loved the game, someone who loved to coach, someone who loved to watch his players move on to achieve their own personal and career goals, and someone who loved to hang out in a hockey rink. You know, there is a saying on a plaque in my den that reads 'Hockey is not a matter of life and death… it is much more important than that.'. I would have to agree. Hockey is my life and I really do love it."

JOHN PERPICH: ST. CLOUD STATE HOCKEY

John Perpich grew up in Hibbing and went on to play hockey for the Gophers from 1972-74, scoring 27 total points. From there, Perpich played professionally, including a stint with the St. Paul Fighting Saints in the late 1970s. Perpich later got into coaching and in 1984 he took over as the head coach at St. Cloud State. Although Perpich would only stay for two seasons in St. Cloud, he led the Huskies to back-to-back winning seasons and renewed interest in Husky hockey. During his tenure, Perpich posted a 30-24-4 record, highlighted by his 1985 second-place finish in the NCHA. The following season the Huskies recorded a 16-11-2 overall record and finished fifth in the league. Perpich left the Huskies in 1986 to become the head coach at Ferris State, a Division I school in Michigan, where he would coach for four seasons. Perpich's career collegiate coaching record would stand at 84-116-21. Perpich later got into scouting and is presently a full-time scout with the NHL's Atlanta Thrashers.

CRAIG DAHL
COLLEGE HOCKEY: ST. CLOUD STATE

Craig Dahl grew up in Albert Lea and graduated from Albert Lea High School in 1971. From there, Dahl attended the University of Minnesota on a football scholarship. He stayed for one season, but later decided to transfer to Pacific Lutheran University in Tacoma, Wash., where he played football under Frosty Westering, graduating in 1976 with a degree in physical education and social sciences. Dahl began collegiate coaching at Bethel College in St. Paul in 1980. In his first five seasons, Bethel was 61-75 overall and the Royals were MIAC champions during his second season as well. The Royals made three consecutive conference playoff appearances under Dahl and eventually won the NAIA consolation title in 1984. Dahl was even named the MIAC Coach of the Year in 1985. From there, Dahl became the head coach at the University of Wisconsin-River Falls for one season before coming to St. Cloud State University to serve as an assistant to Herb Brooks during the 1986-87 season. That next year Dahl took over as head coach at SCSU while Herbie went on to take over as the new head coach of the North Stars. Herbie had taken the program from Division II status to NCAA Division I Independent, and then handed the keys to Dahl. Coach Dahl has been going strong at St. Cloud State ever since.

In fact, Dahl has built the Husky program into a national power. This upcoming season will mark his 23rd overall as a head collegiate coach, having posted a 382-357-47 career record. Dahl has 306 wins with the Huskies; a school record, eclipsing the previous record held by longtime coach Charlie Basch. He currently owns a 306-270-45 record at SCSU and has won 20-or-more games five times in the last seven seasons — including a school record 31 wins in 2001. Dahl has been the constant factor behind a program that continues to improve through 16 seasons of Division I hockey. The Huskies have advanced to the WCHA Final Five eight years running and nine times in the last 10 seasons (1994, 96-99, 2000-03). In 2001 the Huskies brought home their first WCHA hardware by winning the Broadmoor Trophy with a WCHA Final Five win over North Dakota.

The Huskies are now regulars in the NCAA Division I Tournament and are on a roll, making it four straight from 2000-03. (Who knows? Maybe they would have won it all by now had 17 of their best players decided to not leave school early to turn pro in the last seven years!) The 1998 WCHA Coach of the Year, Dahl has also coached five Division I All-Americans, including three in the last four seasons (Mike Pudlick in 2000, Scott Meyer in 2001 and Mark Hartigan in 2002. Hartigan was also a Hobey Baker Award top three finalist and led the nation in goal scoring in 2002.) In addition, SCSU has consistently been ranked among the nation's top 10 teams in the college polls since the 2000-01 season — including a No. 1 national ranking for several weeks in 2001-02.

Exciting hockey is not the only product of Dahl's program. Academics are just as important as winning, as evidenced by the fact that 61 SCSU players have been named to the WCHA All-Academic Team since the Huskies joined the league. Finally, the fans are loving every minute of Dahl's Huskies too. In fact, St. Cloud ranked among the nation's top 10 NCAA Division I programs for attendance in 2003. The Huskies, who set a new school record for average attendance last season, ranked 10th in the nation with an average attendance of 6,333 fans per game.

Craig Dahl is one of the nation's brightest young coaches and it will only be a matter of time before he hoists the hardware in the Granite City. Craig and his wife Lynn have two daughters, Shelby

Lynn and Cassidy Elizabeth, and reside in St. Cloud.

HOW WOULD YOU DESCRIBE YOUR COACHING STYLE? "I think you have to coach to your personality. If you try to be something that you are not, then your players will see through that immediately and lose respect for you. So, my personality is a little more laid back and low-key except when you get into the competition part of the game. I like my guys to follow the two phrases we always talk about in our program: 'work hard and work smart.' As long as they are working hard they are not going to hear too much from me other than the X's and O's. I just look at what we need to do everyday to make sure that we are making progress. The hardest thing I think for a coach to do is to step back and take a long term view and realistically assess what it is you are doing. You have to ask yourself where your program is at and what kind of a year it is going to be. Is it going to be a rebuilding year or are you going to contend for the title this year? Some things you can control, like team morale, while others you can't, like injuries, and it is hard to stay on an even keel when things you can't control happen to you."

HOW DO YOU MOTIVATE YOUR PLAYERS? "I think in this day and age you have to motivate your kids from their standpoint of 'What's in it for me?'. I just try to make sure that they understand that we are trying to help them further their careers, if that is their goal, that we are trying to make them a better player, and that we are trying to teach them some values and principles that they can take with them after hockey. We talk a lot about the psychology of them bettering themselves and the value-inducement type of ideas that they can use down the road. Once they see that you know what you are talking about, then they become intrinsically motivated. That is when you can really help them get better. Beyond that, I constantly clip articles about motivation out of the newspaper and give them to my kids to inspire them. I didn't know if the kids liked that kind of thing, but then at the end of the year I got 100% positive feedback on our end-of-year evaluations about them. I was shocked, but it turns out that our kids do in fact like that kind of thing."

WHO WERE YOUR COACHING MENTORS? "My football coach at Pacific Lutheran, Frosty Westering, he was just a legend. He had a completely different philosophy and approach to sports. It wasn't based on wins and losses, it was based on being the best you could be. He believed that each time you went out there, whether it was at a practice or in a game, that you should try to play to your fullest potential, as hard as you could and as well as you could. He was just a wonderful man and I learned a great deal from him. In fact, after I got to know him, I changed my major from business to education so that I could go into coaching and teaching. Then, after that it was definitely Herbie (Brooks). He really taught me about details and about winning. Spending a year together here at St. Cloud State was an incredible experience. He was such a great coach and good friend."

WHAT ADVICE WOULD YOU HAVE FOR YOUNG COACHES STARTING OUT TODAY? "One of the things that I did when I was younger was to seek out advice from more experienced coaches whenever I could. I called guys like Herb Brooks, Gino Gasparini, Brad Buetow, Mike Sertich and Ed Saugestad to ask them about systems, strategy and about life on the road. It was invaluable. I just think that young coaches, myself included, think they know more than they actually do and get threatened by people who actually do know more and have more experience. So, I would just say ask as much advice that you can from other coaches who you respect. The old guys, those mentors, have been through it all before you and will usually help if you just ask."

LOOKING BACK WHAT ARE YOU MOST PROUD OF IN YOUR CAREER? "I would say one of the things that makes me the most proud is when you have a former player call you up five to 10 years after he's graduated and he tells you how much it meant for him to play for you and that now he understands exactly what you were talking about way back when. That is very special to see and I get great internal gratification from that. Then, externally, I am very proud of starting this program from scratch at the division one level and now to be in the NCAA tournament the last four years has been just amazing. Winning the WCHA Final Five championship was so gratifying because there is nothing like the first time."

WHAT IS THE KEY TO RECRUITING? "You have to work at it every day. Recruiting now is a 12 month process and there is nothing that can take the place of using the phones, beating the bushes and going out and looking at prospects. Everybody knows who the top players are, the real key is to find out who the guys are which might have the potential to be great players down the road. So, you have to talk to a lot of people and find out as much as you can about them by establishing relationships. Then, after physically seeing them play and seeing how big, how fast and strong they are, you have to evaluate whether or not you think they has what it takes to play at the next level. Beyond that you just have to sell those kids on your philosophy and on your school atmosphere. We have had 44 straight sell-outs up here and our fans are just electric, so we need those kids to see that and get excited about playing for us."

HOW DO YOU BUILD TEAM UNITY & CHEMISTRY? "First of all, your one on one communication with your kids is really important. Secondly, I meet with my captains once a week to touch base with them and get their feedback about different things. That gives the players a voice, a say in what is going on, and then they feel like they are more able to lead the others. Then, it is how you treat your players, and I try to treat all of them with respect. The problem with that is that a lot of times players equate respect with playing time and as a coach you don't really view it that way. Instead, as a coach you view playing time with performance and not with personality. This is where the communication factor has to come in."

WHAT MOTIVATES YOU? "Aside from the competition, I genuinely want to see my players get better as players and as people. That is an intrinsic thing with me and it makes me feel like what I am doing is important when I see these young men develop on and off the ice. When they start to develop a value system of their own that I think will help them to be successful later in life, then I get very motivated."

FAVORITE LOCKER ROOM SIGN? "Practice like a champion, approach academics like a champion and play like a champion."

WHAT'S THE BIGGEST THING YOU'VE LEARNED FROM COACHING THAT YOU'VE BEEN ABLE TO APPLY TO YOUR EVERYDAY LIFE? "Working hard and understanding the ups and downs in life. You are going to have good days and bad days, but you can't let the good days be too high or the bad days be too low, you have to stay on an even keel. If your kids understand that you are genuinely trying to help them, then by in large you are going to be successful."

WHAT ARE THE KEY INGREDIENTS TO CREATING A CHAMPIONSHIP TEAM? "Talent is number one. After that you need unity and I think the 2003 Minnesota Wild were a great example of that. Lastly, you need belief. The guys have to believe in your plan and they have to buy into it to be successful."

WHAT'S THE SECRET TO YOUR SUCCESS? "I think you have to surround yourself with good people, and that might mean bringing in an assistant that does well what you don't. Then, you need to be organized. You need to plan your work and then work your plan. Lastly, you need to communicate well not only with your players, but with your administrators and educators who are around you so that they understand what you are trying to do with you program and where your philosophy is. I think the best way to describe my philosophy is that it is 'educational athletics,' not 'professional athletics.' I am not a professional coach of professional athletes, I am a professional coach of college athletes. That is why education, integrity, honesty, responsibility, hard work and values are really so important to me."

WHAT WOULD YOU WANT TO SAY TO YOUR FANS, BOOSTERS, AND ALUMNI WHO HAVE SUPPORTED YOU ALL THESE YEARS? "We have just great, great fans here and they have been super supportive of us through the years. So, thanks to all of them, we couldn't do it without you. Husky hockey is a big source of community pride for these people and I am just proud to be a part of that. Win or lose, it is a big night out on the town up here and that is just a great thing. You know, it is like the Barry White song, "I just can't get enough of your love baby! That is how I feel about our fans up here, I just love them."

HOW DO YOU WANT YOUR COACHING EPITAPH TO READ — HOW DO YOU WANT TO BE REMEMBERED AS A COACH? "I would like to be remembered as a good, honest person who ran his program with integrity and tried to help all of his players become better people."

CHUCK DELICH: AIR FORCE HOCKEY

Chuck Delich, a native of Eveleth, went on to become the all-time leading scorer at the Air Force Academy and one of the top 10 scorers in the history of college hockey. (From 1974-77 Delich scored 156 goals and 123 assists for 279 career points.) Delich then went on to post a career record of 154-197-19 as the head coach of the Academy from 1985-97. Delich had taken over as the head coach for the Falcons from former Eveleth native John Matchefts, and was replaced by Bemidji native, Frank Serratore — making for a true Minnesota hat trick.

MIKE FOLEY
HIGH SCHOOL HOCKEY: ST. PAUL ACADEMY

Mike Foley grew up in St. Paul and graduated from Humboldt High School in 1960. Foley then went on to play college hockey in New York at Colgate University, where he served as the team's captain. After graduating with an English degree in 1964, Foley began his coaching career at a high school in nearby Hamilton, N.Y., while still coaching the Colgate freshman squad. Two years later Foley moved back to Minnesota, where he became an assistant coach at North St. Paul High School. Three years later Foley took over at St. Paul Academy, where he served as the head coach of the Eagles for eight years, winning an Independent League state title along the way. Then, in 1977, Foley, in addition to continuing his teaching at SPA, became as an assistant hockey coach under Herb Brooks at the University of Minnesota. Foley would stay with Herbie for three years and then continue for another five years in Gold Country under head coach Brad Buetow as well. In 1985 Foley left the Gophers to focus on teaching and on running his very successful Summer hockey school, which has been an institution in Minnesota for more than three decades now. In all, Foley has been at SPA for 35 years, teaching English and later also serving as the director of operations at the Academy. Mike presently lives in Mendota Heights with his family.

HOW WOULD YOU DESCRIBE YOUR COACHING STYLE? "I remind myself constantly that as a coach you are an educator, a mentor and a role model. It is important to never forget that this game exists for the kids. The kids aren't there to make you look good, you are there for the kids. Period. When you do that you sort of take a holistic approach and you realize that you are teaching life-long lessons and values. That is what it is all about. I also think that good coaches can put kids from various levels of the game into meaningful roles. Once a coach can sell that kid on playing that role, then he will be able to create a unified team."

HOW DID YOU MOTIVATE YOUR PLAYERS? "Once you identify the roles that each player should play, and make them realize how important that role is to the success of the team, whether it is playing on a checking line or being a penalty killer, then motivation comes easy. They have to know that they are just as important as the kid who scores 50 goals. One of the things I used to do was make written evaluations like every other week for each kid on the team. It was maybe just a paragraph or so and then I would post it in the locker room. It would highlight good things, track progress and then give them things that they could work on. This was a great motivational tool because it specifically gave each kid something to work on. Plus, I encouraged the kids to read the other evaluations as well. This got the other kids involved with understanding everyone's roles on the team. I also feel that to be an effective coach you have to have an eye where you can break down players' skills very specifically and analyze them. Then, you have be able to analyze team systems and be able to break that down as well. The specificity and follow-up of motivating this way was a very valuable tool."

HOW DID YOU BUILD TEAM UNITY & CHEMISTRY? "Chemistry begins with players understanding their roles. You have to be very open about those roles and have a lot of communication. That is the key. As a coach you have to have your hand on the pulse of the team so you don't let problems fester and grow. If you have regular one on one and team meetings with the kids, then that will

help. Again, you have to stress the fact that this is their team. I will also say that you have to earn your kids' respect. You can't operate just out of fear, that won't work. They also need to know that you care about them both on and off the ice as people. Networking those kids to colleges is also something I do to build chemistry, because then your kids know that you really care about them. And you have to care just as much about the bottom-enders as you do the top-enders. I also talk to them about all kinds of things outside of hockey and try to get to know them, that helps too. Hockey is just the means to teaching them about life, and that's what's important."

LOOKING BACK, WHAT ARE YOU MOST PROUD OF IN YOUR CAREER? You know, I have never really liked all of the glitz of coaching, I just liked to coach. I loved the kids and the greatest rewards are when these kids come back long after they graduated to see you and tell you that you made a difference in their lives. That is so gratifying to think that you had an impact on them. I always told my kids that they were always moving. It was just a question of whether they were moving ahead or moving backwards. I wanted to instill in them that they can't stand still in life and that they should always go for their dreams."

HOW DO YOU WANT YOUR COACHING EPITAPH TO READ — HOW DO YOU WANT TO BE REMEMBERED AS A COACH? "That I was someone who really cared about the individual kids. And that the game existed for the kids and that I really existed for the kids as well. That was why I was there and that was why I was getting a paycheck, to totally help those kids. Teaching and coaching has been my life and I am very proud of that."

DAVE LANGEVIN:
MINOR LEAGUE HOCKEY

Dave Langevin, a Hill Murray and University of Minnesota-Duluth graduate who went on to win four Stanley Cup rings as a member of the New York Islanders from 1979-85, went on to pursue a career in coaching, starting first with the Idaho Steelheads of the West Coast Hockey League and later with the South Suburban Steers of the Minnesota Junior Hockey League.

CAL MARVIN: WARROAD LAKERS

One of the biggest reasons why Warroad has been dubbed "Hockeytown, U.S.A.," is due in large part to the efforts of one man, Cal Marvin, and his passion for the game of hockey. Cal has become not only synonymous with the most successful senior amateur hockey team in the country, the Warroad Lakers, but also with Minnesota hockey in general.

Warroad, a small town of some 1,700 people on the shores of the Lake of the Woods, is located just 10 miles south of the Manitoba border at the extreme tip of northwestern Minnesota. The town's biggest employer is Marvin Windows, which employs more than 3,000 locals to build and ship windows throughout the world. The owners of the company, the Marvin family, has been an intricate part of the fabric of the community for nearly a century. And luckily for Warroad hockey fans, Cal never wanted to get too involved with the day-to-day operations and management of his family's business, opting instead to pursue his love of hockey — something that would turn out to be a huge blessing in disguise.

The youngest of six children, Cal Marvin was born in 1924, in Warroad, where he grew up playing hockey on the area lakes and ponds. After high school Cal joined the Marine Corps, where he served in the South Pacific during World War II. After returning home from the service in 1946, Cal, along with several of his buddies decided to approach the University of North Dakota about the possibility of starting a new varsity hockey program at the school. The administration thought it would be a good idea, and with that, Cal went ahead and started the Fighting Sioux hockey program.

Cal spent the next several years recruiting players from around northern Minnesota to come to Grand Forks to play hockey. All the while, Cal decided to start another "senior" team back home in Warroad, which he called the Lakers. That way, Cal and his buddies could play hockey during the week at UND, and come home to play for the Lakers on the weekends.

In November of 1949, a significant event happened in the town of Warroad, the indoor Memorial Arena was opened. Affectionately called the "Gardens" by the locals, the arena was a big boost for the community's hockey programs. Cal had started the fund-raising effort to get the arena built two years earlier, and got much of the labor donated for free. Although the rink had no locker room facilities (the kids used to shower across the street from the rink at the Warroad Creamery after games), it was nonetheless a huge improvement from being outside during the frigid Warroad winters.

By the early 1950s the Lakers were competing in the Northwest Hockey League with Crookston, Roseau, Hallock, Thief River Falls and Grand Forks. Not only were they dominating their own league play, they were also whipping the best college teams in the country at that time as well. They had become regulars on many college schedules, including Murray Armstrong's tough Denver teams, as well as Michigan Tech, North Dakota and Minnesota-Duluth. The one team they didn't play, however, was John Mariucci's Gophers. Maroosh used to say: "Marvin, how dumb do you think I am? It doesn't do us any good if we beat you, and we look bad if we don't!"

In 1955 the Lakers had reached the pinnacle of amateur success by beating the Grand Falls (Montana) Americans to win the U.S. National Intermediate Championship. In addition to winning the Northwest Hockey League title, something else happened that next year that really put Warroad on the map. John Mariucci, the coach of the 1956 U.S. Olympic team, decided to have his squad play the Lakers before heading off to Italy. And, although Warroad lost the game (which was held in Eveleth) by the final of 6-2, nearly every U.S. Olympic team since then has kept that tradition alive by making the trek to Northern Minnesota to play the Lakers.

In 1957 Marvin coached the U.S. National team to a fifth-place finish at the World Championships in Oslo, Norway. His Lakers also became the first American sports team to play in the post-WWII Soviet Union. In 1959 the Lakers won the Ontario/Minnesota Hockey League's "Cranford Cup" title. The team went on to win two more consecutive league titles as they expanded into the international scene that year as well to seek out new competition. In 1960 the U.S. Olympic team (led by Lakers' Billy and Roger Christian) came back to town, where they were beaten by a 6-4 margin. Just a few weeks later, in Squaw Valley, Calif., that same team won the Olympic gold medal. The Lakers had become quite the test for college and Olympic squads. Soon other countries, including Sweden and Norway, were stopping in Warroad to take a crack at these kids.

In addition to serving as the manager of the 1965 U.S. National team, Cal guided his Lakers to Western Canada's "Allan Cup" finals, where they ultimately lost to Nelson, British Columbia. In addition, the team jumped over to the Manitoba Senior Hockey League that next year, where they won titles in 1965, 1969 and 1970. From there, the team continued to play well throughout Canada, winning the Western Canadian Intermediate Championship in 1971, Central Canadian Hockey League title in 1972, and Manitoba/Thunder Bay Intermediate Championship in 1973.

In January of 1985 the Lakers ended their college competition and joined the Southeastern Manitoba Hockey League, where they won titles in 1985, 1987 and 1989. Then, in 1991, the Lakers moved to the Central Amateur Senior Hockey (CASH) League, where they won the 1992 league title en route to advancing to the Allan Cup final-four.

In 1993 Cal's family stepped up to the plate big-time, when his brothers Tot and Jack donated more than a half-million dollars of the $4.5 million price tag for the "new" Warroad Gardens ice arena. The state-of-the-art facility then played host to the 1994 Allen Cup finals (the Stanley Cup of senior amateur hockey), becoming only the second U.S. city ever to do so. From there, the Lakers dynasty just continued to grow as they won the Allen Cup that next year as well.

By now, even though the Lakers were performing well, men's senior hockey seemed to be going by way of the dinosaur. The rise of high school and junior hockey had taken its toll on the leagues, with most folding in the 1980s and '90s. It was also taking its toll on Cal, who was getting tired of constantly battling to find a new league to play in, combined with the ever-increasing expenses of travel throughout Canada. While the Lakers decided to play in the Hanover-Tache League in 1996-97, Marvin painfully announced that after 50 years, it would be the team's final season.

A 50-year reunion was held on March 15th, 1997, the same day that Governor Arne Carlson proclaimed "Cal Marvin Day" throughout the state of Minnesota. It was a fitting celebration to a man who has become the venerable Godfather of hockey in Warroad. The Lakers helped countless kids who were in transition from moving from high school to college, or from college to U.S. National or pro teams. Fully 19 U.S. Olympic and National teams have had former Lakers on their roster, and incredibly, the Lakers never had a losing season in their rich five-decade history. The man behind all of this... of course, Cal Marvin. He has dedicated the better part of his life in the pursuit of helping others. He turned the entire community into a Laker's booster program and was fortunate to have the corporate backing from companies such as Marvin Windows and Christian Brothers Hockey Sticks to keep his dream alive. Arguably, no man has done more for his community with regards to promoting the game of hockey, than has Warroad's Cal Marvin.

Among his many awards and honors, Cal was elected to the United States Hockey Hall of Fame as an administrator in 1982. He is also a member of the Manitoba Sports Hall of Fame, the University of North Dakota Athletic Hall of Fame and the Warroad High School Athletic Hall of Fame. He also received the "Maroosh," an award presented in the name of the late John Mariucci for an individual's contributions to hockey. In addition to his Lakers, Cal operated various motels and restaurants in the community, including his Lake of the Woods Resort called "Cal's," which he ran for more than a quarter century. Presently Cal and his wife Beth reside in Warroad. They have 12 children and numerous grandchildren.

Chuck Grillo grew up in Hibbing and played hockey under George Perpich at Hibbing High School, graduating in 1957. From there, Chuck served in the United States Marine Corps for three years and was stationed in Cuba, Florida, North Carolina and California. Then, from 1962-64 Chuck attended Hibbing Junior College and in 1964 he got a teaching degree from University of Minnesota Duluth, graduating with honors. Grillo's first job was at Bemidji High School, where he taught industrial education and coached hockey and baseball. On the baseball diamond, Grillo's Lumberjacks made seven trips to the State High School Tournament, winning one title in 1973. On the ice, Grillo led his team to four state tournaments, including a runner-up finish in 1974. Grillo would stay in Bemidji until 1976, earning his Masters Degree in Guidance and Counseling from Bemidji State University along the way. He even worked summers with legendary International Falls High School Coach Larry Ross at nearby Bemidji Hockey Camp to stay busy.

From 1976-80 Chuck taught and coached at Rosemount High School. In 1981 he returned home to Northern Minnesota and began the next phase of his career, scouting and teaching hockey. Grillo first started scouting for the New York Rangers and later, in 1988, began working with the Minnesota North Stars as the Director of Pro Scouting. In 1992 he joined the San Jose Sharks, eventually working his way up to Executive Vice President, and Director of Player Personnel. Grillo was responsible for the selection of players to stock a new franchise and his keen knowledge of the game helped to lead the franchise into the playoffs.

In 1996 Chuck also started his own business, Minnesota Hockey Camps, which is located outside of Brainerd in Nisswa. Recognized world wide as one of the finest development camps, many NHL teams have utilized the camp to develop their young players. Young men and women from the professional and amateur ranks train at the Minnewawa Lodge Training Centre and Resort throughout the summer months, giving Chuck and his wife a great sense of purpose in life.

"We will measure our net worth by counting the number of 8x10 pictures of all the success stories in life that have come out of this camp," said Chuck. "MHC is our mission in life and that enhances our real net worth in our society. We've made a life out of hockey; our avocation. We enjoy working with players, coaches and trainers. We've been a part of countless success stories and have had over 30 major award winners in the NHL and over 300 NHL players attend our camp."

Currently, Chuck scouts for the Pittsburgh Penguins and continues to discover and develop the nation's top talent. His list of draftees and players he has helped to develop is a who's who of professional hockey, including the likes of: Pat Falloon, Sandis Ozolinsh, Viktor Kozlov, Yevgeny Nabokov, Derian Hatcher, Roman Turek, Tony Amonte, Brian Leetch, Ulf Dahlen, Mike Richter, David Gagner, Tony Granato and Mark Tinordi, to just name a few.

Chuck and his wife Clairene live in Nisswa and have six children: Robbie, Tracy, Chas, Denise, Rachel and Dean, and many grandchildren. One of the true builders of youth hockey in the state of Minnesota, Chuck is indeed a Minnesota hockey legend.

CHUCK'S MISSION STATEMENT:

To be the best provider of hockey training for athletes, coaches and trainers in the world. To operate the company on a sound financial basis of profitable growth. To reach out to players around the world and make the camp the most respected in hockey. To address the needs of the hockey community through involvement with youth programs and other worthy causes. To empower employees and athletes to *"be as much as you can be"* in a nurturing environment which recognizes unique talents of each individual, respect for the talents of others, and creativity.

HOW WOULD YOU DESCRIBE YOUR COACHING STYLE? "I am fully capable of recognizing the kid that needs a pat on the back, as well as the kid who needs a little prodding. You just need to figure out which buttons to push in each kid because they are all different. You also have to be able to think on your feet and be able to react to the moment. Tough love and discipline are important too, and I think I learned that in the Marine Corps. I tell my kids that I am going to like them as to how we relate to each other. I think you have to accept people for who they are, and then help them try and become what we all believe they can be. You know, to me hockey is a way of life for my whole family. I just love the game and am so proud to be a part of it."

HOW DID YOU MOTIVATE YOUR PLAYERS? "You can run out of gimmicks pretty quickly, so you just have to be real with them. That is what it is all about. Once you are real, then you can talk openly with your kids and encourage them to work towards their potential. I just think that everything is about attitude and you motivate from there. It starts with creating an attitude and then getting your kids to buy into that. Another thing I did that I thought was real affective was to have my kids write down what particular skills they thought were in their own asset category. Once they identified those, then, when they stepped out onto the ice, if they all overachieved in their individual asset categories, then the team would get better. They would get better because we emulate others. I mean if a kid sees another kid overachieving in another asset, whatever that might be, he will instinctively want to emulate that skill and get better himself. Eventually, each kid will improve his weaker skills, while still over-achieving in his asset category. Once that gets going and repeats itself, then that is a very powerful thing."

WHO WERE YOUR COACHING MENTORS? "To me there are coaches and there are mentors, and my mentors were Larry Ross and Herbie Brooks. They are great coaches and great people. You know, I think that every child needs at least three to six mentors out-side of his or her immediate family. Mentors are just so valuable and I can't stress that enough. I know that I have become a mentor to a lot of kids as well, and that is extremely gratifying."

WHAT ARE THE CHARACTERISTICS OF WINNERS? "If kids can sense how you, as the coach, are competing or how you would compete, then I think it is an extension of that. So, I believe if you are a competitor from behind the bench, and show no fear in crit-ical moments while still enjoying the game, the kids will pick up on that and play the same way. Winners believe that they can win and then they go out and get it done. It is an attitude."

LOOKING BACK WHAT ARE YOU MOST PROUD OF IN YOUR CAREER? "The great friendships and relationships that I have made in my lifetime are way better than championships."

HOW DID YOU BUILD TEAM UNITY & CHEMISTRY? "You know, I see all of these gimmicks nowadays with the sports psychol-ogists and the team-building seminars, but I think the best way to build chemistry on your team is to find a coach who has an unbeliev-able passion for the game. The kids will sense that and follow along. The kids have to be able to sense that you are doing things out of love for both the game as well as for them. When they believe that you care about them and have a sincere passion for the game, then that rubs off. You can't fake passion. Once kids sense that, then winning is real easy."

WHAT MOTIVATES YOU? "What has always motivated me is helping people help themselves. That is the number one criteria for me. And, it's about giving back to the sport you love. To me, if you are giving back and helping others, and winning along the way, then that is just gravy."

WHAT ADVICE WOULD YOU HAVE FOR YOUNG COACHES STARTING OUT TODAY? "Well, it certainly isn't about money. If you were to add up the dollars you made based on the hours you put in, it would be scary. So, my advice would be that they better have a passion for the game and truly care about others. They also need to be a detail person and be able to critique themselves on a daily basis. I have seen a lot of coaches start out the right way but then all of a sudden they get too focused on where they want to go individually, and they stop caring about others and forget about the people that helped them out along the way. Sooner or later those coaches will fail. So, if you can stay with those principles, you will have success."

FAVORITE LOCKER ROOM SIGN? "The biggest game of your life is the one you are playing today."

WHAT IS THE BEST PIECE OF ADVICE YOU EVER GOT FROM ANOTHER COACH? "I learned from Herbie that you have to allow young people to express their assets. You can't stifle people. If a kid has got major league assets, you just have to let him play his game. There are certain players that are talented enough, so as a coach you should just spend your time oiling the hinges on the door for them so that they can just go out onto the ice and do their thing."

WHAT ARE THE KEY INGREDIENTS TO CREATING A CHAMPIONSHIP TEAM? "Number one you have got to have a horse or two. Then, you have to have everybody fall in line behind them. You also have to have what I call 'critical moment' players, who step it up in critical moments and play their best. They are spe-cial kids. You know, I have seen teams with great stars lose to teams with a bunch of kids who out-work them. So, you need kids who will play their role and work hard for the good of the team."

WHAT'S THE SECRET TO YOUR SUCCESS? "No short cuts, just a lot of hard work. Beyond that, I would have to say that any suc-cess I have had in my lifetime is tied to my best friend and wife, Clairene Grillo. She's been a real supporter and the reason for the suc-cess of our hockey camp. Most importantly, Clairene has allowed me to live my life. Without this commitment from her, I don't know where I would be today. That is important in any relationship. I also watched her grow as a person while taking over the reins at our camp. Anyone will tell you that she is as much a part of our success as any-one. I would also say that my parents, Dom and Doris Grillo, were put on this earth to serve. They are very special human beings, salt of the earth people, who gave me more love than anyone I've ever met."

HOW DO YOU WANT YOUR COACHING EPITAPH TO READ — HOW DO YOU WANT TO BE REMEMBERED AS A COACH? "I want to earn my tombstone for living my life the way I wanted to live it. I think I was put on this earth to serve and help others, and I think I have made a difference. Also, I would say that I applied more of what I learned on an outdoor rink in Hibbing than I did earning all of those credits for my masters thesis. That was the real world up there and that is how I would like to be remembered."

DEL GENEREAU: ST. SCHOLASTICA HOCKEY

Del Genereau is a Duluth hockey icon. Genereau served as the head hockey coach at Duluth Cathedral High School for eight years and built the program into a prep powerhouse. As head coach at Cathedral he produced a 139-38-5 record and won an impressive four consecutive Minnesota State Catholic High School Hockey League championships in the late 1960s. Genereau was appointed head coach at St. Scholastica in 1972, and after his inaugural season, the Saints joined Bemidji State in the ICHA for the 1974 season. St. Scholastica emerged as ICHA champs in 1976 and went on to win the NAIA national championship. The Saints then went on to win their second straight NAIA national championship in 1977 as well. From 1972-77 Genereau posted a career record of 72-36-3 at St. Scholastica, building the program into a small college power.

LAURA HALLDORSON
WOMEN'S COLLEGE HOCKEY: UNIVERSITY OF MINNESOTA

Laura Halldorson grew up in Plymouth and graduated from Wayzata High School, where she starred in volleyball, basketball and softball, as well as in hockey — where she laced em' up for the "Checkers" club team. Upon graduating in 1981, Halldorson then headed off to star at Princeton University — where the co-captain and all-conference winger led the Tigers to three Ivy League Conference titles. Halldorson graduated from Princeton in 1985 with a degree in psychology and then returned home to coach volleyball, softball and basketball in the Wayzata school district from 1985-87. During that same time Halldorson led her Checkers squad to three national club championships, and even played on the 1987 U.S. National Women's Team. Halldorson then opted to head back East, to pursue her passion of coaching. After serving as an assistant at Princeton for two years, she took over as the head hockey coach at Colby College, where she was later named as the ECAC Co-Coach of the Year in 1996.

Then, in 1996, Halldorson got the opportunity of a lifetime when she was named as the University of Minnesota's inaugural women's head hockey coach. Her job would be to literally build the program from the ground up — from scratch. A tenacious worker, Halldorson wasted little time in assembling her first team — a squad which would eventually finish fourth in the inaugural 1998 AWCHA National Championships. For her efforts, she was named as the first ever American Hockey Coaches Association Women's Coach of the Year. Halldorson then led the Gophers to an impressive 29 wins in her sophomore campaign, capped off by a third-place showing at the National Championships. In her third season, Halldorson led the Gophers to a 4-2 victory over Brown University, to earn the National Championship — the first such coveted hardware in the history of Minnesota women's athletics. She had officially arrived!

After winning the regular season WCHA title and then finishing fifth in the nation in 2001, Halldorson's Gophers came out swinging in 2002 and won their first regular season and tournament WCHA championship. From there, they capped off their season by finishing third at national championship, marking the program's fourth appearance at the nationals. For her effort, Halldorson was again named as National Coach of the Year by the American Hockey Coaches Association. The Lady Gophers again made it back to the Frozen Four in 2003, but lost out in the semi's as the UM-Duluth Bulldogs captured their third straight national title.

Among Halldorson's many coaching awards and accolades, she is a two-time AHCA National Coach of the Year, two-time WCHA Coach of the Year, New England Hockey Writers' Women's Coach of the Year and ECAC Women's Hockey Co-Coach of the Year. In addition, she served as the President of the American Women's Hockey Coaches Association from 1991-94, and also presently serves on the Patty Kazmaier Award committee. The award, emblematic of the nation's top women's college ice hockey player, is named in honor of Patty Kazmaier, a teammate of Halldorson's at Princeton.

At the national level, Halldorson served as the assistant coach on the gold medal-winning team at the 1998 USA Hockey Women's Festival and also served as an assistant coach for the 1999 U.S. Women's Select Team that competed in the Three Nations Cup in Finland. Halldorson was also a head coach at the 1999 USA Hockey Women's Festival and was an assistant coach for the national Under-22 team in 1999. Additionally, she served as an assistant coach with the U.S. Junior National Team in 1995 and worked with USA Hockey's girls' and women's national development camps from 1991-

99. Furthermore, Halldorson was a member of the Women's Olympic Evaluation Committee, helping to choose the team that won the gold medal at the 1998 Winter Olympic Games in Nagano, Japan. She is also a member of the American Hockey Coaches Association, Women's Hockey Coaches Association and Women's Sports Foundation.

Today, the Lady Gophers play in the newly constructed Ridder Arena, the finest women's only hockey facility in the world. And their coach, Laura Halldorson, is leading the charge. Having posted 20-win seasons in each of her six seasons at Minnesota, she is among the very elite in women's college hockey coaching. Her gaudy 160-38-16 career record in Gold Country speaks for itself. A tenacious recruiter and extremely hard worker, Halldorson has earned the respect of her players and peers alike. She is truly a pioneer in a sport that is only going to get much, much bigger in the future. And how great it is that the state of Minnesota is leading the charge.

HOW WOULD YOU DESCRIBE YOUR COACHING STYLE? "I think as a coach you just have to figure out what works best for you personally, and from there you need to figure out what works best for your players. You don't want to go too far away from your personality and style that you have evolved into, but you also want to make sure that you can relate to each team and each player that you coach. I think my style is unique. I am not a big yeller, but I am pretty intense because I am very competitive and I hate to lose. But, I also want to keep things in perspective and I don't have a philosophy of winning at all costs. So, I think it is very important how you go about things and how you conduct yourself. Beyond that I think it is important that we have a program that has class and tries to do things the right way. In terms of my actual game style, I think I just try to stay calm and interact in a positive way with my players."

IF YOU COULD MAGICALLY GO BACK IN TIME TO THE FIRST YEAR YOU WERE A HEAD COACH AND GIVE YOURSELF SOME ADVICE FOR THE FUTURE, KNOWING WHAT YOU KNOW NOW, BACK THEN, WHAT WOULD YOU SAY TO YOURSELF? "I got into coaching because I wanted to have a positive impact on people's lives. But, sometimes you are not always going to be able to help or change people that need help. You just have to accept that are not always going to be able to have things turn out the way you want them to. Sometimes there are things beyond your control and you have to accept that. I have something inside of me that wants to fix situations and problems in people, and when I see things in my players, I feel the urge to jump in and help them change. Sometimes that works and sometimes that doesn't. It is something I have gotten better at, but have had to work at it over the years."

WHAT MOTIVATES YOU? "You know I struggle with the old saying 'you learn more from losing than you do from winning' because I hate to lose. It does, however, force you to push yourself to make changes and tweak what you are doing to get better. That motivates me. I am also motivated by seeing my players do well both on and off the ice."

ON THE STATE-OF-THE-STATE OF GIRLS HOCKEY IN MINNESOTA: "There has a been a lot of growth and positive development within our sport at all levels and that is great to see. Overall, Minnesota has something that no one else in the country has right now, and that is an enormous number of young girls who are playing organized hockey. The high school league is a very unique experience for these kids and it is a really wonderful thing to see happening. I mean it is such a big deal — it gets great support from the schools and so much exposure from the media. In fact, when I tell my friends out East that our state high school championship game is televised and draws about 4,000 fans, they simply can't believe it. We have truly come a long way in the evolution of the game, and I couldn't be happier to see the progress. The girls have come so far and really the sky is the limit."

WHAT'S THE BIGGEST THING YOU'VE LEARNED FROM COACHING THAT YOU'VE BEEN ABLE TO APPLY TO YOUR EVERYDAY LIFE? "I think the biggest thing is having to deal with all kinds of different situations, both good and bad. I guess the goal is to stay on an even keel emotionally and not go up and down like a roller coaster. But that is sometimes easier said than done when you get emotionally attached to your players and to your program. So, that is the challenge. You just need to continue to learn and grow and work on getting better each time out, and that is something that you can apply to your everyday life."

WHAT ARE THE KEY INGREDIENTS TO CREATING A CHAMPIONSHIP TEAM? "Leadership is the most important thing. Beyond that people have to care about each other, they have to be on the same page, they have to buy into the system and the coaching staff, they have to work hard, they have to be unselfish and they have to be humble with no big egos. You just need to have a group of people with a positive attitude that puts the team first and works towards a common goal. All of those clichés and more are really what it is all about."

HOW DO YOU WANT YOUR COACHING EPITAPH TO READ — HOW DO YOU WANT TO BE REMEMBERED AS A COACH? "My goal has always been to have a positive impact on other people's lives. Beyond that I just want to have a first class program that does things the right way, teaches the right things, emphasizes integrity, and is very positive. Having said that, I want to have all that and still be able to have my team vie for a national championship every year. If we can do that then I think I am doing something right. So, when it is all said and done I want to known as some-

one who not only prepared her players for life after college, but gave those players a lasting, positive and memorable experience as members of the Gopher Women's Hockey program."

DEAN TALAFOUS: UNIVERSITY OF ALASKA-ANCHORAGE

Dean Talafous was born in Duluth and went on to play three years of hockey at the University of Wisconsin, where he helped the Badgers win an NCAA title. Talafous turned pro in 1973 and went on to play nearly 500 games in the NHL during the mid-1970s and early 1980s with the Atlanta Flames, Minnesota North Stars and New York Rangers. As a six-foot-four winger, Talafous was also able to create space for himself in the slot and win battles for the puck along the boards. Talafous retired from playing in 1982 to pursue a career in coaching. After spending several years as an assistant under Doug Woog's Gophers at the University of Minnesota, Talafous went on to become the head coach at the University of Wisconsin River Falls in 1989. He would remain at River Falls until 1996, when he took over at the University of Alaska-Anchorage, where he remained until 2001. For his career, Talafous posted a 160-192-40 record.

ROBB STAUBER: GOPHER HOCKEY (GOALTENDING COACH)

Robb Stauber grew up in Duluth and went on to star as a goalie at Duluth Denfeld High School, graduating in 1986. From there, Stauber went on to earn first-team All-American and All-WCHA honors at the University of Minnesota, where, in 1988, he became the first goaltender ever to win the Hobey Baker Award, which honors college hockey's top player. Stauber rewrote the record books in Gold Country and is still the Gopher 's career leader in saves percentage (.906); ranks second in school history for career wins (73), most games played (98) and minutes played (5,717). During Stauber's career at Minnesota, the Gophers posted a 102-34-4 record, back-to-back WCHA Championships in 1988 and 1989, and three-straight NCAA Frozen Four appearances. A draft pick of the Los Angeles Kings, Stauber played professionally for 10 seasons with the Los Angles Kings, Buffalo Sabres, New York Rangers, and Washington Capitals organizations. Stauber was also a member of the 1993 Stanley Cup finalist Kings squad, and led Kings goaltenders in that season in win percentage, saves percentage, and goals-against average. Stauber's best professional season came in 1998, when, as a member of the American Hockey League's Hartford Wolfpack, he posted a 20-10-4 record, 2.41 goals-against average and a .920. saves percentage. He was twice honored as an American Hockey League all-star. Following his playing career, Robb later returned to the University of Minnesota, where he took over as the team's volunteer goaltending coach. With back-to-back national championships in 2002 and 2003, it is clear that Robb is doing a very, very good job in training his Gopher netminders. In addition, Robb also launched his own business, manufacturing and selling his creation called the "Staubar" — the first piece of training equipment designed specifically for goaltenders. Furthermore, Robb also oversees the world renowned Stauber-Ostby Goalie Academy, which organizes and operates goaltender camps year-round in the Midwest. Based in Edina, the Academy is housed in a state-of-the-art facility which hosts professional and amateur goaltenders from around the world. Presently, Robb has two children, Ruby and Jaxson, and resides in Plymouth.

JOHN HARRINGTON
COLLEGE HOCKEY: ST. JOHN'S

John Harrington grew up on the Iron Range and played high school hockey at Virginia under long-time Coach Dave Hendrickson. From there, Harrington went on to star for the University of Minnesota-Duluth from 1975-79. That next year Harrington gained fame as a member of the fabled 1980 U.S. Olympic hockey team which captured the gold medal at the Winter Games in Lake Placid, New York. Harrington played hockey in Lugano, Switzerland for one season in 1981, before returning home as a member of the U.S. National Hockey Team in the 1981, 1982 and 1983 World Hockey Championships. He then completed his international playing career as a member of the 1984 U.S. Olympic Hockey team which competed in Sarajevo, Yugoslavia.

From there, Harrington came home to serve as an assistant coach at Apple Valley High School from 1981-84. His big coaching break came that next year when he became an assistant coach at the University of Denver, where he would serve from 1984-90. In 1990 John came home to serve as an assistant at St. Cloud State University under Coach Craig Dahl. Then, in 1993, Harrington became the head hockey coach and assistant soccer coach at St. John's University, where he has been ever since. In 1996, Harrington guided SJU to its first MIAC regular season title since 1950. In 1997 the Johnnies repeated as MIAC regular season and playoff champions and proceeded to advance to the NCAA Division III hockey final four, bringing home the third-place trophy to boot. Now entering his 11th season in Collegeville, Harrington has guided the Johnnies to an impressive 158-102-21 (.600) career record. The winningest hockey coach in school history, Harrington has led the Johnnies to the MIAC playoffs nine times and the NCAA tournament four times.

Among Harrington's many coaching accolades, he is a three-time MIAC Coach-of-the-Year (1994, 1996 and 2003). In addition, he is a member of the U.S. Hockey Hall of Fame, and also received the Lester Patrick Award in 1980 for outstanding service to hockey in the U.S. He is also a charter member of the U.S. Olympic Hall of Fame, a 1990 inductee into the Minnesota Olympic Hall of Fame and a 2001 inductee into the Minnesota-Duluth Athletic Hall of Fame. Harrington also served as the president of the American College Hockey Coaches Association during the 1999-2000 season. In addition to his collegiate coaching experience, Harrington has served as an assistant coach at the U.S. Junior Olympic Festival (1992) and National Sports Festivals (1990 and 1983). In 1995, Harrington also served as head coach of gold medal-winning Team North at the Olympic Sports Festival in Denver, Colo.

John and his wife Mary presently reside in St. Cloud and have three children: Leah, Patty and Chris — who was a member of the 2003 WCHA All-Rookie team for the two-time NCAA champion Golden Gopher hockey team.

HOW WOULD YOU DESCRIBE YOUR COACHING STYLE? "I think when I started I just tried to emulate the coach that I had the most success under, and that was Herb Brooks. I was also fortunate to play under Bob Johnson and Lou Vairo as well, so I was able to get a lot of great ideas from those guys too. So, from all of their teachings I think I was able to create my own style. It has since evolved, but it still comes down to hard work, respect and good team play. You know at this level you can really make a difference with kids. You are taking somebody who might have a single or partial strength in something, but also has some weaknesses, and then try to develop those things. That is rewarding to see those kids come along

and get better. I love that challenge and that all goes into coaching."

HOW DO YOU MOTIVATE YOUR PLAYERS? "I think you have to get to know your players first of all and then find out what motivates them. Some kids you can take the whip to and others you need to dangle a carrot in front of. You just need to figure out which needs which, then you can motivate them. I let some guys know what I think they can accomplish if they do certain things, and I let other guys know that I expect a lot more out of them, so it really varies from kid to kid. You know, I always tell my kids that 'when I stop talking to you and riding you out on the ice, that is when it is time to worry.' Because, at that point I have found other guys to spend my time on and pay attention to."

WHAT IS THE KEY TO GOOD TIME MANAGEMENT? "You know, I actually teach a time management class up at St. John's and I tell my kids all the time that I should actually be in this class and not teaching it! Really though, it comes down to procrastination. You just have to stay on top of things more than anything else. I am lucky, I am a morning person and I like getting up and getting things done right away. Others can't do that. I also make a lot of lists and then work like crazy to cross things off of them because I know I will be adding to them by the end of the day."

IF YOU COULD MAGICALLY GO BACK IN TIME TO THE FIRST YEAR YOU WERE A HEAD COACH AND GIVE YOURSELF SOME ADVICE FOR THE FUTURE, KNOWING WHAT YOU KNOW NOW, BACK THEN, WHAT WOULD YOU SAY TO YOURSELF? "When I first started out I was way too wound up and way too negative I think. So, I would be much more positive with my players and encourage them more by giving them more pats on the back. I would also get to know each of them better and not just assume I could motivate them all by the same methods. It used to be where a coach could just say 'hey, this is the way I coach, now you adjust to me,' whereas now you can't do that. You have to be able to find out what makes each kid tick and then push the right buttons."

LOOKING BACK WHAT ARE YOU MOST PROUD OF IN YOUR CAREER? "I think that if you work hard at something, sometimes dreams can come true. It happened for me as a player as a member of the 1980 U.S. Olympic team and hopefully will happen again as a coach at St. John's."

WHAT IS THE KEY TO RECRUITING? "It is selling your school and your program first and foremost, particularly at this level, because they are going to carry that with them a lot longer in life than they will hockey. You have to find out what kids are looking for and then sell what you have to offer them along with yourself. That is important. Then, I think it is important too for the entire team to get involved. I like our players to meet the recruits and then get their input too. Sometimes your best salesmen are your players, because they can relate to young kids their own age."

HOW DO YOU BUILD TEAM UNITY & CHEMISTRY? "We do some things together with our kids away from the rink, where we will have get-togethers, movies and dinners and stuff like that. Road trips are particularly good for building chemistry because the guys really get to know each other on the bus and in the hotel at night and that kind of thing. I also always tell everyone on our team that they have a role and that they play a key part in our overall team's success by playing that role, whatever that may be. Then, as a coach, you need to get your kids to buy into that and get them to respect one another's roles on the team. So, all of that helps to get everybody on the same page."

WHAT MOTIVATES YOU? "I love trying to be successful in everything I do. That is my nature. I am not afraid of losing, but I love winning a lot better. I don't like to lose, period. I am also motivated by making players better. As a player myself I didn't think I was a naturally gifted person, so I had to figure out ways to be better than the top players in order to be successful."

WHAT IS THE BEST PIECE OF ADVICE YOU EVER GOT FROM ANOTHER COACH? 'I remember when I was an assistant at Denver and having (Wisconsin Coach) Jeff Sauer tell me one time that I was going to need to learn to lose before I could become a head coach. I was a bad loser early on because I am so competitive, and I have always remembered that."

WHAT ADVICE WOULD YOU HAVE FOR YOUNG COACHES STARTING OUT TODAY? "I think you need to be firm and have discipline with your kids and you need to somehow get them to make a commitment to what they are doing. Hockey isn't always fun, but the satisfaction you get from playing or coaching well is what it is all about. So, as a young coach you need to tell your kids that you are all in this together and that if you are all committed to getting better, then you will have fun."

WHAT'S THE BIGGEST THING YOU'VE LEARNED FROM COACHING THAT YOU'VE BEEN ABLE TO APPLY TO YOUR EVERYDAY LIFE? "There are going to be ups and downs, and you just have to deal with it. Early in my career I let things on the team effect everything else in my life, including things at home and that was bad. So, you need to prepare well, try your best and then just move on. You have to let go of some things so that you can focus on the future. Understanding that has really helped me be a better coach, husband and father."

WHAT ARE THE KEY INGREDIENTS TO CREATING A CHAMPIONSHIP TEAM? "You have got to have talent, first and foremost. I have found that I am a better coach when I have better players and I am not as good of a coach when my players are not as good. It is simple but true. Then, you have to get your players to buy into whatever you are trying to accomplish as a coach. From there, you have to get your players to understand their roles. You know, it is like 'here is what you do best' and 'here is my expectations of you.' You have to tell them that not everybody can be a first liner, but that you need grinders, penalty killers and role players to be successful as a team. Once you have that then things like chemistry and respect follow suit. When all of those things come together anything can happen."

WHAT'S THE SECRET TO YOUR SUCCESS? "I think I have been able to evaluate my players in a hurry and then be able to adapt to what their abilities are in order to build successful teams. So, adaptability would by the key, along with playing to our strengths while developing our weaknesses."

WHAT WOULD YOU WANT TO SAY TO YOUR FANS, BOOSTERS, AND ALUMNI WHO HAVE SUPPORTED YOU ALL THESE YEARS? "I have been at St. John's for 10 years now and I know how much support that all of the parents of the kids have given to me and to this program. So, thanks for supporting your sons and for being there for us, both personally as well as emotionally, and not to mention financially. I really appreciate all of that."

HOW DO YOU WANT YOUR COACHING EPITAPH TO READ — HOW DO YOU WANT TO BE REMEMBERED AS A COACH? "I would say somebody that the players respected, somebody that didn't ask more of his players than he would of himself, and somebody who had some measure of success."

TOM SERRATORE: BEMIDJI STATE HOCKEY

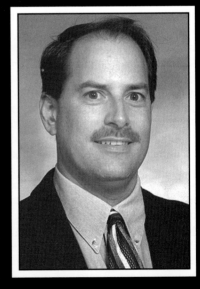

Tom Serratore grew up in Coleraine and went on to play college hockey at Western Michigan University from 1977-79, before earning his degree in physical education from Bemidji State University in 1982. Serratore lettered four years in hockey at the two schools, playing goalie. At BSU, Serratore played in a couple of NCAA III national hockey tournaments for the Beavers, including the 1986 squad which won the national championship. Serratore went on to play two years with the St. Paul Vulcans in the USHL before playing professionally with the Nashville South Stars in the CHL in 1982. He then got into coaching, and went on to coach in the USA Hockey Developmental Program until 1985. From there, Serratore took over as an assistant at the University of North Dakota from 1987-89. After that, Serratore got into junior hockey coaching, and coached both the USHL's Rochester Mustangs, who he led to a national championship, and later the Austin Mavericks, posting a 247-103-6 record along the way. In addition, Serratore also coached at the high school level, first as an assistant at Brainerd High School and later at Henry Sibley High School, where he served as the head coach in 1991. In 1993, Serratore was named as the associate head coach at St. Cloud State University, where, under coach Craig Dahl, he led recruiting efforts and was instrumental in helping the program reach national prominence.

In 1998 Serratore went back to Bemidji State to serve as an assistant under legendary coach, Bob Peters. There, he would play a big part in the transition to Division I hockey and also was involved in building College Hockey America, the nation's newest Division I hockey conference. Then, in 2000, Serratore got his big break when Peters decided to finally step down after becoming the second winningest college hockey coach in history. In the three years since Serratore has been behind the Beaver bench, he has posted a modest 26-32-13 record. In addition, Tom and his brother Frank, head coach at Air Force, are one of just two sets of family members that coach against each other in the same conference in any sport. (Bobby Bowden, the head football coach at Florida State and his son Tommy, the head coach at Clemson, are the others.) Thus far, big brother Frank has bragging rights over his little bro with six wins and a tie, to no losses. With Tom Serratore steering the ship, the Beavers look poised to become a future Division I power in the CHA.

PAUL HOLMGREN
PRO HOCKEY: PHILADELPHIA FLYERS

Paul Holmgren grew up on the East side of St. Paul and was skating by the age of two. Thanks to his father, who flooded the empty lot next door to their house to make a rink every Winter, Paul got plenty of ice-time with his brothers. From there, he skated every chance he got.

"The playground that we played at was four blocks from our house," recalled Holmgren. "In the winter time we didn't have to take our skates off. We'd just put our skates on and skate up to the playground, where the hockey rinks were, then skate home for dinner and skate back up after dinner. My mom did make us put our skate guards on to come in the house though."

Holmgren went on to play on two state high school hockey tournament teams at Harding High School and then played a year of junior hockey for the St. Paul Vulcans under Doug Woog in the Midwest Junior Hockey League. There, Holmgren was selected to be part of a team comprised of a MJHL players which competed in the World Junior Tournament in Leningrad, USSR. In 1974 Holmgren played for one season with the Golden Gophers, under Coach Herbie Brooks. There, the sturdy winger scored 11 goals and tallied 21 assists for 32 points en route to leading the Gophers to the NCAA tournament, where they ultimately lost to Michigan Tech in the Finals.

That following year Holmgren left college to sign with the Minnesota Fighting Saints of the WHA under Coach Glen Sonmor. When the franchise folded in March of 1976, Holmgren, who scored 30 points that season, moved on to play with the NHL's Philadelphia Flyers, who had drafted him the previous year. To finally play in the National Hockey League was a dream come true.

Holmgren would go on to play in the Flyers organization for nine seasons. One of the highlights of his career came in 1980, when the club compiled a 35-game unbeaten streak and made it all the way to the Stanley Cup Finals, before losing to the Islanders. There, despite suffering a knee injury in the final round, Holmgren became the first American-born player ever to record a hat trick in a final-series game. A 30-goal and 35 assist scorer during the regular season, the 6-foot-3, 220-pound bruiser, who also racked up 300+ penalty minutes that year, finished that post-season with 10 goals and 10 assists. In 1984 Holmgren came home to finish his career with his hometown North Stars. That next year, however, he was forced to retire due to a recurring shoulder injury. The two-time NHL All-Star would finish his career with 144 goals and 179 assists for 323 points, as well as 1,684 penalty minutes to boot — this guy was tough!

Philadelphia's legendary General Manager Bobby Clarke called Holmgren the "heart and soul" of the Flyers and described him as "a leader who led by example and played each game as hard as he could. A fearless competitor, he was one of the league's hardest hit-ters. When it came to scoring, he was most dangerous around the goal crease where he specialized in making life miserable for goal-tenders."

From there, Holmgren got into coaching and returned to Philly that next year to serve as an assistant with the Flyers. In 1988 Holmgren, at just 33 years old, was named as the Flyers head coach. He would remain as the team's head coach until 1992, finishing his coaching stint with the Flyers with an overall record of 107-126-31. The following year Holmgren became the head coach of the Hartford Whalers. He would coach the Whalers off and on from 1992 to 1996, before returning to the Flyers organization to serve as the director of pro scouting. He would later take over as the assistant general man-ager under Bob Clarke, a position he currently holds.

One of just a few Americans to have coached in the NHL, Paul Holmgren was an out-standing player and coach. Paul, who is also a black-belt, and his family currently reside in Somerdale, N.J., just outside of Philly, near the team's practice facility.

HOW WOULD YOU DESCRIBE YOUR COACHING STYLE? "My philosophy was to have an aggressive attacking style. When we had the puck we wanted to push the offense and when we didn't have it the idea was simply to get it back as quickly as possible. Of course you have to remember that I was coaching around 15 years ago and the game has changed quite a bit since then. There was a lot more forechecking involved back then than there is today. Also, today if teams don't have the puck they just sort of sit back in a counter-attack mode, and that is certainly not what I preached as a coach."

HOW DID YOU MOTIVATE YOUR PLAYERS? "As a coach you tried to get to know your players as well as you could from a per-sonal standpoint, and then try to get to them that way. Really though, at this level most guys are self-motivated and can do a lot of things on their own. A lot of it for me was getting guys to buy into what we were doing and then caring for one another as players and as friends. That way guys would try and win for their buddy's, their teammates."

WHO WERE YOUR COACHING MENTORS? "I was fortunate enough as a player to play for Doug Woog, Herbie Brooks, Glen Sonmor, Fred Shero and Pat Quinn, in that order. I learned a lot from those guys and would certainly say that much of my coaching style came from bits and pieces of them."

WHAT ARE THE CHARACTERISTICS OF WINNERS? "Winners are players that are willing to make the ultimate sacrifice and commitment to their team."

LOOKING BACK WHAT ARE YOU MOST PROUD OF IN YOUR CAREER? "I am very proud of the fact that I made it to the National Hockey League as a player. Back when I first got into the league their weren't that many American players in the league. So, for me to come out of Harding High School and then to play for the Vulcans and then the Gophers and then a year in the WHA, was an amazing experience all leading up to my time in the NHL. I had to pinch myself then and I still pinch myself now to think about it."

WHAT IS THE KEY TO GOOD TIME MANAGEMENT? "To me it is nothing more than listing what you need to do each day and then following through with a checklist."

HOW DID YOU BUILD TEAM UNITY & CHEMISTRY? "A lot of it is just being together and learning a lot about each other away from the rink as well as at the rink. You have to have your guys spend time together to build chemistry. We tried to do things together as a team beyond practicing and playing, particularly when we were on the road. Whether it was going to dinner, going bowling or going to a movie, we just did stuff together. I have always felt that teams that are close and hang together usually have pretty good success. Chemistry is not something that you can force upon your players, but if you have the right core group of players, then they can help that sense of team unity and togetherness come to life."

WHAT MOTIVATED YOU? "You know, everybody wants to win. It just comes down to doing whatever it is going to take to ultimately achieve that goal. It is also the fear of losing, because nobody likes to lose either."

HOW DID YOU EARN THE RESPECT OF YOUR PLAYERS? "For starters you don't ask them to do things that you yourself don't do. If you ask them to be on time, then make sure that you are on time. If you ask them to work a little harder, then you work a little harder. Players follow the lead of the coach. So, if the coach is on time and puts in his time to make the team better, then players see that and it rubs off on them."

WHAT ADVICE WOULD YOU HAVE FOR YOUNG COACHES STARTING OUT TODAY? "Figure out how you want your team to play after looking at what you have. I think the mistake coaches make today is playing a certain style without having the type of players that can play that style. Just go with what you have got and fill in the pieces to get better."

FAVORITE LOCKER ROOM SIGN? "You play for the logo on the front (of your jersey) and not the name on the back."

WHAT DID IT MEAN FOR YOU TO BE A GOPHER? "I still get goose bumps whenever I think about walking up those old wooden steps at Williams Arena with the school song being played by the band. Then, skating around the ice prior to the game with the fans hanging over the boards and so riled up, that was as good as it got. There was so much enthusiasm there and it was just such a wonderful experience for me. Even though I only played one year for the Gophers, I feel very fortunate that I was able to be a part of it all. It was one of the best times of my life and something I will never forget. I remember losing to Michigan Tech in the Finals, but those were some great memories nonetheless. Now, to see them winning back-to-back championships is really neat. I scout players for the Flyers and I got to see them a bunch over the past few years. As a fan, I still pull for them and it is great to see their success. You know, once a Gopher, always a Gopher."

WHAT'S THE BIGGEST THING YOU'VE LEARNED FROM COACHING THAT YOU'VE BEEN ABLE TO APPLY TO YOUR EVERYDAY LIFE? "I think in whatever you do if you are committed, you work hard and you stick with your plan, then you will be successful."

WHAT ARE THE KEY INGREDIENTS TO CREATING A CHAMPIONSHIP TEAM? "You need some good players and you need some good role players. Then you need depth. You also need to have a group that comes together with a common goal and is willing to commit to that in order to get it done. From there, you need a group of players that, despite obstacles, will stick to the plan that was put in place at the start of the season."

WHAT'S THE SECRET TO YOUR SUCCESS? "I am a hard worker and am a committed person. Beyond that, you know, coaching is a pretty tight fraternity. I can remember when I was coaching the Flyers and could see that the end was near for me. The team was not doing too well and inevitably I was going to go. I just remember a couple of guys calling me up and telling me to hang in there. They told me that it was not the end of the world and sometimes even if you do your best that is not good enough, but that is OK. So, I guess I would just say stick with it and do what you think is right. I did what I felt was right in my heart when I coached and sometimes you lose your job because your team doesn't win. You win and lose as a team, but when things get tough, sometimes the coach has got to go. That is just the reality of this business."

HOW DO YOU WANT YOUR COACHING EPITAPH TO READ — HOW DO YOU WANT TO BE REMEMBERED AS A COACH? "I would like to think that I had an impact on the players' lives that I coached. I made some great friendships along the way and I am grateful for that."

KEN YACKEL: COLLEGE & PRO HOCKEY GOPHERS & MINNEAPOLIS MILLERS

Ken Yackel grew up in St. Paul and graduated as a three-sport star from Humboldt High School in 1949. Yackel then went on to the University of Minnesota, where, in addition to earning All-American honors on the Gopher Hockey team, he also lettered in football and baseball. Behind Yackel, the Gophers reached a pair of NCAA tournament final four berths in both 1953 and 1954 with Yackel being named to the All Tournament Team in 1954. In addition, Yackel also played on the U.S. silver medal-winning hockey team at the 1952 Olympics in Oslo. From there, Yackel went on to play professional with Cleveland and Providence in the American League as well as Saskatoon and St. Paul of the Western League. In 1959 Yackel played with the Boston Bruins, becoming just one of two American-developed players to appear in the NHL in the decade of the 1950's. In the early 1960's Yackel, who had also briefly coached at Edina High School in the late '50s, went on to serve as the player/coach of the IHL's Minneapolis Millers. In 1961 the Millers won the regular season championship as Yackel captured the league scoring championship as the team's player/coach. The following year he scored a career high 50 goals and was named to the league's first all-star team at left wing. In 1963 Yackel coached the Millers to the IHL Finals, where they lost to Fort Wayne, but his 100 points was enough to gain second team all-star honors. In 1965 Yackel served as the head coach the U.S. National Team in the world tournament at Tampere, Finland. Then, late in 1971, Yackel answered the call of his alma mater and filled in as the interim coach for the Gopher's when Glen Sonmor left in midseason to coach the WHA's Fighting Saints. Yackel would post a 7-17 record during his brief tenure behind the Gopher bench. From there, Yackel would remain active in the hockey community not only in his native Minnesota, but also nationally. Later, he was involved in the Mariucci Inner City Hockey Starter Association, a program to encouraged hockey among inner city kids throughout the Twin Cities. In 1986 Yackel was enshrined into the U.S. Hockey Hall of Fame. Yackel, who died in 1991 at just 59, was one of Minnesota's greatest all-around athletes. His legacy lives on today at Ken Yackel Ice Arena on St. Paul's West Side.

WILLARD IKOLA
HIGH SCHOOL HOCKEY: EDINA

Willard Ikola grew up in Eveleth loving hockey. There, he would go on to become another in a long line of incredible goaltenders to come out of the tiny Iron Range town, joining the likes of NHL stars Frank Brimsek, Mike Karakas and Sam LoPresti — all heroes of Ikola. Ike, as he was affectionately, known, went on to play goalie for three undefeated state championship hockey teams at Eveleth High School from 1948-50. From there, he went on to become an All-American goaltender at the University of Michigan, where he led the Wolverines to a pair of national championships in 1952 and 1953. Ikola then went into the Air Force, and while serving in the military, he went on to play on the silver medal-winning 1956 U.S. Olympic team in Cortina, Italy. The coach of that team was fellow Eveleth hockey legend John Mariucci. After playing on the 1957 and 1958 U.S. National Teams, Ike retired from hockey and decided to get into teaching and coaching on a full-time basis.

From there, upon the advice of John Mariucci, Ikola took over as the coach at Edina High School in 1958, replacing former Gopher Ken Yackel, who had just left to sign with the Minneapolis Bruins. There, Ike became synonymous with high school hockey in Minnesota and established himself as one of the greatest hockey coaches in American history. When Braemar Arena was finally built in 1965, a dynasty was about to ensue. Ikola's Edina teams were among the most prolific in state high school hockey tourney history, winning 22 Lake Conference championships, 19 regional playoffs, eight state championships (1969, '71, '74, '78, '79, '82, '84 and '88), and two runner-up's. His 616-149-36 record over 33 years of coaching the Hornets makes him not only the winningest hockey coach in Minnesota state high school history, but also the second all-time winningest coach in the history of high school hockey in America. Ike, with his trademark hounds-tooth hat, retired from coaching in 1991 to join the Minnesota North Stars as a scout and clinic instructor.

Among his many coaching honors and accolades, Ike was enshrined into the U.S. Hockey Hall of Fame, National High School Sports Hall of Fame, University of Michigan Hockey Hall of Fame, Minnesota High School Hockey Coaches Hall of Fame and the Minnesota State High School League Hall of Fame.

A true living legend, Ike is a giant in the world of Minnesota hockey. Willard is presently retired and living in Minnetonka, where he can be seen at the local rink, rooting on his grandsons and granddaughters as they come up the youth hockey ranks.

HOW WOULD YOU DESCRIBE YOUR COACHING STYLE? "I suppose we really worked hard on the fundamentals, and on developing skills. I found out in a hurry that you have got to start out with the basics: passing, receiving, shooting and skating. I was fortunate to play on good teams during my playing career and I was able to draw on a lot of that experience to create my own unique style. Beyond that, I think you had to have a disciplined hockey team in order to be successful. Take penalties for instance. You just can't have bad penalties, particularly away from the puck, it will eventually catch up with you. I strived for that. Conditioning is another thing. You can't be successful if your team is not in top shape. We always tried to develop three lines so that our kids would be well rested and ready to go. Depth was always important to me. A lot of other teams that went with two lines oftentimes had trouble late in games when their kids got too tired. Then, beyond that I always tried to spread the talent to all three lines and not really load up on just one line. I

thought that we would be better off with that strategy. As for style, we were not a real big checking team as much as we were a good passing and skating team. We moved the puck well and we took a lot of pride in just playing the game the way it was supposed to be played. Our teams were usually among the least penalized in the league and I think that all goes back to discipline."

HOW DID YOU MOTIVATE YOUR PLAYERS? "First of all you have to have a good youth feeder program in order to have a successful high school program. That is number one. Then, from there the motivation wasn't very hard. You know, because we had built up such a strong program and had a lot of exposure on television from the state tournament, a lot of kids wanted to play hockey at Edina. That was a big motivation for our kids, they wanted to carry on that tradition and make it back to the state tournament year after year. Being on television is a very powerful thing for kids, and they wanted to get there. So, for me there really wasn't much motivation to do, our kids were pretty self motivated when they got to that level and they wanted to succeed. We just tried to teach them the fundamentals and prepare them to be successful."

WHO WERE YOUR COACHING MENTORS? "Cliff Thompson was my high school coach at Eveleth. He was a marvelous man and really a good teacher. I learned a great deal from him and I really tried to pattern a great deal of my coaching style after him."

IF YOU COULD MAGICALLY GO BACK IN TIME TO THE FIRST YEAR YOU WERE A HEAD COACH AND GIVE YOURSELF SOME ADVICE FOR THE FUTURE, KNOWING WHAT YOU KNOW NOW, BACK THEN, WHAT WOULD YOU SAY TO YOURSELF? "I think early on in my career I was expecting too much and doing some drills that were probably over my kids' heads and just beyond their skill level. It took me a while to realize that and to get back to the basics, and that was one of the smartest things I ever did. You know, in the beginning it was tough. And, on top of all that we were an outdoor program with no arena. We played games inside, but practiced outside and had to deal with the snow and cold, it was tough. To get the skill level up to where it should be like at International Falls or Hibbing or Roseau, which all had indoor arenas at that time, we knew we had a lot of work to do. So, it took a while but we got there. Another thing that was tough for me personally, was the fact that I had been a goaltender and simply didn't know a lot about offensive strategy. I knew a great deal about defense, but I needed some help in teaching things like face-offs and power-plays, so I called guys like John Mayasich for advice. It was a learning process and you got better as you got more years under your belt. Then, I always went to the clinics and if I came away from those with just one or two new things, then I thought it was well worth the time. You know, hockey people are a unique group in the sense that they are friendly and share a lot of things, more so than other coaches I think. Even after those clinics we would go out for beers together and talk even more hockey, and that was special to get to know those guys. And even though you battled those same guys during the season, we all helped each other out to grow the sport. That was what it was all about."

HOW DID YOU BUILD TEAM UNITY & CHEMISTRY? "You know, you watch the kids of course, and you figure out pretty quickly who the hockey players are. I was a junior high school physical education teacher too, so I had the advantage of seeing first hand who the best athletes were coming down the pipeline. I had them in class as well, so you got to see what kind of students they were as well. Then, you saw them in summer camps on top of that and it was a real advantage. By then the kids knew you and trusted you, and that helped to build the chemistry on our teams. The kids grew up together, playing hockey, and by the time they were on the varsity it was like they were family. I even used to ask some of the better kids who they wanted to skate on a line with. Then, when you get that kind of feedback, it really helped. Some of our best lines came about from those recommendations and that worked out really well."

WHAT'S THE BIGGEST THING YOU'VE LEARNED FROM COACHING THAT YOU'VE BEEN ABLE TO APPLY TO YOUR EVERYDAY LIFE? "I would say discipline. Hockey is a game of mistakes and the team that makes the least mistakes is going to win most of the time."

WHAT'S THE SECRET TO YOUR SUCCESS? "It was all about our youth feeder system. We were had more than 100 kids go on to play division one hockey through the years with another eight or so making it in the National Hockey League, and that says a lot. Usually, when we won a state tournament, we would have at least a half a dozen kids that would go on to play division one hockey, and that was a tribute to our feeder program. Nowadays with junior hock-ey that would be unheard of."

WHAT WOULD YOU WANT TO SAY TO YOUR FANS, BOOSTERS, AND ALUMNI WHO HAVE SUPPORTED YOU ALL THESE YEARS? "By the time kids get into our high school program they have been skating for years and years, and that means that a lot of people have contributed to the teaching and coaching of that player. It is a team effort and our program has had success because of all of those people up and down the line who have worked hard in developing our kids. Our youth programs are strong and that is why we have a strong high school program. So, I take my hat off to those people and say thanks. They certainly made my job a lot easier."

HOW DO YOU WANT YOUR COACHING EPITAPH TO READ — HOW DO YOU WANT TO BE REMEMBERED AS A COACH? "We tried to play the game right and we focused on the fundamentals. So, I would hope to be remembered as someone who made a difference with his kids as a coach and teacher, and as someone who ran an honorable program which had a lot of success."

WALTER BUSH: USA HOCKEY

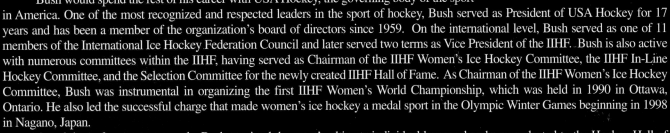

Walter Bush has been involved in hockey virtually his entire life as a player, coach, manager, administrator and team owner. Bush was born in Minneapolis and went on to graduate from Breck High School. From there, Bush played hockey at Dartmouth. While working on his law degree back at the University of Minnesota, Bush kept his skates sharp by playing senior hockey and helping to organize the Central Professional Hockey League (CPHL), in which he served as Owner and President of the Minneapolis Bruins (Boston's minor-league affiliate) from 1963-65.

Bush then became involved in team management, and, after managing the 1959 U.S. National Team that participated in the IIHF World Championship in Prague, Czechoslovakia, he managed the 1964 U.S. Olympic Team too. In addition, Bush also served as President of the Minnesota Amateur Hockey Association for three years as well.

Bush would later lead a group of businessmen in purchasing the NHL's Minnesota North Stars. Bush would serve as the North Stars' first President from 1967-76 and later became Chairman of the Board. Bush spent 17 years in the NHL working with a variety of committees. Bush has also remained active in professional hockey, recently serving as one of two principle owners of the Kentucky Thoroughblades, formerly of the American Hockey League.

Bush would spend the rest of his career with USA Hockey, the governing body of the sport in America. One of the most recognized and respected leaders in the sport of hockey, Bush served as President of USA Hockey for 17 years and has been a member of the organization's board of directors since 1959. On the international level, Bush served as one of 11 members of the International Ice Hockey Federation Council and later served two terms as Vice President of the IIHF. Bush is also active with numerous committees within the IIHF, having served as Chairman of the IIHF Women's Ice Hockey Committee, the IIHF In-Line Hockey Committee, and the Selection Committee for the newly created IIHF Hall of Fame. As Chairman of the IIHF Women's Ice Hockey Committee, Bush was instrumental in organizing the first IIHF Women's World Championship, which was held in 1990 in Ottawa, Ontario. He also led the successful charge that made women's ice hockey a medal sport in the Olympic Winter Games beginning in 1998 in Nagano, Japan.

A recipient of numerous awards, Bush received the sport's ultimate individual honor when he was elected to the Hockey Hall of Fame in 2000. He was also distinguished with the NHL's Lester Patrick Award in 1973 in recognition of his outstanding service to ice hockey in the United States. He was also enshrined in the United States Hockey Hall of Fame in 1980 and, in 1989, was elected to the Minnesota Sports Hall of Fame. In addition, Bush served as a Governor and Vice-Chairman for the Hockey Hall of Fame in Toronto, and was also the Director and member of the Selection Committee for the U.S. Hockey Hall of Fame. Bush is a also member of the Board of Directors of the United States Olympic Committee and is secretary of the U.S. Olympic Foundation. During the XIX Olympic Winter Games in Salt Lake City, Bush received the Olympic Order from the International Olympic Committee, the highest honor given in the Olympic movement. Bush was also named as the NHL's Executive of the Year in 1972 by the Hockey News. Furthermore, in recognition of his immeasurable service to USA Hockey, the organization dedicated its national headquarters as The Walter L. Bush, Jr. Center in June of 1999.

Bush, who resides in Edina, retired as President of USA Hockey in 2003. A man with a true passion for the game of hockey, Walter Bush is a real Minnesota hockey legend.

JACQUES LEMAIRE
PRO HOCKEY: MINNESOTA WILD

Jacques Lemaire grew up in LaSalle, Quebec, loving the game of hockey. As a player, Lemaire would rise up through the ranks and play his entire NHL career with the Montreal Canadiens from 1967-79. There, he was a member of eight Stanley Cup championship-winning teams, including four straight from 1976-79. Known for being a clutch player, the speedy centerman also tallied the Stanley Cup-clinching goals in both the 1977 and 1979 Finals. Lemaire finished his illustrious playing career with 835 points (366 goals, 469 assists) in 853 regular season games, scoring 20 or more goals in each of his 12 seasons in the National Hockey League.

Following his retirement, Lemaire began his coaching career in Switzerland, where he served as player/coach of the Sierre Club. He returned in 1981 to take over as the first head coach of the expansion Longueuil Chevaliers, of the Quebec Major Junior Hockey League, where he guided the team to the Finals in his first season. From there, Lemaire began his NHL coaching career with his old team, the Canadiens. He took over the Habs midway through the 1983 season and guided them to the Wales Conference Finals. The next year, he coached Montreal to the Adams Division championship. Lemaire stepped aside as the head coach following the 1985 campaign, however, and spent the next eight years in the team's front office, playing a big role in both of Montreal's Stanley Cup championships in 1986 and 1993.

In 1993 Lemaire came to the States to take over as the head coach of the New Jersey Devils. Over the next five seasons he would compile a record of 199-122-57 (.602), and guide the Devils to their first-ever Stanley Cup championship along the way in 1994. For his efforts he was awarded the Jack Adams Trophy as the NHL's outstanding head coach. In 1998 Lemaire stepped down once again to serve as a consultant for his Canadiens.

Then, in the Summer of 2000, Lemaire got back into the game and was named as the first-ever head coach of the expansion Minnesota Wild. How would this legendary hockey figure do with a young expansion team? Simply amazing. Playing to sell-out crowds at the newly constructed Xcel Energy Center in St. Paul, Lemaire became an instant fan-favorite for his hard work and no-nonsense gritty style. During the Wild's inaugural year, Lemaire's club set an expansion team record with a nine-game home unbeaten streak (5-0-4-0) and finished with the seventh highest point total (68) for an expansion club in NHL history. During the 2002 season, the Wild finished ahead of their first season's pace by five points and improved their goals and assist production by 75. Then, Lemaire did the improbable in 2003, leading his young Wild all the way to the Stanley Cup semifinals. Sure, they lost a heartbreaking series to the Anaheim Mighty Ducks, but it was one heck of a ride for hockey fans in Minnesota. Lemaire led the third-year Wild to its first postseason appearance and finished with 95 points, a 22-point improvement on 2002. For his efforts, the 57-year-old Lemaire won his second Jack Adams Award as the NHL's Coach of the Year. Overall, Lemaire has guided the Wild to a 93-118-35 record during their first three seasons, and he did it all with one of the lowest payrolls in the league.

Lemaire is the epitome of a player's coach, and is arguably the most respected man in hockey today. With the Wild, he turned a little expansion team into the little-engine-that-could, making believers out of all the nay-sayers along the way. One of the most knowledgeable men in the game, Lemaire has proven that he can coach under any circumstances. Whether he is implementing his now infa-

mous "neutral-zone trap," or trying to get a young player to get better, or even resurrecting a career of an older veteran, Lemaire is a teacher and a motivator. He is also a winner in every sense of the word. Not only does he have his name on the Stanley Cup an incredible 11 times, as both a player and coach, but he also owns a career head coaching record of 340-277-104 in 10 NHL seasons. The 1984 Hall of Fame inductee has also taken seven of the 10 teams he has coached to the post-season, and is set to keep it going for the Wild in 2004 and beyond.

Jacques, who also owns a very successful construction company in Canada, and his wife Mychele have homes in the Twin Cities, Montreal and Sarasota, Fla., where they are avid boaters. They have three children, including two sons, Patrice and Danyk, and one daughter, Magalie.

HOW WOULD YOU DESCRIBE YOUR COACHING STYLE? "I think I am the type of person who will coach the way the players want me to coach. I am a guy who will stick with his ideas and I try to go with what I know. With regards to coaching and how to handle people, I think my players play a big part in that. I mean if they want me to be tougher for instance, then I get tougher. If they want me to ease up on them, then that is what I do depending on how they respond to what I am asking of them. You know, every coach tries to find a way to win. The goal is to win. Period. You also have to work with the type of players that you have. You just have to find a certain way to play which will help the individual to perform. You know, people talk about my defensive philosophy and the 'neutral zone trap' and that kind of thing, and that is OK. But I don't know one coach who doesn't want his players to score. Believe me, scoring is a good thing and it is good for your team. But, you just have to consider what is best for your team and what you can do to get the most success possible from your players. Then, after all that, you have to sell that to your players and get them to buy into it. If things are not going well, then you have to find another route. And if your second route is no good, then you need to find a third. When you run out of routes, you are done as a coach. That's it."

ON MINNESOTA: "The whole experience has been just great for my wife and I. We love it here and it feel that it is very similar to Quebec with regards to the climate, the scenery and the lakes, and it just feels like home. As for being with the Wild, it has been wonderful. It is really more than I ever expected, no doubt. We had a plan and we are very much ahead of our plan now and that makes it a little tougher because now we aren't going to be drafting as low as we were supposed to. So, that makes it tougher for the next season to repeat and to improve on our success. But up to now we have done it and we are going to have to work even harder to get better. Our guys need to step it up. The older guys are being good leaders and the younger guys are following. Hopefully we will be able to continue that success in the years to come. Minnesota is just a great place and they take their hockey very seriously here. There is a lot of great hockey here, from the high schools to the Gophers, and that makes for some very knowledgeable fans."

HOW DO YOU MOTIVATE YOUR PLAYERS? "Every coach has different ways to motivate his players. You know it is hard to explain because there are so many little things that coaches do to try to motivate his guys. It depends a lot on their character and how hard they want to work. That will tell me how to deal with them as a coach. I think most of motivation comes from the players themselves. A player that loves his job, wants to succeed, wants to win and is proud of himself, is easy to motivate."

WHAT ARE THE CHARACTERISTICS OF WINNERS? "Winners are not necessarily guys who have won in the past — they might have just been a part of a good team and have won as a result. A winner is a guy who is very dedicated to his team and is very dedicated to his job. He will do things to help other guys and will lead by example. Basically, a winner is a team player. If you are not a team player then you are not a winner."

IF YOU COULD MAGICALLY GO BACK IN TIME TO THE FIRST YEAR YOU WERE A HEAD COACH AND GIVE YOURSELF SOME ADVICE FOR THE FUTURE, KNOWING WHAT YOU KNOW NOW, BACK THEN, WHAT WOULD YOU SAY TO YOURSELF? "I was too intense when I first started out in coaching. Sometimes I looked at things like there was no tomorrow and that was just too intense. Maybe I was nervous about not having success or not having a team that would perform."

LOOKING BACK WHAT ARE YOU MOST PROUD OF IN YOUR CAREER? "I think being involved in winning organizations, because I have learned a lot from being a part of that. You learn what it takes to win and what you have to do to win."

WHAT IS THE KEY TO GOOD TIME MANAGEMENT? "You just have to stay on top of things all of the time. Every day it seems like you run into one, two, or three problems and you have to detect the problems which could be major ones. You have to correct those first and then go from there. You can't let little problems turn into big problems."

HOW DO YOU BUILD TEAM UNITY & CHEMISTRY? "This is probably the hardest thing to explain. It's kind of funny because to me, coaches, we are all the same. We think alike and maybe the difference is how we relate to our players as individuals and how we relate to the group. To me that is the only difference in coaches. How you sit down and talk to a player and how he understands what you are saying is the key. Then, how is he going to feel afterwards? Then, when that doesn't work, you have to go to plan B and find something else. To me everything you do during every single day is part of creating team unity. It's the way you talk, the way you practice, the way you live your life. Then, from a coaching standpoint, it is also how you correct them and why you correct them because they have to know why in order to improve. You just have to constantly work on building teamwork, then you will have chemistry."

WHAT MOTIVATES YOU? "What makes me really proud is when I look at my team and see that they are playing great as a unit and having success. That really motivates me."

WHAT ADVICE WOULD YOU HAVE FOR YOUNG COACHES STARTING OUT TODAY? "I would say to listen more than you talk, because you will learn a lot."

WHAT'S THE BIGGEST THING YOU'VE LEARNED FROM COACHING THAT YOU'VE BEEN ABLE TO APPLY TO YOUR EVERYDAY LIFE? "How to deal with people. When you have to deal with 23 different characters every year, it gets interesting. You learn when to talk and when to listen."

WHAT ARE THE KEY INGREDIENTS TO CREATING A CHAMPIONSHIP TEAM? "First, I think you have to have players. From there, I would say teamwork and then good management, in that order."

WHAT'S THE SECRET TO YOUR SUCCESS? "I don't think there is any secret. If anything, it is the environment that I have surrounded myself in. All my career I have had great assistants and a great management team. That is a very big thing in my mind. As a result, I always feel comfortable working with those people and that lets me focus on coaching. Also, as a player I learned that when coaches were talking, that was when I needed to be listening. That is how I learned so much and have since been able to pass it along to my players."

WHAT WOULD YOU WANT TO SAY TO YOUR FANS, BOOSTERS, AND ALUMNI WHO HAVE SUPPORTED YOU ALL THESE YEARS? "We have been blessed to have had what happened here in Minnesota. These people lost their team, the North Stars, and they showed great patience in getting another one. The coaches, management and players just really appreciate the fans here because they are really, really good. The players know that the fans here support them and, to a certain point, will accept certain mistakes that they make. I know it will be tougher in the future because of the fact that we are ahead of our plan, but that just means we will have to work harder. Really, I don't think we have to do what we did last year in making it to the conference finals. Repeating that same performance year after year will be tough, and believe me, we are not there yet. We'll have some ups and downs along the way, but we will have to work very hard to keep this level of success. The fans have played a big part in that though, and I would like to thank them for their support. They are behind us and the players feel that. They don't feel the pressure of winning every night and that motivates our guys to play harder and to win for them. Win or lose, as long as they play hard the fans can accept that. The fans realize too that we are a young team and are building for the future. We have a plan. We aren't there yet, but we will be in a few years."

HOW DO YOU WANT YOUR COACHING EPITAPH TO READ — HOW DO YOU WANT TO BE REMEMBERED AS A COACH? "As someone who thought a lot about his players and cared for them. I respect my players because I know what they are going through."

BILL WATSON:
ST. SCHOLASTICA HOCKEY

Bill Watson, a former Hobey Baker winner at the University of Minnesota-Duluth in 1985, went on to serve as the head coach at St. Scholastica, in Duluth, from 1991-93, and later served as an assistant at Western Michigan University. The Powerview, Manitoba, native later moved back to Duluth with his family, where he currently has a successful insurance business.

DON LUCIA
COLLEGE HOCKEY: UNIVERSITY OF MINNESOTA

Don Lucia grew up in Grand Rapids and went on to graduate from Grand Rapids High School in 1977. There, he led his team to a pair of State High School Hockey titles in 1975 and 1976, as well as a pair of third-place finishes in 1974 and 1977. The sturdy defenseman not only earned all-state honors in hockey his senior year, but also on the gridiron as a linebacker on the football team. From there, Lucia, who was later drafted by the Philadelphia Flyers of the National Hockey League, went on to play hockey at the University of Notre Dame. There, Lucia emerged as the team captain with the Fighting Irish, graduating in 1981.

Lucia then got into coaching, with his first job coming at the University of Alaska-Fairbanks, where he served as an assistant from 1981-85. In 1985 he moved over to the University of Alaska Anchorage, where he served as an assistant for two seasons before returning to Fairbanks for his first head position. Lucia served as the head coach at Fairbanks for six years, posting four winning seasons and an overall record of 113-87-10, before leaving the Nanooks in 1993 to take over as the head coach at Colorado College.

At CC Lucia took over the reins of the program that had not experienced a winning season in the previous 13 campaigns. How would he do? Outstanding. Lucia guided the Tigers to a record of 23-11-5 and the WCHA regular-season title in his rookie season — the program's first in 37 years. Lucia was honored at the conclusion of that season with the Spencer Penrose Award as National Coach of the Year. Lucia he didn't stop there though, guiding the Tigers to an unprecedented three straight outright regular-season league titles in his first three years behind the bench. Colorado College won a school-record 33 games in 1996, and made it all the way to the NCAA championship game. For his efforts, Lucia was named WCHA Coach of the Year that same season, and added a second league coach of the year trophy at the conclusion of the 1997 season as well, when he led his Tigers back to the NCAA Frozen Four semi-finals. In all, Lucia would spend six seasons in Colorado Springs, racking up a gaudy 166-68-18 record along the way.

On April 9, 1999, the University of Minnesota announced that Don Lucia would become the 13th head coach in Golden Gopher Hockey history. Nearly three years to the day later, Lucia raised the NCAA Championship Trophy above his head at the Xcel Energy Center in St. Paul. Led by Hobey Baker Award winner Jordan Leopold, and All American Johnny Pohl, the Gophers hung on to beat Maine in one of the greatest Finals in history that year. Amazingly, he would do it again that next year too, making it back-to-back national championships as the Gophers this time beat New Hampshire in the Finals of the Frozen Four in Buffalo, New York.

Lucia, who has posted an awesome 107-48-17 record during his four year tenure with the Gophers, has an overall career record of 386-203-46 over the past 17 seasons. He has established himself as one of the premier collegiate coaches in the nation and has put the Gophers back on top of the hockey world once again. In all, he has coached 12 All-Americans, more than three dozen All-WCHA players, nearly five dozen WCHA All-Academic team members, six Hobey Baker Award finalists and five WCHA Defensive Players of the Year. And, he is one of just six coaches in NCAA history to lead two different teams to the Frozen Four.

Lucia has also been active with USA Hockey for the last decade, having served as head coach of the national-16 team that competed in Finland in 1996, as well as for Team West at the U.S.

Olympic Festival in Denver in 1995. Lucia also served as the president of the American Hockey Coaches Association in 1999.

Don and his wife Joyce live in Plymouth and have four children: Alison, Jessica, Anthony and Mario.

HOW WOULD YOU DESCRIBE YOUR COACHING STYLE? "Number one, I give my assistants a lot of responsibility in what we do and they have a lot of say. I think it is a team effort, it is not just about me, so I want a lot of input from my staff and players. Ultimately, I have the final say in things, but communication is very important to our success. I have always tried to have my teams play on an even keel night in and night out too. I don't think you can get all fired up for Friday night and then have a let down on Saturday, so consistency is also very important to me."

HOW DO YOU MOTIVATE YOUR PLAYERS? "Number one, you have to coach to your own personality. I don't think you can copy what a certain coach does and then try to be the same thing, that is impossible. So, I try to treat my kids fairly. I want them to respect me, but there also has to be a line where they know who is in charge. Then, I try to give the leaders of our team a lot of say in what we are doing. I also think that as I have gotten older as a coach I have begun to realize more and more that you just have to try to make each individual team the best that that particular team can be. And that changes from year to year. My philosophy has always been that I want our team to reach its potential, and I don't ever want my players to play with the fear in that if they make a mistake that they will get benched. Hockey is a game of read and react and you have to play with confidence. When you play with confidence, that is when you play your best."

WHO WERE YOUR COACHING MENTORS? "My father was my high school football coach and he had a big impact on me. Then, Mike Sertich and Jim Nelson were my high school hockey coaches, and I had a lot of respect for those guys too. So, you take pieces of those people who you have been around your whole life and that kind of forms your style. I remember as a kid admiring Bud Grant's calm and cool on the sidelines, and I have always felt that that was a very important quality to have."

ON WINNING BACK TO BACK NCAA CHAMPIONSHIPS: "You know, it is like when I go out recruiting players to come here and I always ask them the question, 'if you could win a national title, whose jersey would you want to be wearing?'. And I certainly feel that way as a coach, that there is no better place to win a title than at the University of Minnesota, because of how much pride there is in this state with Gopher Hockey. I am so happy to be back in Minnesota. This is just an incredible program and it is really a once in a lifetime opportunity to serve as the coach of the Gophers."

IF YOU COULD MAGICALLY GO BACK IN TIME TO THE FIRST YEAR YOU WERE A HEAD COACH AND GIVE YOURSELF SOME ADVICE FOR THE FUTURE, KNOWING WHAT YOU KNOW NOW, BACK THEN, WHAT WOULD YOU SAY TO YOURSELF? "Be more patient, you are not going to change the world."

WHAT ARE THE CHARACTERISTICS OF WINNERS? "Commitment, character, and teamwork."

LOOKING BACK WHAT ARE YOU MOST PROUD OF IN YOUR CAREER? "I would hope that most of the players who have played for me can look back and feel that they were treated fairly, reached their potential and had a great time."

HOW DO YOU BUILD TEAM UNITY & CHEMISTRY? "I don't believe in hazing or rookie initiations. I am big believer that once a player is on the team then everybody should be treated the same. I think that chemistry starts from there."

WHAT MOTIVATES YOU? "I am really into my family and I just try to spend as much time as possible with them as I can. They really motivate me to be the best person that I can be, both on and off the ice."

WHAT ADVICE WOULD YOU HAVE FOR YOUNG COACHES STARTING OUT TODAY? "Coach to your personality, be patient and treat your players like you would want your son to be treated."

WHAT'S THE BIGGEST THING YOU'VE LEARNED FROM COACHING THAT YOU'VE BEEN ABLE TO APPLY TO YOUR EVERYDAY LIFE? "To be disciplined in everything I do."

WHAT ROLE HAS YOUR FAMILY PLAYED IN YOUR SUCCESS? "I couldn't have had the success I have had without the support of my wife. She has had to hold down the fort at home while I have been out coaching and recruiting all across the country and I really appreciate that. Whether it is recruiting dinners or team meals at our house, she has been there and that has made my job so much easier. And, the team has become more of an extended family to my own family, and I think that helps build team unity and chemistry too."

WHAT'S THE BEST PIECE OF ADVICE YOU EVER GOT FROM ANOTHER COACH? "Mike Sertich once told me to 'take care of the game.' And by that he meant that the game is bigger than any one person, any one player or any one coach. So, try to make decisions that benefit our sport."

ON RECRUITING NON-MINNESOTANS: "To me 'Pride on Ice' does not mean an all-Minnesota team, it is taking pride in the hockey program at the University of Minnesota and supporting whoever is wearing a maroon and gold jersey."

WHAT WOULD YOU WANT TO SAY TO YOUR FANS, BOOSTERS, AND ALUMNI WHO HAVE SUPPORTED YOU ALL THESE YEARS? "The people here have been so great to me and my family, and we really appreciate that. This is my fourth coaching job and while they have all been great, it is particularly special to be back in Minnesota and having success. The fans here are so smart and so enthusiastic and that makes our jobs so much easier as coaches. It is so sweet to see that the whole state embraces our hockey program, even though there are four other division one schools here as well. That just does not happen anywhere else and I am very lucky to have that kind of support. It is special. So, I am just on this train ride for a short time and when I get off, somebody else will get on and do a great job as well."

HOW DO YOU WANT YOUR COACHING EPITAPH TO READ — HOW DO YOU WANT TO BE REMEMBERED AS A COACH? "I hope that when it is all said and done that we have turned a lot of boys into men. I also hope that we not only had success, but we had success the right way. It is very important that we graduate our players and that we try to have them all reach their potential. So, as a coach I would hope to be remembered for things like that."

LARRY ROSS:
INTERNATIONAL FALLS HIGH SCHOOL HOCKEY

Larry Ross graduated from Morgan Park High School in his hometown of Duluth in 1940 and from there went on to serve four years in the Navy at the height of World War II. Ross saw action in Sicily, Salerno, North Africa, the Pacific Theatre and the Persian Gulf as a salvage diver. Despite his worldly travels, Ross still found time to play hockey on the Navy team in 1942, and upon his return he played goalie for the amateur St. Paul Seven-Ups for a year. Ross then attended the University of Minnesota, where he emerged as an all-American goaltender in 1951 and 1952. After graduating from the U of M, Ross went on to become a coaching legend at International Falls High School. Ross' Broncos would win 16 conference championships, play in the state hockey tournament 14 times, win six titles, place second twice and third three times. From 1964 through 1966, the Broncos captured three consecutive state titles, going undefeated in 58 straight games along the way to create one of the greatest dynasties in high school hockey history. In all, Ross coached 31 years at the Falls, racking up an amazing 566-169-21 (.749) career record. Ross would retire in 1984 as the state's second all-time winningest hockey coach. (In 1966 Ross was offered the head coaching job at the University of Wisconsin but turned it down to stay in Minnesota.) Dozens and dozens of Ross' former players went on to swell the ranks of college hockey, with eight players later seeing Olympic action and 12 going on the play in the NHL.

In addition, Ross also started the Rainy River Community College hockey program, and for a stretch, ran both teams at the same time. From 1980-84, Ross served as a scout for the NHL's Hartford Whalers, and after his retirement he continued to scout for the Whalers, North Stars and the San Jose Sharks. Among his many honors and accolades, Ross was named coach of the year by the Minnesota Hockey Coaches Association in 1983; in 1985, he was awarded the National High School Special Sports Award by the National High School Athletic Coaches Association; in 1988, he was the recipient of the John Mariucci College Award from the American College Hockey Coaches Association; and in 1988, Ross was inducted into the United States Hockey Hall of Fame. The consummate teacher and coach, Ross even wrote a book entitled "Hockey For Everyone." Ross was not a great motivator amongst his blue collar constitutes, nor did he have a complex psychological theory on strategy either. He just wanted to win and was willing to work hard and pay the price to achieve that. That is why Larry Ross was a winner. In the "Nation's Ice Box," a town of just 8,000 souls, hockey reigned supreme... and Larry Ross was its king. A true hockey legend in every sense of the word, Larry Ross was one of the all-time great ones.

JOHN MATCHEFTS
COLLEGE HOCKEY: COLORADO COLLEGE & AIR FORCE

John Matchefts grew up in Eveleth loving the game of hockey. So good was Matchefts that at the age of just 16 he was invited to play on the 1948 U.S. Olympic hockey team. While high school league rules prevented him from playing on the team, the phenom did go on to lead his Eveleth Golden Bears High School hockey team to three state high school championships from 1947-49, going undefeated along the way. Matchefts learned the game from legendary Eveleth hockey coach Cliff Thompson, who allowed the speedy three-time all-state centerman to be creative out on the ice. It is no wonder that Matchefts held the state record for all-time assists when you consider his linemate was none other that John Mayasich, the leading state tourney goal scorer of all-time. A well-rounded athlete, Matchefts also starred on the football and baseball teams at Eveleth as well.

From there, Matchefts went on to play college hockey at the University of Michigan from 1949-53. There, Matchefts became a two-time All-American en route to leading his Wolverines to a trio of NCAA Championships from 1951-53. Known as the "Fly" because of his speed, agility and maneuverability, Matchefts averaged two points per game at Michigan, with 57 goals and 74 assists in his college career. Upon graduating, Matchefts declined the opportunity to play professional hockey, and instead went on to play on the 1955 U.S. National team. (He also played on the 1951 U.S. National team as well as the 1952 U.S. Olympic team while in college.) Then, in 1956, Matchefts laced em' up for fellow Eveleth native John Mariucci, as a member of the U.S. Olympic team which won a silver medal in Cortina, Italy.

Matchefts then got into coaching and teaching, spending the next three years at Thief River Falls High School in the late 1950s. There, he led his boys to the state high school hockey tournament in 1959. In 1960 he came home to Eveleth to teach and take over as the head coach of the Golden Bears, replacing his mentor, Cliff Thompson. Matchefts led Eveleth to the state tourney in his first season back in Eveleth and wound up coaching the Bears for seven more before going on to take over as the head coach at Colorado College.

John left Eveleth to coach in college because he saw that there were so many kids from Minnesota who could play college hockey, but simply weren't getting a chance to play. So, he went to CC and recruited a bunch of kids from the Iron Range to give them a chance. All of the other coaches in the WCHA were Canadian and were only taking Canadian kids. John Mariucci encouraged him to take the job as well, to help American kids get more opportunities.

Matchefts coached at the old Broadmoor Arena in Colorado Springs from 1966-71, earning WCHA Coach of the Year honors in 1968. In 1972 John left CC, but didn't leave town. That's because that year he headed across town to take over as the head coach of the Air Force Academy, which is also in Colorado Springs. Matchefts would coach at the Academy for 15 years, giving not only Minnesota kids, but American kids, the opportunity to play and get an education at the next level. He took the Academy from a club team to division one status, ultimately retiring from coaching in 1992 with a career record of 207-237-9. Matchefts would remain with the Air Force Academy Athletic Department for several more years, however, before finally retiring for good.

A member of the United States Hockey Hall of Fame, John is retired and presently lives in Colorado Springs. John Matchefts was an extraordinary player, an outstanding coach and a tremendous person.

HOW WOULD YOU DESCRIBE YOUR COACHING STYLE? "I had a lot of exposure to the National Hockey League and Russian hockey early on in my career and that enabled me to develop a concept of how the game should be played. So I just tried to pass on what I knew to the younger people. I was fortunate to grow up in a community like Eveleth where hockey meant so much to the community. We learned the game as kids from the older players and passed it on just like they did. It was a great tradition and I was proud to grow up in that environment. You know, as far as I am concerned, the skills and techniques of hockey have never changed. We have just improved on the team aspect of the game, that is all."

HOW DID YOU MOTIVATE YOUR PLAYERS? "You know, I never really thought about motivating my players, I just thought about teaching them what the basic skills were. Hockey is a magic game when it is played the right way and I just tried to teach my players the fundamentals so that they could play as best as the could. I tried to get them to be self motivated so that I could focus on teaching them."

LOOKING BACK WHAT ARE YOU MOST PROUD OF IN YOUR CAREER? "I was very proud to have come from Eveleth. I was lucky to have played in the state high school hockey tournament and in college and then in the Olympics. All of it was just a marvelous experience."

HOW DID YOU BUILD TEAM UNITY & CHEMISTRY? "I usually just explained to the players what my philosophy was and what the rules and regulations were. If they accepted them they got a uniform and if they didn't then they didn't get one. I explained to them that this was the way it was going to be and this was what I was going to teach. That was it."

WHAT MOTIVATED YOU? "What motivated me started early on when I began coaching at Thief River Falls and Eveleth. When I saw that there were no opportunities for American hockey players to go on and play college hockey, that motivated me to do something about it. So, I got into coaching at the collegiate level and from there I was able to make a difference. I wanted to show the rest of the world that American kids were just as good, and in many cases better, than the Canadian kids. I am very proud of that."

WHAT'S THE SECRET TO YOUR SUCCESS? "I really enjoyed watching division three players become division one players. In other words, watching players develop their skill was what it was all about. My success came from making that happen and that was very gratifying for me to see."

HOW DO YOU WANT YOUR COACHING EPITAPH TO READ — HOW DO YOU WANT TO BE REMEMBERED AS A COACH? "I suppose I would want to be remembered for being able to pass on what skills I was able to learn to other people so that they could improve themselves."

CLIFF THOMPSON:
EVELETH HIGH SCHOOL HOCKEY

Cliff Thompson was an Eveleth hockey institution. Thompson, who attended Minneapolis Central High School, went on to play hockey at the University of Minnesota, graduating in 1925. From there, Thompson took over as the coach of the Eveleth High School hockey team in 1926. The rest, they say, is hockey history. Thompson, who is considered even to this day to be the most celebrated and respected high school hockey coach in our state's history, would create a hockey dynasty that would never be equaled. Under Thompson's direction, Eveleth High School quickly gained a reputation as the team to beat in the state of Minnesota, and before long teams from the Twin Cities were lining up to take a crack at the boys from the Range. Eveleth held strong though, and answered most every challenge given to them.

By 1929, the Golden Bears were riding an unbelievable winning streak, not having lost a game in more than three years against all of the Iron Range and Duluth schools. That year a metro high school all-star team of sorts, called the Cardinals, was assembled by former Minneapolis Miller great Nick Kahler. The Cards, who had won the Minneapolis Recreation title that year, were composed primarily of players from Minneapolis South and West High Schools. The Cards and Bears would do battle that year in front of a packed house at the Minneapolis Arena, with the all-star team edging Eveleth in a thriller by the narrow margin of 2-1. (An idea of the caliber of talent on the ice that night was personified by the fact that six of the 11 Eveleth players and five of the 11 Minneapolis players would later play professional hockey.)

Eveleth's icy reign of terror continued through the 1930s, giving people hope and joy during the years of the Great Depression. One of the reasons for this was due to the fact that people such as coach Thompson made sure that all of his kids had a good pair of skates under their feet, as well as quality protective equipment around them. By the 1940s more and more schools were playing hockey, and it was inevitable that a state-wide tournament would come to fruition. And, in 1945, mainly through the efforts hockey pioneer Gene Aldrich of St. Paul, that's just what happened, when the Minnesota State High School League hosted the first-ever boys state high school tournament at the St. Paul Auditorium.

Thompson led his squad to that first tournament and showed the rest of Minnesota what the people on the Range had known for years — Eveleth was awesome! Led by what many still consider today to be the greatest ever high school hockey line of Pat Finnegan, Wally Grant and Neil Celley, the Golden Bears breezed through the tourney and captured the state's first ever crown. The Golden Bears shut out Granite Falls 16-0 in their first quarterfinal game, and in so doing they set a rather unique record that still stands today: "LEAST STOPS BY A GOALTENDER — ONE, by Eveleth's Ron Drobnick," (On a shot from center ice nonetheless!) Eveleth rolled over St. Paul Washington 10-0 in the semifinal contest, and went on to edge a strong Thief River Falls team 4-3 for the title. Wally Grant, who would later star as a member of the infamous "G" line at the University of Michigan, tallied both the tying and go-ahead goals in that championship game.

That next season, in 1946, Eveleth narrowly missed a repeat title finishing third, only to see one of their own native sons bring home the hardware instead. That's because former Eveleth goaltender Oscar Almquist, a former Golden Bear back in the 1920s, who went on to star at St. Mary's College and later for the St. Paul Saints, coached Roseau High School to its first title. Eveleth would continue its domination at the tourney through 1956. During that 12-year span the Golden Bears won five championships, twice finished as runners-up and claimed three third place finishes. The team earned a berth in the first 12 state tournaments and rode two amazing winning streaks of 79 and 58 games. One era in particular was the greatest possibly in the history of high school sports. That was from 1948 to 1951, when the team posted a perfect 69-0 record over four consecutive undefeated seasons en route to winning four straight titles. Incidentally, Eveleth's unbelievable winning streak ended in 1952 when Iron Range rival Hibbing bested the Golden Bears 4-3 in the title game.

Those incredible Eveleth teams were led by so many outstanding young men, including the likes of John Matchefts and Willard Ikola. But one man stands alone when it comes to "legendary status" in Minnesota high school hockey during that era — John Mayasich, who is arguably the greatest player ever to lace up a pair of skates in Minnesota. Mayasich still holds 10 scoring records in the state tournament including most all-time points (46) and goals (36). But 1951 was the year Mayasich stole the show when he amassed 18 points in three games on 15 goals and three assists, including seven goals in a semifinal win over Minneapolis Southwest. (Of course, Mayasich went on to become an All-American at the University of Minnesota, where he rewrote the Gopher record book, scoring 144 goals and 298 total points. Mayasich then became the only player ever to compete on eight U.S. National or Olympic teams.)

From 1926-58 Thompson guided the Bears and when it was all said and done, he had posted on of the most amazing records in the history of sports: 534-26-9. In addition to coaching the high school team, Thompson also coached the Eveleth Junior College team, where his career record was equally impressive at 171-28-7. In fact, his Junior College squad even garnered the nation's top collegiate ranking on several occasions during the late 1920s, even beating out the likes of Minnesota, Michigan and Yale. (EJC's toughest competition year in and year out was the Eveleth High School team, which often beat them in scrimmages!)

Generations of Eveleth youngsters received hockey instructions from Thompson, and in addition to his giving them the best hockey leadership, he was the object of deep affection that only boys can have for a man as close to them as their coach and teacher. Thompson's legacy is immeasurable. No less than a dozen Eveleth players went on to play in the National Hockey League and virtually all them learned the game from Thompson. (Among them were Frank Brimsek, Mike Karakas, Sam LoPresti and John Mariucci — all Hall of Famers, as well as John Mayasich, John Matchefts and Willard Ikola, who are also legendary hockey figures in Minnesota.)

Among his many coaching honors and accolades, Thompson was made an honorary member of the American Hockey Coaches Association in 1957, one of only a handful of men ever so honored. A true American hero, and a legend in every sense of the word, Cliff Thompson died on June 7, 1974, in Eveleth.

SHANNON MILLER
WOMEN'S COLLEGE HOCKEY: UM-DULUTH

Shannon Miller grew up in Melfort, Saskatchewan, playing hockey. Miller would go on to earn her bachelor's degree in physical education from the University of Saskatchewan in 1985, competing in four Canadian National Championships from 1982-85 along the way. From there, Miller, who also refereed at the college level during that time, would go on to become a police officer in Calgary, Alberta. After seven years in law enforcement, Miller was hired by the Olympic Oval in Calgary, to build the first ever international high performance training program for women's hockey. At the same time, Miller would also get into coaching.

Miller launched her national coaching career as an assistant with the Alberta Women's Hockey Team (18 and under) in 1989 and two years later was part of a club, which captured a gold medal in the first-ever ice hockey competition for women in the Canadian Winter Games. Miller would go on to coach Team Canada for seven years, winning the major competitions for six out of those seven and was the first female head coach to ever coach a women's Olympic hockey team anywhere in the world. In those seven years with the national team, Miller directed Canada to a silver medal in the 1998 Winter Olympic Games and to three consecutive gold medals at Women's World Ice Hockey Championships (1992, 1994 and 1997). Miller also coached Canada to gold-medal finishes at both the 1995 and 1996 Pacific Rim Championships as well as at the Three Nations Cup tournament in 1996 as well.

In 1999 Miller came to the University of Minnesota Duluth, where she became the program's first ever women's hockey coach. Since then, she has simply dominated the sport, literally rewriting the history books as she goes. Miller has led the Lady Bulldogs to three consecutive back-to-back-to-back NCAA Championship titles from 2001-03, becoming the first coach since Gopher Football legend Bernie Bierman some seven decades ago, to win three straight titles in division one sports in Minnesota. The 2003 national title even came at the DECC in Duluth, making it even sweeter. The NCAA title game was simply epic as UMD edged Harvard, 4-3, in double overtime. The win, before more than 5,000 home fans, gave Miller a final record of 31-3-2 for the year as well as a three-peat — making her Bulldogs an official dynasty.

During Miller's illustrious career at UMD, she has compiled an amazing 108-19-13 record for a whopping .818 winning percentage, earning the top spot among all women's college hockey coaches. Miller has guided the Bulldogs into the national tournament every year, capturing the first three NCAA Championship titles ever played. She has also coached the team to two WCHA regular season championships (2000 and 2003) and three WCHA Tournament titles (2000, 2001 and 2003) as well.

Miller and her Bulldog teams have also been invited to the White House on three separate occasions to be honored by President George W. Bush. "I know something about sports and it takes a great coach to win the national title. And this team has an extraordinary coach," said Bush on Miller's accomplishments.

Among Miller's many coaching honors and accolades, in 2001 she was chosen to coach the first ever WCHA All-Star team, which competed with the U.S. Olympic team in a two game series in preparation for the 2002 Olympic Games. In 2000 Miller was selected to serve on the inaugural NCAA women's hockey committee, which plans, organizes and operates the women's NCAA Final Four. (This year she will continue her duties with the committee for a fourth

consecutive season.) Miller was also named as the 2003 American Hockey Coaches Association Coach of the Year as well as the 2000 WCHA Coach of the Year. In addition, for her groundbreaking successes for female sports in Canada, Miller was given the prestigious Canadian Advancement of Women in Sport Award after the 1998 Olympics. Additionally, Miller's been a volunteer member of the Canadian Hockey Association Female Council, president of the Southern Alberta Women's Hockey League and chairperson of the Saskatchewan Female Hockey League. She was also honored in 2003 by the NHL's Calgary Flames organization for her global pioneer work in the game of hockey.

Shannon Miller is an outstanding person and coach. And, as she continues to make hockey history in Duluth, she also continues to make the entire state of Minnesota very proud as well.

In the world of women's college hockey, Shannon Miller is without question, a living legend.

HOW WOULD YOU DESCRIBE YOUR COACHING STYLE? "I definitely have a holistic approach to coaching. The basis for that philosophy is that the athletes are people first and they have a whole world around them that effects how they feel everyday, and therefore the outcome of their performance. If you approach it as they're people and they have many other factors influencing their performance and how they feel that day for training, then you better understand the athlete and therefore you can better motivate them and help them reach their own potential. With regards to the other factors, it's obviously school, family, friends, vehicle situation, finances, all of those kinds of things. So, I actually get quite involved with my athletes as people and work from that approach. Having said that I think that I am a coach who is very flexible regarding my style. I am certainly not tyrannical, but I am also not really passive and quiet when I coach either. Some wonder how I can be so subdued on the bench while others think I am very intimidating, intense and aggressive. I just try to be myself, and that has always been my style."

HOW DO YOU MOTIVATE YOUR PLAYERS? "There are different ways. I mean there is team motivation, when you are trying to motivate your entire team, which is done by talking about what is important to them and stirring their emotions as a group. Then there is individual motivation, which I spend a lot of time on. I look at what is important for each and every person and then figure out how to help them get there. And then you have got to find ways to stir their emotions and push their buttons as individuals. So many people sitting in the room want different things. They want the same outcome with regards to winning, but a lot of them want to get their taking different roads. I am also a very strong motivational coach and that is so important. I mean every team lifts weights, every team has talent, every team has a grinder line, and every team has good goaltending in big games. So when you are that evenly matched physically, it all comes down to psychology and motivation after that."

WHAT IS THE KEY TO RECRUITING? "First of all, you have to figure out what your strengths are and what your niche is. Many of the Big 10 schools have things that we do not have, such as big rinks on campus, the bigger budgets, etc. So you can't try to be something you are not. For us, the key was using our international contacts, as well as my high profile as a former Olympic coach. Then, you have to work very hard and just pay the price. Of course, it also helps if you have an eye for talent."

IF YOU COULD MAGICALLY GO BACK IN TIME TO THE FIRST YEAR YOU WERE A HEAD COACH AND GIVE YOURSELF SOME ADVICE FOR THE FUTURE, KNOWING WHAT YOU KNOW NOW, BACK THEN, WHAT WOULD YOU SAY TO YOURSELF? "I would say to keep the game in perspective and to not take yourself too seriously. The media and public opinion will be involved, there will be all kinds of pressures and hoopla, and there will be people trying to drive you in a certain direction, but the reality is that none of that matters. You need to block all that out and just do what you think is right."

ON DULUTH HOCKEY: "Duluth has just been outstanding. They just love hockey there and the people are so friendly. They have embraced women's college hockey and we are very grateful. Their support has been outstanding and the fact that we were No. 2 in the country for attendance says a lot. Not bad for a team that has only been in existence for only four years!"

LOOKING BACK WHAT ARE YOU MOST PROUD OF IN YOUR CAREER? "With regards to the three national championships I am very proud of our accomplishments. The whole thing has been pretty unbelievable really. It is more than we had ever hoped for, but not more than what we have worked for. Winning the third title here in Duluth this past year was like a fairy tale ending. The best way to sum it up is that there is a very proud feeling here that we made history and we laid an incredible foundation of excellence for women's hockey teams to build on for years to come."

HOW DO YOU BUILD TEAM UNITY & CHEMISTRY? "Chemistry is a very important piece of the puzzle and you have to be very patient with it. It is important not to force it. You need to create the type of environment that will foster team chemistry itself. First of all, before you can have team chemistry, individuals have to be happy. If individuals are happy then they can be happy for their teammate sitting beside them. If everyone is happy and puts the team first, then you can achieve good chemistry."

WHAT MOTIVATES YOU? "It's never the fear of losing. What motivates me is the fact that I am very driven. You know, I come from a family of care-givers and I think coaching falls into that area. The biggest thrill I get is bringing the best out in people and seeing those people stretch themselves so far that they actually reach their potential. That motivates me every day."

WHAT'S THE SECRET TO YOUR SUCCESS? "I think my style is very flexible. I mean you can't really put me in a box. I listen, I am compassionate, I am very driven and most importantly I am committed to excellence."

WHAT WOULD YOU WANT TO SAY TO YOUR FANS, BOOSTERS, AND ALUMNI WHO HAVE SUPPORTED YOU ALL THESE YEARS? "I would say thank you for recognizing the importance of Title IX and opening your arms to a new women's sport that is growing rapidly and gaining worldwide acceptance. Thank you too for your patience in allowing women's hockey to be seen as the little sister to the big brother of men's hockey and letting us grow in a very healthy environment."

HOW DO YOU WANT YOUR COACHING EPITAPH TO READ — HOW DO YOU WANT TO BE REMEMBERED AS A COACH? "I would like to be remembered as somebody who had a holistic approach to coaching, was very compassionate, listened, had patience with people, and in doing so was incredibly successful."

DON JACKSON: NHL ASSISTANT

Don Jackson, a Bloomington Kennedy graduate who played college hockey at Notre Dame, went on to play professionally with the NHLs North Stars, Edmonton Oilers and New York Rangers from 1977-87. Jackson was also a member of two Stanley Cup champion Oilers teams in 1984 and '85. From there, Jackson became an assistant coach in the National Hockey League with the Quebec Nordiques, Pittsburgh Penguins, Chicago Blackhawks and Ottawa Senators, where he has currently been employed since 2001.

WARREN STRELOW: NHL GOALIE COACH

Warren Strelow grew up in St. Paul and went on to earn all-state honors as a goalie at Johnson High School. Following his high school career, Strelow played at the University of Minnesota, and later in the United States Hockey League for Des Moines and the Minneapolis Millers. Strelow then got into teaching and coaching at Mahtomedi High School, where he coached hockey and taught English and social studies for 14 years. Strelow later went on to serve as the goalie coach at the University of Minnesota from 1974-83. During Strelow's eight seasons at Minnesota, the Golden Gophers won three NCAA championships and twice finished runner-up. In addition, Strelow would also serve as the goalie coach for the 1979 U.S. National team as well as the 1980 gold medal winning U.S. Olympic team. In 1983 Strelow began working as a full-time goaltender coach at the professional level, spending six years with the NHL's Washington Capitals and four more with the New Jersey Devils. During those 10 years, Strelow tutored an impressive list of netminders including the likes of Sean Burke, Al Jensen, Pat Riggin, Pete Peeters, Clint Malarchuk, Bob Mason, Craig Billington, Chris Terreri, Corey Schwab and Martin Brodeur — one of his three All-Star protégés.

In 1997 Strelow took over as the goaltender coach of the San Jose Sharks, and has been there ever since. Strelow's positive influence on the team's netminders is evidenced by the career seasons and marked progress posted by several of the team's top goaltenders over the last two seasons, including the 2001 NHL Rookie of the Year winner, Evgeni Nabokov. Known throughout the hockey world for his expertise and results in training young goaltenders, Strelow's main responsibilities with the organization include working on techniques, reinforcing strengths and improving weaknesses of all the Sharks goaltenders.

In addition, Strelow also served as the goaltending coach for the 2002 U.S. Olympic team in Salt Lake City, where his team captured a silver medal. Among Strelow's many coaching awards and accolades, in 1996, he was inducted into the Minnesota High School Hockey Coaches Hall of Fame. Furthermore, for the past 27 years, Warren has operated the nationally renowned Strelow Goalie School in Minnesota, where, during the summer months, netminders of all ages can work on developing all phases of their game.

LOU NANNE
PRO HOCKEY: MINNESOTA NORTH STARS

Lou Nanne grew up in Sault Ste. Marie, Ontario, and went on to play junior hockey with Hall of Famers Phil and Tony Esposito. Originally wanting to go to college to be a dentist, Lou came to Minnesota to play for John Mariucci's Golden Gopher hockey teams from 1961-63. Earning Gopher captain and All-American honors in his senior year, Nanne tallied a career-high 74 points that season, becoming the first defenseman to win a WCHA scoring title. For his efforts the newly naturalized American citizen was named as the league's MVP.

Upon graduating from the University, Lou was drafted by the NHL's Chicago Blackhawks. Nanne got into a contract dispute with the Hawks, however, and ultimately refused to play for them, which led to a five year layoff from pro hockey. While he sat out, he worked for Minneapolis businessman Harvey Mackay's envelope company and also coached the Gopher freshman hockey team for four years as well. During that time, while playing on and off with the USHL's Rochester Mustangs to stay sharp, Nanne also went on to captain the 1968 U.S. Olympic hockey team in Grenoble, coached by former Gopher All-American Murray Williamson. Then, when the NHL expanded, Chicago couldn't "freeze" him anymore because of the new Reserve List. So, Nanne became a free agent and decided to play for Minnesota's new expansion team, the North Stars, where he would emerge as one of the team's first big stars.

Louie quickly earned a reputation as being a good team player for the Stars. Polished at killing penalties, he also developed into a fine checking forward who was often matched against the other teams' top line. Louie, considered as Minnesota's "Ice God," would go on to play defense and winger for the North Stars through 1978, becoming the only player to play with the team in all of the first 11 years of their existence. For his career with the North Stars, including the playoffs, the NHL All-Star tallied 72 goals and 167 assists for 239 points. On the international front, Nanne also captained the 1975 and 1977 USA World National teams, while serving as the assistant captain of Team USA in the 1976 1981, 1984 and 1987 Canada Cup tournaments, as well as in the 1994 World Championships.

Nanne then went from player to coach in 1977-78, and later became the team's general manager that next year as well. Of the players on the 1981 Stanley Cup team, only five were left from the team that Nanne took over in 1978. Louie quickly became known around the league as a shrewd wheeler and dealer of talent. He had clout with the other GM's around the league and parlayed that into his favor. In 1979 he claimed Dave Semenko from Glen Sather's Edmonton Oilers in the expansion draft for the sole purpose of dealing him right back to Sather in a "gentleman's agreement" to leave Neal Broten available for them in that year's upcoming amateur draft. Neal, of course, went on to become a legend in Minnesota. Louie would finished his 24-year career with the Stars as the team president from 1988-90. Bobby Smith would be his first pick while Mike Modano would be his last. As a GM, Louie was one of the best.

As a player, coach, GM, and president of the North Stars, Lou Nanne has one of the most storied careers of any player who has been involved in the game of ice hockey. Nanne also served as a member of the International Committee for USA Hockey, as a member of the NHL Board of Governors, and later served as Vice President of the NHL Players Association.

Although Canadian by birth, Nanne also became a well-known advocate of the Americanization of the NHL. He was one of the first to scout U.S. colleges for American talent and to take an active role in the support of player-development programs, which also included Olympic and international competition. Nanne also wasn't just involved with the North Stars. For his many contributions to USA hockey, Nanne was honored as a recipient of the 1989 Lester Patrick award. And, in addition to being named to the 50 Year WCHA All-Star team, in 1998 Nanne was inducted into the U.S. Hockey Hall of Fame.

Possibly the most recognized hockey figure in the state, "Sweet Lou from the Soo" is extremely well liked and respected by his peers. He had been a fixture with the North Stars from start to finish and is the authority on hockey in Minnesota today. His quick wit, colorful sense of humor and knowledge of the game also landed him several TV commentating jobs, including Stanley Cup playoffs and Finals for "Hockey Night in Canada," CBS and NBC. But his favorite color man gig was covering the annual Minnesota State High School Hockey Tournament, something he did from 1964-2003. Nanne has also gone on to become a very successful businessman as well, serving as an executive vice president with the Minneapolis-based Voyageur Asset Management Company. Later, he even beat prostate cancer. That's Lou, a real winner.

Lou and his wife Francine presently reside in Edina, where Lou is playing plenty of golf and watching his grandkids play a lot of hockey.

HOW WOULD YOU DESCRIBE YOUR COACHING STYLE? "I would say it was a combination of hard work, speed and physical contact. I liked a lot of movement and a lot of motion. I wanted my players to be involved. For instance I wanted them to make themselves available for a pass when they didn't have the puck. Then, when they went to the forecheck I wanted them to make sure that they made contact with the player to take him out. Things like that were important. I just wanted constant motion and contact, that was my style."

HOW DID YOU MOTIVATE YOUR PLAYERS? "I tried to motivate them by making them believe in their abilities and encouraging the strengths that they had. I also wanted to point out the weaknesses that the other teams had so that they could gain confidence and feel like they were a better player. I wanted my guys to play with a lot of confidence, so whatever I could do to help them gain confidence is what I wanted to do to motivate them. I also encouraged them to never give up and never quit on a play because you never know what can happen."

WHO WERE YOUR COACHING MENTORS? "Certainly, John Mariucci was right there. His biggest philosophy was to never get outworked and I tried to follow that as well. John was just a wonderful person and I respected him a great deal."

WHAT ARE THE CHARACTERISTICS OF WINNERS? "Winners have heart. They are willing to make more sacrifices, take more responsibilities and outwork their opponents. They just have something in them where they want to be involved in pressure situations because they are comfortable in their abilities to deliver. They also respect their teammates and their teammates respect them. Winners are unique people and very important to a team's success."

LOOKING BACK WHAT ARE YOU MOST PROUD OF IN YOUR CAREER? "I have had a lot of things that I have been proud of, so no one thing really stands out. I was a player, coach, general manager, president and even a broadcaster, so I was lucky enough to do it all. I mean I was fortunate to have a long career in the NHL, scored some key game-winning goals, and helped our teams advance to the playoffs. Then, as a general manager I was fortunate enough to have a team make it to the Stanley Cup Finals. In college I was able to win a scoring championship as a defenseman, and that was something special too. Maybe the thing I would be most proud of would by the longevity I had in pro hockey by being in the game for 23 years. It was not the individual things, it was the team stuff that was so rewarding."

HOW DID YOU BUILD TEAM UNITY & CHEMISTRY? "You can't really build it yourself as a coach, it just has to come from the players. You can, however, facilitate it by making it fun for them to play with one another. If you constantly keep your players involved and get them into situations where they are comfortable with one another, then that all goes into it. You know, there is a real conflict of opinions with regards to the old question of 'does chemistry come before winning? or does winning come before chemistry?' In other words, is it easier to have chemistry when a team is winning versus losing? I am not sure what the answer is, but I do know that chemistry is critical to a team's success."

WHAT MOTIVATED YOU? "Winning was what motivated me. Anytime I am involved in a competitive situation I just want to win, and that is just me. It wasn't about trophies or money, I just want to beat my opponent in whatever I am doing. It didn't matter if I was playing for a dollar on the golf course or for $50,000 in the Stanley Cup Playoffs, I just wanted to win."

WHAT IS THE KEY TO GOOD TIME MANAGEMENT? "Good organization is the key. Anybody who wants to be successful has to have goals and objectives, but in order to get there you have follow a plan. Following that plan requires a lot of organization."

WHAT ADVICE WOULD YOU HAVE FOR YOUNG COACHES STARTING OUT TODAY? "One of the things I used to tell my coaches when I was a general manager was to not let their emotions get the better of them after a big game. Whether they won or lost, I encouraged them to not make any big decisions right away. Instead, they should sleep on it and come back the next day with a refreshed look. Then, if they feel the same way, go ahead and do it. It is just very important to not let your emotions make a decision for you right after a big game because they may lead you the wrong way."

WHAT'S THE BIGGEST THING YOU'VE LEARNED FROM COACHING THAT YOU'VE BEEN ABLE TO APPLY TO YOUR EVERYDAY LIFE? "The work ethic. It doesn't matter what you are involved in, whether it is playing a game, or working in a field, or selling something, or being a dentist or what have you, if you are willing to work hard you will be successful. Inevitably, if you are consistently willing to work hard, then you will outwork your competition and ultimately win more games than you will lose."

WHAT ARE THE KEY INGREDIENTS TO CREATING A CHAMPIONSHIP TEAM? "First of all you have got to have talent. You are not going to win without talent. Then, speed, hockey sense and discipline are the keys I think. Sure, you can get guys with the biggest hearts in the world, but if they can't skate then you won't win. Then, you have to have chemistry, a cohesiveness where your players will work hard and play together as a team, regardless of how they may or may not feel about one another off the ice. You also need some guys who will lay it out on the line and will not shortchange you on effort. Finally, you won't win with mediocre goaltending."

WHAT'S THE SECRET TO YOUR SUCCESS? "I think it was my commitment to being successful. I worked hard and believed in never giving up, in whatever I was doing. I also never worried about making mistakes. I mean as a general manager I made over 100 trades, so I didn't worry about making a mistake. If I felt it was good for the organization then I did it and didn't worry about what people might say or think or do. I was proud of that."

WHAT WOULD YOU WANT TO SAY TO YOUR FANS, BOOSTERS, AND ALUMNI WHO HAVE SUPPORTED YOU ALL THESE YEARS? "I really appreciate the support and loyalty that we got from them. I also appreciate their knowledge of the game. They always accepted people who worked hard and I respected that. I knew that we could never shortchange our fans, they were too smart and that is why our players enjoyed playing for them. It was a real treat to play and coach for people with so much knowledge, enthusiasm and passion for the game. It was an honor to play here, whether it was with the Gophers or with the North Stars, it meant the world to me."

HOW DO YOU WANT YOUR COACHING EPITAPH TO READ — HOW DO YOU WANT TO BE REMEMBERED AS A COACH? "I would want to be remembered as someone who created an organization that worked hard with a passion, was entertaining and didn't shortchange the fans in any way. I also want to be thought of as someone who always played with the philosophy of never letting anybody beat him because they outworked him."

RIC SCHAFER:
UNIVERSITY OF ALASKA-FAIRBANKS HOCKEY

Ric Schafer grew up in Minneapolis and went on to graduate from Blake High School. From there, Schafer played hockey at Notre Dame under legendary coach Lefty Smith. There, Schafer scored 27 goals and 40 assists for 67 points, and served as the captain of the 1974 Irish team. In 1973, Schafer helped the Irish to a runner-up spot in the WCHA tournament, where they ultimately lost to Wisconsin in the finals. After playing for a year in Switzerland, Schafer came back to Notre Dame to serve as an assistant under Smith. He would remain until 1980, when he left to take over the reins as the first ever head coach at the University of Alaska-Fairbanks. Schafer spent seven seasons with the Nanooks, taking them from Division II status to Division I along the way. In his seven years at Alaska Fairbanks, Schafer compiled a 105-87-3 mark including four consecutive 20-win seasons from 1984-87. Then, in 1987, Schafer returned to South Bend to take over as the head coach of the Irish. He would spend the next eight seasons at Notre Dame, compiling a record of 112-152-15 during that time. During his tenure, the Irish went from Division I independent to a return to the CCHA for the 1992-93 season. Schafer would leave the Irish in 1995 as the program's second all-time winningest coach. Overall, Schafer posted a 217-239-18 career record in his 15 years as a head coach.

DON OLSON
COLLEGE HOCKEY: ST. MARY'S UNIVERSITY

Don Olson grew up in Duluth and went on to play hockey at Denfeld High School, graduating in 1967. From there, Don headed east to play hockey at Harvard. After graduating in 1971, Olson returned to Minnesota to take some time off. Instead, he wound up coaching a peewee team in West Duluth, and before long he found himself serving as an assistant at Duluth Cathedral High School. One year later he became their head coach. He would remain at Cathedral for four years before going on to take over as the head hockey coach at St. Mary's in Winona in 1976. He would be taking over a hockey program which didn't even have an arena, but he was up to the challenge. The nearest arena was 50 miles away in Rochester, which made it tough to recruit. But Olson hung in there and more than 300 wins later, he is still going strong. Olson eventually got his arena built, and with it so too came the kids and the victories. In 1982 he would take over as the school's athletic director but later stepped down in 1999 to focus solely on coaching hockey. In addition, Olson also coached cross country and golf over the years at St. Mary's as well.

On the ice Olson currently boasts a 323-313-30 overall record with St. Mary's and has had a lot of post-season success too. In 1981 he led the Cardinals to an NAIA National Tournament appearance and for his efforts was named as the NAIA Men's Hockey Coach of the Year. In 1988 Olson coached the Cardinals to the MIAC regular-season hockey title, and in 1989 and 1995 he guided them to MIAC post-season hockey titles as well. Through 1996 his SMU men's hockey teams qualified for the MIAC's post-season tournament 10 straight years and in 11 of the last 12.

Among Olson's many coaching accolades and honors, he was named as the MIAC Coach of the Year three times: 1980, 1988 and 1995. In addition, in 1988 and 1989 he was named as the Division III West Region Men's Hockey Coach of the Year. He was also named as one of just six men's hockey coaches nationwide for the 1995 Shrine East West College Hockey Classic. Now entering his 27th season as head hockey coach at St. Mary's, Don Olson has become a Southern Minnesota hockey coaching icon.

HOW WOULD YOU DESCRIBE YOUR COACHING STYLE? "I think my style has evolved over the years but overall I would say that if you are a coach you are also a teacher. While we are definitely trying to develop hockey players in terms of their skill and understanding of the game, it has become more about values and character. In terms of basic philosophy I have always been somewhat of a purest. I believe the real game is still about skill, speed, moving the puck and creating. I also believe in letting my kids play and not having to worry about us reprimanding them for every little mistake. We encourage them to go out and develop their skills and become creative. I have never been a fan of 1-0 games with all the hooking, holding and interfering either. That is not my style at all. Our style is much more about guiding and molding rather than demanding and dictating. You know, at our level here in division three, the competition is changing so much. It is so difficult now, versus say 25 years ago, and I think that is a great thing for Minnesota hockey."

HOW DO YOU MOTIVATE YOUR PLAYERS? "I don't do a lot of yelling and screaming, that is not my personality. I try to motive them by creating good values and by creating a good rapport within the team. I want them to realize that success comes from hard work and by doing things the right way, not by trying to take shortcuts. We

also try to motivate them by peer motivation, where the players do a lot of their own goal-setting and create mission statements. This gets them to get driven internally and also to come together as teammates as well."

WHO WERE YOUR COACHING MENTORS? "In high school I played for Dick Northey, who coached for a lot of years up at Denfeld. He grew up on the Range and played at Michigan State, so he had some pretty good experience. Then, in college at Harvard I played for Billy Cleary and Cooney Weiland, who were both outstanding players and coaches. Finally, I was an assistant coach at Duluth Cathedral under Pat Francisco, who played at UM-Duluth, and he was a great coach too."

IF YOU COULD MAGICALLY GO BACK IN TIME TO THE FIRST YEAR YOU WERE A HEAD COACH AND GIVE YOURSELF SOME ADVICE FOR THE FUTURE, KNOWING WHAT YOU KNOW NOW, BACK THEN, WHAT WOULD YOU SAY TO YOURSELF? "I think as a young coach you have a tendency to think so much about wins and losses. Then, as you get older, your views change on the approach and processes that you take. Too many times you think about the present and sometimes you don't lay the foundational values that you really need. So, maybe I would've tried to define the culture of my program earlier on. Once you create that, then you can instill the work ethic, values and attitude to build a successful program. Then, the successes will come, and not just on the ice either."

LOOKING BACK WHAT ARE YOU MOST PROUD OF IN YOUR CAREER? "We have come a long way here at St. Mary's, from the time I first got here when I had to shovel our rink until now, where we have built a really solid program with a beautiful facility on campus. I am also very proud of the kids we have turned out here, and that has been very rewarding as a teacher and coach."

WHAT IS THE KEY TO RECRUITING? "Over time you need to develop a good reputation for your program, one that is fair with good values and gives kids an honest chance. Then, networking is huge. Being able to have people out there in the high school and youth ranks who will let you know who is out there is invaluable. I tell you it's difficult for us because we don't have scholarships. It's tough but we are trying as hard as we can. Plus, it is so confusing right now with the popularity of junior hockey. That has really changed the landscape with regards to how you recruit and that has made it a very different ballgame. Everybody has to recruit now in order to stay alive. Kids just have so many options coming out of high school now and the rules have definitely changed over the years. We are also trying to identify not only talented kids, but kids with character. We want kids with good work ethics, have good values, are good student-athletes and are going to be good citizens on campus and in the community. I am at the point now where I think that character issues are even more important than skill issues, and that says a lot."

HOW DO YOU BUILD TEAM UNITY & CHEMISTRY? "We try to develop our leaders and stress the team concept. You need to identify those young leaders early on, as freshmen, and work with them to understand their role in the locker room. If they can spot problems, then they can deal with things internally. It is a process, and it varies from season to season. I remember at one point because of all of the kids who had played junior hockey we started to pick up some of their traditions. Things like freshman initiations and a little bit of hazing like making freshmen carry bags and pick up pucks after practice and that kind of thing. But I got away from that after realizing that it was not a good way to build team chemistry and develop a healthy atmosphere. I just think it is a lot harder to build chemistry today than it was 25 years ago, quite honestly. There are a lot of bigger, faster, stronger kids now and they don't all necessarily understand the game as well as you would like them to. In the past a lot of kids loved to play because they had a passion for the game. You know, when I first started at St. Mary's we didn't have an arena so for several weeks we used to have to take a bus every night at 11:00 to Rochester so we could practice. We would get done at 1:00 in the morning and eat sandwiches on the bus ride home, and talk the whole way. It was tough, but what that did was build team unity. The guys who came out for our program just loved the game and didn't have all the benefits of today's kids. There was just a real passion there and the kids really supported each other. As hard as that was, that was a fun time."

WHAT MOTIVATES YOU? "I am motivated to do well for my kids. We have 50 kids in our varsity and junior varsity programs and as their coach I feel that I have a responsibility to do everything that I can to make sure that they have a good experience as members of the St. Mary's hockey family. I think I get my energy and work ethic from that."

WHAT ADVICE WOULD YOU HAVE FOR YOUNG COACHES STARTING OUT TODAY? "I think they need to get into it for the right reasons. They need to create a good foundation and try to realize that as much as they are working with kids, that parents will be involved every step of the way. I would also say to just be true to their own values, that is the most important thing. Don't compromise them for outside pressures, or for the sake of winning games. It's tough. You know I just saw that the average life span of a hockey coach in Minnesota these days was down to something like four and a half years. That is alarming. I just don't think we are going to see too many Tom Saterdahlen's, Willard Ikola's, and Larry Ross' in the future, because there just isn't the longevity there anymore."

WHAT'S THE BIGGEST THING YOU'VE LEARNED FROM COACHING THAT YOU'VE BEEN ABLE TO APPLY TO YOUR EVERYDAY LIFE? "It's about being true to yourself and your values in relationships. It is also about developing people skills and working hard. I have developed a good work ethic as a coach, and that too has translated into my everyday life."

WHAT ARE THE KEY INGREDIENTS TO CREATING A CHAMPIONSHIP TEAM? "You obviously have to have talent, and in hockey there is one position that always stands out and that is goaltending. You need to be solid in goal to make your run. Then, you need to play the whole rink, play defense and create on the offensive side. The bottom line though is that it is not just about skill and talent, but creating good chemistry with a strong work ethic. You know, I have been amazed with the fact that over the past couple of seasons the players on the Wild have so consistently supported their coaching staff. They have completely bought into their system, and seem to have the work ethic to support it. That is unique in sports and if you can create that, then you can win championships. I mean the Wild certainly did not have the talent as some of the other playoff teams, but because they believed in what they were doing it all worked out."

WHAT'S THE SECRET TO YOUR SUCCESS? "I have had so many great assistants and great players who have bought into what we have been trying to do. I think we work hard, are fair, are honest with our players, and in the end we are rewarded for that. I always say to our players to do the right thing and use good judgment. That is the key and I hope in the end we can say we did it the right way as good citizens of the game."

WHAT WOULD YOU WANT TO SAY TO YOUR FANS, BOOSTERS, AND ALUMNI WHO HAVE SUPPORTED YOU ALL THESE YEARS? "It's about the whole journey, and it has been wonderful. When you're in teaching and coaching, the journey is about the people and the relationships, and I have been so fortunate to have been a part of this program. So many parents, supporters, fans and players have touched my life in a positive way and I am very grateful for that. It is because of them that I continue to do this for as long as I have. I still very much enjoy it and I still love being out on the rink with my players. So, thanks to all those people."

HOW DO YOU WANT YOUR COACHING EPITAPH TO READ — HOW DO YOU WANT TO BE REMEMBERED AS A COACH? "I hope I will be remembered as somebody who didn't compromise what he thought was the spirit of the game. I just think there is a purity to the game and I hope I will be remembered as somebody whose teams played with discipline and respect for the game. Hopefully they will say that I gave something back to the game beyond coaching his own team."

MIKE GUENTZEL: GOPHER HOCKEY

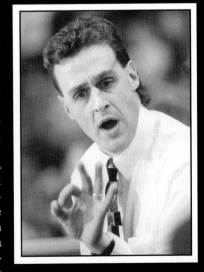

Mike Guentzel grew up in Marble, Minn., and went on to play hockey, football and baseball at Greenway High School, where he graduated in 1981. From there, Guentzel accepted a scholarship to play hockey at the University of Minnesota. There, the defenseman tallied a career total of 87 points in 143 games for the Maroon and Gold and served as team captain in 1985. Following his collegiate career, Guentzel, a 1981 draft pick of the New York Rangers, briefly played professional hockey for the Salt Lake City Golden Eagles of the IHL and the New Haven Night Hawks of the AHL. Guentzel began his coaching career in 1986 as an assistant coach for the St. Paul Vulcans, being promoted to head coach and general manager in 1989. The Vulcans won the 1991 Junior "A" national championship, and the following year Guentzel was honored as the USHL Coach of the Year. Guentzel also served three years as assistant coach with the U.S. National Junior Team as well. From there, Guentzel went on to spend two seasons as head coach and general manager of the Omaha Lancers of the USHL. In his first season, the Lancers won both the regular season and playoff championships. Overall, Guentzel recorded an 89-39-2 record in Omaha, including a 23-11 mark in postseason playoff action. Guentzel then came back to his alma mater to serve as an assistant coach. Now beginning his ninth season on the Golden Gopher hockey staff, Mike Guentzel is widely regarded as one of the top assistant coaches in the country. Mike and his wife Sally presently reside in Woodbury and have three sons: Ryan, Gabe and Jake.

BOB PETERS
COLLEGE HOCKEY: BEMIDJI STATE UNIVERSITY

Bob Peters is not only the winningest coach in the history of Minnesota college hockey, he is also the second winningest coach in the history of all college hockey. That's right, only one coach, Ron Mason of Michigan State, has won more games than Peters. Synonymous with hockey in Minnesota, Peters, who built a 35-year dynasty at Bemidji State, which remains unparalleled in the world of collegiate athletics, has become a coaching legend in the Land of 10,000 Lakes.

A native of Fort Frances, Ontario, Peters went on to star as a goalie at Fort Frances Collegiate High School. A 1960 graduate of the University of North Dakota, Peters spent his college days playing goaltender for the Fighting Sioux. (His son Steve later followed his old man to play between the pipes at UND as well in the late 1980s.) Upon graduating, Peters coached on the high school level for one season before rejoining the UND staff as an assistant coach. In 1964, Peters was named as UND's head coach and during his initial campaign his team won the WCHA championship and finished third at the NCAA Championships. For his efforts Peters earned WCHA Coach of the Year honors. Peters would coach for a total of two years in North Dakota, finishing his reign at UND with a 42-20-1 coaching mark.

In 1966 Peters decided to leave the NCAA Division I school in lieu of a small college program in its early stages of existence — Bemidji State University. "I knew a new arena was going up," Peters would say. "All we needed was a foundation to build on. Every time a new arena goes up, there is another hockey base to build on."

Within two seasons Peters had led BSU to its first NAIA national championship and set the foundation for what would become one of the most dominant programs in college hockey. In all, there would be 27 post season playoff appearances, 15 conference championships, and 13 national championships over the next 35 years under his tutelage. By the time he hung it up in 2001, he had amassed 744 victories as a head coach, 702 coming at Bemidji State alone — making him the first coach to win 700 or more games at a single school. In addition, he still holds national collegiate records for most wins in an unbeaten season (31-0-0 in 1983-84) and the longest unbeaten streak (43 games from Nov. 8, 1983 to Jan. 1, 1985). Peters also owns the distinction of being the only collegiate head coach to have teams reach the final four in each division of national collegiate hockey championships: NCAA-I, NCAA-II, NCAA-III and NAIA. During his tenure, Bemidji State produced more than 80 All-Americans, eight U.S. National Team Players, five Olympians, four NHL players and a host of minor professional players in the U.S. and Europe. Most importantly to Peters, however, is the growing list of Beaver alumni who have gone on to work in the hockey ranks as high school and college coaches, officials and administrators.

Ever the task-master, Peters was a student of the game. His routine behind the bench often included writing notes on his opponents' shooting tendencies, studying the mannerism's of his opposing goalies, and constantly making sure that his boys are skating hard. "When you play a Bob Peters team, you better be ready to skate," said Augsburg Coach Ed Saugestad. "You won't see many teams that go harder for 60 minutes than the Beavers."

A recipient of more than a dozen Coach of the Year awards, Peters was also honored by having the College Hockey America (CHA) regular-season championship trophy, called the "Peters Cup," named in his honor. Peters also served on championship committees for the NAIA and NCAA for over 20 years, and in 2001 was named

as a Hobey Baker Legend of Hockey.

After successfully transitioning his club to the division one level, Peters finally stepped down as the head coach at BSU in 2001. Although he is now retired from coaching, Peters still remains heavily involved in the sport he so dearly loves. His latest challenge is overseeing the continued growth of the upstart College Hockey America conference, having been named as the league's commissioner in the Spring of 2001. In addition, Peters also continues to volunteer and provide administrative assistance to the BSU athletic department. His longtime Bemidji International Hockey Camp is no more, and he is finally getting to spend more time with his wife, kids and grandkids in Bemidji. Hey, if it weren't for Paul Bunyan, this guy would most definitely be Bemidji's biggest legend!

HOW WOULD YOU DESCRIBE YOUR COACHING STYLE? "First and foremost I bring my head and heart to the arena and to the office every day. I don't try to change my personality to emulate anybody else, I just try to be myself. Any success that came my way was not looked for in terms of trying to further my own career. The players really don't care how much you know until you first show how much you care. If they get that feeling, then they will really put forth an extra effort to improve themselves and be a great team person. That is part of it. The other part is that I do believe that there is only one director in a symphonic orchestra, and there is only one head hockey coach. You have to make decisions and stand by those decisions either way. Eleanor Roosevelt once said 'go ahead and do what you think is right because you are going to get criticized for it anyway.'. I also come to the rink totally prepared and organized. I am very demanding. I have a great deal of compassion but I have a great deal of firmness too. I tend to give people a second chance but not usually a third. I tell my kids what our goals our, what my expectations are, and my task is to get every player to play even better than they think they can. When you are dealing with people you have to use your heart, when you are dealing with yourself you have to use your head."

HOW DID YOU MOTIVATE YOUR PLAYERS? "It doesn't matter who has the best players, it matters who has the best team. Again, players don't care how much a coach knows until the coach shows how much he actually cares. They have to have the feeling that you care about them and that your career promotions and advancements aren't relying on them to the point where you are pushing them in order to get promoted. I also feel that people who play for you need to feel important. On top of all that, as a coach you need to have firm expectations. If you expect average or below average, then that is exactly what you will get. That is human nature. This is the bar; this is what I expect; this is what we're working for and this is what I want. Then, you have to ask what is the coach's main objective. If your main objective is to make an athlete play better, then that athlete has to think that he can play better — then he can be motivated. I have also always used this as a policy: 'when you play for me, you play for me forever — you are never forgotten.' I think that my players knew that, and that was all part of motivation."

IF YOU COULD MAGICALLY GO BACK IN TIME TO THE FIRST YEAR YOU WERE A HEAD COACH AND GIVE YOURSELF SOME ADVICE FOR THE FUTURE, KNOWING WHAT YOU KNOW NOW, BACK THEN, WHAT

WOULD YOU SAY TO YOURSELF? "You know, when I first got into this business, I should have been thrown into jail for impersonating a coach. I didn't know what the heck I was doing. I came around though and studied the game very, very hard. So, if I had to say something, I would have said to be more patient early on. That is something I have worked on through the years to get better at."

LOOKING BACK WHAT ARE YOU MOST PROUD OF IN YOUR CAREER? "That we built a program that provided opportunities for so many, many players. So many kids went on to play professionally and so many others got the opportunity to play here and get an outstanding education in the process. We created a great hockey culture here and that is something I am very proud of. We also really worked hard on producing high school hockey coaches and a lot of great teachers and coaches came out of here as a result. You know, longtime coaches like myself, we laid it on the line and 'done our darndest.' I am proud of that. When your players come back and think that they were lucky to play for you, then that makes it all worth while."

WHAT WAS THE KEY TO RECRUITING? "For us it was very different because we had a very limited amount of scholarship money in the beginning. It was infinitesimal. The most we ever had to give was like $4,750 total, for everybody. We later went to division III and Division II, and finally Division I, but in between that time it was tough to recruit. We had to work very hard in the Summer to recruit the top kids and we made the best of it. Really, because I didn't have a full-time assistant to help out, I did most of my recruiting over the telephone. Luckily, I had a lot of former players who were coaching and they were able to help me a great deal in recruiting. It was a year round thing though, after supper at night and on most every weekend. The key was to establish good contacts and to be as visible as possible. You just had to talk to a lot of people and see as many kids as you could. Then, you had to make sure that the parents knew that you were concerned about their sons as people and not just as players. My attitude was that the most precious thing that a parent has is a child, so they had to very comfortable with you as a coach. Beyond that, I looked for kids who played two sports and were captain material. Those were key pieces to the chemistry puzzle."

HOW DID YOU BUILD TEAM UNITY & CHEMISTRY? "I didn't have the luxury of hand-picking my rosters because of the lack of funding that we had for student-athletes. So, I worked as best as I could with the kids that I had to built team unity. First of all, I tried to get all of my kids to feel very comfortable with me by letting them know that I cared about them. The second thing was to make them feel good about each other. To that end it started in my pre-season training program, which was so important. That time really brought our players together. Then, I had a very demanding daily schedule for them, which forced them to work very hard. It made every player come to the conclusion that they were either committed or they weren't committed. You got that by putting objectives and obstacles in their paths, and telling them that this is what it is like if you want to be a champion. I would tell them that they would have to do these things on the ice and off the ice, then they would have an opportunity to achieve success. One of our biggest things that we did to build chemistry was our annual end of pre-season training camp 23 mile hike. It was a challenge that was really rigorous and once they completed it, it bound them together very closely. You know, I used to tell my kids that practice was like religion — you have to take it when you don't want it so you'll have it when you need it. I have always felt that if you can get your kids all on the same page, and maybe that means them being angry at you at times, then they get pretty determined. I did a lot of things like that to bring them together off the ice. Another thing was ice fishing during the Christmas break, where we would all take the day off and go as a team. It was a lot of fun and the guys got to know each other. We would have a big fish fry that night then and those were very memorable events for us. We had

alumni events and golf events too. Overall, the bar was held very high and I set high standards for them. We also did a lot with tradition and history. That is so important. I keep a scrapbook for every season and I shared that with them, along with the great stories. Once the players see that, then they buy into it and want to be a part of it. When a player plays for me he plays for me forever. And when they know that they are wanted, appreciated and never forgotten, then that is a very powerful thing. We created that and I was very proud of that."

WHAT MOTIVATED YOU? "Who motivates the motivator? The answer is the motivator motivates the motivator. What motivates me? Well, I am a self-starter. I read a great deal of history books and biographies about great leaders, whether they are religious, military, political, business, humanitarian or sports related. There are many common bonds that tie those type of people together regardless of what their occupation or profession is. So, I read a great deal about leadership. President Eisenhower said that leadership is something that can be learned, and I would agree. Leadership in all of its forms really motivates me. I am always trying to hone my leadership skills and that drives me to be a better person in whatever I am doing in life."

WHAT ADVICE WOULD YOU HAVE FOR YOUNG COACHES STARTING OUT TODAY? "George Halas, the legendary coach of the Chicago Bears, was once asked 'Why are you successful?' His response was 'If you don't have anything to do, get down to the office and do it.' In other words, you have to put in the time. When you are in the office you are in the environment. You know, the average length of service of a coach is about seven years. Young coaches have to be patient as well as passionate. There is just no substitute for hard work. Any coach that goes in with a 'me-first' attitude, I want him on my schedule, along with all those coaches that shoot par golf in the Summer! This is not a five day a week, eight hour a day job. It is 24/7 and that is the truth. Other than Christmas day, you don't get a lot of time off in this business. Even when you are off, you are thinking and planning and preparing. It can be tough on your family if they are not supportive of you too. So many times I would leave when the kids were still in bed and then I would get home at night and they were back in bed. Then, you are traveling or recruiting on weekends and at night. So, that was tough, but that is what you have to do to be successful in this business. Coaching consumes you, but if you love it, then that is a wonderful thing."

FAVORITE LOCKER ROOM SIGN? "I have millions of quotes from so many great people. But, if I had to pick a couple I would say 'The less than dedicated are the majority in this world,' and the other is 'Summertime soldiers of sunshine patriots — there is no place for them on this team.' You have to be committed year round, totally, whether it is going good or whether it is going bad. Lastly, I would say 'Don't let the bastards grind you down,' which I got from General Vinegar Joe Stillwell. The bastards aren't just people, it could be problems or what have you, and you just can't let that happen."

WHAT'S THE BIGGEST THING YOU'VE LEARNED FROM COACHING THAT YOU'VE BEEN ABLE TO APPLY TO YOUR EVERYDAY LIFE? "Self sacrifice and commitment. I explain that to my players this way: When you have breakfast and you are having bacon and eggs, while the chicken made a commitment… the hog made a sacrifice. When you put it in those terms, they get it pretty quickly."

WHAT ARE THE KEY INGREDIENTS TO CREATING A CHAMPIONSHIP TEAM? "Championship teams start with people. In recruiting you look for good people, for multi-sport athletes and for leaders and captains. Then they have to be committed, great listeners, who work very hard. They need to be able to buy into your plan and that is where it starts. From there, you need players with patience because you can buy everything else at the supermarket except for experience. So, if they are patient, that will all come.

When you combine all of these things, along with me being on their case about doing well in school, and raising holy hell with them when they needed it, and patting them on the back when the needed that too, then that is what it is all about. In my system it takes time and repetition, and you don't see a lot of the rewards until you are a junior or senior. Those players need to see all of those championship banners hanging in our arena too. That goes back to the history and tradition that they are playing for. Consciously or subconsciously, they will want to continue that tradition and be a part of it. Tradition is lasting victory and tradition never graduates. That is what you have to create. They have to know that it is a great, great honor to put on the Bemidji jersey, and that they have earned that. The Montreal Canadiens call their sweaters the 'holy cloth' in French, and they never allow them to touch the floor. That kind of tradition is what I have created here. You earn that green and white jersey before you put it here on and you be proud of it when you have it on."

WHAT'S THE SECRET TO YOUR SUCCESS? "I have never reached that point in life of being so comfortable that I wasn't prepared. I respected every opponent and never, ever took anybody for granted — I never assumed anything. I planned out everything down to the smallest details, but I tried to make that as simple as possible for the players. Sometimes you can over-coach, and I tried not to do that. Beyond that, I worked very hard and I cared for my players."

WHAT WOULD YOU WANT TO SAY TO YOUR FANS, BOOSTERS, AND ALUMNI WHO HAVE SUPPORTED YOU ALL THESE YEARS? "I am so grateful to them. I am also so grateful to my players and what they did for us — not for me, but for the team and for the university. We didn't have scholarship money in my time, and our boys had to buy their own skates until we turned division one. I am so appreciative of that. We had such a high caliber of players in our program and the fans appreciated that too."

HOW DO YOU WANT YOUR COACHING EPITAPH TO READ — HOW DO YOU WANT TO BE REMEMBERED AS A COACH? "I cared about the game and I cared about people. For me, my players always came first. I am just so grateful that I had the opportunity to have the best job in the world. I am so appreciative of the people who came before me, and the tradition and history that came before me, and I am very proud to be able to give back."

FIDO PURPUR: UNIVERSITY OF NORTH DAKOTA HOCKEY

Clifford "Fido" Purpur, a native of Grand Forks, ND, played for USHL's St. Paul Saints from 1946-47. Purpur would go on to coach at the University of North Dakota from 1949-56 and was later enshrined into the U.S. Hockey Hall of Fame.

COACH PETERS' INFAMOUS LIST OF "26 RULES"

1. Never retaliate after receiving a big hit or a cheap shot!
2. Never go off-sides on a 3-on-2 or a 2-on-1.
3. Never carry the puck into your own end except on a power play.
4. Never throw blind passes from behind the opponent's net.
5. Never pass diagonally across the ice in your own zone unless you are 100% certain.
6. Backchecker backchecking between the blue lines on a defensive 3-on-3 should pick up and check the weak side lane unless he has an offensive angle on the puck carrier.
7. Second man go all the way for a rebound.
8. When the defense has the puck at the opponent's blue line, look four places before shooting.
9. Forward in front of opponent's net must face the puck and lean on the stick.
10. Puck carrier skating over center with no one to pass to and no skating room must dump the puck
11. No forward must ever turn his back to the puck at any time.
12. Never check or board an opponent from behind.
13. No player is allowed to position himself more than two zones away from the puck.
14. Never allow our team to be outnumbered in the defensive zone.
15. Delayed penalty on opposition – sixth attacker tactics.
16. Be aware of the clock near the conclusion of a power-play!
17. Backchecking 2-on-2 or 1-on-1, even on a power-play, pick up an open man trailer, or come in behind the defense.
18. Two men in forechecking responsibilities of the third man.
19. Never clear the puck from behind the dots in our zone when you are in a crowd or on your backhand unless 100% sure.
20. Nearest forward to a 1-on-1 boards scrum must support the puck.
21. Don't "dick" with the puck at either blue line… be deliberate!
22. The second forward must always go to the net of offensive attempts and opportunities.
23. Our defensemen must be mobile enough not to get beat 1-on-1, they must have good enough hands to make the quick simple effective breakout pass, and be tough enough to control the corners and the front of the net.
24. Blocking shots: 6 to 8 blocked shots per game will translate into one goal for and one goal against, resulting in two goals.
25. What it takes to be a Beaver hockey player: Hockey is a contact sport, very fast, and very competitive. Games are won with people who have the competitive patience and determination to attack the puck and be there first. People who have these characteristics will play on the winning side 95% of the time, or put it another way, players who quit or arrive late will play on the winning side 5% of the time. We want players who compete and players who dominate the six pits (the four corners and the fronts of the nets). These are the people who will wear our sweater proudly and will get ice time. These are also the people who will experience success and excel at this level!
26. *Here are some other points of emphasis to take note of:*
A. Win defensive zone face-offs.
B. Block out on face-offs won, get to coverage if lost, and know where you go on all face-offs.
C. Use wall or glass to bank pucks.
D. Chip pucks two zones ahead if possible.
E. Always try and be on forehand to make a play. You will always be a threat and the opposition will honor your forehand by playing more soft.
F. If you are in a situation where trouble may occur in offensive zone, cycle behind the net or in corner to get good position.
G. Always finish checks so people are eliminated to get involved in play and to maintain a physical presence.
H. Create a defensive presence so nobody wants to come in front of our net. Make people pay the price!
I. If the puck is at point, go grab a man and get your sticks up. Remember rebound management.

SCOTT SANDELIN: UM-DULUTH HOCKEY

Born and raised in Hibbing, Scott Sandelin capped off his four-year playing career at the University of North Dakota in 1986 by being named as a finalist for the Hobey Baker Memorial Award. Sandelin captained the Fighting Sioux and also earned All-WCHA first team and All-American second team honors that year as well. After graduating with a degree in marketing, Sandelin then went on to play seven years of professional hockey, including National Hockey League stints with the Montreal Canadiens (1986-88), Philadelphia Flyers (1990-91) and Minnesota North Stars (1991-92). Internationally, Sandelin also skated for Team U.S.A. at the 1989 Goodwill Games, the 1986 World Championships and the 1984 World Junior Championships. A nagging back injury, however, forced him to retire prematurely in 1992. From there, Sandelin got into coaching, first with the American Hockey Association's Fargo-Moorhead Express, where he served as coach and general manager. That next year he served as coach and general manager of the Fargo-Moorhead Junior Kings of the Junior Elite Hockey League. Sandelin then headed back to his alma mater, to serve as an assistant coach at UND for six seasons — including the last three as an associate head coach. During his tenure in Grand Forks, North Dakota laid claim to two NCAA titles (1997 and 2000), three WCHA regular season championships (1997-99), two WCHA playoff crowns (1997 and 2000) and earned four straight berths in the NCAA tournament (1997-2000). Sandelin's primary responsibilities with the Fighting Sioux included serving as the team's recruiting coordinator and assisting head coach Dean Blais with all aspects of practice and game preparation. Then, in 2000, Scott came home to take over as the head coach of the University of Minnesota-Duluth Bulldogs. Sandelin inherited a program in a rebuilding phase and has since begun a turn-around that is well on its way. In his four seasons at Duluth, Sandelin has posted a career record of 42-67-12. Generally regarded as one of the more promising young coaches in college hockey, Sandelin, who also currently serves as a vice president of American Hockey Coaches Association, returns for his fifth year behind the Minnesota-Duluth bench in 2003-04. Scott and his wife Wendy have one son, Ryan, and presently reside in Hermantown.

JOHN MAYASICH: U.S. NATIONAL TEAM

John Mayasich has long been regarded as one of the finest amateur hockey players ever produced in the United States, and is without question the greatest player to ever lace em' up in Minnesota. Mayasich grew up playing hockey in Eveleth and went on to lead his Eveleth High School team to an amazing run of four consecutive undefeated state championship seasons from 1948-51. Mayasich set nearly every major high school tournament record during that run, and incredibly, most of them still stand more than 50 years later. Mayasich then headed to the University of Minnesota, where he would join up with another Eveleth hockey legend, Gopher Coach, John Mariucci. There, Mayasich led the Gophers to a couple of NCAA Final Fours, and took college hockey by storm. Before his career was over, the perennial All-American had tallied Gopher records of 298 career points and 144 goals. His totals worked out to an incredible 1.4 goals per game average with nearly three points per game. In his senior year, he had an incredible six-goal game against Winnipeg and also tallied eight points against Michigan that same season. At the end of his playing career with the Gophers, Mayasich fulfilled his military obligations and then went on to star on the 1956 silver medal-winning U.S. Olympic hockey team in Cortina, Italy.

This was the dawn of modern hockey in Minnesota, and Mayasich was rewriting the record books as he went along. He was a "velvety-smooth skater," with a keen, sixth sense into the psyche of the goalie's every move. He is credited as being the first college hockey player to develop the slap shot, a new weapon that instilled fear into an already perplexed group of goaltenders that tried to stop him. John was an artist with his stick and his stick-handling skills were legendary. On power-plays, he could kill penalties by toying with opposing defenses. He used to take the puck and simply weave around the rink without ever passing to a teammate until the penalty had been killed. With amazing ability like that, it's hard to believe that he was often criticized for passing too much.

"The camaraderie was the best, those friendships go back 40 years now," recalled Mayasich on his playing days at the U of M. Playing with the players who I had played against throughout my high school career was really exciting. We had great Gopher players like Dick Meredith, Dick Dougherty, Gene Campbell, Ken Yackel, Wendy Anderson, and Stan Hubbard. I got to see the world through hockey, and the purity of the game is the bond that keeps those friendships together today. It was quite a time to be involved with the Gopher program as it was just taking off back then. It made me proud of the fact that I was there when all of this was happening. Now, to see what the program has grown into today, and to think that maybe, in a small way that I had something to do with it, is incredible. My time at the U of M was great."

Following college, Mayasich went on to play on a record eight U.S. Olympic and National teams. Declining professional hockey opportunities in the then six-team NHL, Mayasich devoted his remaining hockey career to the semi-pro Green Bay Bobcats, where he played and coached. In addition, in 1969, Mayasich was called upon to serve his nation again when he was named as the coach of the U.S. National team. Mayasich received numerous honors during his career, including being the first Minnesotan to be voted into the National High School Athletic Hall of Fame. Then, in 1976 Mayasich had a homecoming of sorts, being inducted into the U.S. Hockey Hall of Fame in his native Eveleth.

"John Mayasich brought college hockey to a new plateau," recalled John Mariucci. "He was the Wayne Gretzky of his time, and if he were playing pro hockey today, he would simply be a bigger, stronger, back-checking Gretzky. The words to describe him haven't been invented. When I say he's the best, that's totally inadequate."

DAVE PALMQUIST
GIRLS HIGH SCHOOL HOCKEY: SOUTH ST. PAUL

Dave Palmquist was born in Hibbing but grew up in Columbia Heights when his father, a Lutheran minister, moved his family to the Twin Cities. Palmquist went on to attend Minnehaha Academy High School, graduating in 1982. From there he played hockey and golf at Bethel College, where he also got a teaching degree. His first job was at his alma mater, Minnehaha Academy, where he became the head boys hockey coach at just 23 years of age. Palmquist taught physical education and coached at the Academy for seven years until leaving in 1994 to take over the girls hockey and boys golf programs at South St. Paul. Palmquist has been with the Packers for nine years now, and has become a girls hockey coaching legend in the process. On the ice his teams have been simply dominant. Not only have his Lady Packers won back-to-back state championships in 2002 and 2003, but they also set a state record by winning 52 straight games along the way. Girls high school hockey is only nine years old in Minnesota, and South St. Paul has already won two titles, one runner-up and two third place finishes. The Packers have also won seven of nine conference titles as well, simply dominating their competition. Palmquist is a two-time coach of the year in 1999 and 2001, and is amongst the winningest girls high school hockey coaches in the state with a 203-32-10 record. Dave Palmquist is without question a girls high school hockey coaching legend in the Minnesota and he is still going strong. Dave and his wife Karen have four children and presently reside in the Twin Cities.

HOW WOULD YOU DESCRIBE YOUR COACHING STYLE? "I think I am a players coach and have always put my players first. I have always tried to bring out the best in them by building them up with confidence and praise. I try to teach them about life too, through their experiences in hockey. My biggest message to the kids has always been to win with pride, to be humble in victory and to be classy in everything they do."

HOW DO YOU MOTIVATE YOUR PLAYERS? "I never try to make the games bigger than they are. I hold that back until February, when we get towards the playoffs. So, we have always had a philosophy in that the games early on are for learning and building, and the ones later in the season are the ones that are really important. I just try to motivate them by encouraging them and getting them to relax and have fun out on the ice. I let them know that my expectations of them are to always get better and to do their best. I just don't try to put a lot of pressure on them until the end of the season, when it really counts."

LOOKING BACK WHAT ARE YOU MOST PROUD OF IN YOUR CAREER? "I am very proud of the relationships that I have developed over the years with my players. To see them after they graduate and to know that they had a positive experience playing for me, then that is great. Hopefully they knew that I cared about them as people and that I was concerned about how they were doing in class as well as on the ice."

IF YOU COULD MAGICALLY GO BACK IN TIME TO THE FIRST YEAR YOU WERE A HEAD COACH AND GIVE YOURSELF SOME ADVICE FOR THE FUTURE, KNOWING WHAT YOU KNOW NOW, BACK THEN, WHAT WOULD YOU SAY TO YOURSELF? "Looking back I would have just told myself to stay the course. Stick with what you believe in and don't ever compromise what you feel in your heart.

Remember that you are in this for the kids and they are what is most important."

WHAT MOTIVATES YOU? "I think the greatest motivator for me is just the passion that I have for hockey and for kids. I love the challenge that comes about every new year and I look forward to good things happening. I am just driven to be successful and really love what I am doing."

WHAT ADVICE WOULD YOU HAVE FOR YOUNG COACHES STARTING OUT TODAY? "I would tell them to be true to themselves. When you know that you are doing what is best for kids, then no matter what criticism may come your way, you can sleep well at night. If you have integrity and a strong value system, then you will be successful in this business."

HOW DO YOU BUILD TEAM UNITY & CHEMISTRY? "We try to come up with a theme every year which embodies the message that it is not about 'me,' but rather the entire team. Then, I just try to preach about the team concept and about how important having a positive attitude is. You know, South St. Paul has such a great hockey tradition and I think the kids feed on that. They know the history and that all goes into building chemistry. I also let them know that no one person is more important than the whole team concept and that has worked well for us over the years."

FAVORITE LOCKER ROOM SIGN? "I just always say to the girls to be first class in everything we do."

WHAT'S THE BIGGEST THING YOU'VE LEARNED FROM COACHING THAT YOU'VE BEEN ABLE TO APPLY TO YOUR EVERYDAY LIFE? "Everyday is a new day and everyday is an opportunity to make a difference in somebody's life. I would also say perseverance because I have learned to work hard and to stick with it."

WHAT ARE THE KEY INGREDIENTS TO CREATING A CHAMPIONSHIP TEAM? "I think for starters you need people who have a real passion for the game. Then, you have to have the players. To be a champion you also need to have some breaks go your way along the way too. I also think that championships start in the locker room. How our kids conduct themselves away from the ice, in the classroom and at home, makes a big difference. When you have winners in the classroom and in their everyday lives, then that really translates onto the ice."

WHAT'S THE SECRET TO YOUR SUCCESS? "I would say the secret to my success has been having good players who care and are passionate about the game. If they can feed off of my passion that I have, then that is great. I would also say that I have a great assistant coach in Pete Edlund, who has been with me since I got here. When you have somebody with you who loves the game as much as you do, then that just makes your program that much better. In addition, I would also say that my faith and family are the two biggest priorities in my life and they keep me strong."

WHAT WOULD YOU WANT TO SAY TO YOUR FANS, BOOSTERS, AND ALUMNI WHO HAVE SUPPORTED YOU ALL THESE YEARS? "We have had a great following of fans who have really taken a lot of pride in our program and that is just wonderful to see. Our community has really backed these girls and that is great. A lot of the old timers who followed the boys for so long are now supporting us and that is great to see too. They follow us around to different games and have been very instrumental in our success. So, thanks to all of them, it really means a lot to me and to our kids."

HOW DO YOU WANT YOUR COACHING EPITAPH TO READ — HOW DO YOU WANT TO BE REMEMBERED AS A COACH? "I would want to be remembered as a man of integrity who always played the game fair and always had respect for his opponents. Hopefully I will be remembered as someone who helped to grow the sport of girls hockey and made it better for them along the way."

BOB GAINEY: MINNESOTA NORTH STARS

Bob Gainey spent his entire 16-year playing career with the Montreal Canadiens, where he was a member of five Stanley Cup champion teams. Gainey took over as the North Stars' head coach in 1990 and that next year he then led team to the Stanley Cup Finals, where they lost in six games to Pittsburgh. Gainey was named general manager in 1992 and served in the dual role through the club's move to Dallas in 1993 through 1996, when he relinquished his head coaching duties. Gainey was inducted into the Hockey Hall of Fame in 1992.

DAVE PETERSON: SOUTHWEST HIGH SCHOOL & OLYMPIC HOCKEY

Minneapolis native Dave Peterson was a true pioneer of Minnesota hockey. Peterson's coaching career began in 1954 as an assistant at Minneapolis North High School. The following year, he was named head coach at Southwest High School, a program he would direct for the next 27 years. Peterson led Southwest to 11 state tournaments (1965, 1968-73, 1975-77 and 1980), and won it all in 1970. For his efforts, he was named as the Coach of the Year on three separate occasions.

From there, Peterson got into international coaching. As a head coach, he directed three U.S. National Teams, as well as several U.S. National Junior and Select Teams. In 1984 Peterson served as an assistant coach to Lou Vairo on the 1984 U.S. Olympic Team. That next year Peterson guided the 1985 U.S. National Team to a fourth place finish at the World Championships in Prague, marking the first time since 1976 that a U.S. team had advanced to the medal round in the World Championships. In 1986, Peterson guided the U.S. National Junior Team to a bronze medal at the World Junior Championships in Hamilton, Ontario. Peterson would then go on to serve as the head coach of the 1988 U.S. Olympic Team at Calgary, as well as the 1992 U.S. Olympic Team which finished fourth at the XVI Winter Games in Albertville, France. With that, Peterson became just the second individual in the history of United States hockey to serve as head coach for two consecutive Olympic Teams.

Peterson retired at the end of 1996 from USA Hockey's national staff after having served as the organization's Director of Coaching and Player Development from 1989-91 and Technical Director from 1992-96. Then, on July 17, 1997, Peterson tragically passed away at the age of just 66. In his memory, USA Hockey established The Dave Peterson Coaches' Goalkeeping Symposium, which is held annually in conjunction with the USA Hockey National Goalie Camp in Colorado Springs, Colorado. In addition, the Minnesota State High School Hockey Coaches Association created an award in his honor which is given annually to a high school coach who has shown great leadership in developing youth hockey either locally or statewide. One of the most experienced international hockey coaches in America, Dave Peterson was one of America's very best.

CONNIE PLEBAN: UM-DULUTH HOCKEY

John "Connie" Pleban was born and raised in Eveleth, where he went on to star on the Eveleth High School team from 1930-32 under legendary coach Cliff Thompson. Pleban then played for Eveleth Junior College before going on to play on professionally. Pleban played for the Baby Ruth national AAU champion team in 1935 (a team which had nine Eveleth natives on its 13-man roster), and was captain and later player-coach of the Eagle River, Wis., Falcons semipro team from 1934-38 as well. Pleban also served as the player-coach of the Eveleth Rangers semi-pro team from 1938-41, and the Marquette, Mich., Sentinels semi-pro team from 1941-42, before entering the service for World War II.

Returning to Eveleth after the war, Pleban moved on as a coach and builder of amateur hockey by serving as the player-coach of the Eveleth Rangers again, and then holding the unique post of player-coach-manager of the 1950 U.S. National which that won the silver medal in London. Pleban then coached the 1952 U.S. Olympic team as well, guiding his boys to a silver medal in Oslo, Norway. In 1955 Pleban took over as the head coach at the University of Minnesota-Duluth, where he would remain for the next five seasons. There, Pleban helped lead the school's transition from small-college to major-college status. In his five-year tenure at UMD, Pleban's Bulldog teams never lost a game in the MIAC and he wound up with an impressive 71-30-5 career record. As a builder of the game, Pleban also successfully solicited NCAA rule-makers to expand body-checking from half to full ice — a move that would forever change the game as we know it today.

Pleban then went on to coach the 1961 U.S. team at the World Tournament in Geneva, as well as the 1962 U.S. team, which won the bronze medal at Colorado Springs. From there, Pleban lived in Duluth, where he helped to organize amateur teams and leagues through the 1960s and '70s, always promoting and advancing the game he loved every step of the way.

MIKE RAMSEY
PRO HOCKEY: MINNESOTA WILD

Mike Ramsey was born in Minneapolis and went on to star on the Minneapolis Roosevelt High School hockey team. From there, Ramsey wore the Maroon and Gold at the University of Minnesota, leading the Golden Gophers to the 1979 NCAA Championship along the way. Ramsey then went on to become the youngest player, at just 18, to play for the fabled 1980 "Miracle on Ice" Olympic team which won the gold medal in Lake Placid, New York.

Ramsey then joined the NHL's Buffalo Sabres, who had drafted him with their number one pick the year before. Ramsey would go on to play for 14 years in Buffalo before being traded to Pittsburgh in 1993. That next year, however, the sturdy defenseman was dealt to the Detroit Red Wings, where, after playing in the Stanley Cup Finals, he would ultimately retire in 1996. In all, Ramsey would play in the NHL for 18 seasons and in 1,070 games he tallied 79 goals and 266 assists for 345 points. He also played in four NHL All-Star Games (1982, 1983, 1985 and 1986) and racked up 1,012 penalty minutes as well. Then, in 1997 Ramsey became an assistant coach with the Sabres. He would remain in Buffalo for three seasons before coming home in 2000 to take over an assistant with the expansion Minnesota Wild under head coach Jacques Lemaire.

At just 41, Ramsey, who is now entering his fourth year with the Wild, is considered to be among the brightest young coaching minds in the game today. In 2003 the Wild made it all the way to the conference finals, becoming the darlings of professional hockey. Mike Ramsey had a lot to do with that success and is doing an outstanding job as the Wild's top assistant.

Among Mike's many honors and accolades, he was named as the Sabres' team MVP in 1987 and also won the Punch Imlach Memorial Award in 1988 for leadership and dedication. In 2001 Ramsey was also inducted into the Buffalo Sabres Hall of Fame. Additionally, Mike was was awarded the Lester Patrick Trophy, for outstanding contributions to American hockey, as a member of the 1980 gold medal winning team. In addition to his Olympic experience, Ramsey also represented the United States at the World Championships in 1982, and at the Canada Cup tournament in both 1984 and 1987 as well.

Presently, Mike and his wife Jill have three children and reside in Chanhassen.

HOW WOULD YOU DESCRIBE YOUR COACHING STYLE? "As a player I thought like a coach. I saw the game like a coach and I always saw myself becoming a coach one day. By no means, however, did that mean I was ready to be a coach yet. I am still learning the ropes. So, as an assistant, my relationship is much different with the players than it is with the head coach. In Jacque's (Lemaire) system, the players know that they can come and talk to any of us anytime. I think the assistants act as a sort of buffer, however, to filter out a lot of stuff before it gets to the top. Sometimes players just feel more comfortable coming to me for certain things and I really enjoy that. My relationship with the players is great because since I played so long in the National Hockey League, I feel like I truly understand what they are thinking and feeling out on the ice. Once you establish that credibility with your players, then you can talk to them much more openly and honestly to help them deal with certain situations."

HOW DO YOU MOTIVATE YOUR PLAYERS? "As an assistant, I think my role is different. I am just one piece of the puzzle for motivating our team. At this level the players motivate themselves. We can help that though by the way we practice, the way we prepare and the work ethic that we instill. Then during games, it comes down to how well the coaches handle their players, as well themselves, behind the bench. That really reflects upon how the players will respond out on the ice. If we look frustrated as coaches, then the players pick up on that and they too become frustrated. So, you have to do a lot of little things to create a good atmosphere where the players can learn from you, but still motivate themselves."

WHAT ARE THE CHARACTERISTICS OF WINNERS? "There are a lot of winners that have never won, and there are a lot of winners who were just in the right place at the right time. I have always found it fascinating when a club wants to bring in a guy just after he's won a Stanley Cup, or a Super Bowl or World Series, because they think he is a winner. I look at that and think to myself, 'you know, that guy was just in the right place at the right time — that's all.' I mean look at someone like Ray Borque. If he hadn't won that Stanley Cup with Colorado his last year, are you going to tell me he is not a winner? That guy is a winner. Period. So, certainly there are common characteristics of winners, but it is different for everybody. And it is different how we define winners too, it is not just about winning. Winners just have that certain quality about them."

HOW DO YOU BUILD TEAM UNITY & CHEMISTRY? "To be a great coach you have to have a lot of great qualities. You've got to know how to motivate players, baby-sit players, know the X's and O's, be able to communicate, teach, handle the press and do about a million other things. So it is tough. But overall you need the right mix of personalities in the room to create good chemistry. That goes all the way back to your management and your scouts and which types of players they are bringing into the locker room. From star players to 'plumbers,' it all comes down to how the coach can mold them into his style — because how he deals with them affects how well they will react both on and off the ice."

WHAT MOTIVATES YOU? "I would probably say the fear of losing. I guess I dislike losing much more than the thrill I get from winning."

HOW DO YOU EARN THE RESPECT OF YOUR PLAYERS? "By respecting them. You have to be honest, fair and work hard at your job."

WHAT'S THE BIGGEST THING YOU'VE LEARNED FROM COACHING THAT YOU'VE BEEN ABLE TO APPLY TO YOUR EVERYDAY LIFE? "Patience and understanding."

WHAT ADVICE WOULD YOU HAVE FOR YOUNG COACHES STARTING OUT TODAY? "You need to become a student of the game. Know the game and work at it. Be a good person. Be respectful of others and treat people how you would want to be treated."

WHAT ARE THE KEY INGREDIENTS TO CREATING A CHAMPIONSHIP TEAM? "You need skill, talent, work ethic, timing and some luck."

WHAT DOES THE TERM LOYALTY MEAN TO YOU? "Loyalty means that you will stick together. If the ship sinks, we all go down together — no one jumps off. That is loyalty. When your team is playing together, that is how it feels. You don't go separate ways and everyone sticks together."

WHAT'S THE SECRET TO YOUR SUCCESS? "I am very simple in my approach. I just try to be a good listener, be realistic, be honest, work hard and try to learn as much as possible. I remember after I won that gold medal in the 1980 Olympics, I just sat back and thought 'wow, everybody should be able to feel what this feels like, it was just awesome.' I think that is why I am coaching. Obviously I get paid to coach, which is a great way to make a living, but when you win, you get that great feeling. It is a different kind of feeling winning as a player and now as a coach, but it is still the best thing in the world. It is such a feeling of accomplishment and it's a real high that is very fulfilling. If you could bottle that and sell it, you would be a billionaire."

ON HIS WILD'S WILD RIDE OF 2003: "What can you say, it was just an amazing story. I mean just for us to make the playoffs as early as we did and the way that we did was so amazing. The entire experience was very special and it was something that I will always remember. It was just special being a part of the original coaching staff right from the start. You could see all of the groundwork being laid for the foundation right from the get-go, and to see that all come to reality was very special. It is a real honor to be a part of this organ-ization. Jacques (Lemaire) is a special person, and his outlook on the game is really outside of the box compared to other coaches. He has a passion for the game and the delivery of his message to the players is like nobody else's. His message has meaning and the players really respect him."

WHAT WOULD YOU WANT TO SAY TO YOUR FANS, BOOSTERS, AND ALUMNI WHO HAVE SUPPORTED YOU ALL THESE YEARS? "I appreciate the fact that so many people have followed my career, that is just amazing to me. From the Gophers to the Olympics to Buffalo to Pittsburgh to Detroit and finally back to Minnesota, it has been a great ride. I just really appreciate their support and would want to thank everyone who has been there for me. It is a real honor to be thought of that way and I am very lucky."

HOW DO YOU WANT YOUR COACHING EPITAPH TO READ — HOW DO YOU WANT TO BE REMEMBERED AS A COACH? "I would want to be remembered as somebody who was respected and who treated his players with respect."

STEVE CARLSON: MINOR LEAGUE HOCKEY

Steve Carlson grew up in Virginia, Minn., and went on to gain notoriety in the game of hockey, both as a player and coach, but more importantly, as an actor. That's right, Steve and his brother Jeff, along with their friend Dave Hanson, would go on to become the legendary "Hanson Brothers" from the movie Slapshot. Steve, Jeff, and their other brother, Jack Carlson, who would go on to become one of the all-time great enforcers with the Minnesota North Stars, were originally signed as a forward line for the minor league Johnstown Jets back in 1974. Their antics then inspired the movie Slap Shot, which starred Paul Newman. While brother Jeff never made it to the NHL, Steve played one season with the Los Angeles Kings. Steve also went on to play for a number of years in the WHA, where, in addition to centering a line with Gordie and Mark Howe in New England in 1978, he also played alongside Wayne Gretzky in Edmonton in 1979 — the last year of the WHA. Steve then went in to coaching and later become an assistant coach with Baltimore in the American Hockey League. The "Hanson Brothers" were reunited in 2001, when Slapshot II was released. And, while the first one was a true classic, it is safe to say that the sequel will not be winning any Oscars any time soon!

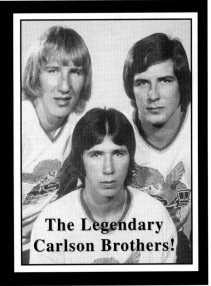
The Legendary Carlson Brothers!

BOB MAY: UNIVERSITY OF NORTH DAKOTA HOCKEY

Dr. Bob May, who coached high school hockey at Minneapolis Roosevelt in the early 1950s, went on to serve as the head coach at the University of North Dakota for two seasons from 1957-59. There, May led the Sioux to a NCAA Division I National Championship in 1959, beating Michigan State, 4-3, in Troy, NY. In addition, May's Sioux placed second in 1958 as well. May would finish his short but illustrious career at UND with a record of 44-17-2 (.714). (The Sioux had no conference affiliation at that point due to the breakup of the WIHL in March of 1958. The WCHA, of which UND was a founding member, would form at the end of the 1959 season.)

May would then go on to become a pioneer in the development and advancement of women's hockey in Minnesota. May was very active with the Checkers, Minnesota's first dominant women's club team in the 1970s. In 1980 the Checkers won the national Open B Division women's title. From there, the Checkers, who were led by Laura Halldorson, who would go on to serve as the Gopher Women's Hockey Coach, and Jill Pohtilla, who would go on to serve as the Augsburg Women's Hockey Coach, went on to win a couple of USA Hockey National Midget titles in the early 1980's, in both the 15-and-under and later in the 19-and-under categories.

MIKE RANDOLPH
HIGH SCHOOL HOCKEY: DULUTH EAST

Mike Randolph grew up in Duluth loving hockey. As a kid he played on a Lower Chester peewee squad which featured four future pro players: Pokey Trachsel, Keith Gilbertson, Chuck Ness, and himself, which ultimately lost in the national tournament to a team from Detroit which featured Marty and Mark Howe. Randolph would go on to play high school hockey at Duluth Cathedral under Coach Del Genereau, graduating in 1970. Cathedral was a high school power at the time and his team won several private/Catholic league titles during that time. Randolph then went on to play in the minor leagues for six years, followed by a stint on the 1976 U.S. Olympic team, of which he was the last player cut from the final roster. Randolph retired at that point and came back to Duluth, where he become an assistant at St. Scholastica — earning his teaching degree along the way. From there Randolph went on to become an assistant with both Gus Hendrickson and Mike Sertich at the University of Minnesota-Duluth. Randolph later became an assistant at Duluth Denfeld High School before coming over to Duluth East in 1987. There, Randolph established himself as one of the premier high school hockey coaches in the nation, winning two state titles (1995 and 1998), finishing second three times and leading his Greyhounds to eight state tournament appearances along the way.

In 2003 Mike was relieved of his coaching duties at Duluth East by school officials in a very publicized, emotional and controversial dispute regarding school fundraising, among other things. In his 15 seasons behind the Greyhound bench, however, Randolph posted an amazing 308-83-10 career record. Randolph continues to teach fourth graders at Stowe Elementary School in Duluth, and, at just 51 years of age, is keeping his coaching options open in the future. Wherever he winds up, one thing will be for sure — they will be winners, because Mike Randolph is a proven winner and an outstanding hockey coach.

HOW WOULD YOU DESCRIBE YOUR COACHING STYLE? "My philosophy when I came into the program was to provide an environment where the kids could excel at a high level. When I first got here I think that the system that was in place had a lot of the best players not playing. It was more of a situation of who their parents were or where they came from. So, that was one of the first things that I wanted to change. We decided to play the best players and provide them an opportunity schedule-wise as well as scrimmage-wise where they could play against the best competition in the state. We also paid close attention to our kids off the rink as well because we wanted our kids who wanted to play beyond high school to have the opportunity to reach their goals both on the ice and in the classroom."

HOW DO YOU MOTIVATE YOUR PLAYERS? "We motivated them by our passion for the game and by our passion to coach and be around kids. We put a lot into it and in turn we asked them to put a lot into it. We usually carried around 37 players on our roster and tried to treat everybody with respect. We always assumed that whoever the kids thought the 37th best player was, was as important as the No. 1 best player. So, we tried to make everybody part of the program and bring them together as a team where they cared about each other."

WHAT ARE THE CHARACTERISTICS OF LEADERS? "Guys who think of the team first. We used to give out a 'we not me' trophy every year and those are the kind of guys who you are looking

for. Some kids lead by example while others are more verbal, and over the years we had some excellent leadership from both kinds of kids. In fact, we had several former captains on our teams go on to become captains on their college teams, and that says a lot about those kids."

LOOKING BACK WHAT ARE YOU MOST PROUD OF IN YOUR CAREER? "I think I am most proud of the number of kids who have graduated from our program, went to college and have gone on to lead successful lives with their own families. It is gratifying to think that in some small way you played a part in that."

HOW DO YOU BUILD TEAM UNITY & CHEMISTRY? "Without chemistry you are not going to go anywhere. So, everyone worked hard and brought what they could to the team. We used to do a lot of different things, like going bowling as a team. Obviously, being in Duluth, we had to travel quite a bit to face the best competition throughout the state, and that meant spending a lot of time traveling on buses. So, we tried to use that time together to build team unity too. Then, we also did an annual fundraiser where the kids sold Christmas wreaths to help the program afford different things. All of those things helped us come together as a team and that was all part of it."

WHAT MOTIVATES YOU? "Just being around the kids was motivation enough for me. You know, I enjoyed practicing so much, that was my favorite part of coaching. Planning practices, organizing practices and running practices with my assistants was so much fun. Winning and losing was never that important to us. What was important was that the kids played hard and had fun, because if they did that then the winning would take care of itself. Ultimately our goal was to get to the state tournament and we knew that in order to get there we had to take it day by day and shift by shift. So, building a good team with good chemistry all went into that and that motivated me."

WHAT ADVICE WOULD YOU HAVE FOR YOUNG COACHES STARTING OUT TODAY? "I remember taking a coaching class from UM-Duluth coach Jim Malosky and he made a statement that stuck with me in the early part of my career. He said 'If I was to coach in this day and age, I would move every five years.' Basically what he felt was that after a five year stay, parents and supporters get real critical of your coaching style. It is at that point he said, that you need to move on. You know, you no longer see the Willard Ikola's of the world nowadays. Those guys with 30 years of coaching at one school are becoming very scarce. And I think one of the reasons for that is because coaching is a lot of time and a lot of headaches for not a lot of money. So my advice would be to just have fun where you are at and enjoy it while it lasts. If you need to move on then do so, but do it for your own reasons so that you can be happy as a teacher and coach."

WHAT'S THE BIGGEST THING YOU'VE LEARNED FROM COACHING THAT YOU'VE BEEN ABLE TO APPLY TO YOUR EVERYDAY LIFE? "Not to get too up and not to get too down, the same is true in life. Beyond that, I have learned to realize that hockey is really important to a lot of kids who are at a very sensitive age, and as a coach you can make a big impression on them."

WHAT ARE THE KEY INGREDIENTS TO CREATING A

CHAMPIONSHIP TEAM? "The biggest thing is chemistry. You have to get everybody working towards a common goal, to believe in each other and to get them to be on the same page. That is very difficult in this day and age with regards to parental involvement. You just have a lot of parents nowadays who think they are coaches and somehow as a coach you have to get the kids to realize that there is only one coach. That can be tough."

WHAT'S THE SECRET TO YOUR SUCCESS? "I think it is a combination of a lot of hard work from our kids and from a lot of dedicated parents. Hockey is important to a lot of parents in this community and that starts at a very young age. The kids get very good coaching all the way up the ladder here and are provided the opportunity to be in an environment where they can be successful. By the time they get to high school, they are very well prepared and that makes my job a lot easier."

WHAT WOULD YOU WANT TO SAY TO YOUR FANS, BOOSTERS, AND ALUMNI WHO HAVE SUPPORTED YOU ALL THESE YEARS? "I can't thank my supporters enough. The support has been unbelievable throughout the years and I have great, great memories of the 15 years that I was at East, as well as with all the other years of coaching that I have in this community. I have been blessed to have been surrounded by great players, great parents, great fans, great friends and a great coaching staff. Not many guys are that fortunate."

ON LEAVING DULUTH EAST, NOT ON YOUR OWN TERMS: "It was brutal. The more I think about it the sicker I get, knowing that people can get by with stuff like that. But I know that I have to move on and get over it. Overall, I would just want to say thanks to all the people for all the great support that they have given my family and I over the years. It has been unbelievable. It has also been a very difficult thing on us. I feel bad for people who have to go through something like this and not have the support that I have been lucky enough to have. The support has been statewide and I am very appreciate of that. It is very touching and very humbling. I just can't thank people enough for that. So, for now I am going to help coach my nine year old son's team and try to have some fun. I have a daughter who is a junior right now as well, and once she graduates then I will look for other opportunities. So, if a head coaching job becomes available, then I will have to evaluate it at that point. I have a good job teaching at an elementary school right now, but know that there is still some good coaching left in me. I love coaching and I would like to think that I have something to offer, so I hope something opens up somewhere along the line."

HOW DO YOU WANT YOUR COACHING EPITAPH TO READ — HOW DO YOU WANT TO BE REMEMBERED AS A COACH? "That I worked hard, was respected both as a coach and as a person, and in some way touched the lives of my kids."

CODDY WINTERS: UNIVERSITY OF PENNSYLVANIA HOCKEY

Frank "Coddy" Winters grew up playing as a rover in the era of seven-man hockey in his hometown of Duluth, around the turn of the century. Winters went on to play semi-professional hockey in Cleveland for nearly 20 years, playing on five championship teams. He also went on to coach hockey at the University of Pennsylvania as well, where he was very influential in starting the program and building it into a division one contender. Though having the opportunity to turn professional, Winters instead preferred to remain an amateur. Many regarded him as one of the greatest American born hockey players. Winters, who was a charter member of the U.S. Hockey Hall of Fame, died in 1944 at the age of 60 in Cleveland.

"BADGER" BOB JOHNSON: COLLEGE, OLYMPIC & PRO HOCKEY

Bob Johnson is a Minnesota hockey legend. Period. A graduate of Minneapolis Central High School, Johnson went on to play left wing for the Gopher Hockey team under coach John Mariucci from 1954 to 1955. (Johnson originally went to North Dakota, but, after failing to crack the Canadian dominated line-up, came home to play for the Minneapolis Millers semi-pro team. There, his player-coach was Mariucci, who also coached the Gophers as well. Maroosh liked what he saw and took the kid in as a transfer.) An outstanding athlete, Johnson would also play baseball for the Gophers as well. In fact, Johnson had originally signed a pro baseball contract with the Chicago White Sox after graduating high school, but instead went into the Service. When he was discharged, he opted instead to try his hand at coaching and teaching. So, he began coaching at the his high school level, first at Warroad, where he taught and coached hockey and baseball. There, he also played hockey for Cal Marvin's infamous Warroad Lakers senior team. Johnson had quite a schedule going in those days, too. Playing with the Lakers on Wednesdays, Saturdays and Sundays while coaching his Warriors on Tuesdays, Thursdays and Fridays, left Monday as his only day to relax. But, he managed. Bob just loved hockey.

A few years later Johnson headed south, to Minneapolis Roosevelt High School, where he won four City Conference titles in six years with the Teddies. Johnson then hit the college scene, taking over the reins at Colorado College in 1963. After four years at C.C., he moved on to the University of Wisconsin, where, in a period of 11 years, he led the Badgers to seven NCAA tournaments, winning three national championships and one runner-up finish. It was there where the 1977 NCAA Coach of the Year recipient was given the nickname, "Badger Bob." Johnson then led the 1976 U.S. Olympic team to a fourth-place finish at Innsbruck, Austria. In addition, Johnson also coached the 1981,1984, and 1987 U.S. teams in the Canada Cup as well as the 1973, 1974, 1975 and 1981 U.S. National Teams as well.

Then, in 1982, Johnson coached the NHL's Calgary Flames for five seasons. In 1990 he took over as coach of the Pittsburgh Penguins, where in his first season, he led the team to a Stanley Cup victory over the Minnesota North Stars. Johnson, who served as Executive Director of USA Hockey for a three-year period, tragically died in 1991 from brain cancer at the age of 60. His gift for inspiring his players and everyone associated with him was recognized when he was inducted into the U.S. Hockey Hall of Fame in 1991 as well as the Hockey Hall of Fame in Toronto in 1992. Badger Bob was one of the greatest hockey coaches ever to hail from Minnesota. A tireless promoter of American hockey, his memory lives on from his now-famous phrase which epitomized his love for the game: "It's a great day for hockey." Bob and his wife Martha had five children, including Mark, who was a member of the 1980 gold medal-winning U.S. Olympic Hockey Team.

DON ROBERTS
COLLEGE HOCKEY: GUSTAVUS

Don Roberts grew up in Appleton and went on to graduate from Appleton High School in 1952, where he starred in football, basketball, track and baseball. From there, Roberts would go on to play football, basketball and baseball at Gustavus, graduating in 1956. Roberts lettered in his first two years in basketball and also won a letter in baseball as a sophomore, but football was his forte. He lettered four years on the gridiron under Coach Hollingsworth, playing on three championship teams and earning all-MIAC honors as a fullback and defensive lineman his senior season.

Then, as a platoon leader in the Marine Corps, Roberts went on to coach baseball and football at Camp Pendleton. Two years later he came back to Gustavus to teach physical education and coach baseball (1960-64), football (1961-65) and even wrestling for a short stint. In 1964 Roberts was asked to take over the hockey program, and by 1966, despite not knowing a thing about hockey, he had produced a conference champion. That, is the sign of a great coach.

Over the next four decades Roberts' hockey teams would go on to win 13 MIAC titles, including eight straight starting in '65, and he only missed postseason play on three occasions. The first coach to ever win 500 games, Roberts also led the Golden Gusties to three national championship finals as well. Don Roberts took a hockey program in its infancy and turned it into a dynasty. For his efforts he was named conference coach-of-the-year on eight different occasions and was also named as both the NAIA and American Hockey Coaches Association Coach of the Year in 1975. In 1993, he received the AHCA's John MacInnes Award for his lifetime commitment to the sport of hockey. More recently he was honored with the creation of the Don Roberts Trophy, which is now awarded annually to the MIAC Conference Champion. In addition to developing 28 All-Americans and 66 All-Conference players, Roberts led the Gusties to a fifth place ranking on the all-time Division III win list as well.

Because he knew so little about the game in the beginning, Don truly became a student of the game. He read whatever he could and talked to whoever would listen. He even traveled with his teams to Europe every few years to play teams over there, and see how they did things across the pond. In all, Roberts would coach the Gusties for a total of 40 years and finished with a career record of 532-278-25. When it was all said and done he had very quietly become the winningest hockey coach in NCAA Division III hockey history. The ultimate tribute, however, came in 1998 when the school renamed Lund Arena as Don Roberts Arena in his honor.

Don and his wife Nancy live in St. Peter and have four children, including two who followed their old man in playing football for the Gusties.

Upon his retirement from the game in 1997, Don reflected: "The winning and the losing, that's something we all do as coaches. Starting the youth hockey program in St. Peter and building the indoor rink at Gustavus are among the most rewarding things I've done. I'll always remember the great friendships I've made and all the traveling I've done because of hockey."

HOW WOULD YOU DESCRIBE YOUR COACHING STYLE? "My philosophy on coaching was that it was the coaches job to put the right people into the right situations so they could be in a position to help the team win. It is also about personal relationships, being able to communicate and working hard. You know, I wanted to be a coach from the time I left high school. I coached a lot of different sports, from

wrestling to baseball to football to basketball to hockey. But I wasn't destined to be a hockey coach. In fact, basketball was my main sport. Gustavus needed a hockey coach though, so I took on that challenge. Hockey was so similar to basketball in my eyes in that it was very easy for me to understand the tactics of it. So, I jumped in and learned as much as I could, reading books and listening to other coaches speak on the subject. It turned out to be a fantastic experience and something that really shaped my life."

HOW DID YOU MOTIVATE YOUR PLAYERS? "I have always been a positive coach and not a negative coach. Being able to motivate by understanding which switch to throw on each individual was the key. I learned great leadership in the Marine Corps and that helped me to understand how to motivate my kids."

IF YOU COULD MAGICALLY GO BACK IN TIME TO THE FIRST YEAR YOU WERE A HEAD COACH AND GIVE YOURSELF SOME ADVICE FOR THE FUTURE, KNOWING WHAT YOU KNOW NOW, BACK THEN, WHAT WOULD YOU SAY TO YOURSELF? "Perseverance is the key in life. You have to be able to stick with something and have the inner desire to get it done. You also have to set reachable, attainable goals. Then, you have to evaluate yourself every so often and try and improve on what you think is important."

WHAT ARE THE CHARACTERISTICS OF LEADERS? "I would say confidence and the ability to communicate."

LOOKING BACK WHAT ARE YOU MOST PROUD OF IN YOUR CAREER? "Seeing these kids go on to become successful businessmen, doctors and lawyers. That is so gratifying as a coach. Just to be a part of their lives means so much. I mean how many jobs do people have where they really get to make a difference in a young person's life? I am very proud of that."

WHAT WAS THE KEY TO RECRUITING? "I depended a lot on the high school coaches because I was too busy teaching and coaching to get out and do a lot of recruiting. They were a very valuable resource and really helped me out a great deal. I also learned a lot about players from their parents. I asked them a lot of questions and tried to get to know them as well. Most importantly though, I relied on my players for recruiting. They knew the high school kids and told them the way it was. Now it is all different with kids playing junior hockey, but that is an entirely different story."

HOW DID YOU BUILD TEAM UNITY & CHEMISTRY? "I think that we created it when we did things like practicing outside and driving together on road trips in buses together. Just getting together in different settings let the kids get to know each other and that helped to build chemistry."

WHAT MOTIVATED YOU? "You know, it was more than just playing. I wanted our kids to come away with a lot more than that. The kids pay to play at this level and I wanted them to have fun, to learn and to go on to become good people."

WHAT ADVICE WOULD YOU HAVE FOR YOUNG COACHES STARTING OUT TODAY? "Enjoy it while it lasts. I miss it, the camaraderie, the locker room, the practices and just the kids. That was a great, great time in my life."

WHAT'S THE BIGGEST THING YOU'VE LEARNED FROM COACHING THAT YOU'VE BEEN ABLE TO APPLY TO YOUR EVERYDAY LIFE? "That there are ups and downs. You win some you lose some, and some get rained out. The toughest thing though is to have the gumption and inner strength to be able to pick yourself up when you face adversity. That transmits over to your team."

WHAT'S THE SECRET TO YOUR SUCCESS? "I realized early on that you have to try to get the very best players that you can. In order to be a good coach you just have to get good players. There is no question about that. I also think that success builds on success. You know, because I had never played hockey, I had to really listen to my players and learn as I went along."

WHAT ARE THE KEY INGREDIENTS TO CREATING A CHAMPIONSHIP TEAM? "The key ingredient is always going to be talent. You have to have enough talent to put the kids in a position to win a championship. The wins and losses will all even out if you have perseverance, but if you can instill confidence in your kids and keep communicating with them then anything can happen."

ON BEING THE WINNINGEST DIVISION III COLLEGE HOCKEY COACH OF ALL TIME: "I have seen a lot of periods of hockey, that is for sure! Really though, that was special. You know, we only play 20 games a season, so that took some time. I think we had just one losing season, and that was my first year back in 1965 when we went 1-14. That was a lot of fun that first year because we were starting something and it grew into something very special."

WHAT WOULD YOU WANT TO SAY TO YOUR FANS, BOOSTERS, AND ALUMNI WHO HAVE SUPPORTED YOU ALL THESE YEARS? "You know, I still communicate with a lot of my alumni and I think I must have 600 or so counting my junior varsity kids. They have been just great to me though and I couldn't even begin to thank them enough for what they have done for me over the years."

HOW DO YOU WANT YOUR COACHING EPITAPH TO READ — HOW DO YOU WANT TO BE REMEMBERED AS A COACH? "Somebody who really enjoyed his job and enjoyed the relationships not only with the players but with his fellow coaches in the MIAC. As a coach you really get involved with these kids' lives and it was nice to know that you made a difference."

MIKE EAVES: WISCONSIN HOCKEY

Mike Eaves, who played for the Minnesota North Stars from 1978-83, took over as the head coach at the University of Wisconsin in 2002, replacing Minnesota native Jeff Sauer. Eaves, who also coached for a year at Shattuck St. Mary's Prep School in Faribault, also served as an assistant at St. Cloud State for one season as well. Eaves, a former All-American at Wisconsin, led the Badgers to the 1977 NCAA title over Michigan. Prior to coming back to Madison, Eaves had previously served as an assistant with the NHL's Calgary Flames, Pittsburgh Penguins and Philadelphia Flyers.

JILL POHTILLA: AUGBURG WOMEN'S HOCKEY

Jill Pohtilla grew up in Plymouth and went on to graduate from Wayzata High School in 1981. Pohtilla then played volleyball and softball at Augustana College (Sioux Falls, S.D.) for three years before transferring to the University of Minnesota, where she graduated in 1987 with degrees in psychology and biology. Pohtilla would then go on to teach and coach volleyball, softball and hockey at Anoka and Champlin Park High Schools, as well as coach volleyball at Minnetonka and Wayzata High Schools. Pohtilla has also played ice hockey on all levels for the past two decades, and was a member of the four-time national champion Minnesota Checkers girls' hockey team. Pohtilla was hired in 1995 as Augsburg's first women's hockey coach, and in that capacity has worked hard to build the sport among colleges and universities in Minnesota. She was instrumental in developing the Midwestern Collegiate Women's Hockey Alliance (MCWHA), and later, was part of the formulation of women's hockey as a varsity championship sport in the Minnesota Intercollegiate Athletic Conference (MIAC) — just the second conference in the nation (and first at the exclusively Division III level) to sponsor the sport.

Pohtilla has also been active on the national women's hockey scene. In 1997 and 1998, she was selected by current U.S. Olympic women's hockey head coach Ben Smith to coach at the U.S. Olympic Women's Hockey Development Camp in Lake Placid, N.Y., coaching teams of 15-16 and 17-18 year olds. In addition, Pohtilla served as the president of the Minnesota Girls' and Women's Hockey Associations in 1990. She was also the secretary/treasurer of the American Women's Hockey Coaches Association as well. Furthermore, Pohtilla was named to the NCAA Division III Women's Hockey National Committee in 2000, which oversees the sport's national championships. A tireless advocate in the development of girls' and women's hockey in Minnesota, Pohtilla was even honored by the Minnesota Coalition to Promote Women in Athletic Leadership in 1998 with its "Breaking Barriers Award" on National Girls and Women in Sports Day.

Now in her ninth season behind the bench at Augsburg, Pohtilla has posted a very impressive 107-64-7 (.621) career record. Known as an outstanding motivator and innovator, Pohtilla is a true pioneer of her sport and amongst the very best of the best in women's college hockey.

TOM SATERDALEN
HIGH SCHOOL HOCKEY: BLOOMINGTON JEFFERSON

Tom Saterdalen grew up in Rochester and went on to graduate from Rochester John Marshall High School. From there, Saterdalen captained the hockey and tennis teams at Bemidji State University, graduating with a teaching degree in 1964. Saterdalen's first teaching and coaching job was in Superior Wis., where, from 1966-70, he won a pair of Wisconsin state hockey titles. After spending a year as an assistant high school hockey coach and head tennis coach at Cloquet, followed by one year as an assistant hockey coach at Bemidji State, Saterdalen then went to the University of Minnesota, where he served as an assistant coach from 1970-72.

Saterdalen's next stop would be at Bloomington Jefferson High School. There, he would teach and coach hockey and tennis, and become a Minnesota coaching legend along the way. On the ice, from 1973 to 2003, Saterdalen's Jaguars won 13 Lake Conference hockey championships and were in the regional hockey finals an amazing 23 out of 26 times. Of those 23 times, the team made it to the state tournament on 15 occasions and won five state championships (1981, 1989, 1992, 1993 & 1994) as well. His three straight titles from 1992-94 was one of the greatest runs in state history. Saterdalen would retire in 2003 as one of the winningest hockey coaches in state history with a career record of 545-167-21. Saterdalen also sent more than 60 players on to play Division I college hockey with 18 moving to the professional ranks, and seven playing in the NHL.

In addition, Saterdalen also served as the tennis coach from 1980-2002, where he won two state titles, eight conference titles and three sectional titles, racking up a 284-102 record along the way.

Among Saterdalen's many coaching honors and accolades, he was the Minnesota High School Tennis Coach of the Year in 1996 and also won four Minnesota High School Hockey Coach of the Year Awards in 1981, 1988, 1993 and 2002. He was also the recipient of a special Coach of the Year award from the National High School Athletic Coaches Association in 1994. In addition, Saterdalen was inducted into the Bemidji State University Athletic Hall of Fame in 1986.

In 2003, after nearly nearly four decades of teaching and coaching, Saterdalen retired as a true Minnesota coaching icon. It would be an incredible legacy for an incredible person. Tom presently resides in Bloomington with his family. In addition, his son, Jeff, also starred on the St. Cloud State University hockey team as well.

HOW WOULD YOU DESCRIBE YOUR COACHING STYLE? "My philosophy is to treat my players like I want to be treated. I tried to be really honest and up front with them and let them know where they stood all the time. I let them know that I cared about them more as a person than as a player. I was also a very positive, upbeat person and I tried to have a lot of fun."

HOW DID YOU MOTIVATE YOUR PLAYERS? "First, we got the kids to really care about each other and we made sure that it was like a family. We tried to create a culture where we had the parents get together and really create a family-type atmosphere. The run we had in the early 1990s, where we won three straight state championships, was amazing and what was even more special about that was the fact that all 16 sets of parents would sit together at those games. I have always said that you can always look at a high school team and see how the players are going to do by how their parents are reacting. If the parents are all sitting together then there is very little selfishness

or very little individualism out on the ice because the parents care about the kids as a team. So, I just tried to always impress upon my kids that the most important thing was the team. And no matter how good people were, the team was over and above everything else. As a result, I think our players shared the puck really, really well and tried to play hard for each other."

WHO WERE YOUR COACHING MENTORS? "I would say my football coach at Rochester John Marshall High School, Lauren Hagge, was someone I learned a great deal from. Then, on the hockey side, I was lucky enough to serve as an assistant under Glen Sonmor, Ken Yackel and Herb Brooks at the University of Minnesota. Those guys were great and that was a wonderful experience. Glen was so upbeat and positive and really emphasized repetition. Then, Ken was just the opposite, he was a teacher who broke everything down into every minute, frame by frame, details. Finally, Herbie kind of put everything together and had his own tough style too. So, I enjoyed my time with all three of those guys and certainly took bits and pieces from all of their styles and put them into my own."

WHAT ARE THE CHARACTERISTICS OF LEADERS? "I think a real leader has to not care about stepping on some people's toes. But he also has to back that up out on the ice. You can't be just a guy that says things without having the game to back it up. Leaders might not be the most popular guys on your team, but they have to be respected."

LOOKING BACK WHAT ARE YOU MOST PROUD OF IN YOUR CAREER? "I would say it was being able to give a lot of kids a lot of chances to really believe in themselves and have a great opportunity to play hockey and be proud of what they have done. It is easy to remember the Mike Crowleys, Tom Kurvers, Mark Parishs and Ben Clymers, but we have had a lot of other great, great kids through the years here too, and I am very proud of that."

IF YOU COULD MAGICALLY GO BACK IN TIME TO THE FIRST YEAR YOU WERE A HEAD COACH AND GIVE YOURSELF SOME ADVICE FOR THE FUTURE, KNOWING WHAT YOU KNOW NOW, BACK THEN, WHAT WOULD YOU SAY TO YOURSELF? "I would say don't be so hard on yourself. When I first started coaching and we played poorly I would always blame myself. Then, I would get down on the kids and work them hard too. I think John Bianchi, who was my assistant for 21 years, said it best when he reminded me that it is the players who play the game and all we can do as coaches is get them ready to play, so don't beat yourself up."

HOW DID YOU BUILD TEAM UNITY & CHEMISTRY? "If coaches treat their players with respect, then players will treat other players with respect. That builds chemistry."

WHAT MOTIVATED YOU? "I wanted to be a great teacher and coach so that I could see kids progress and get a chance. I really just wanted kids to be as good as they can possibly be and that was my driving force."

WHAT ADVICE WOULD YOU HAVE FOR YOUNG

COACHES STARTING OUT TODAY? "They have to be very stubborn and hard headed. They have to try to do what is right and try to be fair with themselves. Then, they certainly can't be afraid to make a stand because they think they are going to be shot down all of the time. I mean in just the second year I was at Jefferson I had a petition go around from the locals to get rid of me, but my administrators backed me up and said that they were behind me 100%. Then, about every five years or so we would have some parents who thought that their kids should be playing more and they got after me. It is very demeaning and it makes you feel bad because you, as a person, want to do what is best for kids and what is best for the team. So, when people are taking shots at you it is tough on your ego. Sure, you make some mistakes and some bad choices along the way, but you have to live with them and move on. Overall, I would just tell them to hang in there. Get involved with the parents and stick to what you believe is right. Then, get involved in building youth programs and do what is best for your program, that is what is going to pay off in the long run. It will take long hours, but there is no shortcut."

WHAT IS THE KEY TO GOOD TIME MANAGEMENT? "Without question it is being organized. Then, you have to have priorities. You know, during my hockey and tennis seasons I probably got a lot more done in my classroom than I did when I wasn't in season because I had to be so unbelievably organized."

FAVORITE LOCKER ROOM SIGN? "The harder you work the luckier you get." & "Passes come from the heart."

WHAT'S THE BIGGEST THING YOU'VE LEARNED FROM COACHING THAT YOU'VE BEEN ABLE TO APPLY TO YOUR EVERYDAY LIFE? "Self direction and being satisfied with yourself and what you do. Now that I have retired I am having so much fun watching hockey, playing tennis and just relaxing. Life is good."

WHAT ARE THE KEY INGREDIENTS TO CREATING A CHAMPIONSHIP TEAM? "First of all you have to get your kids to believe in you and your staff. From there, you have to get them to believe in themselves. Talent doesn't always translate into success. I mean, our 1980 state championship team had 10 kids go on to play division one hockey. Then, even though our 1981 state championship team only had three division one kids, they had this tremendous desire as a team to achieve and never to give up. We won six of seven overtime games that year and tied the other one, so, despite not having a lot of talent, they just played with a lot of heart."

WHAT'S THE SECRET TO YOUR SUCCESS? "Coaching is no different than sales. The harder you work the more success you are going to have, and, once again, there are no shortcuts."

WHAT WOULD YOU WANT TO SAY TO YOUR FANS, BOOSTERS, AND ALUMNI WHO HAVE SUPPORTED YOU ALL THESE YEARS? "It has been a great ride and so much fun. Thanks for all the support, we couldn't have done it without you."

HOW DO YOU WANT YOUR COACHING EPITAPH TO READ — HOW DO YOU WANT TO BE REMEMBERED AS A COACH? "I would like to be remembered as a guy who really cared about kids. Everything has to do with the giving of yourself, the more you can give of yourself, the more you are going to get back — and if you base your philosophy on that you are going to be a rich person."

DOUG PALAZZARI: USA HOCKEY

Doug Palazzari was born and raised in Eveleth, where he grew up loving the game of hockey. Doug's father, Aldo, played hockey in the NHL with Boston and New York back in the 1940s, so it was no wonder that Doug would take to the game. Palazzari went on to play hockey at Colorado College, where he was a mainstay for the Tigers from 1970-74. He led Colorado College in scoring in both 1972 and 1974, earning NCAA All-America, First-Team All-Western Collegiate Hockey Association and WCHA Most Valuable Player honors during those same seasons.

Following his collegiate career, Palazzari spent eight seasons (1974-82) playing professional hockey in the St. Louis Blues' system. He registered 38 points on 18 goals and 20 assists in 108 regular-season games in the National Hockey League, but made his greatest impact while playing for the Salt Lake City Golden Eagles of the Central Hockey League — the Blues' top minor league affiliate at the time. There, Palazzari was twice honored as the CHL's Most Valuable Player (1978 and 1980) and was tabbed as the league's All-Time Greatest Player by The Hockey News in 1997. He also received the AHAUS Outstanding Player Award in 1978 as well. In addition, Palazzari's international playing experience includes being selected as a member of the 1973 and 1974 U.S. National Teams and he also represented the U.S. in the inaugural Canada Cup tournament in 1976.

Palazzari has served in a coaching capacity for USA Hockey on several occasions, most recently in 1991 as head coach for the U.S. Select 16 Team. He also served as an assistant coach for Team South at the 1991 U.S. Olympic Festival, the 1989 U.S. Select 17 Team and for the teams that represented the U.S. at the 1987 Pravda Cup and the 1986 Calgary Cup. Palazzari also spent six seasons serving as an assistant coach at Colorado College, from 1985-91.

Palazzari was named Executive Director of USA Hockey in 1999, signaling yet another important milestone in a lifelong hockey career that has spanned the spectrum from player to coach to administrator. As Executive Director of USA Hockey, Palazzari directs the day-to-day operations of a National Governing Body that provides programs and services to nearly 600,000 ice and inline hockey players, coaches, officials and volunteers nationwide. Prior to being named Executive Director of USA Hockey, Palazzari oversaw the organization's Youth and Education Programs for the previous eight years, most recently as Senior Director.

Among his many honors and accolades, in 2000 Palazzari was inducted into the U.S. Hockey Hall of Fame, back in his hometown of Eveleth, in recognition of his accomplishments at all levels of the sport. Doug and his wife Sara reside in Colorado Springs, Colo., and

JEFF SAUER
COLLEGE HOCKEY: UNIVERSITY OF WISCONSIN

Jeff Sauer was born in Wisconsin but moved to Minnesota at the age of four when his father became the assistant football coach and head hockey coach at St. Paul Central High School. Jeff went on to star on the St. Paul Washington High School hockey and baseball teams, graduating in 1961. From there, Sauer went on to play hockey and baseball at Colorado College, graduating in 1965 with a degree in sociology. After college, Sauer got drafted and went into the Army for two and a half years. Upon his return, he became an assistant at Colorado College under Coach Bob Johnson. Then, in 1968, when Johnson was named as the head coach at the University of Wisconsin, Sauer followed along.

In 1971 Sauer got his big break when he was offered the head coaching job back at Colorado College. At CC, where he would serve as head coach from 1971-82, Sauer won 166 games and was twice named WCHA Coach of the Year. His first award came following his rookie season, and the second followed the 1975 campaign, when his Tigers finished third in the league. After 11 years at Colorado, Sauer was offered the head coaching position at back at the University of Wisconsin. Bob Johnson had moved on to coach in the NHL and Sauer was eager to try his hand at something new.

So, in 1982 Sauer took over the Badger Hockey program and started making history right out of the gates, becoming the first coach in college history to win a national title in his inaugural season. Sauer's second national title came in 1990, when his Badgers went 36-9-1 en route to recording the school's second-winningest season in history. In total, the Badgers would reach the NCAA tournament 12 times under Sauer and also won five WCHA playoff titles as well. He also produced 17 All-Americans in his 20 seasons behind the Badger bench. In addition, many of his players have gone on to play professionally, including the likes of Chris Chelios, Tony Granato, Curtis Joseph, Joseph Mellanby, Pat Richter and Danny Heatley, to name a few. The winningest coach in UW history, Sauer retired in 2002 after 31 years of coaching as the fourth-winningest coach in NCAA history with a career record of 655-532-57. Sauer's list of achievements in college hockey places him among the elite in the coaching ranks. He is not only the winningest coach in Badger history in any sport, but he is the WCHA's most victorious and most tenured coach.

In addition to being one of college hockey's top coaches, Sauer also had a noticeable presence on the international scene as well. He was very active in USA Hockey, the national governing body for U.S. hockey, and was dedicated to the development and promotion of hockey at all levels in the United States. In 2000, Sauer coached the women's team at the Olympic Festival in Lake Placid, N.Y. In 1997, Sauer coached the U.S. Select Team which played at the Tampere Cup in Finland. In 1995, Sauer was chosen to serve as the head coach of the U.S. National Team at the World Championships in Sweden. In 1992, Sauer was an assistant coach for the U.S. at the World Tournament in Prague, Czechoslovakia. At the 1990 Goodwill Games, Sauer served as head coach of Team USA. In 1989, Sauer coached the USA Select Team at the Pravda Cup (Leningrad, U.S.S.R.). Sauer has also coached at the Olympic Festival (1987), served on the U.S. Olympic Hockey Committee (1984), been a member of the NCAA Rules Committee (eight years) and even served as editor of the NCAA's rule book. He did it all!

One of the most-respected coaches in the game, Sauer continues to be a consummate diplomat for the game of hockey. He remains involved at all levels of the game, from instructing kids at summer camps to speaking at high school assemblies to coaching international-level athletes in world tournaments. Sauer was honored in 2002 by USA Hockey, when he received the JOFA/USA Hockey Distinguished Achievement Award given to a U. S. citizen who has made hockey his or her profession and has made outstanding contributions, on or off the ice, to the sport in America. Jeff Sauer is a hockey coaching legend. Period. Jeff and his wife Jamie reside in Middleton, Wis., and have two kids, Chip and Beth.

HOW WOULD YOU DESCRIBE YOUR COACHING STYLE? "I liked to let my players be creative and tried not to structure the talented kids. I just let them play and then tried to structure the other players around those guys. I always put an emphasis on goaltending and on good defense, and then let the players who could get the job done offensively, get the job done. I think I was a laid back coach, but I had a lot of intensity too. It was a very successful philosophy and I enjoyed coaching that way."

HOW DID YOU MOTIVATE YOUR PLAYERS? "I am not a fire and brimstone kind of a guy. It was more about self-motivation for me. I put a lot of responsibility on our captains to help motivate players too. I just think for a kid to have an opportunity to play in the WCHA at such a great program like Wisconsin that he owed it to himself and to his school to go out and give it his best effort night in and night out. I never asked kids to win games, I just asked them to work hard and do the little things that needed to be done in order to help win games."

IF YOU COULD MAGICALLY GO BACK IN TIME TO THE FIRST YEAR YOU WERE A HEAD COACH AND GIVE YOURSELF SOME ADVICE FOR THE FUTURE, KNOWING WHAT YOU KNOW NOW, BACK THEN, WHAT WOULD YOU SAY TO YOURSELF? "I knew when I first started out that I could compete with the big boys, I just needed to work hard and get it done. That was my attitude early on and I kept that through my entire career. You know, I still remember when I was the coach at Colorado College and I was at my first WCHA coaches meeting. I was this 27 year-old kid and came into the room and sat down next to John Mariucci. Across the table was John MacInness, to the left was Amo Bessone, to the right was Bob Johnson and on the other side of the table were Murray Armstrong and Ralph Romano. I mean I was sitting in a room with legends, it was just a who's-who of hockey. So, we went ahead and did the schedule for the league around the table with our calendars open. The other guys kept telling me 'Hey, don't worry we will take care of you kid…'. Well, when the meeting was over I had a grand total of six home games, everything else was on the road. It was a big case of welcome to the league rookie! We fixed it, but I sat back at that moment and really had to think about my future."

LOOKING BACK WHAT ARE YOU MOST PROUD OF IN YOUR CAREER? "I think through it all I was always just myself, a kid from St. Paul. I tried to stay the same type of guy that I was when I grew up. I hope that I would be remembered as someone who was always friendly before and after games, and was always very complimentary and supportive of his players."

WHAT WAS THE KEY TO RECRUITING? "You have to sell yourself, that is how you recruit athletes. Every school has got a good educational format, so it comes down to how well you sell yourself and your program. I know a lot of guys give kids the high-pressure sales job, but that was never me. We never went after 20 players and hoped to get five, we went after a few specific players and tried to get them all. So, overall you have to sell the league, sell yourself and sell your school."

HOW DID YOU BUILD TEAM UNITY & CHEMISTRY? "Chemistry is tough, particularly nowadays with junior hockey becoming so popular. Now, there are an awful lot of 20 and 21 year old freshman coming into the league. I can remember a few years ago having a 17-year-old and a 24-year-old on the same team. That is a big difference. Chemistry, however, is trying to relate the older players to the younger players. It is a magical, special thing between the kids. In 1990 we won the national championship with a team that did not have a ton of talent, but we had great chemistry. Chemistry and leadership are what it is all about."

WHAT IS THE KEY TO GOOD TIME MANAGEMENT? "I never felt that coaching was a nine to five job. It was a job where you went to the office and worked until the job was done. I always felt like during the season I was just constantly working. Whether I was home in bed getting ready to sleep, or what have you, I was thinking about line combinations, or our power play or something. It was always with you. A coaches job is really never done and that was just the nature of the beast."

WHAT MOTIVATED YOU? "It is always fun to win, but to watch players develop, especially at the college level, and see how they went from kids to mature young men, that is what motivated me."

WHAT ADVICE WOULD YOU HAVE FOR YOUNG COACHES STARTING OUT TODAY? "I would just say work as hard as you can and try not to let the pressure get to you. Compete, go hard for 60 minutes on the ice, but then afterwards get to know the other coaches and spend some time with them. That is all part of the experience."

WHAT'S THE BIGGEST THING YOU'VE LEARNED FROM COACHING THAT YOU'VE BEEN ABLE TO APPLY TO YOUR EVERYDAY LIFE? "You know, if you could have just coached, it would have been a great job. I mean nowadays the head coach has to deal with everything from NCAA rules, to recruiting, to admissions, to the media. Would you believe that one summer I think we had close to 20 golf outings? It sounds ridiculous but you have to be at all of those things. At the college level especially, there is so much more involved that the normal person doesn't see. I can remember going into the office early in the morning and by noon your train of thought might have changed five different directions and none of them even involved talking about hockey. I know that after all of that I just couldn't wait to get out from behind the desk and to the rink to play hockey."

WHAT ARE THE KEY INGREDIENTS TO CREATING A CHAMPIONSHIP TEAM? "Talent doesn't win games alone. Again, you need to have chemistry. You also need to have specific types of players, like a good goaltender and some goal scorers. The foot soldiers are important too, and you need leaders to motivate those guys to get better and help the team."

WHAT'S THE SECRET TO YOUR SUCCESS? "Everything that I did as a coach was always with the team first. If the team had success, then the individuals would also have success. You know, I can look at a team picture and nine times out of 10 I can see the focus of the team through the team picture. If the head coach is sitting in the front of the first row, then you know that the coach is the focus of that team. If the coach is in the back row and the team is in front, then you know that the team comes first. For me, I was always in the back of my team photo and I think that says a lot about me as a person and as a coach."

HOW DO YOU WANT YOUR COACHING EPITAPH TO READ — HOW DO YOU WANT TO BE REMEMBERED AS A COACH? "He was fair, had integrity, went out and worked as hard as he possibly could to have success, and hoped that his players enjoyed playing for him. It's not about how many wins I had, it was always about my players' successes and achievements."

NICK KAHLER: MINNEAPOLIS MILLERS & AUGSBURG COLLEGE HOCKEY

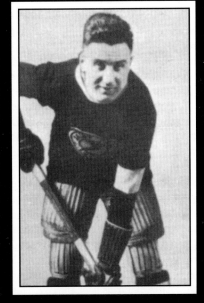

Nick Kahler grew up in Dollar Bay, Mich., in the heart of Michigan's Copper Country, playing hockey around the turn of the century. An outstanding player, Kahler would go to serve as the captain of nearly every team he would play on. After playing professionally in Canada, Kahler went on to join the Duluth Curling Club 1914. From there, Kahler went on to join the St. Paul Athletic Club, where he would serve as a manager, coach and player. In 1916, playing alongside legends Moose Goheen, Tony Conroy and Eddie Fitzgerald, Kahler's A.C. won the coveted McNaughton Cup against Sault Ste. Marie, Mich., and then went on to defeat Lachine, Quebec, for the Art Ross Trophy. Kahler played with the A.C. until 1920 and was even selected to play on the 1920 Olympic Team, but financial obligations precluded his participation. In 1920 Kahler launched the Minneapolis Millers in the United States Amateur Hockey Association. His 1925 team won the league title, but the start of professional hockey in the United States brought a quick end to the Millers by the end of the 1927 season. In addition, Kahler was selected to coach the Augsburg College Team, which was set to represent the United States in the 1928 Olympics. It never happened though, as the decision was ultimately made by United States Olympic Committee chairman, General Douglas MacArthur, to send no team that year to the Winter Games in St. Moritz, Switzerland. Kahler, who would guide the Auggies throughout the early 1930s, achieved great success at the school thanks to the "original" Hanson Brothers: Julius, Lewis, Joe, Oscar and Emil, who made up one of the most lethal brother combinations in college hockey history. Kahler returned to pro hockey for one more season in 1937 as owner of the (now) professional Millers, and saw his team capture the American Hockey Association title. In addition to his hockey interests, Kahler was also a great promoter. He founded Golden Gloves boxing in Minnesota as well as the Northwest Sports Show in Minneapolis. Among his many awards, Kahler was inducted into the Minnesota Sports Hall of Fame in 1962; was awarded the Governor's Public Service Citation and Heritage Award in 1967; and was inducted into the U.S. Hockey Hall of Fame in 1980. Kahler died in 1983 at the age of 91, in Minneapolis.

ED SAUGESTAD
COLLEGE HOCKEY: AUGSBURG

Ed Saugestad grew up in Minneapolis and graduated from South High School in 1955. From there, Saugestad went on to play hockey at Augsburg, where he also served as a hard-nosed tackle on the Auggie football team. In 1958 Saugestad was asked to take over as a playing coach. After graduating with a double minor in physical education and biology in 1959, Saugestad went to attend graduate school at the University of Minnesota, where he got his master's degree. Saugestad then came back to his alma mater in 1964 to teach Biology and coach hockey. He would also serve as an assistant under Edor Nelson on the Auggie football team — a position he would hold for 25 years. (Saugestad would later serve as the school's athletic director from 1981-87 as well.)

Saugestad would lead the hockey Auggies through some dark years in the MIAC, but slowly but surely got better and better over time. By 1971 the Auggies were one of the strongest small college teams in the country, and even went on to beat Gustavus, 8-6, to finish third in the NAIA finals — small college's national championship. In 1973 the program got a huge boost when Augsburg Arena, complete with two rinks, was built on campus. With their new rink, coupled with the addition of a huge new centerman by the name of Stan Blom, the Auggies repeated as MIAC champs in 1978. But they didn't stop there. After beating Ferris State 6-4 in the quarters, and UW-River Falls 10-2 in the semis, Augsburg went on to beat Bemidji State, 4-3, to win the NAIA title. In 1981, led by star winger John Evans, the Auggies won another MIAC title and then advanced on to the NAIA playoffs. There, after beating UW-River Falls, 9-2, and Michigan Deerborn, 7-4, in the semifinals, Augsburg beat UW-Superior, 8-3, to win their second NAIA championship. Once again the Auggies were the best small college team in the land.

After posting an all-time MIAC best 16-0 record (which included averaging nearly eight goals per game), the Auggies made it six MIAC titles in a row in 1982. Then, after beating UW-Eau Claire 7-6, and Michigan Dearborn, 5-4, in the playoffs, Augsburg found themselves back in the NAIA championship game. There, the Auggies went on to beat Bemidji State, 6-3, to finish as back-to-back national champs. The Augsburg program was now a dynasty, and the pride of Minnesota.

Although the Auggies continued to play well in the conference as well as throughout the ranks of Division III, that would be the last MIAC title for the team through the millennium. Aside from advancing to the NCAA D-III Final Four in 1984, the Auggies had a relatively quiet stretch until the mid-1990s. But, for coach Saugestad, whose achievements included garnering three national championships, seven MIAC titles, nine appearances in the NAIA national tournament, one appearance in the NCAA Division III national tournament, and 15 runner-up finishes over his storied career, the best was yet to come. That's because in 1996 Saugestad won his 500th career game, joining an elite fraternity of just 12 other college hockey coaches to have ever done so. After 37 years behind the Augsburg bench, and 24 All-Americans later, the coach retired from the game after that season with a final record of 503-354-21. At the time, his 503 wins ranked him fifth all-time in NCAA Hockey history.

Among Saugestad's many honors and accolades, he earned three NAIA Coach of the Year awards, six MIAC Coach of the Year awards, and the governor of Minnesota even declared an official "Ed Saugestad Day" on February 17, 1996. In 1998, the MIAC even christened the playoff championship traveling trophy as the "Ed

Saugestad Trophy" in his honor. Fittingly the first team to win the Saugestad Cup was Augsburg, that same year. A brilliant tactician and teacher, Ed Saugestad has become synonymous with Augsburg hockey, and will forever be remembered as a true Minnesota hockey coaching legend.

HOW WOULD YOU DESCRIBE YOUR COACHING STYLE? "Mainly what I tried to do was to have a definite system that we followed. I tried to give the guys every bit of help I could in terms of having as much practice time as they needed, or as much help in drills as they needed, so that they could be as good as they could be. I tried to be different too because I thought when you did something completely different it was always very difficult for the other teams to adjust. Believe it or not, one of the best learning tools I ever got was a Russian Red Army play book from when they were here playing one time. I spent some time with the team and was just fascinated by some of the unique things that they did. So, we copied their power play and some other set plays and that was very innovative stuff. After that, I just tried to stay out of my kids' way so that they could play hockey. You know, at the Division III level, you are always a teacher first and a coach second. What I have always tried to do is teach my players that sports, like life, is made of decisions. Decisions come from reactions. Now, my system of playing hockey may not have changed much in 30-some years, but the options have. That's what you teach a player, to use his options."

HOW DID YOU MOTIVATE YOUR PLAYERS? "You know, if you are a jockey on a racehorse and you go to the whip, some horses will go faster, while others will quit. So, you have to know your kids so that you can determine how to motivate them. I always told my kids that I would never insult them, personally, I would just insult the way that they played. I told them never to take that personally, but I thought it was good to point out their errors so that they could learn from them and get better. I never wanted to practice doing the wrong things, and if you let things go by, that is what can happen. I learned long ago that as mad as you get at your kids for not doing something right, they are just as mad at themselves."

WHO WERE YOUR COACHING MENTORS? "I would have to say Ernie Anderson, the basketball coach here at Augsburg, and then Edor Nelson, who I served as an assistant for on the football team for 25 years. The two of them had so much class and really knew how to handle men. They seemed to be able to get the best out of their players with their personalities and not through some elaborate system. I learned a lot from each of them and have a lot of respect for them. After that I really respected John Mariucci, Herbie Brooks and Lou Vairo, they were great, great hockey people."

IF YOU COULD MAGICALLY GO BACK IN TIME TO THE FIRST YEAR YOU WERE A HEAD COACH AND GIVE YOURSELF SOME ADVICE FOR THE FUTURE, KNOWING WHAT YOU KNOW NOW, BACK THEN, WHAT WOULD YOU SAY TO YOURSELF? "Get real organized and plan every move you make. Then, don't second guess yourself, and don't worry so much about what is going to happen."

LOOKING BACK WHAT ARE YOU MOST PROUD OF IN

YOUR CAREER? "I would say being appreciated by my players and by my school. Then, winning the national championship for the first time back in 1978 over Bemidji. That was very, very special. I will never forget when (Gustavus Coach) Don Roberts came over to the bench afterwards and said, 'We did it, the MIAC finally won it!'."

HOW DID YOU BUILD TEAM UNITY & CHEMISTRY? "I always thought that in hockey it came down to which players you had playing together on certain lines. If you find out which guys are buddies and which guys enjoy playing with certain guys, then that helps. But ultimately it comes down to you as the coach to determine which lines will play the best together. Beyond that, we tried to do things off the ice as a group when we could. I just wanted our guys to be friends with one another and to respect one another. If that happened, then they would play well together as a team out on the ice."

WHAT MOTIVATED YOU? "I really enjoyed the practices and just being with the guys. When you retire that is what you miss the most and I bet every coach would say that. That was the fun part of it. I mean how many people get to spend their careers staying in college and never having to go to work? I was lucky."

WHAT ADVICE WOULD YOU HAVE FOR YOUNG COACHES STARTING OUT TODAY? "Just hang in there and don't expect too much too fast. It is a growing process and young coaches are so enthusiastic and want to move onward and upward so fast. So, remember that patience is a virtue."

WHAT IS THE KEY TO GOOD TIME MANAGEMENT? "You know, hockey is really conducive to good time management. When I used to coach football, we used to stay out there for hours on end working on things. Well, in hockey, you only have so much ice time because somebody else is renting the ice every other hour or so. So, that forces you to get organized and to be pretty efficient. I mean when that zamboni driver blows the horn and throws those gates open, your time is up. Period! I used to plan out my drills to the exact minute, otherwise we wouldn't be able to finish. I even videotaped things to find out later just how much time they took and that was helpful in planning structured practices."

WHAT'S THE BIGGEST THING YOU'VE LEARNED FROM COACHING THAT YOU'VE BEEN ABLE TO APPLY TO YOUR EVERYDAY LIFE? "You have to make a plan and stick to it. I was very organized and tried to think through everything I did before I did it. That was important."

WHAT ARE THE KEY INGREDIENTS TO CREATING A CHAMPIONSHIP TEAM? "I was very fortunate to have so many great players here at Augsburg and that is the key to having any good team. That goes back to recruiting, you need good kids. Then, you have to put them on the right lines together, and that goes back to chemistry. I really think that because you only get a very limited number of scoring chances during a game that when your kids have their chance, they need to make the most of it. I really stressed that. We used to put up targets in certain spots on the ice and have our kids shoot and shoot at them to become really accurate. After a while your players buy into that and then they build their confidence up. I never believed in the old 'throw it at the net' philosophy that a lot of other coaches had. I mean could you imagine a basketball coach saying that? I wanted them to believe that they should score every time they shot and to be upset if they didn't. That was how we got our kids to become better scorers."

WHAT'S THE SECRET TO YOUR SUCCESS? "Hockey was all consuming, but I just tried to have fun with it and help as many kids as I could along the way."

WHAT WOULD YOU WANT TO SAY TO YOUR FANS, BOOSTERS, AND ALUMNI WHO HAVE SUPPORTED YOU ALL THESE YEARS? "They were great. They were just absolutely great. A large part of your success is the support you get from around you. Everybody was so enthusiastic at our games and we just appreciated all the support we got from our fans, students, parents and community. When you have great fan support the players feed off of that, and then the fans feed back off of the players reacting to their enthusiasm, and it just snowballs from there."

HOW DO YOU WANT YOUR COACHING EPITAPH TO READ — HOW DO YOU WANT TO BE REMEMBERED AS A COACH? "He tried to do his best for his players so that they could always improve and be successful both on and off the ice."

SERGIO GAMBUCCI: NORTH DAKOTA HIGH SCHOOL HOCKEY

Sergio "Serge" Gambucci grew up in Eveleth loving sports. After graduating from Eveleth High School, Gambucci went on to serve in World War II. When he returned, he attended St. Cloud Teachers College (now St. Cloud State University), where he captained the hockey team and was its top scorer for two seasons. Gambucci continued his hockey career as a top-level amateur player after college and was the player/coach and leading scorer for the Crookston Pirates in 1951 when they won the United States national amateur championship. When his playing career was over, Gambucci turned to coaching and teaching — first at Cathedral High School in Crookston, and then at Central High School in Grand Forks, North Dakota. There, his Grand Forks teams won 10 state high school hockey titles between 1961-78, and he finished his illustrious coaching career with the third-highest winning percentage in U.S. high school hockey history. Among Gumbucci's many honors and accolades, he was been inducted into the Grand Forks Central Athletic Hall of Fame, the Grand Forks Public School Teachers' Hall of Fame, the St. Cloud State University Athletic Hall of Fame and the North Dakota Coaches Association Hall of Fame. In addition, in 1996 Gambucci was enshrined in the coaches category of the United States Hockey Hall of Fame. Gambucci crafted a legendary hockey career out of two basic ingredients: A love for the game of hockey and a conviction that invaluable life lessons could be taught and learned through athletic competition. Upon his retirement, Gambucci was recognized on the floor of the United States Senate by Senator Kent Conrad, who said, "As a teacher and a role model, he inspired thousands of students with a message of integrity and hard work." From Serge to Elio to Gary, the Gambucci name has become synonymous with hockey in Minnesota. Serge and his wife Eleanor had seven children and many grandchildren.

FRANK SERRATORE
COLLEGE HOCKEY: AIR FORCE ACADEMY

Frank Serratore grew up in Coleraine loving hockey. As a goalie Serratore went on to earn all state honors his senior season at Greenway of Coleraine High School and then continued into the junior ranks with the St. Paul Vulcans under coach Doug Woog from 1975-77. After garnering USHL Goaltender Award of the Year honors, Serratore went on to play college hockey for Western Michigan University for two seasons and then finished his career at Bemidji State University in 1982. There, Serratore played hockey and baseball, graduating with his bachelor's degree in physical education and elementary education. Serratore had a brief stint in net with the Nashville South Stars (Central Hockey League) in 1982 before finally hanging up the pads to get into coaching full-time.

Serratore's first job was as the head coach and general manager of the Rochester Mustangs (1985-87), followed by a stint with the Austin Mavericks (1983-85) of the U.S. Junior Hockey League. During his tenure in the USHL, Serratore won three league championships and was runner-up twice while posting a 247-103-6 record. In 1987, he led Rochester to a national championship. While coaching in the USHL, he was named general manager of the year twice and coach of the year once. Serratore's first assistant coaching job at the collegiate level came at the University of North Dakota from 1987-89. That next year Serratore took over as the head coach and general manager of the Omaha Lancers of the USHL. In one season, he took over a last-place team and led them to the USHL regular season and playoff championship. The worst-to-first Cinderella season earned Serratore the USHL General Manager of the Year and the Omaha Sportscasters Sportsman of the Year awards in 1990.

From there, Frank hit the big time, landing the head coaching position at the University of Denver in 1990. He would stay four seasons at DU, leading the Pioneers to a 49-91-9 record along the way. Credited with rebuilding a struggling Pioneer program and drastically improving their attendance, Serratore left DU in 1994 to finish his master's degree in athletic administration and physical education from the University of North Dakota. The next stop on Serratore's coaching carousel came with the IHL's Minnesota, and later Manitoba, Moose, where he served as the head coach and general manager from 1994-96. Serratore led the expansion Moose to a 52-56-16 record in two seasons and in 1995, he led the team to the IHL playoffs, where they lost to the eventual Turner Cup Champion Denver Grizzlies in the first round.

In 1997 Serratore returned to Colorado to take over as the new head coach of the Air Force Academy and he has been there ever since. In his first season, Serratore's disciplined and aggressive style produced more wins than the previous two seasons combined. As he now enters his seventh season with the Falcons, Serratore has posted a 91-113-13 overall record. He is also the only coach in AFA history to lead the team to five consecutive 15-win seasons.

Overall, Serratore's record in 10 seasons as a college head coach is 140-204-22. He is also a good friend to USA Hockey, having served as the head coach of the United States Under-17 Select Team that competed in the Five Nations Tournament in Prievizda, Slovakia, in 2003. In addition, he coached at two USA Hockey Olympic Sports Festivals and has served as a coach at the USA Hockey Development Program since 1985. Serratore is also member of the NCAA Championships Committee and has served on the Hobey Baker Selection Committee as well.

A true friend to hockey, Serratore has the enthusiasm and

energy necessary to win it all. Considered by many to be one of the best and brightest young coaches in the game today, it is just a matter of time before he takes that next step and brings home the hardware.

It is also interesting to note that Frank and his brother Tom, the head coach at Bemidji State University, are one of just two sets of family members that coach against each other in the same conference in any sport. (Florida State football coach Bobby Bowden and his son Tommy, who is the head coach at Clemson, are the others.) Thus far Frank has bragging rights over his little brother with six wins and a tie to no losses.

Frank and his wife Carol have four children, twin boys Thomas and Timothy and daughters, Carly and Carina, and reside in Colorado Springs.

HOW WOULD YOU DESCRIBE YOUR COACHING STYLE? "I think you have to constantly make adjustments. When I first started coaching I was basically an ex-player turned coach. I had a lot to learn. But thanks to what I learned from Bob Peters, at Bemidji State, I was able to formulate a philosophy of my own which incorporated much of the detailed systems that he used. I think I still have a players mentality, but that just helps me to understand the game. I also think you have to constantly make adjustments over time to adapt to how the game changes as well as how the kids change. I think that kids now are much more worldly than they were 15-20 years ago. They responded to the Vince Lombardi, Bobby Knight and Herb Brooks-type of coaches who challenged them and got in their face back then, but I think it is much different now. I don't think that kind of coaching will work in this day and age with these kids. I just think that coaching is always a work in progress and you have to keep with the times as the game changes. If you don't stay in the mainstream with the kids they will just tune you out."

HOW DID YOU MOTIVATE YOUR PLAYERS? "Kids today respond better to praise than they do to criticism. I mean you have to pick your battles, that is for sure. I also think there are a lot of different ways to approach your kids to motivate them. You can't always come at them with high octane, sometimes you have to mix it up a little bit. Sometimes too you have to let the kids figure it out themselves. We always have a pregame meeting and also go over our strategy between periods to go over our objectives for that game. I try to motivate my kids throughout the week though and really try to stay in a routine. I think motivation has to come from the heart and the players can sense if it doesn't."

WHO WERE YOUR COACHING MENTORS? "I never really knew a lot about systems until I played for Bob Peters at Bemidji State. He had a very detailed system on how we play and why we play. We took notes on everything and he was so meticulous about everything. He just made a tremendous impression on me as a player and later as a coach. He taught me so much and was the one who really inspired me to become a coach after playing for him. And that might be his biggest legacy — all of the coaches he has produced. He is a great person. Beyond Bob, I would have to say that I have a great deal of respect for Bob Gernander, Chuck Grillo, Doug Woog and Glen Sonmor. They are all great coaches too, and people that I have a lot of admiration for."

WHAT ARE THE CHARACTERISTICS OF LEADERS? "They have a presence about them. They are able to sell themselves to players and get them to do things that maybe they don't want to do. They can motivate, they are focused, they are strong willed, they are proactive, they learn from their mistakes and the don't quit."

LOOKING BACK WHAT ARE YOU MOST PROUD OF IN YOUR CAREER? "When I look back at all of the kids that I coached who are now coaching themselves, that just makes me feel great. To watch those guys come up and to think that you might have had a small hand in their success both on and off the ice is just very rewarding."

HOW DO YOU BUILD TEAM UNITY & CHEMISTRY? "A lot of it has to do with having the right kind of hard working, unselfish people. Then, you have to have a good environment that is conducive to learning where that can all come together. Chemistry is a funny thing and really varies from year to year, depending on your kids. You just try to get the best kids you can, and get them together in a good atmosphere. Then you just have to hope that they can come together as a team. You know, hockey is truly a cooperative effort. It is not like baseball where an individual can carry a team at the plate. Hockey is a real team game and it doesn't matter how good you are, you are not going to succeed without the help of your teammates. Everybody has a role too, from checkers, to playmakers, special teamers, to scorers, to defenders, and collectively everybody has to do their job in order for the team to succeed. Great teams with great chemistry have that."

WHAT MOTIVATES YOU? "You know, I just love the competition and the team aspect of it all. When the puck drops it is us against them and I live for that. Then, I also think about being a mentor to these kids and making a difference in their lives. After having kids of my own I really look at the kids differently now. It is more than hockey for me now, we are preparing these kids for life and that is a big responsibility that I take very seriously."

ON HOCKEY AND LIFE: You know, hockey is a lot like life, especially for today's kids. And, hockey, for good or bad, has really become a white collar sport because it is so expensive to play. From the equipment to the ice time, it takes a lot of resources to play this game. So, another thing that is interesting to see is how much hockey mirrors life. When these kids go out onto that 200 x 85 ice sheet, their daddy can't buy them a goal. Daddy can't buy them camaraderie with their teammates. Daddy can't buy them a win. These kids have got to go out and earn that themselves and it is a rough, violent sport. So, just like in life, if you don't go out and be proactive, then you are not going to succeed. Good players need to pay the price in the corners; they need to go to the net; they need to work hard, and they need to learn to work with others so that they can be successful. That is what it is all about. You're not going to win every game, but if you do all the right things then the wins will take care of themselves. There are a lot of parallels between hockey and life. That is what makes this game so great for preparing our young people for life."

WHAT'S THE BEST PIECE OF ADVICE YOU EVER GOT FROM ANOTHER COACH? "Bob Peters once told me that if you take care of the little things then the big things will take care of themselves."

WHAT'S THE BIGGEST THING YOU'VE LEARNED FROM COACHING THAT YOU'VE BEEN ABLE TO APPLY TO YOUR EVERYDAY LIFE? "Turning negatives into positives, especially when you are dealt a bad card. You just have to deal with things in a positive way and then move on."

WHAT WOULD YOU WANT TO SAY TO YOUR FANS, BOOSTERS, AND ALUMNI WHO HAVE SUPPORTED YOU ALL THESE YEARS? "Minnesota is such a great place to be from because hockey is so engrained into the culture and it is so important to the people there. So, I am very proud to be from Minnesota and can't thank the people there enough for supporting me and giving me the opportunity to be a part of this great game."

HOW DO YOU WANT YOUR COACHING EPITAPH TO READ — HOW DO YOU WANT TO BE REMEMBERED AS A COACH? "Just like Bob Peters, Bob Gernander, Chuck Grillo, Doug Woog and Glen Sonmor inspired me as both a coach and as a person, I too would hope to inspire as many young people as I can in the same way that those five guys inspired me."

GORDY GENZ: RAMSEY HIGH SCHOOL & HAMLINE HOCKEY

Gordy Genz grew up in St. Paul and went on to lead his Humboldt High School Hockey team to a pair of state tournaments in 1952 and 1953. From there, Genz went on to play football and hockey at Hamline, serving as the team captain on the ice for three years before graduating in 1959. Genz then got into coaching, first at Warroad High School, where he served as the head coach from 1959-62. From there, Genz headed south, to take over as the head coach at Roseville's Alexander Ramsey High School (which later became Roseville Area High School), from 1962-94. There, Genz became a coaching legend. In all, Genz would win more than 500 high school games, six conference championships and take seven teams to the State Tournament. His Alexander Ramsey teams were Region Champions in 1963 and 1965, and the 1973 team was runner-up to Hibbing in the State High School Hockey Championship Game. In addition, Genz was selected by USA Hockey and the U.S. Olympic Committee to serve as an assistant coach to Brad Buetow and the West hockey team at the 1983 National Sports Festival. The West team won the gold medal and many of its members were selected to the 1984 Olympic team. Genz, who retired from high school coaching and teaching after 35 years, came back to Hamline in 1985 to serve as an assistant on the hockey team. Genz's leadership and coaching experience has proven invaluable for the young Pipers. Among his many coaching honors and accolades, in 1995 Genz was the recipient of the Minnesota High School Coaches Association "George Haun Award" for outstanding service and leadership. He is also a member of the Minnesota Hockey Coaches Hall of Fame as well as the Hamline Athletic Hall of Fame. Now in his ninth year as an assistant with the Pipers, Gordy is still having a ball.

MIKE SERTICH
COLLEGE HOCKEY: UM-DULUTH

Born and raised in Virginia, Minn., Mike Sertich was a three-sport standout in hockey, baseball and football at Roosevelt High School in Virginia. After turning down a football scholarship at North Dakota, Sertich went on to play hockey at the University of Minnesota-Duluth, graduating in 1969 with a degree in physical education. From there, Sertich wasted little time in landing his first teaching and coaching job, joining Head Coach Gus Hendrickson at Grand Rapids High School. After building a hockey dynasty with the Indians in the early and mid-1970s, UMD officials persuaded both Hendrickson and Sertich to try their coaching magic at the collegiate level. So, Sertich, who had also been an assistant baseball coach at Grand Rapids, decided to go for it. He would serve as Hendrickson's right-hand man and the Bulldogs' chief recruiter for seven years before accepting the job as UMD's head coach in the spring of 1982.

At UMD Sertich would build a dynasty in the early 1980s, leading his club to the NCAA Finals in 1984, where his Bulldogs ultimately lost a heart-breaker to Bowling Green in quadruple overtime. He followed that up the next year with a return trip to the Final Four, this time losing to R.P.I. in triple overtime. In all, Sertich would spend 18 years as the head coach of the Bulldogs, amassing a 350-328-44 record. He also led UMD to three WCHA titles (1984, 1985, and 1993) as well.

In 2000 Sertich left UMD to become the interim head coach at Michigan Tech. The interim tag would be removed later that season, however, and Sertich would remain with the Huskies for a total of three seasons before retiring from coaching in 2003. While Sertich posted a very modest 25-69-9 record at Tech, his overall career record stands at 375-397-53.

Among Sertich's many coaching honors and accolades, he was named as the American Hockey Coaches Association Division I Coach of the Year (Spencer-Penrose Award) in 1984. In addition, he shares with legendary Michigan Tech Coach John MacInnes the distinction of being the only four-time WCHA Coach of the Year as well. A past president of the American Hockey Coaches Association and member of the NCM Ice Hockey Rules Committee, Sertich was active in an array of coaching endeavors with USA Hockey as well.

One of the nation's most respected coaches, Mike Sertich has earned a reputation for being a great motivator and hockey tactician. Sertich is without question one of the smartest coaches in Minnesota hockey history and on top of that, he is a great guy to boot. Now retired, Mike and his wife Audie presently reside on Island Lake just outside of Duluth, and have three children: Scott, John and Lori.

HOW WOULD YOU DESCRIBE YOUR COACHING STYLE? "Well, Bud Grant has always been one of my heroes, so I guess I stole as much from him as I could. I always felt that as he went, so went his teams. He had great insight, poise and discipline, and that is exactly the same thing that you want out of your team when it comes down to crunch time. Bud also cared a great deal about his players and respected them as well as their individuality. With that he also commanded a lot of respect and was very firm when he needed to be. Then, he enjoyed a good practical joke every now and then, and so do I. Bud just had an uncanny ability to lead and I have always respected and admired that. Bud always put the glory to the players and to the organization. He was never in the front row of the team picture and that says a lot about his ego. You know, I have studied and read a lot about what makes certain coaches successful and that has

always fascinated me. I have read about Bud Grant, Tom Landry, Don Shula, Bobby Knight, Rick Pitino, Dan Gable, Herbie Brooks, and a lot of hockey coaches from both Canada and Europe. I found it so interesting to learn about how these guys dealt with topics like team leadership, chemistry, character, relationships, discipline, values and loyalty. When you combine those ingredients into a winning culture, it is easy to see why those coaches were so successful. Really, you just need to get down to the basics: preparation, focus, execution and repetition. I just always tried to be myself, but I truly believe that what I am is a result of many, many defining moments in my life and that is how I developed my personality and my style both on and off the ice."

HOW DID YOU MOTIVATE YOUR PLAYERS? "I never was one for big pep talks. They make you feel good but they only last about as long as you give them. I tried to do my motivating during the week. First of all I tried to physically prepare them for what was ahead. Then, mentally, I did a lot of work off the ice with a sports psychologist. We did a lot of visualization, focusing, relaxation and breathing exercises. You know, if you had a bad shift, this would help you refocus for your next shift and get back into the game. Each kid is different and you had to figure out which buttons to push on him in order to motivate him. Some kids needed an arm around them while others responded by you being in their face. Some were dealt with privately and others publicly. I think Herbie (Brooks) was the master at figuring all of that out and that was why he was so successful. I sense that the guys who played for him loved him to death, respected him tremendously, but also feared him. So, for me, as far as motivating went, I tried to establish relationships with each kid in order to really find out what he was all about and what excited him. I always made it a point to make eye contact every day with my kids and to talk to each one of them personally. I never liked to be yelled at so I was not a yeller to my kids. I was stern, strict and demanding, but fair. I just wanted my kids to be prepared so that we could be successful as a team. I later learned that I had more success with kids when I just sat back and let them play the game. They enjoyed it more and they knew when they made a mistake. I wanted to correct those mistakes, but maybe that meant waiting until going over the film with them individually afterwards. I wanted to focus on the positives during that time though and really build the kid up so that he could be self motivated through self confidence. Kids had to fit into their roles as well and be team players for the good of the team. I love the saying: 'The game in its purest form is like ballet, unfortunately not all of us are ballerinas.' I have always remembered that."

WHO WERE YOUR COACHING MENTORS? "I think all of us as coaches develop our coaching styles from our mentors and former coaches. I think we are all pirates in this game though and really don't know a lot of us who have any original thoughts. I remember this though. When I first got the job in Duluth the first guy I talked to was Herbie (Brooks). He was great. Then, Dave Hendrickson from Virginia probably taught me as much or more about the game as anybody. Beyond that I got a lot of stuff from European coaches when I spent time over there. I just asked a lot of questions from a lot of people. Bob Johnson was also someone who I respected a lot too. I wasn't afraid to try different things and as a teacher I always wanted to be innovative and never stop learning. In addition, I was a big believer in conditioning, and like Herbie, I spent a lot of time with

Jack Blatherwick (a renowned trainer), who was just brilliant."

IF YOU COULD MAGICALLY GO BACK IN TIME TO THE FIRST YEAR YOU WERE A HEAD COACH AND GIVE YOURSELF SOME ADVICE FOR THE FUTURE, KNOWING WHAT YOU KNOW NOW, BACK THEN, WHAT WOULD YOU SAY TO YOURSELF? "I would tell him to never lose sight of the fact that this is just a game and this will always be a game. It is not life and death. Sure, there is a winner and a loser, that particular night, but the lessons go way beyond that. Also, I would tell him to have as much fun as he could and to work as hard as he could."

HOW DID YOU BUILD TEAM UNITY & CHEMISTRY? "We did a lot of off ice stuff. We had a lot of meetings with a sports psychologist, we had retreats and we just got the kids away from hockey to get to know each other. We really tried to develop a culture to establish our core values and define who we were as a team so we could be successful. I tried to tell them that it was not a right, it was a privilege to play hockey. I look at a guy like Shjon Podein, he is a great example of a kid who refused to be denied. He had a great work ethic, good character, leadership ability and was just the entire package. He is an incredible story. To see him having so much success in the National Hockey League is just wonderful."

WHAT MOTIVATED YOU? "I think there are defining moments in your life when you look at your personality and see how you measure up and how you develop to be what you are. You can look back and find those 10 or 15 moments in your life that did that. Once you recognize that and are comfortable with who you are, then you can become anything you really want. But you have to have that inner confidence, and sports gave me that. It gave me that reinforcement that I was so desperate to get from my father, but never got. So, when I was coaching that was a big thing. I simply did not want to fail in front of my dad and that made me a nervous wreck. He did get to see our success with UMD in the mid-1980s before he died and that was great, but it was tough for me to have him see our games because he made me so nervous. That all went back to when I was a little kid. In the end, I realized that I have to just be me and not anybody else."

WHAT ADVICE WOULD YOU HAVE FOR YOUNG COACHES STARTING OUT TODAY? "First of all I would let every kid play with a puck everyday as much as they could. I really believe strongly in that. I believe in teaching the concept and getting them to understand the concept of the game before they can play it on the rink. And you do that by letting them be creative during practice in a small area. That is where they learn how to play off of each other, how to give-and-go, how to pic, how to free themselves up for a shot. One of the common things you see with kids today is that they are big and strong and they can skate like hell. But I don't know how many of them really know how to play the game and really understand the game. I don't think they realize just how little they actually have the puck on their sticks. You know, I loved watching the 2002 Olympics when they broke down exactly how much time each player had the puck for on TV. It is great for kids to see that a superstar like Joe Sakic touched the puck for about one minute and 20 seconds during the entire game. I remember watching Gretzky play and just being amazed by how he just knew where to go on the ice and that he was always going to places where he anticipated the puck would be. He learned that in his backyard out on the pond. That is how you learn this game and we need more of that. Kids haven't changed but parents have. We just need to give them more time to play, and play other things besides hockey. Does anyone even know that John Mayasich was a great football player? Kids have to be well rounded in order to be happy and successful. Basketball players can practice every day out on the street. Hockey is more difficult because of ice time, but kids need to get out and play outside or else have their coaches give them more free time to be creative and learn amongst

themselves. That is where they learn. Sure, roller hockey is helping, but it is not the same."

WHAT WAS THE KEY TO RECRUITING? "I think you had to get on them early, you had to stay on them hard and you had to be yourself. You had to show the parents as well as the kids those five things: leadership, discipline, direction, relationships and character. Beyond that, I always spoke to the parents. If they were going to entrust their boy with me for the next four years, then that was a big commitment for both of us."

WHAT'S THE BIGGEST THING YOU'VE LEARNED FROM COACHING THAT YOU'VE BEEN ABLE TO APPLY TO YOUR EVERYDAY LIFE? "I think John Wooden said it best, 'Losing is never fatal and winning is never final.' So, I guess I wish I would have enjoyed the wins as much as I spent deploring the losses. My goal in life was to be half the man my dogs thought I was. My labs taught me the true meaning of doing things unconditionally and to serve rather than be served. Once I understood that, it all came together for me."

WHAT ARE THE KEY INGREDIENTS TO CREATING A CHAMPIONSHIP TEAM? "I think you have to have talent, a good culture, trust, honesty, hard work and chemistry – that bond or foxhole mentality where each guy knows that somebody is going to cover his back. It happens when guys are selfless rather than selfish. Character isn't what you do in front of a group, it is what you do when no one else is around."

WHAT'S THE SECRET TO YOUR SUCCESS? "I had great players. I had guys who were selfless. I had a great support staff. I had a chance to be innovative and I took it. I wasn't afraid to try new things and that might have been the secret to my success."

WHAT WOULD YOU WANT TO SAY TO YOUR FANS, BOOSTERS, AND ALUMNI WHO HAVE SUPPORTED YOU ALL THESE YEARS? "I definitely want to thank everybody that has touched my life in so many ways. Certainly I wouldn't be where I am without the support of the people here and obviously the guys who were willing to share ideas with me when I asked, and who helped me to become what I have become. The fans in Duluth are some of the greatest in hockey. They are knowledgeable, they appreciate the effort and they supported us. It is a blue collar, roll up your sleeves kind of mentality up there, and that was how we tried to build the image of our program."

HOW DO YOU WANT YOUR COACHING EPITAPH TO READ — HOW DO YOU WANT TO BE REMEMBERED AS A COACH? "He was a fair guy. That's about it. I think about my life in sports and I realize just how fortunate I have been to find an avenue to find out who I am. Being a teacher and being a coach afforded me an opportunity to touch some lives and I hope I did. I don't think you are measured by wins and losses and trophies and rings. I think you are measured by what you have developed and by the quality of people that you have developed. That is an indication of a great coach."

DAVE LAURION: UNIVERSITY OF ALASKA-FAIRBANKS HOCKEY

Dave Laurion, an International Falls native who played goalie at Notre Dame, coached at the University of Alaska-Fairbanks from 1993-2000, where he posted a career record of 86-147-12.

TERRY SKRYPEK
HIGH SCHOOL & COLLEGE HOCKEY: CRETIN & ST. THOMAS

Terry Skrypek grew up in the Midway area of St. Paul and went to graduate from Cretin High School in 1966 as a multi-sport star. From there, Skrypek played hockey at St. Mary's in Winona, graduating in 1970. Skrypek then went directly from the St. Mary's campus to work at Hill-Murray High School, where he served as the school's head hockey coach for 17 years. During that time he recorded a 325-42-2 record (.883) and led his team to 12 berths in the state high school hockey tournament. His Pioneer teams were state champions in 1983 and state runners-up three other years. Skrypek, who also coached football and baseball, won a state baseball title in 1976 as well. In addition, he taught English at Hill-Murray too. Among his many high school accolades, Skrypek was named as the Minnesota State Coaches' Association Coach of the Year in 1983. In 1987 Skrypek left Hill Murray to take over as the head hockey coach at St. Thomas University. He would end his illustrious high school coaching career as one of the all-time best.

That next year Skrypek led the Toms to the MIAC title and was named conference Coach of the Year. The No. 5 nationally ranked Toms repeated that feat in 1990 and made it all the way to the NCAA Final Eight. In 1991 Skrypek became the first hockey coach in St. Thomas history to win three straight MIAC titles, and his next two teams extended the MIAC streak to five. The 1992 team reached the NCAA quarterfinals, and Skrypek was again named as the MIAC Coach of the Year. The Toms made it six straight in 1994, and reached the NCAA quarterfinals that year as well, where they lost at eventual NCAA runner-up UW-Superior. Incredibly, the 1995 Toms extended the MIAC title streak to seven, but lost in the MIAC tourney finals. UST took third place in 1996 and second in 1997 before recapturing the conference crown in 1999. The 2000 Toms won their first three NCAA games by a combined 23-4 score and became the first MIAC team to reach an NCAA hockey championship game, where they lost a tough 2-1 decision to Norwich, Ver,. The team's 27 wins and .849 winning percentage set school season records, however, while Skrypek was also a finalist for national Coach of the Year honors. In 2002 the Toms were ranked as high as fifth nationally and reached the NCAA playoffs, where they lost 2-1 to eventual champion UW-Superior, and in 2003 they came within an overtime loss of returning to the NCAA playoffs.

Now starting his 16th season as head coach, Terry Skrypek has become synonymous with St. Thomas hockey and has established himself as one of the top collegiate coaches in the country. During his tenure at STU, Skrypek has posted a 303-135-28 overall record, including a stellar 196-44-16 record in the rugged MIAC. The Toms have reached the MIAC playoff championship game 16 times in the 18-year history of the format, and have won the conference title 12 times under his tutelage as well. Skrypek currently ranks in the top 10 among active Division III coaches in wins (303) and winning percentage (.682).

In all, Skrypek has never had a losing season in 33 years of coaching (17 at Hill-Murray and 16 at St. Thomas), and he is still going strong. In fact, things are looking even better than ever for the Toms these days. That is because it was announced in 2003 that St. Thomas Academy and the University of St. Thomas will partner to build a $4 million, 1,100-seat ice hockey arena on the STA campus in Mendota Heights, about 12 miles south of UST's St. Paul campus.

A 2001 inductee into the St. Thomas Athletic Hall of Fame, Terry Skrypek is a hockey coaching legend. In addition to his coach-

ing duties, Skrypek, who received his master's degree in athletic administration in 1991, also teaches in the physical education department at St. Thomas.

Terry currently resides in Little Canada with his wife, Valerie. They have four children, daughters: Heidi, Shannon, and Brianna, all St. Thomas graduates; and son Bryan, who went on to serve as a captain on the Toms' hockey team in 2003 as well.

HOW WOULD YOU DESCRIBE YOUR COACHING STYLE? "Sometimes the confidence that a coach has in himself will show through in his team. So, I am a guy who likes to show his players that I believe in what I am doing and am confident in what I am doing. Then, once you get them to believe in that, and in the system you are trying to get across, then you will have success. Obviously, when you have success, then more and more players buy into that. Eventually you create a winning program and it just continues on and on. Besides that I am a disciplinarian and just encourage my guys to work hard. I believe that it is the small things that are important because they all add up to the big picture. If you pay attention to the details and do the little things right, then it will all come together for your team."

HOW DO YOU MOTIVATE YOUR PLAYERS? "There are so many different ways to motivate. I think the positive way is the best way, personally. Saying the right things at the right times is big too. You have to be very careful with criticism though, and not make it a team thing. I think if you are going to correct somebody then you should do that individually by pulling a player aside and talking to him one on one. There are times when someone might deserve a tongue lashing in front of the entire team, if he embarrasses the entire team or does something stupid, but that is rare. Mostly though, I try to motivate them positively and individually. I like to tell them how good they can be if they do the right things, and that can be very powerful."

WHO WERE YOUR COACHING MENTORS? "I would say my high school coach at Cretin, Ted Joyce, he was a coaching legend who was way ahead of his time. He wasn't the most sophisticated coach, but boy did the guys love playing for him because he was a great human being. Then, I would also say Tim McNeill, who was an assistant at Cretin but then went on to become the head coach at St. Mary's. I followed him down to Winona and had a great time playing for him. He later wound up moving on to Notre Dame, but I enjoyed my time with him a great deal. He was a great coach and a great person. I learned a great deal about hockey and about life from both of those guys, they were great mentors."

LOOKING BACK WHAT ARE YOU MOST PROUD OF IN YOUR CAREER? "The greatest reward I have had is just working with the people who I have worked with. These kids are great and the journey has been amazing. I love coming to work everyday and it is fun. This is a kids game and I am lucky to still just be a kid. Then, as a high school coach, I am proud of the fact that I have won a state baseball title and a state hockey title. Then, as a college coach I am proud of the fact that we made it to the finals of the 2000 division three championships. We didn't win, which was disappointing, but it was great to know that we went farther than any MIAC team had gone before."

WHAT IS THE KEY TO RECRUITING? "At the division III level it is selling education. You have to let them know that it is not just about hockey, it is about going to school and getting a degree. We have a great school and we also have a great hockey program here, so we are very fortunate to have that. Winning attracts good players and we have been very fortunate in that regard."

HOW DO YOU BUILD TEAM UNITY & CHEMISTRY? "Chemistry is really a family thing. You have to treat it like a family and you have to get all the members of your family on the same page, looking out for each other. It comes down to social skills. You have to get your kids together and have them do things together. When they have fun together, then that is where chemistry starts. You need for them to create those bonds, because it will translate out onto the ice. A cohesive team plays together and that is something you constantly have to work at. You also can't just assume it is going to happen either, you really need to work hard at it all the time."

WHAT MOTIVATES YOU? "I just love this game. I have been around it all of my whole life and I loved going to the park as a kid to play as often as I could. I would spend the whole day down there, then come home for supper, eat, and then go back afterwards. That was the way I grew up and I have always just loved this game. You know, I have been coaching for 34 years now and I have enjoyed every aspect of it. Coaching keeps you young and it is still very fun for me."

WHAT ADVICE WOULD YOU HAVE FOR YOUNG COACHES STARTING OUT TODAY? "I think that young coaches should develop their own philosophies and then stick to them. Young coaches have a tendency to compromise themselves and will concede different things. Once they start doing that, it leads to other problems with parents and with kids buying into your program. So, stick with what you believe and be your own person. Then, do what is best for the kids, that is the most important thing."

FAVORITE LOCKER ROOM SIGN? "The harder I work the luckier I become," and "Attitude is everything."

WHAT'S THE BIGGEST THING YOU'VE LEARNED FROM COACHING THAT YOU'VE BEEN ABLE TO APPLY TO YOUR EVERYDAY LIFE? "The biggest thing is never giving up. Things might be down and out, but if you stick with it long enough it will all work out. If you work hard and give it your best effort then things will eventually turn out for you. You really just can't ever give up."

WHAT ARE THE KEY INGREDIENTS TO CREATING A CHAMPIONSHIP TEAM? "For starters you have to have some players with some skills or you are not going to get over that hump. Determination and hard work are also very important, and can overcome skill from time to time, but you need to have it all to win it all. Guys need to put in the extra time and do the extra little things for the good of the team. Then, you need to have a cohesiveness amongst your players where they know that they can depend on each other. If they know that they can depend on each other and have that chemistry, then anything can happen."

WHAT'S THE SECRET TO YOUR SUCCESS? "I am just a middle class guy with a middle class work ethic. I learned hard work from my dad and I have tried to follow that in everything I do. I try to work hard for my team and for my players, that is what is most important. I also try to learn as much as I can from other coaches and from clinics and what have you. In fact, I still have a hand-out that I got from Willard Ikola at my first hockey clinic back in 1972. And I still use it! Those were the golden years of hockey in Minnesota back then and I was just lucky to learn as much as I could from the Willard Ikokas, Larry Rosses, Dave Petersons and Ted Joyces of the world. I was just a sponge and tried to soak it all in, and it helped to define my style even to this day."

WHAT WOULD YOU WANT TO SAY TO YOUR FANS, BOOSTERS, AND ALUMNI WHO HAVE SUPPORTED YOU ALL THESE YEARS? "Thanks for the opportunity. That opportunity was enhanced and was so much fun because of the support I got from so many great people along the way. The years I had at Hill Murray were probably the greatest years of my life and the years here at St. Thomas have been outstanding as well. For me it has been a great ride and I have enjoyed every minute of it."

HOW DO YOU WANT YOUR COACHING EPITAPH TO READ — HOW DO YOU WANT TO BE REMEMBERED AS A COACH? "I would want to be remembered as a humble guy who wasn't seeking out personal fame or glory, but a guy who just wanted to be a part of something that was fun and rewarding, and that he had success doing that."

OSCAR ALMQUIST:
ROSEAU HIGH SCHOOL HOCKEY

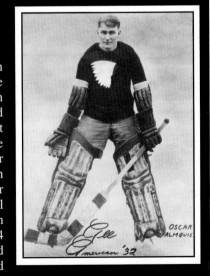

Oscar Almquist grew up in Eveleth playing hockey. Almquist would go on to star on his Eveleth high school team as a goalie from 1923-27. Then, after a two-year stint with Virginia of the Arrowhead Amateur League, Almquist went on to play between the pipes at St. Mary's College in Winona, where, in addition to leading the Redmen to their first MIAC title in 1929, he also earned All-American honors in 1932 and 1933 as well. Almquist then began his professional career, first with the Eveleth Rangers, followed by three all-star seasons with the St. Paul Saints in the American Hockey Association. Almquist went into high school coaching at that point, the career for which he would become legendary. After coaching for a year at tiny Williams High School in 1937, Almquist moved to Roseau, where he began coaching, and also playing for the amateur Cloverleaf's. In 1941 the "Big O" became the team's head coach, a position he would hold until 1967. During this period Roseau High School became a perennial power, winning state titles in 1946, 1958, 1959, and 1961. Under Almquist's tenure, the Rams appeared in the state tourney 14 times, and in addition to the four state championships, finished as runner-ups on four occasions and also won two consolation titles as well. Before retiring to become the school's athletic director and principal, the "Giant of the North" had posted a career record of 404-148-21, including an amazing 49-game winning streak from 1957 through 1959. Long considered as the "Dean of Minnesota High School Hockey Coaches" for his many contributions to the growth of hockey in the state, Oscar Almquist was simply a legend. In recognition of his career achievements, Almquist was made an honorary life member of the American Hockey Coaches Association in 1969. He was also inducted to the Minnesota Hockey Coaches Association Hall of Fame in 1982, as well as the U.S. Hockey Hall of Fame in 1983.

LEFTY SMITH
HIGH SCHOOL & COLLEGE HOCKEY: S. ST. PAUL & NOTRE DAME

Charles "Lefty" Smith grew up in South St. Paul playing hockey on the area lakes and ponds. He can still vividly remember being smitten with the envy after watching the first ever Minnesota High School hockey tournament and wondering why his South St. Paul High School didn't have a team. So, Smith and his buddies circulated a petition around town and in the Fall of 1945, varsity hockey began in South St. Paul. Smith would go on to graduate from St. Thomas in 1951, where he played hockey and baseball for the Tommies. From there, he returned to South St. Paul to serve as an assistant hockey coach in 1953, and then took over the head coaching duties in 1958. The opening of newly constructed Wakota Arena in 1959 brought the program indoors, much to the diligent efforts of Smith. He remained with the Packers until 1968, compiling an impressive career record of 201-69-11, en route to leading his teams to eight state tournament appearances — as well as a pair of runner-up finishes in both 1961 and 1968.

In 1968, another start-up project of sorts beckoned for Lefty's call. The University of Notre Dame was adding varsity hockey and needed a good Minnesotan to run their program. Enter Lefty Smith. So, he packed up and headed east to South Bend, Ind., where he would go on to become the all-time winningest coach in Fighting Irish Hockey history with more than 300 wins over a 19-year span. Under his tutelage, Notre Dame produced six All-Americans and finished second in the Western Collegiate Hockey Association (WCHA) twice (1973 and 1977). In 1982, the Irish moved to the Central Collegiate Hockey Association (CCHA), where Smith guided the Irish to the Great Lakes Invitational Championship and the CCHA championship game, where they ultimately lost to Michigan State. Then, after the University announced that it would no longer sponsor varsity hockey in 1983, Smith remained as the head coach of the program as a club team for one year, and then for three more seasons when it competed as a non-scholarship independent program. The popular head coach retired following the 1987 season with a career record of 307-320-30. More importantly, however, in his 19 seasons at Notre Dame, all 126 players who played for him completed their collegiate eligibility and earned college degrees. Not many college coaches can say that.

Among Smith's many coaching honors and accolades, in 2003 he was honored at the Hobey Baker Award Banquet as a "Legend of Hockey" for his outstanding accomplishments in the game. In addition, he was also named as the WCHA Coach of the Year in 1973. Furthermore, Smith served two years as president of the American Hockey Coaches Association and also coached the Central team at the 1978 U.S. National Sports Festival.

Retiring from coaching in 1987, Lefty became Director of the new Loftus Sports Center complex on the Notre Dame campus, where he remains today coordinating events and activities. Lefty is without question one of the good guys in all of college hockey, and will forever be known as a real pioneer of the game. Lefty and his wife Mary have eight children (five girls and three boys), and presently reside in South Bend.

HOW WOULD YOU DESCRIBE YOUR COACHING STYLE? "I would say my style was a little bit laid back. I liked to have some levity at times and be light-hearted. I think Donny Lucia described it best when he characterized it as somewhat on the light side, yet at the same time there was a line, and don't step over that line." (Lucia, now the Gophers coach, played for Smith at Notre Dame.)

HOW DID YOU MOTIVATE YOUR PLAYERS? "You know, I always felt that if these kids were going to make all of these sacrifices in order to be in college athletics, then they might as well make it worth while and really try to win. The other part of it was making the best use of their God-given talents. So, I just tried to encourage my kids to do their best, have fun and work hard for the good of the team."

WHAT ARE THE CHARACTERISTICS OF LEADERS? "A leader is someone who can get others to listen to him and follow him, and that is done in many different ways. Some lead by their athletic abilities while others lead by their verbal abilities, it just varies."

LOOKING BACK WHAT ARE YOU MOST PROUD OF IN YOUR CAREER? "I would say that there are two things. First, at the time I came out of South St. Paul, all anybody really wanted to do was to graduate from high school and get a job in the meat packing plants. So, because of my involvement in starting the hockey program there, kids could now have the opportunity to get an education and play the game of hockey around the world. It is wonderful to think about all of the great people who have come out that program over the past half century now and to think that I might have had a small part in that. Guys like Terry Abram, who went on to become a coach and later a principal at Anoka High School. That is just great to see, people making a good life for themselves and giving back to their community. You know, I would love to have a championship ring on my finger, don't get me wrong, but these types of things are much more gratifying. Second, in my 19 years at Notre Dame we recruited 126 kids to play hockey with all 126 getting their degrees, and in four years nonetheless. I am very, very proud of that."

WHAT WAS THE KEY TO RECRUITING? "We were lucky here. First, we had a great school with so much tradition and history that it was easy to get kids to come here. Secondly, we had a good product to sell on the ice. Then, kids who come to Notre Dame also know that once they graduate they will be a part of an amazing network in their professional careers and that sells itself. They know that they will get a first class education, play top notch sports, and then go on and have every opportunity to have a good life after school."

HOW DID YOU BUILD TEAM UNITY & CHEMISTRY? "I used to try to get our kids to develop a closeness amongst themselves. We used to get the kids together for dinners, nights-out, alumni games, team trips and we had our kids serve as youth coaching mentors too. So, we did a lot of different things to build chemistry. Beyond that we also tried to recruit people who had similar personalities and, to a certain degree, that helped to get a lot of the same types of kids who could all get along and play well as a team. We never really had a blow-up in my 19 years here either, and that said a lot. I think part of that came from the fact we tried to have somewhat of a father-figure type role with our kids. You know, I have eight kids of my own, so that role was easy for me to fulfill."

WHAT MOTIVATED YOU? "Winning meant that you were enjoying the fruits of your labor. You know, I remember sleeping in the warming shack at our rink back in South St. Paul and waking up in the middle of the night to flood the ice. After a while you started to figure that if you were going to make those kind of sacrifices then you should really get something out of it, and that was winning. Then, in college, you have to have that competitive fire in you that you want to do as well as you can. So, to see the impact you can make on young people's lives is very rewarding."

WHAT IS THE KEY TO GOOD TIME MANAGEMENT? "You have to lay out your plans on a yearly basis, then break them down month by month, week by week and day by day. From there, it is just following the schedule as best as you can. Once you are organized, then it is easy to sit back and draw up your schedules, plan practices and make your line-ups."

WHAT ADVICE WOULD YOU HAVE FOR YOUNG COACHES STARTING OUT TODAY? "Unfortunately, what I see happening today makes me a little bit concerned. I look at the state of Minnesota and I see where the average high school coach lasts approximately five to six years, and that is really sad. The days of the Oscar Almquists, Cliff Thompsons and Willard Ikolas, the real long-term guys, are gone. I think that has gone down the drain because of the fact that the parents have too much control and influence over what is going on. I really think that parents are ruining athletics for kids today and that makes me very sad. I would like to see us drop some of this formality stuff and start going back to the playground mentality of where the kids just get to play and have fun without all of the pressures. I mean as kids we never used to travel outside of the Twin Cities with our team. Today, I go back and see the teams traveling to Toronto, Detroit, Duluth, etc., and I think 'you have got to be kidding!' What they really need is to be able to master the fundamentals. You know, in our day we needed coaching because we didn't know what the hell a break-out was, a fore check was, a power play was, or anything else. Today, what the kids need is to go back and play some shinny, just play for fun outside where they can work on their skills. I think back to Phil Housley, whose father played for me at South St. Paul. Well, I was able to watch Phil develop as a player and could see that he was something special. But you know what? He didn't get any more coaching than anybody else on that team, but the thing that made him great was the fact that he would go back to the outdoor rinks after dinner to play keep-away with the little kids for a few hours. That is where he developed the skills that have made him an NHL All-Star. Nowadays kids don't want to play unless they have a traveling secretary, a house mother, and somebody to tie on their bibs and wipe their noses. That bothers me. So, if I was a young coach today, I would do my best to keep the parents out of the picture. I know that they have to pay the bills and all of that stuff, but you have to let them know that you are the boss of your program."

FAVORITE LOCKER ROOM SIGN? "You know, one of my favorite sayings that we had up was actually a quote from Horace Greeley and it read: 'Fame is a vapor, popularity an accident, riches take wings, those who cheer today will curse tomorrow, only one thing endures — character.' I always liked that. Beyond that we wanted to make our locker room a very fun place, so our signs and so forth were more fun than anything else. Maybe it was a funny pimp on a coach or on a player, just something that made them all feel like they were in the same boat together and that was fun."

WHAT'S THE BIGGEST THING YOU'VE LEARNED FROM COACHING THAT YOU'VE BEEN ABLE TO APPLY TO YOUR EVERYDAY LIFE? "You know, I think back to my days as a kid growing up in South St. Paul and wonder, had it not been for athletics — hockey and baseball, I probably would still be following the cattle at the stockyards looking at the south sides of a bunch of northbound cows. I mean, I was able to get a college education through athletics and it has just given me a tremendous life, so I appreciate that very much. So, I like to explain that to kids who have an opportunity to use their talents to make a better life for themselves, what a wonderful thing that is both for them personally, as well as for their communities. Unfortunately, I think in this day and age we have

gotten away from that and we are now more worried about the financial aspects than anything else and I think that is sad."

WHAT ARE THE KEY INGREDIENTS TO CREATING A CHAMPIONSHIP TEAM? "We never won the whole ball of wax here, so maybe you don't want my answer! Really though, I think it comes down to getting your players into the right positions where they can best help the team. They all have roles to play and when they do that your team is stronger. So, if you are honest with your players, if you are open with them, if you get them to work hard, and if you get the luck of having a hot goaltender, then anything can happen."

WHAT'S THE SECRET TO YOUR SUCCESS? "Dumb luck! I have always been honest with the kids and have always let them know that I was concerned about them as individuals, and not just as athletes."

HOW DO YOU WANT YOUR COACHING EPITAPH TO READ — HOW DO YOU WANT TO BE REMEMBERED AS A COACH? "That I was concerned about each and every player — from the stars to the guys that didn't get to play much — and that somewhere along the line I may have done something to make their lives a little better."

RONN TOMASSONI: HARVARD

Ronn Tomassoni, an Eveleth native and 1980 R.P.I. graduate, spent 17 years as a coach with Harvard (head coach from 1990-99), posting a career record of 140-115-26 along the way. Tomassoni's teams won three consecutive ECAC titles from 1992-94, an ECAC tournament title in 1994, and a Beanpot championship in 1994. His '93 and '94 teams reached the NCAA tournament. In addition, Tomassoni compiled a 106-70-22 record in ECAC play. As an assistant with the Crimson, Tomassoni spent eight years working under legendary coach Bill Cleary. With Tomassoni on the staff, the Crimson advanced to the NCAA Tournament on eight occasions and to the national championship title game three times. They also won the NCAA title in 1989 when they beat the Golden Gophers at the old Civic Center. A two-time finalist for the American Hockey Coaches Association Coach of the Year and real class act, Tomassoni left the team in 1999 to start his own business. He would go on to found Educational Edge, Inc., a company which assists talented students to "gain an edge" through the college admissions process. The company also provides assessments of student's athletic potential and can provide recommendations for athletic development. Ronn presently resides in Duluth.

GLEN SONMOR
PRO & COLLEGE HOCKEY: SAINTS, NORTH STARS & GOPHERS

To say that Glen Sonmor would be an understatement. He is "old-school" down to the bone, and that is what makes him one of the most colorful and popular figures in Minnesota hockey history. Whether he was punching someone's lights out as a player, or teaching the fundamentals of the game as a very successful coach, Glen has been a part of the fabric of Minnesota sports for more than half a century.

Born in 1929 in Moose Jaw, Saskatchewan, Glen Sonmor grew up in Hamilton, Ontario, idolizing hockey greats Maurice "Rocket" Richard and Gordie Howe. A fine athlete, Glen went on to star for his high school football, basketball and baseball teams, while also playing Junior B hockey for his hometown Hamilton Lloyds. By 1948, at the age of 19, Glen had left home to play junior hockey for the Guelph (Ontario) Biltmores, and later the Brandon (Manitoba) Wheat Kings.

Then, in 1949, the 5'11" 165-pounder caught a break by landing a spot on the USHL's Minneapolis Millers roster. Glen, a tough defenseman who was on his way up the hockey ladder, was soon befriended by another tough defenseman who was on his way down. His name was John Mariucci. Maroosh, a former Chicago Blackhawks star back in the 1930s and 40s, took the young Sonmor under his wing, and strongly encouraged him to go back to school and get his degree. Mariucci even got him enrolled at the University of Minnesota, where, over the next several summers and during his off-seasons, Glen would take classes.

Sonmor played for the Millers during the 1949-50 season, scoring an impressive 60 points in only 55 games. He moved on that following year, landing next in Cleveland — home of the New York Rangers' AHL minor league affiliate Barons. Glen bounced back and forth between Cleveland and also with the St. Louis Flyers, until he finally got the call to come play in Madison Square Garden. Scoring just two points in 15 NHL games, however, Sonmor was sent back down to Cleveland one more time. He was called back up to the Big Apple once again in 1954-55, only to be sent back to Ohio after only 13 games in the "show." There, during a successful campaign with the Barons that had yielded him 25 points in only 30 games, on February 27, 1955, during a game against Pittsburgh, something happened that forever changed his life. On a routine play in front of the net, Glen was hit directly in the face by a blistering slapshot from the point. The shot crushed his eyeball, and tragically, he lost the sight in his eye. In an instant, his promising hockey career had abruptly come to a screeching halt. (Ironically, the puck was shot by his old next-door neighbor and childhood pal from Hamilton.)

Devastated, the 25-year-old gathered himself together, and pondered what to do with his life. That next year, Glen's old friend John Mariucci, now the Gophers head hockey coach, invited him to move back to Minnesota, to finish his degree, and coach his freshman squad while he was away coaching the 1956 US Olympic team in Italy. (Athletic Director Marsh Ryman took over the varsity team while he was gone.) Invigorated with a new sense of purpose to his life, Glen worked hard, studied, got his degree in physical education, and started to learn about the science of coaching hockey. One of Sonmor's best skaters that first year on his freshman squad was a kid from the East side of St. Paul by the name of Herb Brooks.

Sonmor left the "U" that next year and took a job coaching for Eddie Shore's Springfield, Mass., American Hockey League team. Later he took over for the St. Catherine's (Ontario) junior team that included future hall of famer Stan Mikita. A year later he wound up

just outside Toronto, as the head coach of Hamilton's West Dale High School. Finally, after thoroughly paying his dues, Sonmor got the head coaching job at Ohio State University, where he would coach and also work towards getting his master's degree. He only stayed their a year though, because that next season, in 1966, he got a call from his old friend John Mariucci, who, upon resigning, had recommended him for his former job as the head coach of the Gophers.

"John stressed the high school player, and the importance of the Minnesota players in particular," said Glen. And that's just what Sonmor did. Glen focused his ideals into the pursuit of winning a national title with all Minnesota kids. Rather than bringing in the older, junior Canadien players, Sonmor instead continued in Mariucci's tradition and recruited the local high school talent. Among those kids were Mike Antonovich and Dean Blais, who would eventually lead the Gophers to a 1971 WCHA title as well as runner-up honors in the NCAA Championship — a very close game they lost to Boston University, 4-2.

One of Glen's defining moments as the ultimate player's coach happened that same year during a Gopher game in Duluth. "There was this one fan who always sat in the same spot, and gave the opposing players hell all game," reminisced Glen. "Well one time this loudmouth reached over and grabbed Mike Antonovich's stick when he was checked over by the boards near him. I was looking for an excuse to nail this idiot, and figured this would be as close as I would get. So, I jumped up from the bench, and beat the snot out of him but good. I knew he wasn't a fighter because he just kept grabbing my shirt, while I bloodied his face. It was a big production, and Herbie (Brooks) even came down to my defense from the press-box. I guess I showed that drunk son-of-a-bitch a thing or two about messing with a Gopher!" After the game, which Minnesota won in overtime on a Ron Peltier wrister, Glen got up on a table in the locker room and, while pumping his clenched fist, he waved his torn shirt around like a victory flag. Behind Glen, it was no surprise that the Gophs nearly went on to win win the national championship that year.

Glen would do anything for his boys. "Once at a tournament in Michigan I saw Glen go above and beyond his call of duty as our coach," recalled Dean Blais. "As we were entering the arena, some fans were mouthing off at us outside. We were going to get into it right there in the street, but Glen came over and said he'd take care of it. He went over to the five guys and BANG-BANG! Two punches, and two guys were laying on the ground. The other three ran, and he calmly walked back over to us and said smiling, 'You know, sometimes it feels good standing up for yourself!'"

Glen ultimately coached the Gophers from 1966-71, en route to posting a 79-82-6 record. He also produced three All-Americans, including Gary Gambucci, Murray McLaughlan and Wally Olds. Incidentally, Sonmor's selection as his freshman coach was a former Gopher All-American by the name of Lou Nanne — a man who would one day return the favor.

In 1971 Sonmor was offered the head coaching position of upstart St. Paul Fighting Saints of the World Hockey Association. Glen was torn, but in the end decided to step down in mid-season from the U of M to lead the Saints. (He was replaced by interim coach Ken Yackel.) Glen remained with the Saints for five years, coaching and serving as the team's GM, until the organization folded in 1977. He then coached the WHA's Birmingham Bulls for a season, before being hired as the new head coach of the North Stars by his old apprentice, Lou Nanne — who had just retired from playing and taken over as the team's new general manager.

Sonmor became a huge fan-favorite at the Met Center, ultimately turning the team around and getting people excited about their Stars. There would be some bumps in the road along the way though for the fiery coach. A couple of times he had to leave coaching because alcohol had gotten the better of him. But, after entering a treatment program, he came back with a new vigor. The highlight of his tenure was surely when he led the Stars to their infamous 1981 Stanley Cup run against the New York Islanders. "I've had a good many thrills in the game, but nothing to equal that," said Sonmor. Glen coached the Stars from 1978-83, briefly in 1984-85 and again in 1987, finishing his tenure with a 174-161-81 overall record for a .516 winning percentage, while also going 36-21 in the playoffs. He remained in the team's front office through 1990, where he continued to contribute, as a coach, assistant general manager and chief scout.

Glen went on to scout for the Philadelphia Flyers in the early 1990s, and in 1994, he became the director of player development for the IHL's Minnesota Moose. After the Moose moved to Winnipeg in 1996, Glen was hired as a scout for the Phoenix Coyotes by his former employee, Bobby Smith, who was now the team's general manager. In 1999 Glen joined the scouting staff of his hometown Minnesota Wild, where he remains today. In addition, Glen has also worked as a radio analyst for Minnesota Golden Gopher hockey games for the past several season as well.

Known as one of the game's great characters, Glen is a Minnesota treasure. Once during a game turned around and asked woman who was heckling him, "Excuse me ma'am, how much do you charge to haunt a three-bedroom house?" Another time after a bad call during a game, Glen popped out his false glass eye and offered it to the ref exclaiming, "Here, you take it, you need it more than I do!" Sonmor's colorful personality has touched many lives in this state. He was the epitome of a players' coach who always stood up for his men in the heat of the battle. Glen wasn't a great X & O guy, rather, he could find talent and get them fired up to take on the world. Somehow, he was able to make his players play better than they ever thought possible. His refreshing honesty, combined with his raw toughness made him a one-of-a-kind in hockey coaching annals. Perhaps the best indicator as to just what kind of guy he is, is reflected in what some of his former players and pals had to say about him:

"He's a unique person with a great personality," said Lou Nanne. "I don't know anybody who enjoys life more than Glen. For what he's gone through, with losing the eye and the alcoholism, he's really got one of the strongest positive attitudes I've seen. He is undoubtedly one of the best coaches to come along in the National Hockey League in the last 20 years. He's been a guy who's done a tremendous amount for hockey in Minnesota. He has been involved on so many levels for 25 years and he's just made a huge contribution here. He's a super person and a great friend."

"From Glen I learned that you can't have all great players on your team," said former player Bill Butters. "He felt that you had to have a few tomahawkers, a few skilled guys, and a good blend of guys with grit and character. He always said though, that you need five or six brutes out there to protect your good guys, and intimidate the other team. Glen had a great vitality for life. When I played for the Stars, Lou Nanne never liked to play me, but Glen did. Lou said to Glen jokingly, 'You have to start looking at Butters with your good eye Glen, so you can see just how bad he really is!'

"One time when I was playing with Jack Carlson for the Fighting Saints, we were losing to Hartford in the playoffs," Butters added. "Glen called us into the locker room to chew our butts. He said 'What the heck is going on out there? Look at you guys. Just look around the room. What do you think you're here for? Your good looks, and hockey ability? Heck no! I want you guys to start a brawl out there, and I don't want it to end! We're going to win this series, and when that puck drops I want this place to go crazy!' Glen thought that you had to intimidate as a coach. He wasn't into skill development for guys like me. I liked that we were on the team for one pur-

pose. I wasn't a great player, but I knew that as long as Glen was in hockey I'd have a job — because he knew that I'd play hard and physical for him."

"Glen was a super motivator, and was the type of guy who would always have fun," said former Gopher Dean Blais. "You'd do anything for him, because his fun attitude rubbed off on his players. He was the most motivating coach I ever played for. He motivated by pure fun."

"I loved Glen, we were from the same mold," said Mike Antonovich. "I went to the 'U' because of him. He taught me a lot about hockey, and about life. We got along so well, he was such a fun loving guy to be around. He would let us scrimmage all practice sometimes. He'd join in too, and play with us. He was just one of the boys. He knew his hockey, and was just a great guy."

"A character, that was Glen," said former Gopher and Fighting Saint Gary Gambucci. "He was such a nice guy, and able to laugh and have fun as well. I remember so many funny stories about Glen, he was one of a kind."

Glen currently resides in Bloomington, where, in addition to scouting for the Wild and doing radio analysis for Gopher Hockey games, he still finds time to enjoy the game of hockey. Glen is a legend in every sense of the word, and that is why everyone loves him.

HOW WOULD YOU DESCRIBE YOUR COACHING STYLE? "I wasn't the best X's and O's coach with regards to systems and strategy, but I had a love for the game. I think that came through in my style. I really wanted my guys to play with a passion and play like hell. If we had to mix it up out there then that is what we had to do sometimes. Hockey is a tough game and I loved every bit of it. I really tried to find specific roles for each of my players so that they had a place on the team. They all wanted to contribute in some way and I wanted them to be able to showcase their talents for the good of the team. So, whatever their role was, I encouraged them to be the best at that so that the team could be successful. When you get your players to buy into that, then you are well on your way because that is what it is all about. Even though my style varied a lot at the various levels that I coached at, some things remained the same. I mean I coached in high school, juniors, college, the minors and in the pros, but as long as you treated your players with respect, were honest with them and cared about them, you would be successful."

HOW DID YOU MOTIVATE YOUR PLAYERS? "You have to be absolutely honest with your players about where they stood on the team. You can't con anybody, you just had to tell them where they stood, good or bad. Once you did that, then you could define specific roles for each player and make them feel important. Whether it was Jack Carlson mixing things up or Timmy Younghans killing penalties, everybody had a role to play for the good of the team. I just tried to motivate each guy individually to do his best and work for the betterment of the team. You just can't say enough about guys like Jack (Carlson), he stood up for his teammates and always had their backs. If anybody wanted to take a run at Dino Cicarelli, Bobby Smith or Neal Broten, and try to intimidate them, then Jack would be right there to let them have it. Big Jack was the ultimate team player and that is why the fans loved him."

ON FIGHTING: "I think I was influenced early on by Freddy Shero, who was a teammate of mine back in Cleveland. He was a quiet, unassuming kind of a guy, but he had a philosophy about the game where fighting was a legitimate strategy. Freddy, of course, went on to become the architect of Philadelphia's 'Broad Street Bullies' during the 1970s. They made fighting a tactic to intimidate their opponents and it worked. If the tempo wasn't going along the way he wanted it to, he would just send out four or five guys to make it into a war. They would just come in waves and beat the other team down until they didn't want to play. I remember back then there was a joke in the league when players would get the 'Philadelphia Flu,' just before they would have to play those guys because no one wanted to play against them and get the crap kicked out of them. Nowadays you couldn't play that way. The rules have changed and really now you couldn't afford to have five guys in the penalty box, it would kill you. So, for me, I enjoyed that kind of style and it was fun. The fans loved it too. I get asked more than anything about that playoff game in Boston back in 1981, where we had something like 409 penalty minutes, that was something else! You know, we had never won a game in Boston up until that point and we had something to prove that night. I remember telling my guys in the locker room that we had to take a stand. So, I told them that the first time that there was any sign of intimidation or taunting, we are going to war and we were going to keep going to war until it was over. I told them I couldn't guarantee that we would win, but I could guarantee them that we would never win in Boston until we made a stand. They bought into it too because I think it was Bobby Smith who was the first guy to drop his gloves, and Bobby was no bruiser, let me tell ya! I was never so proud to see that at one point during the game, there were five fights going on and we were winning them all! You know, the thing that got me in trouble was after the game their coach, Gerry Cheevers, said that we had no character and that I was a thug. So, when those same reporters came over to talk to me and told me what he had said about me, I told them to go back and tell Cheevers to come down between periods of the next game to see me. And I said, 'Oh, and by the way, tell him to bring a f------- basket to carry his head home in!' Hey, we won and that was so much fun. I just couldn't stand seeing other teams try to intimidate our top guys, so I would send out guys like Jack Carlson to keep it straight. We had some others too, like Brad Maxwell, Willie Plett and even Billy Butters, who knew their roles. I loved Billy (Butters) and lobbied hard to get him on our roster with the Stars. My players used to kid around with the media and tell them that the reason they would go out there and mix it up so quickly was so that I didn't jump over the boards and beat them to it!"

WHO WERE YOUR COACHING MENTORS? "I was so appreciative of John Mariucci. He helped me get started in this business, he got me to go to school and get my degree, and he took me under his wing during my career. We were teammates on the old Minneapolis Millers back in 1949 and he was just the best. I will never forget what he told me after that season, he said 'Glen, I have played pro hockey now for 10 years and nearly every one of my teammates was Canadian. You are the first one I have met that actually graduated from high school, so you are going to college, period!' So, he took me down to the University of Minnesota and got me enrolled. I was just a kid, but I listened and started going to summer school.

FRED SHERO: NHL's PHILADELPHIA FLYERS

Fred Shero would go on to become a hockey coaching legend in the National Hockey League with the Philadelphia Flyers and New York Rangers. Shero got his start, however, in the Land of 10,000 Lakes, first with the St. Paul Saints of the International Hockey League, where he coached from 1960-61, and then with the St. Paul Rangers of the Central Professional Hockey League, where he coached from 1963-65. The Winnipeg native, who won the Jack Adams Award as the NHL Coach of the Year in 1974, was known for his toughness and his players were expected to play the same. The fans enjoyed watching Freddie's team's play, because they knew it was going to be action packed. In 1980, Shero received the Lester Patrick Trophy awarded for outstanding service to hockey in the United States. In addition, in a 1999 Philadelphia Daily News poll, Shero was selected as the city's greatest professional coach/manager, beating out legends such as Connie Mack, Dick Vermeil, Greasy Neale, Billy Cunningham, Dallas Green and Alex Hannum. It was a fitting tribute to one of the most innovative coaches in NHL history. Fred died on November 24, 1990.

Then, that changed my life later on when I lost my eye in 1955 when I was just 25 years old and playing pro hockey in Cleveland. I will never forget laying in a hospital in Pittsburgh scared to death. My wife and I had just had our first baby four days earlier and she was still in the hospital back in Cleveland and I didn't know what I was going to do. I knew that my playing career was over and was terrified. Just then John Mariucci called me and said, 'hey kid,' he used to always call me kid, 'don't you worry about a thing, I have arranged for you to come to Minnesota where you can finish your degree and be my freshman coach for the Gophers.' Wow, it was like God had spoken to me. Then to come back to the University, that was just such a great time. John really almost adopted me because he was just so good to me and my family. Then, a few years later when John left to go to the North Stars, he was the one who got me the head coaching job with the Gophers. I had been at Ohio State coaching and getting my masters degree, but was elated to come back to Minnesota. I have been here ever since. And do you know what? I graduated with high distinction as well, which is something I am very proud of. John went to all that work to get me in there and I wasn't going to let him down. So I studied hard and worked my tail off. John and I were friends for so long and he was really a father figure to me as well as my best friend. I say even to this day that every kid in Minnesota who plays college hockey anywhere in this country should say a little prayer to John Mariucci to thank him for all the work he did. So, it was a real privilege to have a mentor like John."

LOOKING BACK WHAT ARE YOU MOST PROUD OF IN YOUR CAREER? "I think it would be my 20 years of sobriety. That was a long journey getting past that, but I was proud of myself for getting clean. I lost my job and then got it back, and that was very special to me. You see, it was no secret that I had my troubles with alcohol early on and I used to think that it had no effect on my coaching, but of course it did. I was blessed to have people who stood by me until I finally came to grips with it. Thank God for Louie Nanne, who had to remove me from coaching when I got so bad back in 1983. It was right there in my contract that I couldn't drink again, and I knew I had messed up. Louie could've been done with me right then and there with no money, no job and no future, but he stuck with me and helped me get help. He saw his friend falling apart and he said he was going to help me, and he stood by me. He had to remove me from coaching, but promised to keep me in the organization if I would get help. So, I went and did what I had to do and got cleaned up. So, I went back to heading up player development and worked my way back. Then, a couple of years later when Bill Mahoney was coaching the Stars, Louie asked me to come back and coach the team again. I had been sober for about two and a half years at that point and couldn't believe my ears. That was such a proud moment for me because it told me that they had faith and confidence in me again. There was a lot of stress in coming back to coaching again, and some people were worried that the pressure might even get me to drink again. But I knew that I had changed my life around by then and would never go down that road again. So, that entire experience was life changing for me and really something that I am proud of accomplishing. I saw the importance of friends and learned to really appreciate those who will stand by you when you screw up. Then, if you are willing to do the right thing, you can come back and live out your dreams while learning some very valuable life lessons."

WHAT ARE THE CHARACTERISTICS OF WINNERS? "As much as anything winners have a passion for what they are doing. They can't fake that. It is more than money, it is the fact that real winners would be playing hard even without any money. It is just in their nature and they are born with that."

WHAT MOTIVATED YOU? "My whole life was sports and I was just so lucky to have the opportunity to live out my dreams. Coaching kids was a wonderful experience and to see them succeed was just great. Sure, I loved the competition and I loved winning, but I also got great satisfaction from seeing my players do their best and then go on to have happy and productive lives after hockey."

WHAT WAS THE BEST ADVICE YOU EVER GOT FROM ANOTHER COACH? "When I was in high school in Canada, we didn't have high school hockey, it was juvenile or midget hockey. So, I played basketball in the winter at school and then played hockey afterwards, at night. Well, we had a pretty good basketball team and I was actually our team's leading scorer. But it was getting to be too much. I can remember finishing basketball practice and then having a car waiting for me to take me to a hockey game. Finally, my high school basketball coach, George Ferris, told me that he was not going to allow me to do both. He knew that I loved both sports but he advised me to quit the basketball team to focus on hockey. He told me that even though I was the star of his basketball team, that their weren't going to be any basketball scouts coming up there to discover any five-foot-ten white point guards any time soon. The scouts were going to be at the hockey rink and that was where I needed to be in order to catch my break. It was tough advice, but he was right and he had a big influence on my life. He told me to decide what you really love to do in life and then go out get the best possible training that you can in that particular field. Then you will find a career you love and it won't even seem like work."

IF YOU COULD MAGICALLY GO BACK IN TIME TO THE FIRST YEAR YOU WERE A HEAD COACH AND GIVE YOURSELF SOME ADVICE FOR THE FUTURE, KNOWING WHAT YOU KNOW NOW, BACK THEN, WHAT WOULD YOU SAY TO YOURSELF? "I would tell that kid that he was about to embark on a wonderful opportunity and a joyous ride, so just enjoy it and take it all in because these are going to be the best years of your life."

WHAT ADVICE WOULD YOU HAVE FOR YOUNG COACHES STARTING OUT TODAY? "Just be yourself and don't try to be anything you aren't because kids can see right through that in a hurry. You can make mistakes along the way, but if you are genuine about what you are trying to do; you treat your kids with respect and dignity; let them know that you appreciate them; find roles for each of them on the team; and you try like heck to win, then you will be successful. Beyond that it is just identifying what you love to do and getting the best possible preparation. Then, don't worry about the money because it will all work itself out."

WHAT'S THE BIGGEST THING YOU'VE LEARNED FROM COACHING THAT YOU'VE BEEN ABLE TO APPLY TO YOUR EVERYDAY LIFE? "You know, my whole life has been sports. I have reached retirement age and have never had a real job. Hey, I don't think I have ever even faxed anything!

WHAT'S THE SECRET TO YOUR SUCCESS? "I wasn't the greatest X's and O's guy, but I cared about my players very, very much and had a real passion for the game of hockey. My players knew that I would be straight forward and honest with them and that they could believe what I was telling them. Sure, I made mistakes, but they were honest mistakes and I think my players knew that. So, I worked hard and did the best I could so that my team would come out on top. I also believed in sticking to things and following through with them. I just believed that you had to take whatever God given talent you had and then use it to the best of your ability. I would also add that having a great sense of humor really helps too. Everybody can use a good laugh every now and then, and that is what really keeps you young at heart."

WHAT WOULD YOU WANT TO SAY TO YOUR FANS, BOOSTERS, AND ALUMNI WHO HAVE SUPPORTED YOU ALL THESE YEARS? "The two words that come to mind for starters are thank you. The fans here were absolutely wonderful. They supported me through thick and thin and I really appreciated that so much. From the Gophers to the Fighting Saints to the North Stars, it was just amazing. I will never forget that Stanley Cup Playoff run back in 1981, it was something I will always look back on and treasure. Fans still stop me on the street to talk to me and are so complimentary, and that just means the world to me."

HOW DO YOU WANT YOUR COACHING EPITAPH TO READ — HOW DO YOU WANT TO BE REMEMBERED AS A COACH? "As somebody who cared a great deal about his players, as somebody who cared very much about winning, as somebody who did the best job he could to help his team win, as somebody who just enjoyed every minute of what he was doing, and as somebody who was very appreciative that he had the chance to do what he loved to do for a living for as long as he did. I had such a great appreciation of what a privilege it was to make my living doing something I loved. That is how I would like to be remembered."

TROY WARD: COLLEGE & PRO HOCKEY

Troy Ward grew up in North St. Paul, and went on to play college hockey at UW-Eau Claire, graduating in 1985. After earning his master's degree in athletic administration in 1987, Ward got into coaching. Ward's start in coaching came at his alma mater, UW-Eau Claire, where he served as the head coach from 1987-90 and as an assistant to Mike Eaves for the 1986-87 season. Ward then moved on to become an assistant coach at the University of Denver from 1990-93, under head coach Frank Serratore. There, Ward was responsible for the weight training and nutrition programs while also coaching the defensemen and special teams. From there, Ward served as the general manager and head coach of the Dubuque Fighting Saints of the Junior A United States Hockey League (USHL). There, he led the Saints to a 63-45-5 mark and coached 18 players who received Division I scholarships in his two seasons. Ward then hit the pro ranks, serving as an assistant coach for the IHL's Indianapolis Ice in from 1995-97, and winning an Eastern Conference Championship along the way. From 1997-2000, Ward served as an assistant coach for the NHL's Pittsburgh Penguins. Then, in 2001, Ward took over as the head coach of the Trenton Titans, where, after leading his boys to a 61-26-4 record and the Northern Conference title, he was named as the ECHL's Coach of the Year. That next year Ward served as the Senior Vice President and Director of Hockey Operations for the East Coast Hockey League, and was in charge of all the league's hockey operations, officiating departments and served as the primary liaison with the NHL, AHL and all other pro leagues. Ward then returned to the collegiate coaching ranks in 2001 to again serve as an assistant coach under head coach Mike Eaves at the University of Wisconsin. Ward has now been involved with hockey at all levels either as a player or coach for 20 years. In addition, Ward is also very active in summer camps, and is also the owner and camp director of the Hockey and Sons Skill Camp. Furthermore, Ward has been involved with USA Hockey's Masters Symposium and Select 16 camps as well. Since 1994 Ward has also been a coach at the C&O High Altitude Hockey Camp in Denver, which is a conditioning camp for professional players. Tom has two sons, Taylor and Nathan, and presently resides in Madison.

TOM WARD
HIGH SCHOOL & COLLEGE HOCKEY: SHATTUCK & GOPHERS

Tom Ward grew up in Richfield loving sports, and why not, his father was a physical education teacher as well as a football and wrestling coach. Tom went on to play football, baseball and hockey at Richfield High School, before going to play hockey and baseball at the University of Minnesota from 1982-86. Ward was then drafted by the Winnipeg Jets and later had his rights traded to his hometown North Stars, but he declined to pursue the game professionally. Ward also had an opportunity to play professional baseball at that time, but opted instead to get right into coaching. From there, Ward put his education degree to work back at his alma mater, Richfield High School, where he taught and coached football, baseball and hockey. Three years later Ward took over as an assistant coach under Mike Guentzel with the St. Paul Vulcans Junior A Hockey team. Ward would later serve as the team's head coach and general Manager for three years when Guentzel moved on to take over the Omaha Lancers. After three years with the Vulcans, Ward then joined Doug Woog as an assistant back with the Golden Gophers. Ward would serve stay with the Maroon and Gold for four years before finally taking over as the head hockey coach at Shattuck St. Mary's Prep Academy in Faribault.

Now entering his fifth season at Shattuck, Ward has definitely made a name for himself in the coaching world. Shattuck is a prep hockey power and consistently churns out division one talent year in and year out. The school has won three out of the five last national championships, with Ward winning two and Andy Murray (who left the program when Ward came in to take over as the head coach of the L.A. Kings) claiming the other. The titles, USA Hockey Midget Tier One, are basically the national championships for high school aged hockey. Shattuck is the only school in Minnesota, however, which plays in this division, with all other high schools playing in the State High School League. Shattuck plays around 75 games per year under this format and, incredibly, the school has lost just a handful of games over the last several years. Playing mostly Canadian and other elite teams from around the country, Shattuck is simply dominant in the sport of hockey. And leading that charge is Tom Ward, whose overall record in the four years that he has been in Faribault is an amazing 216-31-11. Tom and his family presently live in Bloomington, and he commutes to Faribault every day.

HOW WOULD YOU DESCRIBE YOUR COACHING STYLE? "I think my teams are very disciplined, but we are also a very free-wheeling team as far as our style of play. I would describe it as a blend of the European and North American styles in that we like to control the puck and move the puck versus dumping and chasing all of the time. It is a brand of hockey that our kids like to play. We just really stress skill work in practice, that is the key. We work on stick handling, skating and actually teach kids how to check, which I think is a lost art. The bottom line here is that the kids really enjoy our system and have bought into it. As a result, we have been extremely successful. We also really focus on the team concept, and try not to highlight individuals."

WHAT IS THE KEY TO RECRUITING? "You know, we are lucky. For us we don't have to do a lot of hard core recruiting, which is great. I would say 99% of the kids that end up coming here contact us first. It is tough though, with regards to other programs trying to grab our kids even though they are not finished with their eligibility. I don't try to do that to anyone else but at the same time I understand that there is a time and a place for every kid to move on,

whether it is from our program or to our program. We are just lucky to have a great program which attracts good people to us and that we don't have to go out and beat the bushes. That is one of the great luxuries that we have here and we are very fortunate to be in that situation."

HOW DO YOU BUILD TEAM UNITY & CHEMISTRY? "Chemistry is something that we work on here from day one. We stress the fact that no one is bigger than the team in our program and that the team always comes first. We tell the kids that all the individual accolades, awards and honors will come if the team does well and that they are an important part of the team. We try to reinforce to the kids that there is only one puck and each individual has to buy into his role and what he can contribute to the team. Our kids buy into the fact that everybody can bring something different to the team. From the very first try-out we tell the kids that when we take the 20 kids for our prep team (Shattuck's top team), that they are not the 20 most skilled players. It will be the 20 best guys who we think will make the best team. We are not looking to have an all-star team, we are looking to have a team of guys who will accept their role and accept responsibility for doing their part. Because of that, we get a lot of sweat equity out of some of our veteran kids, who, even if they are not top-flight goal scorers, know that if they work hard that there will always be a spot on the roster for them."

ON SHATTUCK: "We're blessed here, that is for sure. I mean you can't make chicken salad out of chicken sh..! We have got really good players here and they are very motivated kids. The school is structured as such where the kids are put into an environment where they are diligent and task oriented. Overall, these are just really good kids from good families and they try very hard to do their best. That environment has also been very conducive in helping a lot of kids move on to advance their academics and athletics at the next level."

WHAT ARE THE KEY INGREDIENTS TO CREATING A CHAMPIONSHIP TEAM? "You've got to have good team oriented players with skill. Then, you've got to have great goaltending and you've got to have luck, because it's not always the team that is the most skillful that wins. Sometimes it comes down to the team that stays away from injuries, or the team that gets the right draw. There are a lot of extraneous circumstances that come into play to win a championship and I learned about that at the U of M. So many times we had such great teams there, and for whatever the reason, sometimes the stars didn't align for us. But hey, that's hockey."

WHAT'S THE SECRET TO YOUR SUCCESS? "Having good players would be first and foremost. Being able to work with good, motivated, skillful players who can buy into a team-first philosophy is what it is all about. I think we have created an atmosphere here where our kids know that they will be counted on to do something special for the team, whether it is to block a shot, win a draw, score a big goal, make a great pass, make a big save or not take a stupid penalty. Hopefully we have been able to get our kids to realize that everyone can do something to help the cause and that has really made our program a big success."

HOW DO YOU WANT YOUR COACHING EPITAPH TO READ — HOW DO YOU WANT TO BE REMEMBERED AS A COACH? "Somebody who was honest, treated his players fairly, really cared about his kids and believed in putting the team first."

DOC ROMNES: GOPHER HOCKEY

Elwyn "Doc" Romnes was a star hockey player at White Bear Lake High School before going on to play college hockey at St. Thomas. Then, in 1930, after playing three years with the semi-pro St. Paul Saints of the AHA, Romnes broke into the NHL at a time when there were just two American-born players in the league. Romnes joined the Chicago Blackhawks and then went on win a pair of Stanley Cups with the team in 1934 and 1938. He would later add one more in 1939, as a member of the Toronto Maple Leafs, where he scored the winning goal in the Leafs only victory over the Bruins in the Stanley Cup Finals. Romnes was always known as a very clean player who followed the rules of the game. In fact, Romnes drew just 46 penalty minutes in 403 games over his career, and in 1936 he even won the Lady Byng Trophy, for sportsmanlike conduct, tallying just six penalty minutes in 48 games. (Romnes remained the only American ever to win the award until Joe Mullen did it 52 years later.) Romnes would retire from the game in 1940 to pursue a career in coaching. He started out at Michigan Tech, serving there from 1941-45. He then got back into playing, leading the Kansas City Pla-Mors to the USHL title in 1946, before hanging it up again for good after that season. From there, Romnes came home to take over as the head coach at the University of Minnesota. Romnes would coach the Gophers from 1947-52 and finished his career in Gold Country with a career record of 52-59. A member of the U.S. Hockey Hall of Fame, Romnes died on July 21, 1984 in Colorado Springs, at the age of 77.

TED BRILL:
GRAND RAPIDS HIGH SCHOOL HOCKEY

Theodore R. "Ted" Brill was a Minnesota hockey giant. The Grand Rapids native did more for the game of hockey in the state of Minnesota than will ever be known. T.R. dedicated more than 40 years of his life to serving the amateur hockey establishment in Minnesota and throughout the United States as a coach, volunteer and administrator. Brill's involvement with amateur hockey began in 1962, when he organized a youth hockey program in Moorhead, where he attended Moorhead State University. For the next 22 years, Brill coached youth hockey, including high school teams, in St. Paul and Grand Rapids. In 1974 he became a member of the board of directors of the Minnesota Amateur Hockey Association (MAHA), a position he held for 29 years. While with MAHA (today known as Minnesota Hockey), Brill served a four-year stint as President from 1980-83, and organized and implemented various coaching-related programs. As the Minnesota Director of USA Hockey's Coaching Education Program from 1974-82, Brill founded and administered the program and its clinics throughout the state. In 2003, Brill celebrated his 25th year as an executive board member of the Minnesota High School Coaches Association. In addition, for the past eight years Brill acted as USA Hockey's High School Section Director, and had also served stints as a member of the USA Hockey Youth and Marketing Councils. Among Brill's many accomplishments, he was named Vice President of the U.S. Hockey Hall of Fame Board of Directors from 1989-95, and was the General Manager of the U.S. National Junior Team at the 1982 International Ice Hockey Federation World Junior Championships in Minnesota. Brill also served on the Minnesota Hockey Foundation Board of Trustees for 13 years, and was closely involved with player development camps as well as USA Hockey Select Festivals and Camps. In 1999, Brill was honored with the Walter Yaciuk Award, presented annually by USA Hockey's Coaching Education Program. On May 5, 2003, T.R. tragically passed away at his home in Grand Rapids, following a long battle with cancer. Fittingly, that Summer, Brill was (posthumously) given the William Thayer Tutt Award, which is presented annually by USA Hockey to a volunteer who, during many years of service, has displayed a selfless dedication to the enhancement of ice hockey at the grassroots level in America. A legend in Minnesota hockey, T.R. will truly be missed.

TOM OSIECKI: BURNSVILLE HIGH SCHOOL
& ST. OLAF WOMEN'S HOCKEY

Tom Osiecki is among the best of the best in the world of high school hockey in Minnesota. A native of St. Paul, Osiecki earned his undergraduate and graduate degrees from the University of St. Thomas in history and physical education, respectively, in 1964 and 1968. After teaching and coaching baseball, hockey and football at St. Agnes High School in St. Paul from 1964-66, Osiecki got into coaching at Burnsville High School, where, from 1966-99, he would guide his Braves to a pair of state championships in 1985 and 1986. In addition, his teams won five consecutive Section I Hockey titles from 1983 to 1987, and another in 1990. In 1996 Osiecki left the boys program at Burnsville, to take over as the girls' hockey coach. He would guide the team for the next three years, leading them to a state runner-up finish in 1996. In addition to coaching high school hockey, Osiecki also served as the varsity girls' badminton coach for five years, from 1994-99, winning four state championships (1996, 1997, 1998, and 1999) along the way. Furthermore, Osiecki was an assistant baseball coach for two years and an assistant football coach for three.

After retiring from teaching in 1999, Osiecki went on to take over as the head women's hockey coach at St. Olaf. Now entering his third year with the Oles, Osiecki is poised to bring the same type of success that he had in Burnsville, down to Northfield. Among his many coaching honors and accolades, Osiecki is a two-time Minnesota State High School Hockey Coach of the Year winner. He was also named to the Minnesota High School Hockey Coaches' Hall of Fame in 1995. In addition, Osiecki also served as a scout for the North Stars and the Dallas Stars from 1990-95 as well. Tom and his wife Bev live in the Twin Cities and have two sons, Matt and Mark, who also had very successful hockey careers.

MURRAY WILLIAMSON
OLYMPIC HOCKEY

Murray Williamson grew up in Winnipeg and grew up playing in the minor hockey systems up in Manitoba. As a 15-year-old he was recruited into the sponsorship system of the Montreal Canadiens, where he competed for three years. In 1952, as an 18-year-old, he coached a neighborhood team to the Manitoba Bantam A championship. Williamson left the St. Boniface Canadian junior system in 1954 to come to Minnesota. There, he attended Eveleth Junior College, where he also played for the Eveleth Rangers in the Thunder Bay Senior League.

In 1955 Williamson came to the University of Minnesota to play for John Mariucci, ultimately earning a All-American honors with the Gophers in 1959. After graduating with a bachelor's degree in business administration, Williamson went on to play semi-pro hockey in the Ontario Hockey Association Senior League. Then, in 1962, Williamson became the player/coach of the USHL's St. Paul Steers, and that next year assumed ownership of the team. Under his tutelage, the Steers became such a power in the league that by 1965 the team was converted into the U.S. National team. It would be the beginning of a very long and illustrious coaching career for Williamson, who, over the years would go on to coach more than 200 international senior matches as well as five National and two Olympic teams.

Williamson, who was now a naturalized U.S. citizen, then coached the U.S. National Hockey Team in the World Championships in Vienna in 1967. Williamson was also doing his part to promote the game for American kids as well. You see, in 1967 there were just three Americans playing in the NHL, so the pinnacle for American players at that time was the Olympic team. Williamson recognized that and gave our boys the opportunity to represent their country in international competition. That next year Williamson became the youngest man to ever coach a U.S. Olympic Hockey team, leading Team USA to the 1968 Winter Games in Grenoble, France. Over the next two years Williamson would guide the U.S. National Teams at the World Championships in both Bern, Geneva, and Bucharest, Hungary. Then, in 1972, Williamson made history when he led the U.S. Olympic Hockey Team to the Silver medal in Sapporo, Japan. With a roster that included the likes of Mark Howe, Robby Ftorek, Huffer Christianson, Lefty Curran and Henry Boucha, the team came from nowhere to shock the hockey world.

In 1974 Williamson organized America's first International World Junior team, a club which would go on to participate in the World Junior Invitational Tournament in Leningrad. Three years earlier Williamson had become the first North American coach ever to visit inside the Russian Army Training Camp in Moscow at the invitation of Anatol Tarasov, the famous Soviet hockey coach. A true student of the game, Williamson learned a great deal from the Russians and applied that knowledge to his own players back home in Minnesota.

Williamson's overall record included more than 130 victories against some of the best competition, home and abroad, and his longevity as a coach of Olympic and National teams ranks second only to the late Walter Brown, former owner of the Boston Bruins. Williamson, who later coached a Swiss team in Geneva, would also go on to start one of the most successful and well respected summer training camps for youth hockey players in the world, Bemidji International Hockey Camp, which, with legendary Bemidji State Coach Bob Peters, he ran from 1967-2000. Literally tens of thousands of kids made the trek to Bemidji to learn the game of hockey

up in the great northwoods and it has long been recognized as the first hockey camp in the world.

After coaching, Murray went on to become a very successful businessman. Presently, he has a lot of investment property in the real estate business and owns several hotels and restaurants throughout the country as well. Murray and his wife reside in the Twin Cities and have two sons who also coach hockey, Kevin and Deano, who played for the Gophers — just like the old man. When it comes to International hockey, Murray Williamson is without a doubt, a coaching legend, and someone who should be thanked for all that he did to promote the game for Americans as well as for Minnesotans. A real student and innovator of the game, Williamson truly made a difference in the world of hockey.

HOW WOULD YOU DESCRIBE YOUR COACHING STYLE? "I didn't really have an overlying philosophy other than total dedication to the team and very hard work. My style was more about intensive training. I went to Russia and spent a lot of time with Anatol Tarasov to learn about training techniques. Back in the late 1960s the Russians were doing things that are commonplace now, but simply unheard of here. I was also very involved with my players and was very concerned about the chemistry of the team. But mostly I was interested in finding new ways to incorporate technical training and conditioning to improve my team. I would add too that I was never really a guy who liked the spotlight, I was more of a background guy and that was certainly part of my style as well."

WHO WERE YOUR COACHING MENTORS? "I think the great Russian coach Anatol Tarasov would be right up there. We became great friends over the years and I really respected his ideas and approach to the game. I mean so many of his conditioning and training techniques, like using two pucks in one drill, were just revolutionary at the time. So, he would certainly be a mentor of mine."

IF YOU COULD MAGICALLY GO BACK IN TIME TO THE FIRST YEAR YOU WERE A HEAD COACH AND GIVE YOURSELF SOME ADVICE FOR THE FUTURE, KNOWING WHAT YOU KNOW NOW, BACK THEN, WHAT WOULD YOU SAY TO YOURSELF? "I would say don't evaluate your talent on skill alone, you need to bring character to the table too. Those guys might not be the best players but they will give you 110% and they have good character, which is what you need to build your team around. It's not the all-stars, it's those guys who really make the difference."

LOOKING BACK WHAT ARE YOU MOST PROUD OF IN YOUR CAREER? "I think the fact that we won a lot of games with great people, many of whom I am still close with today. You know, we recently had a reunion for the 1972 Silver Medal Olympic team down in Florida, and the players all chipped in and got me a solid silver replica of our medal. You know, when I was the coach I never got one, so that meant so much to me. Even 30 years later the chemistry between all those guys is still there and that means a great deal to me."

WHAT WAS THE KEY TO RECRUITING? "Back in my day it was simple: get them out of the Army and get them assigned to your hockey team! It was tough in those days, but you just had to work hard and talk to a lot of people in order to put your team together.

There are no short cuts, you just need to work hard and get out there."

HOW DID YOU BUILD TEAM UNITY & CHEMISTRY? "You know, it was never a planned thing. It was just a gut feeling about how you wanted to put your team together. Certain character guys really made it all come together along with your all-stars and team leaders. A lot of it comes down to how well you pick your team and fit the pieces together. Also, it's like Vince Lombardi said, 'You have got to have total respect for your players and they have got to have total respect for you.' Once you have that, then you have something. I can name a lot of guys out there that played on high profile teams but their egos got in the way and they failed. I mean look at guys like Bud Grant, Jacques Lemaire and even Bob Peters at Bemidji, they are not big ego guys but they were very successful and have such respect from their players. That all goes into building chemistry."

WHAT'S THE BEST PIECE OF ADVICE YOU EVER GOT FROM ANOTHER COACH? "It wasn't specific advice, but John Mariucci taught me a lot. He had a great way with people and had such a great sense of humor. I really miss him, he was great."

WHAT ADVICE WOULD YOU HAVE FOR YOUNG COACH-ES STARTING OUT TODAY? "I think first and foremost you have to really by honest with your kids. You have to just say it like it is and not worry about being politically correct. You have to know the consequences of telling some kid that he is not skating well enough and that you can't use him on your team. That's tough but you just need to be up front, principled and put the team ahead of yourself."

WHAT'S THE BIGGEST THING YOU'VE LEARNED FROM COACHING THAT YOU'VE BEEN ABLE TO APPLY TO YOUR EVERYDAY LIFE? "You can't take your coaching philoso-phies to your social structure. Coaches are dictatorial control guys who run the ship. If you take that attitude to the golf course or to your family you won't last very long."

WHAT'S THE SECRET TO YOUR SUCCESS? "I think it was just total intensity. Living hockey day and night and having a passion to not get beat. I am not sure exactly what defines the parameters I use to define success other than being there and knowing what it takes to win. I think intensity, concentration, preparation and dedication are all things that have gone into it, that is for sure. Things have changed now, but back in my day strength and conditioning were what it was all about for me. Nowadays teams have so many coaches covering every specific position, as well as even having specific strength and recruiting coaches. Back in my day we didn't have all that and you had to wear a lot of hats. So, in order to stay ahead of the competi-tion you had to get the best players, motivate them and respect them. I will also say that I never abused a player either. I chewed a lot of ass, but is was behind closed doors. That was important."

WHAT WOULD YOU WANT TO SAY TO YOUR FANS, BOOSTERS, AND ALUMNI WHO HAVE SUPPORTED YOU ALL THESE YEARS? "Thank you for what you did for me. I would just hope that I did as much for you as you did for me. Thanks too for all the guys who put out and sacrificed for our teams. I would hope that I contributed as much to their lives as they did to mine."

HOW DO YOU WANT YOUR COACHING EPITAPH TO READ — HOW DO YOU WANT TO BE REMEMBERED AS A COACH? "I think that I tried to build the best teams that I could and that I contributed more to our National and Olympic programs, during the toughest of times, than maybe any other coach. I think that our teams were huge contributors to the development and success of not only future National and Olympic programs, but also to our World Junior teams as well."

ANDRE BEAULIEU: ST. MARY'S HOCKEY

Andre Beaulieu was a hockey legend at St. Mary's University. In fact, the speedy winger scored an amazing 233 points in just 63 hockey games with the Cardinals! Beaulieu, who was a phenom back in his native Quebec, came to Winona after starring in the Quebec Junior A League when he was just 15 years old. Beaulieu didn't want to play pro hockey (Montreal had his draft rights), and instead wanted to pursue a life as a teacher and coach. So, Beaulieu worked with his high school counselor to find a college in the States that would be a good fit for him. One of those schools was St. Mary's. "I was looking for a place to go to college," said Beaulieu. "I wanted to learn English badly. I knew I didn't want to end up working in a foundry the rest of my life."

Because he had played professionally for several years in the IHL after playing junior hock-ey, he was ineligible to play NCAA D-I hockey. But, St. Mary's, a member of the NAIA at the time, had no such restrictions. Head coach Max Molock worked out the details and got Andre a student work study job, appropriately enough, helping to build the new rink on campus. Starting from scratch, Beaulieu and his buddies took that summer and built St. Mary's their new outdoor rink — goals and all. St. Mary's then hit the ice in their new rink in 1961 with Beaulieu leading the way. As both player and assistant coach, he scored an amazing 41 points in just 16 games that season. That next season Bob Paradise, a star defenseman from Cretin High School who would later star in the NHL, joined the team. This combo proved to be lethal for St. Mary's, which went on to win back-to-back MIAC title in 1964 and 1965. Thousands of St. Mary's fans would brave the freezing temperatures at the outdoor rink to see the team and its new stars tear up the ice. Beaulieu went on to score 62, 63, and 68 points respectively over his next three years, finishing with an unbelievable 134 goals and 99 assists for 233 points in just 63 games. (That's an average of 3.7 points per game on an outdoor rink!) The four-time all-conference selection once even scored nine goals in a 9-0 win over Augsburg. He finally got some national attention by being featured in Sports Illustrated's "Faces in the Crowd," after scoring 13 goals in a pair of weekend games against St. Olaf and Carleton.

After graduating, Beaulieu went on to become a math teacher and head hockey and tennis coach both at Hill-Murray and at Stillwater High Schools. At Hill-Murray, Beaulieu led his Pioneers to one runner-up and two Minnesota State Independent Hockey Tournament Championships. Beaulieu would later serve as the general manager and coach of the Minnesota Junior Stars of the Midwest Junior 'A' Hockey League, the predecessor to the USHL, during the early 1970s. In his second season with the Junior Stars, Beaulieu led the team to an Anderson Cup championship. Beaulieu's achievements then earned him a spot behind the U.S. National Team bench in 1974, at the World Junior Championships, and then an assistant with the National Hockey League's Minnesota North Stars in 1975. (He would briefly serve as the team's head coach during the 1977-78 season as well.) Later, in the fall of 1978, Beaulieu became the general manager of the USHL's Sioux City Musketeers. Beaulieu, who got into pro scouting after that, currently works with the NHL's New York Rangers as a team scout.

DOUG WOOG
COLLEGE HOCKEY: UNIVERSITY OF MINNESOTA

Doug Woog grew up playing hockey in St. Paul and went on to graduate from South St. Paul High School in 1962. There, he earned all-state hockey honors for an amazing three consecutive years and also starred on the football team as well. Next, Woog fulfilled a life-long dream by accepting a scholarship to play for the University of Minnesota and learn the game from one of the all-time great coaches, John Mariucci. Woog went on to a fabulous career in Gold Country, earning All-American honors his junior season after leading the team in scoring. He was named as captain for his senior season en route to leading the team to a 16-12-0 record, and a second place finish in the WCHA. For his efforts Woog was named the team's MVP. From 1964-66 the speedy center scored 48 goals and 53 assists for 101 career points. Woog went on to graduate with honors from the U of M in 1967.

From there, Woog played for the 1967 U.S. National Team and was a candidate for the 1968 U.S. Olympic team. After that, however, it was off to the real world as he went on to teach geography and coach football and hockey at Hopkins West Junior High School. Then, in the fall of 1968, Woog took a job at his high school alma mater, where he became the head soccer coach as well as an assistant on both the hockey and baseball teams. While coaching at South St. Paul, Woog's soccer program won six conference titles and twice finished as runner-up's for the state championship.

From 1971 through 1977 Woog branched out to coach as much hockey as he could. In the process, he led the St. Paul Vulcans and the Minnesota Junior Stars to a pair of U.S. Junior National titles along the way. During that time, in 1973, Doug fulfilled another dream when he earned his Master's Degree in guidance and counseling from St. Thomas University. In 1978, Woog was chosen to lead the West Team in the U.S. Olympic Festival, where his squad won the gold medal. It would be the beginning of a long relationship with USA Hockey. (At the 1989 Olympic Festival Woog duplicated that feat by winning the gold medal with his South squad. Woog was also the assistant coach of the 1982 U.S. National Junior Team and then served as an assistant coach for the 1984 Olympic team that competed in Sarajevo, Yugoslavia as well. In 1985 Woog coached the U.S. National Junior Team; in 1987 he served as the assistant coach for Team USA in the 1987 Canada Cup; and in 1989 he was the head coach of the of U.S. Select 17 team. In addition, he served as a national committee member for the AHAUS and was chairman of the National Skating Committee for USA Hockey.)

In 1985 the "Wooger" returned to his college alma-mater. There, he guided the Golden Gophers to seven league championships (four regular season and three post-season) over his illustrious 14-year career. During his tenure in Gold Country the Gophers were among the nation's very best, garnering WCHA Final Four/Five and NCAA appearances in 12 of 14 seasons, posting seven 30-win seasons, and appearing in six NCAA Final Fours. He came close to winning it all on several occasions, including the 1989 NCAA Finals, where, had Randy Skarda not hit the pipe in overtime at the old Civic Center versus Harvard, maybe Woog would still be coaching today. In 1999 Woog resigned as the University of Minnesota's head hockey coach to take an assistant athletic director position at the school. He would leave as the program's all-time winningest coach with a gaudy 389-187-40 record (.664).

Today, in addition to his work at the University, Woog is a television analyst for Gopher Hockey games and also runs his own

summer hockey camp in northern Minnesota. Woog has been instrumental in initiating and maintaining youth athletic organizations in his community and is an overall good friend to hockey. Doug Woog achieved great success in Gold Country, and he did it all with Minnesota kids. That alone may have been the single greatest tradition in all of college sports, yet it was something that was constantly used against him as the reason why his teams never won the NCAA championship. Nevertheless, Woog was a great coach, a wonderful person, and a tremendous supporter of Minnesota hockey. In 2002, in addition to his many coaching awards and accolades, Woog was honored by being inducted into the U.S. Hockey Hall of Fame.

Presently, Doug and his wife Jan reside in St. Paul. They have three children: daughter Amy, and sons Steve and Dan — who both played college hockey as well.

HOW WOULD YOU DESCRIBE YOUR COACHING STYLE? "It's experiential. It all starts from the coaches that you played for because as a coach, that is what you know. I learned a lot from several different coaches and that all went into creating my own style. It was a real mixed bag and in retrospect, that was great because I had several different styles to choose from when we played different kinds of teams. I mean the European style was so different than the North American style, and that was all part of it. From there, I just believed in hard work and good teamwork. I believed that you should treat kids the same way you would want your own kid to be treated. You want them to be taught well, you want them to have a chance to win, and you want them to have opportunities to succeed."

HOW DID YOU MOTIVATE YOUR PLAYERS? "You know, that has really evolved. From the time I was coaching in high school until the end of my college coaching days, my style of motivation really changed with the times. I realized that there were a lot of different ways to motivate kids and that helped me become a better teacher. I just loved teaching, that was what it was all about for me.

WHO WERE YOUR COACHING MENTORS? "I learned a great deal from my high school coach, Lefty Smith, and of course from John Mariucci at the University of Minnesota. I also learned a lot about the international style of hockey from Lou Vairo."

IF YOU COULD MAGICALLY GO BACK IN TIME TO THE FIRST YEAR YOU WERE A HEAD COACH AND GIVE YOURSELF SOME ADVICE FOR THE FUTURE, KNOWING WHAT YOU KNOW NOW, BACK THEN, WHAT WOULD YOU SAY TO YOURSELF? "I would say 'Hey, what the heck are you doing here? You should have been an assistant before becoming a head coach!' I was in way over my head when I got this job and that was a big adjustment. I will never forget our first series and thinking that I was being booed by all the fans. I just thought it was going to be a long year, but it turned out they were yelling 'Wooooog!' instead, and everything turned out all right from there."

WHAT DID IT MEAN FOR YOU TO BE A GOPHER? "It was a life-long dream come true for me to be able to play for the Gophers. The fact that we had scholarships was just a means to an end. Back then there weren't that many opportunities for us after college as far as hockey was concerned, what with only six NHL teams and all. So, we played for the love of the game and were happy to get to school to be able to make a living. Yeah, being a Gopher was pretty special."

WHAT ROLE DID YOUR FAMILY PLAY IN YOUR SUCCESS? "They were great. You know, to coach my sons was very special to me. They were good players and it was a great to see them get the opportunity to play college hockey. From there, it was great too that my family was not only very supportive, but that they stayed out of the spotlight. I mean my kids didn't get into any trouble, they didn't do drugs, they were just great kids, and that was big because those are the kinds of distractions that can be detrimental to your career. Really though, I couldn't have asked for more with regards to what they gave me in terms of the freedom of doing what I loved to do. I think back to when I first started out. I was coaching junior hockey, coaching the South St. Paul soccer team, serving as a high school counselor and going to graduate school all at the same time. Then, I had a couple of kids in diapers at that same time, so my wife was a saint. Her support was incredible. So, yeah, I am very lucky to have a great, supportive family."

ON TAKING ONLY MINNESOTA KIDS TO BE GOLDEN GOPHERS: "It all goes back to John Mariucci's dream of giving the American kids a chance to play college hockey. I guess I took that one step further at the University by going after only Minnesota kids. My vision was a tribute and a thank you to Maroosh for all that he did for us. And really, to see that evolution and to give our kids the opportunity, that may be more important to me than coaching for 45 years. A lot of people don't know the history of all this, but it goes way back to American kids just not having the chances to play at the next level. Back in our day there were so few opportunities. Thank God for John Mariucci, who just gave me the chance, because at the time there were very few of them out there for us. Because most of the coaches were Canadian, the vast, vast majority of the scholarships then went to the Canadian kids. Then, even after those kids graduated and went on to play professionally, they took most of those jobs too. It was a double whammy. So, it was tough for our era of players, and I just wanted to make sure that our kids had more opportunities than we did. Was it controversial? No question. But we stuck to it and were proud of our decision. It was nothing against anybody else. It wasn't anti-Canadian by any means, it was just pro-Minnesotan. That's all. John (Mariucci) wasn't anti-Canadian either, he was just anti-older Canadian players, the 22 year old freshmen who competed against our 18-year-old kids. But hey, you know, with a couple of breaks here or there, there is no question in my mind that we would have won some titles along the way with the all-Minnesota rosters. So, do I have any regrets? None."

LOOKING BACK WHAT ARE YOU MOST PROUD OF IN YOUR CAREER? "I am just proud of all the good kids that we have had in our program over the years. None of our kids got into trouble and they have since gone on to do some great things in their lives. That is very rewarding as a coach. Then, to have made so many friendships along the way, and to be so genuinely appreciated by the fans and supporters — that means the world to me."

HOW DID YOU BUILD TEAM UNITY & CHEMISTRY? "We had a lot of traditions that we did which built chemistry. For instance, we used to take some of the seniors hunting every year down in Iowa. We also used to have golf tournaments, social outings, dinners, and even maybe taking the guys to a North Stars game. We wanted to get guys into social situations where they could become friends outside of hockey and that led to better team unity. I think even the dorms helped out too, where the kids lived with one another. The other thing that was because all of the kids were from Minnesota, they had that in common. They all knew of each other, or had played with or against one another at one time or another over the years as well, and that helped too."

WHAT ADVICE WOULD YOU HAVE FOR YOUNG COACHES STARTING OUT TODAY? "There are no shortcuts and once in a while you just have to be lucky. I would also say that coaching opportunities are created when people start talking about you. Your name has got to start to surface and the only way it will surface is by doing well where you are at and then getting out there to be seen. If that means stepping up your level of competition, then so be it, but you need to get noticed to advance in this business. I would also tell them to learn as much as they can from other coaches that they respect. Beyond that, they just have to pay their dues along the way."

WHAT'S THE BIGGEST THING YOU'VE LEARNED FROM COACHING THAT YOU'VE BEEN ABLE TO APPLY TO YOUR EVERYDAY LIFE? "Happiness. I have been so lucky to have had all of the opportunities that I have had. To be able to spend my entire career here in Minnesota was extremely gratifying. I count my blessings for all of the great people that I have been lucky enough to meet and have an impact on in this business, and I really appreciate it. I also haven't had to sell my values or cheapen myself along the way and that makes me happy too."

HOW DO YOU WANT YOUR COACHING EPITAPH TO READ — HOW DO YOU WANT TO BE REMEMBERED AS A COACH? "I would want to be respected by the guys who I respect the most. When you have the respect of the guys who I would call 'champions of their game,' then that is something special. I also want to be thought of as someone who won with dignity and performed with dignity."

THE AUS BROTHERS: PETER & WHITEY
BETHEL & ST. OLAF HOCKEY

Peter and Whitey Aus have been coaching hockey in Minnesota for more than three decades. Peter, who has dedicated much of his life to traveling throughout the United States and Canada working with Christian Athlete Hockey Camps as a power skating specialist, has coached hockey at Bethel College for more than a decade. In 2001, he earned MIAC Coach of the Year honors after the Royals finished in fourth place in the league and advanced to the conference championship series. A former Murray High School and then St. Olaf hockey and football standout, Peter also has more than 30 years of high school coaching experience at both Litchfield and Willmar — where he won two conference championships and was twice named as the Section 5 Coach of the Year in 1985 and again in 1990.

Whitey, also a prep and collegiate standout with the Oles, went on to coach hockey at Roseville High School for 15 seasons before becoming the head coach at St. Olaf from 1976-97. For more than 20 years, Whitey was a fixture in Northfield, earning MIAC and NAIA Coach of the Year honors, as well as becoming the school's all-time winningest coach along the way. In addition, Whitey earned MIAC Coach of the Year honors in 1984 as the coach of the Ole soccer team. He also served as the school's athletic director as well.

Peter Aus

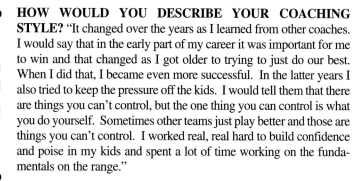

DOUG GALLIGHER
HIGH SCHOOL GOLF: EDINA

Doug Galligher grew up in Aberdeen, S.D., and after graduating from Huron High School, went on to play golf at Northern State College in Aberdeen. From there, Galligher worked summers at Camp Warren, a YMCA camp, where he met a lot of kids from Edina. As a result, he got his first teaching job in 1965 at Valley View Junior High School in Edina. He later went on to teach algebra and geometry at Edina High School, where he became a girls golf coaching legend for 34 years, winning five state titles along the way. One of those titles came in 1997, when Hilary Homeyer won the individual championship. Homeyer later went on to win the 2003 Women's U.S. Open, making Galligher, as well as the state of Minnesota very proud. In addition, Galligher coached girls basketball for 12 years and won a state title with the Hornets in 1988 as well. Galligher also served as the assistant boys track coach under Ed Hendrickson for 12 years, winning several titles with that program too. Galligher retired in 1999 and presently lives in both Lutsen and in Florida.

HOW WOULD YOU DESCRIBE YOUR COACHING STYLE? "It changed over the years as I learned from other coaches. I would say that in the early part of my career it was important for me to win and that changed as I got older to trying to just do our best. When I did that, I became even more successful. In the latter years I also tried to keep the pressure off the kids. I would tell them that there are things you can't control, but the one thing you can control is what you do yourself. Sometimes other teams just play better and those are things you can't control. I worked real, real hard to build confidence and poise in my kids and spent a lot of time working on the fundamentals on the range."

HOW DID YOU MOTIVATE YOUR PLAYERS? "Most of my kids were pretty highly motivated on their own. So, for me it was more of a matter of keeping them going in the right direction. We spent a lot of time on the practice tee watching them hit balls and if a little change was needed, then I stepped in. But for the most part they were very self-motivated. The most important thing that I did was to compliment them when they hit good shots. I wanted to constantly build their confidence, that was the key. I just worked with them on getting the club face square at impact and from there good things would happen. I never tried to overhaul their swings, I just worked with what they had so that they could be consistent. They truly believed in themselves and once kids believe that they can do anything, success in inevitable."

WHO WERE YOUR COACHING MENTORS? "I learned so much from Ed Hendrickson, the legendary Edina track coach who I was an assistant under for 12 years. He taught me so much about how to get kids to play their best. Ed won several state track titles at Edina and was really a coaching legend. His specialty was quarter milers, but he could do it all and really got the best out of his kids. He was just an absolute magician. He started back in 1955 and coached for over 30 years. He also coached the cross country teams at Edina too. You know he was a real tactician with the kids. He was the kind of guy who would give a speech and all of the kids would turn and say 'what in the world is he talking about?' But the one kid that the entire speech was directed to, knew. And that was Ed, he was great."

LOOKING BACK WHAT ARE YOU MOST PROUD OF IN

YOUR CAREER? "I have had a lot of kids who have gone on to become very successful in life and that makes me very proud. I would also say the improvement that some teams and some individuals made during their time with me was very rewarding to see too."

HOW DID YOU BUILD TEAM UNITY & CHEMISTRY? "I never had a No. 1 player, I always moved them around depending on how they were playing. Even back in the mid-1990s when we had Kalen Anderson and Hilary Homeyer dominating every week, I still tried to mix them up to play with the other girls. I thought that was important because not only did it give the girls something to shoot for every week, but it also taught the better players how to play with the No. 5 and No. 6 girls. They then raised the level of play with the lower kids, and it helped to build the entire team up. I always thought it was a total team effort though, and you needed four good scores to win. I impressed on the kids that we had six good golfers who were trying to post those four scores, and that they all needed to step up and play together as a team."

WHAT MOTIVATED YOU? "I always have enjoyed teaching and coaching. For me it was really just a joy to go to practice because our kids were so good to work with. I don't think I ever had a kid who ever showed any form of disrespect, and they worked very hard. They also listened very well and I appreciated that. I had a lot of respect for my kids and I think it was mutual. You know, sometimes if we were really beating an opponent, I told my kids that when the match was over, I always hoped that the girls on that other team went home saying 'I'd rather golf with an Edina girl than anyone else.' That was often our objective, based on how we conducted ourselves on the golf course. We didn't have any temper tantrums because I didn't tolerate them. Nor did I tolerate any inappropriate behavior. Because that not only reflects on the kids but it reflects on the team and the school."

WHAT'S THE BIGGEST THING YOU'VE LEARNED FROM COACHING THAT YOU'VE BEEN ABLE TO APPLY TO YOUR EVERYDAY LIFE? "With my own children, I have been more positive. I have given them more positive reinforcement, given them more confidence in what they do and what they are capable of doing. And, the bottom line is that whatever you do, you need to be happy. If you are not happy, why do it?"

WHAT ARE THE KEY INGREDIENTS TO CREATING A CHAMPIONSHIP TEAM? "Naturally, you have to have some kids with ability. Beyond that, the most important thing is the thought process a kid has where they believe in their mind that they can make this put, or they can hit that shot. And if they didn't, then to know that they could hit the next one. Golf is so mental and the best kids can not only play good golf, but they can handle the mental side of the game. When kids play with confidence, they often play about two levels higher than what they even thought they could have played at."

ON PARENTS: "You know, I don't think I have ever seen a really successful athlete who didn't have very good parental support. That is also important, to have good kids with good backgrounds. I have always felt that if the parents couldn't support the coach, then they should take their kid somewhere else, because it was the kid who was going to pay the price. At that point the kids don't know whether to listen to their parents or the coach, and then they lose their confidence. The conflict that is created then leads to failure or certainly a much lesser performance. So, having parents that are supportive in the right way is very important to each individual and to the team's success."

WHAT'S THE SECRET TO YOUR SUCCESS? "I had a lot of help from other coaches. I never thought that I had all the answers. I was a good listener and never felt that I was above a suggestion which might help my team. I also watched a lot of videotape along the way to get better and I just worked very hard. And, I stressed very hard in practice to be perfect. If we were putting, we wanted to make five out of five, not four out of five, and if we were shooting free throws, we wanted to make 10 out of 10, not eight out of 10. That was very important to me and to the success of our teams."

WHAT WOULD YOU WANT TO SAY TO YOUR FANS, BOOSTERS, AND ALUMNI WHO HAVE SUPPORTED YOU ALL THESE YEARS? "It was a privilege, joy and pleasure for me to work with their daughters and sons. The parents that I had for the most part were just wonderful, so thanks for all your support."

HOW DO YOU WANT YOUR COACHING EPITAPH TO READ — HOW DO YOU WANT TO BE REMEMBERED AS A COACH? "I guess I would like to be remembered as a person who had great respect and as someone who enjoyed working with young people. Hey, it was great and I wouldn't have missed this for the world. It was a wonderful experience and I was so lucky to be a part of a such a great group of kids. We had something very special going here and to see the success of the kids along the way was just tremendous."

BRAD JAMES: GOPHER GOLF

Brad James, originally from Queensland, Australia, played for the Gophers from 1993-96, graduating with honors with a degree in kinesiology and sports management. After serving as an assistant, James took over as the head coach of the Gophers in 2002. That same year he made history en route to leading the Gophers to the NCAA title — making Minnesota the first northern team since Ohio State in 1979 to capture the crown. And, his boys did it in a dramatic fashion. In a tie for 16th place and trailing the leader by 10 shots after two rounds, James' Gophers chipped away at the lead, shooting the third day's top round, a 1-under 283. They were now just three shots behind Georgia Tech for the lead. Minnesota, led by All-Americans Justin Smith and Matt Anderson, then shocked the golf world by firing an amazing 6-under par 278 on the final day to claim the NCAA title by four shots. Regarded as one of the top young golf instructors in the state, as well as one of the hottest coaches in college golf, James and his wife Tanya presently reside in Minneapolis.

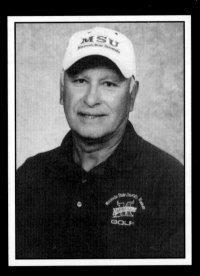

NICK CAMPA: MS-MANKATO WOMEN'S GOLF

Now in his 15th season as Mankato's women's golf coach, Nick Campa has become one of college golf's senior statesmen. Campa, a two-time District Coach of the Year (1998 and 2000) and three-time North Central Conference Coach of the Year (1998, 2000 and 2001), has led five MSU teams to North Central Conference titles (1989, 1995, 1996, 1998 and 2001). Campa has also sent nine teams to the national championship tournament and has placed third in three of those trips (1990, 1991, and 1992). In addition, Campa has coached five individuals to All-American status as well. Under Campa, the Mavericks have won more than 50 tournaments and have emerged as a division II golf power. Campa, who served as the Mankato West Senior High School assistant golf coach and was a junior high coach prior to his arrival at MSU in 1988, was also a captain in the Mankato Fire Department with 25 years of service.

LES BOLSTAD: GOPHER GOLF

New Prague native Les Bolstad has long been considered the godfather of golf in Minnesota. At just age 18, Bolstad became the youngest ever winner of a U.S. Public Links title, when he did so in 1926. As a golfer at the University of Minnesota, Bolstad went on to win two Big Ten titles. Bolstad would also go on to win Minnesota Public Links, State Amateur and State Open titles during his illustrious playing career as well. Bolstad would serve as the U of M's golf coach from 1947-76, and mentored many of the state's most successful golfers, including the legendary Patty Berg. Bolstad was later inducted into the Collegiate Golf Coaches Hall of Fame. In addition, in 1983 the University's Golf Course was renamed in his honor.

NANCY BAKER
COLLEGE GYMNASTICS: GUSTAVUS

Nancy Baker grew up in St. Peter and went on to graduate from Gustavus with a physical education degree in 1956. From there, Baker taught in North Mankato and St. Peter for two years before returning to her alma mater as a professor of physical education in 1958. (She would later get her master's degree at Mankato State University.) At Gustavus Baker would literally start the women's gymnastics program from scratch and then make history along the way. Initially, Baker worked with Bill Watson, the owner of a highly regarded school of gymnastics in Minneapolis, to organize gymnastics workshops for teachers and participants which turned out many of the top coaches and gymnasts in the region during the 1960s. Under Baker's direction, Gustavus sponsored the first women's gymnastics meet in Minnesota back in 1963 and thus began a gymnastics dynasty that remains to this day.

From 1966, when the first state college meet was held, until 1982, when the state meet was no longer held, Baker led Gustavus to 15 titles in 17 appearances. Regional and national competitions commenced in the early 1970s and Baker again had her program at the front of the pack with a second-place finish at the first regional meet and an eighth place finish at the first national meet in 1971. In 1982, the Association for Intercollegiate Athletics for Women (AIAW) hosted its first national championship for small colleges and, sure enough, Gustavus walked away with the title. Baker led her team to seven small college national titles between 1982 and 1992, before finally calling it quits that same year. Her final numbers were simply mind-boggling. In her 30-year coaching career, Baker coached five All-Around National Champions, 14 individual event national champions and 34 All-Americans. Baker led 29 out of 30 teams to the national tournament, and that was when college gymnastics competed with divisions I, II and III all combined together. Gustavus went against the big boys without any athletic scholarships, yet were consistently among the top eight programs in the country.

Among Baker's many honors and accolades, she was named as the Division III National Coach of the Year in 1982, 1984, 1989 and 1992. In addition, Baker has been very involved in the organization and administration of small college gymnastics, having served as gymnastics chairperson for the AIAW, the National Association of Intercollegiate Athletics (NAIA) and the National Collegiate Gymnastics Association (NCGA). Baker's contributions to the athletic department have not been limited to gymnastics either, as she has also coached the swimming team and served as the Director of Women's Athletics from 1970-79.

Since retiring from coaching in 1992, Baker continued to teach classes in the health and exercise science department. She has taught for 43 years at Gustavus, the third longest professorship in the history of the University. She received the Edgar Carlson Award for innovative teaching from the College in 1983 and the College's Community Service award in 1990. Baker has also served 15 years on the St. Peter School Board as well.

An expert in biomechanics, movement and how one moves through space, Baker was not only an amazing teacher, she was one of the true pioneers of women's collegiate athletics. When it comes to women's gymnastics, Nancy Baker is a legend among legends with a truly remarkable legacy.

Nancy and her husband Richard presently reside on a lake outside of St. Peter in Kasota, on *Baker Bay Road*... and yes, they are the Baker's! They have two children, Geri and Pat, both of whom graduated from Gustavus. Now retired, Baker still gets to scratch her musical itch by playing in a swing band with her pals called the "Echo's," playing gigs all over Minnesota.

HOW WOULD YOU DESCRIBE YOUR COACHING STYLE? "I worked with quite gifted students at Gustavus who were at the top of their class both academically and athletically. So, when you have students of great mental ability and also of great athletic ability, because of their genes, that is a win-win combination. My philosophy was to try to develop each child to their maximum ability. When you are dealing with a gifted mind, you never have to tell your students twice because they hear you the first time. So, my expectations of them were to enjoy their athletic experience but I also felt that there was a priority in life that had to balance out. Because I worked for a private institution, when I recruited my kids I told them that God was first, their family was second, academics was third and gymnastics was always fourth. We always had fun in addition to getting the maximum ability out our of our kids, and that was why I think I we were so successful."

HOW DID YOU MOTIVATE YOUR ATHLETES "I was very positive about their strengths. Because I have an expertise in biomechanics I could instruct them where errors may have occurred so that we could work on that so that. Then, they would always have a goal and they could correct that errors immediately so that we could get on to the next goal. The motivation was to say 'where do we want to be by the end of the season?' and the answer was always, the nationals. So, we set short range and long range goals for each student and then worked towards reaching them. It was a program in which success bred success. As soon as an athlete learned one skill, she would go on to master the next, and so on. Every time they attained that goal, the feeling of success was the key to motivation. Then, the support of the entire team was also important. I think that everybody felt a sense of belonging on the team, even if they were on the junior varsity."

LOOKING BACK WHAT ARE YOU MOST PROUD OF IN YOUR CAREER? "I am most proud of the success that my students have had in their lives. It really has nothing to do with their athletic ability. I am also proud of the fact that so many of my former students have gone on to become coaches, I think there are 28 of them and there may be more. Now, all of those women are helping children and that is very rewarding to see."

WHAT WAS THE KEY TO RECRUITING? "Being honest with your students and telling them what your expectations were. If they thought they were going to get away from their moms and dads when they came to college, they were wrong, because I was there. I kept track of them and after they knew what I expected of them, then it was up to them as to whether or not they wanted to be under my tutelage or not."

HOW DID YOU BUILD TEAM UNITY & CHEMISTRY? "Girls are interesting to coach. They just plain clicked because they got along with each other. We had very few temperamental students in all my years and I was lucky for that. One thing we did to create team unity was to always celebrate everybody's birthday, that was extremely important. Then, I would say the first 15 minutes of every practice was spent socializing while we were all stretching, and that helped too to in creating chemistry. We also got away as much as we could and got together socially, which was tough being on a very limited budget. We were like a family though and the girls were like sisters. They really depended on each other and for the most part I think they became sincere friends. I just provided them the opportunity to be together and they took over from there."

WHAT MOTIVATES YOU? "It was the students who motivated me. You know, my biggest job was to unlock the door to the gym. The rest of it just happened."

WHAT ADVICE WOULD YOU HAVE FOR YOUNG COACHES STARTING OUT TODAY? "Don't get lost in the winning and losing because you have to teach children how to win in life. Also, be kind to your students, understand them and listen to them. Then, teach them to say 'please' and 'thank you,' or 'how may I be helpful to you?'. Those are all very important things in life."

WHAT ARE THE KEY INGREDIENTS TO CREATING A CHAMPIONSHIP TEAM? "If you are going to have a championship team then the recruiting is very important because the children need to be taught young. And that really applies to everything. I mean if you are going to learn to read well, you must read early and often. If you are going to play a musical instrument, you better start by the time you are in the third grade. It is just introducing these children early on and taking advantage of those brain cells — because they are just like sponges at that point. Then, encourage them to develop at an orderly progression. In other words, you don't jump to Z before you have ABC mastered. If we do this with everything, and get them hands on, they will learn and they will remember much better later in life. Teaching is just so important and it makes a big difference. It comes back to work ethic and mastering of skills. It is not being No. 1 in the nation, that is not what makes winning. Winning is winning in life, not winning on a court or a field as far as I am concerned. With that philosophy, I have had a heck of a lot of success."

WHAT'S THE SECRET TO YOUR SUCCESS? "I have a solid philosophy. If you care about your students, they feel that and they will give you their maximum effort. Then, you have to have a lot of laughter too."

WHAT WOULD YOU WANT TO SAY TO YOUR FANS, BOOSTERS, AND ALUMNI WHO HAVE SUPPORTED YOU ALL THESE YEARS? "I would thank them for the opportunity of a lifetime. It has been a privilege and a pleasure. Gymnastics has allowed me to see the world and I couldn't be more appreciative of their support."

HOW DO YOU WANT YOUR COACHING EPITAPH TO READ — HOW DO YOU WANT TO BE REMEMBERED AS A COACH? "That I cared about my students, that is how I want to be remembered."

MARTHA NAUSE: MACALESTER GOLF

Martha Nause, a St. Olaf College graduate, recently took over as the head men's and women's golf coach at Macalester College, where big things are expected under her tutelage. Nause, a 22-year LPGA tour veteran who recently retired, had an illustrious professional career. Nause had three tour wins, including a win at the prestigious du Marier Ltd. Classic in 1994, an LPGA major championship. In addition, Nause also won the 1991 Chicago Sun-Times Shoot-Out and the 1988 Planters Pat Bradley International as well. Nause also played on winning teams for the USA against Japan in the Nichirei Cup in 1988, 1991 and 1994 too. In addition, Nause has conducted numerous clinics on all phases of the game of golf and has attended teaching seminars by Manuel de la Torre, PGA Teacher of the Year. A member of the LPGA Player Council, Nause also served as a non-voting member of the LPGA Executive Committee. In 1995 she was the winner of the Heather Farr Player Award, which "recognizes an LPGA tour player who, through her hard work, dedication and love of the game, has demonstrated determination, perseverance and spirit in fulfilling her goals as a player." The first woman inducted into the St. Olaf College Athletic Hall of Fame, Nause is also in the Wisconsin Golf Hall of Fame.

VICTOR DUNDER: DULUTH CENTRAL HIGH SCHOOL SKIING

Long considered to be the father of high school skiing, Victor Dunder Sr. was born in Sweden in 1901. When he was two years old, his family emigrated to America and settled in Two Harbors. Dunder would go on to graduate from Two Harbors High School, where he played basketball and football. Dunder then attended college at the University of Minnesota and was a star guard on the Gopher Basketball team, graduating in 1926. From there, Dunder went on to teach accounting and coach basketball at Stillwater High School. He later moved on to teach and coach in Willmar, and, after earning his master's degree from Iowa State University, accepted a teaching and coaching position at Duluth Central High School. There, Dunder taught physical education and coached football, basketball and even fly casting. In 1931, Dunder organized the first ever high school level ski competition in the United States, the "Arrowhead Ski Tournament," and that next year it was turned into the first Minnesota State High School Ski Tournament. The first state tournament was held at Duluth's Chester Bowl and consisted of just ski jumping, while that next year cross country skiing was added. Dunder's Duluth Central Trojans would dominate the event, and would go on to win four state championship titles. (The program would win 19 in all!) Dunder retired as the athletic director for all of the Duluth Public Schools in 1966 and died in 1983. Victor and his wife Judi had three children: Victor Jr., Mary Beth and Will. A man with a vision, Victor Dunder was an icon in the world of high school skiing.

DEBBIE DRISCOLL
HIGH SCHOOL GYMNASTICS: MAHTOMEDI

Debbie Driscoll grew up in Bloomington and graduated from Bloomington Kennedy High School in 1973. She then went on to graduate from Gustavus, where she got a teaching degree in physical education and health, and also starred on the gymnastics team. Her first teaching and coaching job was at Mahtomedi High School and 26 years later she is still there, going strong. Among her many coaching accolades, Driscoll has taken a team to the state tournament all but five times in her 26 year coaching career and has won an amazing 10 state team titles along the way. She is among the winningest gymnastics coaches of all-time in the state of Minnesota and is a real high school coaching legend. Among her many coaching awards and accolades, in 2002 Driscoll became the first high school coach ever to be inducted into the University of Minnesota Gymnastics Hall of Fame.

HOW WOULD YOU DESCRIBE YOUR COACHING STYLE? "The key is finding what motivates each gymnast. I don't think you can treat them all the same. Sure, you have to have the same rules and guidelines for each of them to follow, but you can't coach them all the same because they respond very differently. That is what I really like about coaching, to try and figure out how to reach each kid and motivate them to be their best. Some of them want a personal relationship with you while others don't want to be talked to outside of the gym."

HOW DO YOU MOTIVATE YOUR PLAYERS? "The truly motivated kid is intrinsically motivated and will motivate herself with just a little bit of a push. Then you have kids who need extrinsic motivation and all the little gimmicks that go along with it. So, I am just positive with all my kids and I try to reinforce what they are doing well. One example that has worked well for me is what I call my 'coupon program.' The way it works is that kids are motivated on small levels based on how they achieve. So, in the process of learning a certain skill, doing well in a meet or achieving a high score at a meet, they can earn a coupon. It is a little piece of paper that says 'you've done good,' and if they earn 25 coupons in a season then they get a free gymnastics tee-shirt. And, believe it or not, my kids are just obsessed with these tee-shirts. I have done this for years and years and my kids just can't get enough of it. So, little things like that I think are great motivational tools."

WHO WERE YOUR COACHING MENTORS? "Nancy Baker was my coach at Gustavus and was a real mentor to me. She did so much to get the sport started and is just such a great person."

LOOKING BACK WHAT ARE YOU MOST PROUD OF IN YOUR CAREER? "It is not so much all the titles, but really it is the kids. When they come back to see me after they graduate, that is so great. When they say 'thanks, you did this for me,' or 'thanks, this was really great,' that is just so neat. I had one girl who I hadn't heard from in 10 years and she wrote me a letter to invite me to her wedding and to tell me that I was so important to her. That is the stuff that means the most to me, that I was a special person in their lives."

HOW DO YOU BUILD TEAM UNITY & CHEMISTRY? "It is tough to get and you don't always have it. I try to get it by motivating my kids to understand that the team win is a lot more important than an individual win. I think that girls can be really competitive and jealous of one another, so you have to make sure that your kids all get

along. I don't encourage my kids to beat one another in competition, I just want them to do their best. I tell them I don't care which girl wins an event, just as long as it is a girl from Mahtomedi."

WHAT MOTIVATES YOU? "I have just always really loved this sport. I teach because it is a great job, but it also affords me the opportunity to coach, and that is what I love doing."

WHAT ADVICE WOULD YOU HAVE FOR YOUNG COACHES STARTING OUT TODAY? "We really need more coaches for our sport. It is hard for women to stay in the field because of their families and commitments. I have been fortunate to have a husband who is also a phys-ed teacher and a coach, so we have worked our seasons around each other. He is very supportive of me and of my career and I am lucky. I have known so many other women coaches who have had to quit because of family commitments, and that is tough. Families are more important, that is for sure. But it is hard to see, because our sport desperately needs new blood. So, for advice I would just say stay with it because our women athletes need more women coaches for women's sports. Try and find a way to make it work. Keep coaching and don't drop out after a few years, stick with it. We need you."

FAVORITE LOCKER ROOM SIGN? "It is not a question of getting rid of the butterflies, it is getting them to fly in formation."

WHAT'S THE BIGGEST THING YOU'VE LEARNED FROM COACHING THAT YOU'VE BEEN ABLE TO APPLY TO YOUR EVERYDAY LIFE? "Discipline. I think you have to be disciplined in athletics, especially in gymnastics. There is just so much that goes into it with the strength conditioning, the fear factor and in setting goals to reach certain skills."

WHAT IS THE KEY TO GOOD TIME MANAGEMENT? "I believe in the saying: 'if you need something done, ask a busy person to do it.' You have to discipline your whole life that way. I also make a lot of lists, otherwise I would never get anything done."

WHAT ARE THE KEY INGREDIENTS TO CREATING A CHAMPIONSHIP TEAM? "You have to have a lot of talent for starters. You know, once you create a winning program it just feeds off of itself though. Once we started winning it just rolled and rolled and rolled. Then, the younger girls want to come out for the team because they see that success. So, it builds upon itself."

WHAT'S THE SECRET TO YOUR SUCCESS? "Dedication and not being afraid to put in the hours. You also have to be committed to the kids because they can tell if you are phony or not."

HOW DO YOU WANT YOUR COACHING EPITAPH TO READ — HOW DO YOU WANT TO BE REMEMBERED AS A COACH? "That I really cared about the girls. My daughter was on the team three years ago and when she graduated it took on new meaning again in that now all of these girls are my kids again. I feel like I have my own kid raised and she is off in the real world, so I have taken on these other kids to be my daughters. That is a wonderful feeling. So, it wasn't just about winning for me, it was about making a difference in my kids' lives — all of my kids."

MILAN MADER
HIGH SCHOOL GYMNASTICS & VOLLEYBALL: LAKEVILLE

Milan Mader was born and raised in Czechoslovakia prior to World War II. His family survived the war and was able to overcome the communist regime. In school, Mader enjoyed long distance running and later went on to compete on the Czech National Track team for seven years. Mader would later attend an institute for teachers in the Czech Republic and got married at the age of 25 in 1968, shortly after the Soviet invasion. That next year he emigrated to the United States and wound up in Minnesota because his brother was at the University of Minnesota doing research. Mader got his first teaching job in the Robbinsdale school district and later wound up teaching and coaching track, volleyball and soccer at Cooper High School. In 1975 his athletic director joked that since he was from Europe, he must know a thing or two about gymnastics. So, he started the gymnastics program there too.

In 1977 the Lakeville girls gymnastics and track coaching position came available and Mader decided it would be a good fit. So, he made the move and has since become a Lakeville coaching legend. Mader would go on to teach junior high physical education within the school district, while coaching at the high school. In gymnastics Mader has built a dynasty where his teams have won 10 state championships. In volleyball, Mader is also a coaching guru, having led the Lakeville volleyball team to eight state tournament appearances and a pair of state runner-up finishes to boot. In fact, Mader is just one of three coaches in state history to win more than 600 games as a high school volleyball coach. His numbers are simply amazing, both in gymnastics as well as in volleyball. Milan Mader is without question a Minnesota coaching legend and is truly among the very best of the very best. Still going strong, Milan presently lives in the Twin Cities with his family.

HOW WOULD YOU DESCRIBE YOUR COACHING STYLE? "I grew up in a much different athletic system. In Czechoslovakia there were no organized athletics in schools, it was all in clubs. In fact, from the time I was 17 to 30 years old, I had only one coach. He instilled good work ethics in me though and I have carried that forward to my kids here too. As for me, I work very hard. It takes time to have a successful program too. Slowly and gradually the program started to become successful here and that was all from the hard work and great dedication from our girls."

HOW DO YOU MOTIVATE YOUR PLAYERS? "I have a very good coaching staff which is very knowledgeable and professional. Gymnastics is a sport of no mistakes with a lot of pressure, and our coaching staff works well with our kids to help them do their best. It is tremendously demanding for them, especially our younger girls who are in the eighth and ninth grade, so we just try to work with them the best that we can so they can achieve their goals. I have such admiration for these girls because of their dedication. They could play other sports and not have to work and train so hard, but they love it and when they feel that way about something, then they can motivate themselves to do well. I believe that our success is not because we have better athletes than anybody else, but because our athletes train harder than anybody else."

LOOKING BACK WHAT ARE YOU MOST PROUD OF IN YOUR CAREER? "I am proud to have planted a good seed in the minds of my kids. To see my kids go on to become successful in life and become good citizens is so gratifying. I always tell my kids that the skills they learn along with their dedication, will make them successful people later in life."

HOW DO YOU BUILD TEAM UNITY & CHEMISTRY? "We always stress the team concept and that it is 'we not me.' We have had so many individual state champions here through the years and sometimes I can't even remember their names or their performances, but I always remember the teams. I never forget our teams."

WHAT MOTIVATES YOU? "Whether it is volleyball or gymnastics, I just love to teach and coach these kids. I have coached a sport in every season since 1974, which is something like 85 straight back-to-back-to-back seasons without a break. So, I work very hard and am motivated by seeing my kids do well. It is my life and I love it. It is not the winning or the success, really, it is just walking into the gym and working with young people. It is certainly not a financial motivation, but I am rich in other ways by having all of these great relationships."

WHAT ADVICE WOULD YOU HAVE FOR YOUNG COACHES STARTING OUT TODAY? "Be honest and stick with it. We don't do it for money, we do it for the love of these kids and we can't forget that. They depend on us to be there for them."

WHAT ARE THE KEY INGREDIENTS TO CREATING A CHAMPIONSHIP TEAM? "You have to have the proper preparation, repetition and work on the details. In gymnastics it comes down to the very little things, so we prepare hard and try to get ourselves ready both mentally and physically. I would also say that in gymnastics it all comes down to the balance beam, that is what makes it or breaks it for you. So, we try to work extra hard on that."

WHAT'S THE SECRET TO YOUR SUCCESS? "I think honesty and hard work. It is the soul of an immigrant to really do anything to survive, and I have worked very hard. Also, we have a great facility here in Lakeville. When we opened this school back in 1993 the superintendent told me that we would have a permanent gymnastics facility and that has meant everything. There are so few in the state, but it helps us tremendously. It is a great commitment to our kids and it has helped us build up our program to what it is today. For the kids, to have their equipment and apparatus up all year round for them to use, that is a very big advantage for us. So many other schools have to take down and put up their equipment between seasons or even between practices, so that has been great for us. It is also nice for the kids in this area who don't have to spend a lot of money to go to private clubs. They can train and work right here and that is so nice. I mean hockey rinks are built for hockey and tennis courts are built for tennis, so it is nice to have someplace just for gymnastics."

WHAT WOULD YOU WANT TO SAY TO YOUR FANS, BOOSTERS, AND ALUMNI WHO HAVE SUPPORTED YOU ALL THESE YEARS? "I am an immigrant and I am very proud to be a citizen of this country. This community has given me a chance and I appreciate that very much."

HOW DO YOU WANT YOUR COACHING EPITAPH TO READ — HOW DO YOU WANT TO BE REMEMBERED AS A COACH? "I was honest and true to the game. I worked very hard and tried my best to help the kids achieve their goals."

FRED ROETHLISBERGER
COLLEGE GYMNASTICS: UNIVERSITY OF MINNESOTA

Fred Roethlisberger grew up in Milwaukee and got into gymnastics at an early age, starting first with the Milwaukee Turners club. Following his prep days, he went on to star at the University of Wisconsin, where he became the first individual to receive the school's Athlete of the Year Award while participating in a sport other than football or basketball. He would earn his bachelor's degree in 1966 and his master's in 1970. From there, Fred went on to captain the 1967 Pan Am Team in Winnipeg, winning gold medals in the all-around, high bar and parallel bars at the competition. That next year Roethlisberger become the second-highest scorer for the U.S. squad in Mexico City at the 1968 Olympic Games.

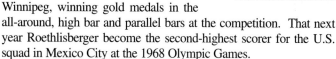
Marie, John & Fred

Roethlisberger then began his illustrious coaching career, first at Wisconsin-Whitewater in 1968. In 1971, he came to the University of Minnesota, where he assisted head coach Pat Bird for one season before being named as the head coach the following season. Since then, he has been a fixture in Minnesota sports, building the Golden Gopher gymnastics program into a Big Ten and national power. Now entering his 32nd season with the program, Roethlisberger has led the Gophers to 11 Big Ten titles (four in the '70s, three in the '80s and four in the '90s). He has also coached a total of 22 All-Americans during his tenure. In addition, his gymnasts have captured 50 individual Big Ten titles and his program has continually produced U.S. National Team members.

Roethlisberger has also been an active figure in the efforts of the U.S. National Team and has participated in a wide variety of international competitions in which he has served as a coach of the U.S. contingent. Furthermore, Roethlisberger was president of the Elite Coaches Association and also served on the USA Gymnastics Men's Program Committee for nine years — three as chairman and five as the board of directors.

Among his many coaching accolades, Roethlisberger has been named the Big Ten Coach of the Year four times (1990, '91, '92 and '95) and the Mideast Region Coach of the Year five times (1972, '78, '89, '90 and '92). The U.S. Gymnastics Federation selected him as their Coach of the Year on four occasions as well (1990, '92, '93 and '95). Additionally, Roethlisberger was inducted into the U.S. Gymnastics Hall of Fame in 1990 as a gymnast, coach and contributor, and also the Wisconsin Sports Hall of Fame as well.

Fred is presently married to Connie Foster, who is the Dean of Education at the University of Wisconsin-River Falls. Together, they have one son, Gus. Roethlisberger also has two children from a previous marriage who went on to become All-American gymnasts at the University of Minnesota. His daughter, Marie, an M.D., was on the 1984 Olympic team as well as the 1983 and 1985 World Championship teams. His son, John, was a three-time Olympian and four-time national all-around champion, and is considered by many to be among the very best gymnasts in U.S. history. In the world of Minnesota gymnastics, Fred Roethlisberger is a legend. The modern patriarch of the sport in the Land of 10,000 Lakes, he is still going strong and making history along the way.

HOW WOULD YOU DESCRIBE YOUR COACHING STYLE? "I think you have to be obsessive compulsive and intense in terms of whatever you want to excel at."

HOW DO YOU MOTIVATE YOUR PLAYERS? "I guess I never really thought about it, I just expect it. I walk into the gym and I expect a lot of hard work. It is really about making known your expectations, and my kids know what I expect of them."

WHAT ARE THE CHARACTERISTICS OF WINNERS? "Aside from having some genetic gifts, it's an obsessive compulsive nature. In gymnastics it is just a dedication to gymnastics and exemplifying hard work."

LOOKING BACK WHAT ARE YOU MOST PROUD OF IN YOUR CAREER? "I am happy for our various championships and for the guys who made National and All-American teams, but there's really no one single thing — it's the culmination of many significant things."

WHAT IS THE KEY TO RECRUITING? "It's kind of like selling cigarettes, some kids catch on to some things and some catch on to others. It's an image thing and there is not a lot of substance there usually. I don't know why kids choose one place over another oftentimes. It's just an impression or a feeling that kids have and you don't know their desires are. You know sometimes they avoid you (your school) because they know you have a no excuses hard work type of atmosphere. Other times they like you (your school) because they think somebody on your team is cool. It is real hard to figure out at times, it really is."

IF YOU COULD MAGICALLY GO BACK IN TIME TO THE FIRST YEAR YOU WERE A HEAD COACH AND GIVE YOURSELF SOME ADVICE FOR THE FUTURE, KNOWING WHAT YOU KNOW NOW, BACK THEN, WHAT WOULD YOU SAY TO YOURSELF? "I would just do it all the same way — going at it hard and with a lot of intensity."

HOW DO YOU BUILD TEAM UNITY & CHEMISTRY? "I don't really worry too much about team unity. It might be nice to have but I think it is overrated for gymnastics. I mean you have unity when everybody does his job. If an individual does his job he basically says 'OK I did my job, now you do your job…', and the next guy says 'OK you did your job, now I am going to do my job…', and so on. It is a shared responsibility for everyone to just do their job, that is what unity is. Really, I just try and have everybody work hard. The people that don't want to work hard simply get pushed to the side. That way everybody is unified because the only people that are left are the ones who want to work hard."

WHAT MOTIVATES YOU? "I think the fear of failure is a big motivator for me. I just sort of latch on to things and become very intense and compulsive about them, and that is how I am with gymnastics."

WHAT ADVICE WOULD YOU HAVE FOR YOUNG COACHES STARTING OUT TODAY? "You have to be intense and you have to make it a lifestyle. It just has got to be a part of your thought process all of the time."

WHAT'S THE BIGGEST THING YOU'VE LEARNED FROM COACHING THAT YOU'VE BEEN ABLE TO APPLY TO YOUR EVERYDAY LIFE? "I think there is more from my everyday life that I apply to coaching. It's a back and forth thing. So, I don't really learn anything from coaching, I think mostly I have learned things from my parents growing up on how to work and how to be honest — all the things that help with coaching."

WHAT ARE THE KEY INGREDIENTS TO CREATING A CHAMPIONSHIP TEAM? "Scoring more points than the other team. I mean you have to take it one guy at a time and one tenth (scores are in tenths of points) at a time to maximize every individual score. That all goes back to how you train them in the gym."

WHAT WOULD YOU WANT TO SAY TO YOUR FANS, BOOSTERS, AND ALUMNI WHO HAVE SUPPORTED YOU ALL THESE YEARS? "We just had our 100 year reunion celebration and I guess what really moved me was seeing how many people that were there who really cared about our program. It was so surprising to see all of the people come out of the woodwork to help save our program this last year with all of their fundraising and genuine support. I appreciate having so many friends, many I didn't know were there. It was very moving to me because I am such an individualistic kind of person. It really made me stop, reevaluate and appreciate how many friends that I have and that the program has as well."

HOW DO YOU WANT YOUR COACHING EPITAPH TO READ — HOW DO YOU WANT TO BE REMEMBERED AS A COACH? "I would hope that my kids had a really good experience being on my teams; learned how to compete; had fun; and that they learned what it meant to invest a lot of effort into something."

VIC GUSTAFSON: GUSTAVUS SWIMMING

Vic Gustafson attended the University of Minnesota from 1936-39 and then finished his schooling at Gustavus in 1942. Then, after serving as an aviator in WWII, he returned to Gustavus in 1945 to teach physical education and coach the swimming team. From there, Gustafson became a Gusty legend, coaching swimming at the school from 1945-77. During his illustrious coaching career in St. Peter, Gustafson earned eight MIAC Championship (1949, 1952, 1955, 1956, 1957, 1958, 1959 and 1960), as well as eight second place conference finishes. Among Gustafson's many coaching awards and accolades, in 1973 he was given the College Swimming Coaches Association of America Distinguished Service Award. In addition, from 1967-77 he served as a member of the NCAA swimming rules committee and was also editor of the NCAA swimming guide for eight years as well. Gustafson also coached other sports at Gustavus through the years as well, including, track, hockey, golf, tennis and cross country. Vic and his wife Betty presently reside in St. Peter and have three children: Jerry, Judy and Jan.

STATE HIGH SCHOOL COACHES HALL OF FAME MEMBERS:

1980 Art Avis, Hutchinson, Wayne Courtney, Mpls. Roosevelt, George Haun, Staples, George "Baldy" Hays, Blue Earth, Stan Nelson, Anoka, Vern Morrison, St. Cloud Tech, George Rose, St. Paul Como, Norman Wagner, Fisher

1981 Ove Berven, Austin, Lloyd Holm, St. Louis Park, George Saunders, Pine City, Earle Teas, Pipestone, Clifford Thompson, Eveleth, Herb Wolf, Fairmont

1982 Oscar Almquist, Roseau, William Broekemeier, Cass Lake, Jerry Eckstein, Plainview, William Hansen, Willmar, John Hermes, Fergus Falls, Burt Munson, Mountain Lake, Herman Woock, Crosby Ironton

1983 Al Halley, Mpls Southwest, A.J. Kramer, Roseau, Ralph Peterson, Plainview, Bob Roy, St. Louis Park, Granville Smith, Park, Arnold Veglahn, St. James

1984 Verne Herman, Plainview, Butzie Maetzold, Hopkins, Ralph Skay, Thief River Falls, Ab Strommen, Park, Louis Todnem, Mankato West

1985 Fred Kellett, Brainerd, Steve Kerzie, Gilbert, John Nett, Winona Cotter, Milt Osterberg, Worthington, Rudy Rauker, Warroad

1986 Bruce Frank, LeSueur, Del Mollberg, Detroit Lakes, William Ochs, Bloomington, Lincoln, K.T. Smith, Breckenridge, Angelo Taddi, Nashwauk-Keewatin

1987 Duane Baglien, Edina, Chester Bisel, Lynd-Butterfield, Herb Claffy, Milaca, John Rengel, Staples, Dick Seltz, Austin

1988 Art Hass, Austin, Jim Hastings, Duluth Central, Dale Scholl, Redwood Falls, Lloyd Stussy, Wells-Easton, Don Swanson, Henry

1989 Jack Conley, Forest Lake, Wayne Dietz, Anoka, Roy Hokkanen, Cotton, Clyde McDonald, St. Paul Harding

1990 Jerry Bernatz, Chatfield, Leo Grossman, Wabasso, Dick Lynch, Silver Bay, Larry Ross, International Falls, Bob Ryan, St. Paul Humbolt, Archie Sailer, Frazee

1991 Ralph Boline, Fosston, Paul Busch, Roseville, Harlan Kirkeby, Lewiston. Tom Mahoney, Fairmont, Max West, Brownton

1992 John Conzemius, Wadena-Deer Creek, Mac Dahl, LaCrescent Les Drechsel, Crookston, Hugo Goehle, Hills-Beaver Creek, Al Wold, Rochester John Marshall

1993 Lloyd, Carlson, Win-E-Mac, John Davies, Crosby-Ironton, Don Fox, Austin Stan Otness, Farmington, Bob Turner, Como

1994 Kermit Aase, Brainerd, Willard Ikola, Edina, Angelo Pergol, Cloquet, Ron Raveling, Columbia Hts., Evar Silvernagle, Rochester

1995 Walter Chapman, John Marshall, Bernard Broderick, St Paul Murray, Richard Lawrence, Eveleth, Kerwin Engelhart, Rochester John Marshall, Tony Thiel, Battle Lake

1996 Malcom Doane, St Cloud Tech, Chuck Elias, Mpls. Central, Jim Gotta, Moorhead, Dave Peterson, Mpls. Southwest, Bill Selisker, Crosby-Ironton

1997 Edgar Braun, Norwood-Young America, Stav Canakes, Edina, Ron Malcom, Anoka, Steve Lipp, Breckenridge, Stanton Thorson, St. Paul Highland Park

1998 Lou Cotroneo, St Paul Johnson ,Pete Herges, Albany, Albert "Bud" Higgins, Austin, Ed Prohofsky, Mpls Marshall U High, Bill Rose, Rothsay

1999 Bill Hare, Greenway Coleraine, Mike Jurabek, Prior Lake, Pat Lanin, Hopkins, Jerry Snyder, Lake City, Richard Traen, Delano

2000 Noel Bailey, Aitkin, Darryl "Skip" Boyum, Northfield, Darien DeRocher, Foley, Jim Muchlinski, Marshall, Harold Schroeder, Blue Earth

2001 Len Olson, Owatonna, George Thole, Stillwater, Steve Kjornes, Westbrook - Walnut, Grove Guido Kauls, Minnehaha Academy, Tink Larson, Waseca

2002 Ken Baumann, Mahnomen, Klemet Haugen, Austin, Jerry Riewer, Staples, Grady Rostberg, Hutchinson, Richard Skoog, Duluth East

ALAN MERRICK
PRO SOCCER: MINNESOTA KICKS & STRIKERS

Alan Merrick grew up in Birmingham, England, where he loved to play soccer and cricket as a kid. Merrick was a tremendous athlete as a youngster and quickly moved up through the ranks as a soccer star. In 1968 Merrick represented England in the 1968 Junior World Cup in France, and then went on to play as a defender for nearly a decade in the English Premier Division — the country's top professional circuit. In the mid-1970s Alan moved across the pond to play professional soccer. He would ultimately wind up in the Land of 10,000 Lakes, where he became the captain of the upstart Minnesota Kicks, an NASL franchise which had just been relocated from Denver. A playoff run that year saw the Kicks eventually lose to Pele's New York Cosmos, but it appeared that pro soccer was here to stay. From 1977-81, Merrick led the Kicks to several division titles, all the while entertaining the countless thousands of fans who came out to support them at old Metropolitan Stadium in Bloomington. The club averaged nearly 23,000 fans per game during one stretch, which was among the highest attendance in the league.

In 1979 the Kicks switched over to play in the NASL Indoor League before eventually folding in 1981. Merrick would later play for the US National Team which was called "Team America," the U.S. Olympic team in training. In 1984 the Ft. Lauderdale Strikers moved to Minnesota, and the team was renamed as the Minnesota Strikers. At the conclusion of the 1984 season, however, the Strikers left the NASL and moved to the MISL Indoor League. Merrick would go on to serve as the head coach of the Strikers for all four years of the club's existence and was even named Soccer Digest's MISL Coach of the Year on two different occasions. Then, in 1988, and after a 107-97 overall record, the franchise folded. Pro soccer wouldn't return again until 1994, when the Minnesota Thunder hit the grass, playing in the USISL. Meanwhile, Merrick went on to become a soccer legend in Minnesota. Over the past 20 years, he has been part of thousands of clinics and coaching sessions, greatly impacting the sport throughout the Midwest. Merrick is regarded as a master coach holding the USSF and Canadian "A" licenses, as well as the English F.A. Coaching Badge and the NSCAA Premier Classification. Alan is presently the head coach of the University of Minnesota Men's Soccer Club team and also owns the Alan Merrick Soccer Academy in Lakeville, which operates clinics nationwide.

HOW WOULD YOU DESCRIBE YOUR COACHING STYLE? "I would describe my style, in a word, as creative. It was a whole new environment from which to play in, let alone coach from, because we went from playing outdoors on a large grass field, to playing indoors on a hockey sized rink with Astroturf. Our situation was such that we were an outdoor team that suddenly was confronted with the fact that we had to change over to play indoors. There were no longer 11 players on a side, and really the players had never played in that type of environment before. So, it was being creative with the roster of players that I inherited, many of whom were not suited for the indoor game. But, because they were brought to Minnesota to play outdoor soccer with the Strikers, their was a loyalty there to not jettison these guys away. It was a difficult transition. I had to manufacture ways for keeping players in an environment that didn't embarrass them. I watched an awful lot of film and tried to put in plays and systems that allowed all of our players to succeed."

WHAT ARE THE CHARACTERISTICS OF LEADERS? "I think they can put themselves into many different environments and then come together as pieces of a jigsaw puzzle. They need to be multifaceted; they need to have experienced it; they need to be real; and when they can project that to their teammates, then they will respect them.

LOOKING BACK WHAT ARE YOU MOST PROUD OF IN YOUR CAREER? "I was never ejected from a game and never had a red card. I respected the game as a player, respected it as a coach and I continue to respect it. The game is bigger than any one individual and any one team. I have never forgotten that."

HOW DID YOU BUILD TEAM UNITY & CHEMISTRY? "One of the first things I did was to create a committee which was comprised of several different players, usually including a senior pro, an American, and a European, who then served as a sort of leadership group. They were the ones who then did the disciplining on the team and if they couldn't handle it then I would step in. That brought a lot of unity immediately because I threw the ball back in their court. Sure, I was the ogre in many instances, but they policed themselves and questioned their own efforts and commitment. They even devised a disciplinary code as well as a fining system which they kept and did whatever they wanted to do with. They either gave that money to charity or donated it to a cause. It was up to them. Beyond that, all of the guys just got on the same page so that everyone could better understand what each other was doing. That way an individual wouldn't blame someone else for a mistake. We would also look at the film and analyze what went wrong and then try to fix it without blaming anyone. Like Minnesota, it was kind of a 'no fault' situation where we were all in it together."

WHAT MOTIVATED YOU? "I had always been on winning teams as a player and that transcended into my coaching. My motivation was also to just make it here. You see, I originally came here to Minnesota for a one month vacation. Then, after being here, I decided that this was a great place to live and raise my kids. So, I sold my property back in England and made a determination that I was going to make my new life here. That was a lot of pressure and certainly played a part in my motivation to be successful."

WHAT ADVICE WOULD YOU HAVE FOR YOUNG COACHES STARTING OUT TODAY? "Be patient and pay your dues.

FAVORITE LOCKER ROOM SIGN? "I don't believe in rah-rah, it makes the hairs on the back of my neck stand up. You do that after the fact and not before. Talk is cheap and I feel that you simply have got to go out there and perform."

WHAT'S THE BIGGEST THING YOU'VE LEARNED FROM COACHING THAT YOU'VE BEEN ABLE TO APPLY TO YOUR EVERYDAY LIFE? "Humility. You're only as good as your last good performance and you have got to sustain that without resting on your laurels."

WHAT'S THE SECRET TO YOUR SUCCESS? "It was creating the appropriate environments for players to succeed. It was also being realistic and knowing that there were going to be good times and bad times in any given game or any given season."

HOW DO YOU WANT YOUR COACHING EPITAPH TO READ — HOW DO YOU WANT TO BE REMEMBERED AS A COACH? "He made the game enjoyable for his players and allowed them to succeed. I also want to be regarded as somebody with substance."

PAT HAWS: ST. JOHN'S SOCCER

Pat Haws, a 1972 graduate of St. John's, will begin his 26th season as the Johnnies' head coach in 2003. One of the nation's winningest soccer coaches and the winningest in Minnesota college soccer history, Haws owns a 269-100-38 career record. In addition, Haws has posted a 177-53-26 record in the MIAC and has won six conference titles to boot. Haws was named as the MIAC Coach of the Year in 1986 and 1989 and was also the NCAA Division III Midwest Region Coach of the Year in 1986. Haws is the first soccer coach in MIAC history to win more than 200 games and coached his 400th career match in 2002. Haws took over the Johnnies soccer program in 1978 and since then his teams have finished in first or second place 14 times. At one stretch during the 1980s, SJU ranked seventh among all Division III teams in the nation with a .772 winning percentage. In NCAA Division III tournament play, SJU received playoff bids in 1986, 1989 and 1990. In addition, in 1986 and 1989, St. John's reached the Division III quarterfinals, only to lose both games by one goal each. In addition to becoming a soccer legend, Haws also started St. John's swimming and diving program. In fact, Haws was the program's first and only coach in the first 25 seasons of the sport in Collegeville, and built the program from the ground up before stepping down in 1998. Simply put, Pat Haws is among the very best of the best, and is still going strong.

DAVID GEATZ: GOPHER TENNIS

David Geatz grew up in Grand Forks, N.D., and went on to become one of the finest players in North Dakota tennis history. A three-time North Dakota High School state singles champion, Geatz finished his prep career undefeated in 103 matches. Honored as the North Dakota Athlete of the Year as a junior, he also claimed three state open singles titles. Then, as a freshman at New Mexico State, Geatz was conference runner–up in doubles and the league singles champion the following year. After transferring to New Mexico, he qualified for the NCAA Championships in singles. Geatz also claimed the WAC title in doubles his junior year as well. Following college, Geatz played in Europe as a pro, winning eight tournaments. (Geatz received his master's degree in sports administration in 1985 and his PhD in 1991 from New Mexico.)

In 1982 Geatz became the head coach at the University of New Mexico, posting a 121-65 record from 1982-87. That next year Geatz came to Minnesota, where he has been ever since. In his first season, he led the team to a 21-9 season, the Big Ten Championship and a berth in the NCAA Tournament. Since then, he has been dominant. Geatz has guided the Gophers to five Big Ten Championships in his 15 seasons at the helm and racked up nearly 300 wins along the way. In addition, he has been named Big Ten Coach of the Year three times (1991, 1992 and 1994) and was named Region IV Coach of the Year in 1994 and 2000. Overall, in 18 seasons as a collegiate head coach, Geatz's teams have put together 20-win seasons on 11 occasions and he has over 400 career wins. Geatz has also coached several student-athletes who went on to compete in the pro circuits as well. David and his wife Pam reside in Minneapolis and have one son, D.J., who was a freshman on the University of Nebraska Men's Tennis Team in 2002-03.

CHARLIE BANKS: DULUTH CENTRAL HIGH SCHOOL SKIING

Charlie Banks grew up in the 1930's in the Chester Bowl area of Duluth. It was there that Scandinavian immigrants taught Banks the Alpine and Nordic disciplines, lessons which would form the foundation of a lifelong passion. Banks went on to win the State Cross Country Skiing championship in 1942 at Duluth Central High School and then went into teaching and coaching. Banks would go on to teach and coach at Duluth Central High School for 27 years, leading his kids to two state championships along the way. In addition, he created a 10-kilometer trail system behind his home where many ski events were held, including the Erik Judeen Memorial Classic in 1960 and the USSA Junior Nationals in 1967. Banks was a lifelong member of USSA and active in promoting jumping and Nordic events in the Duluth area from the 1960's until his death in 1998. A tireless worker, Banks would drive his kids out to his trail 20 miles from the school, train, eat his supper, and then drive the kids back to Duluth where he would teach night school. All that, while he was raising four daughters of his own, teaching high school, and always making time to groom the trails. Banks' legacy will include the Erik Judeen Memorial Classic race, which is now over 40 years old; the Korkki Nordic Ski Center, which flourishes on the scenic trails he handcrafted with an axe and grub hoe back in 1954; and lastly a memorial fund that was established in his name that now assists cross country programs at area high schools. In the world of skiing, Charlie Banks was a an icon who truly made a difference.

BUZZ LAGOS
PRO & HIGH SCHOOL SOCCER: THUNDER & ST. PAUL ACADEMY

Buzz Lagos grew up in New Jersey and went to college at Providence, where he played freshman basketball. Believe it or not, Buzz didn't even play soccer in high school, he was a runner instead. Buzz got his degree in mathematics and wound up going to graduate school at the University of Minnesota. It was there that he began playing soccer. Buzz got his first job teaching math and coaching soccer at St. Paul Academy (SPA). There, he flourished as a coach, posting an amazing 256-55-35 career record and winning four state high school soccer titles along the way. Lagos' teams were dominant and were in the final four nearly every year he coached there. In all, Lagos taught Math at SPA for 25 years and coached the soccer team for 20 of those years — becoming one of the winningest high school soccer coaches in state history. At SPA Lagos also coached several future soccer stars, including his son, Manny Lagos, who went on to

play professionally in the first division. (In 2001 Manny led the San Jose Earthquakes to the Major League Soccer title.) Other future stars included Tony Sanneh, who went on to play on the U.S. National Team, and Amos Magee, who played for the MLS' Tampa Bay Mutiny.

Buzz became Minnesota's first coach to earn a U.S. Soccer Federation "A" license in 1978, and later put that to good use in 1990 when he co-founded the Minnesota Thunder, a professional A-League soccer franchise which plays its home game at the 15,000-seat National Soccer Center in Blaine. Fourteen years later, he is still going strong as the team's head coach. Among his many highlights with the Thunder included coaching his son, Manny, from 1990-96, and also leading his club to an A-League title in 1999. In addition, the club's appearance in the 2003 A-League Finals was their sixth in eight seasons along with 1994, 1995, 1998, 1999 and 2000. Among Lagos' many coaching accolades, he was named as the USL Coach of the Year in 1995, and was also selected to coach the 1999 A-League All-Star Game in Virginia Beach, Va., as well as the 1996 USL All-Star Game in Blaine. Prior to coaching the Thunder, Lagos helped coach the men's club team at the University of Minnesota and also scouted for the Minnesota Kicks back in the late 1970s and early 1980s as well.

Buzz would love nothing more than to turn his Thunder into an MLS franchise, but he knows that in order to move up to the next level he will need to get a new stadium — which isn't such a popular thing these days in the Land of 10,000 Lakes. A real soccer legend, Buzz, and his wife Sarah, presently reside in St. Paul, and have eight children and 22 grandchildren.

HOW WOULD YOU DESCRIBE YOUR COACHING STYLE? "I would say, in a word, cooperative. I try to work with my players in trying to get them to play their best and thereby making the team the best possible team it can become. I wouldn't call my style confrontational or dictatorial, nor would I call it laid back. But, I am in charge and I am the boss, make no mistake about that. I use my experiences to make the decisions, but I work with the players and realize that their input is very valuable. I would say my strengths include good organization, generating good ideas on how to play, how to make things fun and how to make it competitive. You know, I have always had that ability to have fun with my kids while staying competitive. We could all be laughing while working our butts off at the same time. That is what competition is all about."

HOW DO YOU MOTIVATE YOUR PLAYERS? "I have always felt that the key to motivation is good preparation. We train hard and get our players to push themselves to reach their highest level of potential. Fitness is key with me and I think once an athlete can train at the highest level, and is physically prepared, then motivation becomes pretty easy. I just set high expectations for them to be their best. You get their tempo up and appeal to their sense of responsibility, their pride, and you get them to play. There is not much more to it than that."

WHAT IS THE KEY TO GOOD TIME MANAGEMENT? "Being the coach of a team, as is being the member of a team, makes time management much easier because you have such a strong sense of responsibility to that team. So, that forces you to get organized, to be on time, and to focus because you want that team to be successful. After all, you don't want to be the one who holds them back. It really comes down to team motivation and the fact that everyone counts on everyone else for the team to do well. It is great when you get to a point where the team is so important that guys overlook their own bad habits and go beyond themselves to rise above it all."

WHAT ARE THE CHARACTERISTICS OF LEADERS? "Generally I have found that leaders have good character with high integrity, honesty, good communications skills, a solid work ethic and a positive attitude."

HOW DO YOU BUILD TEAM UNITY & CHEMISTRY? "I think it is important for your players to try and be friends on and off the field, because that builds chemistry. Whether that comes from non-soccer events like barbecues or playing golf as a group, that all goes into it. I also think it is important to get a lot of player involvement with regards to decision making. That is a valuable thing, to give them some ownership for the team. Then, I just feel that it is important to be a coach who is open and listens to his players. Sometimes it is a challenge to deal with all of the different nationalities and ethnicity's, but I really enjoy that aspect of soccer. It is very diverse and much more interesting. As far as chemistry goes, it is not so much about their diverse cultures or personalities, it is more about their diverse playing styles — that is where it gets challenging as a coach, to try and merge them together."

WHAT ADVICE WOULD YOU HAVE FOR YOUNG COACHES STARTING OUT TODAY? "You know, I think it is important to actually play this game, and stay in touch with what is happening out on the field. Even if you are not a top player, you need to play with the kids and be out there to get a sense of the game from that level. Beyond that, it is getting your soccer coaching education and that happens through experience — at all levels of the game, from kids to high school to coaching licensing courses. Then, I would strongly recommend going overseas to coach and learn the game. I lived in Uruguay for six months with my family in 1983 and that was an amazing experience. You need to always be a student of the game, and always try and have fun with it, that is very important."

WHAT'S THE BIGGEST THING YOU'VE LEARNED FROM COACHING THAT YOU'VE BEEN ABLE TO APPLY TO YOUR EVERYDAY LIFE? "There is a lot of intuition in my ability to coach and that has translated into my everyday life as well. The other thing would be organizational skills, which are certainly key for both coaching and in life."

WHAT ARE THE KEY INGREDIENTS TO CREATING A CHAMPIONSHIP TEAM?
"Number one would be getting good players, because you have to have talent. Then you have to have good chemistry and leadership from players with high character. Once you have that, then you have to mix them together with on-the-field training, as well as some off-the-field events, which brings your team together, and that all translates into success."

WHAT'S THE SECRET TO YOUR SUCCESS?
"I would have to say intuition and organization."

ON THE FUTURE OF SOCCER IN MINNESOTA:
"You know, we had a lot of success here over the years with the Kicks, Strikers and now the Thunder. It continues to grow in popularity at the high school level, but at the college level for boys, we have a lot of work to do. While most colleges have women's programs at the division one, two or thee levels, there are hardly any opportunities for young men. The MIAC schools offer men's soccer, but there are no public colleges in Minnesota where a young boy can go and play varsity soccer. That, in my opinion, is a tragedy and should be changed."

WHAT WOULD YOU WANT TO SAY TO YOUR FANS, BOOSTERS, AND ALUMNI WHO HAVE SUPPORTED YOU ALL THESE YEARS?
"I have to say first that I recognize that I wouldn't be where I am now without all the wonderful support that I have gotten through the years. I would say thanks to all of those people for their support and encouragement, it means a lot. I would also say that I consider myself to be very lucky to have been able to have the opportunity to be in the vanguard of this growth of soccer in our state. And, while I have been in the forefront for much of that growth, I would like to acknowledge so many others who have put in just as many hours as I have and have been just as dedicated with the same amount of enthusiasm. That is why soccer continues to grow and get better, because of all of the volunteers, coaches, parents and kids who make the game what it is today. I just really appreciate what they have all done. In addition, I would also like to thank my wife, Sarah, who has been such a supportive and valuable partner in my life.

HOW DO YOU WANT YOUR COACHING EPITAPH TO READ — HOW DO YOU WANT TO BE REMEMBERED AS A COACH?
"The thing I am most proud of is when my players have an enjoyable experience and are able to reach for their full potential as an individual and in the team context."

TOM VINING: ROSEVILLE HIGH SCHOOL TENNIS

Tom Vining is a high school tennis coaching legend. Vining first began coaching tennis at Brooklyn Center High School in 1968, after graduating from Minnesota State Mankato, where he played on the Maverick tennis team. After spending two years in the military, Vining got a job teaching English at Alexander Ramsey High School in 1971, and later became the head boys tennis coach that following Spring. Then, in the Fall of 1974, Vining became the coach of the newly created Ramsey girls tennis team. Since then, he went on to become the first high school tennis coach in Minnesota to earn 1,000 total victories (boys and girls). In 2002, and after 29 years, Vining retired from Roseville High School with a career record of 502-173. (Ramsey merged with Kellogg to form Roseville High School in the mid-1980s.) Then, in 2003, after 33 seasons with the boys, Vining retired with 504-224 mark. Although his teams never won a state championship, Vining regularly made appearances in the girls tournament, winning seven consecutive Section 3AA championships in one stretch, and 14 in all. In addition, his Raiders twice reached the Class AA state finals as well. Sure, the private schools are dominant in tennis and sure, Edina has won 40 championships since 1966 (19 in boys and 21 in girls), but the reality is that many of the kids who play for those schools learned that game via private lessons, and had more opportunities to spend their summers competing in U.S. Tennis Association tournaments. For guys like Vining, and others, like Bob Pivec, who won more than 900 matches at Coon Rapids, they weren't as fortunate to have their kids play all year round. Vining finished his illustrious career as the winningest coach in state history and as a true high school tennis coaching legend.

DENNIS DALE: GOPHER SWIMMING & DIVING

Dennis Dale graduated from the University of Minnesota with a bachelor's degree in business administration and physical education in 1967. That same year, the Gophers finished 10th at the national meet and Dale placed seventh in the 100 meter backstroke and led off the ninth-place 400 medley relay unit en route to garnering All-America honors. From there, Dale got into high school teaching and coaching at Burnsville High School, where over 12 years he would build the boys' and girls' swimming programs into a perennial state powerhouse. Dale's teams would win four state championships and he was honored as the state Coach of the Year in each of his final four seasons. While there, Dale also coached more than 20 prep All-Americans and a number of Junior Olympic finalists as well. In 1985 Dale came back to his alma mater to take over as the Gopher's head swimming and diving coach. Since then, he has become an institution.

Now entering his 19th season as the head coach of the Gopher program, Dale has been the driving force behind the University of Minnesota's resurgence onto the national collegiate swimming and diving scene. Minnesota has consistently finished among the top 10 at the NCAA Championships during this past decade, and much of that success has to do with Dale's ability to motivate and lead by example. Minnesota has placed among the top three in the Big Ten team race each of the past 13 seasons and has also won four Big Ten titles under Dale. Prior to winning the title in 1996, Minnesota had not won a conference title in 70 years! Under Dale's direction, Minnesota clinched the USA National Championship in April of 1998 at the U of M's Aquatic Center. Dale also led the Gopher Swim Club to a second-place finish at the 1991 Long Course Senior Nationals, where former U of M swimmer and All-American Del Cerney won Minnesota's first national title in more than 20 years in the 50 freestyle.

Behind Dale, the Gophers have posted a 137-26 overall record and for his efforts he has been honored as a five-time Big Ten Coach of the Year. Competing at the nationally renowned Aquatic Center, the Gophers have a first class facility for a first class program. In addition, Dale has also been involved in coaching on the international scene. He served as an assistant coach of the Brazilian National Team at the 2000 Olympic Games in Sydney, Australia; was an assistant coach of the 1998 U.S. Goodwill Games Team; was a member of the 1993 & 1995 Olympic Festival Coaching Staff; and coached the West team to victory at the 1995 Olympic Festival.

JOHN LEANEY
COLLEGE SOCCER: MACALESTER

John Leaney grew up in England, loving the sport of soccer. He went on to play "football" at Manchester University in England, and then got into coaching and teaching physical education at a school in England. His first big coaching gig came at the University of California, San Diego, where he built the women's program into a national power, and led them to the Final Four in 1986. That next year he came to Minnesota, to first take over as the Macalester men's soccer coach, and later the women's. He has since been coaching the men for 17 years, and the women for 15, making soccer history along the way.

Since his arrival at Macalester, he has simply dominated his competition. His first Macalester men's team went 10-4-2 and since then Leaney has led the Scots to seven MIAC crowns and eight NCAA playoff appearances. Mac won its third straight MIAC title in 1999 and then placed second in 2000 before capturing the MIAC title again in 2001 and 2002. He has been honored as MIAC Coach of the Year seven times and in 1990 and 1997 was named West Region Coach of the Year. The Scots have compiled an impressive 193-63-29 slate under Leaney for a winning percentage of .728 and have defeated some of the top programs in the country under his tutelage as well. Leaney also helped develop the school's first seven All-America players, five conference Most Valuable Players, as well as five professional soccer players.

On the women's side Leaney has been just as impressive. The Mac ladies have gone 202-48-16 in 14 seasons under Leaney for a winning percentage of .789. Macalester has captured six MIAC championships during his tenure (1992, 1997, 1998, 1999 , 2000 and 2001), and has allowed just five goals in league play over the last six seasons. Since the start of the '96 season, Leaney and the Scots have gone 116-15-9 (.861) while out-scoring their opponents 372-57. The 1998 NCAA Division III Coach of the Year, Leaney has been honored as conference and region coach of the year numerous times. In addition, he has developed 11 All-Americans, five conference MVPs and four Umbro Select All-Star Classic participants. Under Leaney, the Scots have made 10 appearances in the NCAA playoffs, including the 1998 national championship team which beat the College of New Jersey. The team had made the playoffs for seven straight seasons, before falling short in 2002, and also reached at least the national quarterfinals four times in the last seven years.

Combined, the Macalester men's and women's soccer teams have gone 395-111-45 under Leaney for an amazing .758 winning percentage. His teams have claimed 13 MIAC titles and been selected for the NCAA playoffs 17 times. He has coached a conference Player of the Year 11 times, as well as 17 All-Americans and 31 All-Region players. Simply put, John Leaney is a college soccer coaching legend and he has single handedly built the men's and women's soccer programs at Macalester College into national powers. Now entering his 18th season in St. Paul, Coach Leaney is still going strong and shows no signs of slowing down.

HOW WOULD YOU DESCRIBE YOUR COACHING STYLE? "I am actually a very simple coach. My coaching style comes down to this, 'what does it take to win a game?'. Some people have a negative connotation with that and think it is a 'win at all cost' philosophy, but it is not. I just think you have to have a winning attitude. We form our team strategy and tactics based on winning each particular game. We also don't really pay a lot of attention to our opponents, where a lot of other coaches do. My philosophy is that if

we do what we are good at doing, then they have to pay attention to us, and our defense is designed for everybody and not any one team in particular. You see, I am a great believer that you are in every game that you play if you play good defense. So, we start with basic fundamentals on defense and go from there. I was an attacking kind of player myself, so I have always wanted to be creative on offense, while maintaining a solid defense."

HOW DO YOU MOTIVATE YOUR PLAYERS? "I believe that players should be self-motivated, and if they are not then I am not really keen on trying to invent something for them. I also believe that you cannot have the same level of talk for every game because there are big games and there are games that are not so big. You can't fool intelligent players by pretending that a game is big when it in reality it is not. So, you need to find other ways to motivate. Sometimes I just remind them about how bad they will feel if they lose an upcoming game and don't prepare properly for it. I don't dwell on negativity, but I think that style works. That also gives me the opportunity to save those big time speeches for the big time games. You see, I do not believe that a player goes out onto the field and doesn't try, and I do not believe that a player goes out to deliberately do anything wrong. So, I do not believe in yelling at them. I think that men and women are different, because I coach both, but most certainly I get so much more out of women players by showing disappointment rather than anger. You have to work with each group differently, but the principles are the same."

IF YOU COULD MAGICALLY GO BACK IN TIME TO THE FIRST YEAR YOU WERE A HEAD COACH AND GIVE YOURSELF SOME ADVICE FOR THE FUTURE, KNOWING WHAT YOU KNOW NOW, BACK THEN, WHAT WOULD YOU SAY TO YOURSELF? "Oh, I was so awful then! As a young coach I was pretty impetuous. I used to think that if a player was potentially very good, then I would play them. My reason for doing that was that I figured that they were only going to be better anyway, so why not just put them in there. But, that was a big mistake because a lot of them floundered and struggled, which ultimately hurt their confidence. So, now I am very careful about bringing players in. They have to absolutely have to be ready to play. It is all about their maturity, before their ability level. Timing is everything and that is something I have gotten a lot better at in my later years."

LOOKING BACK WHAT ARE YOU MOST PROUD OF IN YOUR CAREER? "I am most proud of our phenomenal graduation record. Beyond that, our national championship in 1998 was very, very special. The way that we did that was even more special than the actual victory itself. All of the teams that we beat were better than us and it was just a massive overachievement. It was done with team chemistry and it was just a great group of kids. We did it with fantastic student athletes who got great grades and did everything they were supposed to do in college. Now, to see those kids as they are getting older, it is great to feel like I am someone that they still look up to."

WHAT IS THE KEY TO RECRUITING? "The key to recruiting is being honest. If you are absolutely honest with the kids then they respect that. As a salesman selling your program, I have always felt that being honest was the best policy, even if you lose some kids in the process. I don't lie to them about what they can expect here and that is important to me. I also believe that your best recruiters are your kids because they tell it like it is."

HOW DO YOU BUILD TEAM UNITY & CHEMISTRY? "I don't think you can. I think what you can do, however, is to create an environment for it. To try to make chemistry doesn't work. But, if you create an environment where people are on the same page and they have the same goals, then it is a happy, positive environment that people want to belong to. I also believe in humor, which builds unity within a group. In addition, I firmly believe that at the end of a game it is over. Period. There is no crying. There is no dwelling on it. I tell my players that by the time they are out of that shower I don't want to see anybody talking negatively or being downcast. If you put a lot of those things together, you create an environment where everybody is really happy to get along, you involve everything about team concepts and not on individuals, you talk about people helping the team and that the team comes first, then you have got a great start for team chemistry. If you allow or encourage individuals to only go after their own goals, then it won't work. You can't just make chemistry, but you can create a positive environment with positive team goals. The bottom line is that good people make good team chemistry. In fact, I do not recruit people who are not good people. And I don't mean people who are good athletically, I mean people who are genuinely like other people and want to work with other people in a positive way. I avoid recruiting negative players at all costs. I call anybody and everybody when I am recruiting to find out about people's characters, it is just that important to me. I have always said that you can have one bad apple in your group, but if you have two or three, they tend to link cells like a cancer and spread throughout your team. I also tell our kids that they are responsible for their teammates, themselves and their school, so they shouldn't do anything that would ever be detrimental to those things. That is really our only rule and the players respect that."

WHAT MOTIVATES YOU? "The fact that we shouldn't be doing what we are doing. The fact that we are an academic institution first, with some immense hurdles to overcome to be on the same playing field as some other institutions, not necessarily in Minnesota, which maybe are not as strict with everything that they do. The fact that we do everything that we can do to never miss classes gives us a tremendous disadvantage. Other schools have more practice time than us and that hurts us too. But, we are in school to learn and that is most important. We are a private, very highly academic, expensive school, so given that, it is amazing that we are a national championship program. We can go up against the big dogs and win, and that is great."

WHAT ADVICE WOULD YOU HAVE FOR YOUNG COACHES STARTING OUT TODAY? "First of all, don't coach until you have finished playing. You learn so much from playing and you can't short change yourself there. There are so many impetuous youngsters who want to get into coaching but still have a lot of good playing in them. They want it and they want it now, and they don't understand that playing teaches you far more about the game than any coach can. So, play at the highest level that you can for as long as you can, then think about coaching. Secondly, don't think that you have to have everyone like you. You are the coach and you have to be true to yourself. Then, earn the respect of your players and remember that it isn't just given to you."

FAVORITE LOCKER ROOM SIGN? "Play to our strengths and cover our weaknesses"

WHAT'S THE BIGGEST THING YOU'VE LEARNED FROM COACHING THAT YOU'VE BEEN ABLE TO APPLY TO YOUR EVERYDAY LIFE? "No matter how good you think you can be, there are going to be setbacks. In life you can never think that everything is going to be sweet roses. So, you have to be prepared that something can happen."

WHAT ARE THE KEY INGREDIENTS TO CREATING A CHAMPIONSHIP TEAM? "Team chemistry is far more important than it is made out to be. Many have said that you can't win without it. Secondly, you have to have talent. Owners and athletic directors sometimes think that coaches can work miracles, but you really have to have talent. The best coaches know how to get the best out of poor talent, but you need some players to win."

WHAT'S THE SECRET TO YOUR SUCCESS? "There are three things you have to do be a successful division III coach, and coaching is the third. Recruiting, unfortunately, is first, particularly at our school. It is tough because there are so many good schools that these kids can go to and we oftentimes have to recruit against the Ivy Leagues, which is very difficult. Second, is the ability to communicate with your players. If you can can't relate to them and talk to them, it doesn't matter how much talent you have. You have to get them to play for you. That requires encouraging your players and really getting to know them."

WHAT WOULD YOU WANT TO SAY TO YOUR FANS, BOOSTERS, AND ALUMNI WHO HAVE SUPPORTED YOU ALL THESE YEARS? "I am really thankful that so many of my players and our supporters stay in touch with me. I would just say thank you to them for their support, it means a great deal to me and to the program."

HOW DO YOU WANT YOUR COACHING EPITAPH TO READ — HOW DO YOU WANT TO BE REMEMBERED AS A COACH? "I would like to be remembered as someone who did everything he could to make his players' experiences positive ones and that he worked really hard to do his best — both on and off the field. I have had so many great relationships with my kids through the years and was even a surrogate father to some of them at times."

PAT LAMB:
CARLETON WOMEN'S TENNIS

Pat Lamb spent 31 years at Carleton, teaching, serving as administrator and coaching tennis. On the court, Lamb's teams won three straight MIAC titles from 1985-87 and won 8 of 10 Associated Colleges of the Midwest Tennis Titles. Lamb was named NCAA Division III Coach of the Year in 1987 and was inducted into Minnesota Tennis Hall of Fame in 1992. Lamb, who also served as the women's athletics director at Carleton from 1972-85, was instrumental in developing women's varsity athletics at Carleton, in Minnesota and in Midwest.

Lori Meyer grew up in Storm Lake, Iowa, and went on graduate from Upper Iowa University in 1982, where she lettered in volleyball, basketball and softball. Meyer then came to Minnesota State Mankato as a graduate assistant on the women's softball team, where she also got her masters degree in sports administration as well. In 1984 Meyer was named as the team's head coach and she has been going strong ever since. Now entering her 20th season as the head softball coach with the Mavericks, she owns a 577-402-3 (.589) lifetime coaching record, which ranks 17th on the all-time NCAA Division II coaching list for wins. Meyer has twice guided the Mavs to NCC titles (1987 and 1989) and her 1987 team won the NCAA Eastern Regional and then went on to finish third at the national tournament. In all, Meyer has coached 11 All-Americans and MSU teams have won 25 or more games in a season in 13 of her 19 seasons as head coach. A three-time Midwest Regional Coach of the Year recipient, and six-time NCC Coach of the Year recipient (1986, 1987, 1989, 1995, 1997 and 2003), Meyer is MSU's all-time winningest softball coach. In addition to coaching, Meyer also teaches a class in Human Performance at MSU as well. In the world of college softball, Lori Meyer is as good as it gets and is a real coaching legend.

HOW WOULD YOU DESCRIBE YOUR COACHING STYLE? "With regards to handling kids, my philosophy has had to change over the past two decades because I think the kids have really changed. I just think that kids are not as mentally tough nowadays. You have to motivate each kid differently and that is a process year in and year out. My intensity has not changed through the years, but how I portray that intensity has changed a lot. Back when I first started out I raised my voice a lot and maybe even used to get in the face of a kid every now and then, but I don't think you can do too much of that now. As for style, on defense I would describe my style as aggressive. On offense I also like to be aggressive. If I have got kids with speed then I like to hit and run, bunt and run, and suicide squeeze. I am not afraid to get kids thrown out at home, I think you have to force the play. I want to challenge that outfielder to come up and field the ball cleanly, throw the strike to home plate and see if that catcher can hang on to apply the tag. If they can do all that and get our guy out then I am OK with my decision to run and be aggressive."

HOW DO YOU MOTIVATE YOUR PLAYERS? "When you have a team of 16 kids you have got to figure out how to motivate each and every one of your kids differently. Some kids you can maybe raise your voice with, while others need a soft voice and a pat on the back. It really varies. You have to challenge them to improve and get better, and you need to give them discipline too. I also think though that most of the motivation should come from within. I mean they have got to want to go out there and get it done."

IF YOU COULD MAGICALLY GO BACK IN TIME TO THE FIRST YEAR YOU WERE A HEAD COACH AND GIVE YOURSELF SOME ADVICE FOR THE FUTURE, KNOWING WHAT YOU KNOW NOW, BACK THEN, WHAT WOULD YOU SAY TO YOURSELF? "To remember that coaching is all about people skills and to treat people the way I would want to be treated. It's not the wins and losses that they're going to remember, it's the relationships and life lessons that they learn and take away."

LOOKING BACK WHAT ARE YOU MOST PROUD OF IN YOUR CAREER? "Getting the most out of my teams and watching my kids reach their potential as players has been very rewarding. I would also say getting to the national tournament final four early on in my career was pretty special too."

WHAT IS THE KEY TO RECRUITING? "The key is being able to use your people skills to find good talent, good citizens and good student athletes. You have got to sell your program and good recruiting is very critical towards the success of a program. You also need horses in order to compete with the top programs. Overall though, I would say that honesty and integrity are the biggest things in recruiting."

HOW DO YOU BUILD TEAM UNITY & CHEMISTRY? "I think this is very, very critical. I have had teams that maybe weren't as talented but they had great chemistry and they always seemed to go a little bit further than a talented team with no chemistry. Maybe I am wrong, but I think it is harder for a team of women to create chemistry than it is for men. Females will tend to be a little bit more petty and there is a little bit more back-biting going on with them versus with the guys. Men will usually just get whatever it is off of their chest and then move on, and that means problems or issues don't linger around for as long. Overall though, you really have to work at chemistry. You have to be very up front and very honest with kids nowadays. I think kids want to know where they stand on a team and I think you as a coach need to constantly give them feedback throughout the season to let them know how they are doing and what they need to improve on. Then, you have to have your goals clearly defined for your program. When your kids know what your team is all about, then they can be a part of it and buy into it. Finally, people have to accept their roles on the team. That can be tough because each of those 16 kids was a star in high school and now only nine of them can be starters. No one likes to ride the pines and that can be tough."

WHAT MOTIVATES YOU? "The thrill of competition is the main thing, but I also love watching kids come here and improve. To see them grow as people and then realize the they are going to go out and lead our world one day in the future is very motivating."

WHAT ADVICE WOULD YOU HAVE FOR YOUNG COACHES STARTING OUT TODAY? "I always remember an old saying: 'People will forget what you say, people will forget what you did, but people will never forget how you made them feel.' When I started here at just 24, I got that slogan from the athletic director who took a chance on me and I have never forgotten it. As far as advice goes though, I would say that coaching is a job with long hours, but it is a very rewarding job. I also think there is a fine line for young coaches just starting out who are very young and might want to become friends with their student athletes who are probably around the same age. I just think you can't go there, you really can't be friends with your players, it just doesn't work. You also have to be honest with kids and remember that they are human beings. I would just say treat them like you would want to be treated."

FAVORITE LOCKER ROOM SIGN? "I like Bill Bradley's saying: 'You can't buy heart, you gotta play from within.'"

WHAT'S THE BIGGEST THING YOU'VE LEARNED FROM COACHING THAT YOU'VE BEEN ABLE TO APPLY TO YOUR EVERYDAY LIFE? "I would say people skills and communication skills, because in coaching to be successful you have got to constantly be communicating whether it is to your staff or to your team."

WHAT ARE THE KEY INGREDIENTS TO CREATING A CHAMPIONSHIP TEAM? "It starts from the leadership at the top, from the coaching staff on down. You need to have good talent, discipline, team chemistry, and players who are driven with a good work ethic."

WHAT'S THE SECRET TO YOUR SUCCESS? "I would say my work ethic, my passion for the game, my intensity, my people skills, my desire to learn and the fact that I really care about my student athletes."

HOW DO YOU WANT YOUR COACHING EPITAPH TO READ — HOW DO YOU WANT TO BE REMEMBERED AS A COACH? "I would want to be remembered as a caring coach who cared about her student athletes. I would also hope to be thought of as someone who demanded excellence, taught discipline and had a great work ethic."

DENNIS JOHNSON: ST. BEN'S SOFTBALL

Denny Johnson grew up in St. Cloud and played football, basketball and baseball at St. Cloud Tech High School. From there, Johnson went on to play basketball for three years at St. Cloud State University, graduating in 1976 with a degree in English. Johnson then went into teaching and coaching and in 1983 became the head basketball coach at St. Cloud Cathedral, where he would remain until 1986. The next stop for Johnson would be at nearby St. Ben's, where he would take over as the school's head softball coach and assistant basketball coach. Since taking over the softball program 17 years ago, Johnson's overall record sits at a very solid 369-166-3 (.689). The second winningest coach of all-time in the MIAC, Johnson has also posted the top winning percentage in the conference over the last 10 seasons as well. Among Johnson's many coaching honors and accolades, in 2003 he was named as the Assistant Coach of the Year by AFLAC. The criteria for the award is based on longevity, expertise, contributions to the school and community, and special achievements throughout their careers. Over 350,000 assistant coaches across the nation were nominated.

LISA BERNSTEIN: GOPHER SOFTBALL

Lisa Bernstein is now the winningest softball coach in Gopher history. Bernstein played softball at the University of Arizona from 1983-86. A four-year starting catcher, Bernstein batted .257 with 47 RBI and ranked sixth on the all-time putout list with 561 at the end of her career. Her senior year, Bernstein was a Pacific-10 all-conference selection and a second-team all-region pick. She was also an Academic All-America honorable mention recipient and a two-time most valuable player for the Wildcats. Bernstein came to Minnesota in 1991 after serving as an assistant coach for five years at Arizona. During that time, Arizona recorded a 249-88 record, played in five NCAA tournaments and won the 1991 national championship. (Bernstein also earned her master's degree in exercise and sports sciences from U of A in 1989 as well.) With the Gophers, Bernstein has made history. With 430 wins, she has posted a .590 winning percentage and her Gophers have qualified for four NCAA Tournaments in 1996, 1998, 1999 and 2002. In 1999 Bernstein promoted her assistant coach, Julie Standering, to co-head coach. Julie, who was a teammate of Bernstein's at Arizona, focuses on recruiting while Bernstein focuses on the day-to-day operations of the program. Bernstein and Standering are both excellent teachers of the game. Bernstein focuses on hitting, outfield and catching, while Standering's on-the-field duties include infield, left-handed slap hitting, baserunning, conditioning and agility. Their commitment, enthusiasm, work ethic and passion for the game have helped to build a well-respected program at the U of M. They have coached six All-Americans, 28 all-region picks, eight first-team, 15 second-team and five third-team All-Big Ten selections over the past 11 seasons. Over the last 12 years, Bernstein and Standering have averaged over 35 wins per season and have had 10 winning seasons, including the last eight in succession. In addition, they are both experienced clinicians, teaching softball players throughout the country. Bernstein and Standering also co-own North Country Softball Camps and Clinics, which conducts camps and clinics annually throughout the state of Minnesota. In 2000 the Gopher softball program got a huge boost when the 1,000-seat Jane Sage Cowles Stadium opened on campus — one of the finest in the country. With the two-heads-are-better-than-one approach, these Gophers are getting it done and making Minnesota very proud along the way.

BOB MERTZ
HIGH SCHOOL SOFTBALL: NEW ULM CATHEDRAL

Bob Mertz grew up on a farm in Siegel Township, just outside of New Ulm, and went on to graduate from New Ulm Cathedral High School in 1967. From there, Mertz went on to attend Minnesota State Mankato, where he got a teaching degree in Math. Mertz them came home to begin a coaching and teaching career which has now spanned three decades in the New Ulm Area Catholic School System. As the head coach at New Ulm Cathedral for the past 24 years, Mertz, who has an amazing record of 437-85 (.837%), is the winningest softball coach in Minnesota state high school history. Mertz has also won four state championships (1993, 1994, 1995 & 2003) and appeared in seven state tourneys along the way. A student of the game in every sense of the word, Bob Mertz is a legend in the world of girls softball. And, he is still going strong!

HOW WOULD YOU DESCRIBE YOUR COACHING STYLE? "I grew up on a farm, so I guess discipline and hard work are just a part of who I am. I believe in the fundamentals and think that defense is very important. I am also a disciplinarian in that I think things should be done right. I would describe my style as very aggressive. We just run, run, run and go, go, go and try to make few mistakes. I also believe in slap bunting and just take a real aggressive philosophy to hitting and generating runs. The kids have really bought into that as well and seem to like that style of play. That makes things a lot easier for me as a coach too, when you get kids that want to be out there and are having fun playing the game."

HOW DO YOU MOTIVATE YOUR PLAYERS? "The confidence has got to come from them, I just try to help them achieve their best. My goal every season is to try and get as much out of these kids as I can. As a coach I sort of hang the carrot over them of that I am never really satisfied with their efforts. That way they know that they can always improve and get better. They reach for that carrot, but I always pull it away and ask them for a little bit more. I just want to get more and more out of them and I want them to never be satisfied with being good. I want them to be great and want them to try and do their very best. You know, I also don't like one sport athletes. I encourage our kids to play other sports and want them to be well rounded. When you have kids who are good athletes with a diverse background, then they are much easier to motivate because they are already students of the game and are more receptive to learning."

WHAT ARE THE CHARACTERISTICS OF WINNERS? "Work ethic, believing in yourself, confidence and the feeling that they really want to succeed. It comes from the heart."

LOOKING BACK WHAT ARE YOU MOST PROUD OF IN YOUR CAREER? "New Ulm has such a rich baseball and softball tradition and that is something that we have worked very hard to create. Our community embraces it and gives us so much support. We have a great summer softball program here and we just get the kids excited about the sport at an early age. We have great assistant coaches in our program too, they have been a part of our program for 20 years and that helps a great deal to build continuity. We make it a family thing and it is great to see generations of kids wanting to play softball here. That is very special."

HOW DO YOU BUILD TEAM UNITY & CHEMISTRY? "I tried not to do too much with captains. Instead our seniors are our captains and I leave it up to them to carry on the tradition that we have created here at Cathedral. I tell them that I can't do it myself, so I leave it up to them to help me teach the younger players. They help me build chemistry and I think it is such an important thing with the kids. With it, you can do anything, it is just a very powerful thing. It is about not being selfish and always putting the team first. Once you have that then you will have a winning program. The other thing is that here, in a small town, these kids grow up with each other and many of them play organized ball for 10-12 years together. That really helps in building chemistry when the kids already know each other and like each other."

WHAT'S THE SECRET TO YOUR SUCCESS? "Hard work is so important and I just think you'll never get anything without it. You have to have fun though, that is also important."

WHAT WOULD YOU WANT TO SAY TO YOUR FANS, BOOSTERS, AND ALUMNI WHO HAVE SUPPORTED YOU ALL THESE YEARS? "Thanks for the memories. I have had some great times here and just appreciate all of their support. They have been so great to me and my family and that means a great deal to me. We have had a lot of success here and that is because of the good people who have been a part of this program."

HOW DO YOU WANT YOUR COACHING EPITAPH TO READ — HOW DO YOU WANT TO BE REMEMBERED AS A COACH? "He gave it his all; he got the most out of his players; he got the most out of himself; and he had a lot of fun along the way."

DAN BLANK:
ST. MARY'S SOCCER

Dan Blank is a local legend in college soccer circles. Blank has led St. Mary's University to seven Minnesota Intercollegiate Athletic Conference titles, qualified for the NCAA tournament seven times and coached 15 All-American athletes. The three-time MIAC Coach of the Year also sports an impressive career record of 231-96-23. Blank is truly a Cardinal coaching icon.

CHARLIE WHITBRED
HIGH SCHOOL SOFTBALL: PARK COTTAGE GROVE

Charlie Whitbred graduated from Park Cottage Grove High School and then went on to attend the University of Minnesota. Whitbred briefly played hockey for the Gophers, but later transferred to play at Lakewood Junior College. Whitbred got into teaching and coaching after that, back at his alma mater and has since gone on to become the second all-time winningest girls high school softball coach in state history with more than 400 wins. His Park Cottage Grove High School Wolfpack have been to the state tournament eight times now, winning one state title in 1993 and twice finishing runner-up in 1992 and 1999. Whitbred has been coaching girls softball for 22 years and is among the game's senior statesmen. Whitbred has also coached boys soccer for the past 17 years at Park and has taken his teams to the state tournament five times there as well. One of his former players, Donnie Gramenz, now plays for the Minnesota Thunder. Whitbred has also coached girls hockey for the past eight years and even coached boys hockey prior to that as well. The man has simply done it all, and done it all very, very well. He is truly a Park coaching legend.

HOW WOULD YOU DESCRIBE YOUR COACHING STYLE? "When I first started coaching I really wanted to win and sometimes winning was maybe a little more important than the kids. But the older I got and the more I coached and got to know the kids, the better I got. My philosophy is to still to try and win, but to do what is best for the program and what is best for the kids. I try to play everybody and try to keep everybody happy, that is real important. We have been lucky though and it has all worked out. We just have a great program here."

HOW DO YOU MOTIVATE YOUR PLAYERS? "Some kids you can chew their butt out a little bit and others you can just look at them and that will be enough, it really varies from kid to kid. Sometimes you can take a kid out of a game for an inning or two to let them think about a mistake or something and then get them back in there. There are a lot of ways and everybody is different. You have to be able to read each particular kid and then find out what motivates them as an individual."

LOOKING BACK WHAT ARE YOU MOST PROUD OF IN YOUR CAREER? "I am just proud of all of the great kids who we have had come through our program over the years. To see what they have done for the program is just tremendous. Then, to see some of your kids go on to play in college, that is very rewarding too. Like Laura Peters, who went on to earn All-Big 10 Honors at the U of M, that is great. I think we have had at least a half a dozen who have gone on to earn scholarships at the division one level and a whole bunch of others who played at D-II and D-III."

HOW DO YOU BUILD TEAM UNITY & CHEMISTRY? "If you have a good mix of kids then that helps. We just try to create an environment where the juniors and seniors can help the freshmen and sophomores. That is how you build a solid program. Then, the girls hang out a lot together too and that is big for creating chemistry as well. If they are friends off the field, then they will be friends on the field and that is where it starts. It helps too that I coach in the Summers, because a lot of those same kids then go on to play varsity softball. Once you already know the kids, then it makes it a lot easier to get along and to build that chemistry."

WHAT MOTIVATES YOU? "To see all the girls grow up and go to college and get married and then have families is wonderful. To get e-mails or calls or to see your former students in the community and talk to them is also very rewarding. It is just great to watch them grow up and move on to bigger and better things in life. I mean just a while ago we got our house toilet-papered by the girls from the 1993 state championship team who were having a reunion party, and that was a riot. Those girls are still close to this day and as a coach that really makes you feel great."

WHAT ADVICE WOULD YOU HAVE FOR YOUNG COACHES STARTING OUT TODAY? "I would recommend that they find a mentor. Then, try to get a handle on the parental pressures that will come. Parents will call and wonder why their kid is not playing, so you have to be ready for that. Then, don't lie to the kids. Talk to them and be very honest with them on what they need to work on. Kids and parents appreciate that."

WHAT'S THE BIGGEST THING YOU'VE LEARNED FROM COACHING THAT YOU'VE BEEN ABLE TO APPLY TO YOUR EVERYDAY LIFE? "Athletics are like life. You are competing every day not only for a position on the team but for a position in the job field or what have you. The competition has taught me a lot about life and about how to be successful."

WHAT ARE THE KEY INGREDIENTS TO CREATING A CHAMPIONSHIP TEAM? "You can't win without good players. You have to have quality players and we have been lucky enough to have had some great kids over the years. If you have a successful program then the younger kids can watch the older kids and learn from them. That is how it all starts. Once you have a program like that then you will have kids coming into the gym to work out and they will want to play in the Summer too. The kids are what makes the program, it is not so much the coach. You just need to give them the opportunity and the environment to play in."

WHAT'S THE SECRET TO YOUR SUCCESS? "I have been able to adapt to changes and that has made me pretty versatile. You know, in the old days you could be a lot tougher and a little more verbally abusive I suppose. Now, it is totally different and you have to really change with the times in order to stay successful in this business."

WHAT WOULD YOU WANT TO SAY TO YOUR FANS, BOOSTERS, AND ALUMNI WHO HAVE SUPPORTED YOU ALL THESE YEARS? "They have been great. I would just say thanks for your support, we couldn't do it without you."

HOW DO YOU WANT YOUR COACHING EPITAPH TO READ — HOW DO YOU WANT TO BE REMEMBERED AS A COACH? "I would want to be remembered as a coach whose kids respected him. I also want to be known as somebody who worked very hard and was a winner."

TIM DALY
HIGH SCHOOL SWIMMING: MINNETONKA

Tim Daly grew up in Bloomington and went on to swim at Bloomington Lincoln High School. From there, Daly swam at the University of Minnesota, where he set the 200 freestyle record — a mark which held for 10 years. Daly's first coaching job was back at Lincoln High School, where he coached the girls swim team in 1980. Daly wound up coaching the Edina West boys team later that same season, only to see the two Edina schools consolidate that year. So, he went back to Bloomington Lincoln, where he coached both the girls and boys squads. But, as luck would have it, Lincoln closed that next year.

So, from there Daly went to Minnetonka High School, first as an assistant, and then as the head coach shortly thereafter. Daly began coaching the girls and boys at Minnetonka in 1982 and has since gone on to become a coaching legend, winning seven state titles on the boys side along the way. Among his many coaching honors and accolades, in 1991 Daly's boys team set a national record in the 200 medley. In addition, Daly has also had players qualify for the state tournament in every year except for the first season of his amazing coaching career. And, unlike most coaches, Tim is not a teacher in the schools either, which makes it tougher to recruit kids for his teams. In addition to coaching, Tim also works as a financial advisor with G.E. Financial and lives in Mound.

HOW WOULD YOU DESCRIBE YOUR COACHING STYLE? "I would say I have a hard, caring attitude I guess. I care a lot about my kids but they know that I have high expectations for them on the way they should conduct themselves. I want them to behave themselves and respect their teammates as well as their facility. Those are all important things that go into developing your own style."

HOW DO YOU MOTIVATE YOUR PLAYERS? "With swimming it is a little easier than in other sports in that you can see right away if someone is doing better or worse based on the clock. The clock is the ultimate motivator in this sport. I just try to get them to work together and try their hardest. I push them to be better than they were the day before and that is how we do it."

LOOKING BACK WHAT ARE YOU MOST PROUD OF IN YOUR CAREER? "Aside from all the records I guess I am proud of the fact that I have done this for so long and that I still enjoy it. We have had so many kids go on to compete in college and that is rewarding to see too. I mean to see kids like Matt Taylor, who went to the U of M, or Jeff Dragsten, who went on to compete at Stanford, is so great. Working with these kids and watching develop as people has been so much fun."

HOW DO YOU BUILD TEAM UNITY & CHEMISTRY? "I think that goes back to respect. My kids don't have to hang out with each other away from the pool, but when they are together I want them to get along and respect one another. I try to treat everybody the same too. I mean if kids mess up then I hold them out of meets, even the top kids. So, we may lose a meet here or there because somebody messed up. But, sooner or later kids seem to understand what we are doing. That way we don't have a lot of internal problems. I make it clear as to what my expectations are at the beginning of the season with both the students as well as with their parents. That makes for a smooth season. I will say, however, that with the boys it is a lot eas-

ier. The girls can be tougher. You can have a great team make-up one year and then have the worst the next, so it is much harder to figure that out. That is one of the biggest reasons why I got out of coaching the girls. They can either be the most fun to coach or the worst, depending on what you have to work with. Boys, on the other hand, say what is on their mind, get it off their chests, and move on. So, chemistry is tough, but you just have to always work at it."

WHAT MOTIVATES YOU? "To be able to work with kids and even turn them around if they are heading down the wrong road is very rewarding. When their parents come up and tell me that their kids have changed for the better, then that is great to see."

WHAT ADVICE WOULD YOU HAVE FOR YOUNG COACHES STARTING OUT TODAY? "I would tell them to go to clinics and learn from the best coaches. Then, don't be afraid to try something new."

WHAT'S THE BIGGEST THING YOU'VE LEARNED FROM COACHING THAT YOU'VE BEEN ABLE TO APPLY TO YOUR EVERYDAY LIFE? "I would say setting goals and planning for outcomes. That has always been so important to me whether it is in athletics or in business or in life."

WHAT ARE THE KEY INGREDIENTS TO CREATING A CHAMPIONSHIP TEAM? "I think your kids have to want it, and that means more than one person. Then, that feeling has to spread. It never just happens. You have to create that winning environment from the beginning of practice and work hard to achieve it. I was very fortunate to have some of the best swimmers in the country on my teams in the early 1990s. That attitude just spread throughout the program and when you have that, younger kids see it and want to come out for the team. Then, with all of the other summer programs, community teams, USS teams, and what have you, we have just a great area of competition here — from Wayzata to St. Louis Park to Minnetonka. That was great and the kids sort of thrived off of each other to get better."

WHAT'S THE SECRET TO YOUR SUCCESS? "Just caring about my kids and having a plan of attack for success. I get my kids to think that they can win the state meet instead of other kids who just wish that they can. Then, my biggest thing is to get my kids to swim their fastest at the state meet. That is where it counts and that is one of the reasons why we have been so successful. I stress the importance of doing well throughout the season, but come tournament time, I really want them to perform their absolute best. That is very important."

WHAT WOULD YOU WANT TO SAY TO YOUR FANS, BOOSTERS, AND ALUMNI WHO HAVE SUPPORTED YOU ALL THESE YEARS? "I would just say thanks for their support, it has been great."

HOW DO YOU WANT YOUR COACHING EPITAPH TO READ — HOW DO YOU WANT TO BE REMEMBERED AS A COACH? "You know, I would rather be remembered for what my swimmers have done. I would say though that I have gotten a lot more from them than they have gotten from me."

MELLANIE PUSATERI
GIRLS HIGH SCHOOL SWIMMING: EDINA

Mellanie Pusateri grew up in Dubuque Iowa and graduated from Wahlert High School in 1986. From there, Pusateri went on to swim competitively at the College of St. Catherine's, graduating in 1990. Pusateri then spent the next two years working at the University of Minnesota, doing research, and also substitute teaching. Her first teaching and coaching job out of college was at Edina High School, teaching physical education and serving as an assistant coach on the girls swimming team. There, Pusateri served under Traci Bergo, who had won several state championships in the late 1980s. Pusateri served as an assistant from 1992-98 and then took over as head coach in 1998. Pusateri wasted little time making a name for herself as the head coach either, winning three straight state titles and grabbing a runner-up spot in her first four years with the Hornets.

An avid marathon and triathlon runner, Pusateri continues to build on one of the strongest girls swimming programs in the country, and is considered to be amongst the very best and brightest young coaching minds in her sport. Mellanie and her husband Ryan have one son, William, and presently reside in Minneapolis.

HOW WOULD YOU DESCRIBE YOUR COACHING STYLE? "I try to encourage all of my athletes, not just my top kids. We have had a lot of success because we always have a well balanced program with good kids on the upper and lower ends of the spectrum. We are also grades seven through 12, which gives the younger kids the opportunity to really blend in with the older kids and learn as they come up. We don't make any cuts at our level either, which is nice. Participation is the basis of our program. Our kids, because they are year round swimmers, are committed and want to achieve success. So, between the participation we have and the determination of our kids, I think that is why we have a successful program."

HOW DO YOU MOTIVATE YOUR PLAYERS? "I think most of our kids are self-motivated and their motivation comes from within. As a coach I try to motivate my kids by talking about the history of the program and by encouraging them to do their best. I just try to build on their confidence and then go from there. The kids know the rich history of Edina swimming and they want to be a part of that, so in that sense we are very lucky."

LOOKING BACK WHAT ARE YOU MOST PROUD OF IN YOUR CAREER? "I am so proud of all the athletes that I have coached who went on to swim competitively at the next level. I am also very proud of all my kids who continue to live a healthy lifestyle. Given the fact that I am a physical educator as well as a coach, I just want to encourage women, in particular, to feel good about themselves and to lead a healthy and productive life."

HOW DO YOU BUILD TEAM UNITY & CHEMISTRY? "Cohesiveness is critical in our program. We try to create it by not only working hard in practice, but we do a lot of team functions and social events outside of the pool. We do a lot of team building activities too, such as teaming up an older swimmer with a younger swimmer, so they get to know each other and can learn from one another. Things like that really make a difference and that all translates into success in the pool."

WHAT MOTIVATES YOU? "I love to see the success of the girls in our program. I love to see them set goals and achieve them. So, I am totally motivated by them and by their achievements."

WHAT ADVICE WOULD YOU HAVE FOR YOUNG COACHES STARTING OUT TODAY? "I would tell them to make sure that they enjoy their athletes. Then, I would tell them to get to know and respect their community, because they will need to know their community as well as they know their athletes. That is so important."

WHAT'S THE BIGGEST THING YOU'VE LEARNED FROM COACHING THAT YOU'VE BEEN ABLE TO APPLY TO YOUR EVERYDAY LIFE? "I don't think you can control every situation. Life sometimes throws you a curve ball and you just have to learn how to deal with that when it comes. By understanding that, I think you can have success in your personal life as well. You just can't be too structured, regimented or narrow minded, you have to take whatever comes your way."

WHAT ARE THE KEY INGREDIENTS TO CREATING A CHAMPIONSHIP TEAM? "You obviously have to have talent. There needs to be some ability there or you aren't going to get too far. Then, you have to have a good support system with the parents, the administration and with the community. You also need to have a coaching staff that works together to help achieve the team's goal, which is the state championship. We set our goals very high here and we try to achieve them every year."

WHAT'S THE SECRET TO YOUR SUCCESS? "I don't think there is any secret. I am successful because I enjoy what I do and I am motivated by what I do."

WHAT WOULD YOU WANT TO SAY TO YOUR FANS, BOOSTERS, AND ALUMNI WHO HAVE SUPPORTED YOU ALL THESE YEARS? "I feel very lucky to be a part of the Edina system, we have a great youth program and we have a great history and tradition here. The community is really behind us and our entire coaching staff really appreciates that. The administration has been outstanding as well, and that helps us so much. So, thanks to everyone, especially the parents for giving us so much support, they are wonderful."

HOW DO YOU WANT YOUR COACHING EPITAPH TO READ — HOW DO YOU WANT TO BE REMEMBERED AS A COACH? "I would want to be remembered as someone who enjoyed what she did. I enjoyed all of my athletes, I enjoyed my job and I wouldn't have done it if I didn't love it."

WALTER HOOVER:
ROWING & CREW

Walter Hoover, a Duluth native who was considered one of the great oarsmen of his time, coached the U.S. Olympic Rowing team to five medals at the Summer Games of 1956.

JEAN FREEMAN
COLLEGE SWIMMING: UNIVERSITY OF MINNESOTA

Jean Freeman grew up loving to swim and went on fulfill a childhood dream by becoming a member of the University of Minnesota's swimming and diving team from 1968-72. Upon graduating, Freeman served as a Gopher assistant coach in 1972-73 before being named as the program's head coach that next season. Since then, Freeman has taken the program to new heights.

Having posted winning records in 20 consecutive seasons, Freeman has coached more than five dozen swimmers to All-America status and over 100 swimmers have garnered All-Big Ten honors during her reign as well. Perhaps Freeman's biggest year came in 1999, when the Gophers won their first-ever Big Ten championship. Freeman earned her fourth Big Ten Coach of the Year award that year and was also named as the recipient of the National Collegiate and Scholastic Swimming Trophy, awarded by the College Swimming Coaches Association of America. The award is the highest of its kind in the United States and is presented annually to an individual for having contributed in an outstanding way to swimming as a competitive sport and healthful recreational activity at schools and colleges. Freeman was the first female to win the award in its 41-year history. So, how would she top that? She won a second straight Big Ten title that next year too.

Known for her coaching philosophy which centers on what she calls the "total person concept," in which academics are emphasized as much as athletics, Freeman has gained the respect of her student-athletes, as well as her colleagues. She has made the most of the state-of-the-art Aquatic Center as well, a facility that Freeman feels is the best in the nation available on a regular basis to a Division I school. Freeman earned her 200th career victory in 2001 and has led the Gophers to an upper-division finish in the Big Ten Conference 19 of the last 24 seasons. In addition, Minnesota teams have placed at the NCAA championships in each of the last 17 years and are regularly ranked as a top-20 squad in the nation — occasionally cracking the top 10.

Among her many coaching accolades, Freeman has an endowed scholarship named after her, and was also inducted into the Minnesota Women's Athletics Hall of Fame in 2000. In 1995, Freeman was named as one of just three women to Team Speedo, a national advisory board for swimming and diving. She also received an award from the College Swim Coaches Association of America (CSCAA), recognizing excellence in college coaching and service to the coaching. In addition, Freeman was also inducted into the Minnesota Swim Coaches Association Hall of Fame in 1992.

Active in state and national organizations, Freeman was named senior chair of Minnesota USS and to the board of the College Swim Coaches Association in 1997. She also served a four-year term on the NCAA Men's and Women's Swimming Committee. Freeman has coached nationally and internationally as well. In 1992, she was the assistant coach on the women's USS Junior National Team that won the Quebec Cup. Furthermore, Freeman helped coach the West team to a gold medal at the 1991 U.S. Olympic Festival.

Now entering her 31st season as the head coach at Minnesota, Freeman has not only built a competitive swimming and diving program in Gold Country, she has accomplished a feat much more difficult: maintaining that program among the nation's elite year after year. In the world of women's college swimming, Jean Freeman is truly a legend.

HOW WOULD YOU DESCRIBE YOUR COACHING STYLE? "I try to figure out what makes each individual tick. I look at their personalities, I look at why they compete, I look at why they go to school and , I look at why they are in the sport. When I can figure those things out I am a much better coach. Also, I would add that our program is continually getting more well known as a great place to be on a winning team. I let kids know that if they come here that they will get faster as a swimmer, get better as a diver and you will graduate on time. That is what we are all about."

HOW DO YOU MOTIVATE YOUR PLAYERS? "I think the best athletes are intrinsically motivated. If my kids don't know why they are doing something, I find it important to try and get them to figure out why they are doing it. You sort of have to tap into what their passions are and then go from there as far as motivation. I just try to make connections with them on a personal level as much as I can."

IF YOU COULD MAGICALLY GO BACK IN TIME TO THE FIRST YEAR YOU WERE A HEAD COACH AND GIVE YOURSELF SOME ADVICE FOR THE FUTURE, KNOWING WHAT YOU KNOW NOW, BACK THEN, WHAT WOULD YOU SAY TO YOURSELF? "To keep balance and focus as much as possible in your life. I find that a lot of young kids today think that they have to do too much at once. So, I just like having them make a list of everything and then encourage them to focus on just doing certain things in year one, year two or what have you. Otherwise they get overwhelmed with all of their interests and things that they want to do. So, they need to combine a focus with balance, and that will help them to be better student-athletes."

WHAT ARE THE CHARACTERISTICS OF WINNERS? "A person who is not afraid to go after something, can admit that it's fun to beat people and who can take pride in themselves as an athlete. That is a winner."

WHAT'S THE BEST PIECE OF ADVICE YOU EVER GOT FROM ANOTHER COACH? "To not worry and to not take all of your worries home with you."

LOOKING BACK WHAT ARE YOU MOST PROUD OF IN YOUR CAREER? "The number of individuals who have done so well both athletically and academically. Those are very good alum's. They come back and they help out and are very proud to have been a part of our program. That's what I am most proud of."

WHAT WAS THE KEY TO RECRUITING? "Oh, I wish I knew! I think letting them know what you have to offer. Then it is spending a lot of time just hitting enough people by phone calls or letters. It's like they say in the business world, 'it's who you know.' So, you have to have a lot of contacts out there in the field who are willing to recommend your program via word of mouth. That really helps."

HOW DID YOU BUILD TEAM UNITY & CHEMISTRY? "Rather than thinking of it in terms of building chemistry, I think of it as a byproduct of teaching respect — respect for themselves, for their teammates, for what you are trying to accomplish as a team, and for who they are trying to represent."

WHAT'S THE KEY TO GOOD TIME MANAGEMENT? "I think it is your goal setting. I mean if you focus in on your goals then you will spend you time wisely."

WHAT MOTIVATES YOU? "When I see people get over a hurdle it makes up for all the hard times in my life. Seeing people gain confidence and moving on to the next thing that they are doing in their life is motivating to me. Plus, what I do is fun and I enjoy my job."

WHAT ADVICE WOULD YOU HAVE FOR YOUNG COACHES STARTING OUT TODAY? "Be true to themselves and don't try to be someone else when they are coaching."

FAVORITE LOCKER ROOM SIGN? "I have left that up to our captains and they take care of all that, it is entirely up to them to put up things that they think are important and motivating to the team."

WHAT'S THE BIGGEST THING YOU'VE LEARNED FROM COACHING THAT YOU'VE BEEN ABLE TO APPLY TO YOUR EVERYDAY LIFE? "That you need to be happy and enjoy what you are doing. You have to just enjoy the process. If you wait your life away for that big moment, like the Big Ten's or the NCAA's in our case, it's going to be very tough day to day. So, you need to enjoy each step along the way."

WHAT ARE THE KEY INGREDIENTS TO CREATING A CHAMPIONSHIP TEAM? "I would say that the kids need to have respect for themselves and for their teammates and then have a willingness to be consistent at working hard."

WHAT'S THE SECRET TO YOUR SUCCESS? "We enjoy winning, it's no secret! Winning is also a byproduct of pulling together and having fun. That has always been our focus, we don't talk a lot about winning, we talk about doing the things that we need to do to be better people and to be better athletes. Once you do that, then the wins will come."

WHAT WOULD YOU WANT TO SAY TO YOUR FANS, BOOSTERS, AND ALUMNI WHO HAVE SUPPORTED YOU ALL THESE YEARS? "Thanks, it's always fun to have people that understand what you are doing. It is very rewarding to know that so many people care and that they think enough of our program to support us and our athletes."

HOW DO YOU WANT YOUR COACHING EPITAPH TO READ — HOW DO YOU WANT TO BE REMEMBERED AS A COACH? "I cared about people, I enjoyed what I did and I did a good job."

JOHN MADURA: HIGH SCHOOL DIVING

John Madura has been coaching diving for 34 years now, and is amongst the best in the business. The Austin native went on to dive for the Gophers in the mid-1960s before coming to Mounds View High School to serve as the orchestra teacher and diving coach. An accomplished cellist, Madura was named as the Minnesota Music Educator of the Year in 1988. Presently, Madura coaches girls diving in the Fall and boys in the Winter for three different metro schools: Mounds View, Irondale and Spring Lake Park/St. Anthony. In all, Madura has coached 16 state champions and 23 All-Americans. And, for six straight years (1986-91), a Mounds View girl won the state championship under his tutelage — including his daughter, Stacy, who won it in 1988. In addition, Madura's brother, Tom, has coached diving at Prior Lake for 29 years as well.

DAVE HAUCK: ST. OLAF SWIMMING

Dave Hauck is a legend in the world of college swimming. Hauck is a graduate of Gustavus Adolphus College, where he was an MIAC freestyle sprint champion and record holder. Hauck then went on to complete his master's degree in physical education from Bemidji State University. From there, Hauck got into teaching and coaching. Now in his 35th year at St. Olaf as a professor in the physical education department, Hauck has coached the Ole men's swimming program for 27 years and the women's for 12. Along the way, he has made history.

During Hauck's 27 years as the men's coach, his teams have compiled 27 straight winning seasons. In addition, the men's team has a dual meet record of 211-67, including a 135-10 conference record (100-1 since 1981). They have won 22 MIAC championships, including 20 consecutive wins from 1981-99. At the national championships, the men have finished in the top-10, 10 times and the top-five, five times. Fully 57 athletes have earned all-American status and three have become national champions in 14 different events. In 1987, Hauck was honored as the NCAA Division III Men's Swimming Coach of the Year.

On the women's side, Hauck's Oles have recorded a 91-20 dual meet record, including a 76-1 mark in the MIAC. They have won 10 of the last 12 MIAC championships and have two top-5 and two top-10 finishes at the national championships as well. In addition, five women have become national champions and 42 have earned all-American honors. In his first year coaching the women's team, Hauck was recognized as the 1989 NCAA Division III Women's Swimming Coach of the Year.

Among his many coaching awards and accolades, Hauck is a member of the Gustavus Adolphus Athletic Hall of Fame and was recently honored as a distinguished alumni. In 1993, he was inducted into the Minnesota Swimming Hall of Fame, and he also currently holds a prominent positions on the College Swim Coaches Forum as well as the College Swim Coaches Association (CSCAA). Then, in 2000, Hauck was honored by the CSCAA as the recipient of the Richard E. Steadman award. Steadman was the former president of the CSCAA, was a leader in the International Swimming Hall of Fame and exhibited a caring and loving relationship for his fellow coaches and athletes throughout his career. The award is conferred annually to a swimming or diving coach in high school, club or university ranks who, in the opinion of the International Swimming Hall of Fame and the CSCAA Forum, has done the most to spread joy and happiness throughout the sport of swimming & diving.

Dave and his wife Mary presently reside in Northfield and have three children. One of them, Bob, has served as the co-coach at St. Olaf with his old man for the past 15 years. Bob returned to the program as a coach in 1988, after a successful swimming career under his father which culminated in 1987. That year the Haucks were named Division III Coach and Swimmer of the Year. Since then, the father-son dynamic duo has developed one of the most unique programs in the country. Their coaching combination creates a family atmosphere bringing innovation, expertise, and experience to the swimming and diving program.

GARY AASEN
HIGH SCHOOL TENNIS: EDINA

Gary Aasen grew up in Fridley and went on to star on the tennis team at Fridley High School, graduating in 1982. From there, Aasen played tennis at the University of Minnesota, where he emerged as one of the program's top players. Aasen first got into coaching while at the U of M, serving as an assistant coach with the Gophers during and after his playing career. After graduating from the U of M, Aasen never taught in the public school system, rather, he has been a full-time tennis coach his entire life.

Then, in 1994, Aasen came to Edina High School, where he has since become one of the top tennis coaches in the state. Aasen has led the Hornets to five state championships during his tenure in Edina (1995, 1998, 2000, 2002 and 2003), and taken the tennis world by storm. Sure, he inherited one of the nation's elite high school tennis programs, but Aasen's unique coaching style and motivational tactics have clearly set him apart from the pack. He is a proven winner and has the hardware to prove it. In addition to coaching the Hornets, Gary also works at several local country clubs doing clinics and running tennis programs. Tennis, is clearly this man's life, and why not? He is among the very best of the best and is still going strong.

HOW WOULD YOU DESCRIBE YOUR COACHING STYLE? "I tend to be very goal oriented. You know, I almost consider all of our matches prior to the playoffs to be practice matches. So, even though we might be playing for a conference title or in a weekend tournament, those are all matches that are used as prep for the real matches coming up. It is a matter of perspective I think in that we are building during the year, using everything we can during that time to build up towards something. So, it deals with prepping a team for what might happen and what could happen, and seeing if we can stay on track towards that."

HOW DO YOU MOTIVATE YOUR PLAYERS? "Edina is an enigma. The average kid I get is extremely motivated already by the time they get here. So, that is not the hard piece at Edina. The hardest piece at Edina might be picking the right goals and using that motivation to get to the right level of play. Or, it might be to improve a certain shot, or to improve as a doubles team, or whatever it may be. So, typically the motivation there is pretty high. These guys know that we are going to be able to contend for a state title; they know that they might be one of the better individuals in the state; and they know that there is a lot of tradition and history here. I think that gives them a lot of motivation right out of the gate. It may be more of a matter of channeling that energy so it is not much about competing against each other with regards to battling for positions on the team, but rather towards the team's goals and needs."

HOW DO YOU BUILD TEAM UNITY & CHEMISTRY? "I think it is putting each individual player in a position where they may be able to accomplish more than they thought was possible as a group, as opposed to just an individual. So, if the group concept becomes a uniting factor, then they will become a good team. But that comes from them, and it is very tricky because it may or may not happen. I just think that if you put them in front of enough scenarios where they can see that they need each other, then they might become a better team and the chemistry will develop."

WHAT MOTIVATES YOU? "To continually see if you can get the maximum effort out of a group of high school kids, that is what motivates me."

WHAT ADVICE WOULD YOU HAVE FOR YOUNG COACHES STARTING OUT TODAY? "You need to decide why you are there and what you want to accomplish early on. Then, stick with it and don't get sidetracked by winning or losing. Just hang in there and build something special over time. That is how you go about creating a winning program for years to come."

FAVORITE LOCKER ROOM SIGN? "We have a big board above our door at our training facility which has every state and individual champion listed on it. Just to look at that tradition and history is a big motivating factor to our kids I think."

WHAT'S THE BIGGEST THING YOU'VE LEARNED FROM COACHING THAT YOU'VE BEEN ABLE TO APPLY TO YOUR EVERYDAY LIFE? "First, I think that preparation is everything in terms of business or sports or whatever. The better prepared you are the more success you will have. Secondly, don't get distracted by the small stuff. Just keep on track and keep focused on the big picture and what really matters. You know, when I go into a season I am trying to get people to play better and to build chemistry. I am rarely trying to win a state title. If I am successful at those things though, then the latter will follow."

WHAT ARE THE KEY INGREDIENTS TO CREATING A CHAMPIONSHIP TEAM? "You have to have realistic goals as a team and individual goals for your players. Then, you have to have a flat out time commitment from your kids. There is really no substitution for hard work. Then, everyone needs to be on the same page and everyone needs to know that everyone else is there for the same reasons."

WHAT'S THE SECRET TO YOUR SUCCESS? "I think it is trying to get the maximum effort that I can absolutely get out of each of my kids."

WHAT WOULD YOU WANT TO SAY TO YOUR FANS, BOOSTERS, AND ALUMNI WHO HAVE SUPPORTED YOU ALL THESE YEARS? "You know tennis is obviously different than say football or basketball, where you can pack the stadium, but our fans are great. They are really an unheralded motivating factor for us by just being there. Their support goes an awful long way and we appreciate that. We don't thank them enough, but our tradition was built on that support."

HOW DO YOU WANT YOUR COACHING EPITAPH TO READ — HOW DO YOU WANT TO BE REMEMBERED AS A COACH? "I would want to be remembered as someone who always tried to help every individual player grow as a person and as a player as much as they possibly could. And, I would also want to be remembered as someone who always made his best attempt at fielding the best team which he could field in any given year."

STEVE PAULSEN
GIRLS HIGH SCHOOL TENNIS: EDINA

Steve Paulsen grew up in Northfield and went on to play tennis at nearby St. Olaf College, where he earned All-American honors. Paulsen then went on to teach and coach tennis at Faribault High School for a year, followed by a year in Minneapolis as well. Paulsen then got out of teaching in 1986 and went to work for Northwest Athletic Clubs, where he has been employed ever since, teaching and running tennis clinics. In between, Paulsen has gone on to run tennis programs at several prestigious local country clubs including Oak Ridge, Woodhill and Olympic Hills.

Paulsen later took over as the head coach of the Edina boys tennis program in 1988 and over the next five years he won four state titles. That next year Paulsen coached both the boys and girls squads, and in 1993 he made the switch, becoming exclusively the Edina girls coach. The Edina girls program was a dynasty at the time and had won 14 state titles in a row from 1978-91 under Ted Greer and Chuck Anderson, who later moved on to take over at Stillwater High School. Paulsen jumped right in though, and picked up where Anderson had left off by proceeding to win the program's 15th straight title in 1992. Since then, Paulsen has gone on to win an incredible six more state championships, and shows no signs of slowing down either. Steve Paulsen is among the elite tennis coaches in the state of Minnesota and is simply one of the best in the business.

HOW WOULD YOU DESCRIBE YOUR COACHING STYLE? "I am not a big yeller and I would say that I am pretty laid back. I would pattern myself after Bud Grant and not after Mike Ditka, put it that way! At the same time I have high expectations for my kids and I try to hold them to some pretty high standards as well. We work very hard but we also try to have fun. You know, when you are winning it is fun, so we are lucky to have that kind of program where we are fortunate enough to do both."

HOW DO YOU MOTIVATE YOUR PLAYERS? "I would say that most of my kids are pretty well self-motivated by the time they get here, but the competition within the team in it of itself is great motivation for them. I also try to sit down with my kids one-on-one and challenge them by setting goals with them."

LOOKING BACK WHAT ARE YOU MOST PROUD OF IN YOUR CAREER? "I am most proud of the quality of kids who have come out of the Edina tennis program over the years. Then, when they come back to say hi or to see a match, that is just great to see. So, if they feel good enough to come back and support us, then that makes me very proud."

IF YOU COULD MAGICALLY GO BACK IN TIME TO THE FIRST YEAR YOU WERE A HEAD COACH AND GIVE YOURSELF SOME ADVICE FOR THE FUTURE, KNOWING WHAT YOU KNOW NOW, BACK THEN, WHAT WOULD YOU SAY TO YOURSELF? "From a coaching standpoint, I have learned a ton over the years. I would say though, that I would probably have tried to have been a better communicator with my kids early on. That is something that I have tried to work on."

HOW DO YOU BUILD TEAM UNITY & CHEMISTRY? "First is trust and then I would say respect. We do a lot of things together as a team in our program, where our No. 1 player will play with our

No. 15 player. Things like that do a lot to help kids gain respect for one another. I also think that we are fairly unique in that we do a lot of things with the varsity and junior varsity together too. We compete together in certain events and all of that helps to create chemistry I think. You know, at Edina sometimes the tennis gets in the way of the old social calendar, but that is all part of the experience here. The better the friends the kids are, then the more chemistry you will have."

WHAT MOTIVATES YOU? "I love to see the kids improve. From a team standpoint, it really motivates me to see the kids come together as a group. That is just great to see and is very intrinsically rewarding to me. Certainly, the winning is great, but to do it in such a way where the kids are having a good time and developing friendships, then that is wonderful."

WHAT ADVICE WOULD YOU HAVE FOR YOUNG COACHES STARTING OUT TODAY? "Be honest and stick to your principles. You have to be honest and open to not only the kids but to the parents too. That is important."

WHAT'S THE BIGGEST THING YOU'VE LEARNED FROM COACHING THAT YOU'VE BEEN ABLE TO APPLY TO YOUR EVERYDAY LIFE? "I would say that I have learned from the kids who I coach about the discipline it takes to succeed. Also, the direct communication is huge. Being open and honest with everyone, especially when things are not going well, is a very big thing that I have carried into my personal life too."

WHAT ARE THE KEY INGREDIENTS TO CREATING A CHAMPIONSHIP TEAM? "Aside from the internal motivation from your athletes, I would say they have to work at their game all year long. That is absolutely critical at this level. Certainly, I am very blessed to have the talent, but my kids work extremely hard during the off-season and I am the beneficiary of that."

WHAT'S THE SECRET TO YOUR SUCCESS? "Great kids who want to be there and a great tradition at Edina High School. I have a great J.V. coach and great support from the school and fans. I really owe all of my success to the kids and for how much they work at it in the off-season. They are so dedicated to tennis and it really shows."

WHAT WOULD YOU WANT TO SAY TO YOUR FANS, BOOSTERS, AND ALUMNI WHO HAVE SUPPORTED YOU ALL THESE YEARS? "The parents at Edina sometimes get a bad rap. But I have to say that they have been unbelievably supportive to me and my program over the years. They go so far out of their way to help their kids and to help me and I really appreciate that. They make my job a blast and if they weren't that way I probably wouldn't be here for as long as I have been."

HOW DO YOU WANT YOUR COACHING EPITAPH TO READ — HOW DO YOU WANT TO BE REMEMBERED AS A COACH? "As someone who stuck to his standards and was morally and ethically sound in his teaching and coaching. I don't stand for nonsense on the court and even though we have been pretty successful though the years, that is probably even more important to me than even the winning."

Chuck Anderson grew up in Virginia, Minn., and went on to attend Virginia High School in the early 1950s, where he played hockey and tennis. The reason he played tennis in high school was because they didn't have a high school baseball team. So, he took up tennis and played American Legion baseball in the Summers. Anderson then went on to play hockey and tennis at Hamline University. There, he got a teaching degree and wound up getting his first teaching and coaching job in Elk River in 1958. He stayed five years, teaching American history, health and phys-ed, and also started the hockey and tennis programs at the school as well. From there, Anderson headed south, to the Lake Conference, to set up shop at Robbinsdale Cooper High School. Anderson taught and coached at the school from 1963-76, winning a state boys tennis title in 1970.

In 1976 Anderson abruptly resigned from coaching. It was a decision based upon a ruling that the school board had made which stated that freshmen could not play varsity tennis. So, at that point Anderson and his wife decided to let their four kids have the option of either staying in the Twin Cities, or heading south to Blue Earth, where they could live with their aunt, uncle and grandma. The kids decided to see how tennis was in Southern Minnesota, and they packed their bags. The tennis coach in Blue Earth, Hal Schroeder, was among the winningest in state history, so Anderson knew that his boys would be in good hands.

Anderson wanted to keep coaching, however, so, while he continued to teach at Cooper, he coached tennis at several other schools, including Breck, Macalaster and St. Cloud State University. Then, in 1983, Anderson took over as the head girls tennis coach at Edina High School. He stayed for 10 years, claiming nine state titles along the way — even winning more than 200 consecutive matches at one point.

In 1993 Anderson left Edina to take over at Stillwater High School, where he has been coaching the boys and girls programs ever since. He retired from teaching at Robbinsdale Cooper that same year and is having fun now just coaching. Anderson has since gone on to win one state title at Stillwater, and one runner-up finish as well. Anderson has transformed Stillwater's boy's and girl's programs, getting more than 100 kids to try out for the team every year. While Anderson was too modest to acknowledge his all-time career record, he has surpassed Tom Vining on the all-time wins list, and Vining has over 1,000 career wins in both boys and girls tennis. So, one can only assume he is the all-time winningest coach in Minnesota girls high school tennis history. The fact that Chuck is too modest to know his own record says volumes about the type of person he is. A man of great integrity and character, Chuck Anderson is a true Minnesota tennis coaching legend.

HOW WOULD YOU DESCRIBE YOUR COACHING STYLE? "It is about the kids. All they have to do is try and I will take them as far as they want to go and as far as their talent will enable them to go. Then, I was always a big advocate of letting the best kids play. The idea was that the best kids were going to give your team the best chance at winning, whether they were in ninth grade or even in seventh grade. Kids accept that, it is just the adults who have problems with it. You know, when my son was a freshman in Blue Earth, they beat Minnetonka, who had David Wheaton on their team, for the state championship. If it had been up to the parents at some schools, that freshman wouldn't have been able to play. Many felt that he took away a position from a hard working senior, well to that I say baloney.

Tennis is a unique game and I always felt that the best players should be out there giving your team its best opportunity to win, regardless of age. Period. In fact, I may even run for the school board in the future just to have a say in that."

HOW DO YOU MOTIVATE YOUR PLAYERS? "By being a good role model and working hard. The kids see how hard I work and the hours I put in and that rubs off. I still play competitively, so the kids will see me stay after practice and hit an extra 100 serves or things like that, and that is just leading by example I suppose. I try to do that both on and off the court by living a good life."

LOOKING BACK WHAT ARE YOU MOST PROUD OF IN YOUR CAREER? "I am proud of the number of lives I have touched over the years. The idea that I have furnished so many kids with the knowledge to play a lifetime sport is very gratifying. I would also add that I am very proud of the accomplishments of my four children too. They are just great, great kids."

HOW DO YOU BUILD TEAM UNITY & CHEMISTRY? "I relied on the kids for chemistry. I just told them that it was their team and it was all up to them. I have even had captains on state championship teams that never even played a single match. Leadership is very important to a team's success and really that can take many forms."

WHAT MOTIVATES YOU? "The end product I guess, that I am doing something worthwhile. Tennis keeps me young. I may be getting older, but I refuse to grow up."

WHAT ADVICE WOULD YOU HAVE FOR YOUNG COACHES STARTING OUT TODAY? "Don't go on an ego trip and remember that you are not bigger than your program. I would also tell them to accept anybody that offers help and advice and not to be intimidated. Finally, don't play politics."

FAVORITE LOCKER ROOM SIGN? "Winners never quit and quitters never win."

WHAT'S THE BIGGEST THING YOU'VE LEARNED FROM COACHING THAT YOU'VE BEEN ABLE TO APPLY TO YOUR EVERYDAY LIFE? "If you give it your best effort then things will work out."

WHAT ARE THE KEY INGREDIENTS TO CREATING A CHAMPIONSHIP TEAM? "You have to have talent. Then, you have to have good practice habits. You know, I never cancelled practice, ever. And that says a lot. We were very dedicated and we worked very hard."

WHAT'S THE SECRET TO YOUR SUCCESS? "Hard work. There aren't that many secrets to tennis. Be diligent and be reliable. Say what you are going to say and do what you are going to do. Be accountable and be responsible. That's it."

ON HIS FOUR BOYS: "I have got four great kids (Greg, Chris, Miles & Roger) and they were the best thing that ever happened to me. I would drive down to Blue Earth to get them every weekend and bring them back up to the Twin Cities, but it was worth every second of it. They never gave me any grief in their lives and they were just such good people. I am so proud of them. Not only did they win 12 state tennis titles between them, but they also have eight college degrees between them. (Chris and Miles went on to become captains at St. Cloud State, Greg was a captain at Indiana University and Roger went on to become the captain at the University of Minnesota.) And do you know what? They never asked me for a dollar. I am just a teacher and coach, but I think I am the richest guy in the world. (Roger, the youngest of the four and who is now a doctor, set a national record by winning 206 matches in high school.) You know, they have won 12 state championships between them, and I only have 11, so I would like to win at least one more so that I can tie them before I walk away."

WHAT WOULD YOU WANT TO SAY TO YOUR FANS, BOOSTERS, AND ALUMNI WHO HAVE SUPPORTED YOU ALL THESE YEARS? "It has been a heck of a trip! Stay in touch! You know I have had so many great kids. I coached a kid who caught the first touchdown pass for the Miami Dolphins in the Super Bowl and I have also coached kids who are doing time in the Stillwater prison. It has really been a heck of a trip!"

HOW DO YOU WANT YOUR COACHING EPITAPH TO READ — HOW DO YOU WANT TO BE REMEMBERED AS A COACH? "He did a good job."

LARRY SUNDBY: ST. CLOUD STATE WOMEN'S TENNIS

Larry Sundby is a St. Cloud State tennis coaching legend. Over the past 16 seasons Sundby has posted a 275-113 career record en route to winning three North Central Conference women's tennis titles to boot (1988, 1990 and 1991). Sundby has been coaching high school and college tennis for 25 years now and his overall record stands at 406-156. Among his many coaching awards and accolades, Sundby was voted as the North Central Conference Coach of the Year in 1988 and 1991, and was recognized as the Minnesota High School Girl's Class AA Tennis Coach of the Year in 1992 as well. Sundby is also a professor emeritus of accounting at St. Cloud State University as well.

STEVE WILKINSON: GUSTAVUS TENNIS

Steve Wilkinson is a Gustavus coaching legend. Period. A native of Sioux City, Iowa, Wilkinson played collegiate tennis at the University of Iowa, where he lettered for three seasons and finished second in No. 1 doubles at the Big Ten Championships his senior season. From there, Wilkinson would wind up in St. Peter, where he recently completed his 33rd season as the head coach of the men's tennis team at Gustavus. Wilkinson has built a dynasty in St Peter, as his Gusties have won 30 of the past 33 MIAC tennis titles (including 15 straight) and have compiled an astonishing conference dual match record of 283-1 (.996). Since Wilkinson took over the Gustavus tennis program, his teams have won two NCAA Division III titles (1980 and 1982), six national championships in doubles, and four national titles in singles. The winningest active coach in Division III college tennis, Wilkinson's career record is an astonishing 747-227 (.767). In addition, Wilkinson has been named the NAIA National Coach of the Year twice (1974 and 1984) and the NCAA Division III Coach of the Year three times (1983, 2001, 2003).

Still very active playing tennis, Wilkinson has been ranked No. 1 in the United States in the 45, 50, and 55 and over divisions. He has also represented the United States in the Dubler Cup, Perry Cup and Austria Cup, winning the world championship in Montevideo, Uruguay, in 1989 and finishing second in Berlin, Germany, in 1992.

Wilkinson has also been very involved in several national tennis organizations and has served on the executive committees of the United States Professional Tennis Association, the Intercollegiate Tennis Association, and the United States Tennis Association. In addition, from 1980-93, Wilkinson served on the Intercollegiate Tennis Association Executive Committee representing Division III. Among his many awards and accolades, Wilkinson was inducted into the Iowa Tennis Hall of Fame in 1974, the Northern Tennis Association Hall of Fame in 1983 and the Missouri Valley Hall of Fame in 1999. Furthermore, since 1977 Wilkinson has directed Tennis and Life Camps, helping nearly 2,000 students each summer develop tennis skills and a sportsmanlike approach to athletics. Along with coaching, Wilkinson, who received an MBA in finance and a PhD in Asian Religions, presently teaches sports ethics at Gustavus.

BUD BJORNARAA
BOYS HIGH SCHOOL TRACK & FIELD: APPLE VALLEY

Bud Bjornaraa grew up on a farm in rural Northwestern Minnesota near the small community of Oaklee. There, he played football and ran track and field at Oaklee High School under Coach Roy Hokkenon. As a senior, Bud earned all-state honors in football and was offered a scholarship to play at the University of Minnesota. After his freshmen year Bud wanted a change of scenery, so he transferred to the University of North Dakota. (Bud's freshman teammates would go on to win the national championship in 1960 under Murray Warmath.)

Bud's educational background would include degrees in physical education, coaching and industrial technology. Bjornaraa got his first teaching and coaching job in Isle, Minn., and then spent several years in Wisconsin, before winding up at Richfield High School, where he spent six years as well. In 1976 Bjornaraa moved on to Apple Valley, where he coached the Apple Valley High School boys track team from 1976-99 — winning eight state championships and 12 sectional championships along the way. Bjornaraa also served as an assistant on the football team as well. Incredibly, in all the years he was there, his track teams never finished lower than second place in the conference or in the section, and even won 17 consecutive conference crowns at one point. It was a dynasty. In all Bud coached both track and field and football for a total of 39 years. His overall career coaching record in track & field was an astonishing 361-69. Among his many coaching accolades, Bud was the 1986 Track & Field Coach of the Year as well as the 1994 Assistant Football Coach of the Year. Additionally, in 1999 he was named as the NSCA National and State Strength Coach of the Year.

After retiring, Bud went on to become a motivational speaker and expert in the subjects of strength conditioning, weight training, speed development, jump improvement, and weight management. Additionally, Bud has also performed over 100 clinic presentations, authored numerous journal and magazine articles on strength and conditioning, while remaining active with local and national associations and programs. Bjornaraa has even written several books on the subjects. Bud has devoted his entire professional career to physical education and coaching, and has truly made a difference. In the world of high school track and field, Bud Bjornaraa is a legend.

HOW WOULD YOU DESCRIBE YOUR COACHING STYLE? "I was a details guy and was real hands-on too. I was a planner and just expected the very best. I always emphasized practice time too. Some people practice and practice, but they practice the wrong things with the wrong techniques and habits. Then those bad habits become engrained and it is tough to break them. I was pretty hard core and regimented, but I also think I was fair. I also thought my practices were difficult, but were usually good learning experiences with a lot of challenges and variety to make them enjoyable. I guess I was always a fixed point in a changing universe. Kids always knew what they were going to get when they got me as a teacher or as a coach. I also was the first one there and the last one to leave, so if kids wanted to stay late and work on something I would be there for them. I was committed and had a real passion for training. We all were, I mean I had the same assistants with me for more than 20 years. From there, winning just sort of fell into place."

WHAT WAS THE KEY TO RECRUITING? "I always felt that I never wanted to let any good kids get away. I was relentless when it came to getting kids involved. I just kept after kids to come and try out for my teams and eventually they would give in and they would usually have a good experience when it was all said and done. I can even remember kids at one time or another crying because they wanted to quit my team so bad and I just wouldn't let them. And some of them wound up being state champions. I just don't give up on people and I try to push them to be their best."

HOW DID YOU MOTIVATE YOUR PLAYERS? "I enjoyed training, particularly because you could deal with people more of on a one on one basis, and then you could get into their heads a little bit to help mold them as human beings. I also always tried to line up the toughest competition for our kids, because I wanted to prepare them for the best. Whether it was Stillwater, White Bear Lake, Mounds View or even Fargo South (N.D.), we wanted to play the best of the best so that we could always get better."

HOW DID YOU BUILD TEAM UNITY & CHEMISTRY? "Chemistry sort of develops itself. Just surround yourself with the right people and it will fall into place. You may have to pull some people aside from time to time to keep everything in order, but overall I think that everyone wants to be successful, regardless of who they are or what they are doing. So, if they have an opportunity to be a part of a successful program that has a good tradition, then they will be willing to make some changes in order to get better. We also did little things like before every practice we would have a little fireside chat. It could be 10 minutes or 45 minutes, depending on what issues came to mind during the day. That certainly built unity as well. You know, a sport is merely a sport, win or lose the sun is going to come up the next day. But, there are some valuable lessons to be learned along the way."

WHAT'S THE BIGGEST THING YOU'VE LEARNED FROM COACHING THAT YOU'VE BEEN ABLE TO APPLY TO YOUR EVERYDAY LIFE? "Never give up, be consistent with what you do, and do things in moderation."

WHAT'S THE SECRET TO YOUR SUCCESS? "The way I have always tried to coach and teach is to help people, but not do too much for them. I think if we do too much for people we actually do them an injustice because we handicap them. They have to take ownership in what they do and that is important."

WHAT WOULD YOU WANT TO SAY TO YOUR FANS, BOOSTERS, AND ALUMNI WHO HAVE SUPPORTED YOU ALL THESE YEARS? "I would have to give one huge thank you to everybody who believed in me for starters. So many people supported me through thick and thin over the years and that really meant a great deal to me."

HOW DO YOU WANT YOUR COACHING EPITAPH TO READ — HOW DO YOU WANT TO BE REMEMBERED AS A COACH? "I would hope a bunch of things including: persistent, consistent, knowledgeable, multi-faceted, believed strongly in preparation and training, believed in the journey more than the destination, loved working with people, patient, good listener, demanding, fair and made things enjoyable."

ROY GRIAK
TRACK & FIELD/CROSS COUNTRY: UNIVERSITY OF MINNESOTA

Roy Griak grew up in Duluth and graduated from Morgan Park High School in 1942. He then went on to run both cross country and track and field at the University of Minnesota for the Golden Gophers. Griak earned his bachelor's degree in education from the U of M in 1949 and then added a master's degree in 1950. From there, Griak went on to teach at Nicollet High School and then in the Mankato Public School system, before beginning his teaching and coaching career at St. Louis Park High School in 1953. Griak's college coaching career would come a decade later, when he came back to his alma mater to take over the reigns of the Gopher program in 1963, replacing his former coach Jim Kelly. Over the next three decades, Griak would become a track and field legend in Gold Country.

Griak led the Golden Gophers to Big Ten cross country titles in 1964 and 1969. His 1968 cross country squad finished second at the Big Ten meet, and placed fourth and the NCAA Championships. In addition to three Big Ten titles, his cross country squad produced three second-place and seven third-place finishes at league meets. Griak also added a Big Ten track & field title to his resume in 1968 as well. Overall, Griak coached a total of 47 cross country and track and field All-Americans in his tenure, including three NCAA Champions. His athletes collected 60 Big Ten individual titles too.

When Griak stepped off the track for the last time in 1996, Minnesota honored its legendary coach by naming the nation's largest annual cross country meet, formerly the Minnesota Invitational, after him. Griak then became the administrative assistant for the cross country and track & field teams at the U of M, a position he currently holds. Griak has also been inducted into the Drake Relays Coaches' Hall of Fame in 1993, the U of M Hall of Fame in 1996 and the United States Track Coaches Hall of Fame in 2001. Griak has two sons, Seth and Jason, and presently resides in Plymouth.

HOW WOULD YOU DESCRIBE YOUR COACHING STYLE? "When you are working with young people I think one of the biggest things you need to consider is being fair to everybody. I think I was always stern, but fair. I also felt that if I put in the time, exemplify the enthusiasm and work hard, then the athletes will follow suit. I also care about my kids both on and off the field. It has never been 'my way or the highway.' Pure and simple, that has been my philosophy and it has worked."

HOW DID YOU MOTIVATE YOUR PLAYERS? "I think motivation is an intrinsic thing. It is not a matter of you coaching them, rather it is self motivation. Sure, you have to have the tools for them to respond properly in a game situation, but overall if you prepare them well and give them the tools, then that in my eyes is motivation."

IF YOU COULD MAGICALLY GO BACK IN TIME TO THE FIRST YEAR YOU WERE A HEAD COACH AND GIVE YOURSELF SOME ADVICE FOR THE FUTURE, KNOWING WHAT YOU KNOW NOW, BACK THEN, WHAT WOULD YOU SAY TO YOURSELF? "I wanted to be the best teacher possible and I did everything I possibly could to make that happen. I read, went to clinics, listened to people and even copied whatever I could from other coaches who also had success."

WHAT ADVICE WOULD YOU HAVE FOR YOUNG COACHES STARTING OUT TODAY? "Be enthusiastic. Love what you do. Care about your individuals. Try to learn as much as you can. Motivate yourself to be a better person. Stay in good physical condition too. I think you need to look the part and if you emulate physical fitness then your kids will follow suit."

WHAT WAS THE KEY TO RECRUITING? "Getting on the phone and working real hard at it. Minnesota was a difficult place to recruit in because of the cold weather. But, you could also use that to your advantage as well. I just tried to turn all of the negatives into positives and work real hard on selling our program's rich history."

HOW DID YOU BUILD TEAM UNITY & CHEMISTRY? "By caring and letting my kids know that they were a big part of our program. Whether they were stars or just another young man who was coming out to practice, I tried to make him feel good about what he did that day. Whatever he could accomplish that day, I would always try and be there to pat him on the back and say 'hey, you're doing great.'"

WHAT MOTIVATED YOU? "I really enjoy watching young people grow and develop into higher levels of achievement. For me to see a young freshman and to know that with a lot of teaching and hard work, where that person would be in four years, was a wonderful feeling. That was my motivation."

WHAT'S THE BIGGEST THING YOU'VE LEARNED FROM COACHING THAT YOU'VE BEEN ABLE TO APPLY TO YOUR EVERYDAY LIFE? "Take care of your health. Being around young people keeps you young."

FAVORITE LOCKER ROOM SIGN: "Motivation is self-determination."

WHAT ARE THE KEY INGREDIENTS TO CREATING A CHAMPIONSHIP TEAM? "In this day and age it is all about recruiting. Years ago it was about hard work and development, but now you have to recruit good kids. It is a completely different ballgame today."

LOOKING BACK, WHAT ARE YOU MOST PROUD OF IN YOUR CAREER? "The continued friendships that I have with the athletes which I have built through the years. You know, I never made a lot of money coaching, but it enriched my life in so many other ways that I truly believe I am a rich man today."

WHAT'S THE SECRET TO YOUR SUCCESS? "Enthusiasm and a love of my sport."

WHAT WOULD YOU WANT TO SAY TO YOUR FANS, BOOSTERS, AND ALUMNI WHO HAVE SUPPORTED YOU ALL THESE YEARS? "If the past, present and future scholar athletes who have been a part of the program here at the University of Minnesota believe that they have accomplished their highest potential, then that would be a feather in any coaches cap."

HOW DO YOU WANT YOUR COACHING EPITAPH TO READ — HOW DO YOU WANT TO BE REMEMBERED AS A COACH? "He cared for his athletes."

GERI DIRTH
GIRLS HIGH SCHOOL TRACK & FIELD: APPLE VALLEY

Geri Dirth grew up in Delhi, Iowa, and attended Maquoketa Valley High School, where she played basketball, track and softball. Dirth then went on to play basketball at Luther College, graduating in 1977 with degrees in physical education and psychology. From there, Dirth taught and coached at the high school level in Iowa for four years before coming to Apple Valley High School in 1980. There, Dirth went on to teach phys-ed and coach everything from track to cross country to basketball. For the past 24 years, however, track has been her thing. Dirth has very quietly gone on to establish herself as one of the preeminent track coaches in state history. In all, Dirth has won seven True Team state track titles and five MSHSL track titles. In 2003 her squad went 85-3, proof that she shows no signs of slowing down. In addition, Geri's husband, Rod, teaches math and coaches the boys track and field team at Apple Valley as well. Rod took over the program from Bud Bjornaraa, one of the all-time legends in Minnesota track. Geri and Rod met at Luther, where they each ran track, and have been together ever since. Geri's teams have made the most True Team appearances in state history, and she is still going strong. An outstanding motivator and a true friend to the sport of track and field, Geri Dirth is one of Minnesota's very best.

HOW WOULD YOU DESCRIBE YOUR COACHING STYLE? "I try to get my athletes to believe in themselves. Also, I try to treat them as people first, then as students and athletes second. I want them to be positive and to always think that the glass is half full rather than half empty."

HOW DO YOU MOTIVATE YOUR PLAYERS? "By caring about them, getting to know them and trying to realize that each one of them has different needs and different ways of achieving success. I really take pride in trying to get to know them and in welcoming them into our track family. I just want them to feel united as a tight group in this big school and let them know that we are always there for them. When I say 'we' I mean my assistant coaches, who are just awesome, I can't say enough about them."

IF YOU COULD MAGICALLY GO BACK IN TIME TO THE FIRST YEAR YOU WERE A HEAD COACH AND GIVE YOURSELF SOME ADVICE FOR THE FUTURE, KNOWING WHAT YOU KNOW NOW, BACK THEN, WHAT WOULD YOU SAY TO YOURSELF? "Do what you love and love what you do. You have to, to put this much time and energy into it."

WHAT ARE THE CHARACTERISTICS OF WINNERS? "You know, I hardly ever use that word. I prefer to say champion instead because a champion is someone who knows that they have gone out there and given it their best. But there are a lot of people who are going to go out and give it their best and not be the No. 1 winner. So, I very seldom ever talk about winning, I say let's go out there and be champions. Now, as far as champions go, I think their characteristics are that they are prepared to take advantage of their opportunities when they come along. They are prepared physically, mentally, emotionally and spiritually, and that is why they are champions."

LOOKING BACK WHAT ARE YOU MOST PROUD OF IN YOUR CAREER? "All of the lives that I have touched. When athletes come back 10 years later and say thanks or credit you for believ-

ing in them when they were just kids, that is wonderful. For instance, I look at Shani Marks, she was a perfect example. She went on to become the Big 10 champion in the Triple Jump at the U of M. She recently wrote an article talking about how grateful she was to me and my assistants for helping her get to where she is at now. I remember one day she didn't want to run track anymore and I just sat her down and told her that she had so much God given talent and that she just needed to stick it out and do her best. Now, here she is on her way to competing in the 2006 Summer Olympics. It just makes me so proud."

HOW DO YOU EARN THE RESPECT OF YOUR ATHLETES" "From the very get-go I tell them that I will respect them if they respect me. I think respect is so important in our program. I just want our kids to be good to each other, believe in themselves, have a passion for the sport, be students of the sport, take pride in their community, treat each other fair and honest, and have fun."

HOW DO YOU BUILD TEAM UNITY & CHEMISTRY? "Sometimes it is tough because track and field can be a very individual sport, but we try to do a lot of team building things early in the year. We mix different athletes into different events and really encourage all of them to get to know each other. I also always talk to them as people. For instance I might tell them, 'OK, today I want you to go home and be a better daughter — do something totally unexpected for your parents.' Then the next day I might talk about being better students and that they should do something beyond what they normally do in the classroom that day. Or about being a better friend, to do something nice for a friend. Finally, I talk about being a better athlete, and we build from there. I think my psychology background has me drawing a lot more on the mental side of things. I mean, when I used to coach basketball I had each player close their eyes and shoot 10 free throws in their head before they went to bed. We visualize a lot with our team and that helps. We put on some nice classical music, like George Winston, and relax while we do a lot of mental preparation so that they feel like they have been there before. I also have a theme for every season too, like this year's was 'Victory is Gold.' That helps us focus too. I also reinforce to them that this is their moment and that they need to achieve it, enjoy it, do the best they can, be proud of who they are, make good decisions and be a class act."

WHAT'S THE BIGGEST THING YOU'VE LEARNED FROM COACHING THAT YOU'VE BEEN ABLE TO APPLY TO YOUR EVERYDAY LIFE? "Now that I have children growing up I look at things a little bit differently. I think that every moment is important for these athletes and I know that I want to coach them the same way I would want my children to be coached. I feel like I have become much more aware of my athletes' needs and wants since I have a daughter who is on my team now. It's a cool thing because I just try and treat all of my athletes like they were my own."

WHAT ARE THE KEY INGREDIENTS TO CREATING A CHAMPIONSHIP TEAM? "Positive thinking. You have to realize that there are going to be some definite emotional ups and downs. You also have to realize that whenever God closes a door he also opens a window. Some things happen and we have no control over them, but yet there are reasons for them and hopefully somewhere down the line some good things will come from that experience."

WHAT'S THE BEST PIECE OF ADVICE YOU EVER GOT FROM ANOTHER COACH? "To pick your battles. There are some issues that don't have a lot of substance to them and we should learn to just let those go and not take them personally. You can't be in control of everything these 14-18 year-olds are doing."

WHAT WOULD YOU WANT TO SAY TO YOUR FANS, BOOSTERS, AND ALUMNI WHO HAVE SUPPORTED YOU ALL THESE YEARS? "I can't thank the Apple Valley community enough, they have been so wonderful. The parents, the youth programs, the supporters, just everybody. I wouldn't change my world for anything right now, I am just very lucky to be a part of all of this."

HOW DO YOU WANT YOUR COACHING EPITAPH TO READ — HOW DO YOU WANT TO BE REMEMBERED AS A COACH? "That my enthusiasm was contagious; my positiveness; for trying to bring out the best in every athlete; and for caring for the total person."

KENT STAHLY: HAMLINE TRACK & FIELD

Kent Stahly, a native of St. Paul, coached track and cross country for a total of 44 years. Stahly served as Hamline's track and field coach for 35 of those years and even started the school's first cross country team. During his years at Hamline, Stahly's teams won nine straight MIAC Track Championships from 1974-83, and won MIAC Cross Country Championships in 1973, 1975 and 1977. Stahly also coached 87 individual NCAA Division III All-Americans and 14 NAIA All-Americans as well. In addition, Stahly coached Mike Manders to NCAA Division I All-American status too. Furthermore, Stahly also founded the popular Hamline Relays, which would become a fixture in the world of Minnesota track and field. He is a Hamline coaching legend.

AL HALLEY: SOUTHWEST HIGH SCHOOL CROSS COUNTRY & TRACK & FIELD

Albert Halley grew up in Kansas and graduated from the University of South Dakota in 1926. Halley went on to teach math for four years in Emery, S.D., and three years in Durand, Wis., before moving to Minneapolis. There, Halley taught and served as an assistant coach in basketball and track at Washburn High School from 1933-40. In 1940, Halley moved over to the newly opened Minneapolis Southwest High School, where he would become a coaching legend. There, Halley helped start Minnesota's high school cross country program in 1943. In addition to coaching cross country for 28 years at Southwest, Halley also coached basketball for eight years, track for 21 years, and even served as an assistant principal for eight more. Later he served as the first president of the State Track Coaches Association in 1959. Halley's numbers were astonishing. His boys' cross country teams won 14 state titles from 1946-70. In addition, Halley's track teams won three state titles (1946, '55, and '56) as well as 14 Minneapolis City Championships. Halley also coached numerous individual state champions, including a kid named Pete Aurness, who would go on to become known as the famous actor, Peter Graves. One of the winningest coaches of all-time, Halley's contributions as a high school track and cross country coach in the state of Minnesota rank second to no one. Simply put, the man was a legend. A true pioneer in academics and athletics, Al Halley died in 1986 at the age of 82.

BOB BONK: FAIRMONT HIGH SCHOOL TRACK & FIELD and CROSS COUNTRY

Bob Bonk graduated from Blue Earth High School in 1967 and then went to earn teaching and master's degrees from Minnesota State Mankato. From there, Bonk's first gig was at Windom High School, from 1971-73. Then, in 1973, he came to Fairmont High School, where he has gone on to become a coaching icon. Bonk has taught math and coached cross country and track at Fairmont now for 31 years. In fact, he pulls quadruple duty — serving as the head coach for both the boys and girls track and cross country programs. Over the past three decades, his numbers have been incredible. In cross country, his girls have won one MSHSL AA Cross Country title (1988), while his boys won an A title (1989) as well. In track, his girls teams have won five state True Team titles, including four in a row from 1998-2001, while the boys also won the 1998 True Team state title as well. A six-time state coach of the year, Bonk's boys cross country winning percentage is at .80%, while his girls are at .86%. In addition, Bonk has won a combined total of 63 South Central Conference championships: (17 boys CC), (18 girls CC) (10 boys Track) & (18 girls track). Still going strong, Bob Bonk is an outstanding teacher, coach and person — and a true Minnesota coaching legend.

BOB HOISINGTON: MINNEAPOLIS CENTRAL & SOUTHWEST HIGH SCHOOLS TRACK & FIELD

Bob Hoisington, who grew up in Pine Island and went on to become a track star at Carleton College, later coached at Minneapolis Central High School for 14 years, and then at Southwest High School for anther 16, retiring after more than 30 years of teaching math and coaching. In all, he won seven MSHSL Team Championships, finish with three runner-ups, and produce 36 Individual Champions. A seven-time Minneapolis Coach of the Year, Hoisington won 22 Minneapolis City Track/Cross Country Championships and seven Twin City Indoor Track Championships too. His dual meet track record at Central was an astounding 107-8. A five-time Minnesota State Coach of the Year, Hoisington is also enshrined into no less than seven Halls of Fames. Known for his work ethic and strong values, Bob Hoisington is a real Minnesota track and field legend.

ROSS FLEMING
HIGH SCHOOL TRACK & FIELD: MOUNDS VIEW

Ross Fleming grew up in Mountain Lake and graduated from Mountain Lake High School in 1978. From there, Fleming went on to run track and cross country at Bethel College, graduating with a degree in physical education in 1982. Fleming then went on to teach at Sunnyside Elementary School. In 1985 Fleming got his first track coaching gig at Columbia Heights High School. He stayed one year before taking over as the head track & cross country coach at Mounds View High School in 1986. Fleming would replace Bob Stewart, who, despite stepping down, has since stayed on to serve as Fleming's top assistant. Together, the dynamic duo have made history.

Ross Fleming (R) & Bob Stewart (L)

Since starting at Mounds View High School Fleming has built a dynasty. And, because he didn't initially work at the high school until many years later, he has never been able to directly recruit there — making his success with the program even that much more amazing. From 1998-2003, his Mustangs won six straight True Team championships in Class AAA, and won three MSHSL state titles as well. His teams have also earned a second place finish along with three thirds too. Since taking over the program in 1986, Fleming's teams have consistently dominated the conference and region. (In track there is a separate individual tournament, which is called 'true team' and it is sponsored by the state coaches association. Then there is also a state team title, which is a different title altogether that is sponsored by the state high school league. In true team competition, each member of the 36 member high school squad scores points, with the totals going towards a single true team title. Only individuals and relays qualify for the state meet, however, not teams. Then, the top nine teams [the top eight teams plus one at-large team] get together to compete at the state true team meet.)

A two-time coach of the year recipient, Fleming, who later began teaching at Mounds View High School in 2003, has a true passion for his sport and is clearly one of the young guys carrying the torch for the future. Driven, hard working and determined, Fleming has achieved his success by no accident. He has created a winning program that can rival any in the country. He is among the very best of the very best and continues to make Minnesota proud.

HOW WOULD YOU DESCRIBE YOUR COACHING STYLE? "The simple thing in education is that kids come first. So, we just say whatever is best for the kids, that is the way we are going to do it. I think my coaching staff's philosophy is that we believe a lot can be accomplished if nobody cares who gets the credit. I think egos are a double edged sword. I think you have to have an ego because you want to be associated with success, but you don't want it to get in the way of the team. You know, we rarely talk about winning. We just emphasize the fundamentals and ingredients to be successful. Our kids are definitely confident though and they know that whoever they are competing against on a given day will probably have to run the perfect meet to beat them. So, we have a positive expectancy to be the best. I can't say that they expect to win every time, but that is kind of the way they feel I guess. They just expect to win and if it doesn't happen it didn't mean that we let down, it meant that somebody else was simply better."

HOW DO YOU MOTIVATE YOUR PLAYERS? "Motivation is a simple thing. I think you can get anything you want out of this life if you help enough other people get what they want. For me, helping kids reach their goals is what it is all about and motivating them always comes back to the team concept. I also write my kids a very personal letter from the heart every year, to encourage them and to keep them focused. I always remember the quote from (Oregon track legend) Steve Prefontaine: 'Some people race to see who is the fastest… we race to see who has the most guts.' You know, I also have four retired teachers as assistant coaches with around 140 years of experience behind them, and that is just great for our kids too."

HOW DO YOU BUILD TEAM UNITY & CHEMISTRY? "No one person is any more special than the next guy on my teams. Chemistry is built on a sense of fairness for me. I really don't treat our No. 1 shot-putter who holds the all-time state record any different than I treat our no. 7 shot-putter. We just treat the kids as people. Sure, some of them are better than others: faster, stronger, and what have you, but we reward loyalty and hard work."

WHAT'S THE SECRET TO YOUR SUCCESS? "I hate to lose. I also want to make sure that when we are up on an opponent, that they have no chance of coming back. I am not the kind of guy who enjoys a 2-1 baseball game, if I am watching the Twins I want them to win 12-0. To me that is fun. It's not like I'm talking about running up the score, but at the same time when you have got somebody down, you want to make sure that they don't any thoughts about coming back to get you later. You just have to keep the pressure on and I thrive on that. I think when we keep the pressure on the other team then we don't feel it ourselves. We just keep at it."

HOW DO YOU WANT YOUR COACHING EPITAPH TO READ — HOW DO YOU WANT TO BE REMEMBERED AS A COACH? "He had passion for what he did. It is all about the kids and that was what he was all about."

An excerpt from Fleming's 2003 team letter:

"I'd like you to forget for a moment that we are going for (state title) No. 6. That is a burden that you lifted this Winter and Spring when you worked hard and performed magnificently. It is just a number. For this team, this particular group of guys, we're going for our first one. Take care of this ONE. Consider it an advantage that we've had so much success over the years. It's your inheritance. What you do with it is up to you. The other Mounds View champions had obstacles and worthy opponents. They prevailed. If they could do it so can you. Claim your place in the unparalled Mounds View Track tradition. Take that thought captive. None of our opponents can share in that. Only you know what it's like. They are in awe of you. They want what you have but don't know how to capture that sense of confidence and pride. Continue to compete with poise and precision. Others may try hard, but you know how to go beyond the effort. There is something extra inside each of you that manifests itself when called upon. You have ambition and drive. You compete with a need to enforce the momentum of your will on the inertia of circumstance. Embrace our tradition. It will carry you to a level of performance that exceeds anything you've done before."

"Some succeed because they are destined to; most succeed because they are determined to." — *Anatole France.*

TIM MILES: ST. JOHN'S TRACK & FIELD and CROSS COUNTRY

As an athlete at St. John's, Tim Miles was an All-MIAC performer in cross country. There, in addition to winning the MIAC six-mile run championship, he also finished as the runner-up in the steeplechase event in track in 1976. After receiving his master's degree in forestry from the University of Minnesota in 1979, Miles returned to St. John's in 1979 to serve as the head coach of the cross country and track and field programs. Now, a quarter of a century later, Miles has produced a winning program that has finished among the MIAC's top two squads in 20 of the past 24 seasons and have won seven MIAC titles (1981, 1982, 1983, 1996, 1997, 1998 and 1999) along the way. At the national level, Miles' teams have gained 14 top 15 finishes at the NCAA Division III meet and have produced 14 All-Americans. The Johnnies have also qualified as a team for the national meet 18 times since 1979. Miles' track and field teams have also consistently finished among the best in the MIAC and at the NCAA level. In fact, his teams have produced 38 Division III All-America performances since 1980 as well. Tim Miles is among the best of the best and is still going strong up in Collegeville.

RANDY SMITH: UM-MOORHEAD WOMEN'S TRACK & FIELD

Randy Smith reached some remarkable heights as an NCAA Division I national champion high jumper at the University of Kansas. Smith, who was once ranked third in the United States and 10th in the world, was named head women's track coach at The University of Minnesota Moorhead in 1979. Over the next 15 years Smith would build a division III powerhouse. Smith has guided the Lady Dragons to 10 Northern Sun Intercollegiate Conference Indoor and Outdoor team titles, and 280 All-NSC individual awards. Smith also produced four consecutive national relay titles in the 4 X 800, and a national hurdle champion as well. In all, Smith developed 11 national champions, 27 All-Americans and 72 national place winners. Under Smith's guidance, the Dragons finished in the top 10 four times at national indoor meets and also logged two top 10 outdoor performances. Smith resigned as head coach of the Dragons in 1994, as a true track and field legend — both as a competitor and coach.

BILL THORNTON: ST. OLAF TRACK & FIELD and CROSS COUNTRY

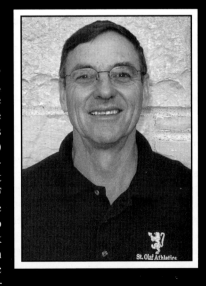

Bill Thornton graduated from the University of Kansas with a physical education degree in 1963 and then received his master's degree from the University of Arkansas in 1964. From there, Thornton got into teaching and coaching. He would eventually wind up at St. Olaf, where he would become a cross country coaching icon. Now entering his 33rd year as the head coach of the Oles track & field and cross country programs, his statistics are amazing. During his tenure he has coached 96 Midwest Conference and Minnesota Intercollegiate Athletic Conference (MIAC) champions, and 29 NCAA Division III, and one NCAA College Division All Americans, including five National champions. Of the conference champions, 13 are MIAC record holders — eight indoors and five outdoors. A strong believer in coaching education, Thornton also holds USAT&F Level I and II Coaching Certifications as well as Bronze and Silver Level Certification in the Pole vault. His Level II Certifications are in the event areas of jumps and throws. Thornton is a also member of the United States Track Coaches Association and the NCAA Division III Track Coaches Association, where he has served as the secretary since 1984. Since 1985 he has been involved in the United States Olympic Festivals, sponsored by the United States Olympic Committee, serving as a travel coordinator, and most recently as an assistant commissioner for men's athletics. A 1996 Sabbatical Leave enabled Thornton the opportunity to serve as co-manger of equipment and co-supervisor of field of play for the centennial Olympic Games in Atlanta. Ranked as an associate professor of physical education, his teaching expertise includes a variety of activity classes as well as exercise physiology, and lifeguard training. In addition, Thornton has carried his strong beliefs in teaching and coaching education and served as a clinician at numerous clinics around the country. Bill and wife Merrell have two sons, both of whom are coaches of track & field in Minnesota — Mark, who is at Northfield High School and also serves as an assistant at St. Olaf, and Paul, who is at St. Mary's University.

RON MASANZ
COLLEGE TRACK & FIELD: UM-MOORHEAD

Ron Masanz grew up in South St. Paul and went on to play in the third ever state high school hockey tournament in 1947 at South St. Paul High School. From there, Masanz played football at the University of Minnesota, where he was a reserve center. After graduating from the U of M, Masanz began working as an assistant coach back at South St. Paul High School. Then, in 1951, he went into the Marine Corps, where he coached football in Jacksonville, Fla. (One of his players was none other than the Splendid Splinter himself, Ted Williams.) Masanz's first teaching and coaching job was in Graceville, Minn, followed by a 12-year stint at Morris High School, where he taught and coached track and football. Masanz then moved to the University of Minnesota-Moorhead in 1968, where he was recruited to be the assistant football coach under Ross Fortier. The head track coach position, according to Masanz, "was just something that came with the job…"

By 1972 the Dragons had secured their first Northern Intercollegiate Conference track title, and things were just getting warmed up. The dynasty that ensued was nothing short of amazing. Masanz would lead his Dragons to 28 NIC Indoor and Outdoor team championships. He also developed 322 conference individual and relay champions. And, he tutored 49 All-Americans and 69 NAIA and NCAA Division II national place winners. In addition, Masanz led the Dragons to a 50-meet home indoor winning streak in Alex Nemzek Hall from 1970-81. Masanz would coach Moorhead Track and Field for a total of 19 years before hanging up the cleats in 1986. (He also coached football for nine seasons as well.) Masanz then came out of retirement in 1990 for one more year, winning both the indoor and outdoor NSIC conference championships before hanging it up one more time. Since that time, he has been an active contributor to the athletic department and is frequently called upon for advice.

Among his many coaching awards and accolades, Masanz was named as the NAIA District IV Coach of the Year seven times. In addition, he was elected to the NAIA Track Hall of Fame in 1985, the Dragon Hall of Fame in 1991, and the Northern Sun Intercollegiate Conference Hall of Fame in 2000. Masanz also served as NAIA national representative at the 1984 Olympic Games in Los Angeles, and was a member of the United States Track and Field Hall of Fame selection committee as well. Masanz is also involved with the Winged Foot Club, an organization of former UM-Moorhead men's track & field and cross-country athletes which provides scholarships and equipment for the school. Then, in 2000, the Winged Foot Club established the $250,000 Ron Masanz Endowment, which will be used each year for student-athlete scholarships for men and women participating in Dragon track & field and cross-country. Oh yeah, they also renamed the track after him too. Not bad!

Under Masanz's leadership the Dragon Track and Field program grew to both regional and national prominence. A relentless worker, Masanz wouldn't quit chasing his dreams until the Dragons had reached every reasonable goal in sight. With only one losing season in 40 years of coaching, he simply never quit. An amazing coach and an amazing person, Ron Masanz is a track and field coaching legend. And he is still going strong! At 75 Ron still runs three miles every day and swims every other day. He and his wife run regularly together and even run the Grandma's Marathon 5K every year as well. Ron is even planning a trip to the 2004 Summer Olympics in Athens, where he is planning on running the original marathon route from the first Olympiad. Ron and his wife have five children and presently reside in Park Rapids.

HOW WOULD YOU DESCRIBE YOUR COACHING STYLE? "You know, I never ran track a day in my life and I couldn't beat a turtle, so I just sort of learned as I went along. I think if you asked most of my kids over the past 40 years they would say it was pretty hard-nosed. We may not have had the best talent, but we were going to be successful because there were not too many teams that were in better physical condition and were more motivated than we were. It all comes down to making kids believe. You have to have some talent, but you can overcome some of that if your kids believe in themselves."

HOW DID YOU MOTIVATE YOUR PLAYERS? "There is no such word as can't in my vocabulary. I just didn't want anybody to think that they couldn't do something. So, we went into every meet thinking we could win it. It didn't take long for the kids to buy into that philosophy and it just grew from there. From there, we had the kids make three commitments to the program: a physical commitment, a mental commitment and a spiritual commitment. Now for the spiritual commitment, I didn't care if they were Hindu, Muslim, Catholic, Jewish, Lutheran, or even atheists, I just wanted them to have a spiritual side for them to focus on. Now, because track and field is not so much a team sport, I tried to make it a team concept anyway — like in football. So, we would have our sprinters, our long distance runners, our hurdlers, our throwers, or what have you, become a team together. They all hung out together, contributed to each other's growth together and supported each other. Another thing I did was that I tried to congratulate every kid at the end of each race, right on down to the guy who finished last. I never cut anybody either, unless they did something awfully bad. I told my kids that if they stuck with me for four years that I could almost guarantee them a trip to the national championship — and I fulfilled that promise about 85% of the time over my tenure. My philosophy was that if you stayed at it long enough, and didn't give up, and didn't say can't, it could be done."

LOOKING BACK WHAT ARE YOU MOST PROUD OF IN YOUR CAREER? "We did a good job and people recognized that. All we did was work hard and we just outworked our competition. As a result we were always invited to the Big 10 and Big 12 meets against the top division one schools in the nation. The only reason we got invited was because we had quality kids. We weren't going to beat them because we didn't have the numbers, but it was an honor to be there with them. I mean we couldn't even give kids scholarships, we could only get them jobs working in food service. I think my kids had good experiences here though and that makes me proud too. To see them contributing now, after they have graduated, means an awful lot too. Another thing that I did that I was proud of was my 24-hour open door policy with my kids, both at my office and at home. I mean had kids call me at three in the morning to tell me that their dad died and they didn't have any money to get home. So, you get up and drive them home, and talk to them and comfort them. We were a family. I just tried to be a decent guy that's all. I am also proud of the endowment fund named in my honor, and also that they renamed the track after me. I will never forget my father's face when he saw that. He was a butcher at the packing house his whole life and when he saw my name on that track his eyes lit up and he said 'What the heck is this?!'. So, that was great. It has all been great."

WHAT WAS THE KEY TO RECRUITING? "You just have to

get out and see a lot of people. One year I went to 312 high schools in Minnesota to recruit, and that was when the little schools were still independent and not all combined like they are today. Of course, I could recruit for both track and football, because at Moorhead we allowed our kids to play two sports — which doesn't happen everywhere, but it was tough. You just had to keep at it and work hard."

HOW DID YOU BUILD TEAM UNITY & CHEMISTRY? "I stressed the team aspect. What I did, because we didn't have a very big staff, was to assign the juniors and seniors to be the event leaders. That way those guys would help to coach the freshmen and sophomores. I even set up individual team schedules at practice for each separate group of athletes. I trusted them to work hard and it paid off. So, it was putting that all together and then making them believe, that was how we created team unity."

FAVORITE LOCKER ROOM SIGN? "The Three D's: Determination, Dedication and Desire"

WHAT ARE THE KEY INGREDIENTS TO CREATING A CHAMPIONSHIP TEAM? "It starts with attitude. You have to have the right chemistry and attitude. If you can motivate people and make them believe, then you can win championships, no problem."

WHAT'S THE SECRET TO YOUR SUCCESS? "Hard work. My parents came from the old country. My mother was from Austria and my father came from Germany, and they knew the meaning of hard work. Other than that I just tried to treat kids like I wanted to be treated. I also put the time in and worked hard. The key thing for us was conditioning and we ran 440's (now it is 400 meters, not yards) until they came out of their ears. We had one kid that took a bet and ran all the way up here one weekend from St. Paul along I-94. Our kids were in shape, no question! Beyond that I was organized to the Nth degree and that was critical for our success too."

WHAT WOULD YOU WANT TO SAY TO YOUR FANS, BOOSTERS, AND ALUMNI WHO HAVE SUPPORTED YOU ALL THESE YEARS? "Thank you for believing in what we were trying to do. I loved every minute of it and to tell you the truth I miss coaching terribly and wish I could do it all again. I find myself following kids around the country to support them and to watch them compete. That is how I stay involved in the sport. I have been out of it for 17 years now, but still keep in touch with a lot of my kids. In fact, my wife and I send out over 500 Christmas cards every year to a lot of them. My wife even sends out little red Dragon shoes to our former athletes when they have babies. We are still all family. They are grown and have families now and have successful careers — that is just great to see. I miss the kids, I just loved them."

HOW DO YOU WANT YOUR COACHING EPITAPH TO READ — HOW DO YOU WANT TO BE REMEMBERED AS A COACH? "Here lies a guy who worked hard and didn't believe that it couldn't be done."

LYNNE ANDERSON: GOPHER TRACK & FIELD

Lynne Anderson, of Andover, a two-time Olympian discuss thrower in 1976 and 1980, has coached the women's and men's throw teams at the University of Minnesota since 1980. During her 22 years of coaching, Anderson has produced 23 All-Americans and over two dozen Big Ten titles. She was also the assistant coach of the 1997 World Cup Team and has presented numerous throw clinics both nationally and in Minnesota.

JOE SWEENEY: ST. THOMAS WOMEN'S CROSS COUNTRY & TRACK & FIELD

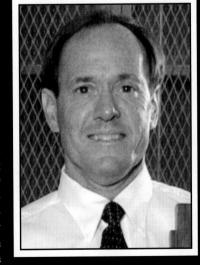

Joe Sweeney grew up in Chicago and went on to become a standout distance runner for the Tommies in the late 1970s. From there, Sweeney would get into coaching and eventually wound up back at St. Thomas as the head coach of the women's cross country and track & field teams. Nearly a quarter of a century later, Sweeney has built one of NCAA Division III's most successful cross country and track and field programs. The numbers are impressive. Under Sweeney, the Lady Toms have posted three consecutive impressive MIAC team championship winning streaks, including 14 outdoor track titles from 1985-98; nine indoor track titles from 1989-97; and nine cross country titles from 1981-89. Incredibly, UST has earned 48 MIAC team championships out of 63 contested in cross country, indoor track and outdoor track. Sweeney has also coached 19 individual national champions (two in cross country and 17 in track & field), and nearly 125 All-Americans as well. He also has 16 top-seven national team finishes in cross country (five championships and five runner-ups), and is the only coach in Minnesota to win an NCAA track relay championship (4x100 in 1997). In addition, Sweeney has had top-five national team placings in cross country, indoor and outdoor track in 25 of a possible 62 times. Furthermore, UST has had a cross country All-American or a team in the national meet 21 out of 23 seasons. Sweeney was named National Coach of the Year in track and field in 1995 and has been honored as MIAC Coach of the Year several times as well. An outstanding coach and an outstanding person, Joe Sweeney has created a dynasty at St. Thomas and has done it with quality people whom he cares deeply for. Sweeney's teams have been filled with excellent students and active members of the campus scene, which is very important to him. A real legend, Joe and wife Kathleen reside in New Brighton and have five children.

BUD MYERS: MANKATO CROSS COUNTRY

Earl "Bud" Myers grew up in St. Joseph, Mich., and went on to teach and coach track and field at Minnesota State Mankato from 1948-79. Over his 31 year tenure, Myers captured a combined 25 Northern Intercollegiate (NIC) and North Central Conference (NCC) titles. Myers' cross country teams reached the national meet for 23 consecutive years and, in addition to gaining a pair of second-place finishes in 1960 and 1968, finished lower than 10th only twice during that span. Myers also coached the MSU football team for four years, from 1949-52, during which they won three conference titles. Myers even served as the president of the National Collegiate Track Coaches Association from 1969-72 as well. Myers, after which MSU's fieldhouse is named, is also member of the MSU and NIC Halls of Fame.

LARRY RUSS: ST. THOMAS TRACK & FIELD

Larry Russ was a practicing chiropractor when he was hired at St. Thomas in 1969 to coach the men's cross country and track and field teams. Russ coached track and field at UST until 1980 (when Mark Dienhart replaced him), and also cross country (including a pair of women's teams in 1977-78) until retiring in 1993. His 1984 and 1986 men's cross country teams won NCAA Division III team championships, and his 1985 team won the National Catholic Championship meet by outrunning Division I powers Villanova and Notre Dame. During his tenure at UST, Russ coached 23 All-Americans, including 1982 national champion Nic Manciu. In addition, from 1975-92 Russ' teams qualified for the nationals 17 out of 18 times, and they placed in the top seven in Division III in 11 of 13 years from 1978-90 as well. Under Russ, the Tommies have won 13 MIAC titles, including 10 in row from 1984-93. Larry Russ is a true Tommy coaching legend.

BILL HUYCK: CARLETON CROSS COUNTRY

Bill Huyck graduated from Carleton College in 1953 and went on to become a coaching legend with the Knights. During his illustrious career in Northfield, Huyck led Carleton to the 1980 cross country national championship, the only national title in school history. In addition, he led the cross country team to 12 Midwest Conference titles and also coached Dale Kramer, one of greatest Division III cross country and track runners of all time. Furthermore, Huyck won a total of 10 Midwest Conference titles as the head indoor track coach as well.

LEFTY WRIGHT: ST. LOUIS PARK HIGH SCHOOL TRACK & FIELD

Lefty Wright, a Minnetonka native, went on to serve as the head cross country coach at St. Louis Park High School from 1964-69. In addition, he also served as the assistant track coach from 1958-69 as well. Although Wright didn't coach for a very long period of time at the high school level, he certainly made the most of his time in the spotlight. Wright's cross country teams won one state title in 1961, finished second in 1963 and 1968, and came in third in 1964 and 1969. Additionally, his track teams won four state titles in 1962, 1963, 1965 and 1966 — not bad considering the guy only coached for six seasons! Furthermore, Wright was a region/section cross country meet director for 32 years and gave 33 years of service to the Minnesota State High School League in both cross country and track meets in a wide variety of responsibilities. Wright has also been an official for numerous championship events and provided training for officials at multiple track and field clinics.

GARY WILSON: GOPHER WOMEN'S CROSS COUNTRY and TRACK & FIELD

Gary Wilson grew up in Lyndonville, N.Y., and went on to compete in cross country and track & field at Cortland State, N.Y., captaining all three teams as a senior. From there, Wilson got into coaching. His first gig was at the University of Wisconsin-LaCrosse, where he built the program into a Division III powerhouse. There, Wilson coached the women's teams to three consecutive national track and field championships and one national cross country title. UWL finished in the top five at cross country nationals in six of Wilson's eight years with the program. He also coached the Wisconsin-LaCrosse men's track and field team for seven years, coaching both the men's and women's teams in 1982 and 1983. In all, his teams at UWL won 21 conference titles.

From there, Wilson came to Minnesota, and now entering his 19th season in Gold Country, he has become a coaching icon. Wilson has guided the Lady Gophers to five consecutive trips to the NCAA meet and placed 25th at the 2001 NCAA Cross Country Championships. In each of the last five seasons, the Gophers have finished in fourth-place or higher at the Big Ten Championships. In addition, the Gopher cross country team has finished in the upper half of the conference 13 of the past 14 seasons and has been ranked among the nation's top 25 teams in 12 of the past 15 seasons. The 1989 squad made its first trip to the NCAA meet since 1983 and Wilson's achievements were recognized by his fellow coaches as he was named 1989 Region IV Coach of the Year after guiding the Gophers to a second-place finish at the regional championships. In 1991, Wilson led the Gophers back to the national championships, and their 17th-place finish was the team's highest since 1983, a finish his team duplicated 1999. In all, Wilson has led Minnesota to seven NCAA cross country championship meets and has coached 42 women track and field All-Americans as well as 12 women cross country All-Americans. (He has also coached 25 men track and field All-Americans too.)

Wilson is also very involved in the growth of his sport. He served as the president of the Women's Intercollegiate Cross Country Coaches Association in 1994 and 1995. He also served as the Region IV representative on the national committee from 1987-91. Other accomplishments in his highly distinguished career include coaching the U.S. junior team that participated at the 1993 World Cross Country Championships in Amorebieta, Spain, and the World Junior Track and Field Championships in Sydney, Australia, in 1996.

Wilson is also considered to be one of the foremost authorities in the United States on distance training. Not only has he produced many national-class runners, he is also a teacher of coaches. Wilson served as the national curriculum coordinator for endurance events in the USATF Coaching Education Program from 1984-93. He also teaches a number of schools, does clinics at the Olympic Training Center every year, and is often sought after to speak at camps and clinics throughout the country.

Gary Wilson is among the most respected coaches in the country and he should be commended for encouraging his kids to be all-around people, stressing both academics and athletics. Gary and his wife Suzy reside in Stillwater and have three children: Ben, Laura, and Adam.

PHIL LUNDIN: GOPHER TRACK & FIELD

Phil Lundin earned his bachelor's degree in physical education from Augsburg College in 1974, where he was the captain of his football and track teams. Lundin went on to earn his master's degree in physical education from the University of Minnesota in 1976, and then got into teaching and coaching. Lundin's first gig was at Burnsville High School, where he taught physical education and health, and was the assistant cross country and track & field coach for 12 years. While there, he helped build the Blaze into a state powerhouse in the tough Lake Conference and also helped to lead the cross country teams to three straight Class AA state titles from 1978-80. He also won the state track and field title in 1978 as well.

From there, Lundin came to the University of Minnesota, where he would first serve as an assistant before later taking over as the head track and field coach from the legendary Roy Griak. Since then, Lundin has built the Gopher program into a national contender through a lot of hard work and also through his ability to recruit. In fact, one of the reasons he is so successful recruiting in the Scandinavian countries is due to the fact that he speaks three Scandinavian languages. Lundin's tenure in Gold Country has been filled with many outstanding accomplishments. He has led the team to three Big Ten championships, including back-to-back outdoor titles in 1998 and 1999 and the program's first ever indoor title in 1998. The Gophers have finished no lower than fourth in any of the Big Ten meets with Lundin as head coach and have placed either first or second at the outdoor championships in six of his seven seasons at the helm. In addition, Lundin's student athletes have earned 45 All-America certificates, 65 Big Ten Conference Gold Medals and 68 Academic All-Big Ten awards.

Among his many coaching awards and accolades, in 1998 Lundin was named as the 1998 Big Ten Indoor Coach of the Year and was the unanimous choice for Outdoor Coach of the Year after leading Minnesota to their first title in 30 years. He would make it two Big Ten Outdoor Coach of the Year awards in a row in 1999 as well. Lundin has established Minnesota as a perennial title contender and, despite working in a cold weather climate, has found a way to get it done. Phil and his wife Sue presently reside in Apple Valley and have two children, Dan and Teresa.

DIANNE GLOWATZKE
COLLEGE VOLLEYBALL: ST. CLOUD STATE

Dianne Glowatzke grew up in Chaska and went on to graduate from Chaska High School in 1964. From there, Glowatzke went on to play volleyball and basketball at Minnesota State Mankato, becoming a pioneer of sorts in women's intercollegiate athletics. Glowatzke received a teaching degree in physical education and health from MSU and then went on to get her first teaching and coaching job at Annandale High School. Glowatzke stayed nine years at Annandale before coming to St. Cloud State in 1977, where she coached volleyball and softball. She would eventually give up her softball duties, however, to focus solely on volleyball.

Glowatzke would then go on to become a volleyball coaching legend at St. Cloud State, retiring 26 seasons later at the end of the 2002 season with a 527-418 career record. Glowatzke won one NSIC title along the way, and also led her squad to a regional tournament in 1995 in which they wound up in the elite eight nationally. Only the second person to coach volleyball in the history of Husky athletics, Glowatzke ranks among the top 10 in career wins in NCAA Division II volleyball. She retired after the 2002 season and now resides in Santa Fe, New Mexico.

HOW WOULD YOU DESCRIBE YOUR COACHING STYLE? "There are many spectrums of coaching, but I would say that the emphasis has to be on the student-athletes and that the things we do as coaches is all for the betterment of those people. You know, I just read Hilary Clinton's new book and she talked in terms of the discipline of gratitude. That is something that I think we all need to remember and hopefully something we can pass on to our athletes as well. Also, I think that when teams do well, it is the athletes and not the coaches, who deserve the credit."

HOW DID YOU MOTIVATE YOUR PLAYERS? "I put the emphasis on my kids to be the best that they could possibly be in whatever they did. I encouraged them to work as hard as they could and then they would be able to determine their own outcomes. Volleyball was a team sport, so as long as everybody worked as hard as they could, then the team would be successful. Then, all coaches have their own little ways of pushing their players, and that is important too. You have to push athletes differently because they are all different types of people. Some will respond to positive reinforcement whereas others need to be pushed. I believed in treating everybody according to their personality, so finding that out was the key. It is a system of trial and error, but once you find out what it is with that particular individual, then you will have success."

LOOKING BACK WHAT ARE YOU MOST PROUD OF IN YOUR CAREER? "I am proud of how I helped so many young people mature because that to me was the most important thing you could ever do."

WHAT WAS THE KEY TO RECRUITING? "So many things factored into recruiting, from the success of your program to your university environment, to the types of kids that you have. Your kids were also great recruiters too. Then, as coaches, we made a big impression on the kids as well, so you were really selling yourself to them. They had to feel comfortable with you in order for them to want to come to school and play for you."

HOW DID YOU BUILD TEAM UNITY & CHEMISTRY? "Some years you had it and others you didn't. Each year the personality of your team was different depending on the kids you had. The big thing with chemistry for me was the selection of captains. They are so important with team chemistry. They have to be able to communicate with the coaches but their peers have to trust them. Good captains can help motivate the entire team because they put a different kind of peer pressure on their teammates that you can as a coach. I think they are the most important members of the team, so I always tried to get the best people that I could to serve that role."

WHAT MOTIVATED YOU? "The love of sports motivated me. My dad really wanted to have a boy and he got me instead, so I was raised as a tomboy. Ever since I was a little girl I have just loved sports and loved the competition. Sure, winning is nice, but just to be able to compete and have fun is really what motivates me."

WHAT ADVICE WOULD YOU HAVE FOR YOUNG COACHES STARTING OUT TODAY? "Make sure that you have discipline. I think athletes will tell you, especially after they have left your program, that the rules, discipline and expectations that you had were very helpful to them later in life. So, it is important to have that and even though they might not be thrilled about it at the time, they will appreciate it later on."

WHAT'S THE BIGGEST THING YOU'VE LEARNED FROM COACHING THAT YOU'VE BEEN ABLE TO APPLY TO YOUR EVERYDAY LIFE? "To be able to sit down and evaluate myself the same way I evaluate my kids — that has carried over into my personal life. We don't ask ourselves enough who we are, where we are going and what we want to do in this world. So, that is one of the things that I have really taken away from athletics."

WHAT ARE THE KEY INGREDIENTS TO CREATING A CHAMPIONSHIP TEAM? "You need good athletes from a physical standpoint who are technically sound. Then, you need athletes who are mentally tough. Beyond that you need good coaching and a good school environment which offers a lot of support. Parents are also important, as is the support of the community at large. You need all of those things to be successful."

WHAT'S THE SECRET TO YOUR SUCCESS? "I could be fairly easy-going, yet I had great expectations for the athletes that I coached. They understood that I believed in them and cared for them though and that was very important to me."

WHAT WOULD YOU WANT TO SAY TO YOUR FANS, BOOSTERS, AND ALUMNI WHO HAVE SUPPORTED YOU ALL THESE YEARS? "I would just say thank you for all your support. I would also say thanks to all of our athletes who have given so much of themselves for this program."

HOW DO YOU WANT YOUR COACHING EPITAPH TO READ — HOW DO YOU WANT TO BE REMEMBERED AS A COACH? "I would want to be remembered as a coach was fair and cared about her athletes as people."

CAROL HOWE-VEENSTRA
COLLEGE VOLLEYBALL: ST. BEN'S

Carol Howe-Veenstra grew up in Crosby Ironton and went on to graduate from Crosby Ironton High School in 1971. From there, she went on to get her degree in physical education from Minnesota State University Moorhead in 1975, where she also starred on the volleyball team. After college Carol's first teaching and coaching job was at St. Cloud Technical high school. There, she led her girls to the region finals in seven of the 10 years she was at the helm, and also guided her teams to four state tournament appearances as well. In 1983 Howe-Veenstra got her master's degree in physical education from St. Cloud State University. Two years later she took over as the head volleyball coach at the College of St. Benedict. For 15 years Carol coached the ladies at St. Ben's, racking up a career record of 342-142 along the way. From 1986-94, and again in 1997, St. Ben's was selected for NCAA postseason competition. Carol has also served as the school's athletic director for the past 15 years as well, a position she assumed full-time since stepping down as head coach. Among her many coaching accolades, Carol was the MIAC Coach of the Year in 1989 and 1997, and was also the Central Region Coach of the Year in 1986 and 1990 as well. Additionally, she is a member of the UM-Moorhead, St. Cloud Technical High School, and Minnesota High School Volleyball Coaches Halls of Fames. Carol and her husband Steve have one son and live in St. Cloud.

HOW WOULD YOU DESCRIBE YOUR COACHING STYLE? "What I really loved about coaching volleyball was that you focused so much on the team aspect. The success of the team was so centered on knowing your role and contributing to your fullest extent. I really felt strongly about playing with intensity, playing with a passion and about making a commitment to discipline. Those were the trademarks of the teams that I coached."

HOW DID YOU MOTIVATE YOUR PLAYERS? "I think the main thing was to make sure that we were all striving for the same goals and had similar values about what we wanted out of our season. We had to then ask ourselves 'why we are here?' and 'what are we trying to accomplish?'. We also needed to have fun, that is so important to a team's success. We worked on all of this a lot in practice, because that is where it all started. From there I tried to motivate with a lot of positive reinforcement and with a lot of verbal intensity. I tried to make things very competitive and game-like in practice, but I also tried to make it fun. I wanted our kids to constantly improve themselves so that they could build their confidence and ultimately help the team to get better and better."

LOOKING BACK WHAT ARE YOU MOST PROUD OF IN YOUR CAREER? "There are so many great games, great highlights and great comebacks that I remember, but it is the relationships with my kids that mean the most to me. When your kids stay in touch with you and come back and visit you, that is so special. It is great to follow them as they continue to develop their careers, and when they make you a part of that, then that is another kind of victory that I am just as proud of."

WHAT WAS THE KEY TO RECRUITING? "The key to recruiting is really believing in what you have to offer and then finding a really good fit with a high school student athlete. You have to know the school, know your program and know who you are to be suc-

cessful. I think that over time it became more clear to me as to which types of athletes that I might be more successful with, so I tried to recruit them if I could. Then, it comes down to building relationships and making connections."

HOW DID YOU BUILD TEAM UNITY & CHEMISTRY? "There were so many things involved in building chemistry and in team building. We had retreats, we went camping, had cook-outs, we had discussions together and we just tried to understand each other as people. That way, when it came time to interact out on the floor, we could get the job done. It all comes back to respect, and if we respect one another, then we will be successful together as a team. I also believe very strongly in discipline and that helped to raise our standards immensely."

WHAT MOTIVATED YOU? "It is the excitement of that next challenge. It is asking our team 'how good can we be?' or 'how strong can we be?'. There was just an incredible amount of pride that I had in my team and that the team had in themselves and in the program. I loved preparing, I loved the details and I loved the practices. Getting a good recruiting class and putting all the pieces together each year was so exciting and that really motivated me to be my best."

WHAT ADVICE WOULD YOU HAVE FOR YOUNG COACHES STARTING OUT TODAY? "Look to find a mentor who can help you decide which of the details are most important. Then, when you are feeling a little lost in the shuffle, or criticized, or your plan isn't working, you will have someone who will listen to you and help you sort through it all."

WHAT'S THE BIGGEST THING YOU'VE LEARNED FROM COACHING THAT YOU'VE BEEN ABLE TO APPLY TO YOUR EVERYDAY LIFE? "I have learned to appreciate a much bigger variety of people, learning styles, and different kinds of competitiveness. I have also learned patience, which helps me in my administrative role as well as in my personal life to have those experiences with so many different student-athletes because they all have different gifts that they bring."

WHAT ARE THE KEY INGREDIENTS TO CREATING A CHAMPIONSHIP TEAM? "You need talent and you need people who want to compete."

WHAT'S THE SECRET TO YOUR SUCCESS? "You have to learn and study the game, and then you have to work very, very hard and believe in what you are doing."

WHAT WOULD YOU WANT TO SAY TO YOUR FANS, BOOSTERS, AND ALUMNI WHO HAVE SUPPORTED YOU ALL THESE YEARS? "No matter what the outcome, our fans and our family were just wonderfully supportive of us. Even when we weren't performing at our best, they weren't afraid to let us know and we appreciated that."

HOW DO YOU WANT YOUR COACHING EPITAPH TO READ — HOW DO YOU WANT TO BE REMEMBERED AS A COACH? "As somebody who was very passionate, intense and cared a great deal about the people she worked with."

Gretchen Koehler was born and raised in Winona and went on to attend both Winona High School as well as Winona State University. At the time, Winona State had no teams for women, but she participated in almost all sports on a club or intramural level in what used to be called "pay days," where teams just scrimmaged one another informally for competition. Koehler was a well rounded athlete and was good at softball, field hockey, basketball, tennis, volleyball, swimming, track and even bowling. She could do it all. Koehler was a multi-sport athlete who just didn't have the opportunities that girls have today. Koehler was, however, inducted into the Hall of Fame at Winona State as a tennis player, where she was able to compete in a sanctioned school sport. Koehler went on to receive her teaching degree in physical education. Her first teaching job was at Davenport West High School, in Iowa, where she stayed for two years. From there, she went on to graduate school at the University of Iowa to get her master's degree. In 1968 Koehler came to Gustavus and wound up staying until 2003, becoming a women's coaching legend along the way. At Gustavus she posted a 548-355-10 all-time career record from 1969-76, 1978-89 and 1991-96 (she left four different times to go on sabbatical). She also won four MIAC championships along the way. She most certainly would have won more too, had the MIAC had a championship prior to 1982 — when the league started championships for women. Koehler coached the Gusties for 27 years and is among the winningest college volleyball coaches in the country. Koehler also taught a variety of subjects within the Health and Exercise Science and Physical Education Departments at Gustavus as well. A great teacher and coach, Koehler retired in 2003 as one of the best in the business.

HOW WOULD YOU DESCRIBE YOUR COACHING STYLE? "I think I was real pragmatic and I liked to try new things. That worked particularly well for me because I came into the business at a point when things were changing all the time. I found that when I came in I had to go to camps just so that I could learn skills that I could then teach to my own players. So, I was always willing to learn and try new things. Other than that I think I was more of a player-centered coach. I liked to coach the players during practice but I like the leadership of my players to come out on the floor during games. I relied on my captains and on my upperclassmen a lot for that. I oftentimes wouldn't even go out to the huddle after I called a time out. I just called time out to stop the momentum sometimes. I didn't have anything earth shaking to say to them, so I just let them talk it out amongst themselves. They knew what they had to do and they knew if they messed up, so I let my leaders take care of that. My players enjoyed that style I think and we had a lot of success with it."

HOW DID YOU MOTIVATE YOUR PLAYERS? "They had the internal motivation already. They loved to play and they loved the sport. So, it really wasn't me dragging them out there and telling them to get going. I think most of it was internal because they just loved volleyball, and that is why they came out for the team. I never thought of having to use a tactic to motivate my kids, they truly loved the game and that was enough. Sure, when they got tired and those kinds of things, then we would have competitions to keep them going, but overall it was up to them."

LOOKING BACK WHAT ARE YOU MOST PROUD OF IN YOUR CAREER? "I think the individual players and how they have grown as people because of their involvement in sports. I remember getting a call from a former player who just had a baby and she told me that she remembered the stress-management breathing exercises that I had taught her and she was able to use them while she was in labor. Stuff like that is so much fun and makes me very proud. It is a whole life thing, and volleyball is just a small part of it. There was much more to life than volleyball and if I could give them some life skills about leadership, accepting defeat, being gracious when you win, and even about things like healthy eating, then that makes it all worth while. I was developing a whole person when I coached, not just a volleyball player who knew how to spike a ball."

WHAT WAS THE KEY TO RECRUITING? "The key to recruiting for me was finding kids who were interested in Gustavus first. Believe it or not, I never left campus to recruit. I would get names of kids from other people and then contact the kids directly. I never went out and contacted the players first, and that has all changed since I have retired. I don't know if you could operate like that anymore, but it was sure nice for me during my years there. I just stressed academics first and it was no different for me. I was a full-time professor and then the volleyball coach, not a full-time volleyball coach and also a professor. So, I practiced what I preached."

HOW DID YOU BUILD TEAM UNITY & CHEMISTRY? "Chemistry comes from the leadership of your upperclassmen. We used to always have a theme for each season and that worked well for goal setting. Then, we would also have an upperclassmen partner up with a new player to get to know them. When you have people doing things together and they become friends, then that builds chemistry. I really went out of my way to make sure that all of my players got to know each other off of the court and that helped build team unity too."

WHAT MOTIVATED YOU? "I love sports, I love being active and I love working with young people. To be able to give young people an opportunity to utilize their love of sports and help them get better in life, that motivates me."

WHAT ADVICE WOULD YOU HAVE FOR YOUNG COACHES STARTING OUT TODAY? "Don't take yourself so seriously and let the kids enjoy the game. I mean I used to dress up for Halloween and actually sit on the bench in my costume. I told my kids that it would probably be worth at least five points just from having the other team be so distracted from looking at me instead of watching the game. Hey, we were serious about competition, but we enjoyed ourselves and had fun along the way. That was important. You know, nowadays it is so important for coaches to feel like they have to win, and that is sad to me. It used to be about having fun, learning, improving and playing for the love of the game. If you did that, the wins would come."

WHAT'S THE BIGGEST THING YOU'VE LEARNED FROM COACHING THAT YOU'VE BEEN ABLE TO APPLY TO YOUR EVERYDAY LIFE? "I think that in winning and losing you have to realize that sometimes things go right and sometimes things go wrong. That is true for everything in life. You are not going to win 100% of the time, nor will you lose 100% of the time. Sports gives you that perspective, even though you try to push the envelope to only have the positives. There are going to be negatives along the way and that is just part of life. So if you take it in the right perspective and aren't so serious about everything, then you will be much happier and healthier."

WHAT ARE THE KEY INGREDIENTS TO CREATING A CHAMPIONSHIP TEAM? "You have got to have the horses for starters. You don't win anything with mediocre athletes. Then, they have to know the basics and have to be able to play together. I had some outstanding athletes and would really be nowhere without them. Hey, I didn't win any of those 500-plus games. I never set foot on the court and I did not score one point. My players did that and they were great. My job was to put together a system where they could play well in and be happy in. And I wasn't always successful either, but I learned from my mistakes and always tried to get better."

WHAT'S THE SECRET TO YOUR SUCCESS? "Just being who I am. I had my own unique personality and seemed to gel with a lot of people who made a difference in my career. So, thanks to my parents for my upbringing, my humor and for being pragmatic and caring people."

WHAT WOULD YOU WANT TO SAY TO YOUR FANS, BOOSTERS, AND ALUMNI WHO HAVE SUPPORTED YOU ALL THESE YEARS? "We have had some great fans, especially the parents of our players. When I think of all the meets that they traveled to, they were just such great supporters. And whether we won or lost they told us that we played well. They helped to support my philosophy and whatever I was trying to teach my players at the time and I really appreciated that. They always found the positives, even when we lost, and that was wonderful."

HOW DO YOU WANT YOUR COACHING EPITAPH TO READ — HOW DO YOU WANT TO BE REMEMBERED AS A COACH? "May she have a Bud Light up in heaven! We used to always joke about drinking beer and smoking because you were not allowed to drink or smoke if you were part of an athletic team at St. Ben's. So, maybe I would light up a Marlboro and crack open a cold one! No, I am just kidding. You see, I just always tried to have fun. That might be something I would say in the huddle in the middle of a tight match to loosen up the kids. That way they were laughing and could then relax and just play. I loved telling jokes and that made it fun for everybody. Really though, I guess I would like to be remembered as a coach who cared about her players and taught them lifelong lessons, not just volleyball, or tennis, or basketball, or golf, or softball, or cross country, or swimming or bowling — because I coached all of those sports at one time or another. Anything the kids wanted to do, I wanted to help them do it. So, if there were 10 kids

who wanted to run cross country, I helped them get that going. That was me and I hope I made a difference in doing that."

PATRICK LANIN: HOPKINS CROSS COUNTRY SKIING

Patrick Lanin is a Hopkins skiing legend. Lanin, who grew up on the Iron Range, graduated from Virginia High School in 1957, Virginia Junior College in 1959, and then the University of Minnesota in 1966 — where he competed in track and cross-country for the Gophers. Lanin's teaching and coaching career began at Hopkins in the Fall of 1966, where he taught ninth grade science. Lanin would go on to coach track and cross-country running for 30 years and cross-country skiing for 27 years at Hopkins. Later, he coached for three years at Brainerd as well. Lanin's ski coaching career began when Hopkins added a second high school and needed another cross country ski coach. Lanin had not skied prior to that, but learned from the grand master, Norm Oakvik, and two-time state Nordic ski champion, Tim Heisel. Lanin applied the same basic training patterns that he had used for cross-country running to Nordic skiing and it worked. At Hopkins, Lanin's ski teams won 17 sectional championships, 19 conference championships, and seven state championships — including seven individual state champions and three individual runners up. A real legend, Lanin was elected to the Minnesota Ski Coaches Association Hall of Fame in 1982, the Minnesota High School Coaches Association Hall of Fame in 1999 and the Minnesota Running and Track Hall of Fame in 2000. After retiring from teaching, Lanin won the US Master's Cross-Country Skiing Championships in 1999 and 2000. Also an avid runner, Lanin has competed in over 500 races from the 400 meters to the Marathon. Patrick and his wife Emily have three children and presently live on a 125 acre plot on the shores of Camp Lake, about 25 miles southeast of Brainerd — complete with ski trails and bike trails.

400 WINS CLUB MEMBERS: (HIGH SCHOOL VOLLEYBALL)

1. Donna Briton-Hawkins	Belle Plaine
2. Milan Mader	Lakeville
3. Gail Nucech	Hibbing
4. Kathy Frederickson	Moose Lake
5. Walt Weaver	Apple Valley
6. Susan Alstrom	Buffalo Lake-Hector
7. Pete Beckerman	USC
8. Steve Dickhudt	Concordia Academy
9. Deb Harvey	Hayfield
10. Karin Schumaker	Moorhead
11. Doug Smith	Columbia Heights

LINDA LARSON: UM-DULUTH VOLLEYBALL

Linda Larson grew up in Chicago and graduated from Northeastern Illinois University in 1971. Larson later joined the University of Minnesota-Duluth staff in 1975 as UMD's Coordinator of Women's Athletics. The following year, she became UMD's volleyball, women's basketball and softball coaches. In her six seasons at the volleyball helm, Larson compiled a record of 278-57 (.830) and guided the Bulldogs to three AIAW Division II National Tournament appearances, including a fifth place finish in 1980. And, in 1977 and 1978 her Bulldogs posted back-to-back 59-6 seasons. Her volleyball coaching accomplishments also list five consecutive Minnesota AIAW state championships and the inaugural three NSIC titles (1979-81). Larson, who coached just one season of softball with the Bulldogs (1977), spent seven years as the head women's basketball coach as well. During her tenure (1976-80 & 1981-84), the Bulldogs amassed a 110-85 record, including a 20-10 mark in 1983. After leaving the coaching ranks for good in 1984, Larson continued in her role as Women's Athletic Coordinator and Senior Woman Administrator. Then, in 2002, Larson retired after 27 years of service as a coach and administrator at UMD. Among her many coaching honors and accolades, Larson was the recipient of the 1999 President's Award for Outstanding Service to the University of Minnesota system. In addition, Larson served as the chair of the Commission on Women at UMD. The Commission later created the Linda M. Larson Outstanding Woman of the Year Award in her honor, which is given annually to a UMD faculty or staff member. Fittingly, Larson, a longtime advocate of female sports, was the inaugural recipient.

CHET ANDERSON
COLLEGE WRESTLING: BEMIDJI STATE UNIVERSITY

Chet Anderson grew up loving sports in White River, South Dakota. Anderson would become a football star at White River High School and then go on to play college football at the University of South Dakota, where he would eventually get his teaching degree. Just prior to graduating, however, Chet was called into active duty and spent five years overseas in World War II. There, he oversaw 130 men as an infantry company commander and even led his company into the occupation of Japan at the end of the war. At the onset of the war, while Chet was in Fort Ord, Calif., he played on a military football team with many players who had been playing in the NFL. He learned a great deal about the game while playing on the team, and many of those lessons would influence his coaching style years later. Anderson came home to finish college at USD after the war and from there he got his master's degree in education from the University of Minnesota.

Anderson's first teaching job, nine years after he started college, was at Anoka High School, where he coached football for four years and won a Suburban Conference title. From there, he taught two years in a parochial school in Iowa, and after that he came to Bemidji State in 1955. Anderson would teach physical education and health at BSU for 26 years, and coach everything from football to wrestling to tennis for the Beavers as well. While he had great success coaching football at BSU for 10 years, winning three conference titles from 1957-59 and posting a 43-34-5 career record, it was on the matt where Anderson became a real coaching legend. Anderson stepped aside as football coach following the 1965 season to concentrate on wrestling, where the Beavers were becoming a force among the nation's small colleges. Anderson guided the Beaver grapplers to several NAIA second-place finishes and coached four NAIA collegiate champions in 1971, 1975, 1976 and 1978 as well. His program also produced countless all-conference and all-Americans too. In all, he coached wrestling at Bemidji State for 26 years and would coach wrestling for a total of 34 years before finally retiring in 1981. While Anderson was elected to the NAIA Wrestling Hall of Fame in 1975, his greatest honor, however, came in 1996, when the football stadium at Bemidji State was renamed as Chet Anderson Stadium in his honor.

HOW WOULD YOU DESCRIBE YOUR COACHING STYLE? "I think I was very honest and very organized. I would say my philosophy to the game stemmed from my desire to have my players understand how I wanted the game to be played in every way. I had a plan for each player and for where he was going and what he wanted to be. I was an officer in World War II and went through military training to become an infantry company commander, so that training really prepared me for coaching. I was disciplined and expected the same from my kids. I wanted my teams to be very optimistic. I wanted them to leave the field at practice the night before a big game believing that they were going to win. I didn't want them to be overconfident, but I wanted them to put forth their best effort so we could win. I always wondered how you could say you were a good team if you always placed yourself as an underdog and every game you won was an upset. I was totally against the 'Gloomy Gus' approach."

HOW DID YOU BUILD TEAM UNITY & CHEMISTRY? "I think team unity comes from a loyalty to the school, a loyalty to the community and a loyalty to the team itself. So, I tried to build chem-istry on my teams by being very honest and very focused on being something in life. I wanted them to have goals and then I wanted them to reach for those goals. I also wanted my team members to be friends and to bond together. That is where good team unity comes from. You just need to stress that the team comes first, no matter what, and individuals come second. Ideally, you try to build a setting which is like a family, with everyone working together towards a common goal. Captains were very important in building chemistry and I relied on them heavily."

WHAT ARE YOU MOST PROUD OF IN YOUR CAREER? "Aside from all of the great kids that I had in my programs through the years, I would say that my biggest thrill as far as on the field went was when we took the team down to South Dakota and beat my alma mater, the University of South Dakota, very soundly. That meant a great deal to me and was right up there."

WHAT MOTIVATED YOU? "My military experience was extraordinary. The dedication that you have to have is unlike anything else. You see, in the military sense, as a commanding officer you were responsible for your men and to your men. That was a 24 hour a day responsibility that truly motivated you to be the best you could be. I tried to carry that with me in life to always be strong and take care of my men."

WHAT ADVICE WOULD YOU HAVE FOR YOUNG COACHES STARTING OUT TODAY? "I think coaches need to see their kids as more than just athletes, or tools to play and win ball-games, and as people — with futures. I think that they need to have an objective not just for their team and for winning, but specifically for their individual players. They need to help those individuals to succeed in life and to be something. If they coach them in that direction with good, hard discipline, then they will not only be successful, but they will also be producing young men and women into the community who will in turn be successful and productive people. That is important. Then, I would add too that it is very important for young coaches not to pamper their favorite players, because that will cause resentment with the other kids. Beyond that, listen to your assistants and back them up. But always remember it is the head coach who must take the responsibility and blame."

WHAT'S THE BIGGEST THING YOU'VE LEARNED FROM COACHING THAT YOU'VE BEEN ABLE TO APPLY TO YOUR EVERYDAY LIFE? "I think I have had a life with direction, a life with very good friends and a life with solid discipline. I think those things are indelible."

WHAT ARE THE KEY INGREDIENTS TO CREATING A CHAMPIONSHIP TEAM? "First of all you have to have ability, and beyond that there has to be cohesiveness, friendships and loyalty. You know, I don't feel that teams really play for coaches. I feel that teams play for themselves, for their teammates, for their school and for their community. That binding of the individuals together is the main ingredient for winning I think."

WHAT'S THE SECRET TO YOUR SUCCESS? "I always felt that practice never ended on the practice field. So, after practice I would go through the locker room and compliment players and try to

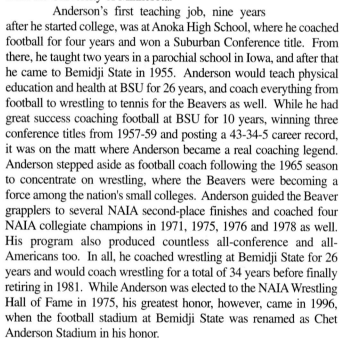

tell them things to work on for the future. That was important and it kept me in touch with the kids on a one-to-one basis. I also ran highly organized practices to utilize everyone's practice time to the fullest. There was no standing around for me, I wanted practice to be short, maybe an hour and a half, but very precise. I wrote out the plans on the bulletin board so every player knew what would take place that day and how much time would be spent doing each drill."

WHAT WOULD YOU WANT TO SAY TO YOUR FANS, BOOSTERS, AND ALUMNI WHO HAVE SUPPORTED YOU ALL THESE YEARS? "I always wanted the fans to see the game not in terms of wins and losses, rather I wanted them to appreciate the team effort. I hoped that they would cheer for our teams, not one individual at a time, but as a team — a whole unit. I always strived to have our teams represent our community and I wanted them to make the people very proud. So, thanks for all of their support, we appreciate it."

HOW DO YOU WANT YOUR COACHING EPITAPH TO READ — HOW DO YOU WANT TO BE REMEMBERED AS A COACH? "I would want to be remembered as somebody who was a role model. I always wanted to be a role model and I hope to be judged for that in every way. Maybe that was from my military background, but I always wanted to live a life that was exemplary and I wanted my team to respect me for that. In turn, I hope that many of them would live that way as well. I hope too that my kids knew that I was always concerned and cared for them, for their futures, and that I always considered them to be part of my family."

TOP 15 ALL-TIME WINNINGEST COACHES (HIGH SCHOOL WRESTLING)

1. Virg Vagle, Paynesville
2. Bill Sutter, Goodhue
3. Scot Davis, Owatonna, Hutchinson, Bird Island
4. Ron Malcolm, Anoka, Worthington
5. Ken Droegemueller, Osseo, Worthington
6. Gary Hindt, Wabasso
7. Bill Demaray, Apple Valley, Richfield
8. Greg Greeno, St. Michael-Albertville
9. Don Dravis, Staples
10. Rick Kelvington, Olivia
11. Jim Short, Simley
12. Bob Board, Coon Rapids
13. Richard Chakolis, Minneapolis North
14. Luverne Klar, Mankato, Mankato West
15. Gary Rettke, Spring Lake Park

MIKE HEBERT: GOPHER VOLLEYBALL

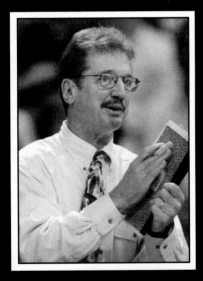

One of the winningest volleyball coaches in the nation, Mike Hebert continues to make history at the University of Minnesota. After graduating from the University of California-Santa Barbara in 1966, Hebert began his coaching career at the University of Pittsburgh, where, from 1976-79, he compiled a 129-52 mark with the women's team and a 60-21 record as the men's coach. In building the program, Hebert won the EAIAW Eastern Region Coach of the Year award in 1978 and 1979.

From 1980-83, Hebert coached the women's team at New Mexico, establishing a 60-57 record and advancing to the NCAA regional championships in 1981 with a 26-17 mark. Hebert was named the Intermountain Athletic Conference Coach of the Year in 1980 as well. Hebert would then go on to spend 13 years at Illinois, making history along the way. While at Illinois, Hebert led the Illini to four Big Ten titles and 11 consecutive NCAA tournament appearances, including the Mideast Regional seven times and the NCAA semifinals in 1987 and 1988. Hebert also posted an impressive 323-127 (.718) record, and finished in the upper half of the Big Ten for 11 consecutive seasons as well.

In 1996 Hebert came to Gold Country. Now entering his eighth season guiding the Gophers, he has turned the program into a national power. In Hebert's seven years at Minnesota (1996-2002), the Gophers are 173-66 (.724), 93-47 (.664) in the Big Ten, and have participated in six NCAA Tournaments. Hebert has also guided the Gophers to the big dance in six of his seven years at Minnesota. Three times (1999, 2000 & 2002) in the last four years the Gophers advanced to the Sweet 16, and in all of the NCAA appearances, Minnesota made it into the second round. The Gophers have also been among the top 12 nationally in attendance in all seven seasons. In 2002 Hebert's team became the first in the program's history to win the Big Ten title. Hebert, who also produced 13 All-Americans at the U of M, has also led the team to three second place or higher finishes in his seven years as well. Now in his 27th year of coaching, Hebert has compiled a 712-318 (.691) record, making him one of the winningest volleyball coaches in history.

Hebert has also been active coaching on the international scene too. In 1987, Hebert served as head coach of the U.S. women's team that competed at the World University Games in Yugoslavia. He was the assistant coach of the U.S. women's team at the 1981 World University Games in Romania and served as a head coach of the North team at National Sports Festival VI in 1985. In 1988, Hebert was the head coach of the U.S. National "B" team, which included squad members training for the 1992 Olympic team. He also served as head coach of the U.S. women's team competing at the 1991 World University Games in Sheffield, England, and at the 1991 Pan American Games in Havana, Cuba. In addition, Hebert traveled to the 1989 Canada Cup and 1990 Cuba Cup as part of a series of assignments with the U.S. National Team. Additionally, in 2002, Hebert coached the U.S. National Team at the Pan American Games.

Among his many coaching honors and accolades, Hebert has twice been named Big Ten Coach of the year at Minnesota and has received the award five times overall. Hebert was named National Coach of the Year in 1985 as well. In addition, Hebert served as the president of the American Volleyball Coaches Association from 1985-88. Furthermore, in 1998, Hebert joined the coaching staff of the USA Men's National Team as an advisory member.

A true living legend, Hebert is also the author of two books, including a co-written autobiography entitled "The Fire Still Burns." Mike and his wife Sherry presently reside in Minneapolis and have two daughters, Becky and Hillary.

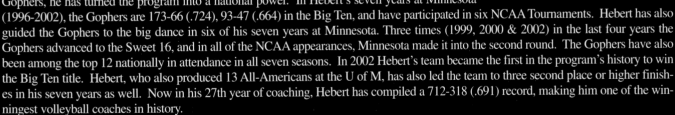

BILL DEMARAY
HIGH SCHOOL WRESTLING: APPLE VALLEY

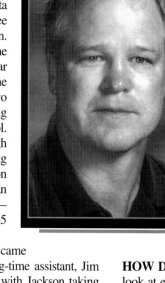

Bill Demaray has spent the better part of three decades devoted to the sport of wrestling. Demaray grew up in Casselton, N.D., and graduated from Casselton High School in 1968. From there, Demaray went on to attend North Dakota State University, where he got his teaching degree and was a two-time NCAA wrestling champion. Demaray's first teaching job was in Fargo, for one year at an elementary school, followed by a year at Fargo South High School. From there, he moved to Minnesota, where he spent the next two year teaching physical education and coaching wrestling and football at Richfield High School. In 1976 Demaray moved on to Apple Valley High School, where he started the school's wrestling program. Over the next 20 years he would go on to lead his teams to six state titles, compiling an amazing record of 407-70-4 along the way — complete with 18 individual champions and 45 place winners.

In 1995 Bill took a year off and then came back to serve as a co-head coach with his long-time assistant, Jim Jackson. That next year the two flip-flopped, with Jackson taking over and Demaray becoming his assistant. Together they went on to win another five more state championships for a grand total of 11. In addition to their 11 state titles, they have won six runner-ups and two thirds as well. They have also made 21 state tournament appearances, including 20 in a row. Their conference record over the past 26 years also stands at 190-4-1 (97.7%), and they have won 13 Lake and eight Missota Conference titles along the way. The numbers are simply astonishing. Apple Valley's total record over the past 26 years now stands at 624-73-7 (89.1%). Even their junior varsity is awesome, posting a 499-59-2 (89.3%) record during that time as well.

As an assistant, Demaray also won two state titles on the football team as well. A member of the North Dakota State University and Minnesota Wrestling Coaches Halls of Fames, Coach Demaray is a high school wrestling legend. Bill and his wife, Sharon, have two sons, Chad and Matt, who both were captains of Eagle wrestling teams as well. Matt, however, was also a two-time NCAA champion and became just the second Minnesota wrestler to win a National Open Freestyle Tournament in 1992 — a feat he repeated in 1993, 1994, and 1995.

The success of the Apple Valley Wrestling program goes back to its coaches, Demaray, Jackson and Dalen Wasmund. In addition to Demaray's accolades, Jackson is also a coaching prodigy. The 2002 National Coach of the Year, 2001 National High School Wrestling Coach of the Year and the 2001 Minnesota Wrestling Man of the Year, Jackson graduated from Oelwein (Iowa) High School and then went on to wrestle at Luther College, where he was a three-time NCAA Division III National Qualifier. In his seven seasons as Apple Valley's head coach, Jackson has compiled a gaudy record of 226-9-3, complete with 16 individual state champions, as well as 39 all-state and 10 academic all-state wrestlers. Jackson and his wife June reside in Lakeville with their daughter, Taylor Anne.

The third coach at Apple Valley is Dalen Wasmund, who currently teaches math at Apple Valley High School. Wasmund was an All-American at the University of Minnesota, where he won a Big Ten title. Wasmund also wrestled internationally as a two time National Champion, Olympic Festival Champion, World Cup silver and bronze medallist, two time U.S. Olympic alternate, and two time U.S. World Team member. Wasmund also coached the Minnesota Storm national freestyle and Greco teams for more than a decade as well. Before joining the Apple Valley coaching staff, Wasmund was

the head coach at Eagan High School, where he helped to build the youth through high school programs. Dalen and his wife Catherine have three sons: Neil, Bryce, and Ryan.

This incredible coaching tri-fecta is a proven winner and shows no signs of slowing down. Apple Valley High School has become synonymous with wrestling and that reputation goes back to the top, with its three great coaches. Here is some more of what the patriarch of that program, Coach Demaray, had to say:

HOW WOULD YOU DESCRIBE YOUR COACHING STYLE? "I think that success is achieved through learning and that learning is the key to success. So, everything needs to be structured around the kids and the people involved in your program, all learning and working together. Through that they enjoy whatever it is you are working towards."

HOW DO YOU MOTIVATE YOUR PLAYERS? "You have to look at each individual. Everybody is different so I try to motivate each person by understanding where they are at as people. From there I try to put them in a position where you can compliment their positives and eliminate their negatives by dealing with them in a one-on-one environment."

LOOKING BACK WHAT ARE YOU MOST PROUD OF IN YOUR CAREER? "The opportunity that I have to work with kids and maybe make a contribution towards their lives is very rewarding. To be able to provide them with great experiences and help them learn, that is real positive for me."

HOW DO YOU BUILD TEAM UNITY & CHEMISTRY? "You build chemistry by developing an attitude where they set a goal and are working towards that goal. Once they make a commitment to that and can see that they are achieving success through the learning process, that just builds on itself. Then, when you have successful people learning and enjoying what they are doing with other people who are doing the same thing, you have a positive attitude — which translates into chemistry."

IF YOU COULD MAGICALLY GO BACK IN TIME TO THE FIRST YEAR YOU WERE A HEAD COACH AND GIVE YOURSELF SOME ADVICE FOR THE FUTURE, KNOWING WHAT YOU KNOW NOW, BACK THEN, WHAT WOULD YOU SAY TO YOURSELF? "I would tell myself to just be patient and make decisions based on what is good for people."

WHAT MOTIVATES YOU? "I have been blessed with so many positive things in my life that, for me, I really enjoying giving back to people and sharing whatever I have through my experiences with them. I am just motivated by helping people and am grateful to have that opportunity."

WHAT ADVICE WOULD YOU HAVE FOR YOUNG COACHES STARTING OUT TODAY? "They have to really think through why they are there. If they want to be successful and they want to help people, then they need to not worry so much about winning and losing. Instead, they should be more concerned with developing an environment where kids can learn. Once you have that, then success will follow quickly. If kids are learning then they are having fun, and if they are having fun, then they will be successful."

FAVORITE LOCKER ROOM SIGN? "I will study and get ready and maybe my chance will come." — Abraham Lincoln

WHAT'S THE BIGGEST THING YOU'VE LEARNED FROM COACHING THAT YOU'VE BEEN ABLE TO APPLY TO YOUR EVERYDAY LIFE? "I have learned over time that everybody is different and that what can motivate one person might not necessarily motivate another. So, you need to address individual needs. I think that can not only be applied to coaching but also in dealing with people in whatever profession you are in. You just need to treat people with respect and understand that people are different. Once you do that, then you will be successful in whatever you do. If you only worry about wins, then your career will be short-lived."

WHAT ARE THE KEY INGREDIENTS TO CREATING A CHAMPIONSHIP TEAM? "First you have to have a sound philosophy. You have to show people that you care and are committed to what you are doing. If they know you care, then you can encourage them as well as criticize them in a positive way to try to get them to improve. You have to develop positive relationships. There are no shortcuts in success, you have to be willing to work hard and have a strong work ethic. Now, to have a successful program, you have to have continued success at a high level over a period of time. To have a successful team, you have to have a philosophy as to why you are there. Are you there to win X number of games, or are you there to develop an atmosphere of learning where kids are going to get better and have fun? I have always believed that through the learning process you will enjoy what you are doing and also be successful."

WHAT'S THE SECRET TO YOUR SUCCESS? "I think I am a caring person and I have always had a strong work ethic."

WHAT WOULD YOU WANT TO SAY TO YOUR FANS, BOOSTERS, AND ALUMNI WHO HAVE SUPPORTED YOU ALL THESE YEARS? "I would just say thanks. I have been really blessed and I appreciate all the support that I have received as a coach and as a person. It has been so enjoyable working with young people and helping them to get better in whatever they do."

HOW DO YOU WANT YOUR COACHING EPITAPH TO READ — HOW DO YOU WANT TO BE REMEMBERED AS A COACH? "I would want to be remembered as a person who cared and was very proud to help other people."

BUCKY MAUGHAN: UM-MOORHEAD WRESTLING

Arthur "Bucky" Maughan grew up in Canonsburg, PA, and went on to wrestle at Moorhead State University at the 115-pound category. There, Maughan became the only Dragon to ever win a Division I individual National Championship. Maughan, who had transferred to MSU from Indiana University, also won a pair of NAIA national championship at 123 pounds as well. Maughan then went on to coach at North Dakota State University in 1964, where he would become a legend. In fact, he is still going strong. Maughan, only the second wrestling coach in the school's history, has gone on to guide the Bison to a 394-112-11 record over the past 39 years, including four NCAA Division II National Championships (1988, 1998, 2000 and 2001) along the way. Among his many coaching honors and accolades, Maughan is member of the Dragon, NAIA and NSIC Halls of Fame.

MIKE MARCINIAK: CLOQUET HIGH SCHOOL CROSS COUNTRY SKIING

Mike Marciniak is a legend in cross country skiing circles and has been involved with the sport for more than a half century. Marciniak grew up in Cloquet and graduated from Cloquet High School in 1956, where he starred on the school's cross country team. Marciniak then went on to win a pair of MIAC titles in 1957 and 1958 at the University of Minnesota-Duluth. In 1958 Marciniak was named to the F.I.S. training squad under the direction of legendary coach Sven Wick, and in 1959 Marciniak skied in the North American Championships at Steamboat Springs, Colorado. In 1964 Mike joined Joe Nowak, Cloquet's head ski coach, and took over the cross-country program. His cross-country teams would play a major role in the 11 State titles won by Cloquet between 1965 and 1976.

Marciniak has had a major influence on cross-country skiing in the Central Division of the United States Ski Association. He was also the junior national coach from 1965 until 1993. One of his highlights from his tenure as junior coach was the second place finish of the Older Junior Boys relay in 1981 in Steamboat Springs. That team included his son Kevin, who went on to attain NCSA All-American status at Northern Michigan University. In 1982 the Older Junior Boys won the relay in Lake Placid and the Junior II Boys were second as well. The Junior Boys team included Mike's youngest son, Patrick. Marciniak spent 15 of those years as Junior Chairman of the CUSSA cross-country division. Marciniak was later awarded with three Central Division Presidential Awards for his work in the division. Marciniak hosted nearly 25 tryout or Central Division Championship races at Cloquet's Pine Valley. In addition, Marciniak was a U.S. Ski Team Regional Coach in 1969. In 1985 he also helped coach the U.S. Polar Cup Team in the Scandinavian race series in which athletes from the Eastern and Central Divisions were involved.

As Marciniak's coaching and competitive years began to wind down, he began to focus on his work as a technical delegate. In addition, since the early 1990's Marciniak has been a member of Cloquet's Park Board, where he represents the interests of Pine Valley — Cloquet's ski area, and ensures that Cloquet has state of the art grooming equipment. Marciniak was employed by Minnesota Power as a Customer Service Representative from 1962 until his retirement in 1995. In 1986 Marciniak was inducted into the Ski Coaches' Hall of Fame. A Nordic legend, Mike Marciniak is among the best of the best, and someone who truly gave back to the sport he loved.

RUMMY MACIAS
COLLEGE WRESTLING: MINNESOTA STATE MANKATO

Rometo "Rummy" Macias grew up in Davenport, Iowa, and went on to wrestle at the University of Iowa, graduating in 1948. In 1950 Macias came to Minnesota State Mankato, where he would inaugurate the MSU wrestling program. Nearly four decades later, Macias would leave MSU as a wrestling coaching legend. Macias simply dominated the wrestling competition in Minnesota during his tenure at Mankato and created a dynasty in the process. From 1950-88 Macias would lead MSU to three national titles (NAIA championships in 1958 and 1959 and a NCAA College Division title in 1965), eight Northern Intercollegiate Conference championships, and one North Central Conference title. In addition, Macias had 93 of his wrestlers attain all-America status (19 were national individual champions, 62 captured NIC individual championships and 12 won NCC individual titles.)

Macias also served two stints as MSU's golf coach, winning four NCC team titles and one NIC title along the way. In addition, Macias served as an assistant coach with the MSU football program as well. Among his many coaching honors and accolades, Macias has been inducted into seven Halls of Fame: MSU, NCC, NIC, NAIA, Amateur Wrestling, Minnesota Wrestling Coaches and the NCAA Division II Wrestling Association. Furthermore, he won several conference and national coach of the year awards, as well as an NCC Golf Coach of the Year too. He was even honored by the National Wrestling Hall of Fame with a Lifetime Service Award, in recognition of his dedication to the development of leadership and citizenship in young people through the sport of wrestling. Upon retiring from coaching at Mankato in 1988, Macias moved to Florida, where he lives in Singer Island with his wife, Ruth. There, in addition to teaching golf at a local country club, Macias also serves as the wrestling coach at nearby Cardinal Newman High School and even runs a wrestling camp as well. A real classic, Rummy Macias is without question a wrestling coaching legend in the state of Minnesota.

HOW WOULD YOU DESCRIBE YOUR COACHING STYLE? "I taught from a scientific standpoint and really emphasized mechanics, physics and leverage. Really, athletics are nothing more than angles, inertia, momentum and inert gravity. So, I think you have to understand the mechanical nuances of a human being and then teach from there. There is no forceful motion involved, it's all scientific. The ones that coach the forceful way are short-lived. That was my feeling."

HOW DID YOU MOTIVATE YOUR PLAYERS? "It was just a do or die type of attitude that I had. I set the examples myself and was very strict on the way I coached. I always felt that if you could succeed in wrestling then you could succeed in everyday life, and that has been proven hundreds of times by individuals who I have coached. In other words, we showed them how to live, how to be dedicated and we taught by example for them to become better citizens. As a result, they learned self esteem, confidence, character and really everything an individual needs to know to be successful in everyday life. That was my philosophy on motivation."

WHAT ARE THE CHARACTERISTICS OF WINNERS? "An individual who works hard towards his or her goal. Winners set their goals high and fear no one along the way."

WHAT ARE THE CHARACTERISTICS OF LEADERS? "A people person with honesty and good character who can stimulate and get along with others."

LOOKING BACK WHAT ARE YOU MOST PROUD OF IN YOUR CAREER? "That I came to Mankato State with a lot of happiness and determination and I left happy. I was able to carry on a good camaraderie with all my colleagues, faculty and co-workers, and can honestly say that I never had one enemy or a person that I held a grudge against."

WHAT WAS THE KEY TO RECRUITING? "You had to show your recruits that you could compete against the best. For me though, I had the jump on everybody. You see, I was just in the right place at the right time in being one of the early settlers of wrestling in the state. Coming up from Iowa I was able to stimulate the individuals in Southern Minnesota and get them excited about wrestling. Before long that area became a hotbed for wrestling talent and we tapped into that from the beginning. We got our program up and running and without scholarships we were still able to compete against the best. We just got them to believe and were able to convince them that they could do anything. Before long, all of our kids were out recruiting and telling other kids about our program. I promised them good competition and success after graduation. I was able to land a lot of big recruits that way and we had a very successful program for a number of years as a result."

HOW DID YOU BUILD TEAM UNITY & CHEMISTRY? "Wrestling is probably the number one sport for camaraderie. Oftentimes, after an individual wrestles, win or lose, the two wrestlers become friends. That is unique in sports. Wrestling is different because you are out there all alone and there is nobody to help you. We stuck together as a team though and really supported one another. Sure, we did things off the mat together too, and that all goes into building chemistry. But mostly, it comes from the kids themselves, that is the key — to get good kids who like each other and enjoy competing as a team together."

WHAT MOTIVATED YOU? "As a youngster I had goals in life and I was determined to reach the top by hard work. So, when I achieved a lot of that success as a young man at Iowa, I was able to carry a lot of that over into my coaching. I have always worked hard and have been motivated by success. I am also motivated by seeing my kids do well both on and off the mat."

WHAT ADVICE WOULD YOU HAVE FOR YOUNG COACHES STARTING OUT TODAY? "Honesty, integrity, hard work and leading by example to show your kids what it takes to become a champion. I also think it comes down to personality. Today you have to be a people person, a promoter and a salesman in order to be successful. You also have to be a good listener too. And try not to use the word 'I' so much, use 'we' instead. That is important."

FAVORITE LOCKER ROOM SIGN? "A little more effort will make you a champion."

WHAT'S THE BIGGEST THING YOU'VE LEARNED FROM COACHING THAT YOU'VE BEEN ABLE TO APPLY TO

YOUR EVERYDAY LIFE? "Hard work. I can do anything I want to if I put my mind to it and work towards that goal. I have always tried to convince my kids not to be the vice president, but to be president. Every individual that I coached had some good thing about them, and working towards that will make them a champion."

WHAT ARE THE KEY INGREDIENTS TO CREATING A CHAMPIONSHIP TEAM? "Unity, setting goals and working towards those goals, stressing character, integrity, not allowing cursing and a lot of hard work. All of those things went into it. Once you got the ball rolling and started having success, the recruits came pouring in and pretty soon you had an outstanding program which expected success year in and year out."

WHAT'S THE SECRET TO YOUR SUCCESS? "Convincing my wrestlers that they could win by working hard and practicing what I taught them. If they can become convinced that they can win with what you are teaching them, then that will translate into success. Once they believe that they can compete against the best competition in the country, then you have got something. My philosophy was this: No matter what kind of background you came from, I believed the tougher you had it in life, the more successful you would be."

WHAT WOULD YOU WANT TO SAY TO YOUR FANS, BOOSTERS, AND ALUMNI WHO HAVE SUPPORTED YOU ALL THESE YEARS? "It wasn't just one person, it was a combination of many, many people. I learned as I coached and I have hundreds and hundreds of people to thank in the city of Mankato. So, thanks too to all my former wrestlers who helped to make my success at Mankato State."

HOW DO YOU WANT YOUR COACHING EPITAPH TO READ — HOW DO YOU WANT TO BE REMEMBERED AS A COACH? "I gave it all I had and I hope that every wrestler that I coached learned something to make him a better person in life. Our alumni program is over 600 strong now and they have been so wonderful to us. I just want our program to keep going and keep growing. It makes me very proud to say that I was a part of that."

FINN GRINAKER: CONCORDIA WRESTLING

Finn Grinaker graduated from Concordia in 1948, where he played football, basketball track and golf. From there, the Halstad native would go on to coach at the college for nearly four decades. Grinaker founded and for 29 years coached the wrestling program at Concordia, winning an MIAC title and inspiring 18 All-America performances in the process. He was also a head coach in basketball for two years, head golf coach for 20 years and an assistant football coach for 39 years under coaches Christiansen and Christopherson as well. One of the most respected coaches and professors in Concordia's history, Grinaker became the backbone of the physical education department through his farsighted curriculum, innovations and dedication to excellence in his teaching. He retired in 1988 as a real Concordia coaching icon.

JOE NOWAK: CLOQUET HIGH SCHOOL SKI JUMPING

Joe Nowak grew up in Duluth and graduated from Duluth Cathedral High School in 1946. After graduating from high school, Joe attended Duluth Junior College and two years later he joined the military. While stationed in Germany, Joe was able to continue his jumping career even winning the Army Championships in Germany, and setting a hill record in the process. After his discharge, Joe returned to Duluth and enrolled at UM-Duluth, graduating in 1958 with a science degree. The UMD placement office then informed him that Cloquet was looking for a science teacher and also had a ski coaching vacancy. Jackpot! Joe was hired in the spring of 1958 and started his coaching career the next winter, where would coach all three disciplines: jumping, cross-country and slalom.

Nowak learned to ski at Duluth's Chester Bowl and went on to become one of America's top jumpers. In 1946 he finished second in U.S. Nationals in Steamboat Springs, Colorado, and from 1951-59 he had several top 10 finishes in U.S. National rankings. Locally, Nowak was a four-time Duluth City Ski Champion, two-time Duluth Invitational Champion (Fond du Lac 70 meter) and set the hill record in 1954 with a 226 foot jump. In addition, Nowak won the 1951 Central U.S Championships held in Chicago, edging out Norwegian, Arfinn Bergman, who won the Gold at the Olympics in Oslo, Norway, that next year. Nowak would compete in three Olympic and World Team trials, but his bids to make the teams all fell short.

At Cloquet High School, Joe was doing well, but his program quickly outgrew its facilities. So, in 1961, Joe found a 40 acre tract of land called Pine Valley on the south side of Cloquet which looked perfect. It had room for downhill, a big landing area for a ski jump, and the hilly terrain would make a challenging cross-country trail. The land was donated to the park system, and all of the steel for the jump was donated by the DM&IR Railroad. The area would open in 1963 with Joe taking the first ride off the new jump. Pine Valley would host the jumping and cross-country portions of the state meet from 1971-76.

The opening of Pine Valley in 1963 coincided with Cloquet High School winning its fourth state championship in skiing, and the first for Nowak. Scores were based on the performance of slalom, jumping, and cross-country teams. Under Nowak, however, Cloquet would go on to win a total of 13 team titles (1965-1971, 1973-1976 and the jumping titles in 1977 and 1978). The high school league dropped jumping in 1979, however. In addition, Nowak coached individual state jumping champions in eight different seasons and was also was the jumping coach for Mike Randall, who went on to compete in the 1984 Olympics in Sarejevo, Yugoslavia.

With budget cuts hitting hard in the 1980s, skiing became tougher and tougher for schools to afford. Joe later divided his $300 coaches salary three ways between two other coaches who took over the cross-country and slalom disciplines. That way, Nowak could focus on his true passion, jumping. Joe would later donate his salary back to the school in order for the program to just stay afloat. Joe finally retired as a teacher in 1983, and his high school coaching career ended that next year as well. He would continue to coach jumpers in the Cloquet Ski Club, however, a club he created back in the 1960s in order to build interest in the sport. In 1978 Nowak was inducted into the Minnesota Ski Coaches' Hall of Fame. A true pioneer in his sport, Nowak was a ski coaching legend in Minnesota. Once offered a coaching position with Team U.S.A., he turned it down to stay close to home on Lake Nichols — where he presently resides.

J ROBINSON
COLLEGE WRESTLING: UNIVERSITY OF MINNESOTA

Since taking over the University of Minnesota's wrestling program 18 years ago, Head Coach J Robinson has built one of the strongest and most respected programs in the nation. Originally from San Diego, Calif., Robinson grew up loving the sport of wrestling and went on to star for his Mount Miguel High School squad, graduating in 1964. From there, Robinson went on to wrestle at Oklahoma State University and then wrestled internationally, competing on two World teams — placing fourth in 1970 and fifth in 1971. Robinson also represented his country in the 1972 Olympic Games as a member of Team U.S.A. In all, Robinson would capture four national wrestling titles during his amateur career, two in freestyle and two in Greco-Roman.

After graduating from OSU with a degree social studies in 1969, Robinson began his coaching career with the Cowboys as a graduate assistant. He then went on to serve as a captain in the U.S. Army's First Cavalry Division in Vietnam from 1971-72. Upon returning home, Robinson joined the University of Iowa's staff as a graduate assistant and was later promoted to an assistant in 1976. He would go on to serve as an assistant coach at Iowa from 1976-84, helping to lead the Hawks to seven NCAA and eight Big Ten crowns. In addition, Robinson served as an interim head coach during the 1984 Big Ten and NCAA championship season as well. From there, Robinson was offered the head coaching position at Minnesota, and he has been making history in Gold Country ever since.

In his first season, the Gophers finished the year without winning a Big Ten dual match. That was about to change in a big, big way. In 1999 Minnesota went undefeated in conference duels and won the Big Ten title, breaking Iowa's 25-year conference title winning streak. In 2001 Robinson won his first national championship with 10 All-Americans by his side. Then, in 2002, his Gophers went 19-0 in duels and did it again — making it back-to-back national championships and creating a dynasty in the process. Robinson's Gophers came close to making it three in a row in 2003 as well, winning their third Big 10 title, but came up just short to Oklahoma State in the NCAA finals to finish as national runner's up.

Robinson enters the 2003-04 season with a 256-86-3 overall record, including an awesome 124-16-0 mark over the last six seasons. He is as close to wrestling royalty as it gets in Minnesota and has single-handedly turned the Gopher Wrestling program into one of the nation's elite. Robinson is a phenomenal motivator, an amazing recruiter, a true player's coach, and has built this program from the ground up. One of the most modest people you will ever meet, Robinson attributes much of his success to his coaching staff of Marty Morgan, Mark Schwab and Joe Russell. Robinson is a winner and the numbers speak for themselves.

During his tenure at Minnesota, more than three dozen wrestlers have earned more than five dozen All-America honors. In addition, he has also coached five NCAA individual titleists as well, with Marty Morgan winning it in 1991, Tim Hartung winning it in 1998 and 1999, Brock Lesnar taking it home in 2000, and Luke Becker and Jared Lawrence doing it in 2002. Robinson has also coached more than two dozen Big Ten Champions and has led his teams to top-six conference finishes in 16 of his 17 seasons, including four straight from 1999-2003.

Regarded as one of the top coaches in the nation by student-athletes and peers alike, Robinson has also coached at the national and international levels as well. He served as an assistant coach on four consecutive U.S. Olympic squads from 1976 to 1988, and then as the head coach for the U.S. at the 1983 Pan American Games. Among his many awards and honors, Robinson was named as the 1998 and 2001 Dan Gable National Coach of the Year, and the 2001 National Wrestling Coaches Association Coach of the Year. In addition, Robinson was awarded the 2001 Amateur Wrestling News Man of the Year award for his work and support of wrestling at all levels. Robinson is also a five -time Big Ten Coach of the Year as well.

A brilliant tactician and teacher, Robinson's teams are consistently nationally ranked because he knows how to recruit and attract the top talent from around the world to the U of M. As a result, he has emerged as one of the top college coaches in the nation. Presently, J and his wife Sue reside in Plymouth with J's daughter, Jordan. J's son Jeb is a student at Iowa.

HOW WOULD YOU DESCRIBE YOUR COACHING STYLE? "I think my style has evolved over the years. I mean 10 to 15 years ago I was probably more authoritative than I am now. I probably see more of the big picture now than I did back then. When you are younger you just sort of plow straight ahead, but now I see 10 different shades of gray. I know that I can be hard on my guys, but at the same time I try to look at the human side of things too."

HOW DO YOU MOTIVATE YOUR PLAYERS? "I think it starts with the type of people that you recruit. Good people listen, take direction well and can be motivated easily. Plus, if you can get quality kids into your program that are already self motivated, then all you have to do is motivate them at certain times — like when things are not going well. Overall, it really helps to start out with a pretty motivated person, because it is tough to motivate someone who doesn't want to be motivated."

WHO WERE YOUR COACHING MENTORS? "My high school coach was Ned Blass, and he was a two-time national champion at Oklahoma State. He was the reason I went to college at OSU, and was a great guy. He had a real impact on me as an athlete. That defined in me that I wanted to be the best. Then, my college coach, Myron Roderick taught me that you have to have a philosophy about wrestling. He said that everything has to be grounded and it is all kind of interconnected. Then, as an assistant coach at Iowa, I would certainly say working with Dan Gable was a great experience. We brought two completely different coaching styles together. One was very organized, philosophical and by the book, while the other was more of a free-for-all. When the two came together we kind of had the best of both worlds and I learned a great deal in that environment which really helped to shape my coaching ideology today."

ON WORKING WITH IOWA LEGEND DAN GABLE: "Dan used to always say a simple thing in that you can always do more. Because his standards were so high, and because he had achieved so much success, he was just able to help his kids reach a new level. He had so much respect and credibility that it was kind of like whatever he said was the law. Overall though, he was very adaptive. He never really forced his style on anybody, instead he tried to build on what guys already had. Then, I would have to say that the premier thing about Gable was his emphasis on conditioning. The philosophy at Iowa was to constantly search for the best, most efficient way to win."

IF YOU COULD MAGICALLY GO BACK IN TIME TO THE FIRST YEAR YOU WERE A HEAD COACH AND GIVE YOURSELF SOME ADVICE FOR THE FUTURE, KNOWING WHAT YOU KNOW NOW, BACK THEN, WHAT WOULD YOU SAY TO YOURSELF? "I would probably say to be more flexible and to try and listen to few more viewpoints."

HOW DO YOU EARN THE RESPECT OF YOUR PLAYERS? "What I try to do to get close with my guys is I try to enter their world more than they enter mine. Instead of them always coming to me, I try and do stuff with them on their level and on their terms. I go to their houses, their parties, and basically go to places where they are comfortable. That way you can bond with them and get to know them. I also work with a lot my kids in summer wrestling camps, where it is not a coaching relationship — just friends. We even do things socially together like take trips and stuff where we are just friends. So you get to interact at a much different level, and that has just been great."

HOW DO YOU BUILD TEAM UNITY & CHEMISTRY? "People will do more for their friends than they'll ever do for somebody they just don't know. Social settings build chemistry. Period. One thing we did was to eliminate apartment living and put all of our freshmen and sophomores into a dormitory on campus. They all live together there and as a result, they all bond with each other. You even see the sophomores start to take care of the freshmen and so on, and eventually you build bonds between classes of kids. This way it is an ongoing process and everybody sort of belongs to a big family. I think I am great friends with a lot of my kids and that is great. I think that is a very scary place for a lot of other coaches though. They feel that they have to build a wall between their players in order to be respected, but I don't believe in that. I think you respect people for who they are and not by what they do. You just have to set boundaries early on and things just take care of themselves from there."

WHAT IS THE KEY TO GOOD TIME MANAGEMENT? "You know the old saying: 'People spend 80% of their time focusing on things that don't really matter, as opposed to spending 80% of their time focusing on the 20% of things that really do matter.' You can't do everything, so they key in life is knowing not only what, but when to prioritize."

WHAT MOTIVATES YOU? "Motivation comes from the inside. I think it is a combination of helping kids achieve their dreams and working towards achieving mine at the same time. I think they are intertwined because the sooner you can help a kid realize his dream, the sooner you are as a coach to realizing yours. And if you are realizing your dreams, then you are winning and making progress along the way. It's much more of a 'we' than an 'I' attitude and that is very important. It requires a little parenting and teaching, but if you can help kids achieve goals that you as a coach never reached, then that is special."

WHAT ADVICE WOULD YOU HAVE FOR YOUNG COACHES STARTING OUT TODAY? "I would tell them to develop a philosophy of what they are trying to do as early as possible. A lot of young coaches understand the technical stuff, but they don't always understand why they are doing certain things. When you understand why you are doing certain things, then it becomes much easier for you to connect all the other dots in creating a successful program. There are four areas to be a good athlete: strength, technique, conditioning and mental attitude, so when you have a solid philosophy you can connect all of these dots together to make everything stronger."

WHAT'S THE KEY TO RECRUITING? "Having a lot of money (laugh and pause…) Really though, I think the key to recruiting is selling a dream. Every kid you recruit wants to be a champion, they are not just there to participate. So, we focus on the fact that sure, we have an outstanding program, but winning is very, very important."

WHAT'S THE BIGGEST THING YOU'VE LEARNED FROM COACHING THAT YOU'VE BEEN ABLE TO APPLY TO YOUR EVERYDAY LIFE? "You can expect people to do things, but if you don't teach them the skills, no matter how bad you want them to do it, they will never do it. So, you have got to think in terms of 'does this person have the necessary skills or can I teach or motivate this person to acquire the necessary skills?'"

DO YOU HAVE A FAVORITE LOCKER ROOM SIGN? "We always have three goals: we want to dominate, we want to be aggressive and we want to have fun. I always figured if we did those things then the winning would take care of itself."

LOOKING BACK, WHAT ARE YOU MOST PROUD OF IN YOUR CAREER? "I am proud of the journey — the people I have met and the relationships I have developed over the years."

WHAT DOES IT MEAN FOR YOU TO BE A GOPHER? "It is a very special thing. I came here 17 years ago and I am going to retire as a Gopher. I started out as a Cowboy, then I was a Hawkeye, but they are going to bury me as a Gopher. It's a great tradition and I am very honored to be a part of it."

WHAT'S THE SECRET TO YOUR SUCCESS? "Perseverance and flexibility. You know, coming to Minnesota when they weren't very good to begin with and then going through that whole process to get to where we are now, is what it is all about. The journey is what this has all been about and it has been a great ride, that is for sure. I mean you wake up every morning to try and get to the top of the mountain, and for me it was sweet to finally get there on my own."

WHAT WOULD YOU WANT TO SAY TO YOUR FANS, BOOSTERS, AND ALUMNI WHO HAVE SUPPORTED YOU ALL THESE YEARS? "I would like to say thank you to all the people who stuck by me during the lean years and when things weren't going our way. I think loyalty is a huge issue and I am grateful to our fans who have believed in me and supported me through the years. Then, when you do finally win the big one, it is so special to share that moment with all of those people who have been there for you. I was so proud to share those two wrestling titles with the state of Minnesota and with all of our wrestling fans. For two years they were able to say that they were the best and that was just a great feeling. Seeing their pride and happiness is special and I am so proud to be a part of that. It makes me want to win a lot more of them too."

HOW DO YOU WANT YOUR COACHING EPITAPH TO READ — HOW DO YOU WANT TO BE REMEMBERED AS A COACH? "He made a difference in our lives, and not just in wrestling. Also, I would say too that I am just one of a bunch of guys who came here with a dream and made it happen."

BILL SIMPSON: STILLWATER HIGH SCHOOL CROSS COUNTRY SKIING

Bill Simpson is a legend in the world of high school skiing. In all, Simpson would rack up 13 state championship titles, 11 state runner-up titles, 38 section championship titles and 38 conference championship titles over his illustrious 25 year coaching career. In the process, he created one of the largest, most inclusive cross country ski programs in the state, which just may very well be one of the largest high school ski programs in the country. Although he retired in 2000, Bill continues to work with the Stillwater ski program as a volunteer coach.

JEFF SWENSON
COLLEGE WRESTLING: AUGSBURG

Jeff Swenson is an Auggie Wrestling coaching legend. Period. Swenson grew up loving sports and in 1975 he came to Augsburg to wrestle and play football. On the mat, Swenson produced a 102-17 record, earning NAIA All-American honors three times (1977-79) and winning the national title at 167 pounds in 1979. On the gridiron, Swenson was a dominant linebacker, earning four letters for the Auggies and leading the team in the tough MIAC. For his efforts, Swenson earned the school's senior Honor Athlete award. From there, Swenson, who earned degrees in health and physical education, and later got his master's degree in health from the University of Minnesota in 1982, became an assistant coach with both the Auggie wrestling and football teams.

In 1980 Swenson served one year as an assistant under Auggie wrestling coach John Grygelko, and then assumed the head coaching duties in 1981. Since then, Swenson has gone on to build a small college wrestling dynasty. Under Swenson, Augsburg has won eight NCAA Division III wrestling national championships in the last 13 years, including three in a row from 2000-02, along with a runner-up finish in 2003. (Both the three straight titles and eight overall titles are NCAA Division III records.) Augsburg's streak of dominance in small-college wrestling includes finishing either first or second nationally 13 times in the last 14 years, as well as finishing in the top four every year since 1989. In addition, Swenson has led his program to 20 MIAC crowns, and produced 130 All-Americans and 28 individual national champions as well. Now entering his 22nd season with Augsburg (Swenson left Augsburg to coach at Rosemount High School from 1985-86), Swenson's collegiate coaching record stands at an unbelievable 280-35, and is among the best in the nation.

And Swenson is just as proud of his team's success in the classroom as he is of their success on the wrestling mat. In 1999 Augsburg had 71 Scholar All-Americans and earned the Division III academic national championship with a team grade-point average of 3.48. The 1998 Auggies finished second in the nation with a team GPA of 3.37, as did the 2000 Auggies, with a team GPA of 3.40.

Among his many coaching accolades, including numerous conference coach of the year awards, in 2001 Swenson was named Lutheran College National Coach of the Year (all sports) from Lutheran Brotherhood, and in 2002, he earned National College Coach of the Year honors (all divisions) from Wrestling USA Magazine. In addition, in 1999 Swenson was inducted into the Augsburg Athletic Hall of Fame.

In addition to serving as the Men's Wrestling Head Coach, Swenson also serves as the Interim Assistant Dean for Athletics and Recreation at Augsburg as well. In this role, he supervises the men's and women's intercollegiate athletic departments, the athletic facilities department, and the college's intramural athletic program. Now entering his 25th season as a coach, Jeff Swenson is still going strong. He is simply one of the best of the very best at what he does, and continues to make Minnesota proud.

HOW WOULD YOU DESCRIBE YOUR COACHING STYLE? "I would say that I am an organized, systematic, demanding motivator."

HOW DO YOU MOTIVATE YOUR PLAYERS? "I try to motivate our student athletes with a logical approach. I try to read people and have had good success with that. The key is learning what motivates each individual because you can't motivate everyone the same

way. While we attempt to treat everybody fairly, quite honestly we don't treat everybody the same because everybody is different. One thing we do that I am very proud of, however, is that we include our entire team in everything we do. For instance, every year after Christmas we take a very expensive trip to Florida and we include the entire roster of around 35 guys. We include our entire team in all of our competitions as well, so that almost everybody can get a full schedule of matches. We always talk about 35 guys going in the same direction, and 35 guys helping one another for the good of the team. All 35 guys will earn varsity letters, all 35 guys will get national championship rings and all 35 guys will be in the team picture at nationals — even though only one guy represents us in each weight class. That is how we motivate our kids to be team players and to push themselves to be the best they can be."

IF YOU COULD MAGICALLY GO BACK IN TIME TO THE FIRST YEAR YOU WERE A HEAD COACH AND GIVE YOURSELF SOME ADVICE FOR THE FUTURE, KNOWING WHAT YOU KNOW NOW, BACK THEN, WHAT WOULD YOU SAY TO YOURSELF? "Never compromise what you believe in."

WHAT ARE THE CHARACTERISTICS OF LEADERS? "That is a real tough question, because I think every leader has their own characteristics. Take my four captains for this upcoming season: the first one is outgoing, friendly, very organized and is a real take the bull by the horn type; the second is very quiet and doesn't say boo, works out extremely hard, and he leads by example; the third one is fabulous in the wrestling room, he has a magnetic personality, has knowledge beyond his years and the kids really respond to him, but he needs to learn how to be a good leader off the mat; then the fourth captain needs to develop more self confidence to be the great leader that he can be, but as a former valedictorian he leads in the classroom. So, leaders come in all shapes and sizes and have many different characteristics. That's why we usually have several captains instead of just one each season, because that way we just get that much more leadership."

LOOKING BACK WHAT ARE YOU MOST PROUD OF IN YOUR CAREER? "I would say I am most proud of our alumni and what they are doing now. I am real proud of the fact that I have been able to have the opportunity to be a part of their lives. I hope I have made a difference in their lives in a positive way, and they have become better people because of that. Now, 25 years later, it is just mind boggling to think about all of our alumni who are out there doing great things in the world."

WHAT IS THE KEY TO RECRUITING? "Being proud of the product that you are selling and having a successful product. You have to remember that you are providing a service for families."

HOW DO YOU BUILD TEAM UNITY & CHEMISTRY? "We talk a lot about accepting everybody for who we are and about finding the positives in individuals as opposed to the negatives. We talk about how everybody has something unique to offer and contribute to our team and that is what team chemistry is. Then, it goes back to including all 35 guys in nearly everything we do. We build team unity by being together and by encouraging each other to be our best."

WHAT MOTIVATES YOU? "I think what motivates me is knowing that I have made a difference in my kids' lives; knowing that I have made their lives better; knowing that I had something to do with them graduating from college and then getting a job; and knowing that through a great wrestling experience that they have become a better person."

WHAT IS THE KEY TO GOOD TIME MANAGEMENT? "I think planning ahead is the key. I put together 'to-do' lists every night and just try to stay on top of everything as best I can. Beyond that I make up job descriptions for everything, and emphasize good communication between everybody. Things will get done if you tell people how to do them and when to do them. One of the things I learned from Dan Gable (Iowa's legendary wrestling coach) is to plan in reverse. Everything we do, including our wrestling schedules, I do in reverse order. So, last year I started out by planning a trip to the national tournament on March 6th and just worked my way back. You also have to also visualize to be successful, and I do that."

WHAT ADVICE WOULD YOU HAVE FOR YOUNG COACHES STARTING OUT TODAY? "Make sure you can live a balanced life and make sure you don't try to do too much. I would also say that no high school wrestling coach should ever coach a Spring sport. You just get spread too thin. Overall, I just think that wrestlers are real needy athletes and they need your attention year-round."

FAVORITE LOCKER ROOM SIGN? "My favorite saying is 'One percent improvement every day' which means that this year we can get 132 % better from October 21st to March 6th. Then, in our wrestling room we have a sign that reads: 'To be a champion: practice like a champion, handle academics like a champion and behave socially like a champion.' Beyond that, we have a saying: 'The pursuit of excellence while building men,' and that saying is on the backs of our tee-shirts as well."

WHAT'S THE BIGGEST THING YOU'VE LEARNED FROM COACHING THAT YOU'VE BEEN ABLE TO APPLY TO YOUR EVERYDAY LIFE? "To do things at the highest possible level and never give anything less than 100%."

WHAT ARE THE KEY INGREDIENTS TO CREATING A CHAMPIONSHIP TEAM? "Good leadership with the coaches and good leadership with your captains. Then, it is developing a work ethic amongst your team and being able to have the student athletes to incorporate those things."

WHAT'S THE SECRET TO YOUR SUCCESS? "I think it is focusing on the journey and not the destination. We just want to focus on improving all the time, no matter what we do. We go over our evaluation sheets from the year before several times throughout the season and then try to work on making things better for the next year. Whether it is an academic plan, a weight training plan, a cardiovascular training plan, or a practice plan — we document it and evaluate it. You know, another thing is that we don't talk about winning at all in our practice room. The kids have goals to be national champs and to beat this guy or that guy in a dual, and I don't think you can prevent that. I mean the internet has made it all but impossible to shelter athletes from knowing about their opponents. But, our program is not win oriented, it is goal oriented and improvement oriented. When you have that, winning takes care of itself."

WHAT WOULD YOU WANT TO SAY TO YOUR FANS, BOOSTERS, AND ALUMNI WHO HAVE SUPPORTED YOU ALL THESE YEARS? "I would just say thanks for supporting us and for being there for us. We couldn't have done it without you. We have just great fans at Augsburg. We always have the largest crowd at nationals and we appreciate that so much. The Augsburg Wrestling program is not about me, it is about the kids. You know, as successful as our program has been, people don't always know who the head coach at Augsburg is, and I am flattered to hear that. In fact, I consider that to be one of the greatest compliments that we could receive, because it means that this hasn't been about me, it is always about the kids and the program."

HOW DO YOU WANT YOUR COACHING EPITAPH TO READ — HOW DO YOU WANT TO BE REMEMBERED AS A COACH? "He made a positive difference and made the lives of his student athletes better."

DOUG REESE: UM-MORRIS WRESTLING

Doug Reese is now in his 13th season as the head wrestling coach at the University of Minnesota-Morris, where he has made quite a splash in the world of wrestling. As a competitor, Reese won a silver medal in the 1993 Master's World Freestyle Championships in Toronto at 130 kilos. Reese, who teaches in the Wellness, Sports Science Department at UM-Morris, is known worldwide for his scientific approach to training, along with developing strong mental skills in his athletes. Reese has produced 25 national champions, 122 All-Americans, 31 Academic All-Americans, 16 U.S. National Team members, and 10 U.S. World Team Members.

Reese, who is also a member of the USA Wrestling national coaching staff, served for eight years on the Board of Directors of USA Wrestling, the National Governing Body of Wrestling in the United States. During his term of service, Reese was Chairperson of the Women's Wrestling Committee, and also served on the Coaches Council Executive Board, the International Exchange Committee, and the Steering Committee. Reese is also a current member of the U.S. National Freestyle Wrestling Coaching Staff. Reese has made 14 trips overseas to Europe and Latin America coaching elite U.S. teams. In addition, Reese has coached in five world championships as well as the Pan-Am Championships in the past seven years. Reese was even the fourth coach in the United States to earn Gold Level Coaching Certification from USA Wrestling.

Reese is also executive director of To The Next Level, a non-profit organization committed to helping athletes and coaches reach their true potential on and off the field of play. TTNL runs camps and clinics and is currently using Olympic Solidarity grants from the International Olympic Committee to teach sports management training, and to teach coaches how to coach affectively. Reese also serves as the Assistant to the Athletic Director at UMM, and is the faculty sponsor of the Fellowship of Christian Athlete huddle on campus.

VIRG VAGLE
HIGH SCHOOL WRESTLING: PAYNESVILLE

Virg Vagle grew up in Lake Bronson, way up in the northwest corner of the state, and attended high school in Fargo. There, Vagle played football, baseball, basketball and track — their was no wrestling program for him to participate in. Vagle then went on to Augsburg, where he played football, graduating from college in 1965. At that time, wrestling was just getting started in many high schools across the state. So, when Vagle got his first job in Paynesville, he became the assistant coach on the newly created wrestling team. One year later, Vagle took over as the head coach and he has been there ever since, making history along the way. Since then, Vagle has become a high school coaching legend. In fact, Vagle is No. 1 all-time in career wins in Minnesota with an amazing 644-133-6 record. In addition, he has won four state championships, made numerous trips to the state tournament and is still going strong. The recipient of numerous coach of the year awards, Virg Vagle is simply one of the best of the best and a true Minnesota wrestling coaching legend.

HOW WOULD YOU DESCRIBE YOUR COACHING STYLE? "I try to put a lot of energy into what I do and I try to get the kids to do the same. There is a lot of dedication on both sides as well as a commitment, and that is important. I have always felt that there is no free ride in our program as well. Everybody needs to work hard to accomplish their goals and we have tried to instill that attitude into our kids over the years. We have also tried to make it a lot of fun for them, which is very important too."

HOW DO YOU MOTIVATE YOUR PLAYERS? "We just try to really get involved with the kids and try to make wrestling an important aspect of their life. Maybe not the most important aspect, but certainly one of the most. We encourage them to work very hard and to try to get them to put a lot into it. We also encourage the team concept and have had a lot of success with our kids buying into that. Then, we just go to work and try to accomplish as much as we can."

LOOKING BACK WHAT ARE YOU MOST PROUD OF IN YOUR CAREER? "Watching young kids mature and grow up in a positive environment is very rewarding. To see them have a little more quality in their lives than they might have had otherwise, that is something I take a lot of pride in. Then, being able to establish a program here at Paynseville that has maintained a high level of competition over such a long period of time, that is great too. It wasn't that we were just up there in the rankings for two or three years either, we have consistently maintained a strong program in the state for a lot of years. We have just had a lot of great kids come through here and that is what has made us so successful."

HOW DO YOU BUILD TEAM UNITY & CHEMISTRY? "This has been a real key for us here at Paynesville through the years. You know, a lot of schools that have wrestling programs think of the sport as an individual one, whereas here we really look at it as a team sport. Our kids look at it that way too, and that has really helped us to be successful. From there, we have built the friendships, the camaraderie and the winning attitude amongst the players and coaches."

WHAT MOTIVATES YOU? "I have just always loved athletics. I loved it as a kid and I love it as an adult. I love the competition too. But it is more than that. I mean you know you are going to win and

you know you are going to lose too, so it is watching the kids grow up and see them succeed. To see those kids with a few rough edges that maybe mature and grow a little bit more than they would've otherwise, without athletics in their life, is the biggest motivating factor for me. To see that happen makes me stick with it. Believe me, if it was just about wins and losses, I would've burned out years ago."

WHAT ADVICE WOULD YOU HAVE FOR YOUNG COACHES STARTING OUT TODAY? "Don't expect to win all the time. You have to see yourself through the tough times. The thrill of victory is great, but the only way you are going to last for an extended period of time in this business is to know how to handle the ups and the downs. Handling the downs is the most important thing you can do. That is how you get your kids to stay motivated and focused so that your team can rise above it all and be successful."

WHAT'S THE BIGGEST THING YOU'VE LEARNED FROM COACHING THAT YOU'VE BEEN ABLE TO APPLY TO YOUR EVERYDAY LIFE? "Athletics prepares you for life. When you get defeated and knocked down, you just have to stay focused, get back on track and get ready to try again — because the good times will come if you work hard. You just can't give up. The will-power and determination that you use in athletics will always be relevant in your everyday life."

WHAT ARE THE KEY INGREDIENTS TO CREATING A CHAMPIONSHIP TEAM? "Well, you have to have some talent for starters. Then, you have to have some luck and you have to have some dedicated kids. The kids also have to have the mental and physical dedication to make it through the difficult times and to be successful. Then, you need to have camaraderie and chemistry too, that is also very important."

WHAT'S THE SECRET TO YOUR SUCCESS? "There is no secret. We have just been fortunate along the way. We have tried to see ourselves through the tough times and then get right back on track. We have not let the tough times derail us and we have also really enjoyed the good times too. That is very important. That is a big motivator for you as well as for your kids."

WHAT WOULD YOU WANT TO SAY TO YOUR FANS, BOOSTERS, AND ALUMNI WHO HAVE SUPPORTED YOU ALL THESE YEARS? "Without them we never would have had that amount of success that we have had, so thanks. Any success or credit that I have gotten over the years I want to share with all of them. They, the whole community, the athletes, the fans, the parents, the supporters, have helped earn any honors that I have gotten along the way. I hope they have enjoyed it as much as I have and I honestly think that they have."

HOW DO YOU WANT YOUR COACHING EPITAPH TO READ — HOW DO YOU WANT TO BE REMEMBERED AS A COACH? "He gave to the sport and to the young people that he had a chance to coach. He treated them fair and tried to motivate them to be a little bit better people than what they would have been without athletics in their lives."

JOHN ELTON: ST. JOHN'S WRESTLING

John Elton grew up in the Twin Cities and graduated from Bloomington Lincoln High School in 1976. There, Elton placed second at the Minnesota State High School Wrestling Tournament as a 145-pounder. As a collegiate wrestler, Elton was a four-year standout for the Johnnies and captured a National Catholic Championship during his senior season. Elton also qualified for the NCAA tournament at 150-pounds in 1979 and 1980 as well as at the NAIA tournament in 1977 and 1978. Elton would go on to graduate with honors from St. John's in 1980 and then got into coaching. Now beginning his 23rd season as head wrestling coach at St. John's University in 2003-04, John Elton has emerged as one of the best in the business. He currently boasts an impressive 261-96-5 dual meet record, and he ranks first among SJU coaches for most dual meet wins in a career. SJU teams have posted an impressive .748 winning percentage during the Elton era and have won 10 or more dual meets 17 times. For his efforts, Elton has been named MIAC Coach-of-the-Year in 1984, 1993, 1995 and 1997. At the national level, SJU has qualified athletes to the NCAA Division III tournament in 18 of the past 19 seasons, including 18 NCAA All-Americans and 26 Scholar All-Americans. John and his wife Joan presently reside in St. Cloud and have two children.

THE STERNER BROTHERS: MIKE & JOHN
SOUTHWEST STATE & UM-MOORHEAD

The Sterner brothers are practically wrestling royalty in the Land of 10,000 Lakes. Known for their intensity and competitiveness, they have become legendary figures in the world of Minnesota wrestling. Here is their story: Mike & John Sterner, twin brothers, were born in Sheridan, Wyo., and raised in Sioux Falls, S.D. They then went on to star in football, wrestling and track, graduating from Boys Town (Neb.) High School in 1957. From there, the two wound up together at South Dakota State University, where they both played football and wrestled.

At SDSU Mike played right guard and nose tackle in football and wrestled at 177 pounds. He was named the 1961 North Central Conference Most Valuable Lineman and was a co-captain of the 1961 squad which finished 8-2 and tied the University of Northern Iowa for the NCC championship. Mike was also named as the Jackrabbits' Most Valuable Wrestler following both his junior and senior seasons.

John, meanwhile, went into the Army after high school, and then went on to join Mike at SDSU a year later. There, he lettered three times in football and wrestling, and was an All-North Central Conference selection in both sports as a senior.

From there, Mike, who is older than John by 15 minutes, first taught and coached at the Flandreau (S.D.) Indian School, then returned to South Dakota State as a graduate assistant in football and wrestling. He completed his master's degree at SDSU and then moved north, teaching and coaching three years at Hettinger, N.D. Mike then came to Southwest State University in 1969 to serve as the head wrestling coach from 1969-98. At SSU, Mike coached 47 NAIA and NCAA All-Americans, including two NAIA National Champions and one NCAA II National Champion. His Mustangs won six NIC Championships, achieved several top 10 finishes in the NAIA meet, and posted a 255-206 record during his tenure. In addition, Mike was named NIC Coach of the Year seven time and was inducted into the NAIA Hall of fame in 1991 as well. Mike also coached 17 years of Mustang football, including four as the head coach from 1973-76. Mike would later get his doctorate from BYU and serve as the chairman of SSU's Department of Health and Physical Education.

Mike and his wife, Karen, an assistant professor of education at SSU, have two children, Michelle and John. John, meanwhile, is SSU's only national champion in wrestling, winning the 190-pound division in 1989. He also played four years of football at SSU and was a key member of the 1987 team which earned the school's first NAIA Division I playoff berth as well. John would later serve as his father's assistant coach, and ultimately take over as the head coach at SSU — where he presently remains.

Brother John, meanwhile, first started out coaching as a graduate assistant back at SDSU for one year, and then began his teaching and coaching career in 1963 at Chariton (Iowa) High School. There, he led his team to a third place finish at the 1964 Iowa State High School Wrestling Tournament. John later coached St. Mary's High School in New England, N.D, to the 1969 North Dakota State Class B Championship, and was honored as North Dakota State Class B Coach of the Year that season as well. John would build a stellar five-year prep dual meet record of 71-7-0 at the school. John later moved to Stevens High School in Rapid City, S.D, that next year to serve as the school's head football coach. Three years later he joined the South Dakota Tech staff and served as wrestling coach for four seasons, posting a 24-8-0 mark, before the sport was discontinued. In 1978 John accepted a teaching and coaching position in the public school system in Rapid City. Ten years later, he came to MSU Moorhead, where he took over the Dragon Wrestling team in 1988.

John hit the ground running at MSU and his teams would go on to capture six consecutive Northern Sun Intercollegiate Conference championships during a remarkable run from 1995-2000, and made a lot of noise on the regional and national levels during that time as well. In 1997 MSU placed 11th at the NCAA II nationals. Then, in 1999 MSU earned their sixth straight NSIC title — also placing third in the North Central regional tournament, and sending five wrestlers to the 2000 NCAA Division II Championships. In 15 years of collegiate coaching, John recorded an impressive 149-96-2 career mark. In addition to his dual meet success, the Dragons flourished in post-season competition as well, dispatching 54 representatives to NAIA National Championships and 21 to NCAA Division II showdowns. The Dragons also garnered 24 All-American awards, including a national championship and nine Academic All-America recipients. In addition, John also spent 10 years as an assistant with the football Dragons as well. John and his wife JoAnn have one daughter, Kay.

AFTERWORD BY JOHN GAGLIARDI

John Gagliardi is a living legend. Period. He is presently the second winningest coach in college football history with 400 career wins and is just nine wins away from surpassing former Grambling Coach Eddie Robinson to take over as No. 1.

Coach Gagliardi's story is a fascinating one, which began in the small coal mining town of Trinidad, Colorado. That is where John was born and raised as the fifth of nine children. Gagliardi grew up loving sports and went on to become the captain of his Trinidad Catholic High School football team. It was there that John also got his first taste of coaching. It all started when his high school football coach, Dutch Clark, was called to service in World War II. You see, without a coach, the school was just going to drop the football program. Most of the young men in the area had been called into action overseas, and there was no one available to take over. So, Gagliardi talked the administration into letting him do the coaching. They agreed and John took over the reins at the age of just 16, serving as the player-coach for his senior year.

Gagliardi agreed to coach the team again that next year after he had graduated. He worked at his father's body shop and enrolled in Trinidad Junior College on the side. Even at that young age people could see he had a gift for teaching, working with young people, and instilling in them a winning attitude. Three years later John enrolled at Colorado College, where he continued to coach at nearby St. Mary's High School. His teams would win a total of three conference titles under his tutelage, and in 1946 he even led his Tigers to the Colorado Parochial School state title game.

After graduating from Colorado College in 1949, the 22-year-old got his first college coaching position at Carroll College, a small Catholic liberal arts school in Helena, Mont. The college, thinking about dropping football because of losing seasons and lack of interest, took a gamble on the young Gagliardi which would pay off big-time. Gagliardi would coach not only the football program at Carroll, but also the basketball and baseball programs as well. Inheriting an athletic program in disarray, he turned things around in

a hurry. On the gridiron he led the football team to a 24-6-1 record, claiming three straight conference titles along the way. On the hardwood, Gagliardi's basketball teams claimed two conference titles and even upset national power Gonzaga in 1953.

Before long, Gagliardi's success drew the attention of another small Catholic college — St. John's University of Collegeville, Minnesota. St. John's needed a coach to succeed the mythical Johnny "Blood" McNally, a former Green Bay Packer and Duluth Eskimo great who is a charter member of the Pro Football Hall of Fame. SJU had not won a conference title in 15 years, and needed to get it turned around. So, the monks at St. John's made John an offer he couldn't refuse — raising his current salary from $2,400 to $4,200. Meanwhile, Blood offered Gagliardi his own gloomy prediction: "Nobody could ever win at Saint John's." Despite Blood's less than encouraging words, John accepted the job and headed west to Collegeville to begin the next journey of his life in the shadows of beautiful Lake Sagatagan.

John immediately quieted the skeptics by winning the Minnesota Intercollegiate Athletic Conference (MIAC) title that fall with the help of his first great halfback, Jim Lehman. Lehman, the father of Minnesota golfing great Tom Lehman, went on to lead the country in scoring that year as well. It would be the first of more than 50 seasons to come on the gridiron. John would later go on to turn around the Johnnies' track and hockey teams as well, proving that his unique coaching methods and motivational skills could make any team a winner. The rest, they say, is history.

John Gagliardi has built one of the nation's top NCAA Division III programs at St. John's. The attitude and winning tradition he instills in his players is unprecedented. Among this seventime national Coach of the Year's many achievements are his three small college national championships. The first came in 1963, when his Johnnies edged Prairie View A&M of Texas, 33-27, in the Camellia Bowl at Sacramento, Calif. The second came two years later, when the Johnnies crushed Linfield College of Oregon, 35-0. (Amazingly the Johnnies' defense allowed just 27 points to be scored against them that entire season!) St. John's then added their third title in 1976, when they beat Towson State of Maryland, 31-28.

As a collegiate coach Gagliardi's numbers are simply astonishing. His teams have won 24 conference titles and have appeared in 41 post-season games. In the past 39 years, SJU has been nationally ranked 37 times and they own a 28-13 post-season record to boot. In addition, from 1962-64 SJU owned the nation's longest winning streak, with 20 wins. And, in 1993, SJU averaged 61.5 points per game, setting a record that may never be broken. Among his numerous awards and achievements, in 1993 the NCAA honored Gagliardi by naming the Division III equivalent of the Heisman Trophy after him. The Gagliardi Trophy is now given annually to the nation's top NCAA Division III football player. What's amazing is that his teams are just getting better and better. In fact, in 2000 St. John's made the national title game, and followed that up with a pair of national semifinal appearances in both 2001 and 2002.

Now entering his 55th season on the sidelines, Gagliardi's success is attributable to more than mere football strategy and tactics. He is an astute judge of talent. He creates a fun environment filled with high expectations, and he concentrates on methods and practices that truly focus on winning. John Gagliardi has built a legacy that is unrivaled in college football, and what's frightening for all the other MIAC schools is that he may just be getting his second wind as he prepares for his emotional journey to football immortality.

With so many records and so many success stories, John Gagliardi has truly earned the title of football legend. Here is a man who has touched countless lives and truly made a difference in this world — making us all so proud. So, who better to talk about the next 100 years of Minnesota coaches than the soon-to-be winningest coach in the history of college football, our very own John Gagliardi:

"Coaches are special people," said Gagliardi. "They do such a great job in handling our young men and women and they do it because

they love kids. I especially admire the coaches at the junior high and high school levels who teach a full course load on top of everything else. They have a really tough job to do, these people, and they don't make a lot of money doing it either. I think if you were to translate a dollar figure per hour with regards to how much they work, it would be just pennies per hour. Just think of the time they put in after school, at nights and on weekends for games. It is a labor of love for these men and women and that is special. Their commitment is oftentimes unappreciated but they get satisfaction out of making a difference in those kids' lives. I have been fortunate enough to meet a lot of great coaches in Minnesota, at all different levels, and I continue to be impressed at the quality of people they are. We should be very, very proud of our coaches here, because they are doing a great job."

"I also think our coaches are doing a tremendous job of getting their athletes prepared to play and compete. Especially high school coaches, they are doing a darn good job in my opinion because each year we continue to get a whole crop of players who can play football as well as any place in the country. And they are excelling in the classroom too. That is what's so good to see. I think that they are doing a fine job of getting more and more athletes onto the next level as well. Now, personally, that is something I am not too concerned about. I just want our guys to get a good education, have fun, compete and win."

"Now, if some players are good enough to move onto the next level and play professionally, then more power to them. But that is not my main goal, getting them into the pro ranks. I just feel that at this level, Division III, there are just a rare few who will ever get the chance to compete at that level. I don't care if you graduate from the University of St. John's, the University of Minnesota or the University of Notre Dame, it is a long-shot to make it in the National Football League, and that is just reality. What I am much prouder of, is when they make it in other ways at the next level — both professionally as well as academically, either as a teacher or coach. For instance, a few years ago our star halfback was accepted to medical school at the prestigious Mayo Clinic in Rochester. Others have gone on to become a president of a university, a state supreme court justice, prominent attorneys, successful businessmen, a bishop, college professors and what have you. That is amazing to me. We get guys that go on to incredible careers here, and that to me is wonderful."

"As far as recruiting goes, I have always figured that as long as we could get the best kids locally, from right around here, then we could compete with anybody. That, in my opinion, is another tribute to our local coaches. Our starting line-up in most years has always consisted of small town players who came from within a 50 mile driving distance of Collegeville. We get good guys from good families and that has been our base of student-athletes. I know this though, we play teams in the post-season from around the country, and I have found that our kids can play with anybody. Those same small town guys are just as good as anybody else and that says a lot about our high school programs in Minnesota. I think we are doing an outstanding job and the coaches can take a lot of that credit."

"The game is changing though, that is for sure. First of all, the size of the players now is just incredible. When I first got into coaching most of the linemen weren't even 200 pounds. I used to think that guys over 210 or 220 were absolute giants. Now, we have running backs bigger than that and many of the linemen are well over 300 pounds. I think it won't be long before the linemen will be over 400 pounds. It is crazy, but that is the way the game has gone. And these guys are not fatsos who can't move out there either, they are athletes who can run and can hit. It is a whole different world today from when I started out, and the thought of 'Bigger - Faster - Stronger' really has a whole new meaning."

"With regards to the state-of-the-state of Minnesota sports, I think we are in great hands. There are a lot of changes taking place right now, but overall things look pretty good. Are we ever going to get our stadium issues resolved with the Vikings and Gophers? I don't know, but I sure hope so. You know, football is a weird game. You start when it is so ungodly hot and then finish when it is so ungodly cold. No wonder they want a new stadium with a retractable roof! Sports are important to our community though and it would be a shame if they couldn't get this ironed out. We need to make sure that future generations of sports fans have teams to root for here."

"As for the fans, what can I say — they have been extraor-

dinary. They are very loyal to Johnny football and that has been great to see. We have actually been the leaders in attendance for all of Division III football for quite some time now and that just shows you how much our fans care. The atmosphere up here is just terrific on game day. In fact, in 1999 Sports Illustrated even did a feature called 'Game Day USA' about college football's top 10 dream destinations, and we were included amongst Clemson, Ohio State, Army, Florida, Notre Dame, Texas A&M, Washington, Nebraska and Stanford. Can you believe that? Wow! What a great honor that was. Unbelievable. NFL Films even came here and did a piece for ESPN called 'Men of Minnesota.' It included Vikings' stars Cris Carter and Paul Krause, and then myself. How do you explain that? I just can't even comprehend how they can put little St. John's in the same category as those guys, but they did and boy was I flattered as heck. Really, you kind of feel like you should at least have the decency to be dead before you get all this amazing recognition!"

"One of the best parts about coaching is that you get to meet a lot of great people. Over the past 50 or so years I have had the privilege of being in so many people's lives and that has been so special to me. I am truly one of the luckiest guys in the world. How else would I meet so many great individuals. I think about guys like Tom Burnet, my former quarterback, who said 'Let's Roll!' and led the heroic charge on September 11th to prevent those terrorists from hijacking that airplane into Washington D.C. Or how about Bill Clemens, who founded Bankers Systems here in St. Cloud which employed several thousands of people. I saw him start from nothing and build an empire, and then he was so generous with his money as a philanthropist. He helped St. John's so much and we are so grateful to people like that. I just think wow, how would I ever meet some of these great people and become friends with them if I weren't the coach of this program. People like Bud Grant, Senator Gene McCarthy or Johnny Blood — it has been just amazing. I am truly very lucky.

"As for the future, it looks very bright. I am excited about this upcoming season and it will definitely be one to remember. I can't thank the fans in this state enough for having supported me all these years. It is a real honor to be a coach. It has been great to teach these guys and watch them grow into men. I have been coaching now for more than five decades and to see what some of them have done with their lives is just incredible. Hopefully that will be my legacy."

John Gagliardi with Eddie Robinson, the man he is about to pass to become the all-time winningest coach in the history of college football.

INDEX

BIBLIOGRAPHY

1. Ross Bernstein: Interviews from over 200 Minnesota sports personalities

2. "Gopher Hockey by the Hockey Gopher," by Ross Bernstein, Mpls, MN, 1992.

3. "55 Years - 55 Heroes" A Celebration of Minnesota Sports, by Ross Bernstein, Mpls, MN, 2002.

4. "Fifty Years - Fifty Heroes" A Celebration of Minnesota Sports, by Ross Bernstein, Mpls, MN, 1997.

5. "Frozen Memories: Celebrating a Century of Minnesota Hockey," by Ross Bernstein, Mpls., MN, 1998.

6. "Pigskin Pride: Celebrating a Century of Minnesota Football," by Ross Bernstein, Mpls., MN, 1999.

7. "Pigskin Pride: Celebrating a Century of Minnesota Football," by Ross Bernstein, Mpls., MN, 2000.

8. "Hardwood Hereos: Celebrating a Century of Minnesota Basketball," by Ross Bernstein, Mpls., MN, 2001.

9. "Batter-Up!: Celebrating a Century of Minnesota Baseball," by Ross Bernstein, Mpls., MN, 2002.

10. "The Hall: Celebrating the History and Heritage of the U.S. Hockey Hall of Fame," by Ross Bernstein, Mpls., MN, 2002.

11. The Minnesota Vikings Media Guides (various 1962-2003)

12. The Minnesota Twins Media Guides (various 1962-2003)

13. The Minnesota North Stars Media Guides (1968-1993)

14. The Minnesota Timberwolves Media Guides (1989-2003)

15. The Minnesota Wild Media Guides (2000-2003)

16. The Minnesota Kicks Media Guide

17. The Minnesota Strikers Media Guide

18. University of Minnesota Men's Athletics Media Guides: (various) Football, Basketball, Hockey, Baseball, Track & Field, Golf, Swimming & Diving, Wrestling, Gymnastics and Tennis

19. University of Minnesota Women's Athletics Media Guides: Basketball, Volleyball, Track & Field, Golf, Swimming & Diving, Soccer, Gymnastics, Softball and Tennis

20. NCC & NSIC Media Guides: Bemidji State, Moorhead State, UM-Duluth, UM-Morris, Concordia-St. Paul, Winona State, St. Scholastica, Southwest State, UM-Crookston, Minnesota State Mankato, St. Cloud State,

21. MIAC Media Guides: Augsburg, Bethel, Carlton, Concordia, Gustavus, Hamline, Macalaster, St. Ben's St. John's, St. Mary's, St. Olaf and St. Thomas

22. NSIC Web-Site & Corresponding Member Web-Pages (Men's & Women's)

23. NCC Web-Site & Corresponding Member Web-Pages (Men's & Women's)

24. MIAC Web-Site & Corresponding Member Web-Pages (Men's & Women's)

25. MSHSL Media Guides (various 1945-2002)

26. "Minnesota Vikings"- Professional Team Histories

27. "Minnesota Timberwolves" - Professional Sports Teams Histories

28. "Minnesota Twins" - Professional Sports Teams Histories

29. "Dallas Stars" - Professional Team Histories

30. "HickokSports.com," Web-Site

31. gophersports.com (various locales within site)

32. mshsl.com

33. usoc.org

34. startribune.com

35. pioneerplanet.com

36. espn.com

37. mscsports.com

38. augsburg.edu

39. varsityonline.com

40. cnnsi.com

41. pigskinpost.com

42. hickocksports.com

43. St. Paul Saints Website

44. Air Force Academy web-site

45. University of Nebraska-Omaha web-site

46. Northern League.com

47. Minnesota History Center Online Archives

48. "Hubert H. Humphrey Metrodome Souvenir Book": compiled by Dave Mona. MSP Pubs., Inc.

49. "The Official NBA Encyclopedia," by Jan Hubbard, Doubleday Pub., NY, 2000.

50. "The Lakers: A Basketball Journey," by Roland Lazenby, St. Martin's Press, NY, 1983.

51. "The History of Minnesota State High School Basketball Tournaments," by Ed Simpkins, 1964.

52. "A Century of Women's Basketball," by Joan Jult & Marianna Trekell, Reston, VA, 1991.

53. "Duluth Sketches of the Past," by Bruce Bennett.

54. "Basketball's Original Dynasty," by Stew Thornley, Nodin Press, 1989.

55. "Gopher Glory," by Steve Pearlstein, Layers Publishing, Minneapolis, 1995.

56. "The Encyclopedia of Pro Basketball Team Histories," by Peter Bjarkman, Carrol & Graf Pub, NY, 1994.

57. "Gopher State Greatness," by Joel B. Krenz, Richtman's Publishing, 1984.

58. "The Association for Pro Basketball Research," Web-Site

59. "The Roots: Early Professional Leagues," by Robin Deutsch and Douglas Stark.

60. "Gustavus Athletics: A Century of Building the Gustie Tradition," by Lloyd Hollingsworth, Gustavus Press, 1984.

61. "Chisholm's McDonald on verge of 800th basketball victory," by John Millea, Star Tribune, Jan. 17, 2003.

62. "A man of many jackets," By Jimmy Patterson, The Coffin Corner Volume XV, 1993.

63. "Sonmor, The scrapper who led Gophers, the Fighting Saints & the Stars has mellowed," by Bruce Brothers, Pioneer Press.

64. "High school baseball: Two coaches for the ages," John Millea, Star Tribune, May 20, 2003.

65. "The Great American Hockey Dilemma," by Murray Williamson (Ralph Turtinen Publishing, 1978).

66. "Called to Serve," by Tom Porter

67. "Verdict of the Scoreboard," by Ade Christenson

68. "Gold Glory": by Richard Rainbolt: Ralph Turtinen Publishing, 1972

69. "Basketball Stars," by Nick Dolin, Chris Dolin & David Check: Black Dog and Leventhal Publishes, 1997

70. "The 100 Greatest Pitchers of All Time": Barnes & Noble

71. "The Harmon Killebrew Story": by Hal Butler: Juliann Messner Publishing

72. "A Thinking Man's Guide to Pro Hockey": by Eskenazi, Gerald, E. P. Dutton, 1972.

73. "The Hockey Encyclopedia": by Fischler, Stan, and Shirley Fischler, Macmillan, 1983.

74. "Unstoppable": The Story of George Mikan, the First NBA Superstar: by George Mikan and Joseph Oberle, published by Masters Press, Indianapolis, 1997.

75. "The Kid From Cuba" by James Terzian, Doubleday Press

76. "Twenty Five Seasons": The First Quarter Century With the Minnesota Twins by Dave Mona and Dave Jarzyna: Mona Publications.

77. "Rod Carew": by Marshall Burchard, Longman, Can., 1978

78. "Sid!" The Sports Legends, the Inside Scoops, and the Close Personal Friends: by Sid Hartman and Patrick Reusse, Voyager Press, 1997.

79. The Winfield Foundation publication

80. "Season of Dreams": by Tom Kelly and Ted Robinson: Voyageur Press

81. "Kent Hrbek": by Jerry Carpenter & Steve Dimeglio: Abdo and Daughters, 1988

82. The U.S. Hockey Hall of Fame Handbook

83. High Minnesota State High School Hockey Tournament Media Guides, various: (1945-2003)

84. "One Goal: A Chronicle of the 1980 US Olympic Hockey Team": by John Powers and Art Kaminsky: Harper Row, 1984

85. "Tarkenton": by Jim Klobuchar and Fran Tarkenton: Harper Publishing, 1976

86. "Winfield" - A Player's Life, by Dave Winfield with Tom Parker: WW Nortan, 1988

87. "Gagliardi of St John's": The Coach, the Man, the Legend: by Don Riley and John Gagliardi: R. Turtinen Publishing

88. North Stars Media Guides (various 1970s - 1990s)

89. "Before the Dome," by David Anderson: Nodin Press, 1993

90. "On to Nicollet," by Stew Thornley, Nodin Press, 1988

91. "Basketball's Original Dynasty," by Stew Thornley, Nodin Press, 1989

92. "The Christian Story": Christian Brothers, Inc. Press Release Information

93. "Minn. Trivia," by Laurel Winter: Rutledge Hill Press, 1990

94. "Minnesota Awesome Almanac," by Jean Blashfield: B&B Publishing, 1993

95. "Gopher Sketchbook," by Al Papas, Jr.: Nodin Press, 1990

96. "NCAA Championships": The Official 2001 National Collegiate Championships Records

97. The Star Tribune Minnesota Sports Hall of Fame publication

98. "Can You Name That Team?" by David Biesel

99. "The Autumn Warrior," by Mike Wilkinson, 1992

100. "The Vikings: The First 15 Years."

101. "Obsession: Bill Musselman's Relentless Quest to Beat the Best "- by Heller: Bonus Books

102. Twins Yearbook: 30th Anniversary Edition - 1991

103. "Purple Hearts and Golden Memories," by Jim Klobuchar: Quality Sports Pub, 1995

104. "Gustavus Athletics," by Lloyd Hollingsworth, Gustavus Adolphus Press, St. Peter, MN., 1984.

105. "Scoreboard," by Dunstan Tucker & Martin Schirber, St. John's Press, Collegeville, MN, 1979.

106. "Awesome Almanac Minnesota," by Jean Blashfield, B&B Publishing, Fontana, WI, 1993.

107. "The Encyclopedia of Sports," by Frank Menke, AC Barnes Pub., Cranbury, NJ, 1975.

108. "My lifetime in sports," by George Barton, Stan Carlson Pub., Minneapolis, 1957.

109. "Professional Sports Teams Histories," by Michael LaBlanc, Gale Pub., Detroit, MI, 1994.

110. "The Encyclopedia of North American Sports History," by Ralph Hickock, 1992.

111. "Concordia Sports - The First 100 Years" by Vernon Finn Grinaker, Concordia Website.

112. "Sports Leagues & Teams," by Mark Pollak, McFarland and Co. Pub., Jefferson, NC, 1996.

113. "Before the Dome," by David Anderson: Nodin Press, 1993.

114. Star Tribune Article by Curt Brown - March 11, 1993 (An Investment of 26 Years Yields Nothing But Memories)

115. Minnesota Almanacs - various throughout 1970s

116. "Baseball: The Early Years," by H. Seymour, 1960.

117. "An Informal History of The Northern Baseball League,' By Herman D. White & Walter H. Brovald, Gryphon Press, St. Paul, 1982.

118. "The Northern League," By R. Arpi & Joe Block.

119. "The Northern League: Proud Tradition," by David Kemp, www.northernleague.com.

120. "The Rise of Baseball in Minnesota," By Cecil Monroe, MN History, June 1938.

121. "The History of Minnesota Football," The General Alumni Assoc. of Minn., 1928.

122. "The Minnesota Huddle," by Stan Carlson, Huddle Publishing Co., Minneapolis, 1937.

123. "A History of St. Thomas Football," by Mike E. Minor (1981), St. Thomas Media G., 1999.

124. "Augsburg Football History," by Don Stoner, SID, Augsburg, 1999.

125. "The Husky Tradition: A History of Men's Athletics at St. Cloud State," by John Kasper.

126. "True Hearts & Purple Heads," by Jim Klobuchar, Ross & Haines, Inc. Mpls., 1970.

127. "The Super Bowls," by Tim Klobuchar and Michael Rand, Star Tribune, January 24, 1999.

128. "Minnesota's Vikings: The Scrambler and the Purple Gang" by Bob Rubin, Prentice Hall, Englewood Cliffs, NJ, 1973.

129. "The Complete Story of the NFL," by Turner Publishing, Atlanta, 1994.

130. "Big Ten Football," by Mervyn Hyman & Gordon White Jr., MacMillan Pub., NY, 1977.

131. "Fifty Years At Memorial Stadium," by Dave Shanna, Alumni News, September 1974.

132. "The Other Side of the Glacier," Bud Grant.

133. "Carleton: the first century," by Leal Headley and Merrill Jarchow, Carelton, 1992.

134. "40 Years of State Football Recalled," by Ted Peterson, "Minn. Football Journal," 1969.

135. "Kirby Puckett": by Bob Italia: Abdo and Daughters, 1992

136. Star Tribune article: Kirby Puckett Weekend, May 23, 1997

137. Pioneer Press: Dick Siebert article: "Siebert Built "U" Baseball" by Charley Hallman

138. University of Minnesota Sports News: "Making His Mark Through Effort and Intelligence," by Len Levine

139. "Players of Cooperstown": Publishing International

140. "Frank Viola": by Jerry Carpenter And Steve Dimeglio: Abdo and Daughters, 1988

141. Twins Magazine: "Home for Good" - Terry Steinbach article by Jim Bohem, July 1997

142. Twins Magazine: "Baseball Pioneers" article by Mark Engebretson, July 1997

143. College Hockey Magazine: "Don Roberts Bids Farewell to Gustavus ," by Jim Rueda, Mankato Free Press.

144. "Kirby Puckett, I Love This Game": by Kirby Puckett: Harper Collins, 1993

145. "Lexington Park: Campy, The Duke, The Babe, and Oh, That Coliseum!," By Patrick Reusse

146 Sports Illustrated: North Stars article, June 1, 1981

147. "The NHL Stanley Cup Centennial," by Dan Diamond

148. Tribune: Tarkenton article , Dec 29, 1975

149. Star Tribune: Bud Grant article, Jan 7, 1986

150. Tribune: Mariucci article, March 13-14, 1984

151. Duluth News: UMD Hockey article, March 25, 1984

152. Sports Illustrated: Rod Carew article, July 16, 1977

153. Ivory Tower: "The Coach Behind the Comeback," by Peter Vanderpoel, 1953

154. Ambassador Magazine: "Leveling the Playing Field," by Curt Brown, July, 1996.

155. "The Encyclopedia of Pro Basketball Team Histories," by Peter Bjarkman, Carrol & Graf Pub, NY, 1994.

156. "Minn. Timberwolves," by Richard Rambeck, Creative Education Pub., Mankato, 1993.

157. Strasen, Marty (et. al.). Basketball Almanac, 1993—94. NY: Publications International, 1994.

"55 YEARS • 55 HEROES"
A CELEBRATION OF MINNESOTA SPORTS

Minnesota's wonderful sports history comes to life in "55 Years – 55 Heroes." Each year, going back 55 years, features one of the greatest moments in the world of Minnesota sports. That event is then tied into an interview and biography of a home-town or home-grown hero. While some chapters feature detailed historical accounts, interviews, extensive quotes and game summaries, others focus on different aspects of that particular event or person. With a Foreword by Bud Grant and an Afterword by Kent Hrbek, the book is both entertaining as well as insightful. Featured in it are literally hundreds of this past half century's greatest professional, minor league, amateur, collegiate and high school teams, along with countless biographies and stories of their star players — all chronicled in one amazing package. While some of those players accounts are inspirational, others are simply hilarious. Hundreds of wonderful pictures, stories, and tons of personal memories from the heroes themselves dot the canvas of this epic tale. From the Minneapolis Lakers and Minneapolis Millers title teams of the 1950s; to the Gopher Football Rose Bowl teams of the 1960s; to the Purple People Eaters and Gopher Hockey championship squads of the 1970s; to the Cinderella North Stars and World Champion Twins of the 1980s; to the upstart Timberwolves and Gopher basketball teams of the 1990s; to the rejuvenated Twins and Hockey Gophers of this new millennium — its all here.

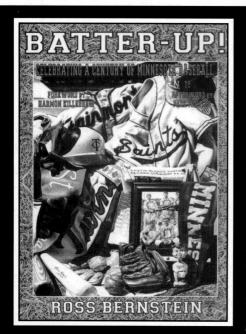

"BATTER-UP!"
CELEBRATING A CENTURY OF MINNESOTA BASEBALL

Minnesota's incredible baseball history comes to life in "Batter-Up! With a Foreword by Harmon Killebrew and an Afterword by Paul Molitor, the book is both entertaining as well as insightful. Featured in it are literally thousands of this past century's greatest professional, minor league, amateur, collegiate and high school teams, along with hundreds of biographies and stories of their star players. From the Twins to the Gophers, and from the Duluth Dukes to the Fargo-Moorhead Red Hawks — its all here. Learn about what it was like to play town team baseball in the old Southern Minny League of the 1950s; or how much fun it must have been to spend a holiday double-header at both Nicollet and Lexington Parks watching the St. Paul Saints and Minneapolis Millers do battle. Not only is there a complete history of the state high school tournament, there are even chapters on Minnesota's MIAC, NSIC and NCC college and university teams as well. In addition, there are also features on the evolution of the women's game, town-ball, the minor leagues, Negro Leagues, American Legion & VFW, Little League and more than 400 pictures to boot. Batter-Up! has captured the pure essence of just what the sport of baseball means to so many of us and pays homage to the countless men and women who have made the game what it is today. From Kent Hrbek to Harmon Killebrew and from Kirby Puckett to Paul Molitor, "Batter-Up!" truly celebrates one of our states greatest treasures — the sport, lifestyle and state-of-mind of baseball.